Frommer's
Costa Rica 2016

By Eliot Greenspan

Published by
FROMMER MEDIA LLC

Copyright © 2016 by Frommer Media LLC. All rights reserved. No part of this publication may be reproduced, stored in a retrieval system, or transmitted in any form or by any means, electronic, mechanical, photocopying, recording, scanning or otherwise, except as permitted under Sections 107 or 108 of the 1976 United States Copyright Act, without the prior written permission of the Publisher. Requests to the Publisher for permission should be addressed to Support@ FrommerMedia.com.

Frommer's is a registered trademark of Arthur Frommer. Frommer Media LLC is not associated with any product or vendor mentioned in this book.

ISBN 978-1-62887-204-0 (paper), 978-1-62887-205-7 (e-book)

Editorial Director: Pauline Frommer
Editor: Karen Fitzpatrick
Production Editor: Heather Wilcox
Cartographer: Roberta Stockwell
Cover Design: Howard Grossman
For information on our other products or services, see www.frommers.com.

Frommer Media LLC also publishes its books in a variety of electronic formats. Some content that appears in print may not be available in electronic formats.

Manufactured in China

5 4 3 2 1

HOW TO CONTACT US

In researching this book, we discovered many wonderful places—hotels, restaurants, shops, and more. We're sure you'll find others. Please tell us about them, so we can share the information with your fellow travelers in upcoming editions. If you were disappointed with a recommendation, we'd love to know that, too. Please write to Support@FrommerMedia.com

FROMMER'S STAR RATINGS, ICONS & ABBREVIATIONS

Every hotel, restaurant and attraction listed in this guide has been ranked for quality and value. Here's what the stars mean:

★ Recommended
★★ Highly Recommended
★★★ A must! Don't miss!

AN IMPORTANT NOTE

The world is a dynamic place. Hotels change ownership, restaurants hike their prices, museums alter their opening hours, and busses and trains change their routings. And all of this can occur in the several months after our authors have visited, inspected, and written about, these hotels, restaurants, museums and transportation services. Though we have made valiant efforts to keep all our information fresh and up-to-date, some few changes can inevitably occur in the periods before a revised edition of this guidebook is published. So please bear with us if a tiny number of the details in this book have changed. Please also note that we have no responsibility or liability for any inaccuracy or errors or omissions, or for inconvenience, loss, damage, or expenses suffered by anyone as a result of assertions in this guide.

CONTENTS

LIST OF MAPS

ABOUT THE AUTHOR

Eliot Greenspan is a poet, journalist, musician, and travel writer who took his backpack and typewriter the length of Mesoamerica before settling in Costa Rica in 1992. Since then, he has worked steadily as a travel writer, food critic, freelance journalist, translator, and personal travel planner, while continuing his travels in the region. In addition to this book, he has authored "Frommer's Belize," "Frommer's Cuba," "Frommer's Ecuador," "Frommer's Guatemala," "Costa Rica For Dummies," and "Costa Rica Day by Day."

DEDICATION

I'd like to dedicate this edition, with love, appreciation and gratitude, to Warren Greenspan, November 26, 1932–January 11, 2011.

—Eliot Greenspan

ACKNOWLEDGMENTS

I say this every year, but I continue to be eternally grateful to Anne Becher and Joe Richey, who were instrumental in getting me this gig—muchas gracias. I'd also like to thank my parents, Marilyn and Warren Greenspan, who showed unwavering love, support, and encouragement (well, one out of three ain't bad) when I chose words and world-wandering over becoming a lawyer or a doctor. Jody and Ted Ejnes (my sister and brother-in-law) deserve a mention; they risked life and limb—literally—leading to two important tips that may help you save yours. (I now believe Ted, and he may have actually almost stepped on a crocodile.) Both Giovana Longhi Garita and Maria Jose Longhi Garita did extensive and meticulous fact checking—my hat's off to their OCD family genes. Finally, all my love to Maria Jose, Fabrizio and Patitas, who continue to accompany me on this journey.

—Eliot Greenspan

THE BEST OF COSTA RICA

Costa Rica continues to be one of the hottest vacation and adventure-travel destinations in Latin America, and for good reason. The country is rich in natural wonders and abundant biodiversity. Costa Rica boasts a wealth of unsullied beaches for sun-bathing and surfing, jungle rivers for rafting and kayaking, and spectacular cloud forests and rainforests with ample opportunities for bird-watching, wildlife viewing, and hiking. In addition to the trademark eco- and adventure-tourism offerings, you will also find luxury resorts and golf courses, plush spas, and some spectacular boutique hotels and lodges.

Having lived in Costa Rica for over 22 years, I continue to discover new spots, adventures, restaurants, and lodgings. In this chapter, I select the very best of what this unique country has to offer.

COSTA RICA'S best AUTHENTIC EXPERIENCES

- **Taking a Night Tour in a Tropical Forest:** Most Neotropical forest dwellers are nocturnal, so nighttime tours are offered at most rainforest and cloud forest destinations throughout the country. Some of the better spots for night tours are **Monteverde** (p. 372), **Tortuguero** (p. 519), and **Drake Bay** (p. 471).

- **Soaking in a Volcanic Hot Spring:** Costa Rica's volcanoes have blessed the country with a host of natural hot spring spots. From the opulent grandeur of **Tabacón Grand Spa Thermal Resort** (p. 351) to the more humble options around **Rincón de la Vieja** (p. 222) to the remote hot river pools at **Rio Perdido** (p. 226), all offer mineral-rich, naturally heated waters to soothe what ails you.

Poás Volcano National Park.

PREVIOUS PAGE: **A red-eyed tree frog in Tortuguero.**

Tabacón Hot Springs.

o **Spotting a Resplendent Quetzal:** The iridescent colors and long, flowing tail feathers of this aptly named bird are breathtaking. This extremely endangered species can still be regularly sighted in the **Monteverde Cloud Forest Biological Reserve** (p. 371) and the **San Gerardo de Dota** region (p. 459).

o **Meeting Monkeys:** Costa Rica's rain- and cloud forests are home to four species of New World Monkeys—howler, capuchin, squirrel, and spider. I can't guarantee you'll see one or more, but your odds are good if you visit **Monteverde** (p. 365), **Tortuguero** (p. 512), **Manuel Antonio** (p. 417), or the **Osa Peninsula** (p. 468).

LEFT: Resplendent Quetzal on Savegre Mountain; RIGHT: Squirrel monkey in Manuel Antonio National Park.

3

- **Zipping Through the Treetops:** You'll find zip-line canopy tours all over Costa Rica. In most cases, after a bit of a hike, you strap on a harness and zip from treetop to treetop while dangling from a cable. Chapter 5, "The Best Special-Interest Trips & Tours."

- **Pouring on the Salsa Lizano:** Whether you're eating at a *soda* (diner) or having breakfast at the Four Seasons, be sure to try some Salsa Lizano, a tangy, tamarind-based sauce that's used on everything from salad to rice and beans to grilled meats and poultry.

Zip-lining through the cloud forest of Monteverde.

- **Playing in a Pickup Football (Soccer) Game:** You'll find informal, friendly *fútbol* matches all across the country. You can head to **La Sabana Park** (p. 135) and find one just about any weekend or afternoon. But I prefer to jump into a game on the beach, with some simple sticks stuck in the sand as goal posts.

- **Touring a Coffee Plantation:** World renowned and highly coveted, you can enjoy freshly brewed Costa Rican coffee at the source all across the country. Go deeper and learn how the bean is grown and processed. Coffee tours are offered around the Central Valley and outside Monteverde. See chapters 7 and 10.

- **Eating at a Soda:** The Costa Rican equivalent of a diner, *sodas* are simple, family-run restaurants serving local standards. You'll find them in every town and city in the country. Order a *casado* (blue plate special), a bowl of *olla de carne* (beef stew), or a plate of *gallo pinto* (rice and beans). **Soda Tapia** (p. 149) in San José, **Soda Carolina** (p. 489) in Puerto Jiménez, and **Soda Tamara** (p. 551) are a few classics you'll come across as you travel the country, but you'll find one or more in every town and city in Costa Rica.

COSTA RICA'S best PLACES TO SEE WILDLIFE

- **Santa Rosa National Park** (northeast of Liberia, in Guanacaste): One of the largest and last remaining stands of tropical dry forest in Costa Rica, Santa Rosa National Park is a great place for all sorts of wildlife viewing. The sparse foliage, especially during the dry season, makes observation that much easier for novice naturalists. See p. 227.

- **Monteverde Cloud Forest Biological Reserve** (in the mountains northwest of San José): There's something both eerie and majestic about walking around in the early-morning mist surrounded by bird

Baby Leatherback Turtle heading to sea.

calls, animal rustlings, and towering trees hung heavy in broad bromeliads, flowering orchids, and hanging moss and vines. The reserve has a well-maintained network of trails, and the community is truly involved in conservation. See p. 371.

o **The Río Sarapiquí Region** (north of San José btw. Guanacaste in the west and the Caribbean coast in the east): Protected tropical forests climb from the Caribbean coastal lowlands up into the central mountains, affording you a glimpse of a plethora of life zones and ecosystems. **Braulio Carrillo National Park** borders several private reserves, and here you'll find a variety of ecolodges, to suit any budget. See "Puerto Viejo de Sarapiquí," in chapter 10.

o **Manuel Antonio** (near Quepos on the central Pacific Coast): The reason this place is so popular and renowned? Monkeys! The national park here is full of them, even the endangered squirrel monkeys. White-faced capuchin monkeys are quite common here, and have been known to rifle through backpacks in search of a snack. See "Manuel Antonio National Park," in chapter 11.

o **Osa Peninsula** (in southern Costa Rica): This is Costa Rica's most remote and biologically rich region. **Corcovado National Park,** the largest remaining patch of virgin lowland tropical rainforest in Central America, takes up much of the Osa Peninsula. Jaguars, crocodiles, and scarlet macaws all call this place home. Whether you stay in a luxury nature lodge in **Drake Bay** or outside of **Puerto Jiménez,** or camp in the park itself, you will be surrounded by some of the most lush and most intense jungle this country has to offer. See chapter 12.

o **Tortuguero Village & Jungle Canals** (on the Caribbean coast, north of Limón): Tortuguero has been called Costa Rica's Venice, but it actually has more in common with the South American Amazon. As you explore the narrow canals here, you'll see a wide variety of herons and other water birds, three types of monkeys, three-toed sloths, and caimans. If you come between June and October, you could be treated to the awe-inspiring spectacle of a green turtle nesting—the small stretch of Tortuguero beach is the last remaining major nesting site of this endangered animal. See "Exploring Tortuguero National Park," in chapter 13.

COSTA RICA'S best ECOLODGES & WILDERNESS RESORTS

Ecolodge options in Costa Rica range from tent camps with no electricity or hot water and communal, buffet-style dining to some of the most

Tropical Beach in Corcovado National Park.

luxurious accommodations in the country. See "Responsible Tourism" on p. 78 for more info on sustainable travel to Costa Rica.

o **Arenal Observatory Lodge** (near La Fortuna): Originally a research facility, this lodge now features comfy rooms with impressive views of Arenal Volcano. Excellent trails lead to nearby lava flows and a remote jungle waterfall. Toucans frequent the trees near the lodge, and howler monkeys provide the wake-up calls. See p. 352.

o **Monteverde Lodge & Gardens** (Monteverde): One of the original ecolodges in Monteverde, this place has only improved over the years, with great guides, updated rooms, and lush gardens. The operation is run by the very dependable and experienced Costa Rica Expeditions. See p. 380.

o **La Paloma Lodge** (Drake Bay): If your idea of the perfect nature lodge is one where your front porch provides prime-time viewing of flora and fauna, this place is for you. If you decide to leave the comfort of your porch, the Osa Peninsula's lowland rainforests are just outside your door. See p. 473.

o **Bosque del Cabo Rainforest Lodge** (Osa Peninsula): Large, unique, and cozy private cabins perched on the edge of a cliff overlooking the Pacific Ocean and surrounded by lush rainforest make this one of my favorite spots in the country. See p. 486.

o **Lapa Ríos** (Osa Peninsula): This was one of Costa Rica's first luxury ecolodges to gain interational acclaim, and it remains one of the best. The attention to detail, personalized service, and in-house guides and tour leaders are all top-notch. See p. 487.

o **Playa Nicuesa Rainforest Lodge** (Golfo Dulce): This lodge is by far the best option on the Golfo Dulce. Set in deep forest, the individual bungalows here are a perfect blend of rusticity and luxury, and the guides, service, and surrounding wildlife are all superb. See p. 497.

- **Tortuga Lodge** (Tortuguero): This is another of the excellent ecolodges run by Costa Rica Expeditions, and features a beautiful riverfront restaurant and swimming pool. The canals of Tortuguero snake through its maze of lowland primary rainforest. The beaches here are major sea-turtle nesting sites. See p. 521.
- **Selva Bananito Lodge** (in the Talamanca Mountains south of Limón): This is one of the few lodges providing direct access to the southern Caribbean lowland rainforests. You can hike along a riverbed, ride horses through the rainforest, climb 30m (100 ft.) up a ceiba tree, or rappel down a jungle waterfall here. See p. 529.

COSTA RICA'S best HOTELS

- **Hotel Grano de Oro** (San José): San José boasts dozens of colonial-era mansions that have been converted into hotels, but few do it like Grano de Oro with its luxurious accommodations and professional service. All the guest rooms have attractive hardwood furniture, including antique armoires in some rooms. When it's time to relax, you can soak in a hot tub or have a drink in the rooftop lounge while taking in San José's commanding view. See p. 142.

- **Finca Rosa Blanca Coffee Plantation & Inn** (Heredia): If the cookie-cutter rooms of international resorts leave you cold, perhaps this unusual inn will be more your style. Square corners seem to have been prohibited here in favor of turrets, and curving walls of glass, arched windows, and semicircular built-in couches. It's set into a lush hillside and surrounding organic coffee farm, just 20 minutes from San José. See p. 190.

The Finca Rosa Blanca Organic Coffee Plantation and Eco Boutique Hotel.

- **Hotel Capitán Suizo** (Tamarindo): With a perfect beachfront setting, spacious rooms, lush gardens and grounds, and a wonderful pool, this is easily the best option in Tamarindo, and one of the best along the whole Gold Coast. See p. 272.
- **Florblanca Resort** (Playa Santa Teresa): The individual luxury villas at this intimate resort feature massive living rooms and private balconies. The service, spa and food are all outstanding, and the resort is spread over a lushly planted hillside, steps away from Playa Santa Teresa. See p. 309.

Arco Iris Lodge, Monteverde.

o **Hidden Canopy Treehouses** (Monteverde): The individual cabins here are set on high stilts and nestled into the surrounding cloud forest canopy. All abound in brightly varnished local hardwoods. The refined, yet convivial vibe is especially palpable in the afternoon over tea or cocktails, when guests enjoy the main lodge's sunset view. See p. 379.

o **Arco Iris Lodge** (Monteverde): This small lodge is set on an expansive piece of property, but within easy walking distance of everything in Santa Elena. And it's the best deal in the Monteverde area to boot. The owners are extremely knowledgeable and helpful. See p. 381.

o **Arenas del Mar** (Manuel Antonio): The whole resort is set amidst old-growth rain forest on a hilly piece of land abutting two distinct beaches. With large rooms, the best of which offer panoramic coastline views from a wrap around balcony equipped with a sunken Jacuzzi. It has a beautiful little spa, and the best beach access and location in Manuel Antonio. See p. 430.

o **Playa Negra Guesthouse** (Cahuita): Located just across a dirt road from a long desolate section of Playa Negra, the individual Caribbean-style bungalows here are cozy and beautifully done, with full kitchens and gingerbread trim. The grounds are a riot of tropical flowers and tall palm trees, and the whole operation has an intimate and refined ambience. See p. 537.

o **Cariblue Bungalows** (Playa Cocles): Try to get one of the private wooden bungalows here. If you do, you might be so happy and comfortable that you won't want to leave. This small Caribbean coast resort is surrounded by tall rainforest trees. Just 90m (300 ft.) or so away, however, are the warm waves of the Caribbean Sea. See p. 558.

COSTA RICA'S best RESTAURANTS

o **Grano de Oro Restaurant** (San José): This elegant boutique hotel has an equally fine restaurant serving contemporary fusion dishes and decadent desserts made with fresh local ingredients. The open-air seating in the central courtyard is delightful, surrounded by potted palms and ornate stained glass windows. See p. 147.

o **Abbocato** (Playa Panamá): The dynamic husband-wife chef team here serves up two unique nightly tasting menus—one Asian, one Mediterranean—executed with skill and creativity. See p. 239.

o **Ginger** (Playa Hermosa): Serving an eclectic mix of traditional and Pan Asian–influenced tapas, this sophisticated little joint is taking this part of Guanacaste by storm. A list of creative cocktails complements the inventive dishes. See p. 239.

o **Papaya** (Brasilito): Housed in a simple, unassuming roadside hotel, this lively little restaurant serves fusion cuisine, using the region's freshest fish and seafood and other local ingredients, influenced by Asian and Latin American styles. See p. 255.

o **Pangas Beach Club** (Tamarindo): Executive chef Jean-Luc Taulere had a long, successful run over in Playa Flamingo, before moving to this relaxed, elegant restaurant. He combines his Catalan heritage, with classical French training, fresh local ingredients and a mix of local, fusion and Asian influences. See p. 275.

o **Lola's** (Playa Avellanas): With a perfect setting on the sand and excellent hearty fare, Lola's gets my vote for the best casual beachfront restaurant in the country. The ocean-loving namesake mascot—a pet pig—just adds to the restaurant's quirky charm. See p. 278.

o **Playa de los Artistas** (Montezuma): This place has the perfect blend of refined Mediterranean cuisine and beachside funkiness. There are only a few tables, so get here early. Fresh, grilled seafood is served in oversized ceramic bowls and on large wooden slabs lined with banana leaves. See p. 305.

o **Gingerbread** (Nuevo Arenal): This world fusion restaurant almost qualifies as dinner theater and participation is encouraged. At times, it feels equal parts bread and circus. Chef Eyal is outspoken and outgoing, engaging diners in lively discussions on food, the arts, politics and current events. Don't come here for a romantic meal in a quiet corner, but do come for some fun and fine dining. See p. 364.

o **Café Caburé** (Monteverde): In addition to the eclectic world cuisine served here, these folks have a delicious, wide ranging and very tempting selection of homemade chocolate treats. I love the casual open-air seating on this second-floor wooden balcony, and the ability to take a Chocolate Tour (p. 377) or visit the Bat Jungle (p. 376) after my meal. See p. 382.

- **Graffiti Resto Café & Wine Bar** (Playa de Jacó): From the small sushi bar in one corner to the graffiti-painted walls, this place is full of surprises. Pan Asian cuisine is blended with the chef's Alabama roots and New Orleans training, whipping up wonders out of local ingredients and spices. See p. 412.

- **Milagro** (Manuel Antonio): A casually elegant little place, Milagro has made a name for itself in the Manuel Antonio area. A humble coffee shop, breakfast joint, and lunch stop, things get kicked up a notch at night with a creative Nuevo Latino menu that takes full advantage of the freshest local ingredients available. See p. 436.

- **La Pecora Nera** (Puerto Viejo): You'll be surprised to find such fine Italian cuisine in a tiny surfer town on the remote Caribbean coast. Your best bet here is to allow yourself to be taken on a culinary rollercoaster ride with a mixed feast of the chef's nightly specials and suggestions. See p. 561.

COSTA RICA'S best FAMILY DESTINATIONS

- **La Paz Waterfall Gardens** (near Varablanca and the Poás Volcano): This multifaceted attraction features paths and suspended walkways set alongside a series of impressive jungle waterfalls. Kids will love the variety and vibrancy of the various offerings, from the hummingbird, wild cat, and reptile exhibits to the impressive power of the waterfalls. See p. 181.

- **Playa Hermosa:** The protected waters of this Pacific beach make it a family favorite. Just because its waters are calm, however, doesn't mean it's boring. I recommend staying at the beachfront **Hotel Playa Hermosa Bosque del Mar** (p. 237) and checking in at **Aqua Sport** (p. 235), where you can rent sea kayaks, sailboards, paddleboats, beach umbrellas, and bicycles.

- **Playa Tamarindo:** This surf town has a bit of something for everyone. It's a great spot for kids to learn how to surf or boogie-board, and a host of tours and activities to please the entire family are available. **Hotel Capitán Suizo** (p. 272) has an enviable location on a calm section of beach, plus spacious rooms and a great pool for kids and adults alike, with a long sloping shallow entrance. See "Playa Tamarindo & Playa Langosta," in chapter 8.

- **Arenal Volcano:** This adventure hot spot offers a nearly inexhaustible range of activities for families of all ages. From gentle safari floats to raging white water rafting, and from flat easy hikes over hanging bridges to challenging scrambles over cooled off lava flows, you're sure to find something that fits the interests, abilities and activity level of every member of the family. See "Arenal Volcano & La Fortuna," in chapter 10.

o **Monteverde:** This area not only has the country's most famous cloud forest, but also offers up a wide variety of attractions and activities. After hiking through the reserve, you should be able to keep everyone happy and occupied riding horses; squirming at the serpentarium; or visiting the Monteverde Butterfly Garden, Frog Pond, Bat Jungle, and Orchid Garden. See "Monteverde," in chapter 10.

o **Playa de Jacó:** Jacó's streets are lined with souvenir shops, ice-cream stands, and inexpensive eateries. Activity options range from surf lessons and bungee jumping to a small-boat cruise among the crocodiles on the Tárcoles River. **Club del Mar Condominiums & Resort** (p. 410) is accommodating to families with small children. See "Playa Herradura & Playa de Jacó," in chapter 11.

o **Manuel Antonio:** This national park has a bit of everything: miles of idyllic white sand beaches, myriad wildlife (with almost guaranteed monkey

TOP: **Surfing in Hermosa;** BOTTOM: **Waterfall at La Paz waterfall gardens.**

Playa Tamarindo.

sightings), and plenty of active-tour options. Of the many lodging options, **Hotel Sí Como No** (p. 432), with its spacious tropical suites, two pools, water slide, and nightly movies, is probably your best bet. See "Manuel Antonio National Park," in chapter 11.

COSTA RICA'S best BEACHES

With more than 1,200km (750 miles) of shoreline on its Pacific and Caribbean coasts, Costa Rica offers beachgoers a wealth of riches.

- **Santa Rosa National Park:** You'll have to four-wheel-drive or hike 13km (8 miles) from the central ranger station to reach these remote beaches, but you'll probably have the place almost to yourself. In fact, the only time it gets crowded is in October, when thousands of olive ridley sea turtles nest in one of their yearly *arribadas* (arrivals). See p. 227.

- **Playa Nacascolo:** With silky, soft white sand, this is the best stretch of beach on the Papagayo Peninsula. The waters here are protected from ocean swells and are great for swimming. See "Playa Hermosa, Playa Panamá & Papagayo," in chapter 8.

- **Playa Avellanas:** Just south of Tamarindo, this white-sand beach has long been a favorite haunt for surfers, locals, and those in the know. Playa Avellanas stretches on for miles, backed largely by protected mangrove forests. This beach is home to **Lola's** (p. 278), perhaps my favorite beachfront restaurant in the country.

- **The Beaches Around Playa Sámara:** Playa Sámara is nice enough, but venturing just slightly farther afield, you'll find two of the prettiest beaches along the entire Pacific Coast. **Playa Carrillo** is a long crescent of palm-backed white sand located just south of Sámara, while **Playa Barrigona** is a hidden gem tucked down a rugged dirt road to the north. See "Playa Sámara," in chapter 9.

- **Playa Montezuma:** This tiny beach town at the southern tip of the Nicoya Peninsula retains a funky sense of individuality, with plenty of isolated spots to lay down your towel or mat. While still a favorite of the backpacker, fire spinners and Hula Hoop crowd, you can also find upscale beachfront lodgings and fine dining restaurants. Nearby, you'll find two impressive waterfalls, one of which empties into an oceanfront pool and the other surrounded by thick forest, as well as the **Cabo Blanco** and **Curú** wildlife preserves. See "Playa Montezuma," in chapter 9.

TOP: **Playa Manuel Antonio;** BOTTOM: **A surf class in Santa Teresa.**

- **Malpaís & Santa Teresa:** With just a smattering of luxury lodges, surf camps, and assorted hotels and hostels, this is the place to come if you're looking for miles of deserted beaches and great surf. See "Malpaís & Santa Teresa," in chapter 9.

- **Manuel Antonio:** Manuel Antonio National Park was the first beach destination to become popular in Costa Rica, and its beaches are still idyllic. The views from the hills approaching the park offer captivating views over thick primary rainforest to the Pacific ocean. This is also one of the few remaining habitats for the endangered squirrel monkey. See "Manuel Antonio National Park," in chapter 11.

Playa Montezuma.

o **Punta Uva & Manzanillo:**
These beaches deliver true
Caribbean splendor, with turquoise waters, coral reefs, and
palm-lined stretches of nearly
deserted white-sand beach.
Tall coconut palms line the
shore, providing shady respite,
and the water is usually quite
calm and good for swimming.
See "Cahuita, Puerto Viejo &
the Beaches of Costa Rica's
Southern Caribbean Coast," in
chapter 13.

Punta Uva Beach on the Caribbean Coast.

COSTA RICA'S best ADVENTURE SPORT EXPERIENCES

o **Mountain Biking the Back Roads of Costa Rica:** The lack of infrastructure and paved roads here that most folks bemoan is a huge boon
for mountain bikers. The country has endless back roads and trails to
explore. The area around La Fortuna and Lake Arenal is my favorite
destination for mountain biking with its widely varied terrain. See
p. 344.

o **Rafting the Pacuare River** (near Turrialba): Arguably the best and
most beautiful river for rafting in Costa Rica, the class III/IV Pacuare
winds through primary and secondary forests, and features one

breathtaking section that passes through a narrow steep gorge. For a real treat, take the 2-day Pacuare River trip, which includes an overnight at a lodge or tent camp on the side of the river. See p. 111.

o **Surfing & Four-Wheeling Guanacaste Province:** From Witch's Rock at Playa Naranjo near the Nicaraguan border to Playa Nosara, more than 100km (60 miles) away, you'll find scores of world-class surf spots. In addition to the two mentioned, try a session at Playa Grande, Punta Langosta, and playas Negra, Avellanas, and Junquillal. Or find your own secret spot. See chapter 8.

o **Trying the Adventure Sport of Canyoning:** While every canyoning tour is unique, it usually involves hiking along and through the rivers and creeks of a steep mountain canyon, with periodic breaks to rappel down the face of a waterfall, jump off a rock into a jungle pool, or float down a small rapid. See chapters 8, 10, and 11.

o **Battling a Billfish off the Pacific Coast:** Billfish are plentiful all along Costa Rica's Pacific Coast, and boats operate from Playa del Coco down to the Golfo Dulce. Costa Rican anglers hold world records for both blue marlin and Pacific sailfish. Go to Quepos (just outside Manuel Antonio) for the best après-fish scene, or head down the Osa Peninsula or Golfo Dulce if you want some isolation. See chapter 8, 9, 11 and chapter 12.

o **Windsurfing or Kitesurfing on Lake Arenal:** With steady gale-force winds (at certain times of the year), the stunning northern end of Lake Arenal has become a major international windsurfing and kitesurfing hot spot. See chapter 10.

Rafting the Pacuare River.

A canyoning tour.

Windsurfing on Lake Arenal.

- **Diving off the Shores of Isla del Coco** (off the Pacific Coast): Legendary among treasure seekers, pirate buffs, and scuba divers, this small island is surrounded by clear Pacific waters, and its reefs are teeming with life (divers regularly encounter large schools of hammerhead sharks, curious manta rays, and docile whale sharks). See p. 289.

- **Hiking Mount Chirripó** (near San Isidro de El General on the central Pacific Coast): The highest peak in Costa Rica, hiking to Mount Chirripó's 3,724m (12,215-ft.) summit takes you through a number of distinct bioregions, ranging from lowland pastures and a cloud forest to a high-altitude *páramo*, a tundralike landscape with stunted trees and morning frosts. See "San Isidro de El General: A Base for Exploring Chirripó National Park," in chapter 11.

COSTA RICA'S best DAY HIKES & NATURE WALKS

- **Lankester Gardens:** If you want a really pleasant but not overly challenging day hike, consider a walk among the hundreds of distinct species of flora on display here. The trails meander from areas of well-tended open garden to shady natural forest, plus there's a highly regarded orchid collection. See p. 201.

- **Rincón de la Vieja National Park:** This park has trails through a variety of ecosystems. My favorite hike is down to the Blue Lake and Cangrejo Falls, where you'll find a pristine turquoise pool fed by a rushing jungle waterfall. You can also hike up to two craters and a crater lake here, while the Las Pailas loop is ideal for those seeking a less strenuous hike. See p. 221.

- **Arenal National Park:** Arenal National Park has several excellent trails that visit a variety of ecosystems, including rainforest, secondary forest, savanna, and, my favorite, old lava flows. Most of them are on the relatively flat flanks of the volcano, so there's not too much climbing involved. See "Arenal Volcano & La Fortuna," in chapter 10.

- **Monteverde Cloud Forest Biological Reserve:** Take a guided tour in the morning to familiarize yourself with the cloud forest, and then spend the afternoon (your entrance ticket is good for the entire day) exploring the reserve on your own. Off the main thoroughfares, Monteverde reveals its rich mysteries with stunning regularity. Even without a guide you should be able to enjoy sightings of a wide range of unique tropical flora and fauna, and maybe even spot a Resplendent Quetzal on your own. See p. 371.

- **La Selva Biological Station:** La Selva has an extensive and well-marked network of trails. You'll have to reserve in advance and take the guided tour if you aren't a guest at the lodge. But the hikes are led by very informed naturalists, so you might not mind the company. See p. 391.

- **Corcovado National Park:** The park has a well-designed network of trails, ranger stations, and camping facilities. Most of the lodges in Drake Bay and Puerto Jiménez offer day hikes through the park, but if you really want to experience it, you should hike in and stay at one or more of the campgrounds. See "Puerto Jiménez: Gateway to Corcovado National Park," in chapter 12.

- **Cahuita National Park:** Fronted by the Caribbean and an idyllic beach, the trails are flat and well-maintained through thick lowland forest. They are parallel to the beach, so you can hike out on the trail and back along the beach, or vice versa. White-faced and howler monkeys are common, as are brightly colored land crabs. See p. 532.

COSTA RICA'S best BIRD-WATCHING

- **Spotting Hundreds of Marsh & Stream Birds along the Río Tempisque Basin:** A chief breeding ground for gallinules, jacanas, and limpkins, it is a common habitat for many heron and kingfisher species. Options include visits to **Palo Verde National Park** (p. 74), **El Viejo Wetlands** (p. 253), and **Rancho Humo** (p. 319).

- **Looking for 300-Plus Species of Birds in La Selva Biological Station:** With an excellent trail system through a variety of habitats, from dense primary rainforest to open pasturelands and cacao plantations, this is one of the finest places for bird-watching in Costa Rica. With such a variety of habitats, the number of species spotted runs to well over 300. See p. 391.

o **Sizing up a Jabiru Stork at Caño Negro National Wildlife Refuge:** Caño Negro Lake and the Río Frío that feeds it are incredibly rich in wildlife and a major nesting and gathering site for aquatic bird species. These massive birds are getting less common in Costa Rica, but this is still one of the best places to spot one. See p. 75.

o **Catching a Scarlet Macaw in Flight over Carara National Park:** Macaws are noisy and colorful birds that spend their days in the park but choose to roost in the evenings near the coast. They arrive like clockwork every morning and then head for the coastal mangroves around dusk. These daily migrations give birders a great chance to see these magnificent birds in flight. See p. 75.

o **Looking for a Resplendent Quetzal in the Cerro de la Muerte:** Serious bird-watchers won't want to leave Costa Rica without seeing one of these iridescent green wonders. See "Where to See Quetzals in the Wild: Cerro de la Muerte & San Gerardo de Dota" in chapter 11.

o **Spotting Hundreds of Species at Wilson Botanical Gardens:** With more than 7,000 species of tropical plants and flowers, the trails of this research facility are fabulous for bird-watching. Hummingbirds and tanagers are plentiful, but the bounty doesn't end there—over 360 species of birds have been recorded here. See "Golfito: Gateway to the Golfo Dulce," in chapter 12.

o **Taking Advantage of the Caribbean's Best Birding at Aviarios Sloth Sanctuary of Costa Rica:** If it flies along this coast, chances are that you'll spot it here; more than 330 species of birds have been seen so far. In the afternoon, large flocks of several heron species nest here. See p. 535.

Collared Aracari Toucan eating fruit in La Selva Biological Station.

2

COSTA RICA IN CONTEXT

*P*ura Vida! (Pure Life!) is Costa Rica's unofficial national slogan, and in many ways it defines the country. You'll hear it exclaimed, proclaimed, and simply stated by Ticos from all walks of life, from children to octogenarians. It can be used as a cheer after your favorite soccer team scores a goal, or as a descriptive response when someone asks you, "¿Como estas?" ("How are you?"). It is symbolic of the easygoing nature of this country's people, politics, and personality.

Costa Rica itself is a mostly rural country with vast areas of protected tropical forests. It is one of the biologically richest places on earth, with a wealth of flora and fauna that attracts and captivates biologists, photographers, ecotourists, and casual visitors alike.

Often called the "Switzerland of Central America," Costa Rica is, and historically has been, a sea of tranquility in a region that has been troubled by turmoil for centuries. For more than 100 years, it has enjoyed a stable democracy and a relatively high standard of living for Latin America. The literacy rate is high, as are medical standards and facilities. Perhaps most significant, at least for proud and peace-loving Costa Ricans, is that this country does not have an army.

COSTA RICA TODAY

Costa Rica has a population of a little more than five million, more than half of whom live in the Central Valley and are considered as urban. Some 94 percent of the population is of Spanish or otherwise European descent, and it is not at all unusual to see fair-skinned and blond Costa Ricans. This is largely because the indigenous population in place when the first Spaniards arrived was small and thereafter was quickly reduced to even more of a minority by wars and disease. Some indigenous populations still remain, primarily on reservations around the country; the principal tribes include the Bribri, Cabécar, Boruca, and Guayamí. In addition, on the Caribbean coast and in the big cities is a substantial population of English-speaking black Creoles who came over in the late 19th and early 20th centuries from the Antilles to work on building the railroad and on the banana plantations. Racial tension isn't palpable, but it exists, perhaps more out of historical ignorance and fear rather than an organized or articulated prejudice.

PREVIOUS PAGE: **Playa Manuel Antonio.**

Where There Is a Tico, There Is Freedom

In 1989, on a visit to Costa Rica, Uruguayan President Julio María Sanguinetti famously declared: *"Donde hay un costarricense, esté donde esté, hay libertad,"* which is roughly translated in the title above.

Personally, I get a kick out of the version co-opted by a local condiment company in its advertising campaign, which states, "Where there is a Tico, there is Salsa Lizano." I find it to be equally true.

In general, Costa Ricans are a friendly and outgoing people. While interacting with visitors, Ticos are very open and helpful. Time has relative meaning to Ticos. Although most tour companies and other establishments operate efficiently, don't expect punctuality, in general.

In a region historically plagued by internal strife and civil wars, Costa Ricans are proud of their peaceful history, political stability, and relatively high level of development. However, this can also translate into arrogance and prejudice toward immigrants from neighboring countries, particularly Nicaraguans, who make up a large percentage of the workforce on the banana and coffee plantations.

Roman Catholicism is the official religion of Costa Rica, although freedom to practice any religion is guaranteed by the country's constitution. More than 75 percent of the population identifies itself as Roman Catholic, while another 14 percent are part of a number of evangelical Christian congregations. There is a small but visible Jewish community as well. By and large, a large section of Ticos are religiously observant, if not fervent, though it seems that just as many lead quite secular lives.

Costa Rica is the most politically stable nation in Central America, and it has the largest middle class. Even the smallest towns have electricity, the water is mostly safe to drink, and the phone system is relatively good and very widespread. Still, the gap between rich and poor is wide, and there are glaring infrastructure needs. The roads, hospitals, and school systems have been in a slow but steady state of decay for decades, with no immediate signs that these matters will improve anytime soon.

Banana plantation.

Tourism is the nation's true principal source of income, surpassing cattle ranching, textiles, and exports of coffee, pineapples, bananas, and Intel microchips. More than two million tourists visit Costa Rica each year, and over half the working population is employed in the tourism and service industries. Ticos whose fathers and grandfathers were farmers and ranchers find themselves hotel owners, tour guides, and waiters. Although most have adapted gracefully and regard the industry as a source of new jobs and opportunities for economic advancement, restaurant and hotel staff can seem gruff and uninterested at times, especially in rural areas. And, unfortunately, an increase in the number of visitors has led to an increase in crime, prostitution, and drug trafficking. Common sense and street savvy are required in San José and in many of the more popular tourist destinations.

The global economic crisis definitely hit Costa Rica. Tourism took a noticeable hit, especially in 2009 to 2010. But it has bounced back nicely. More importantly, perhaps, since credit has historically been so tight, there was never a major mortgage or banking crisis in the country. Today, Costa Rica continues to be a culturally and biologically rich yet diminutive Central American nation struggling to meet the economic and development needs of its population. It seems to be moving in the right direction, even though that movement is maddeningly slow most of the time.

THE MAKING OF COSTA RICA

Early History

Little is known of Costa Rica's history before its colonization by Spanish settlers. The pre-Columbian Indians who made their home in this region of Central America never developed the large cities or advanced culture that flowered farther north in what would become Guatemala, Belize, and Mexico. There are no grand pyramids or large Mayan cities in Costa Rica. However, ancient artifacts indicating a strong sense of aesthetics have been unearthed from scattered excavations around the country. Ornate gold and jade jewelry, intricately carved grinding stones, and artistically painted terra-cotta objects point to a small but highly skilled population.

Spain Settles Costa Rica

In 1502, on his fourth and last voyage to the New World, Christopher Columbus anchored just offshore from present-day Limón. Whether he actually gave the country its name—"the rich coast"—is open to debate, but the Spaniards never did find much gold or minerals to exploit here.

The earliest Spanish settlers found that, unlike settlements to the north, the native population of Costa Rica was unwilling to submit to slavery. Despite their small numbers, scattered villages, and tribal

top: **Cartago's Basilica;** bottom: **Juan Santamaría Memorial Park in Alajuela.**

differences, they fought back against the Spanish until they were overcome by superior firepower and European diseases. When the fighting ended, the European settlers in Costa Rica found that very few Indians were left to force into servitude. The settlers were thus forced to till their own lands, a situation unheard of in other parts of Central America. Few pioneers headed this way because they could settle in Guatemala, with its large native workforce. Costa Rica was nearly forgotten, as the Spanish crown looked elsewhere for riches to plunder and souls to convert.

It didn't take long for Costa Rica's few Spanish settlers to head for the hills, where they found rich volcanic soil and a climate that was less oppressive than in the lowlands. **Cartago,** the colony's first capital, was founded in 1563, but it was not until the 1700s that additional cities were established in this agriculturally rich region. In the late 18th century, the first coffee plants were introduced, and because these plants thrived in the highlands, Costa Rica began to develop its first cash crop.

Unfortunately, it was a long and difficult journey transporting the coffee to the Caribbean coast and then onward to Europe, where the demand for coffee was growing.

From Independence to the Present Day

In 1821, Spain granted independence to its colonies in Central America. Costa Rica joined with its neighbors to form the Central American Federation; but in 1838, it withdrew to form a new nation and pursue its own interests. By the mid-1800s, coffee was the country's main export. Free land was given to anyone willing to plant coffee on it, and plantation owners soon grew wealthy and powerful, creating Costa Rica's first elite class. Coffee plantation owners were powerful enough to elect their own representatives to the presidency.

This was a stormy period in Costa Rican history. In 1856, the country was invaded by **William Walker,** a soldier of fortune from Tennessee who, with the backing of U.S. President James Buchanan, was attempting to fulfill his grandiose dreams of presiding over a slave state in Central America (before his invasion of Costa Rica, he had invaded Nicaragua and Baja, California). The people of Costa Rica, led by their own president, Juan Rafael Mora, marched against Walker and chased him back to Nicaragua. Walker eventually surrendered to a U.S. warship in 1857, but, in 1860, he attacked Honduras, claiming to be the president of that country. The Hondurans, who had had enough of Walker's shenanigans, promptly executed him.

Until 1890, coffee growers had to transport their coffee either by oxcart to the Pacific port of Puntarenas or by boat down the Río Sarapiquí to the Caribbean. In the 1870s, a progressive president proposed a railway from San José to the Caribbean coast to facilitate the transport of coffee to European markets. It took nearly 20 years for this plan to reach fruition, and more than 4,000 workers lost their lives constructing the railway, which passed through dense jungles and rugged mountains on its journey from the Central Valley to the coast. Partway through the project, as funds were dwindling, the second chief engineer, Minor

The Little Drummer Boy

Costa Rica's national hero is Juan Santamaría. The legend goes that young Juan enlisted as a drummer boy in the campaign against William Walker (see above). On April 11, 1865, when Costa Rican troops had a band of Walker's men cornered in a downtown hostel in Rivas, Nicaragua, Santamaría volunteered for a nearly certain suicide mission to set the building on fire. Although he was mortally wounded, Santamaría was successful in torching the building and driving Walker's men out, where they were swiftly routed. Today, April 11 is a national holiday.

Keith, proposed an idea that not only enhanced his fortunes, but also changed the course of Central American history. Banana plantations would be developed along the railway right of way (land on either side of the tracks). The export of this crop would help to finance the railway, and, in exchange, Keith would get a 99-year lease on 1,976,000 hectares (800,000 acres) of land with a 20-year tax deferment. The Costa Rican government gave its consent, and in 1878 the first bananas were shipped from the country. In 1899, Keith and a partner formed the **United Fruit Company,** a business that eventually became the largest landholder in Central America and caused political disputes and wars throughout the region.

> ### The Last Costa Rican Warrior
>
> "Military victories, by themselves, are not worth much. It's what is built from them that matters."
>
> —José "Pepe" Figueres

In 1889, Costa Rica held what is considered the first free election in Central American history. The opposition candidate won the election, and the control of the government passed from the hands of one political party to those of another without bloodshed or hostilities. Thus, Costa Rica established itself as the region's only true democracy. In 1948, this democratic process was challenged by **Rafael Angel Calderón,** who had served as the country's president from 1940 to 1944. After losing by a narrow margin, Calderón, who had the backing of the communist labor unions and the Catholic Church, refused to concede the country's leadership to the rightfully elected president, **Otillio Ulate,** and a civil war ensued. Calderón was eventually defeated by José "Pepe" Figueres. In the wake of this crisis, a new constitution was drafted; among other changes, it abolished Costa Rica's army so that such a revolution could never happen again.

In 1994, history seemed to repeat itself—peacefully this time—when **José María Figueres** took the reins of government from the son of his father's adversary, Rafael Angel Calderón. In 2001, Otton Solís and his new Citizen's Action Party (PAC) forced the presidential elections into a second round, opening a crack in a two-party system that had become seemingly entrenched for good. Although Solís himself finished third and didn't make it to the run-off, his upstart Citizen's Action Party won quite a few deputy slots.

The battered traditional two-party system was further threatened in 2004, when major corruption scandals became public. Two former presidents were arrested (Miguel Angel Rodríguez and Rafael Angel Calderón), and another (José María Figueres) fled to Switzerland. All were implicated, as well as a long list of high-level government employees and deputies, in various financial scandals or bribery cases. Both Calderón and Rodríguez were convicted and sentenced to jail time, while charges have been dropped against Figueres.

President John F. Kennedy visited Costa Rica in March 1963. Upon his arrival, the Irazú Volcano woke up and erupted, after more than two decades of dormancy. Soot and ash reached as far as San José, where the soon-to-be-assassinated leader addressed students and political figures.

In 2010, Costa Rica elected its first female president, **Laura Chinchilla,** who was a vice-president in the outgoing Arias administration. While on April 6, 2014, former University professor Luis Guillermo Solis of the opposition Citizen's Action Party won a run-off presidential election by a landslide over longtime San José mayor Johnny Araya. So far, Solis's presidency has been a mixed bag. He's had trouble moving legislation forward, and divisions within his own ruling coalition have been a large part of that problem. Longstanding structural issues have hampered attempts at addressing infrastructure and revenue problems.

ART & ARCHITECTURE

For a small and provincial country, Costa Rica has vibrant scenes in all the major arts—music, literature, architecture, dance, and even film.

Art

Unlike Guatemala, Mexico, or even Nicaragua, Costa Rica does not have a strong tradition of local or indigenous arts and crafts. The strong suit of Costa Rican art is European and Western influenced, ranging from neoclassical to modern in style.

Early painters to look out for include **Max Jimenez, Manuel de la Cruz, Teodorico Quiros,** and **Francisco Amighetti.** Of these, Amighetti is the best known, with an extensive body of expressionist-influenced work. Legends of the local modern art world include **Rafa Fernández, Lola Fernández,** and **Cesar Valverde.** Valverde's portraits are characterized by large planes of bold colors. While artists making waves and names for themselves today include **Fernando Carballo, Rodolfo Stanley, Lionel Gonzalez, Manuel Zumbado,** and **Karla Solano.**

Sculpture is perhaps one of the strongest aspects of the Costa Rican art scene, with the large bronze works of **Francisco "Paco" Zuñiga** among the best of the genre. Zuñiga's larger-than-life castings include exaggerated human proportions that recall Rodin and Botero. Meanwhile, the artists **José Sancho, Edgar Zuñiga,** and **Jiménez Deredia** are all producing internationally acclaimed pieces, many of monumental proportions. You can see examples by all these sculptors around the country, as well as at San José's downtown **Museo de Arte**

Pre-Columbian foundations at Guayabo National Monument.

Costarricense ★★ (p. 133). I also enjoy the whimsical works of **Leda Astorga,** who sculpts and then paints a pantheon of plump and voluptuous figures in interesting, and at times, compromising, poses.

You'll find the country's best and most impressive museums and galleries in San José (p. 128), and to a lesser extent in some of the country's larger and more popular tourist destinations, like Manuel Antonio and Monteverde.

Architecture

Costa Rica lacks the large-scale pre-Columbian ceremonial ruins found throughout much of the rest of Mesoamerica. The only notable early archaeological site is **Guayabo** (p. 206). However, only the foundations of a few dwellings, a handful of carved petroglyphs, and some road and water infrastructure are still visible here.

Similarly, Costa Rica doesn't have the same large and well-preserved colonial-era cities found throughout much of the rest of Latin America. The original capital of **Cartago** (p. 196) has some old ruins and a few colonial-era buildings, as well as the country's grandest church, the **Basílica de Nuestra Señora de los Angeles (Basilica of Our Lady of the Angels)** ★ (p. 199), which was built in honor of the country's patron saint, La Negrita, or the Virgin of Guadalupe. Although the sculpture of the Virgin was discovered here in 1635, the church itself wasn't inaugurated until 1924.

Colonial-Era Remnant or Crime Deterrent?

Most Costa Rican homes feature steel or iron grating over the doors and windows. I've heard more than one tour guide say this can be traced back to colonial-era architecture and design. However, I'm fairly convinced it is a relatively modern adaptation to the local crime scene.

In downtown San José, Barrio Amón and Barrio Otoya are two side-by-side upscale neighborhoods replete with a stately mix of architectural stylings, with everything from colonial-era residential mansions, to Art Deco apartment buildings, and modern high-rise skyscrapers. One of the standout buildings here, inspired by the Eiffel Tower, is the **Metal School (Escuela Metalica),** which dates to the 1880s, and was shipped over piece-by-piece from France, and erected in place

On much of the Caribbean coast, you will find mostly wooden houses, built on raised stilts to rise above the wet ground and occasional flooding. Some of these houses feature ornate gingerbread trim. Much of the rest of the country's architecture is pretty plain. Most residential houses are simple concrete-block affairs, with zinc roofs.

A few modern architects are creating names for themselves. **Ronald Zurcher,** who designed the luxurious **Four Seasons Resort** (p. 236) and several other large hotel projects, is one of the shining lights of contemporary Costa Rican architecture.

Museo de Arte Costarricense.

The Basilica de Nuestra Señora de los Angeles in Cartago.

COSTA RICA IN POPULAR CULTURE

Books

Though Costa Rica's literary output is sparsely translated and little known outside of Costa Rica, there are some notable authors to look out for, especially if you can read in Spanish.

Some of the books mentioned below might be difficult to track down in U.S. bookstores, but you'll find them all in abundance in Costa Rica. A good place to check for many of these titles is at a well-stocked gift shop, or any branch of **Libreria Internacional** (www.libreriainternacional. com; 𝄐 **800/542-7374**), which has storefronts at most major modern malls, and several other stand-alone locations around the country.

GENERAL INTEREST For a straightforward, albeit somewhat dry, historical overview, there's **"The History of Costa Rica,"** by **Ivan Molina** and **Steven Palmer.** For a more readable look into Costa Rican society, pick up **"The Ticos: Culture and Social Change"** by **Richard, Karen,** and **Mavis Biesanz,** an examination of the country's politics and culture. Another work worth checking out is **"The Costa Rica Reader: History, Culture, Politics,"** a broad selection of stories, essays, and excerpts edited by Steven Palmer and Ivan Molina.

To learn more about the life and culture of Costa Rica's Talamanca coast, an area populated by Afro-Caribbean people whose forebears emigrated from Caribbean islands in the early 19th century, look for **"What Happen: A Folk-History of Costa Rica's Talamanca Coast"** by **Paula Palmer.** This book is a collection of oral histories taken from a wide range of local characters.

FICTION "Costa Rica: A Traveler's Literary Companion," edited by **Barbara Ras** and with a foreword by **Oscar Arias Sánchez,** is a broad and varied collection of short stories by Costa Rican writers, organized by region of the country. Entries include works by many of the country's leading literary lights. Availability of Costa Rican fiction in English is very limited, if you're lucky, you might find a copy of **"Stories of Tatamundo,"** by **Fabian Dobles,** or **"Lo Peor/The Worst,"** by **Fernando Contreras.**

Young readers will enjoy **Kristin Joy Pratt**'s **"A Walk in the Rainforest,"** an introduction to the tropical rainforest written by Ms. Pratt when she was still in high school. Young children will also like the beautifully illustrated **"The Forest in the Clouds,"** by **Sneed Collard** and **Michael Rothman,** and **"The Umbrella." Pachanga Kids** (www.pachangakids.com) has published several illustrated bilingual children's books with delightful illustrations by **Ruth Angulo,** including **"Mar Azucarada/Sugar Sea"** by **Roberto Boccanera** and **"El Coyote y la Luciernaga/The Coyote and the Firefly"** by **Yazmin Ross,** which (full disclosure) I translated, and which includes a musical CD that also features your humble author's singing. Another bilingual children's book worth checking out is **"Zari & Marinita: Adventures in a Costa Rican Rainforest,"** the story of the friendship between a morpho butterfly and a tropical frog.

One of the most important pieces in the Costa Rican canon, **Carlos Luis Fallas**'s 1941 tome **"Mamita Yunai"** is a stark look at the impact of the large banana giant United Fruit on the country. More recently, **Fernando Contreras** takes up where his predecessor left off in **"Unico Mirando al Mar,"** which describes the conditions of the poor, predominantly children, who scavenge Costa Rica's garbage dumps.

NATURAL HISTORY I think that everyone coming to Costa Rica should read **"Tropical Nature"** by **Adrian Forsyth** and **Ken Miyata.** My all-time favorite book on tropical biology, this is a wonderfully written and lively collection of tales and adventures by two Neotropical biologists who spent quite some time in the forests of Costa Rica.

Mario A. Boza's beautiful **"Costa Rica National Parks"** has been reissued in an elegant coffee-table edition. Other worthwhile coffee-table books include **"Rainforests: Costa Rica and Beyond"** by **Adrian Forsyth,** with photographs by **Michael** and **Patricia Fogden,** **"Costa Rica: A Journey Through Nature"** by **Adrian Hepworth,** **"Osa: Where the Rainforest Meets the Sea"** by **Roy Toft** (photographer) and **Trond Larsen** (author).

For an introduction to a wide range of Costa Rican fauna, there's **"The Wildlife of Costa Rica: A Field Guide"** by **Fiona Reid, Jim Zook, Twan Leenders,** and **Robert Dean,** or **"Costa Rica: Traveller's Wildlife Guides"** by **Les Beletsky.** Both pack a lot of useful information into a concise package and make great field guides for amateur naturalists and inquisitive tourists.

"A Guide to the Birds of Costa Rica," by **F. Gary Stiles** and **Alexander Skutch,** is an invaluable guide to identifying the many birds you'll see during your stay. This classic faces competition from the more recent **"Birds of Costa Rica,"** by **Richard Garrigues** and **Robert Dean.** Bird-watchers might want a copy of **"A Bird-Finding Guide to Costa Rica"** by **Barrett Lawson,** which details each country's bird-watching bounty by site and region.

For a fairly complete list of field guides, check out **www.zona tropical.net**.

Film

Costa Rica has a budding and promising young film industry. Local feature films like Esteban Ramirez's **"Caribe"** (2004), about the confrontation between environmentalists and oil developers on Costa Rica's Caribbean coast and **"Gestación (Gestation)"** (2009), a tale of teenage love and pregnancy, are both out on subtitled DVD. **"El Camino (The Path)"** by filmmaker **Ishtar Yasin Gutiérrez** was screened at the Berlin Film Festival, while **Paz Fabrega**'s **"El Viaje"** (2015) was shown to rave reviews at the 2015 Tribeca Film Festival. Released in 2010, **Hilda Hidalgo**'s **"Del Amor y Otros Demonios (Of Love and Other Demons)"** is a compelling treatment of Gabriel García Márquez's novel of the same name. The comic-thriller **"Tropix"** (2004) is one of the few Costa Rican-produced feature films in English.

If you want to see Costa Rica used simply as a backdrop, the major motion picture productions of **"1492"** (1992) by **Ridley Scott** and starring Gerard Depardieu and Sigourney Weaver; **"Congo"** (1995), featuring Laura Linney and Ernie Hudson; **"The Blue Butterfly"** (2004) with William Hurt; and **"After Earth"** (2013), a critical disaster featuring Will Smith and directed by M. Night Shyamalan, all feature sets and scenery from around the country. Serving as more than a mere visual backdrop, Costa Rica appears prominently in the seminal surfer flick **"Endless Summer II"** (1994).

The small **Costa Rican Film and Video festival** (www.centrode-cine.go.cr) is each November in San José.

Music

Several musical traditions and styles meet and mingle in Costa Rica. The northern Guanacaste region is a hotbed of folk music that is strongly influenced by the *marimba* (wooden xylophone) traditions of Guatemala

Marimba players by the entrance to the bazaar at Puerto Limón.

and Nicaragua, while also featuring guitars, maracas, and the occasional harp. On the Caribbean coast, you can hear traditional calypso sung by descendants of the original black workers brought over to build the railroads and tend the banana plantations. Roving bands play a mix of guitar, banjo, washtub bass, and percussion in the bars and restaurants of Cahuita and Puerto Viejo.

Costa Rica also has a healthy contemporary music scene. The jazz-fusion trio **Editus** has won two Grammy awards for its work with Panamanian salsa giant (and movie star) **Rubén Blades. Malpaís,** the closest thing Costa Rica had to a super-group, suffered the sudden and tragic loss of its lead singer, but still has several excellent albums out, and remaining members have been known to play together from time to time.

You should also seek out **Cantoamérica,** which plays upbeat dance music ranging from salsa to calypso to merengue. Jazz pianist, and former Minister of Culture, **Manuel Obregón** (also a member of Malpaís) has several excellent solo albums out, including **"Simbiosis"** (2011), on which he improvises along with the sounds of Costa Rica's wildlife, waterfalls, and weather; as well as his work with the **"Papaya Orchestra,"** a collaboration and gathering of musicians from around Central America.

Local label **Papaya Music ★★★** (www.papayamusic.com) has done an excellent job promoting and producing albums by Costa Rican musicians in a range of styles and genres. Their offerings range from the Guanacasteca folk songs of **Max Goldemberg,** to the boleros of **Ray**

Tico, to the original calypso of **Walter "Gavitt" Ferguson.** You can find their CDs at gift shops and record stores around the country, as well as at airport souvenir stores.

Classical music lovers will want to head to San José, which has a symphony orchestra, youth symphony, opera company, and choir. The local symphony sometimes features the works of local composers like **Benjamin Guitiérrez** and **Eddie Mora.** On occasion, small-scale music festivals will bring classical offerings to some of the beach and inland tourist destinations around the country.

Bars and discos around the country spin salsa, merengue, and cumbia, as well as more modern grooves that include house, electronic, trip-hop, and reggaeton.

EATING & DRINKING

While Costa Rican cooking can be fairly simple and plain, creative chefs have livened up the dining scene in San José and at most of the major tourist destinations, and some are serving modern takes on classic Costa Rican food.

Outside of the capital and the major tourist destinations, your options get very limited very fast. In fact, many destinations are so remote that you have no choice but to eat in the hotel's restaurant. At remote jungle lodges, the food is usually served buffet- or family-style and can range from bland to inspired, depending on who's doing the cooking, and turnover is high.

If you see a restaurant billing itself as a *mirador,* it means it has a view. If you are driving around the country, don't miss an opportunity to dine with a view at some little roadside restaurant. The food might not be all that great, but the view and scenery will be.

At even the more expensive restaurants, it's hard to spend more than $50 per person unless you really splurge on drinks. It gets even cheaper outside the city and high-end hotels. However, if you really want to save money, Costa Rican, or *típico,* food is always the cheapest nourishment available. It's primarily served in *sodas,* Costa Rica's equivalent of diners. At a *soda,* you'll have lots of choices: rice and beans with steak, rice and beans with fish, rice and beans with chicken, or, for vegetarians, rice and beans. You get the picture.

I have separated restaurant listings throughout this book into three price categories, based on the average cost of a meal per person, including tax and service charge: **Expensive,** more than $30 (C15,900); **Moderate,** $15 to $30 (C7,950–C15,900); and **Inexpensive,** less than $15 (C7,950). (Note, however, that individual items in the listings—entrees, for instance—do not include the sales or service taxes.) Keep in mind that an additional 13 percent sales tax applies, as well as a 10 percent service charge. Ticos rarely tip, but that doesn't mean that you shouldn't.

TICO etiquette & CUSTOMS

In general, Costa Ricans are easygoing, friendly, and informal. That said, Ticos tend to be conservative and try to treat everyone very respectfully. Moreover, in conversation, Ticos are relatively formal. When addressing someone, they use the formal *usted* in most instances, reserving the familiar *vos* for close friends, family, and children or teenagers.

Upon greeting or saying goodbye, both sexes shake hands, although across genders, a light kiss on one cheek is common.

Proud of their neutrality and lack of armed forces, everyday Costa Ricans are uncomfortable with confrontation. What may seem like playful banter or justified outrage to a foreign tourist may be taken very badly by a Tico.

In some cases, especially in the service industry, a Tico may tell you what he or she thinks you want to hear, just to avoid a confrontation—even if he or she knows there's little chance of follow-through or ultimate customer satisfaction. I've also had, on more than one occasion, Ticos give me wrong directions, instead of telling me they didn't know the way.

The two words mentioned at the start of this chapter—*pura vida*—will go a long way to endearing you to most Ticos. In conversation, *pura vida* is used as a greeting, exclamation, adjective, and general space filler. Feel free to sprinkle a *pura vida* or two into your conversations with locals. I'm sure it will be well received. For more tips on talking like a Tico, see "Some Typical Tico Words & Phrases" on p. 586.

Tico men dress conservatively. It is very rare to see Costa Rican men wear short pants except at the beach. In most towns and cities, while accepted, tourists will stand out when wearing short pants, sandals, and other typical beach, golf, or vacation wear. Costa Rican women, on the other hand, especially young women, do tend to show some skin in everyday, and even business, situations. Still, be respectful in your dress, especially if you plan on visiting churches, small towns, or local families.

Women, no matter how they dress, may find themselves on the receiving end of whistles, honks, hoots, hisses, and catcalls. For more information on this manifestation of Costa Rican machismo, see "Women Travelers," on p. 582.

Punctuality is not a Costa Rican strong suit. Ticos often show up anywhere from 15 minutes to an hour or more late to meetings and appointments—this is known as *la hora tica,* or "Tico time." That said, buses and local airlines, tour operators, movie theaters, and most businesses do tend to run on a relatively timely schedule.

If the service was particularly good and attentive, you should probably leave a little extra.

Meals & Dining Customs

Rice and beans are the bases of Costa Rican meals—all three of them. At breakfast, they're called *gallo pinto* and come with everything from eggs to steak to seafood. At lunch or dinner, rice and beans are an integral part of a *casado* (which translates as "married" and is the name for the local version of a blue-plate special). A *casado* usually consists of cabbage-and-tomato salad, fried plantains (a banana-like fruit), and a

A typical *casado*.

chicken, fish, or meat dish of some sort. On the Caribbean coast, rice and beans are called "rice 'n' beans," and are cooked in coconut milk.

Dining hours in Costa Rica are flexible but generally follow North American customs. Some downtown restaurants in San José are open 24 hours; however, expensive restaurants tend to be open for lunch between 11am and 3pm and for dinner between 6 and 11pm.

APPETIZERS   Known as *bocas* in Costa Rica, appetizers are served with drinks in most bars. Often the *bocas* are free, but even if they aren't, they're very inexpensive. Popular *bocas* include *gallos* (tortillas piled with meat, chicken, cheese, or beans), *ceviche* (a marinated seafood salad), tamales (stuffed cornmeal patties wrapped and steamed inside banana leaves), *patacones* (fried green plantain chips), and fried yuca.

SANDWICHES & SNACKS   Ticos love to snack, and a large variety of tasty little sandwiches and snacks are available on the street, at snack bars, and in *sodas*. *Arreglados* are little meat-filled sandwiches, as are *tortas*, which are served on little rolls with a bit of salad tucked into them. Tacos, tamales, *gallos* (see above), and *empanadas* (turnovers) also are quite common.

MEAT   Costa Rica is beef country, having converted much of its rainforest land to pastures for raising beef cattle. Consequently, beef is cheap

Chifrijo: King of Costa Rican Bocas

Without a doubt, Costa Rica's most popular and famous *boca* is a bowl of *chifrijo*. The name is a phonetic abbreviation of its two most important ingredients: *chicharrones* (fried pork bellies) and *frijoles* (beans). A proper bowl of *chifrijo* will also have rice, pico de gallo (a tomato-based salsa), a few slices of avocado, and come adorned with some tortilla chips for scooping up all that goodness.

The creation was the brainchild of Miguel Cordero, who began serving it in his family bar in Tibas in the early 1980s. The dish quickly spread like wildfire and can now be found in restaurants and bars around the country. Cordero had the foresight to trademark his dish, and in 2014 began taking legal action against competitors for trademark infringement. Thanks to Cordero's trademark claims, restaurant and bar owners have had to scramble. In most cases, you can still usually find *chifrijo* on the menu, only it might be called *frichijo*, or *hochifri*, or some other variation on the theme.

and plentiful, although it might be a bit tougher—and cut and served thinner—than it is back home. One typical local dish is called *olla de carne,* a bowl of beef broth with large chunks of meat, local tubers, and corn. Spit-roasted chicken is also very popular here and is meltingly tender. Lamb is very sparsely used in Costa Rican cooking, although finer restaurants often have a lamb dish or two on the menu, usually imported from New Zealand.

A plate of Chifrijo.

SEAFOOD Costa Rica has two coasts, and, as you'd expect, plenty of seafood is available everywhere in the country. *Corvina* (sea bass) is the most commonly served fish and is prepared in numerable ways, including as *ceviche.* (**Be careful:** In many cheaper restaurants, particularly in San José, shark meat is often sold as *corvina.*) You should also come across *pargo* (red snapper), *dorado* (mahimahi), and tuna on some menus, especially along the coasts. Although Costa Rica is a major exporter of shrimp and lobster, both are relatively expensive and in short supply here.

A traditional appetizer of ceviche.

VEGETABLES On the whole, you'll find vegetables surprisingly lacking in the meals you're served in Costa Rica—usually nothing more than a little pile of shredded cabbage topped with a slice or two of tomato. For a much more satisfying and filling salad, order *palmito* (hearts of palm salad). The heart (actually the stalk or trunk of these small palms) is first boiled and then chopped into circular pieces and served with other fresh vegetables, with salad dressing on top. If you want something more than this, you'll have to order a side dish such as *picadillo,* a stew or purée of vegetables with a bit of meat in it.

Plátanos (plantains) are giant relatives of bananas and are technically considered a fruit, but they are really more like vegetables and require cooking before they can be eaten. Green plantains have a very starchy flavor and consistency, but they become as sweet as candy as they ripen, especially when fried. Yuca (manioc root or cassava in English) is another starchy staple root vegetable in Costa Rica.

Coconut, Straight Up

Throughout Costa Rica (particularly on the coastal road btw. Limón and Cahuita), keep your eye out for roadside stands selling fresh, green coconuts, or *pipas* in Spanish. Green coconuts have very little meat, but are filled with copious amounts of a slightly sweet, clear liquid that is extremely refreshing.

According to local legend, this liquid is pure enough to be used as plasma in an emergency situation. Armed with a machete, the *pipa* seller will cut out the top and stick in a straw. In the best of cases, the *pipa* will have been cooled over ice. The entire thing should cost around C500.

One more vegetable worth mentioning is the *pejibaye,* a form of palm fruit that looks like a miniature orange coconut. Boiled *pejibayes* are frequently sold from carts on the streets of San José. When cut in half, a *pejibaye* reveals a large seed surrounded by soft, fibrous flesh. You can eat it plain, but it's usually topped with a dollop of mayonnaise.

FRUITS   Costa Rica has a wealth of delicious tropical fruits. The most common are mangoes (the season begins in May), papayas, pineapples, melons, and bananas. Other fruits include *marañón,* which is the fruit of the cashew tree and has orange or yellow glossy skin; *granadilla* or *maracuyá* (passion fruit); *mamón chino,* which Asian travelers will immediately recognize as rambutan; and *carambola* (star fruit).

DESSERTS   *Queque seco,* literally "dry cake," is the same as pound cake. *Tres leches* cake, on the other hand, is so moist that you almost need to eat it with a spoon. Flan is a typical custard dessert. It often comes as either *flan de caramelo* (caramel) or *flan de coco* (coconut). Numerous other sweets are available, many of which are made with condensed milk and raw sugar. *Cajetas* are popular handmade candies, made from sugar and various mixes of evaporated, condensed, and powdered milk. They

Starfruit in Alajuela's public market.

Fresh mango in a fruit market in San Jose.

are sold in differing-size bits and chunks at most *pulperías* (general stores) and streetside food stands.

Beverages

Frescos, refrescos, and *jugos naturales* are my favorite drinks in Costa Rica. They are usually made with fresh fruit and milk or water. Among the more common fruits used are mangoes, papayas, blackberries, and pineapples. You'll also come across *maracuyá* (passion fruit) and *carambola* (star fruit). Some of the more unusual frescos

Witch's Rock Pale Ale from Volcano Brewing Company.

are *horchata* (made with rice flour and a lot of cinnamon) and *chan* (made with the seed of a plant found mostly in Guanacaste—definitely an acquired taste). The former is wonderful; the latter requires an open mind (it's reputed to be good for the digestive system). Order *un fresco con leche sin hielo* (a *fresco* with milk but without ice) if you're avoiding untreated water.

If you're a coffee drinker, you might be disappointed here. Most of the best coffee has traditionally been targeted for export, and Ticos tend to prefer theirs weak and sugary. Better hotels and restaurants are starting to cater to gringo and European tastes and are serving up superior blends. If you want black coffee, ask for *café negro;* if you want it with milk, order *café con leche.*

For something different for your morning beverage, ask for *agua dulce,* a warm drink made from melted sugar cane and served either with milk or lemon, or straight.

WATER   Although water in most of Costa Rica is safe to drink, bottled water is readily available and is a good option if you're worried about an upset stomach. *Agua mineral,* or simply soda, is sparkling water in Costa Rica. If you like your water without bubbles, request *aqua mineral sin gas,* or *agua en botella.*

BEER, WINE & LIQUOR   The German presence in Costa Rica over the years has produced several decent beers, which are fairly inexpensive. Most Costa Rican beers are light pilsners. Almost all mass produced beers are either produced or imported by one single company, Florida Ice & Farm. The most popular brands are Bavaria, Imperial, and Pilsen. I personally can't tell much of a difference between any of them. Licensed local versions of Heineken and Rock Ice are also available.

You can find imported wines at reasonable prices in the better restaurants throughout the country. You can usually save money by ordering a Chilean or Argentine wine over a Californian or European one.

Craft Beer Boom

Costa Rica has seen an amazing boom in craft beers and places to drink them in the past few years. **Costa Rica's Craft Brewing Company** (www.beer.cr; ✆ **2249-0919**) has led the way. Their Libertas Golden Ale and Segua Red Ale are available at more and more restaurants and bars around the country, and can be purchased at larger supermarkets. These folks offer tours of their brewery and have a small brew pub at their main facility in Ciudad Colon, a western suburb of San Jose. Other brews and breweries to look for include Ambar by **Cervecera del Centro** (www.cerveceradelcentro.com); Majadera Pale Ale and Japiendin Tropical Ale from **Treinta y Cinco** (www.treintaycinco.com); and Witch's Rock Pale Ale and Gato Malo Dark Ale by the **Volcano Brewing Company** (www.volcanobrewingcompany.com) in Tamarindo.

Costa Rica distills a wide variety of liquors, and you'll save money by ordering these over imported brands. The national liquor is *guaro,* a crude cane liquor that's often combined with a soft drink or tonic. When drinking it straight, it's customary to follow a shot with a bite into a fresh lime covered in salt. If you want to try *guaro,* stick to the **Cacique** brand.

Several brands and styles of coffee-based liqueurs are also produced in Costa Rica. **Café Rica** is similar to Kahlúa, and you can find several types of coffee cream liqueurs. The folks at **Café Britt** produce their own line of coffee liqueurs, which are quite good and available in most supermarkets, liquor stores, and tourist shops.

Costa Ricans also drink a lot of rum. The premier Costa Rican rum is **Centenario.**

TIPS ON SHOPPING IN COSTA RICA

Costa Rica is not known for shopping. Most of what you'll find for sale is pretty run-of-the-mill mass-produced souvenir fare. So scant are its handicraft offerings that most tourist shops sell Guatemalan clothing, Panamanian appliquéd textiles, El Salvadoran painted wood souvenirs, and Nicaraguan rocking chairs. Still, Costa Rica does have a few locally produced arts and handicrafts to look out for, and a couple of towns and villages with well-deserved reputations for their unique works.

Perhaps the most famous of all towns for shopping is **Sarchí ★** (p. 192), a Central Valley town filled with handicraft shops. Sarchí is best known as the citadel of the colorfully painted Costa Rican **oxcart,** reproductions of which are manufactured in various scaled-down sizes. These make excellent gifts. (Larger oxcarts can be easily disassembled and shipped to your home.) A lot of furniture is also made in Sarchí.

Up in Guanacaste, the small town of **Guaitíl** (p. 276) is famous for its pottery. A host of small workshops, studios, and storefronts ring the

Artist's workshop in Sarchí.

town's central park (which is actually a soccer field). Many of the low-fired ceramic wares here carry ancient local indigenous motifs, while others get quirky modern treatments. You can find examples of this low-fired simple ceramic work in many gift shops around the country, and even at roadside stands all across Guanacaste.

You might also run across **carved masks** ★★★ made by the indigenous **Boruca** people of southern Costa Rica. The small Boruca villages where these masks are carved are off the beaten path, but you will find them for sale at some of the better gift shops around the country. These full-size wood masks come in a variety of styles, both painted and unpainted, and run anywhere from $20 to $150, depending on the quality of workmanship. *Tip:* Don't be fooled. You'll see scores of mass-produced wooden masks at souvenir and gift shops around Costa Rica. Many are imported from Mexico, Guatemala, and Indonesia. Real Boruca masks are unique indigenous art works, and the better ones are signed by their carvers.

In addition to the masks, quite a bit of Costa Rican woodwork is for sale, but it's mainly mass-produced wooden bowls, napkin holders, placemats, and the like. A couple of notable exceptions include the work of **Barry Biesanz** ★★ (p. 154), whose excellent hardwood creations are sold at better gift shops around the country, and the unique, large-scale sculptures created and sold at the **Original Grand Gallery** (p. 354), in La Fortuna.

Coffee remains my favorite gift item. It's a great deal, it's readily available, and Costa Rican coffee is some of the best in the world. See the "Joe to Go" box on p. 153 for tips on buying **coffee** in Costa Rica.

Stop! Be Careful of What You Buy!

International laws prohibit trade in endangered wildlife, so don't buy any plants or animals, even if they're readily for sale. Do not buy any kind of sea-turtle products (including jewelry); wild birds; lizards, snakes, or cat skins; corals; or orchids (except those grown commercially). No matter how unique, beautiful, insignificant, or inexpensive it might seem, your purchase will directly contribute to the further hunting of these species.

In addition, be careful when buying wood products. Costa Rica's rainforest hardwoods are a finite and rapidly disappearing resource. Try to buy sustainably harvested woods, if at all possible.

A few other items worth keeping an eye out for include reproductions of **pre-Columbian gold jewelry** and **carved-stone figurines.** The former are available as either solid gold, silver, or gold-plated. The latter, although interesting, can be extremely heavy.

Across the country you'll find hammocks for sale. I personally find the Costa Rican **hammocks** a little crude and unstable. The same vendors usually have single-person hanging chairs, which are strung similarly to the full-size hammocks and are a better bet.

It's especially hard to capture the subtle shades and colors of the rainforests and cloud forests, and many a traveler has gone home thinking that his or her digital camera contained the full beauty of the jungle, only to see dozens of bright-green and random blurs when viewing the photos on a larger screen. To avoid this heartache, you might want to pick up a good **coffee-table book** or at least some **postcards** of the sights you want to remember forever and send them to yourself. For recommendations of coffee-table books, see "Costa Rica in Popular Culture" (p. 29).

Contemporary and **classic Costa Rican art** is another great option, both for discerning collectors and those looking for a unique reminder of their time in the country. San José has the greatest number of galleries and shops, but you will find good, well-stocked galleries in some of the more booming tourist destinations, including Liberia, Manuel Antonio, Jacó, and Monteverde. Throughout the book, I list my favorite galleries, and you can check out "Art & Architecture" (p. 26) for a list of some of the country's more prominent artists.

Finally, one item that you'll see at gift shops around the country is **Cuban cigars.** Although these are illegal to bring into the United States, they are perfectly legal and readily available in Costa Rica.

WHEN TO GO

Costa Rica's high season for tourism runs from late November to late April, which coincides almost perfectly with the chill of winter in the United States, Canada, and Great Britain, and includes Christmas, New

Year's, Easter, and most school spring breaks. The high season is also the dry season. If you want some unadulterated time on a tropical beach and a little less rain during your rainforest experience, this is the time to come. During this period (and especially around the Christmas holiday), the tourism industry operates at full tilt—prices are higher, attractions are more crowded, and reservations need to be made in advance.

Local tourism operators often call the tropical rainy season (May through mid-Nov) the "green season." The adjective is appropriate. At this time of year, even brown and barren Guanacaste province becomes lush and verdant. I personally love traveling around Costa Rica during the rainy season (but then again, I'm not trying to flee cold snaps in Canada). It's easy to find or at least negotiate reduced rates, there are far fewer fellow travelers, and the rain is often limited to a few hours each afternoon (although you can occasionally get socked in for a week at a time). **A drawback:** Some of the country's rugged roads become downright impassable without four-wheel-drive during the rainy season.

Weather

Costa Rica is a tropical country and has distinct wet and dry seasons. However, some regions are rainy all year, and others are very dry and sunny for most of the year. Temperatures vary primarily with elevations, not with seasons: On the coasts, it's hot all year; in the mountains, it can be cool at night any time of year. Frost is common at the highest elevations (3,000–3,600m/9,840–11,808 ft.).

Average Daytime High Temperatures & Rainfall in San José

	JAN	FEB	MAR	APR	MAY	JUNE	JULY	AUG	SEPT	OCT	NOV	DEC
TEMP (°F)	75	76	79	79	80	79	77	78	79	77	77	75
TEMP (°C)	24	24	26	26	27	26	25	26	26	25	25	24
DAYS OF RAIN	1.3	1.5	2.2	4.2	11.5	14.5	13.7	14.5	18.1	17.9	8.6	2.3

Generally, the **rainy season** (or "green season") is from May to mid-November. Costa Ricans call this wet time of year their winter. The **dry season,** considered summer by Costa Ricans, is from mid-November to April. In Guanacaste, the dry northwestern province, the dry season lasts several weeks longer than in other places. Even in the rainy season, days often start sunny, with rain falling in the afternoon and evening. On the Caribbean coast, especially south of Limón, you can count on rain year-round, although this area gets less rain in September and October than the rest of the country.

In general, the best time of year to visit weather-wise is in December and January, when everything is still green from the rains, but the sky is clear.

Holidays

Because Costa Rica is a Roman Catholic country, most of its holidays are church-related. The biggies are Christmas, New Year's, and Easter, which are all celebrated for several days. Keep in mind that Holy Week (Easter week) is the biggest holiday time in Costa Rica, and many families head for the beach. (This is the last holiday before school starts.) Also, there is no public transportation on Holy Thursday or Good Friday. Government offices and banks are closed on official holidays, transportation services are reduced, and stores and markets might also close.

Official holidays in Costa Rica include **January 1** (New Year's Day), **March 19** (St. Joseph's Day), Thursday and Friday of Holy Week, **April 11** (Juan Santamaría's Day), **May 1** (Labor Day), **June 29** (St. Peter and St. Paul Day), **July 25** (annexation of the province of Guanacaste), **August 2** (Virgin of Los Angeles's Day), **August 15** (Mother's Day), **September 15** (Independence Day), **October 12** (Discovery of America/Día de la Raza), **December 8** (Immaculate Conception of the Virgin Mary), **December 24** and **25** (Christmas), and **December 31** (New Year's Eve).

Calendar of Events

Some of the events listed here might be considered more of a *happening* than an event—there's not, for instance, a Virgin of Los Angeles PR Committee that readily dispenses information. If you don't see a contact number listed, your best bet is to call the **Costa Rican Tourist Board (ICT)** at ✆ **866/COSTA RICA** in the U.S. and Canada, or 2223-1733 in Costa Rica, or visit **www.visitcostarica.com**.

JANUARY

Copa del Café (Coffee Cup), San José. Matches for this international event on the junior tennis tour are held at the Costa Rica Country Club (www.copacafe.com; ✆ **2228-9333**). First week in January.

Fiestas of Palmares, Palmares. Perhaps the largest and best organized of the traditional *fiestas*, it includes bullfights, a horseback parade *(tope)*, and many concerts, carnival rides, and food booths (www.fiestaspalmares.com). First 2 weeks in January.

Fiestas of Santa Cruz, Santa Cruz, Guanacaste. This religious celebration honors the Black Christ of Esquipulas (a famous Guatemalan statue), featuring folk dancing, marimba music, and bullfights. Mid-January.

Fiesta of the Diablitos, Rey Curré village near San Isidro de El General. Boruca Indians wearing wooden devil and bull masks perform dances representative of the Spanish conquest of Central America; there are fireworks displays and an Indian handicrafts market. Late January.

MARCH

Día del Boyero (Oxcart Drivers' Day), San Antonio de Escazú. Colorfully painted oxcarts parade through this suburb of San José, and local priests bless the oxen. Second Sunday in March.

National Orchid Show, San José. Orchid growers throughout the world gather to show their wares, trade tales and secrets, and admire the hundreds of species on display. Contact the Costa Rican Tourist Board for the current year location and dates. Mid-March.

APRIL

Holy Week. Religious processions are held in cities and towns throughout the country. Week before Easter.

Juan Santamaría Day, Alajuela. Costa Rica's national hero is honored with parades, concerts, and dances. April 11.

MAY

Carrera de San Juan. The country's biggest marathon runs through the mountains, from the outskirts of Cartago to the outskirts of San José. May 17.

JULY

Fiesta of the Virgin of the Sea, Puntarenas. A regatta of colorfully decorated boats carrying a statue of Puntarenas's patron saint marks this festival. A similar event is held at Playa de Coco. Saturday closest to July 16.

Annexation of Guanacaste Day, Liberia. Tico-style bullfights, folk dancing, horseback parades, rodeos, concerts, and other events celebrate the day when this region became part of Costa Rica. July 25.

AUGUST

Fiesta of the Virgin of Los Angeles, Cartago. This is the annual pilgrimage day of the patron saint of Costa Rica. Many people walk from San José 24km (15 miles) to the basilica in Cartago. August 2.

Día de San Ramón, San Ramón. More than two dozen statues of saints from various towns are brought to San Ramón, where they are paraded through the streets. August 31.

SEPTEMBER

Costa Rica's Independence Day, celebrated all over the country. One of the most distinctive aspects of this festival is the nighttime marching band parades of children in their school uniforms, who play the national anthem on steel xylophones. September 15.

International Beach Clean-Up Day. This is a good excuse to chip in and help clean up the beleaguered shoreline of your favorite beach. Third Saturday in September.

OCTOBER

Fiesta del Maíz, Upala. At this celebration of corn, local beauty queens wear outfits made from corn plants. October 12.

Limón Carnival/Día de la Raza, Limón. A smaller version of Mardi Gras, complete with floats and dancing in the streets, commemorates Columbus's discovery of Costa Rica. Week of October 12.

NOVEMBER

All Souls' Day/Día de los Muertos, celebrated countrywide. Although it is not as elaborate or ritualized as in Mexico, most Costa Ricans take some time this day to remember the dead with flowers and trips to cemeteries. November 2.

DECEMBER

Fiesta de los Negritos, Boruca. Boruca Indians celebrate the feast day of their patron saint, the Virgin of the Immaculate Conception, with costumed dances and traditional music. December 8.

Día de la Pólvora, San Antonio de Belén and Jesús María de San Mateo. Fireworks honor Our Lady of the Immaculate Conception. December 8.

Las Posadas. Countrywide, children and carolers go door-to-door seeking lodging in a reenactment of Joseph and Mary's search for a place to stay. Begins December 15.

El Tope and Carnival, San José. The streets of downtown belong to horses and their riders in a proud recognition of the country's important agricultural heritage. The next day, those same streets are taken over by carnival floats, marching bands, and street dancers. December 26 and 27.

Festejos Populares, San José. Bullfights and a pretty respectable bunch of carnival rides, games of chance, and fast-food stands are set up at the fairgrounds in Zapote (www.festejospopulares.com). Last week of December.

SUGGESTED COSTA RICA ITINERARIES

C osta Rica is a compact yet varied destination with numerous natural attractions and a broad selection of exciting sights, scenery, adventure activities, and ecosystems. On a trip to Costa Rica, you can visit rainforests, cloud forests, and active volcanoes, and walk along miles of beautiful beaches on both the Pacific and Caribbean coasts. Adventure hounds will have their fill choosing from an exciting array of activities, and those looking for some rest and relaxation can soak in hot springs, get a volcanic mud wrap and massage, or simply grab a chaise lounge and a good book. Costa Rica's relatively small size makes visiting several destinations during a single vacation both easy and enjoyable.

The fastest and easiest way to get around the country is by small commuter aircraft. Most major destinations are serviced by regular commuter or charter airline companies. However, this does imply using San José or Liberia as periodic transfer hubs. If your connections don't line up, you may end up having to tack on nights in either of these cities at the start, end or in the middle of your trip. Luckily, sufficient flights and internal connections make this an infrequent occurrence.

Getting around Costa Rica by car is another excellent option. Most major destinations are between 2 and 5 hours from San José by car, and many can be linked together in a well-planned and convenient loop. For example, one popular loop links Arenal Volcano, Monteverde, and Manuel Antonio. However, be forewarned that the roads here are often in rough shape, many major roads and intersections are unmarked, and Tico drivers can be reckless and rude. See "By Car" under "Getting Around," in chapter 14 for more information on driving in Costa Rica.

The itineraries in this chapter are specific blueprints for fabulous vacations, and you can follow them to the letter. You might also decide to use one or more of them as an outline and then fill in some blanks with other destinations, activities, and attractions that strike your fancy from the rest of this book.

COSTA RICA REGIONS IN BRIEF

Costa Rica rightfully should be called "Costas Ricas" because it has two coasts: one on the Pacific Ocean and one on the Caribbean Sea. These two coasts are as different from each other as are the Atlantic and Pacific coasts of North America.

PREVIOUS PAGE: **A tourist zip-lining.**

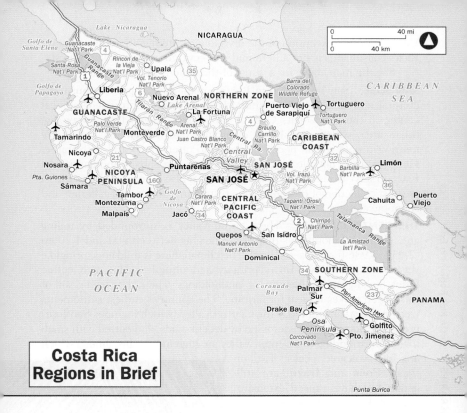

Costa Rica Regions in Brief

Costa Rica's **Pacific coast** is the most extensive, and is characterized by a rugged (although mostly accessible) coastline where forested mountains often meet the sea. It can be divided into four distinct regions—Guanacaste, the Nicoya Peninsula, the Central Coast, and the Southern Coast. There are some spectacular stretches of coastline, and most of the country's top beaches are here. This coast varies from the dry, sunny climate of the northwest to the hot, humid rainforests of the south.

The **Caribbean coast** can be divided into two roughly equal stretches. The remote northeast coastline is a vast flat plain laced with rivers and covered with rainforest; it is accessible only by boat or small plane. Farther south, along the stretch of coast accessible by car, are uncrowded beaches and even a bit of coral reef.

Bordered by Nicaragua in the north and Panama in the southeast, Costa Rica is only slightly larger than Vermont and New Hampshire combined. Much of the country is mountainous, with three major ranges running northwest to southeast. Among these mountains are several volcanic peaks, some of which are still active. Between the mountain ranges are fertile valleys, the largest and most populated of which is the Central

Valley. With the exception of the dry Guanacaste region, much of Costa Rica's coastal area is hot and humid and covered with dense rainforests.

See the map above for a visual of the regions detailed below.

SAN JOSÉ San José is Costa Rica's capital and its primary business, cultural, and social center—it sits fairly close to the country's geographical center, in the heart of its Central Valley (see below). It's a sprawling, urban area, with a population of around one million. Its streets are narrow, in poor repair, poorly marked and often chock-full with traffic. However, a few notable parks, like the Parque La Sabana and Parque del Este, do serve to lessen the urban blight. San José is home to the country's greatest collection of museums, fine restaurants and stores, galleries, and shopping centers.

THE CENTRAL VALLEY The Central Valley is surrounded by rolling green hills and mountains that rise to heights between 900 and 1,200m (2,952–3,936 ft.) above sea level. The climate here is mild and springlike year-round. It's Costa Rica's primary agricultural region, with coffee farms making up the majority of landholdings. The rich volcanic soil of this region makes it ideal for farming. The country's earliest settlements were in this area, and today the Central Valley (which includes San José) is densely populated, crisscrossed by decent roads, and dotted with small towns. Surrounding the Central Valley are high mountains, among which are four volcanic peaks. Two of these, **Poás** and **Irazú,** are still active and have caused extensive damage during cycles of activity in the past 2 centuries. Many of the mountainous regions to the north and to the south of the capital of San José have been declared national parks (Tapantí, Juan Castro, and Braulio Carrillo) to protect their virgin rainforests against logging.

GUANACASTE The northwestern corner of the country near the Nicaraguan border is the site of many of Costa Rica's sunniest and most popular **beaches,** including **Playa del Coco, Playa Hermosa, Playa Flamingo, Playa Conchal, Tamarindo,** and the **Papagayo Peninsula.** Scores of beach destinations, towns, and resorts are along this long string of

Tamarindo at sunset.

Playa Flamingo.

coastline. Because many foreigners have chosen to build beach houses and retirement homes here, Guanacaste has experienced considerable development over the years. You won't find a glut of Cancún-style high-rise hotels, but condos, luxury resorts, and golf courses have sprung up along the coastline here. Still, you won't be towel-to-towel with thousands of strangers. On the contrary, you can still find long stretches of deserted sands. However, more and more travelers are using Liberia as their gateway to Costa Rica, bypassing San José and the central and southern parts of the country entirely.

With about 165cm (65 in.) of rain a year, this region is by far the driest in the country and has been likened to west Texas. Guanacaste province is named after the shady trees that still shelter the herds of cattle roaming the dusty savanna here. In addition to cattle ranches, Guanacaste has semiactive volcanoes, several lakes, and one of the last remnants of tropical dry forest left in Central America. (Dry forest once stretched all the way from Costa Rica up to the Mexican state of Chiapas.)

PUNTARENAS & THE NICOYA PENINSULA   Just south of Guanacaste lies the Nicoya Peninsula. Similar to Guanacaste in many ways, the Nicoya Peninsula is nonetheless somewhat more inaccessible, and thus much less developed and crowded. However, this is already starting to change. The neighboring beaches of **Malpaís** and **Santa Teresa** are perhaps the fastest growing hot spots anywhere along the Costa Rican coast.

As you head south from Guanacaste, the region is similar in terms of geography, climate, and ecosystems, but begins to get more humid and moist. The forests are taller and lusher than those found in Guanacaste. The Nicoya Peninsula itself juts out to form the Golfo de Nicoya (Nicoya Gulf), a large, protected body of water. **Puntarenas,** a small fishing city, is the main port found inside this gulf, and one of the main commercial ports in all of Costa Rica. Puntarenas is also the departure point for the regular ferries that connect the Nicoya Peninsula to San José and most of mainland Costa Rica.

THE NORTHERN ZONE This inland region lies to the north of San José and includes rainforests, cloud forests, hot springs, the country's two most active volcanoes (**Arenal** and **Rincón de la Vieja**), **Braulio Carrillo National Park,** and numerous remote lodges. Because this is one of the few regions of Costa Rica without any beaches, it primarily attracts people interested in nature and active sports. **Lake Arenal** has some of the best windsurfing and kitesurfing in the world, as well as several good mountain-biking trails along its shores. The **Monteverde Cloud Forest,** perhaps Costa Rica's most internationally recognized attraction, is another top draw in this region.

THE CENTRAL PACIFIC COAST Because it's the most easily accessible coastline in Costa Rica, the central Pacific coast has a vast variety of beach resorts and hotels. **Playa de Jacó,** a beach just an hour or so drive from San José, attracts many sunbirds, charter groups, and a mad rush of Tico tourists every weekend. It is also very popular with young surfers, and has a distinct party vibe. **Manuel Antonio,** one of the most emblematic destinations in Costa Rica, is built up around a popular coastal national park, and caters to people looking to blend beach time and fabulous panoramic views with some wildlife viewing and active adventures. Heading south, past Manuel Antonio, you will encounter a wild coastal region where thick rainforests coat steep hillsides that lead down to the undeveloped and virtually undiscovered beaches of Dominical, Matapalo, Uvita and beyond. This region is also home to the highest peak in Costa Rica—**Mount Chirripó**—a beautiful summit, where frost is common.

THE SOUTHERN ZONE This hot, humid region is one of Costa Rica's most remote and undeveloped. It is characterized by dense rainforests, large national parks and protected areas, and rugged coastlines. Much of the area is uninhabited and protected in **Corcovado, Piedras Blancas,** and **La Amistad** national parks. A number of wonderful nature lodges are spread around the shores of the **Golfo Dulce** and along the **Osa Peninsula.** There's a lot of solitude to be found here, due in no small part to the fact that it's hard to get here and hard to get around. But if you like your ecotourism authentic and challenging, you'll find the southern zone to your liking.

THE CARIBBEAN COAST Most of the Caribbean coast is a wide, steamy lowland laced with rivers and blanketed with rainforests and banana plantations. The culture here is predominantly Afro-Caribbean, with many residents speaking an English or Caribbean patois. The northern

Corcovado.

section of this coast is accessible only by boat or small plane and is the site of **Tortuguero National Park,** which is known for its nesting sea turtles and riverboat trips. The towns of **Cahuita, Puerto Viejo,** and **Manzanillo,** on the southern half of the Caribbean coast, are increasingly popular destinations. The beautiful beaches and coastline here, as yet, have few large hotels. This area can be rainy, especially between December and April.

Sea turtle crawling from the beach to the sea in Tortuguero National Park.

COSTA RICA HIGHLIGHTS

The timing is tight, but this itinerary packs a lot into a typical weeklong vacation. This route takes you to a trifecta of Costa Rica's primary tourist attractions: Arenal Volcano, Monteverde, and Manuel Antonio. You can explore and enjoy tropical nature, take in some beach time, and experience a few high-adrenaline adventures.

DAY 1: ARRIVE & SETTLE INTO SAN JOSÉ

Arrive and get settled in **San José.** If your flight gets in early enough and you have time, head downtown and tour the **Museos del Banco Central de Costa Rica (Gold Museum)** ★★ (p. 130)

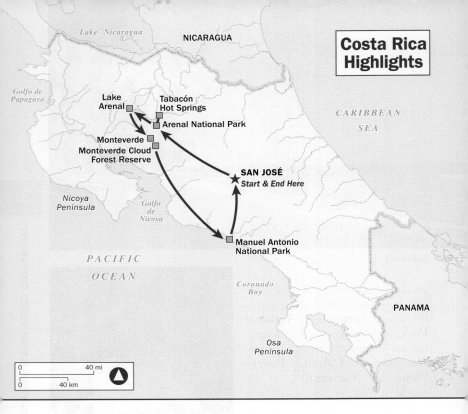

and the nearby **Museo de Jade Marco Fidel Tristán (Jade Museum)** ★ (p. 133).

☕ Fresh Fruit

As you walk around town, stop at one of the roadside stands or kiosks selling small bags of precut and prepared fruit. Depending on the season, you might find mango, pineapple, or papaya on offer. If you're lucky, they'll have *mamon chino*, an odd-looking golf ball-size fruit you might also know as *rambutan* or *litchi* nut.

Head over to the **Teatro Nacional (National Theater;** p. 158). If anything is playing that night, buy tickets for the show. For an elegant and delicious dinner, I recommend **Grano de Oro Restaurant** ★★★ (p. 147), a refined restaurant serving contemporary tropical cuisine with strong French, Italian and Fusion influences. Tables and chairs are set in and around an open-air central courtyard in this elegant neoclassical downtown hotel.

Streets of San José.

DAY 2: HOT STUFF ★★

Rent a car and head to the Arenal National Park and the **Arenal Volcano ★★** area. Hike the **Sendero Coladas (Lava Flow Trail) ★★**, which will take you onto and over a cooled-off lava flow. Spend the evening in the natural hot springs at the **Tabacón Grand Spa Thermal Resort ★★★** (p. 351), working out the kinks from the road and hike. (The

Tabacón Grand Spa Thermal Resort.

volcano may be technically dormant right now, but the natural hot springs are still working just fine.) I recommend reserving a massage or spa treatment in advance.

DAY 3: ADVENTURES AROUND ARENAL, ENDING IN MONTEVERDE ★★

Spend the morning doing something adventurous around Arenal National Park. Your options range from white-water rafting to mountain biking to horseback riding and then hiking to the Río Fortuna Waterfall. My favorite is the **canyoning** adventure offered by **Desafío Expeditions ★★** (p. 337). Allow at least 4 hours of

53

daylight to drive around **Lake Arenal** to **Monteverde.** Stop for a break at the **Lucky Bug Gallery** ★★ (p. 361), along the road between Tabacón and Nuevo Arenal, and an excellent place to shop for gifts, artwork, and souvenirs. Once you get to Monteverde, settle into your hotel and head for a drink and dinner at **Trio ★★★**.

DAY 4: MONTEVERDE CLOUD FOREST BIOLOGICAL RESERVE ★★★

Wake up early and take a guided tour of the **Monteverde Cloud Forest Biological Reserve ★★★** (p. 371). Spend the afternoon visiting several of the area's attractions, which might include any combination of the following: the **Butterfly Garden** ★ (p. 376), **Orchid Garden** ★★ (p. 377), **Monteverde Serpentarium** ★ (p. 376), **Frog Pond of Monteverde**, and the **Bat Jungle ★★★** (p. 376).

DAY 5: FROM THE TREETOPS TO THE COAST ★★★

Use the morning to take one of the **zip-line canopy tours** here. I recommend **Selvatura Park** ★★ (p. 374), which has a wonderful canopy tour, as well as other interesting exhibits. Be sure to schedule the tour early enough so that you can hit the road by noon for your drive to **Manuel Antonio National Park.** Settle into your hotel and head for a **sunset drink** at **Agua Azul** ★★ (p. 435), which offers up spectacular views over the rainforest to the sea. You can drop your car off at any point now and just rely on taxis and tours.

Hiking through Monteverde Cloud Forest.

DAY 6: MANUEL ANTONIO ★★

In the morning, take a boat tour of the **Damas Island estuary** (p. 425), and then reward yourself for all the hard touring so far with an afternoon lazing on one of the beautiful beaches inside **Manuel Antonio National Park ★★** (p. 417). If you just can't lie still, be sure to hike the loop trail through the rainforest here and around **Cathedral Point ★★**. Make reservations at **Milagro ★★★** (p. 436) for an intimate and relaxed final dinner in Costa Rica.

DAY 7: SAYING *ADIÓS*

Fly back to **San José** from the small Quepos airstrip. The short 20-minute flight should get you there in plenty of time to connect with your departing flight home. If you have extra time in the morning, feel free to head back into Manuel Antonio National Park, do some souvenir shopping, or simply relax by your hotel pool. You've earned it.

THE BEST UNDISCOVERED COSTA RICA

Despite Costa Rica's popularity and booming tourism industry, plenty of places are still off the beaten track. And believe me, you'll be richly rewarded for venturing down the road less traveled. Start your trip off with a rental car, which you can turn in after Montezuma. After that, you'll want to fly to Golfito and then arrange for a boat ride to Playa Zancudo.

DAY 1: RINCÓN DE LA VIEJA NATIONAL PARK

Not nearly as popular as the Arenal Volcano, the **Rincón de la Vieja volcano,** along with its namesake **national park ★★** (p. 219), is an underexplored gem. The park features challenging and rewarding hikes, sulfur hot springs, volcanic mud deposits, and stunning jungle waterfalls. My favorite hike here is a vigorous 2-hour trek to **Blue Lake and La Cangrejo Waterfall ★★** (p. 221), which leads to a beautiful forest waterfall emptying into a postcard-perfect turquoise lake. This is a great spot for a picnic lunch and a cool dip. If you have time and energy afterward, finish up with the relatively short and gentle **Las Pailas Loop ★**, which showcases the volcanic fumaroles and mud pots here.

DAY 2: HORSES, HIGH WIRES & HOT SPRINGS

You did plenty of hiking yesterday, so start this day off with something a little different. **Hacienda Guachipelín ★★** (p. 224) offers a range of adventure activities, including horseback riding, river tubing, two zip-line canopy tours, and a waterfall rappel canyoning

Playa Manuel Antonio in Manuel Antonio National Park.

tour (see p. 105 for more about canyoning), in addition to a gorgeous set of natural hot mineral springs set along the side of a jungle river.

DAY 3: GOING DEEP DOWN UNDER

Sitting on top of a massive cave system, **Barra Honda National Park** ★ (p. 319) is Costa Rica's top spot for spelunking. On a typical tour here, you'll descend into the depths of the **Terciopelo Cave** and visit the waterfalls and pools of **La Cascada.** After your visit here, drive to nearby **Playa Sámara,** about an hour away.

🍽 Gusto Beach
With tables set in the sand, and palm trees lit with rope lighting, **Gusto Beach** ★★ serves up excellent Italian fare, as well as fresh grilled fish and meats. See p. 323.

DAY 4: BEAUTIFUL BEACHES

The Nicoya Peninsula has many of the same charms and nearly as many miles of beach as Guanacaste, but far fewer crowds. Although the beach at **Playa Sámara** is nice enough, I recommend heading to neighboring gems **Playa Barrigona** ★★ (p. 318) and **Playa Carrillo** ★★ (p. 317). While in the area, be sure to sign up for an ultralight flight with the folks at the **Flying Crocodile** (p. 318).

DAYS 5 & 6: MONTEZUMA

Montezuma is a great place to mix more beach time with wildlife sightings and visits to some impressive waterfalls. While you can certainly hike to the foot of the **Montezuma Waterfall** ★★ (p. 299), I prefer visiting it as part of the **Waterfall Canopy Tour** ★ (p. 300). I recommend taking a horseback tour to

The Best Undiscovered Costa Rica

Barra Honda National Park 3
Hacienda Guachipelín 2
Montezuma 7
Pavones & Tiskita
   Jungle Lodge 9
Playa Barrigona 4
Playa Carillo 6
Playa Sámara 5
Playa Zancudo 8
Rincón de la Vieja
   National Park 1
Wilson Botanical Gardens 10

El Chorro Falls ★ (p. 299). If you time it right, you can ride home along the beach as the sun sets.

While in Montezuma, visit the **Cabo Blanco Absolute Nature Reserve** ★★ (p. 300), the country's first officially protected area. The main trail inside this park, **Sendero Sueco,** leads to the gorgeous and almost always deserted beach **Playa Balsita.** A trip to Cabo Blanco Nature Reserve can easily be combined with a **kayaking and snorkel tour** to the little cemetery island located just off the village of **Cabuya.**

🍲 Playa de los Artistas
Fresh grilled fish and other Mediterranean fare are the specialty at **Playa de los Artistas** ★★★. If you're limber, slide onto a tatami mat set around one of the low tables closest to the water. See p. 305.

Cangrejo Waterfall.

Waterfall at the Rincon de la Vieja National Park.

DAYS 7, 8 & 9: PLAYA ZANCUDO

You'll want to finish off this itinerary at one of Costa Rica's most remote and undiscovered beach towns. Playa Zancudo is a sleepy little town on a narrow strip of land set between the Golfo Dulce and a saltwater mangrove lagoon. While here, you can go **sportfishing** (p. 494), head over to nearby **Pavones** (p. 502) for a surf session, or take an organized tour with **Zancudo Boat Tours** (p. 500).

One of the better day trips heads southward to **Tiskita Jungle Lodge ★★** (p. 504), which has a wonderful network of trails through the rainforests and fruit orchards of its private reserve. Any wannabe botanist will also want to allot enough time for a visit to the **Wilson Botanical Gardens ★★★** (p. 493), the most impressive botanical gardens in the entire country.

🍺 Sol y Mar ★★

Sol y Mar is a quintessential beach bar. Stop by for a drink, meal, or friendly game of horseshoes. See p. 502.

THE BEST COSTA RICA ADVENTURES

Costa Rica is a major adventure-tourism destination. The following basic itinerary packs a lot of adventure into a single week; if you want to do some surfing, mountain biking, or kayaking, just schedule some more time in. If you're into windsurfing or kiteboarding, you'll definitely want to visit Lake Arenal between December and March.

Rio Fortuna Waterfall, Eco Termales Hot Springs and Tabacon Grand Spa Thermal Resort

Tabacón Hot Springs

La Fortuna

Seluatura Park

Monteverde Cloud Forest Reserve

Pacuare River Rafting Tour

SAN JOSÉ Start & End Here

Lake Nicaragua

NICARAGUA

CARIBBEAN SEA

Golfo de Papagayo

Nicoya Peninsula

Golfo de Nicoya

PACIFIC OCEAN

Coronado Bay

PANAMA

Osa Peninsula

The Best Costa Rica Adventures

DAY 1: STARTING IN SAN JOSÉ

You'll probably have a little time to explore and enjoy **San José.** Head first to the **Plaza de la Democracia ★** (p. 151), where you'll find the **Museos del Banco Central de Costa Rica ★★** (p. 130) and the **Teatro Nacional** (p. 158). Take a break for an afternoon coffee at **Alma de Café ★** (p. 146) inside the Teatro Nacional. For a typical Costa Rican dinner with a spectacular view of the city lights, head to **Tiquicia** (p. 177), which is in the hills above Escazú.

DAYS 2 & 3: GET WET & WILD

Take a 2-day white-water rafting expedition on the **Pacuare River** with **Ríos Tropicales ★★** (p. 216). You'll spend the night at their remote riverside lodge. When you finish running the Pacuare, they will transport you (as part of the trip package) to **La Fortuna ★★.**

Sunset in Coco Beach, Guanacaste.

DAY 4: WATERFALLS TWO WAYS

Go waterfall rappel canyoning with **Desafío Expeditions** ★★ (p. 337) in the morning, and then hop on a horse or a mountain bike in the afternoon and be sure to stop at the **Río Fortuna Waterfall** ★ (p. 343). Take the short hike down to the base of the falls and take a dip in one of the pools there. In the evening, check out the hot springs at **Eco Termales** ★★ (p. 349).

DAY 5: GETTING THERE IS PART OF THE FUN & ADVENTURE

Arrange a **taxi-to-boat-to-horse** transfer over to **Monteverde** with **Desafío Expeditions** ★★ (p. 337). Settle in quickly at your hotel and take a zip-line **canopy tour** in the afternoon. I recommend **Selvatura Park** ★★, which is located near the **Santa Elena Cloud Forest Reserve.** Finally, if you've got the energy, take a **night tour** through either the Santa Elena or Monteverde Cloud Forest Reserve.

DAY 6: MONTEVERDE CLOUD FOREST BIOLOGICAL RESERVE ★★★

Wake up early and head back to take a daytime guided tour of the **Monteverde Cloud Forest Biological Reserve ★★★.** Be sure to bring a packed lunch. After the guided tour, spend the next few hours continuing to explore the trails through the cloud forest here. See if you can spot a **quetzal** (p. 103) on your own. Then transfer back to San José.

Teatro Nacional, San José.

DAY 7: SQUEEZE IN A SOCCER GAME BEFORE SPLITTING

Unfortunately, you'll most likely be on an early flight home from **San José.** If you have a few hours to kill, head for a **hike** or **jog** around Parque La Sabana or, better yet, try to join a **pickup soccer game** (p. 135) here.

COSTA RICA FOR FAMILIES

Costa Rica is a terrific destination for families. If you're traveling with very small children, you might want to stick close to the beaches, or consider a large resort with a children's program and babysitting services. But for slightly older kids and teens, particularly those with an adventurous streak, Costa Rica is a lot of fun. Youngsters and teens, especially those with strong adventurous and inquisitive traits, will do great here. The biggest challenges to families traveling with children are travel distances and the logistical trials of moving around within the country, which is why I recommend flying in and out of Liberia and basing yourself in Guanacaste.

DAY 1: ARRIVE IN GUANACASTE

Fly directly into **Liberia.** From here it's a drive of 30 to 45 minutes to any of the area's many beach resorts, especially around the **Papagayo Peninsula.** I recommend the **Four Seasons**

Resort ★★★ (p. 236) or the **Andaz Peninsula Papagayo Resort ★★★** (p. 236). Both have excellent children's programs and tons of activity and tour options. Alternatively, **Hotel Playa Hermosa Bosque del Mar ★★★** (p. 237) is a lovely beachfront boutique hotel on a quiet and calm section of Playa Hermosa.

DAY 2: GET YOUR BEARINGS & ENJOY YOUR RESORT

Get to know and enjoy the facilities and activities offered up at your hotel or resort. Spend time on the beach or at the pool. Build some sand castles, or get involved in a pickup game of beach volleyball or soccer. In the afternoon, go on a **sail and snorkel cruise.** If you choose a large resort, check out the **children's program** and any scheduled **activities** or **tours** that particularly appeal to anyone in the family. Feel free to adapt the following days' suggestions accordingly.

DAY 3: RAFTING ON THE COROBICÍ RIVER

The whole family will enjoy a **rafting tour** on the gentle Corobicí River. **Rios Tropicales ★★** (p. 216) offers leisurely trips that are appropriate for all ages, except infants. In addition to the slow float and occasional mellow rapids, there'll be plenty of opportunities to watch birds and other wildlife along the way. If you're here between late September and late February, book a **turtle tour** (p. 112) at nearby **Playa Grande** for the evening. The whole family will be awe-struck by the amazing spectacle of a giant leatherback turtle digging a nest and laying its eggs.

A sailboat cruise on the Pacific Ocean.

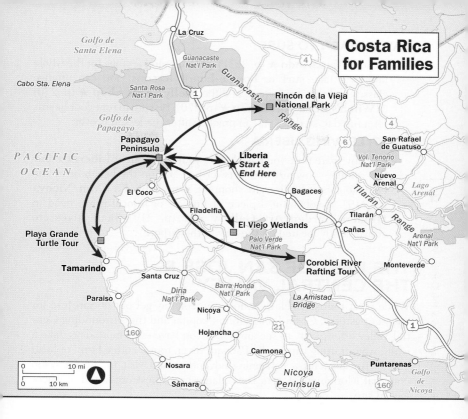

Costa Rica for Families

DAY 4: EL VIEJO WETLANDS ★★

Located about an hour or so drive from the Guancaste beaches, **El Viejo Wildlife Refuge & Wetlands ★★** (p. 253) is a fabulous day-trip destination. Set on a massive old farmstead bordering Palo Verde National Park, this private reserve offers up some of Guancaste's best wildlife viewing, with boat trips on the Tempisque river and safari-style open Jeep tours through surrounding wetlands, as well as a host of other cultural and adventure tour options. Lunch is served in a beautiful, century-old farm building.

DAY 5: HACIENDA GUACHIPELÍN ★

It's time to head for the hills, which are mostly volcanoes in this neck of the woods. Book a full-day Adventure Pass outing to **Hacienda Guachipelín** (p. 224), near **Rincón de la Vieja National Park.** Older and more adventurous children can go river tubing, do a **horseback ride,** or take one of the zip-line **canopy tours.** Younger children should get a kick out of visiting the working farm and cattle ranch, butterfly garden, and serpentarium here.

DAY 6: LEARN TO SURF

Head to **Tamarindo ★** (p. 263) for the day and arrange for the whole family to take **surf** or **boogie-board lessons.** You can arrange classes and rent equipment at either **Kelly's Surf Shop ★** (p. 270) or **Witch's Rock Surf Camp ★** (p. 270). Be sure to rent your boards for a full day, so that you can practice after the lesson is over.

DAY 7: LEAVING LIBERIA

Use any spare time you have before your flight out of **Liberia** to buy last-minute souvenirs and gifts, or just laze on the beach or by the pool. Your best bet for gift shopping is probably **La Gran Nicoya** (p. 219). If you want a piece of fine art or a local print, head to **Hidden Garden Art Gallery ★★** (p. 219). Both stores are conveniently located on the way to the airport.

THE BEST OF SAN JOSÉ & THE CENTRAL VALLEY

While most tourists seek to almost immediately get out of San José for greener pastures, Costa Rica's vibrant capital and the surrounding Central Valley offer plenty to see and do. If you have even more days, take a white-water rafting trip on the Pacuare River, tour a coffee farm, or head out to Turrialba for a canyoning adventure and visit to the Guayabo National Monument, Costa Rica's largest and best excavated archaeological site.

DAY 1: GETTING TO KNOW THE CITY

Start your day on the **Plaza de la Cultura.** Visit the **Museos del Banco Central de Costa Rica ★★** (p. 130), and see if you can get tickets for a performance that night at the **Teatro Nacional** (p. 158). From the Plaza de la Cultura, stroll up Avenida Central to the **Museo Nacional de Costa Rica (National Museum) ★★** (p. 132).

☕ Restaurante Nuestra Tierra

It's a bit of a tourist trap, sure, but this Costa Rican-themed restaurant is very, very conveniently located, and does serve up dependable local cuisine. Order a *casado* (the local blue-plate special) for lunch. It will come served on a banana leaf spread over a large platter, by a waiter or waitress in traditional rural garb from a bygone era. See p. 145.

After lunch, head over to the nearby **Museo de Jade Marco Fidel Tristán (Jade Museum) ★★** (p. 133). As soon as you're finished taking in all this culture, some shopping at the open-air stalls at the **Plaza de la Democracia** (p. 151) is in order.

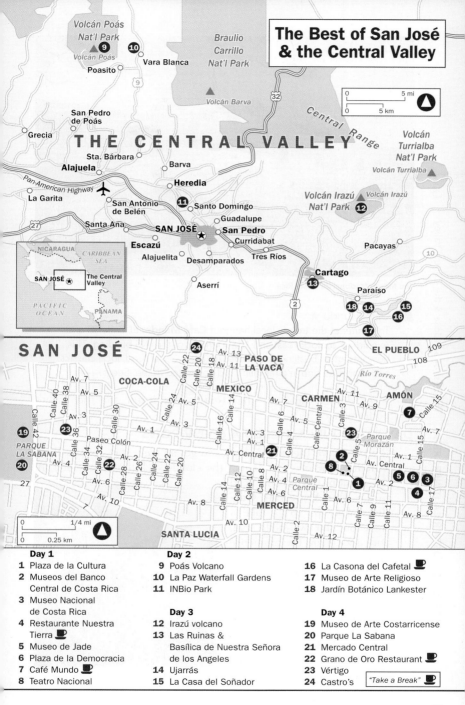

The Best of San José & the Central Valley

Day 1
1 Plaza de la Cultura
2 Museos del Banco Central de Costa Rica
3 Museo Nacional de Costa Rica
4 Restaurante Nuestra Tierra ☕
5 Museo de Jade
6 Plaza de la Democracia
7 Café Mundo ☕
8 Teatro Nacional

Day 2
9 Poás Volcano
10 La Paz Waterfall Gardens
11 INBio Park

Day 3
12 Irazú volcano
13 Las Ruinas & Basílica de Nuestra Señora de los Angeles
14 Ujarrás
15 La Casa del Soñador

16 La Casona del Cafetal ☕
17 Museo de Arte Religioso
18 Jardín Botánico Lankester

Day 4
19 Museo de Arte Costarricense
20 Parque La Sabana
21 Mercado Central
22 Grano de Oro Restaurant ☕
23 Vértigo
24 Castro's   "Take a Break" ☕

The Museo Nacional de Costa Rica.

☕ Café Mundo ★
Try dinner at the trendy local hangout **Café Mundo,** at Calle 15 and Avenida 9, 3 blocks east and 1 block north of the INS building. This busy and often bustling spot serves up a mix of bar food, local classics and World Cuisine in a rambling old converted home. See p. 147.

After dinner, head to the **Teatro Nacional** for the night's performance.

DAY 2: ALAJUELA, HEREDIA & ENVIRONS

Rent a car for the next 2 days, and get an early start for the **Poás Volcano ★★** (p. 182), before the clouds sock the main crater in.

After visiting the volcano, head to **La Paz Waterfall Gardens ★★** (p. 181). Take a walk on the waterfall trail, and also enjoy the immense butterfly garden and lively hummingbird garden. This is a good place to have lunch. On your way back to San José, you'll be making a loop through the hills of **Heredia,** with a stop at **INBio Park ★★** (p. 189). In addition to being a fascinating natural-history

Hummingbird in La Paz Waterfall Gardens.

museum, INBio Park also has a wonderful collection of intriguing animal sculptures by Costa Rican artist José Sancho.

DAY 3: CARTAGO & THE OROSI VALLEY

You'll still have that rental car. Start today off taking in the scenery from 3,378m (11,080 ft.) at the top of the **Irazú volcano ★★** (p. 200). After admiring the view and hiking the crater trail, head down into the country's first capital city, visiting **Las Ruinas ★** (p. 198) and the **Basílica de Nuestra Señora de los Angeles ★★★** (p. 199), on your way out to the Orosi valley. As you drive the loop road around Lake Cachí, stop in **Ujarrás** (p. 202) to see the ruins of Costa Rica's oldest church, and to check out the sculpture offerings at **La Casa del Soñador** (p. 203).

🍽 La Casona del Cafetal
Set on expansive grounds overlooking Lake Cachí, this place serves good, traditional Costa Rican fare. If the weather's nice, grab an outdoor patio table with a view. See p. 204.

After lunch, be sure to visit the **Museo de Arte Religioso ★** (p. 203) in the town of **Orosi** (p. 201) itself. On your way home, stop at **Jardín Botánico Lankester ★★** (p. 201), one of the top botanical gardens in the country. Upon returning to San José, you can return the rental car and rely on taxis in the city, as it's much easier and less stressful than dealing with downtown traffic.

DAY 4: MORE CITY SIGHTS & SHOPPING

Spend this day further exploring the capital. Start by heading out on Paseo Colón to the **Museo de Arte Costarricense (Costa Rican Art Museum) ★★** (p. 133). Be sure to spend some time in their wonderful open-air sculpture garden. After visiting the museum, take a stroll around the expansive downtown **Parque La Sabana** (p. 135). Intrepid travelers can also do some shopping at the **Mercado Central ★** (p. 155).

🍽 Grano de Oro Restaurant
For your final dinner, splurge a bit and head to the elegant **Grano de Oro Restaurant ★★★**, located inside the boutique hotel of the same name. See p. 147. Serving up sophisticated contemporary cuisine using the freshest local ingredients, this is arguably the best restaurant in the city.

After dinner take a late-night turn on the dance floor at **Castro's ★** (p. 159) or **Vértigo ★★** (p. 160).

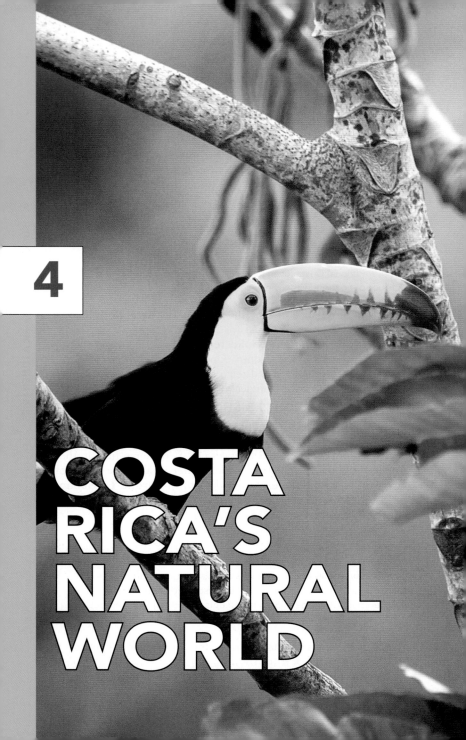

4

COSTA RICA'S NATURAL WORLD

Costa Rica occupies a central spot in the isthmus that joins North and South America. For millennia, this land bridge served as a migratory thoroughfare and mating ground for species native to the once-separate continents. It was also where the Mesoamerican and Andean pre-Columbian indigenous cultures met.

In any one spot in Costa Rica, temperatures remain relatively constant year-round. However, they vary dramatically according to altitude, from tropically hot and steamy along the coasts to below freezing at the highest elevations. These variations in altitude, temperature, and precipitation give rise to a wide range of ecosystems and habitats, which are described in "Costa Rica's Ecosystems," below.

For its part, the wide variety of ecosystems and habitats has blessed the country with a unique biological bounty. More than 10,000 identified species of plants, 880 species of birds, 9,000 species of butterflies and moths, and 500 species of mammals, reptiles, and amphibians are found here. For detailed information on some of the more common or evocative representatives of Costa Rica's flora and fauna, see "Costa Rican Wildlife," p. 81.

Thankfully, for both visitors and the local flora and fauna alike, nearly one-quarter of Costa Rica's entire landmass is protected either as part of a national park or private nature reserve. This chapter includes descriptions of the most important national parks and bioreserves in the country.

THE LAY OF THE LAND
Costa Rica's Ecosystems
RAINFORESTS

Costa Rica's **rainforests** are classic tropical jungles. Some receive more than 508cm (200 in.) of rainfall per year, and their climate is typically hot and humid, especially in the lowland rainforests. Trees grow tall and fast, fighting for sunlight in the upper reaches. In fact, life and foliage on the forest floor are surprisingly sparse. The action is typically 30m (98 ft.) up, in the canopy, where long vines stream down, lianas climb up, and bromeliads grow on the branches and trunks of towering hardwood trees.

Some of the more indicative rainforest tree species include the parasitic strangler fig and the towering ceiba, which can reach some 60m (196 ft.). Mammal species that call the Costa Rican rainforests home include the jaguar, three-toed sloth, all four native monkey species, and Baird's Tapir, while some of the more prominent birds you might spot are the Harpy eagle, Scarlet Macaw, and the Chestnut-mandibled toucan.

FACING PAGE: **Rainbow toucan.**

You can find these lowland rainforests along the southern Pacific coast and Osa Peninsula, as well as along the Caribbean coast. **Corcovado, Cahuita,** and **Manuel Antonio** national parks, as well as the **Gandoca–Manzanillo Wildlife Refuge,** are fine examples of lowland rainforests. Examples of mid-elevation rainforests include the **Braulio Carillo National Park** and the forests around **La Selva** and the **Puerto Viejo de Sarapiquí** region, and those around the **Arenal Volcano** and **Lake Arenal** area.

Smiling baby brown-throated three-toed sloth in the mangrove.

TROPICAL DRY FORESTS

In a few protected areas of Guanacaste (chapter 8), you will still find examples of the otherwise vanishing **tropical dry forest.** During the long and pronounced dry season (late Nov to late Apr), no rain relieves the unabated heat. In an effort to conserve much-needed water, the trees drop their leaves but bloom in a riot of color: Purple jacaranda, scarlet *poró,* and brilliant orange flame-of-the-forest are just a few examples. Then during the rainy season, this deciduous forest is transformed into a lush and verdant landscape.

Other common dry forest trees include the Guanacaste, with its broad, shade canopy, and distinctive pochote, whose trunk is covered with thick, broad thorns.

Because the foliage is less dense than that found in cloud forests and rainforests, dry forests are excellent places to view a variety of wildlife. Howler monkeys are commonly seen in the trees, and coatimundi, puma, and coyote roam the ground. Costa Rica's remaining dry forests are most prominently found in **Santa Rosa, Guanacaste, Rincón de la Vieja,** and **Palo Verde** national parks.

CLOUD FORESTS

At higher altitudes, you'll find Costa Rica's famed **cloud forests.** Here the steady flow of moist air meets the mountains and creates a nearly constant mist. Epiphytes—resourceful plants that live cooperatively on the branches and trunks of other trees—grow abundantly in the cloud forests, where they must extract moisture and nutrients from the air. Because cloud forests are found in generally steep, mountainous terrain, the canopy here is lower and less uniform than in lowland rainforests, providing better chances for viewing elusive fauna.

The remarkable **Resplendent Quetzal** is perhaps the most famous and sought-after denizen of Costa Rica's cloud forests, but you'll also find a broad and immense variety of flora and fauna, including a dozen or more hummingbird species, wild cats, monkeys, reptiles, and amphibians. **Orchids,** many of them epiphytic, thrive in cloud forests, as do mosses, ferns, and a host of other plants, many of which are cultivated and sold as common household plants throughout the rest of the world.

Costa Rica's most spectacular cloud forest is the **Monteverde Cloud Forest Biological Reserve** (p. 371), but you can also explore Monteverde's neighbor, the **Santa Elena Cloud Forest Reserve** (p. 372), or, much closer to San José, the **Los Angeles Cloud Forest Reserve** (p. 103).

MANGROVES & WETLANDS

Along the coasts, primarily where river mouths meet the ocean, you will find extensive **mangrove forests, wetlands,** and **swamps.** Mangroves, in particular, are an immensely important ecological phenomenon. Around the intricate tangle of mangrove roots exists one of the most diverse and rich ecosystems on the planet. All sorts of fish and crustaceans live in the brackish tidal waters. Many larger salt water and open-ocean fish species begin life in the nutrient rich, and relatively safe and protected environment of a mangrove swamp.

Mangrove swamps and wetlands are havens for and home to scores of water birds: **cormorants, magnificent frigate birds, pelicans, kingfishers, egrets, ibises,** and **herons.** The larger birds tend to nest up high in the canopy, while the smaller ones nestle in the underbrush. And in the waters, **caimans** and **crocodiles** cruise the maze of rivers and unmarked canals.

Mangrove forests, swamps, and wetlands exist all along both of Costa Rica's coasts. Some of the prime areas that can be explored by tourists include the areas around the **Sierpe river mouth** and **Diquis**

Resplendent Quetzal.

Magenta-throated Woodstar.

The Irazú Volcano in Cordillera Central.

delta near **Drake Bay** (p. 463), the **Golfo Dulce** (p. 490) in the southern zone, **Palo Verde National Park** and the **Tempisque river** basin in Guanacaste (chapter 8), and the **Gandoca–Manzanillo Wildlife Refuge** on the Caribbean coast (chapter 13).

PÁRAMO

At the highest reaches, the cloud forests give way to **elfin forests** and **páramos.** More commonly associated with the South American Andes, a páramo is characterized by a variety of tundralike shrubs and grasses, with a scattering of twisted, windblown trees. Reptiles, rodents, and raptors are the most common residents here, and since the vegetation is so sparse, they're often easier to spot. **Mount Chirripó, Chirripó National Park** (p. 453), and the **Cerro de la Muerte** (**Mountain of Death;** p. 459) are the principal areas of páramo in Costa Rica.

VOLCANOES

Costa Rica is a land of high volcanic and seismic activity. The country has three major **volcanic mountain ranges,** and many of the volcanoes are still active, allowing visitors to experience the awe-inspiring sight of steaming **fumaroles,** sky-lighting **eruptions,** and intense **lava flows** during their stay. In ecological terms, cooled-off lava flows are fascinating laboratories, where you can watch pioneering lichen and mosses eventually give way to plants and shrubs, and eventually trees and forests.

The top spot to see volcanic activity is, hands-down, the **Arenal Volcano** (chapter 10). Another reliable place to see steady volcanic activity, in the form of mud pots, fumaroles, and hot springs, is in the **Rincón de la Vieja National Park** (p. 221). Closer to San José, the **Poás** (p. 182) and **Irazú volcanoes** (p. 200) are both currently active, although relatively quiet.

COSTA RICA'S TOP NATIONAL PARKS & BIORESERVES

Costa Rica has 34 national parks and reserves, protecting more than 12 percent of the country. Scores of other private reserves bring the total protected area up to some 23 percent of the national territory. Many of these national parks are undeveloped tropical forests, with few services or facilities available for visitors. Others, however, offer easier access to their wealth of natural wonders.

Most of the national parks charge a $12 to $15 per-person per-day fee for any foreigner, although Chirripó National Park costs $18 per day and Isla del Coco is $50 per day. Costa Ricans and foreign residents continue to pay much, much less. At parks where camping is allowed, an additional charge of around $2 per person per day usually applies.

This section is not a complete listing of all of Costa Rica's national parks and protected areas, but rather a selective list of those parks that are of greatest interest and accessibility. You'll find detailed information about food and lodging options near some of the individual parks in the regional chapters that follow.

If you're looking for a camping adventure or an extended stay in one of the national parks, I recommend **Santa Rosa, Rincón de la Vieja, Chirripó,** or **Corcovado.** Any of the others are better suited for day trips or guided hikes, or in combination with your travels around the country.

For more information, call the national parks information line at ℂ **1192,** or the main office at ℂ **2283-8004.**

The Central Valley

GUAYABO NATIONAL MONUMENT
This is the country's only significant pre-Columbian archaeological site. It's believed that Guayabo supported a population of about 10,000 people some 3,000 years ago. The park is set in a forested area rich in flora and fauna, although the ruins are quite small and limited when compared to sites in Mexico, Guatemala, and South America. **Location:** 19km (12 miles) northeast of Turrialba, which is 53km (33 miles) east of San José. See p. 206.

A petroglyph at Guayabo National Monument.

IRAZÚ VOLCANO NATIONAL PARK ★ Irazú Volcano is the highest (3,378m/11,080 ft.) of Costa Rica's four active volcanoes and a popular day trip from San José. A paved road leads right up to the crater, and the lookout also has a view of both the Pacific and the Caribbean on a clear day. The volcano last erupted in 1963 on the same day U.S. President John F. Kennedy visited the country. The park has picnic tables, restrooms, an information center, and a parking area. **Location:** 55km (34 miles) east of San José. See p. 200.

POÁS VOLCANO NATIONAL PARK ★★ Poás is the other active volcano close to San José. The main crater is more than 1.6km (1 mile) wide, and it is constantly active with fumaroles and hot geysers. I slightly prefer Poás to Irazú because Poás is surrounded by dense cloud forests and has some nice gentle trails to hike. Although the area around the volcano is lush, much of the growth is stunted due to the gases and acid rain. On January 8, 2009, a 6.1 magnitude earthquake struck Costa Rica, with its epicenter very close to Poás. The park was closed for several days, and an uptick in volcanic activity was noted. The park still sometimes closes when the gases get too feisty. The park has picnic tables, restrooms, and an information center. **Location:** 37km (23 miles) northwest of San José. See p. 182.

Guanacaste & the Nicoya Peninsula

PALO VERDE NATIONAL PARK A must for bird-watchers, Palo Verde National Park is one of Costa Rica's best-kept secrets. This part of the Tempisque River lowlands supports a population of more than 50,000 waterfowl and forest bird species. Various ecosystems here include mangroves, savanna brush lands, and evergreen forests. The park has camping facilities, an information center, and some rustic, dorm-style accommodations at the Organization for Tropical Studies (OTS) research station here. **Location:** 200km (124 miles) northwest of San José. Be warned that the park entrance is 28km (17 miles) off the highway down a very rugged dirt road; it's another 9km (5½ miles) to the OTS station and campsites. For more information, call the OTS (www.threepaths.co.cr; ✆ **2524-0607**). See chapter 8.

RINCÓN DE LA VIEJA NATIONAL PARK ★★ This large tract of parkland experiences high volcanic activity, with numerous fumaroles and geysers, as well as hot springs, cold pools, and mud pots. You'll find excellent hikes to the upper craters and to several waterfalls. You should hire a guide for any hot-spring or mud-bath expeditions; inexperienced visitors have been burned. Camping is permitted at two sites, each with an information center, a picnic area, and restrooms. **Location:** 266km (165 miles) northwest of San José. See p. 219.

SANTA ROSA NATIONAL PARK ★ Occupying a large section of Costa Rica's northwestern Guanacaste province, Santa Rosa has the country's largest area of tropical dry forest, important turtle-nesting sites, and the historically significant La Casona (p. 227) monument. The beaches are pristine and have basic camping facilities, and the waves make them quite popular with surfers. An information center, a picnic area, and restrooms are at the main campsite and entrance. Additional campsites are located on almost always deserted and entirely undeveloped beaches here. **Location:** 258km (160 miles) northwest of San José. For more information, you can call the park office at ✆ **2666-5051.** See p. 227.

The Nicoya Peninsula

BARRA HONDA NATIONAL PARK Costa Rica's only underground national park, Barra Honda features a series of limestone caves that were once part of a coral reef some 60 million years ago. Today the caves are home to millions of bats and impressive stalactite and stalagmite formations. Only Terciopelo Cave is open to the public. A camping area, restrooms, and an information center are here, as well as trails through the surrounding tropical dry forest. **Location:** 335km (208 miles) northwest of San José. See p. 319.

Monteverde Cloud Forest Biological Reserve.

The Northern Zone

ARENAL NATIONAL PARK ★★   This park, created to protect the eco-system that surrounds Arenal Volcano, has a couple of good trails, and a prominent lookout point that is extremely close to the volcano. The main trail here will take you through a mix of transitional forest, rainforest, and open savanna, before an invigorating scramble over a massive rock field formed by a cooled-off lava flow. **Location:** 129km (80 miles) northwest of San José. See p. 339.

CAÑO NEGRO NATIONAL WILDLIFE REFUGE ★   A lowland swamp and drainage basin for several northern rivers, Caño Negro is excellent for bird-watching. A few basic cabinas and lodges are in this area, but the most popular way to visit is on a combined van and boat trip from the La Fortuna/Arenal area. **Location:** 20km (12 miles) south of Los Chiles, near the Nicaraguan border. See chapter 10.

MONTEVERDE CLOUD FOREST BIOLOGICAL RESERVE ★★★   This private reserve might be the most famous patch of forest in Costa Rica. It covers some 10,520 hectares (26,000 acres) of primary forest, mostly mid-elevation cloud forest, with a rich variety of flora and fauna. Epiphytes thrive in the cool, misty climate. The most renowned resident is the spectacular Resplendent Quetzal. The park has a well-maintained trail system, as well as some of the best-trained and experienced guides in the country. Nearby you can visit both the Santa Elena and Sendero Tranquilo reserves. **Location:** 167km (104 miles) northwest of San José. See p. 371.

Central Pacific Coast

CARARA NATIONAL PARK ★★   Located just off the highway near the Pacific coast, on the road to Jacó, this is one of the best places in Costa

Rica to see scarlet macaws. Several trails run through the park, including one that is wheelchair accessible. The park is comprised of various ecosystems, ranging from rainforests to transitional forests to mangroves. **Location:** 102km (63 miles) west of San José. See p. 399.

CHIRRIPÓ NATIONAL PARK ★★ Home to Costa Rica's tallest peak, 3,761m (12,336-ft.) Mount Chirripó, Chirripó National Park is a hike, but on a clear day you can see both the Pacific Ocean and the Caribbean Sea from its summit. In addition to the summit, a number of trails here lead to beautiful rock formations and small lakes—all well above tree line. **Location:** 151km (94 miles) southeast of San José. See p. 453.

MANUEL ANTONIO NATIONAL PARK ★★ Though relatively small, Manuel Antonio is the most popular national park and supports the largest number of hotels and resorts. This lowland rainforest is home to a healthy monkey population, including the endangered squirrel monkey. The park is best known for its splendid beaches. **Location:** 129km (80 miles) south of San José. See p. 417.

The Southern Zone

CORCOVADO NATIONAL PARK ★★★ The largest single block of virgin lowland rainforest in Central America, Corcovado National Park receives more than 508cm (200 in.) of rain per year. It's increasingly popular but still very remote. (It has no roads; only dirt tracks lead into it.) Scarlet macaws live here, as do countless other Neotropical species, including two of the country's largest cats, the puma and the endangered jaguar. Camping facilities and trails are throughout the park. **Location:** 335km (208 miles) south of San José, on the Osa Peninsula. See p. 480.

The Caribbean Coast

CAHUITA NATIONAL PARK ★★ A combination land and marine park, Cahuita National Park protects one of the few remaining living coral reefs in the country. The topography here is lush lowland tropical rainforest. Monkeys and numerous bird species are common. **Location:** On the Caribbean coast, 42km (26 miles) south of Limón. See p. 532.

TORTUGUERO NATIONAL PARK ★★ Tortuguero National Park has been called the Venice of Costa Rica due to its maze of jungle canals that meander through a dense lowland rainforest. Small boats, launches, and canoes carry visitors through these waterways, where caimans, manatees, and numerous bird and mammal species are common. The extremely endangered great green macaw lives here. Green sea turtles nest on the

A boat tour leaving Tortuguero village.

beaches here every year between June and October. The park has a small but helpful information office and some well-marked trails. **Location:** 258km (160 miles) northeast of San José. See p. 517.

HEALTH, SAFETY & ETIQUETTE IN THE WILD

Much of what is discussed here is common sense. For more detailed information, see "Staying Healthy," in chapter 14. Although most tours and activities are safe, risks are involved in any adventure activity. Know and respect your own physical limits before undertaking any strenuous activity. Be prepared for extremes in temperature and rainfall and for wide fluctuations in weather. A sunny morning hike can quickly become a cold and wet ordeal, so it's usually a good idea to carry along some form of rain gear when hiking in the rainforest, or to have a dry change of clothing waiting at the end of the trail. Be sure to bring along plenty of sunscreen when you're not going to be covered by the forest canopy.

If you do any backcountry packing or camping, remember that it really *is* a jungle out there. Don't go poking under rocks or fallen branches. Snakebites are very rare, but don't do anything to increase the odds. If you encounter a snake, stay calm, don't make any sudden movements, and *do not* try to touch the snake. Also avoid swimming in major rivers unless a guide or local operator can vouch for their safety. Although white-water sections and stretches in mountainous areas are generally safe, most mangrove canals and river mouths in Costa Rica support healthy crocodile and caiman populations.

Bugs and bug bites will probably be your greatest health concern in the Costa Rican wilderness, and even they aren't as big of a problem as you might expect. Mostly, bugs are an inconvenience, although mosquitoes can carry malaria or dengue (see "Staying Healthy," in chapter 14, for more information). A strong repellent and proper clothing minimize both the danger and the inconvenience; you might also want to bring along some cortisone or Benadryl cream to soothe itching. *And remember:* Whenever you enter and enjoy nature, you should tread lightly and try not to disturb the natural environment. The popular slogan well known to most campers certainly applies here: "Leave nothing but footprints; take nothing but memories." If you must take home a souvenir, take photos. Do not cut or uproot plants or flowers. Pack out everything you pack in, and *please* do not litter.

Searching for Wildlife

Animals in the forests are predominantly nocturnal. When they are active in the daytime, they are usually elusive and on the watch for predators. Birds are easier to spot in clearings or secondary forests than they are in primary forests. Unless you have lots of experience in the Tropics, your best hope for enjoying a walk through the jungle lies in employing a trained and knowledgeable guide. (By the way, if it's been raining a lot and the trails are muddy, a good pair of rubber boots comes in handy. These are usually provided by the lodges or at the sites, where necessary.)

Here are a few helpful hints:

- **Listen.** Pay attention to rustling in the leaves; whether it's monkeys up above or *pizotes* (coatimundi) on the ground, you're most likely to hear an animal before seeing one.

- **Keep quiet.** Noise will scare off animals and prevent you from hearing their movements and calls.

- **Don't try too hard.** Soften your focus and allow your peripheral vision to take over. This way you can catch glimpses of motion and then focus in on the prey.

- **Bring binoculars.** It's also a good idea to practice a little first to get the hang of them. It would be a shame to be fiddling around and staring into space while everyone else in your group oohs and aahs over a magnificent quetzal.

- **Dress appropriately.** You'll have a hard time focusing your binoculars if you're busy swatting mosquitoes. Light, long pants and long-sleeved shirts are your best bet. Comfortable hiking boots are a real boon, except where heavy rubber boots are necessary. Avoid loud colors; the better you blend in with your surroundings, the better your chances are of spotting wildlife.

- **Be patient.** The jungle isn't on a schedule. However, your best shots at seeing forest fauna are in the very early morning and late afternoon hours.

- **Read up.** Familiarize yourself with what you're most likely to see. Most nature lodges and hotels have a copy of a few wildlife field guides, although it's always best to have your own. A good all-around book to use is Carrol Henderson's "The Field Guide to the Wildlife of Costa Rica."

RESPONSIBLE TOURISM

Costa Rica is one of the planet's prime ecotourism destinations. Many of the hotels, isolated nature lodges, and tour operators around the country are pioneers and dedicated professionals in the sustainable tourism field. Many other hotels, lodges, and tour operators are honestly and earnestly jumping on the bandwagon and improving their practices, while still others are simply "green-washing," using the terms "eco," "green," and "sustainable" in their promo materials, but doing little real good in their daily operations.

In 2014, Costa Rica was ranked 54th globally in the Environmental Performance Index (EPI; http://epi.yale.edu). This is not a particularly impressive feat given the country's image and marketing strategy. Despite its reputation, the substantial amount of good work being done, and ongoing advances being made in the field, Costa Rica is by no means an ecological paradise free from environmental and social threats. Untreated sewage is dumped into rivers, bays, oceans, and watersheds at an alarming rate. Child labor and sexual exploitation are common, and certain sectors of the tourism trade only make these matters worse.

Over the last decade or so, Costa Rica has taken great strides toward protecting its rich biodiversity, however. Thirty years ago, it was difficult to find a protected area anywhere, but now more than 11 percent of the country is protected within the national park system. Another 10 to 15 percent of the land enjoys moderately effective preservation as part of private and public reserves, Indian reserves, and wildlife refuges and corridors. Still, Costa Rica's precious tropical hardwoods continue to be harvested at an alarming rate, often illegally, while other primary forests are clear-cut for short-term agricultural gain. Many experts predict that Costa Rica's unprotected forests could be gone within the early part of this century.

Recycling is beginning to gather momentum in Costa Rica. More and more you will see separate bins for plastics, glass, and paper on town and city streets, at national parks, and at the country's more sustainable hotels and restaurants. Your hotel will be your best bet for finding a place to deposit recyclable waste, especially if you choose a hotel that has instituted sustainable practices.

While you can find hotels and tour operators using comprehensive sustainable practices all across Costa Rica—even in the San José metropolitan area—a few prime destinations are particular hot spots for sustainable tourism practices. Of note are the remote and wild Osa Peninsula and Golfo Dulce area of southern Costa Rica, the rural northern zone that includes both Monteverde and the Arenal Volcano and Lake Arenal attractions, and the underdeveloped Caribbean coast, with the rainforest canals of Tortuguero, Cahuita National Park, and the Manzanillo-Gandoca Wildlife Refuge.

In addition to focusing on wildlife viewing and adventure activities in the wild, ecolodges in these areas tend to be smaller, often lacking televisions, air-conditioning, and other typical luxury amenities. The more remote lodges usually depend largely or entirely on small solar and hydro plants for their power consumption. That said, some of these hotels and lodges provide levels of comfort and service that are quite luxurious.

In Costa Rica, the government-run tourism institute (ICT) provides a sustainability rating of a host of hotels and tour agencies under its **Certificate of Sustainable Tourism Program (CST).** You can look up the ratings at the website www.turismo-sostenible.co.cr.

Bear in mind that this program is relatively new and the list is far from comprehensive. Many hotels and tour operators in the country haven't completed the extensive review and rating process. Moreover, die-hard ecologists find some of these listings and the criteria used somewhat suspect. Still, this list and rating system is a good start, and is improving and evolving constantly.

A parallel program, **"The Blue Flag,"** is used to rate specific beaches and communities in terms of their environmental condition and practices. The Blue Flags are reviewed and handed out annually. Current listings of Blue Flag-approved beaches and communities can be found at www.visitcostarica.com.

See individual chapters for recommendations on the hotels and lodges that I consider leaders in sustainable tourism practices in Costa Rica. As I mentioned earlier, more and more hotels are continuing to adopt sustainable and ethical tourism practices.

While sustainable tourism options are widespread in Costa Rica, organic and sustainably grown fruits and vegetables (as well as coffee) are just beginning to become available. Very few restaurants feature organic produce, although that is starting to change.

If you're not booking your hotel, tours, and transportation by yourself, you might want to consider using a tour agency that has earned high marks in this area. In Costa Rica, **Horizontes ★★** (www.horizontes. com; ✆ **888/786-8748** in the U.S. and Canada, or 2222-2022 in Costa Rica) has garnered particularly high marks from several rating agencies and organizations. Other exemplary operators include **Costa Rica Expeditions ★★** (www.costaricaexpeditions.com; ✆ **2257-0766**) and **Costa Rica Sun Tours ★** (✆ **866/271-6263** in the U.S. and Canada, or 2296-7757 in Costa Rica).

In addition, those looking for a taste of what many think "the real" Costa Rica should consider booking through **ACTUAR ★★** (www.actuar costarica.com; ✆ **866/393-5889** in the U.S., or 2290-7514 in Costa Rica). This organization groups together a network of small, rural lodges and tour operators. In many cases, accommodations are quite rustic. Bunk beds and thin foam mattresses are common. However, all the hotels, lodges, and tour operators are small-scale and local. In many cases, they are family operations. If you want a true taste of typical, rural Costa Rica, traveling with ACTUAR is a great way to go.

Finally, another great way to make your tourism experience more sustainable is to volunteer. For specific information on volunteer options in Costa Rica, see "Study & Volunteer Programs," in chapter 4, "The Best Special-Interest Trips."

Beyond the country's hotels, tour operators, and volunteer options, it's worth noting here that the local commuter airline **Nature Air** (www. natureair.com; ✆ **800/235-9272** in the U.S. and Canada, or 2299-6000) has been a pioneer in the field. In 2004, Nature Air became the first certified carbon-neutral airline on the planet, and it continues to supplement its own sustainable practices with contributions to reforestation and conservation programs.

COSTA RICAN WILDLIFE

For such a small country, Costa Rica is incredibly rich in biodiversity. With just .03 percent of the earth's landmass, the country is home to some 5 percent of its biodiversity. Whether you come to Costa Rica to check 100 or more species off your lifetime list, or just to escape from the rat race for a week or so, you'll be surrounded by a rich and varied collection of flora and fauna.

In many instances, the prime viewing recommendations should be understood within the reality of actual wildlife viewing. Most casual visitors and even many dedicated naturalists will never see a wild cat or elusive kinkajou. However, anyone working with a good guide should be able to see a broad selection of Costa Rica's impressive flora and fauna. The information that follows is meant to be a selective introduction to some of what you might see.

Scores of good field guides are available; two of the best general guides are **"The Field Guide to the Wildlife of Costa Rica,"** by Carrol Henderson, and **"Costa Rica: Traveller's Wildlife Guides,"** by Les Beletsky. Bird-watchers will want to pick up one or both of the following two books: **"A Guide to the Birds of Costa Rica,"** by F. Gary Stiles and Alexander Skutch, and **"Birds of Costa Rica,"** by Richard Garrigues and Robert Dean. Other specialized guides to mammals, reptiles, insects, flora, and more can be found at Zona Tropical (www.zona-tropical.net), which is a Costa Rican-based publishing house that specializes in field guides and wildlife books.

See also "Bugs, Bites & Other Wildlife Concerns" in chapter 14.

FAUNA

Mammals

Costa Rica has nearly 250 species of mammals. Roughly half of these are bats. While it is very unlikely that you will spot a wildcat, you have good odds of catching a glimpse of a monkey, coatimundi, peccary, or sloth, and any number of bats.

Jaguar

Jaguar (Panthera onca) This cat measures from 1 to 1.8m (3½–6 ft.) plus tail and is distinguished by its tan/yellowish fur with black spots. Often called simply *tigre* (tiger) in Costa Rica. Jaguars are classified as nocturnal, although some say it would be more accurate to describe them as crepuscular, most active in the periods around dawn and dusk. **Prime Viewing:** Major tracts of primary and secondary forest in Costa Rica, as well as some open savannas; the greatest concentration

Ocelot

Baird's Tapir

Three-Toed Sloth

Mantled Howler Monkey

Red-Backed Squirrel Monkey

is in Corcovado National Park (p. 480) on the Osa Peninsula. However, jaguars are endangered and extremely hard to see in the wild.

Ocelot (Leopardus pardalis) Known as *manigordo*, or "fat paws," in Costa Rica, the tail of this small cat is longer than its rear leg, which makes for easy identification. Ocelots are mostly nocturnal, and they sleep in trees. **Prime Viewing:** Forests in all regions of Costa Rica, with the greatest concentration found on the Osa Peninsula.

Baird's Tapir (Tapirus bairdii) The Baird's Tapir is the largest land mammal in Costa Rica. An endangered species, tapirs are active both day and night, foraging along riverbanks, streams, and forest clearings. It is called *danta* or *macho de monte* in Spanish. **Prime Viewing:** Tapirs can be found in wet forested areas, particularly on the Caribbean and south Pacific slopes.

Three-Toed Sloth (Bradypus variegates) The larger and more commonly sighted of Costa Rica's two sloth species, the three-toed sloth has long, coarse, brown-to-gray fur and a distinctive eye-band. Each foreleg has three long, sharp claws. Except for brief periods to defecate, these slow-moving creatures are entirely arboreal. **Prime Viewing:** Low- and middle-elevation forests in most of Costa Rica. While sloths can be found in a wide variety of trees, they are most commonly spotted in the relatively sparsely leaved Cecropia (p. 93).

Mantled Howler Monkey (Alouatta palliate) The highly social mantled howler monkey, or *mono congo*, grows to 56cm (22 in.) in size and often travels in groups of 10 to 30. The loud roar of the male can be heard as far as 1.6km (1 mile) away. **Prime Viewing:** Wet and dry forests across Costa Rica. Almost entirely arboreal, they tend to favor the higher reaches of the canopy.

Red-Backed Squirrel Monkey (Saimiri oerstedii) The smallest and friskiest of Costa Rica's monkeys, the red-backed squirrel monkey, or *mono titi,* is also its most endangered. Active in the daytime, these monkeys travel in small to midsize groups. Squirrel monkeys do not have a prehensile (grasping) tail. **Prime Viewing:** Manuel Antonio National Park and Corcovado National Park.

Central American Spider Monkey (Ateles geoffroyi) Known as both *mono araña* and *mono colorado* in Costa Rica, the spider monkey is one of the more acrobatic monkey species. A large monkey (64cm/25 in.) with brown or silvery fur, it has long thin limbs and a long prehensile tail. It is active both day and night, and travels in small to midsize bands or family groups. **Prime Viewing:** Wet and dry forests across Costa Rica.

Coatimundi (Nasua narica) The raccoonlike coatimundi can adapt to habitat disturbances and is often spotted near hotels and nature lodges. Active both day and night, they are social animals, often found in groups of 10 to 20. Coatimundi are equally comfortable on the ground and in trees. In Costa Rica, most folks refer to this animal by its indigenous name *pizote*. **Prime Viewing:** Found in a variety of habitats across Costa Rica, from dry scrub to dense forests, on the mainland as well as the coastal islands.

Coatimundi

Paca (Agouti paca) The paca, known as *tepezquintle* locally, is a nocturnal rodent that feeds on fallen fruit, leaves, and tubers it digs from the ground. It features dark brown to black fur on its back, usually with three to five rows of white spots. Its belly fur tends to be lighter in color. However, since this species is nocturnal, you're more likely to see its cousin, the diurnal agouti or *guatusa*, which in addition to being smaller, is of a lighter brown coloring, with no spots. **Prime Viewing:** Most often found near water throughout many habitats of Costa Rica, from river valleys to swamps to dense tropical forest.

Tayra (Eira Barbara) This midsize rodent is in the weasel family. Tayras run from dark brown to black, with a brown to tan head and neck. Long and low to the ground, they have a long, bushy tail. It is called *tolumuco* or *gato de monte* in Costa Rica. **Prime Viewing:** Tayras are found across the country, in forests as well as plain areas, and in trees and on the ground.

Collared Peccary (Tayassu tajacu) Called *saino* or *chancho de monte* in Costa Rica, the collared peccary is a black or brown piglike animal that travels in groups and has a strong musk odor. **Prime Viewing:** Low- and middle-elevation forests in most of Costa Rica.

Northern Tamandua (Tamandua Mexicana) The Northern Tamandua, or collared anteater (*oso hormiguero* in Spanish), grows up to 77cm (30 in.) long, not counting its thick tail, which can be as long as its body. It is active diurnally and nocturnally. **Prime Viewing:** Low- and middle-elevation forests in most of Costa Rica.

White-Faced Monkey (Cibus capucinus) Known as both *mono cariblanca* and *mono capuchin* in Costa Rica, the white-faced or capuchin monkey is a midsize species (46cm/18 in.) with distinct white fur around its face, head, and forearms. It can be found in forests all around the country and often travels in large troops or family groups. **Prime Viewing:** Wet and dry forests across Costa Rica.

Birds

Costa Rica has more than 880 identified species of resident and migrant birds. The variety of habitats and compact nature of the country make it a major bird-watching destination.

Jabiru Stork

LEFT: **Keel-Billed Toucan**; RIGHT: **Scarlet Macaw**

Jabiru Stork (Jabiru mycteria) One of the largest birds in the world, this stork stands 1.5m (5 ft.) tall and has a wingspan of 2.4m (8 ft.) and a 30cm-long (1-ft.) bill. An endangered species, the jabiru is very rare, with only a dozen or so nesting pairs in Costa Rica. **Prime Viewing:** The wetlands of Palo Verde National Park and Caño Negro Wildlife Reserve are the best places to try to spot the jabiru stork. The birds arrive in Costa Rica from Mexico in November and fly north with the rains in May or June.

Keel-Billed Toucan (Ramphastos sulfuratus) The rainbow-colored canoe-shape bill and brightly colored feathers make the keel-billed toucan a favorite of bird-watching tours. The toucan can grow to about 51cm (20 in.) in length. Aside from its bill coloration, it is similar in shape and coloring to the chestnut-mandibled toucan. Costa Rica also is home to several smaller toucanet and aracari species. **Prime Viewing:** Lowland forests on the Caribbean and north Pacific slopes, up to 1,200m (4,000 ft.).

Scarlet Macaw (Ara macao) Known as *guacamaya* or *lapa* in Costa Rica, the scarlet macaw is a long-tailed member of the parrot family. It can reach 89cm (35 in.) in length, including its long pointed tail. The bird is endangered over most of its range, mainly because it is coveted as a pet. Its loud squawk and rainbow-colored feathers are quite distinctive. **Prime Viewing:** Carara National Park, Corcovado National Park, and Piedras Blancas National Park.

Resplendent Quetzal (Pharomchrus mocinno) Arguably the most spectacular bird in Central America, the Resplendent Quetzal, of the trogon family, can grow to 37cm (15 in.). The males are distinctive, with bright red chests, iridescent blue-green coats, yellow bills, and tail feathers that can reach another 76cm (30 in.) in length. The females lack the long tail feathers and have a duller beak and less pronounced red chest. **Prime Viewing:** High-elevation wet and cloud forests, particularly in the Monteverde Cloud Forest Biological Reserve and along the Cerro de la Muerte.

Resplendent Quetzal

Magnificent Frigate Bird (Fregata magnificens) The magnificent frigate bird is a naturally agile flier, and it swoops (unlike other seabirds, it doesn't dive or swim) to pluck food

Magnificent Frigate Bird

Montezuma's Oropendola

Scarlet Rumped Tanager

Osprey

Violet Sabrewing

from the water's surface—or more commonly, it steals catch from the mouths of other birds. **Prime Viewing:** Often seen soaring high overhead, along the shores and coastal islands of both coasts.

Montezuma's Oropendola (Psarocolius Montezuma) Montezuma's oropendola has a black head, brown body, a yellow-edged tail, a large black bill with an orange tip, and a blue patch under the eye. These birds build long, teardrop-shaped hanging nests, often found in large groups. They have several distinct loud calls, including one that they make while briefly hanging upside down. **Prime Viewing:** Low and middle elevations along the Caribbean slope, and some sections of eastern Guanacaste.

Scarlet Rumped Tanager (Ramphocelus costaricensis) With a striking scarlet red patch on its backside, this is one of the most commonly sighted tanagers in Costa Rica. It is known locally as *sargento* or *sangre de toro*. For true ornithologists, a reclassification has divided the Costa Rican scarlet rumped tanagers into two distinct species, Passerini's Tanager, which is found on the Caribbean slope and lowlands, and Cherrie's Tanager, which is found along the Pacific slope and lowlands. **Prime Viewing:** Throughout the country, in lowland and mid-elevation areas.

Osprey (Pandion haliatus) This large (.6m/2-ft.-tall, with a 1.8m/6-ft. wingspan) brownish bird with a white head is also known as *gavilan pescador,* or "fishing eagle." In flight, the osprey's wings "bend" backward. **Prime Viewing:** Found in lowland coastal areas and wetlands throughout Costa Rica; seen flying or perched in trees near water. A small population is resident year-round, although most are winter migrants, arriving September to October and departing April to May.

Violet Sabrewing (Campylopterus hemileucurus) The largest hummingbird found in Costa Rica, the violet sabrewing shines a deep purple when the sun strikes it right. Its beak is long, thick, and gently curving. **Prime Viewing:** Mid- and higher-elevation cloud forests and rainforests countrywide.

Roseate Spoonbill (Ajaia ajaja) The roseate spoonbill is a large water bird, pink or light red in color and with a large spoon-shaped bill. Also known as *garza rosada* (pink heron). The species almost became extinct in the United States because its pink wing feathers were used to make fans. **Prime Viewing:** Found in low-lying freshwater and saltwater wetlands nationwide, although rare along the Caribbean coast and plains. Common on the Pacific coast, north-central lowlands, and in the Golfo de Nicoya and Golfo Dulce areas.

Cattle Egret (Bubulcus ibis) The cattle egret is a snow-white bird, with a yellow bill and irises, and black legs. It changes color for the breeding season: A yellowish buff color appears on the head, chest, and back, and a reddish hue emerges on the bill and legs. **Prime Viewing:** Found near cattle, or following tractors, throughout Costa Rica.

Boat-Billed Heron (Cochlearius cochlearius) The midsize boat-billed heron (about 51cm/20 in.) has a large black head, a large broad bill, and a rusty brown color. **Prime Viewing:** Throughout the country, near marshes, swamps, rivers, and mangroves.

Laughing Falcon (Herpetotheres cachinnans) The laughing falcon is also known as the *guaco* in Costa Rica. It gets its name from its loud, piercing call. This largish (56cm/22-in.) bird of prey's wingspan reaches an impressive 94cm (37 in.). It specializes in eating both venomous and nonvenomous snakes but will also hunt lizards and small rodents. **Prime Viewing:** Throughout the country, most commonly in lowland areas, near forest edges, grasslands, and farmlands.

Mealy Parrot (Amazona farinose) Called *loro* or *loro verde*, this large, vocal parrot is common in lowland tropical rainforests on both coasts. Almost entirely green, it has a touch of blue on the top of its head, and small red and blue accents on its wings. *Loro* means parrot, and *verde* means green, so you and locals alike may confuse this parrot with any number of other local species. **Prime Viewing:** Lowland rainforests on the Caribbean and Pacific coasts.

Ferruginous Pygmy Owl (Glaucidium brasilianum) Unlike most owls, this small (about 38cm/15-in.) grayish brown or reddish brown owl is most active during the day. **Prime Viewing:** In wooded areas, forest edges, and farmlands of low and middle elevations along the northern Pacific slope.

Clay-Colored Robin (Turdus grayi) In a country with such a rich variety of spectacularly plumaged bird species, this plain brown robin is an unlikely choice to be Costa Rica's national bird. However, it is extremely widespread and common, especially in urban areas of the Central Valley, and it has a wide range of pleasant calls and songs. Known locally as the *yiguirro*, it has uniform brown plumage, with a lighter brown belly and yellow bill. **Prime Viewing:** Low and middle elevations nationwide, especially in clearings, secondary forests, and amid human settlements.

Amphibians

Frogs and toads are actually some of the most beguiling, beautiful, and easy-to-spot residents of tropical forests. Of the 175 species of amphibians, a solid 85 percent are frogs.

Marine Toad (Bufo marinus) The largest toad in the Americas, the 20cm (8-in.) wart-covered marine toad is also known as the cane toad, or *sapo grande* (giant toad). Females are mottled in color, while males

Marine Toad

Red-Eyed Tree Frog

Green and Black Poison Dart Frog

are uniformly brown. These voracious toads have been known to eat small mammals, other toads, lizards, and just about any insect within range. They have a very strong chemical defense mechanism. Glands spread across their back and behind their eyes secrete a powerful toxin when threatened. **Prime Viewing:** Despite the misleading name, this terrestrial toad is not found in marine environments, but can be found in forests and open areas throughout Costa Rica.

Red-Eyed Tree Frog (Agalychnis callidryas) The colorful 7.6cm (3-in.) red-eyed tree frog usually has a pale or dark green back, sometimes with white or yellow spots, with blue-purple patches and vertical bars on the body, orange hands and feet, and deep red eyes. This nocturnal amphibian is also known as the gaudy leaf frog or red-eyed tree frog. **Prime Viewing:** This arboreal amphibian is most frequently found on the undersides of broad leaves, in low- and middle-elevation wet forests throughout Costa Rica. If you don't find this beautiful, distinctive-looking frog in the wild, you will certainly see its image on T-shirts and postcards.

Green and Black Poison Dart Frog (Dendrobates auratus) Also called the harlequin poison dart frog, the small green and black poison dart frog ranges between 2.5 and 4cm (1–1½ in.) in length. It has distinctive markings of iridescent green mixed with deep black. **Prime Viewing:** On the ground, around tree roots, and under fallen logs, in low- and middle-elevation wet forests on the Caribbean and southern Pacific slopes.

Reptiles

Costa Rica's 225 or so reptile species range from the frightening and justly feared fer-de-lance pit viper and massive American crocodile to a wide variety of less terrifying turtles and lizards. *Note:* Sea turtles are included in the "Sea Life" section below.

Fer-de-Lance

Fer-de-Lance (Bothrops atrox) Known as *terciopelo* in Costa Rica, the aggressive fer-de-lance can grow to 2.4m (8 ft.) in length. Beige, brown, or black triangles flank either side of the head, while the area under the head is a vivid yellow. These snakes begin life as arboreal but become increasingly terrestrial as they grow older and larger. **Prime Viewing:** Predominantly lower elevation forests, but has spread to almost all regions up to 1,300m (4,265 ft.), including towns and cities in agricultural areas.

Mussurana (Clelia clelia) This bluish black, brown, or grayish snake grows to 2.4m (8 ft.) in length. While slightly venomous, this snake has rear fangs and is of little danger to humans. In fact, it is prized and protected by locals, since its primary prey happens to be much more venomous pit vipers, like the fer-de-lance. **Prime Viewing:** Open forests, pastures, and farmlands across Costa Rica.

Tropical Rattlesnake (Crotalus durissus) Known as *cascabel* in Costa Rica, this pit viper has a triangular head, a pronounced ridge running along the middle of its back, and (of course) a rattling tail. It can reach 1.8m (6 ft.) in length. **Prime Viewing:** Mostly found in low elevation dry forests and open areas of Guanacaste.

Mussurana

Basilisk (Basiliscus vittatus) The basilisk can run across the water's surface for short distances on its hind legs, holding its body almost upright; thus its alternate name, "Jesus Christ lizard." **Prime Viewing:** In trees and on rocks located near water in wet forests throughout the country.

Tropical Rattlesnake

American Crocodile (Crocodylus acutus) Although an endangered species, environmental awareness and protection policies have allowed the massive American crocodile to mount an impressive comeback in recent years. While these reptiles can reach lengths of 6.4m (21 ft.), most are much smaller, usually less than 4m (13 ft.). **Prime Viewing:** Near swamps, estuaries, large rivers, and coastal lowlands, countrywide. Guaranteed viewing from the bridge over the Tárcoles River, on the coastal highway to Jacó and Manuel Antonio.

Basilisk

Litter Skink (Sphenomorphus cherriei) This small, brown lizard has a proportionally large head and neck, and short legs. A black stripe extends off the back of its eyes and down its sides, with a yellowish area below. **Prime Viewing:** Common on the ground and in leaf litter of low- and middle-elevation forests throughout the country.

Boa Constrictor (Boa constrictor) Adult boa constrictors (*bécquer* in Costa Rica) average about 1.8 to 3m (6–10 ft.) in length and weigh over 27kg (60 lb.). Their coloration camouflages them. Look for patterns of cream, brown, gray, and black ovals and diamonds. **Prime Viewing:** Low- and middle-elevation wet and dry forests, countrywide. They often live in the rafters and eaves of homes in rural areas.

LEFT: **American Crocodile;** RIGHT **Litter Skink**

Green Iguana (Iguana iguana) Despite its name, the green iguana comes in a range of coloring. Individuals can vary in color, ranging from bright green to a dull grayish green, with quite a bit of red and orange mixed in. Predominantly arboreal, it often perches on a branch overhanging a river and will plunge into the water when threatened. **Prime Viewing:** All lowland regions of the country, living near rivers and streams, along both coasts.

Slender Anole (Anolis [norops] limifrons) This thin, olive-colored lizard can reach 5.1cm (2 in.) in length. There are some 25 related species of *anolis* or *norops* lizards. **Prime Viewing:** Lowland rainforests nationwide.

Sea Life

Boasting over 1,290km (780 miles) of shoreline on both the Pacific and Caribbean coasts, Costa Rica has a rich diversity of underwater flora and fauna.

Whale Shark

Green Turtle

Leatherback Sea Turtle

Whale Shark (Rhincodon typus) Although the whale shark grows to lengths of 14m (45 ft.) or more, its gentle nature makes swimming with them a special treat for divers and snorkelers. **Prime Viewing:** Can occasionally be spotted off Isla del Caño, and more frequently off Isla del Coco.

Green Turtle (Chelonia mydas) A large sea turtle, the green turtle has a teardrop-shaped carapace that can range in color from dull green to dark brown. Adults reach some 1.5m (4.9 ft.) and weigh an average of 200kg (440 lb.). **Prime viewing:** Caribbean coast around Tortuguero National Park, from July through mid-October, with August through September their peak period.

Leatherback Sea Turtle (Dermochelys coriacea) The world's largest sea turtle (reaching nearly 2.4m/8 ft. in length and weighing more than 544kg/1,200 lb.), the leatherback sea turtle is now an endangered species. Unlike most other turtle species, the leatherback's carapace is not a hard shell, but rather a thick, leathery skin. **Prime Viewing:** Playa Grande, near Tamarindo, is a prime nesting site from early October through mid-February; also nests off Tortuguero in much lesser numbers from February through June, peaking during the months of March and April.

Olive Ridley Sea Turtle

Humpbacked Whale

Olive Ridley Sea Turtle (Lepidochelys olivacea) Also known as *tortuga lora*, the olive ridley sea turtle is the most common of Costa Rica's sea turtles, famous for its massive group nestings, or *arribadas*. **Prime Viewing:** Large *arribadas* occur from July through December, and to a lesser extent from January through June. Playa Nancite in Santa Rosa National Park and Playa Ostional, north of Nosara, are the prime nesting sites.

Bottle-Nosed Dolphins

Humpback Whale (Megaptera novaeangliae) The migratory humpbacked whale spends the winters in warm southern waters and has been increasingly spotted close to the shores of Costa Rica's southern Pacific coast. These mammals have black backs and whitish throat and chest areas. Females have been known to calve here. **Prime Viewing:** Most common in the waters off Drake Bay and Isla del Caño, from December through April.

Bottle-Nosed Dolphin (Tursiops truncates) A wide tail fin, dark gray back, and light gray sides identify bottle-nosed dolphins. Dolphins grow to lengths of 3.7m (12 ft.) and weigh up to 635kg (1,400 lb.). **Prime Viewing:** Along both coasts and inside the Golfo Dulce.

Moray Eel (Gymnothorax mordax) Distinguished by a swaying serpent-head and teeth-filled jaw that continually opens and closes, the moray eel is most commonly seen with only its head appearing from behind rocks. At night, however, it leaves its home along the reef to hunt for small fish, crustaceans, shrimp, and octopus. **Prime Viewing:** Rocky areas and reefs off both coasts.

Manta Ray (Manta birostris) The manta is the largest species of ray, with a wingspan that can reach 6m (20 ft.) and a body weight known to exceed 1,360kg (3,000 lb.). Despite its daunting appearance, the manta is quite gentle. If you are snorkeling or diving, watch for one of these extraordinary and graceful creatures. **Prime Viewing:** All along the Pacific coast.

Brain Coral (Diploria strigosa) The distinctive brain coral is named for its striking physical similarity to a human brain. **Prime Viewing:** Reefs off both coasts.

Invertebrates

Creepy-crawlies, biting bugs, spiders, and the like give most folks the chills. But this group, which includes moths, butterflies, ants, beetles, bees, and even crabs, features some of the most abundant, fascinating, and easily viewed fauna in Costa Rica. In fact, Costa Rica has over 300,000 recorded species of invertebrates, with more than 9,000 species of butterflies and moths alone.

Blue Morpho

Leafcutter Ants

Golden Silk Orb-weaver

Blue Morpho (Morpho peleides) The large blue morpho butterfly, with a wingspan of up to 15cm (6 in.), has brilliantly iridescent blue wings when opened. Fast and erratic fliers, they are often glimpsed flitting across your peripheral vision in dense forest. **Prime Viewing:** Countrywide, particularly in moist environments.

Leafcutter Ants (Atta cephalotes) You can't miss the miniature rainforest highways formed by these industrious red ants carrying their freshly cut payload. The ants do not actually eat the leaves, but instead feed off a fungus that grows on the decomposing leaves in their massive underground nests. **Prime Viewing:** Can be found in most forests countrywide.

Golden Silk Orb-Weaver (Nephila clavipes) The common Neotropical golden silk spider weaves meticulous webs that can be as much as .5m (2 ft.) across. The adult female of this species can reach 7.6cm (3 in.) in length, including the legs, although the males are tiny. The silk of this spider is extremely strong and is being studied for industrial purposes. **Prime Viewing:** Lowland forests on both coasts.

Mouthless Crab (Gecarcinus quadratus) The nocturnal mouthless crab is a distinctively colored land crab with bright orange legs, purple claws, and a deep black shell or carapace. **Prime Viewing:** All along the Pacific coast.

Sally Lightfoot Crab (Grapsus grapsus) Known simply as *cangrejo* or "crab," this is the most common crab spotted in Costa Rica. It is a midsize crab with a colorful carapace that can range from dark brown to deep red to bright yellow, with a wide variation in striations and spotting. **Prime Viewing:** On rocky outcroppings near the water's edge all along both coasts.

Mouthless Crab

Sally Lightfoot Crab

FLORA
Trees

Although it's hard work and easy to be confused, it's often rewarding to be able to identify specific trees within a forest. The following are some of the more prominent and important tree species you are likely to see in Costa Rica.

Ceiba (Ceiba pentandra) Also known as the kapok tree, the ceiba tree is typically emergent (its large umbrella-shape crown emerges above the forest canopy), reaching as high as 60m (197 ft.); it is among the tallest trees of Costa Rica's tropical forest. The ceiba tree has a thick columnar trunk, often with large buttresses. Sometimes called the silk cotton tree in English, the ceiba's seed pod produces a light, airy fiber that is resilient, buoyant, and insulating. Throughout history this fiber has been used for bedding, and as stuffing for pillows, clothing, and even life jackets. Ceiba trees may flower as infrequently as once every 5 years, especially in wetter forests. **Prime Viewing:** Tropical forests throughout Costa Rica.

Guanacaste (Enterolobium cyclocarpum) The Guanacaste gives its name to Costa Rica's northwestern-most province, and is the country's national tree. With a broad and pronounced crown, the Guanacaste can reach heights of over 39m (130 ft.), and its trunk can measure more than 1.8m (6 ft.) in diameter. Guanacaste is prized as a shade tree, and is often planted on pasture lands to provide relief to cattle from the hot

Ceiba

Guanacaste

LEFT: **Cecropia**; RIGHT: **Strangler Fig**

tropical sun. **Prime Viewing:** Low elevation forests and plains throughout Costa Rica. Most commonly viewed in the open plains and savannas of Guanacaste.

Strangler Fig (Ficus aurea)   This parasitic tree gets its name from the fact that it envelops and eventually strangles its host tree. The *matapalo,* or strangler fig, begins as an epiphyte, whose seeds are deposited high in a tree's canopy by bats, birds, or monkeys. The young strangler then sends long roots down to the earth. The sap is used to relieve burns. **Prime Viewing:** Primary and secondary forests countrywide.

Cecropia (Cecropia obtusifolia)   Several Cecropia (trumpet tree) species are found in Costa Rica. Most are characterized by large, handlike clusters of broad leaves, and a hollow, bamboolike trunk. They are "gap specialists," fast-growing opportunists that can fill in a gap caused by a tree fall or landslide. Their trunks are usually home to Aztec ants. **Prime Viewing:** Primary and secondary forests, rivers, and roadsides, countrywide.

Gumbo Limbo (Bursera simaruba)   The bark of the gumbo limbo is its most distinguishing feature: A paper-thin red outer layer, when peeled off the tree, reveals a bright green bark. In Costa Rica, the tree is called *indio desnudo* (naked Indian). In other countries, it is the "tourist tree." Both names refer to its reddish, flaking outer bark. The bark is used as a remedy for gum disease; gumbo limbo–bark tea allegedly alleviates hypertension. **Prime Viewing:** Primary and secondary forests, countrywide.

Flowers & Other Plants

Costa Rica has an amazing wealth of tropical flora, including some 1,200 orchid species, and over 2,000 bromeliad species.

Guaria Morada (Cattleya skinneri) The guaria morada orchid is the national flower of Costa Rica. Sporting a purple and white flower, this plant is also called the "Easter orchid" as it tends to flower between March and April each year. **Prime Viewing:** Countrywide from sea level to 1,220m (4,000 ft.). While usually epiphytic, it also is found as a terrestrial plant.

Guaria Morada

LEFT: Heliconia; RIGHT: Hotlips

Heliconia (Heliconia collinsiana)   More than 40 of the world's species of tropical heliconia are found in Costa Rica. The flowers of this species are darkish pink in color, and the underside of the plant's large leaves are coated in white wax. **Prime Viewing:** Low to middle elevations countrywide, particularly in moist environments.

Hotlips (Psychotria poeppigiana)   Related to coffee, hotlips is a forest flower that boasts thick red "lips" that resemble the Rolling Stones logo. The small white flowers (found inside the red "lips") attract a variety of butterflies and hummingbirds. **Prime Viewing:** In the undergrowth of dense forests countrywide.

Ornamental Red Ginger (Alpinia purpurata)   The red ginger plant has an impressive elongated red bract, often mistaken for the flower. Small white flowers actually emerge out of this bract. Originally a native to Indonesia, it is now quite common in Costa Rica, and is used as both an ornamental plant and cut flower. **Prime Viewing:** Countrywide, particularly in moist environments and gardens.

Poor Man's Umbrella (Gunnera insignis)   The poor man's umbrella, a broad-leaved rainforest ground plant, is a member of the rhubarb family. The massive leaves are often used, as the colloquial name suggests, for protection during rainstorms. **Prime Viewing:** Low- to middle-elevation moist forests countrywide. Commonly seen in Poás National Park and Braulio Carrillo National Park.

LEFT: Red Ginger; RIGHT: Poor Man's Umbrella

5

THE BEST SPECIAL-INTEREST TRIPS

Active and adventure travelers will have their hands full and hearts pumping in Costa Rica. From scuba diving with white tip sharks and manta rays off Isla de Caño to kiteboarding over the white caps on Lake Arenal, opportunities abound. And Costa Rica is not just for thrill seekers. You can enjoy a cloud forest tree top for the sight of a quetzal, or spend some time with a local family learning the language.

This chapter lays out your options, from tour operators who run multiactivity package tours that often include stays at ecolodges, to the best places in Costa Rica to pursue active endeavors (with listings of tour operators, guides, and outfitters that specialize in each). I also list some educational and volunteer travel options for those of you who desire to actively contribute to the country's social welfare, or assist Costa Rica in the maintenance and preservation of its natural wonders. For information on Costa Rica's top national parks and private reserves, see p. 72.

ORGANIZED ADVENTURE TRIPS

Because many travelers have limited time and resources, organized ecotourism or adventure-travel packages, arranged by tour operators in either Costa Rica or the United States, are a popular way of combining several activities. Bird-watching, horseback riding, rafting, and hiking can be teamed with, say, visits to Monteverde Cloud Forest Biological Reserve and Manuel Antonio National Park.

Traveling with a group has several advantages over traveling independently: Your accommodations and transportation are arranged, and most (if not all) meals are included in the package cost. If your tour operator has a reasonable amount of experience and a decent track record, you should proceed to each of your destinations quickly without snags and long delays. You'll also have the opportunity to meet like-minded souls who are interested in nature and active sports. Of course, you'll pay more for the convenience of having all your arrangements handled in advance.

In the best cases, group size is kept small (10–20 people), and tours are escorted by knowledgeable guides who are either naturalists or biologists. Be sure to ask about difficulty levels when you're choosing a tour. Most companies offer "soft adventure" packages that those in moderately

PREVIOUS PAGE: **Surfing in Tamarindo.**

good, but not phenomenal, shape can handle; others focus on more hard-core activities geared toward only seasoned athletes or adventure travelers.

Costa Rican Tour Agencies

Because many U.S.-based companies subcontract portions of their tours to established Costa Rican companies, some travelers like to cut out the middleman and set up their tours directly with these companies. That means that these packages are often less expensive than those offered by U.S. companies, but it doesn't mean they are cheap. You're still paying for the convenience of having your arrangements handled for you.

Scores of agencies in San José offer a plethora of options. These agencies can arrange everything from white-water rafting to sightseeing at one of the nearby volcanoes or a visit to a butterfly farm. Although it's generally quite easy to arrange a day trip at the last minute, other tours are offered only on set dates or when enough people are interested. Contact a few of the companies before you leave home and find out what tours they might be doing when you arrive. These local operators tend to be a fair share less expensive than their international counterparts, with 10-day tours generally costing in the neighborhood of $1,500 to $4,000 per person, not including airfare to Costa Rica.

ACTUAR ★★ (www.actuarcostarica.com; © **866/393-5889** in the U.S., or 2290-7514 in Costa Rica) is a great option for budget travelers and anyone looking to get a taste of real, rural Costa Rica. These folks bring together a network of small, rural lodges and tour operators. In many cases, accommodations are quite rustic. Bunk beds and thin foam mattresses are common. However, all the hotels, lodges, and tour operators are small-scale and local. In many cases, they are family operations.

Coast to Coast Adventures ★ (www.ctocadventures.com; © **2280-8054**) has a unique excursion involving no motor vehicles. The company's namesake 12-day trip spans the country, with participants traveling on rafts, by mountain bike, and on foot. Custom-designed trips (with a minimum of motorized transport) of shorter duration are also available. They also offer family-friendly adventure tours and student tours.

Costa Rica Expeditions ★★ (www.costaricaexpeditions.com; © **2221-6099**) offers everything from 10-day tours covering the entire country to 3-day/2-night and 2-day/1-night tours of Monteverde Cloud Forest Biological Reserve and Tortuguero National Park, where they run their own lodges. It also offers 1- to 2-day white-water rafting trips and other excursions. Its tours are some of the most expensive in the country, but it is the most consistently reliable outfitter as well (and its customer service is excellent). If you want to go out on your own, Costa Rica Expeditions can supply you with just transportation from place to place.

Costa Rica Sun Tours ★ (www.crsuntours.com; ☎ **866/271-6263** in the U.S. and Canada, or 2296-7757 in Costa Rica) offers a wide range of tours and adventures and specializes in multiday tours that include stays at small country lodges for travelers interested in experiencing nature.

Horizontes Nature Tours ★★, Calle 32 between Avenidas 3 and 5 (www.horizontes.com; ☎ **888/786-8748** in the U.S. and Canada, or 2222-2022 in Costa Rica), is not a specifically adventure-oriented operator, but it offers a wide range of individual, group, and package tours, including those geared toward active and adventure travelers, as well as families and even honeymooners. The company hires responsible and knowledgeable guides, and is a local leader in sustainable tourism practices.

Shameless Plug

In late 2012, I opened my own boutique travel agency, **Costa Rica Custom Trips** (www.costaricacustomtrips.com; ☎ **970/306-6112** in the U.S., or 2282-4973 in Costa Rica), specializing in customized itineraries and personalized trip planning.

International Tour Operators

These agencies and operators specialize in well-organized and coordinated tours. Many travelers prefer to have everything arranged and confirmed before arriving in Costa Rica, and this is a good idea for first-timers and during the high season. ***Be warned:*** Most of these operators are not cheap, with 10-day tours generally costing in the neighborhood of $3,000 to $5,000 per person, not including airfare to Costa Rica.

U.S.-BASED TOUR OPERATORS

Abercrombie & Kent ★★ (www.abercrombiekent.com; ☎ **800/554-7016**) is a luxury-tour company that offers upscale trips around the globe, and it has several tours of Costa Rica on its menu. It specializes in 8-day highlight tours hitting Monteverde, Arenal, and Tortuguero, and also has an excellent family tour. Service is personalized and the guides are top-notch.

Costa Rica Experts ★ (www.costaricaexperts.com; ☎ **800/827-9046** or 773/935-1009) offers a large menu of a la carte and scheduled departures, as well as day trips and adventure packages, and has decades of experience organizing tours to the country.

Nature Expeditions International ★ (www.naturexp.com; ☎ **800/869-0639**) specializes in educational and "low intensity adventure" trips tailored to independent travelers and small groups. These folks have a steady stream of programmed departures or can customize a trip to your needs.

Overseas Adventure Travel ★★ (www.oattravel.com; ℂ **800/ 955-1925**) provides good-value natural-history and "soft adventure" itineraries with optional add-on excursions. Tours are limited to a maximum of 16 people and are guided by naturalists. All accommodations are in small hotels, lodges, or tent camps, and they offer up very good bang for your buck.

Southern Explorations ★ (www.southernexplorations.com; ℂ **877/784-5400**) has a range of nature and adventure-oriented guided excursions, as well as set itinerary self-guided tours, for individuals, groups, and families.

Tauck ★★ (www.tauck.com; ℂ **800/788-7885**) is a soft-adventure company catering to higher-end travelers. They offer various Costa Rica options, including a family tour, and Costa Rica–Panama Canal package.

In addition to these companies, many environmental organizations, including the **Sierra Club** (www.sierraclub.org; ℂ **415/977-5522**) and the **Smithsonian Institute** (www.smithsonianjourneys.org; ℂ **855/ 330-1542**), regularly offer organized trips to Costa Rica.

U.K.-BASED TOUR OPERATORS

Imaginative Traveller (www.imaginative-traveller.com; ℂ **44/147-385-2316** outside the U.K.) is a good-value operator specializing in budget student, group, and family travel. Their offerings in Costa Rica focus on nature and adventure travel, and often include other countries in Central America. These trips range in duration from 12 to 32 days.

Journey Latin America ★ (www.journeylatinamerica.co.uk; ℂ **020/3432-9325** in the U.K.) is a large British operator specializing in Latin American travel. They offer a range of escorted tours around Latin America, including a few that touch down in Costa Rica. They also design custom itineraries, and often have excellent deals on airfare.

ACTIVITIES A TO Z

Each listing in this section describes the best places to practice a particular sport or activity and lists tour operators and outfitters.

Adventure activities and tourism, by their very nature, carry certain risks and dangers. Over the years, there have been several deaths and dozens of minor injuries in activities ranging from mountain biking to whitewater rafting to canopy tours. Here, I try to list only the most reputable and safest of companies. But you should know your limits and abilities, and don't try to exceed them.

Biking

Costa Rica has several significant regional and international touring races each year, but as a general rule the major roads are dangerous and inhospitable for cyclists. Roads are narrow and without a shoulder, and

PLANNING A COSTA RICAN wedding

Getting married in Costa Rica is simple and straightforward. In most cases, all you need are current passports. You'll have to provide some basic information, including a copy of each passport, your dates of birth, your occupations, your current addresses, and the names and addresses of your parents. Two witnesses are required to be present at the ceremony. If you're traveling alone, your hotel or wedding consultant will provide the required witnesses.

Things are slightly more complicated if one or both partners were previously married. In such a case, the previously married partner must provide an official copy of the divorce decree.

Most travelers who get married in Costa Rica do so in a civil ceremony officiated by a local lawyer. After the ceremony, the lawyer records the marriage with Costa Rica's National Registry, which issues an official marriage certificate. This process generally takes between 4 and 6 weeks. Most lawyers or wedding coordinators then have the document translated and certified by the Costa Rican Foreign Ministry and at the embassy or consulate of your home country within Costa Rica before mailing it to you. From here, it's a matter of bringing this document to your local civil or religious authorities, if necessary.

Because Costa Rica is more than 90 percent Roman Catholic, arranging for a church wedding is usually easy in all but the most isolated and remote locations. To a lesser extent, a variety of

denominational Christian churches and priests are often available to perform or host the ceremony. If you're Jewish, Muslim, Buddhist, or a follower of some other religion, bringing your own officiant is a good idea.

Tip: Officially, the lawyer must read all or parts of the Costa Rican civil code on marriage during your ceremony. This is a rather uninspired and somewhat dated legal code that, at some weddings, can take as much as 20 minutes to slog through. Most lawyers and wedding coordinators are quite flexible and can work with you to design a ceremony and text that fits your needs and desires. Insist on this.

Most of the higher-end and romantic hotels in Costa Rica have ample experience in hosting weddings. Many have an in-house wedding planner. Narrowing the list is tough, but I'd say the top choices include **Hotel Punta Islita** (p. 322), **Villa Caletas** (p. 402), **Makanda by the Sea** (p. 433), **Florblanca Resort** (p. 309), and the **Four Seasons Resort** (p. 236). If you want a remote, yet luxurious, rainforest lodge to serve as host and backdrop, try **La Paloma Lodge** (p. 473), **Bosque del Cabo Rainforest Lodge** (p. 486), or **Lapa Ríos** (p. 487).

If you're looking for service beyond what your hotel can offer, or if you want to do it yourself, check out www.weddings.co.cr, www.weddingscostarica.net, www.liquidweddings.com, www.costaricaweddingcelebrations.com, or www.tropicaloccasions.com.

most drivers show little care or consideration for those on two wheels. The options are much more appealing for mountain bikers and off-track riders. If you plan to do a lot of biking and are very attached to your rig, bring your own. However, several companies in San José and elsewhere rent bikes, and the quality of the equipment is improving all the time. I list rental shops in each of the regional chapters that follow.

The area around **Lake Arenal** and **Arenal Volcano** wins my vote as the best place for mountain biking in Costa Rica. The scenery's great, with primary forests, waterfalls, and plenty of trails. And the hot springs at nearby Tabacón Grand Spa Thermal Resort are a perfect place for those with aching muscles to unwind at the end of the day. However, the new **Río Perdido ★★** (www.rioperdido.com; ☏ **888/326-5070** in the U.S. and Canada, 2673-3600) offers many of the same attractions, including incredible hot springs. But it also features the country's best specifically designed and built mountain bike park, with an extensive network of trails and different level circuits. Finally, **Hacienda Guachipelin** (p. 224) also has an extensive network of bike trails and some excellent rental bikes. See chapters 8 & 10 for full details.

TOUR OPERATORS & OUTFITTERS

Bike Arenal ★ (www.bikearenal.com; ☏ **866/465-4114** in the U.S. and Canada, or 2479-9020) is based in La Fortuna and specializes in 1-day and multiday trips around the Arenal area.

Coast to Coast Adventures ★ (www.ctocadventures.com; ☏ **2280-8054**) offers mountain-biking itineraries among its many tour options.

Lava Tours (www.lava-tours.com; ☏ **8836-8258**) conducts a variety of fixed-date-departure and custom mountain-bike tours all over Costa Rica.

Bird-Watching

With more than 850 species of resident and migrant birds identified throughout the country, Costa Rica abounds with great bird-watching sites. Lodges with the best bird-watching include **Savegre Lodge,** in Cerro de la Muerte, off the road to San Isidro de El General (quetzal sightings are almost guaranteed); **La Paloma Lodge** (p. 473) in Drake Bay, where you can sit on the porch of your cabin as the avian parade goes by; **Arenal Observatory Lodge** (p. 352), on the flanks of Arenal Volcano; **La Selva Biological Station** (p. 391), in Puerto Viejo de Sarapiquí; **Aviarios del Caribe** and **Selva Bananito Lodge** (p. 529), both just north of Cahuita; **Lapa Ríos** and **Bosque del Cabo,** on the

---

Ruta de los Conquistadores

Each year, Costa Rica hosts what many consider to be the most challenging and grueling mountain-bike race on the planet. **La Ruta de los Conquistadores** (The Route of the Conquerors; www.adventurerace.com) retraces the path of the 16th-century Spanish conquistadores from the Pacific Coast to the Caribbean Sea—all in 4 days. The race usually takes place in mid-November, and draws hundreds of competitors from around the world.

Osa Peninsula; **Playa Nicuesa Rainforest Lodge** (p. 497), along the Golfo Dulce; **La Laguna del Lagarto Lodge** (p. 357), up by the Nicaraguan border; and **Tiskita Lodge** (p. 504), down by the Panamanian border.

Some of the best parks and preserves for serious birders are **Monteverde Cloud Forest Biological Reserve** (for Resplendent Quetzals and hummingbirds); **Corcovado National Park** (for scarlet macaws); **Caño Negro Wildlife Refuge** (for wading birds, including jabiru storks); **Wilson Botanical Gardens** and **Las Cruces Biological Station,** near San Vito (the thousands of flowering plants here are bird magnets); **Guayabo, Negritos,** and **Pájaros Islands biological reserves** in the Gulf of Nicoya (for magnificent frigate birds and brown boobies); **Palo Verde National Park** (for ibises, jacanas, storks, and roseate spoonbills); **Tortuguero National Park** (for great green macaws); and **Rincón de la Vieja National Park** (for parakeets and curassows). Rafting trips down the **Corobicí and Bebedero rivers** near Liberia, boat trips to or at **Tortuguero National Park,** and hikes in any cloud forest also provide good bird-watching opportunities.

In San José, your best bets are to head toward the lush grounds and gardens of the **University of Costa Rica,** or to **Parque del Este,** a little farther east in the foothills just outside of town.

COSTA RICAN TOUR AGENCIES

Costa Rica Expeditions ★★ (www.costaricaexpeditions.com; ☏ **2221-6099**) and **Costa Rica Sun Tours** ★ (www.crsuntours.com; ☏ **866/271-6263** in the U.S. and Canada, or 2296-7757 in Costa Rica) are well-established companies with very competent and experienced guides who offer a variety of tours to some of the better birding spots in Costa Rica.

INTERNATIONAL TOUR OPERATORS

Costa Rican Bird Route ★★ (www.costaricanbirdroute.com; ☏ **608/698-3448** in the U.S. and Canada) is a bird-watching and conservation effort that has created several bird-watching specific itineraries, which they offer up as guided tours, or self-guided adventures.

Field Guides (www.fieldguides.com; ☏ **800/728-4953** in the U.S. and Canada) is a specialty bird-watching travel operator. Its 16-day tour of Costa Rica covers a lot of ground, and group size is limited to 12.

Tropical Birding ★ (www.tropicalbirding.com; ☏ **800/348-5941** in the U.S. and Canada), specializing in birding tours around the world, happens to be based in Ecuador. These folks excel at small group tours, with highly skilled guides, and run periodic trips to Costa Rica.

Victor Emanuel Nature Tours ★★ (www.ventbird.com; ☏ **800/328-8368** in the U.S. and Canada) is a well-respected, longstanding small group tour operator specializing in bird-watching trips.

WHERE TO SEE THE resplendent quetzal

Revered by pre-Columbian cultures throughout Central America, the Resplendent Quetzal has been called the most beautiful bird on earth. Ancient Aztec and Maya Indians believed that the robin-size quetzal protected them in battle. The males of this species have brilliant red breasts; iridescent emerald green heads, backs, and wings; and white tail feathers complemented by a pair of iridescent green tail feathers that are more than .5m (1¾ ft.) long.

The belief that these endangered birds live only in the dense cloud forests cloaking the higher slopes of Central America's mountains was instrumental in bringing many areas of cloud forest under protection as quetzal habitats. (Since then, researchers have discovered that the birds do not, in fact, spend their entire lives here.) After nesting between March and July, Resplendent Quetzals migrate down to lower slopes in search of food. These lower slopes have not been preserved in most cases, and now conservationists are trying to salvage enough lower-elevation forests to help the quetzals survive.

Although for many years **Monteverde Cloud Forest Biological Reserve** was *the* place to see quetzals, throngs of people crowding the reserve's trails now make the pursuit more difficult. Other places where you can see quetzals are in the **Los Angeles Cloud Forest Reserve** near San Ramón, in **Tapantí National Wildlife Refuge,** and in **Chirripó National Park.** Perhaps the best place to spot a quetzal is at one of the specialized lodges located along the **Cerro de la Muerte** between San José and San Isidro de El General.

WINGS ★ (www.wingsbirds.com; ✆ **866/547-9868** in the U.S. and Canada) is a specialty bird-watching travel operator with more than 30 years of field experience. Group size is usually between 4 and 16.

Camping

Heavy rains, difficult access, and limited facilities make camping a challenge in Costa Rica. Nevertheless, a backpack and tent will get you far from the crowds and into some of the most pristine and undeveloped nooks and crannies of the country. Camping is forbidden in some national parks, so read the descriptions for each park carefully.

If you'd like to participate in an organized camping trip, contact **Coast to Coast Adventures ★** (www.ctocadventures.com; ✆ **2280-8054**).

In my opinion, the best places to pop up a tent on the beach are in **Santa Rosa National Park** and **Ballena Marine National Park.** At both spots you're likely to have miles and miles of unspoiled beach at your feet, and very few fellow campers around. The best camping trek is, without a doubt, a hike through **Corcovado National Park,** a wild and rugged area and the single largest expanse of lowland tropical rain forest in Central America.

Canopy Tours

Canopy tours are all the rage in Costa Rica, largely because they are such an exciting and unique way to experience tropical rainforests. It's estimated that some two-thirds of a typical rainforest's species live in the canopy (the uppermost, branching layer of the forest). From the relative luxury of Rain Forest Aerial Tram's high-tech funicular to the rope-and-climbing-gear rigs of zip-line operations, a trip into the canopy will give you a bird's-eye view of a Neotropical forest. Canopy-tour operations are now in or close to nearly every major tourist destination in the country. See the individual destination chapters for specific recommendations on canopy tours.

Most canopy tours involve strapping yourself into a climbing harness and being winched up to a platform some 30m (100 ft.) above the forest floor, or doing the work yourself. Many of these operations have a series of treetop platforms connected by taut cables. Once up on the first platform, you click your harness into a pulley and glide across the cable to the next (slightly lower) platform, using your hand (protected by a thick leather glove) as a brake. When you reach the last platform, you usually rappel down to the ground. (Don't worry—they'll teach even the most nervous neophyte.)

Although this can be a lot of fun, do be careful because these tours are popping up all over the place and there is precious little regulation of the activity. Some of the tours are set up by fly-by-night operators (I don't list any of those). Be especially sure that you feel comfortable and confident with the safety standards, guides, and equipment before embarking. Before you sign on to any tour, ask whether you have to hoist yourself to the top under your own steam, and then make your decision accordingly. Most canopy tours run between $45 and $65 per person.

Top Canopy Tours

Arenal Hanging Bridges, Arenal Volcano area (p. 342)

Canopy Safari, Manuel Antonio (p. 427)

Cartagena Canopy Tour, Northern beach area, Guanacaste (p. 269)

Chiclets Tree Tour, Playa Hermosa (p. 407)

Congo Trail Canopy Tour, Northern beach area, Guanacaste (p. 243)

Hacienda Guachipelín, Rincón de la Vieja, Guanacaste (p. 224)

Hacienda Pozo Azul, Puerto Viejo de Sarapiquí (p. 386)

Rainforest Aerial Tram Atlantic, en route to Puerto Viejo de Sarapiquí (p. 165)

Rio Perdido, Bagaces area, near the Miravalles Volcano (p. 226)

Selvatura Park, Monteverde area (p. 374)

Sky Adventure, Arenal Volcano area (p. 342) and Monteverde area (p. 375)

Vista Los Sueños Canopy Tour, Playa Herradura (p. 399)

Waterfall Canopy Tour, Montezuma (p. 300)

Witch's Rock Canopy Tour, Papagayo Peninsula, Guanacaste (p. 236)

monkey BUSINESS

No trip to Costa Rica would be complete without at least one monkey sighting. Home to four distinct species of primates, Costa Rica offers the opportunity for one of the world's most gratifying wildlife-viewing experiences. Just listen for the deep guttural call of a howler or the rustling of leaves overhead—telltale signs that monkeys are in your vicinity.

Costa Rica's most commonly spotted monkey is the white-faced or **capuchin monkey** (*mono cara blanca*), which you might recognize as the infamous culprit from the film "Outbreak." Contrary to that film's plot, however, capuchins are native to the New World Tropics and do not exist in Africa. Capuchins are agile, medium-size monkeys that make good use of their long, prehensile tails. They inhabit a diverse collection of habitats, ranging from the high-altitude cloud forests of the central region to the lowland mangroves of the Osa Peninsula. It's almost impossible not to spot capuchins at Manuel Antonio (chapter 11), where they have become a little too dependent on fruit and junk-food feedings by tourists. Please do not feed wild monkeys (and try to keep your food away from them—they're notorious thieves), and boycott establishments that try to attract both monkeys and tourists with daily feedings.

Howler monkeys (*mono congo*) are named for their distinct and eerie call. Large and mostly black, these monkeys can seem ferocious because of their physical appearance and deep, resonant howls that can carry for more than a mile, even in dense rainforest. Biologists believe that male howlers mark the bounds of their territories with these deep, guttural sounds. In the presence of humans, however, howlers are actually a little timid and tend to stay higher up in the canopy than their white-faced cousins. Howlers are fairly common and easy to spot in the dry tropical forests of coastal Guanacaste and the Nicoya Peninsula (see chapter 8).

Even more elusive are **spider monkeys** (*mono araña*). These long, slender monkeys are dark brown to black and prefer the high canopies of primary rainforests. Spiders are very adept with their prehensile tails but actually travel through the canopy with a hand-over-hand motion frequently imitated by their less graceful human cousins on playground monkey bars around the world. I've had my best luck spotting spider monkeys along the edges of Tortuguero's jungle canals (see chapter 13), where howlers are also quite common.

The rarest and most endangered of Costa Rica's monkeys is the tiny **squirrel monkey** (*mono tití*). These small, brown monkeys have dark eyes surrounded by large white rings, white ears, white chests, and very long tails. In Costa Rica, squirrel monkeys can be found only at Manuel Antonio (see chapter 11) and the Osa Peninsula (see chapter 12). These seemingly hyperactive monkeys are predominantly fruit eaters and often feed on bananas and other fruit trees near hotels in both of the above-mentioned regions. Squirrel monkeys usually travel in large bands, so if you do see them, you'll likely see quite a few.

Canyoning Tours

Canyoning tours are even more exhilarating than canopy tours, in my opinion. Hardly standardized, most involve hiking down along a mountain stream, river, and/or canyon, with periodic breaks to rappel down the face of a waterfall, or swim in a jungle pool. The best canyoning operations in Costa Rica are offered by **Pure Trek Canyoning** ★★ (p. 342) and **Desafío Expeditions** ★★ (p. 337), both in La Fortuna; **Explornatura** ★★ (p. 206), in Turrialba; and **Psycho Tours** ★★★ (p. 478), outside Puerto Jiménez. The latter is arguably my favorite adventure tour in the country, combining waterfall rappelling with the chance to free climb a massive strangler fig tree and then jump off into the abyss connected by a single rope running through a pulley above your head. Previous experience and prime physical condition aren't requisite.

Diving & Snorkeling

Many islands, reefs, caves, and rocks lie off the coast of Costa Rica, providing excellent spots for underwater exploration. Visibility varies with season and location. Generally, heavy rainfall tends to swell the rivers and muddy the waters, even well offshore. Rates run from $70 to $150 per person for a two-tank dive, including equipment, and $35 to $75 per person for snorkelers. Most of the dedicated dive operators listed throughout this book also offer certification classes.

Banana plantations and their runoff have destroyed most of the Caribbean reefs, although **Isla Uvita,** just off the coast of Limón, and **Manzanillo,** down near the Panamanian border, still have good diving. Most divers choose Pacific dive spots such as **Isla del Caño, Bat Island,** and the **Catalina Islands,** where you're likely to spot manta rays, moray eels, white-tipped sharks, and plenty of smaller fish and coral species. But the ultimate in Costa Rican dive experiences is 7 to 10 days on a chartered boat, diving off the coast of **Isla del Coco** (see p. 289).

Snorkeling is not incredibly common or rewarding in Costa Rica. The rain, runoff, and wave conditions that drive scuba divers well offshore tend to make coastal and shallow-water conditions less than optimal. If the weather is calm and the water is clear, you might just get lucky. Ask at your hotel or check the different beach listings in this book to find snorkeling options and operators up and down Costa Rica's coasts. The best snorkeling experience to be had in Costa Rica is on the reefs off **Manzanillo Beach** in the southern Caribbean coast, particularly in the calm months of September and October.

DIVING OUTFITTERS & OPERATORS

In addition to the companies listed below, check the listings at specific beach and port destinations in the regional chapters.

Aggressor Fleet Limited ★★ (www.aggressor.com; ✆ **800/348-2628** in the U.S. and Canada) runs the 36m (118-ft.) *Okeanos Aggressor* on regular trips out to Isla del Coco.

Diving Safaris de Costa Rica ★★ (www.costaricadiving.net; ✆ **2670-0603**) is perhaps the largest, most professional, and best-established dive operation in the country. Based out of Playa Hermosa, this outfitter is also a local pioneer in Nitrox diving.

Undersea Hunter ★★ (www.underseahunter.com; 🕿 **800/203-2120** in the U.S., or 2228-6613 in Costa Rica) offers the *Undersea Hunter* and its sister ship, the *Sea Hunter,* two pioneers of the live-aboard diving excursions to Isla del Coco.

Top Fishing Lodges

Aguila de Osa Inn, Drake Bay (p. 473)
Río Colorado Lodge, at the Barra del Colorado National Wildlife Refuge (p. 511)
Silver King Lodge, at Barra del Colorado (p. 512)
The Zancudo Lodge, in Playa Zancudo (p. 501)

Fishing

Anglers in Costa Rican waters have landed over 100 world-record catches, including blue marlin, Pacific sailfish, dolphin, wahoo, yellowfin tuna, *guapote,* and snook. Whether you want to head offshore looking for a big sail, wrestle a tarpon near a Caribbean river mouth, or choose a quiet spot on a lake to cast for *guapote,* you'll find it here. You can raise a marlin anywhere along the Pacific coast, while feisty snook can be found in mangrove estuaries along both coasts.

Many of the Pacific port and beach towns—Quepos, Puntarenas, Playa del Coco, Tamarindo, Flamingo, Golfito, Drake Bay, Zancudo—support large charter fleets and have hotels that cater to anglers; see chapters 7 and 9 to 12 for recommended boats, captains, and lodges. Fishing trips usually range between $400 and $2,500 per day (depending on boat size) for the boat, captain, tackle, drinks, and lunch, so the cost per person depends on the size of the group.

Costa Rican law requires all fishermen purchase a license. The cost ranges from $15 to $50 depending upon the length of the license and whether it covers salt-water or fresh-water fishing, or both. All boats, captains, and fishing lodges listed here and throughout the book will help you with the technicalities of buying your license.

Costa Rica Outdoors ★ (www.costaricaoutdoors.com; 🕿 **800/ 308-3394** in the U.S. and Canada or 2231-0306 in Costa Rica) is a well-established operation founded by local fishing legend and outdoor writer Jerry Ruhlow, specializing in booking fishing trips.

Golfing

Costa Rica is not one of the world's great golfing destinations. Currently, seven regulation 18-hole courses are open to the public and visitors. These courses offer stunning scenery, and almost no crowds. However, be prepared—strong seasonal winds make playing most of the Guanacaste courses very challenging from December through March.

The most spectacular course is at **Four Seasons Resort** ★★★ (p. 236), but it is open only to hotel guests. Greens fees run $250.

Another very lovely option is the **Reserva Conchal** course ★★ at the **Westin Playa Conchal Resort & Spa** (p. 253) up in Guanacaste. Greens fees here are $150, including a cart. With advance notice and depending on available tee times, this course is currently open to guests at other area hotels with advance reservations.

Hacienda Pinilla ★★ (p. 269) is an 18-hole links-style course located south of Tamarindo. This might just be the most challenging course in the country, and the facilities, though limited, are top-notch. Currently, the course is open to golfers staying at hotels around the area, with advance reservations. Greens fees run around $200 for 18 holes, including a cart.

The **Papagayo Golf & Country Club** ★ (p. 243), on the outskirts of Playa del Coco, offers up a full 18-hole course, with a pro shop, driving range, and rental equipment. It costs $100 in greens fees, including a cart.

Another major resort course is at the **Los Sueños Marriott Ocean & Golf Resort** ★★ in Playa Herradura (p. 401). Greens fees, including a cart, run around $150 for the general public, and guests pay slightly less.

Down along the Central Pacific coast, south of Dominical, the **San Buenas Golf Resort** (www.sbgr.com) has 9 holes. Greens fees, including a cart, run around $45 for 9 holes, or $65 if you play around the course twice.

Currently, the best option for golfers staying in and around San José is **Parque Valle del Sol** ★ (www.vallesol.com; ℭ 2282-9222; p. 172), an 18-hole course in the western suburb of Santa Ana. Greens fees are $99, including a cart.

Golfers who are interested in a package deal that includes play on a variety of courses, should contact **Costa Rica Golf Adventures** ★ (www.golfcr.com; ℭ 888/536-8510 in the U.S. and Canada) or **Tee Times Costa Rica** (www.teetimescostarica.com; ℭ 866/448-3182 in the U.S. and Canada).

Hang Gliding, Paragliding & Ballooning

Paragliding is taking off (pardon the pun) in the cliff areas around Caldera, just south of Puntarenas, as well as other spots around the Central Pacific coast. If you're looking to paraglide, check in with the folks at **Grandpa Ninja's B&B** (www.paraglidecostarica.com; ℭ 908/545-3242 in the U.S. and 8950-8676 in Costa Rica). This place caters to paragliders, and offer lessons or tandem flights. Lessons run around $60 per day, including equipment, while a 20 minutes tandem flight with an experienced pilot will run you around $95.

Serendipity Adventures ★ (www.serendipityadventures.com; ℭ 888/226-5050 in the U.S. and Canada, or 2556-2222 in Costa Rica) will take you up, up, and away in a hot-air balloon near Arenal Volcano. A basic flight costs around $385 per passenger, with a two-person minimum, and a five-person or 800-pound maximum.

Horseback Riding

Costa Rica's rural roots are evident in the continued use of horses for real work and transportation throughout the country. Visitors will find that horses are easily available for riding, whether you want to take a sunset trot along the beach, ride through the cloud forest, or take a multiday trek through the northern zone.

Most travelers simply saddle up for a couple of hours. Rates run between $15 to $30 per hour, depending upon group size and the length of the ride, with full day rides running around $60 to $90, usually including lunch and refreshments.

Rock Climbing

Although this is a nascent sport in Costa Rica, the possibilities are promising, with several challenging rock formations close to San José and along the Cerro de la Muerte, as well as great climbing opportunities on Mount Chirripó.

Spas & Yoga Retreats

Overall, prices for spa treatments in Costa Rica are generally less expensive than those in the United States or Europe, although some of the fancier options, like the Four Seasons or Tabacón Grand Spa Thermal Resort, rival the services, facilities, and prices found anywhere on the planet.

The **Four Seasons Resort ★★★** (p. 236) on the Papagayo Peninsula has ample and luxurious facilities and treatment options, as well as scheduled classes in yoga, Pilates, and other disciplines.

Florblanca Resort ★★★ (p. 309) in Santa Teresa has some of the most beautiful boutique spa facilities that I have ever seen. Two large treatment rooms are set over a flowing water feature.

Luna Lodge ★★ (p. 488) is a very remote lodge located on a hillside overlooking Playa Carate, on the border with Corcovado National Park. Individual rooms and tents offer up views over the rain forests, and the road from Puerto Jimenez literally ends here. These folks run a fairly full schedule of dedicated yoga and wellness programs and have a good little spa on-site.

Pranamar Villas & Yoga Retreat ★★★, Santa Teresa (p. 311), is an upscale, beachfront resort, with a large Balinese-inspired open air-yoga space, and delicious spa-cuisine focused restaurant. A range of daily classes are offered, and a steady stream of visiting teachers and groups use the spot for longer retreats and seminars.

Samasati ★, Puerto Viejo de Talamanca (p. 545), is an intimate yoga retreat set amidst dense forest on a hillside overlooking the Caribbean sea. Accommodations range from budget to rustically luxurious.

Tabacón Grand Spa Thermal Resort ★★★, Tabacón (p. 351), is a top-notch spa with spectacular hot springs, lush gardens, and a volcano view. A complete range of spa services and treatments is available at reasonable prices.

Xandari Resort & Spa ★★, Alajuela (p. 184), is a luxury boutique hotel with distinctive contemporary architecture, abundant art works and it's own little "spa village" that offers up top-notch treatments and services. This is a good choice if you're looking for a day or two of pampering, or for day treatments while staying in San José.

Surfing

Significant sections of the movie "Endless Summer II" (1994), the sequel to the all-time surf classic, were filmed in Costa Rica. All along Costa Rica's immense coastline are point and beach breaks that work year-round. **Playas Hermosa, Jacó,** and **Dominical,** on the Central Pacific coast, and **Tamarindo** and **Playa Guiones,** in Guanacaste, are mini surf meccas. **Salsa Brava** in Puerto Viejo is a steep and fast wave that peels off both right and left over shallow coral. It has a habit of breaking boards, but the daredevils keep coming back. Beginners should stick to the mellower sections of **Jacó** and **Tamarindo**—surf lessons are offered at both beaches. Crowds are starting to gather at the more popular breaks, but you can still stumble onto secret spots on the **Osa** and **Nicoya peninsulas** and along the northern **Guanacaste** coast. Costa Rica's signature wave is still at **Playa Pavones,** which is reputed to have one of the longest lefts in the world. The cognoscenti, however, also swear by **Playa Grande, Playa Negra, Matapalo, Malpaís,** and **Witch's Rock.** An avid surfer's best bet is to rent a dependable four-wheel-drive vehicle with a rack and take a surfin' safari around Guanacaste.

If you're looking for an organized surf vacation, contact **Tico Travel** (www.ticotravel.com; ✆ **800/493-8426** in the U.S. and Canada), or check out **www.crsurf.com.** For swell reports, general surf information, live wave-cams, and great links pages, point your browser to **www.surfline.com.** Although killer sets are possible at any particular spot at any time of the year, depending upon swell direction, local winds, and distant storms, in broad terms, the northern coast of Guanacaste works best from December to April; the central and southern Pacific coasts from April to November; and the Caribbean coast's short big-wave season is December through March. Surf lessons, usually private or in a small group, will run you anywhere from $20 to $40 per hour, including the board.

White-Water Rafting, Kayaking & Canoeing

Whether you're a first-time rafter or a world-class kayaker, Costa Rica's got some white water suited to your abilities. Rivers rise and fall with the rainfall, but you can get wet and wild here even in the dry season. Full-day rafting trips run between $75 and $110 per person.

The best white-water rafting ride is still the scenic **Pacuare River;** although there has been talk about damming it to build a hydroelectric plant, the project has thankfully failed to materialize. If you're just experimenting with river rafting, stick to Class II and III rivers, such as **Reventazón, Sarapiquí, Peñas Blancas,** and **Savegre.** If you already know which end of the paddle goes in the water, you'll have plenty of Class IV and V sections to run.

Die-hard river rats should get **"Chasing Jaguars: The Complete Guide to Costa Rican Whitewater,"** by Lee Eudy, a book loaded with photos, technical data, and route tips on almost every rideable river in the country.

Canoe Costa Rica (www.canoecostarica.com; ℂ **2282-3579**) is the only outfit I know of that specializes in canoe trips; it works primarily with custom-designed tours and itineraries, although it does have several set departure trips each year.

Aventuras Naturales ★★ (ℂ **888/680-9031** in the U.S., or 2225-3939 in Costa Rica) is a major rafting operator that runs daily trips on the most popular rivers in Costa Rica. Its **Pacuare Jungle Lodge** ★★★ (p. 207) is very plush, and a great place to spend the night is on one of its 2-day rafting trips.

Exploradores Outdoors ★ (www.exploradoresoutdoors.com; ℂ **646/205-0828** in the U.S. and Canada, or 2222-6262 in Costa Rica) is another good company run by a longtime and well-respected river guide. They run the Pacuare and Reventazón rivers, and even combine a 1-day river trip with onward transportation to or from the Caribbean coast, or the Arenal Volcano area, for no extra cost.

Río Locos (www.whiteh2o.com; ℂ **2556-6035**) is a small company based in Turrialba. They are a good option for hard-core kayakers, small custom group tours, and those who find themselves in Turrialba.

Ríos Tropicales ★★ (www.riostropicales.com; ℂ **866/722-8273** in the U.S. and Canada, or 2233-6455 in Costa Rica) is one of the major operators in Costa Rica, with tours on most of the country's popular rivers. Accommodations options include a very comfortable lodge on the banks of the Río Pacuare for the 2-day trips.

Windsurfing & Kiteboarding

Windsurfing is not very popular on the high seas here, where winds are fickle and rental options are limited, even at beach hotels. However, **Lake Arenal** is considered one of the top spots in the world for high-wind boardsailing. During the winter months, many of the regulars from Washington's Columbia River Gorge take up residence around the nearby town of Tilarán. Small boards, water starts, and fancy gibes are the norm. The best time for windsurfing on Lake Arenal is between December and March. The same winds that buffet Lake Arenal make their way down to **Bahía Salinas** (also known as Bolaños Bay), near La

IN SEARCH OF turtles

Few places in the world have as many sea-turtle nesting sites as Costa Rica. Along both coasts, five species of these huge marine reptiles come ashore at specific times of the year to dig nests in the sand and lay their eggs. Sea turtles are endangered throughout the world due to over-hunting, accidental deaths in fishing nets, development on beaches that once served as nesting areas, and the collection and sale (often illegally) of their eggs. International trade in sea-turtle products is already prohibited by most countries (including the U.S.), but sea-turtle numbers continue to dwindle.

Among the species of sea turtles that nest on Costa Rica's beaches are the **olive ridley** (known for their mass egg-laying migrations, or *arribadas*), **leatherback, hawksbill, green,** and **Pacific green turtle.** Excursions to see nesting turtles have become common, and they are fascinating, but please make sure that you and/or your guide do not disturb the turtles. Any light source (other than red-tinted flashlights) can confuse female turtles and cause them to return to the sea without laying their eggs. In fact, as more development takes place on the Costa Rican coast, hotel lighting may cause the number of nesting turtles to drop. Luckily, many of the nesting beaches have been protected as national parks.

Here are the main places to see nesting sea turtles: **Santa Rosa National Park** (near Liberia, olive ridleys nest here from July–Dec, and to a lesser extent from Jan–June), **Las Baulas National Marine Park** (near Tamarindo, leatherbacks nest here from early Oct through mid-Feb), **Ostional National Wildlife Refuge** (near Playa Nosara, olive ridleys nest from July–Dec, and to a lesser extent from Jan–June), and **Tortuguero National Park** (on the northern Caribbean coast, green turtles nest here from July through mid-Oct, with Aug–Sept their peak period. In lesser numbers, leatherback turtles nest here from Feb–June, peaking during Mar and Apr).

See the regional chapters for descriptions of the resident turtles and their respective nesting seasons, as well as listings of local tour operators and companies that arrange trips to see sea turtles nesting.

Cruz, Guanacaste, where you can get in some good windsurfing. Both spots also have operations offering lessons and equipment rentals in the high-action sport of kiteboarding. Board rentals run around $55 to $85 per day, while lessons can cost between $50 to $100 for a half-day private lesson. See "La Cruz & Bahía Salinas," in chapter 8, and "Along the Shores of Lake Arenal," in chapter 10, for details.

STUDY & VOLUNTEER PROGRAMS

Language Immersion

As more people travel to Costa Rica with the intention of learning Spanish, the number of options for Spanish immersion vacations increases. You can find courses of varying lengths and degrees of intensiveness, and many that include cultural activities and day excursions. Many of these schools have reciprocal relationships with U.S. universities, so, in some cases, you can even arrange for college credit. Most Spanish schools can arrange for homestays with a middle-class Tico family for a total-immersion experience. Classes are often small, or even one-on-one, and can last anywhere from 2 to 8 hours a day. Listed below are some of the larger and more established Spanish-language schools, with approximate costs. Most are in San José, but schools are also in Monteverde, Manuel Antonio, Playa Flamingo, Malpaís, Playa Nosara, and Tamarindo. A 1-week class with 4 hours of class per day, including a homestay, tends to cost between $420 and $630. (I'd certainly rather spend 2 weeks or a month in one of these spots than in San José.)

Adventure Education Center (AEC) Spanish Institute ★ (www.adventurespanishschool.com; ✆ **800/237-2730** in the U.S. and Canada, or 2787-0023 in Costa Rica) has branches in Dominical and Turrialba, and specializes in combining language learning with adventure activities.

Centro Panamericano de Idiomas (CPI) ★ (www.cpi-edu.com; ✆ **877/373-3116** in the U.S., or 2265-6306) has three campuses: one in the quiet suburban town of Heredia, another in Monteverde, and one at the beach in Playa Flamingo.

Costa Rican Language Academy ★ in San José (www.spanish andmore.com; ✆ **866/230-6361** in the U.S., or 2280-1685 in Costa Rica) has intensive programs with classes held Monday to Thursday to give students a chance for longer weekend excursions. The academy also integrates Latin dance and Costa Rican cooking classes into the program.

Escuela D'Amore ★ (www.academiadamore.com; ✆ **877/434-7290** in the U.S. and Canada, or 2777-0233 in Costa Rica) is situated in the lush surroundings of Manuel Antonio.

Wayra Instituto de Español (www.spanish-wayra.co.cr; ✆ **2653-0359**) is a longstanding operation located in the beach town of Tamarindo.

Alternative Educational Travel

Adventures Under the Sun ★★ (www.adventuresunderthesun.com; ✆ **866/897-5578** in the U.S. and Canada, or 2289-0404 in Costa Rica) is a Costa Rican-based outfit specializing in adventure and volunteer-focused teen travel. Their strong suit is organizing custom group itineraries, but they also run periodic "summer day camps" and set itineraries.

Costa Rica Rainforest Outward Bound School ★★ (www.crrobs.org; ✆ **800/676-2018** in the U.S., or 2278-6062 in Costa Rica) is the local branch of this well-respected international adventure-based outdoor-education organization. Courses range from 2 weeks to a full semester, and offerings include surfing, kayaking, tree climbing, and learning Spanish.

Eco Teach (www.ecoteach.com; ✆ **800/626-8992** in the U.S. and Canada) works primarily to facilitate educational trips for high school and college student groups. Trips focus on Costa Rican ecology and culture. Costs run around $1,600 to $2,200 per person for a 10-day trip, including lodging, meals, classes, and travel within the country. Airfare to Costa Rica is extra.

The **Institute for Central American Development Studies** ★ (www.icads.org; ✆ **2225-0508**) offers internship and research opportunities in the areas of environment, agriculture, human rights, and women's studies. An intensive Spanish-language program can be combined with work-study or volunteer opportunities.

The **Monteverde Institute** ★ (www.mvinstitute.org; ✆ **2645-5053**) offers study programs in Monteverde and also has a volunteer center that helps in placement and training of volunteers.

The **Organization for Tropical Studies** ★★ (www.threepaths.co.cr; ✆ **919/684-5774** in the U.S., or 2524-0607 in Costa Rica) represents several Costa Rican and U.S. universities. This organization's mission is to promote research, education, and the wise use of natural resources in the Tropics. Research facilities include La Selva Biological Station near Braulio Carrillo National Park and Palo Verde, and the Wilson Botanical Gardens near San Vito. Housing is provided at one of the research facilities. The wide variety of programs range from full-semester undergraduate programs to specific graduate courses (of varying duration) to tourist programs. (These are generally sponsored/run by established operators such as Costa Rica Expeditions or Elderhostel.) Programs range in duration from 3 to 10 days, and costs vary greatly. Entrance requirements and competition for some of these courses can be demanding.

Sustainable Volunteer Projects

Below are some institutions and organizations that are working on ecology and sustainable development projects in Costa Rica.

APREFLOFAS (Association for the Preservation of the Wild Flora and Fauna; www.apreflofas.or.cr; ✆ **2240-6087**) is a pioneering local conservation organization that accepts volunteers and runs environmentally sound educational tours around the country.

Asociación de Voluntarios para el Servicio en las Areas Protegidas ★ (**ASVO;** www.asvocr.org; ✆ **2258-4430**) organizes volunteers to work in Costa Rican national parks. A 2-week minimum commitment is required, as is an ability to adapt to rustic conditions, remote locations, and a basic ability to converse in Spanish. Housing is provided at a basic ranger station; a $245 weekly fee covers lodging, logistics, and food, which is standard Tico fare.

Sea Turtle Conservancy (www.cccturtle.org; ✆ **800/678-7853** in the U.S. and Canada, or 2278-6058 in Costa Rica) is a nonprofit organization dedicated to sea turtle research, protection, and advocacy. Formerly known as the **Caribbean Conservation Corporation,** their main operation in Costa Rica is headquartered in Tortuguero, where volunteers can aid in various scientific studies, as well as nightly patrols of the beach during nesting seasons to prevent poaching.

Global Volunteers (www.globalvolunteers.org; ✆ 800/487-1074 in the U.S. and Canada) is a U.S.-based organization that offers a unique opportunity to travelers who've always wanted a Peace Corps–like experience but can't make a 2-year commitment. For 2 to 3 weeks, you can join one of its working vacations in Costa Rica. A certain set of skills, such as engineering or agricultural knowledge, is helpful but by no means necessary. Each trip is undertaken at a particular community's request, to complete a specific project. However, *be warned:* These "volunteer" experiences do not come cheap. You must pay for your transportation as well as a hefty program fee, around $2,700 for a 2-week program.

Habitat for Humanity International (www.habitatcostarica.org; ✆ 2296-3436) has offices in Costa Rica and sometimes runs organized Global Village programs here.

Vida (www.vida.org; ✆ 2221-8367) is a local nongovernmental organization working on sustainable development and conservation issues; it can often place volunteers.

MEDICAL & DENTAL TOURISM

Costa Rica is an increasingly popular destination for dental and medical tourists. Facilities and care are excellent, and prices are quite low compared to the United States and other private care options in the developed world. Travelers are coming for everything from a simple dental checkup and cleaning while on vacation to elective cosmetic surgery or a triple heart bypass operation. In virtually every case, visitors can save money on the overall cost of care. In some cases, the savings are quite substantial.

The country's two top hospitals have modern facilities and equipment, as well as excellent doctor and nursing corps, many of whom speak English. **Clínica Bíblica,** Avenida 14 between Calles Central and 1 (www.clinicabiblica.com; ✆ 2522-1000), is conveniently close to downtown while the **Hospital CIMA** (www.hospitalcima.com; ✆ 2208-1000) is in Escazú on the Próspero Fernández Highway, which connects San José and the western suburb of Santa Ana. The latter has the most modern facilities in the country. An annex of the Hospital CIMA has even opened in the outskirts of Liberia, close to the beaches of Guanacaste.

The United States embassy in Costa Rica maintains a fairly comprehensive list of recommended doctors, dentists, and other specialists at **http://costarica.usembassy.gov/medical.html**.

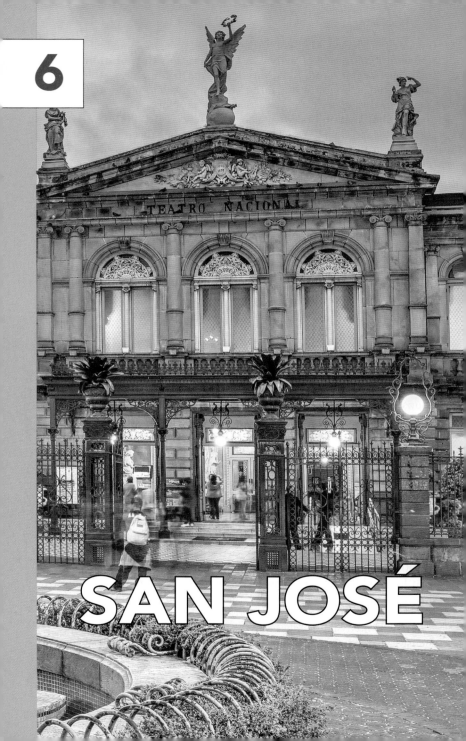

6

SAN JOSÉ

F or as long as I've written this book, my advice has been to get in and out of San José as quickly as possible. In most cases, this remains good counsel. Still, San José is the country's only major urban center, with varied and active restaurant and nightlife scenes, several museums and galleries worth visiting, and a steady stream of theater, concerts, and other cultural events that you won't find elsewhere in the country.

At first blush (and even after having lived here for decades), San José can come across as little more than a chaotic jumble of cars, buses, buildings, and people. The central downtown section of the city exists in a near-constant state of gridlock. Antiquated buses spewing diesel fumes and a lack of emission controls have created a brown cloud over the city's sky. Sidewalks are poorly maintained, narrow and overcrowded, and street crime is a perennial problem. Most visitors quickly seek the sanctuary of their hotel room and the first chance to escape the city.

Founded in 1737, San José was a forgotten backwater of the Spanish empire until the late 19th century, when it boomed with the coffee business. At 1,125m (3,690 ft.) above sea level, San José enjoys springlike temperatures year-round and its location in the Central Valley—the lush Talamanca Mountains rise to the south, the Poás, Barva, and Irazú volcanoes to the north—makes it both stunning and convenient as a base of exploration

This chapter helps you plan whatever time you intend for the capital and ease your way through the pitfalls inherent in such a rough-and-tumble little city.

San José's Top Sustainable Hotels
Aurola Holiday Inn (p. 139)
Crowne Plaza Corobicí (p. 142)
Hotel Grano de Oro (p. 142)

THE best SAN JOSÉ EXPERIENCES

○ **Taking In the Riches at the Gold Museum:** With more than 2,000 pieces spread over three floors, the Gold Museum provides a fascinating look into the pre-Columbian artistry that inspired colonial-era quests, conquests, and excesses. See p. 130.

FACING PAGE: **National Theater of Costa Rica in San José.**

- **Catching a Show at the National Theater:** Completed in 1897, and fronting the downtown Plaza de la Cultura, the National Theater is a beautiful and well-preserved turn-of-the-20th-century theater. It features a stunning marble entryway, a series of marble sculptures, and intricate paintings and murals throughout. It also hosts concerts, theater performances, and special events. See p. 158.

Sculpture in the National Theater.

- **Basking in Tropical Opulence at a Boutique Hotel:** Throughout the late 18th and early 19th centuries, newly rich coffee barons built beautiful mansions around downtown San José. Today, many of these have been converted into charming boutique hotels. See "Where to Stay," p. 138.

- **Visiting the Costa Rican Art Museum and La Sabana Park:** Inhabiting the country's first airport terminal building, the Costa Rican Art Museum houses the country's greatest art collection—from colonial times to the present. Just outside its doors lies La Sabana Park, where you can spend the afternoon relaxing in the grass or practicing any number of sports and activities, alongside some newly made Tico friends. See p. 133 and 135.

- **Getting Out on the Dance Floor:** San José is teeming with dance clubs, and most nights the city's dance floors are packed to overflowing. Choose between an old-school salsa dance hall with a live band, or a more contemporary club blasting the latest electronica. See p. 159.

ORIENTATION

Arriving

BY PLANE

Juan Santamaría International Airport (www.fly2sanjose.com; ☏ **2437-2626** for 24-hr. airport information; airport code SJO) is near the city of Alajuela, about 20 minutes from downtown San José. A taxi into town costs between C15,000 and C29,000, and a bus is only C555.

The Alajuela–San José buses run frequently and will drop you off anywhere along Paseo Colón or at a station near the Parque de la Merced (downtown, btw. calles 12 and 14 and avs. 2 and 4). There are two separate lines: **Tuasa** (𝄢 **2442-6900**) buses are red; **Station Wagon** (𝄢 **2442-3226**) buses are yellow/orange. At the airport, the bus stop is directly in front of the main terminal, beyond the parking structure. Be sure to ask whether the bus is going to San José, or you'll end up in Alajuela. If you have a lot of luggage, you probably should take a cab.

Most car-rental agencies have desks and offices at the airport, but if you're planning to spend a few days in San José itself, I think a car is a liability. (If you're heading off immediately to the beach, though, it's much easier to pick up your car here than at a downtown office.)

Tip: Chaos and confusion greet arriving passengers the second they step out of the terminal. You face a gauntlet of aggressive taxi drivers, shuttle drivers waving signs, and people offering to carry your bags. Fortunately, the official airport taxi service (see below) has a booth inside the calm area just before the terminal exit. And official airport porters also hang out in this area. Still, there's often really nowhere for them to have to carry your bags to because the line of waiting taxis and shuttles is just steps away. Keep a very watchful eye on your bags: Thieves have historically preyed on newly arrived passengers and their luggage. You should tip porters about C200 to C300 per bag.

In terms of taxis, you should stick with the official airport taxi service, **Taxis Unidos Aeropuerto** (www.taxiaeropuerto.com; 𝄢 **2221-6865**), which operates a fleet of orange vans and sedans. They have a kiosk in the no man's land just outside the exit door for arriving passengers. Here they will assign you a cab. These taxis use meters, and fares to most downtown hotels should run between C14,000 and C28,000. Despite the fact that Taxis Unidos has an official monopoly at the airport, you will usually find a handful of regular cabs (in traditional red sedans) and "pirate" cabs, driven by freelancers using their own vehicles. You certainly could use either of these latter options ("pirate" cabs tend to charge a dollar or two less), but I highly recommend using the official service for safety and standardized prices.

You have several options for **exchanging money** when you arrive at the airport. An ATM in the baggage claim area is connected to both the PLUS and Cirrus networks. A **Global Exchange** (www.globalexchange.co.cr; 𝄢 **2431-0686**) money exchange booth is just as you clear Customs and Immigration. It's open whenever flights arrive; however, they exchange at more than 10 percent below the official rate. A branch of **Banco de San José** is inside the main terminal, on the second floor across from the airline check-in counters, as well as a couple more ATMs up there. Most taxis and all rental-car agencies accept U.S. dollars. See "Money & Costs," in chapter 14, for more details.

Tip: There's really no pressing need to exchange money the minute you arrive. Taxis Unidos accepts dollars. You can wait until after you settle into your hotel, and see if the hotel will give you a good rate of exchange, or use one of the many downtown banks or ATMs.

If you arrive in San José via small commuter or charter airline, you might find yourself at the **Tobías Bolaños International Airport** in Pavas (© **2232-2820;** airport code SYQ). This small airport is on the western side of downtown San José, about 10 minutes by car from the center. The airport has no car-rental desks, so unless you have a car or a driver waiting for you here, you will have to take a cab into town, which should cost between C10,000 and C20,000.

BY BUS

If you're coming to San José by bus, where you disembark depends on where you're coming from. (The different bus companies have their offices, and thus their drop-off points, all over downtown San José. When you buy your ticket, ask where you'll be let off.) Buses arriving from Panama pass first through Cartago and San Pedro before letting passengers off in downtown San José; buses arriving from Nicaragua generally enter the city on the west end of town, on Paseo Colón. If you're staying here, you can ask to be let off before the final stop.

BY CAR

For the fearless among you arriving by car, you'll enter San José via the Interamerican Highway. If you arrive **from Nicaragua and the north,** the highway brings you first past the airport and the city of Alajuela, to the western edge of downtown, right at the end of Paseo Colón, where it hits Parque La Sabana (La Sabana Park). The area is well marked with large road signs that direct you either to downtown (centro) or to the western suburbs of Rohrmoser, Pavas, and Escazú. If you're heading toward downtown, follow the flow of traffic and turn left on Paseo Colón.

For those of you entering **from Panama and the south,** things get a little more complicated. The Interamerican Highway first passes through the city of Cartago and then through the San José suburbs of Curridabat and San Pedro before reaching downtown. This route is relatively well marked, and if you stick with the major flow of traffic, you should find San José without any problem.

Visitor Information

The **Costa Rican National Tourism Chamber** (**CANATUR;** www.canatur.org; © **2440-1676**) has a desk at the Juan Santamaría International Airport, the baggage claims area, just before Customs. You can pick up maps and brochures, and they might even lend you a phone to make or confirm a reservation. It's usually open for all arriving flights.

This is one of the most confusing aspects of visiting Costa Rica in general, and San José in particular. Although downtown San José often has street addresses and building numbers for locations, they are almost never used. Addresses are given as a set of coordinates such as "Calle 3 between avenidas Central and 1." It's then up to you to locate the building within that block, keeping in mind that the building could be on either side of the street. Many addresses include additional information, such as the number of meters from a specified intersection or some other well-known landmark. (These "meter measurements" are not precise but are a good way to give directions to a taxi driver. In basic terms, 100m = 1 block, 200m = 2 blocks, and so on.) These landmarks are what become truly confusing for visitors to the city because they are often simply restaurants, bars, and shops that would be familiar only to locals.

Things get even more confusing when the landmark in question no longer exists. The classic example of this is "the Coca-Cola," one of the most common landmarks used in addresses in the blocks surrounding San José's main market. The trouble is, the Coca-Cola bottling plant that it refers to is no longer there; the edifice is long gone, and one of the principal downtown bus depots stands in its place. Old habits die hard, though, and the address description remains. You might also try to find someplace near the *antiguo higuerón* ("old fig tree") in San Pedro. This tree was felled over a decade ago. In outlying neighborhoods, addresses can become long directions, such as "50m (½ block) south of the old church, then 100m (1 block) east, then 20m (two buildings) south." Luckily for visitors, most downtown addresses are more straightforward.

Oh, and if you're wondering how letter carriers manage, well, welcome to the club. Some folks actually get their mail delivered this way, but most people and businesses in San José use a post office box. This is called an *apartado* and is abbreviated "Apdo." or "A.P." in mailing addresses.

City Layout

Downtown San José is laid out on a grid. *Avenidas* (avenues) run east and west, while *calles* (streets) run north and south. The center of the city is at **Avenida Central** and **Calle Central.** To the north of Avenida Central, the avenidas have odd numbers beginning with Avenida 1; to the south, they have even numbers beginning with Avenida 2. Likewise, calles to the east of Calle Central have odd numbers, and those to the west have even numbers. The main downtown artery is **Avenida 2,** which merges with Avenida Central on either side of downtown. West of downtown, Avenida Central becomes **Paseo Colón,** which ends at Parque La Sabana and feeds into the highway to Alajuela, the airport, Guanacaste, and the Pacific coast. East of downtown, Avenida Central leads to San Pedro and then to Cartago and the Interamerican Highway heading south. **Calle 3** takes you out of town to the north, onto the Guápiles Highway that leads to the Caribbean coast.

The Neighborhoods in Brief

San José is divided into dozens of neighborhoods, known as *barrios*. Most of the listings in this chapter fall within the main downtown area, but you'll need to know about a few outlying neighborhoods. In addition, the nearby suburbs of Escazú and Santa Ana are so close that they could almost be considered part of San José. For more information on these towns, see chapter 7.

DOWNTOWN In San José's busy downtown, you'll find most of the city's museums, as well as a handful of small urban parks and open-air plazas, and the city's main cathedral. Many tour companies, restaurants, and hotels are located here. Unfortunately, traffic noise and exhaust fumes make this one of the least pleasant parts of the city. Streets and avenues are usually bustling and crowded with pedestrians and vehicular traffic, and street crime is most rampant here. Still, the sections of Avenida Central between calles 6 and 7, as well as Avenida 4 between calles 9 and 14, have been converted into pedestrian malls, greatly improving things on these stretches.

BARRIO AMÓN/BARRIO OTOYA These two picturesque neighborhoods, just north and east of downtown, are the site of the greatest concentration of historic buildings in San José. Some of these have been renovated and turned into boutique hotels and atmospheric restaurants. If you're looking for character and don't mind the noise and exhaust fumes from passing cars and buses, this neighborhood makes a good base for exploring the city.

A colonial-era building in San José.

LA SABANA/PASEO COLÓN   Paseo Colón, a wide boulevard west of downtown, is an extension of Avenida Central and ends at Parque La Sabana. It has several good, small hotels and numerous restaurants. This is also where several of the city's car-rental agencies have their in-town offices. Once the site of the city's main airport, the Parque La Sabana (La Sabana Park) is San José's largest public park, with ample green areas, sports and recreation facilities, the National Stadium, and the Museo de Arte Costarricense (Costa Rican Art Museum).

SAN PEDRO/LOS YOSES   Located east of downtown San José, Los Yoses is an upper-middle-class neighborhood that is home to many diplomatic missions and embassies. San Pedro is a little farther east and is the site of the University of Costa Rica. Numerous college-type bars and restaurants are all around the edge of the campus, while more upscale and refined restaurants and boutique hotels can be found in the residential sections of both neighborhoods.

GETTING AROUND
By Bus

Bus transportation around San José is cheap—the fare is usually somewhere around C195 to C475—although the Alajuela/San José buses that run in from the airport cost C555. The most important buses are those running east along Avenida 2 and west along Avenida 3. The **Sabana/**

A bus stop in San José.

Cementerio bus runs from Parque La Sabana to downtown and is one of the most convenient buses to use. You'll find a bus stop for the outbound Sabana/Cementerio bus near the main post office on Avenida 3 near the corner of Calle 2, and another one on Calle 11 between avenidas Central and 1. This bus also has stops all along Avenida 2. **San Pedro** buses leave from the end of the pedestrian walkway on Avenida Central between calles 9 and 11, and take you out of downtown heading east.

You pay as you board the bus. The city's bus drivers can make change, although they don't like to receive large bills. Be especially mindful of your wallet, purse, or other valuables, because pickpockets often work the crowded buses.

By Taxi

Although taxis in San José have meters *(marías)*, the drivers sometimes refuse to use them, particularly with foreigners, so you'll occasionally have to negotiate the price. Always try to get them to use the meter first (say *"ponga la maría, por favor"*). The official rate at press time is C640 per kilometer (½ mile). If you have a rough idea of how far it is to your destination, you can estimate how much it should cost from this figure. Wait time is charged at C3,650 per hour, and is pro-rated for smaller increments.

Depending on your location, the time of day, and the weather (rain places taxis at a premium), it's relatively easy to hail a cab downtown. You'll always find taxis in front of the Teatro Nacional (albeit at high prices) and around the Parque Central at Avenida Central and Calle Central. Taxis in front of hotels and the El Pueblo tourist complex usually charge more than others, although this is technically illegal. Most hotels will gladly call you a cab, either for a downtown excursion or for a trip back out to the airport. You can also get a cab by calling **Coopetaxi** (© 2235-9966), **Coopeirazu** (© 2254-3211), **Coopetico** (© 2224-7979), or **Coopeguaria** (© 2226-1366). **Cinco Estrellas Taxi** (© 2228-3159) is based in Escazú but services the entire metropolitan area and airport, and claims to always have an English-speaking operator on call.

On Foot

Downtown San José is very compact. Nearly every place you might want to go is within a 15-by-4-block area. Because of traffic congestion, you'll often find it faster to walk than to take a bus or taxi. Be careful when walking the streets any time of day or night. Flashy jewelry, loosely held handbags or backpacks, and expensive camera equipment tend to attract thieves. **Avenida Central** is a pedestrian-only street from calles 6 to 7, and has been redone with interesting paving stones and the occasional fountain in an attempt to create a comfortable pedestrian mall. A similar pedestrian-only walkway runs along **Avenida 4,** between calles 9 and 14.

By Train

San José has sporadic and minimal urban commuter train service, and it is geared almost exclusively to commuters. There are three major lines. One line connecting the western neighborhood of Pavas with the eastern suburb of San Pedro passes right through the downtown, with prominent stops at, or near, the U.S. Embassy, Parque La Sabana, the downtown court area, and the Universidad de Costa Rica (University of Costa

Pedestrians walking along Avenida Central.

Rica) and Universidad Latina (Latin University). This train runs commuter hours roughly every hour between 5 and 8:30am and 4 and 7:30pm.

Another line runs between downtown San José and Heredia. This train runs roughly every 30 minutes between 5:30 and 8am, and 3:30 and 7:30pm.

And a third line runs between downtown San Jose and Cartago. This train runs roughly every 30 minutes between 6:30 and 8am, and between 3:30 and 7:30pm. This later route is potentially useful for tourists, but again, the train is predominantly for local commuters, and not geared towards tourists. You cannot purchase tickets in advance, and trains often fill up, leaving you waiting 30 minutes or more for the next train.

Fares range from C420 to C550, depending on the length of your ride.

By Car

It will cost you between $45 and $150 per day to rent a car in Costa Rica (the higher prices are for 4WD vehicles). Many car-rental agencies have offices at the airport. If not, they will usually either pick you up or deliver the car to any San José hotel. If you decide to pick up your rental car in downtown San José, be prepared for some very congested streets.

Car-Rental Advice

If you plan to rent a car, I recommend reserving it in advance from home. All the major international agencies and many local companies have toll-free numbers and websites. Sometimes you can even save a bit on the cost by reserving in advance. Costa Rica's car-rental fleet is not sufficient to meet demand during the high season when rental rates run at a premium. Sometimes this allows agencies here to gouge last-minute car-rental shoppers.

The following companies have desks at Juan Santamaría International Airport, as well as offices downtown: **Adobe Rent A Car** (www.adobecar.com; ✆ 2542-4800), **Avis** (www.avis.com; ✆ 800/633-3469 in the U.S. and 800/879-2847 in Canada, or 2293-2222 central reservation number in Costa Rica), **Budget** (www.budget.com; ✆ 800/472-3325 in the U.S. and Canada, or 2255-4240 in San José), **Dollar** (www.dollar.com; ✆ 800/800-6000 in the U.S. and Canada, or 2257-1585 in San José), **Hertz** (www.hertz.com; ✆ 800/654-3131 in the U.S. and Canada, or 2221-1818 in San José), **National Car Rental** (www.nationalcar.com; ✆ 877/222-9058 in the U.S. and Canada, 2221-4700 in San José), and **Payless Rent A Car** (www.paylesscar.com; ✆ 800/729-5377 in the U.S. and Canada, or 2432-4747 in Costa Rica).

Dozens of other smaller, local car-rental agencies are in San José, and most will arrange for airport or hotel pickup or delivery. Some of the more dependable local agencies are **Hola! Rent A Car** (www.hola.net; ✆ **2520-0100**); **Toyota Rent A Car** (www.toyotarent.com; ✆ **2256-5713**); and **Vamos Rent A Car** ★★ (www.vamosrentacar.com; ✆ **800/950-8426** in the U.S. and Canada, or 2432-5258 in Costa Rica). Vamos gets especially high marks for customer service and transparency.

For more advice on renting cars, see "Getting Around: By Car," in chapter 14.

[Fast FACTS] SAN JOSÉ

ATMs/Banks You'll find an extensive network of banks and ATMs around San José. Banks are usually open Monday through Friday from 9am to 4pm, although many have begun to offer extended hours. Post offices are generally open Monday through Friday from 8am to 5:30pm, and Saturday from 7:30am to noon. Due to crime directed at folks just as they are withdrawing cash from an ATM, some of the banks have taken to disabling their ATM networks at night.

Dentists Call your embassy, which will have a list of recommended dentists. Bilingual dentists often advertise in the *Tico Times*. Because treatments are so inexpensive in Costa Rica, dental tourism has become a popular option for people needing extensive work.

Doctors Contact your embassy for information on doctors in San José, or see "Hospitals," below.

Drugstores San José has countless pharmacies and drugstores. Many of them deliver at little or no extra cost. The pharmacy at the **Hospital Clínica Bíblica,** Avenida 14 between calles Central and 1 (✆ **2522-1000**), is open daily 24 hours, as is the **Hospital CIMA** pharmacy (✆ **2208-1080**) in Escazú. **Farmacia Fischel** (www. fischel.co.cr; ✆ **800/347-2435** toll-free in Costa Rica) has scores of branches around the metropolitan area.

Embassies & Consulates See chapter 14.

Emergencies In case of any emergency, dial ✆ **911** (which should have an English-speaking operator); for an ambulance, call ✆ **1028;** and to report a fire, call ✆ **1118.**

Hospitals **Clínica Bíblica,** Avenida 14 between calles Central and 1 (www.clinicabiblica.com; ✆ **2522-1000**), is conveniently close to downtown and has several English-speaking doctors. The **Hospital CIMA** (www.hospital cima.com; ✆ **2208-1000**), located in Escazú on the Próspero Fernández Highway, which connects San José and the western suburb of Santa Ana, has the most modern facilities in the country.

Internet Access Internet cafes are all over San José. Rates run between C600 and C5,300 per hour. Many hotels have their own Internet cafe or allow guests to send and receive e-mail. And many have added Wi-Fi, either for free or a small charge.

Maps The information desks at the airport are usually stocked with decent maps of both Costa Rica and San José. Also try **Librería Lehmann,** Avenida Central between calles 1 and 3 (✆ **2522-4848**); and **Librería Universal,** Avenida Central and calles Central and 1 (✆ **2222-2222**). Perhaps the best map to have is the waterproof country map of Costa Rica put out by **Toucan Maps** (www. mapcr.com), which can be ordered directly from their website or any major online bookseller.

Police Dial ✆ **911** or 2295-3272 for the police. They should have someone available who speaks English.

Post Office The main post office (*correo*) is on Calle 2 between avenidas 1 and 3 (www.correos.go.cr; ✆ **2223-9766**). See "Mail," on p. 576, for more information.

Restrooms Public restrooms are rare to nonexistent, but most big hotels and public restaurants will let you use their restrooms. Downtown, you can find public restrooms at the entrance to the Museos del

Banco Central de Costa Rica (p. 130).

Safety Pickpockets and purse slashers are rife in San José, especially on public buses, in the markets, on crowded sidewalks, near hospitals, and lurking outside bank offices and ATMs. Leave most of your money and other valuables in your hotel safe, and carry only as much as you really need when you go out. If you do carry anything valuable with you, keep it in a money belt or special passport bag around your neck. Day packs are a prime target of brazen pickpockets throughout the city. One common scam involves someone dousing you or your pack with mustard or ice cream. Another scamster (or two) will then quickly come to your aid—they are usually much more interested in cleaning you out than cleaning you up.

Stay away from the red-light district northwest of the Central Market. Also be advised that the Parque Nacional is not a safe place for a late-night stroll. Other precautions include walking around corner vendors, not between the vendor and the building. The tight space between the vendor and the building is a favorite spot for pickpockets. Never park a car on the street, and never leave anything of value in a car, even if it's in a guarded parking lot. Don't even leave your car unattended by the curb in front of a hotel while you dash in to check on your reservation. With these precautions in mind, you should have a safe visit to San José. Also, see "Safety," in chapter 14.

Time Zone   San José is on Central Standard Time (same as Chicago and St. Louis), 6 hours behind Greenwich Mean Time. For the exact time (in Spanish), call ℂ **1112.**

Useful Telephone Numbers   For directory assistance, call ℂ **1113;** for international directory assistance, call ℂ **1024.**

Weather   The weather in San José (including the Central Valley) is usually temperate, never getting extremely hot or cold. May through November is the rainy season, although the rain usually falls only in the afternoon and evening.

EXPLORING SAN JOSÉ

Most visitors to Costa Rica try to get out of the city as fast as possible so they can spend more time on the beach or off in the rainforests. But San José has some of the best and most modern museums in Central America, with a wealth of fascinating pre-Columbian artifacts. Standouts include the Museo de Jade Marco Fidel Tristán (Jade Museum) and the Museo de Arte Costarricense (Costa Rican Art Museum), featuring a fine collection of Costa Rican art, and a large and varied, open-air sculpture garden.

Just outside San José in the Central Valley are also several great things to see and do. With day trips out of the city, you can spend quite a few days in this region. See chapter 7 for additional touring ideas.

The Top Attractions
DOWNTOWN SAN JOSÉ

Catedral Metropolitana (Metropolitan Cathedral) ★ CATHE-
DRAL   San José's principal Catholic cathedral was built in 1871. Rather plain from the outside, the large neoclassical church features a

Downtown San Jose taken from the Jade Museum.

"Tico" sculptures in San José.

mix of stained-glass works, and assorted sculptures and bas-reliefs. It also has a wonderfully restored 19th-century pipe organ. A well-tended little garden surrounds the church and features a massive marble statue of Pope Juan Paul II carved by celebrated Costa Rican sculptor Jorge Jiménez Deredia, who also has a work at the Vatican. The cathedral is just across from the downtown Parque Central (Central Park).

Av. 2 and Calle Central. © **2221-3820.** Free admission. Mon–Sat 6:30am–6:30pm; Sun 6:30am–9pm.

Centro Nacional de Arte y Cultura (National Center of Art and Culture) ★ CULTURAL COMPLEX   Housed in what was formerly the National Liquor Factory (FANAL), this complex of museums

and performance spaces is also home to the Ministry of Culture. The best museum here is the Museum of Contemporary Art and Design (MADC), which has several very large exhibition spaces and features rotating shows of predominantly local and regional artists, with the occasional exhibition from the rest of the world. The theaters, as well as the central courtyard amphitheater, host a wide range of cutting-edge Costa Rican drama, dance, and musical performances. The complex takes

Museo Nacional de Costa Rica.

San José

PASO DE LA VACA

COCA-COLA

MEXICO

PARQUE LA SABANA

Paseo Colón

Coca-Cola
Bus Terminal

MERCED

Av. Central

Av. 17
Av. 15
Av. 13
Av. 11
Av. 7
Av. 5
Av. 7
Av. 5
Av. 3
Av. 5
Av. 3
Av. 1
Av. 3
Av. 1
Av. 2
Av. 2
Av. 4
Av. 4
Av. 6
Av. 6
Av. 8
Av. 10
Av. 10

RESTAURANTS
Alma de Cafe **28**
Café Mundo **17**
Cafeteria 1930 **25**
Del Mar **20**
Grano de Oro Restaurant **9**
Kalú Café **45**
La Esquina de Buenos Aires **34**
Machu Picchu **6**
Mantras Veggie Café **46**
Olio **44**
Park Café **1**
Restaurante Nuestra Tierra **39**
Sapore Trattoria **12**
Soda Tapia **4**
Sofía Mediterranea **43**
Tin Jo **36**
Vishnu **24, 35**
Whapin' **47**

ATTRACTIONS
Catedral Metropolitano **27**
Centro Nacional de Arte y Cultura **18**
Mercado Central **10**
Museo de Arte Costarricense **3**
Museo de Jade Marco Fidel Tristán **33**
Museo de Los Niños **11**
Museo Nacional de Costa Rica **40**
Museos del Banco Central de Costa Rica **29**
Spirogyra Butterfly Garden **13**
Teatro Melíco Salazar **26**
Teatro Nacional **28**

up a full city block between the Parque España and Parque Nacional, and just a half-block away from the Jade Museum (p. 133).

Calle 13, btw. avs. 3 and 5. www.madc.ac.cr. ☏ **2257-7202.** Admission $3, free for children and seniors, and free on Mon for everybody. Mon–Sat 9:30am–5pm.

Museos del Banco Central de Costa Rica (Gold Museum) ★★

MUSEUM   A trove of some 1,600 gold pieces dating from 500 b.c.e. to 1500 c.e., is the primary lure here; visitors are usually bowled over by the intricate workmanship on the mostly small to downright teeny gold items. Interestingly, gold was used in many forms, from cast animal figurines to jewelry to functional pieces. But the museum goes beyond the

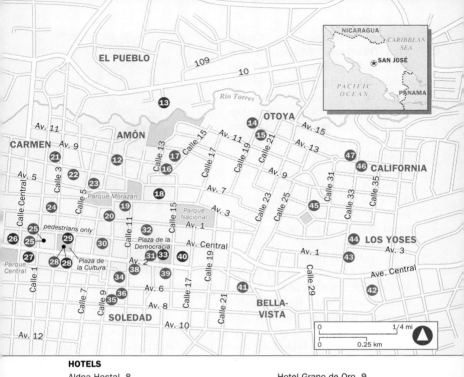

HOTELS

Aldea Hostal **8**
Aurola Holiday Inn **23**
Costa Rica Backpackers **41**
Crowne Plaza Corobicí **2**
Gran Hotel Costa Rica **25**
Hostel Pangea **21**
Hotel Aranjuez **14**
Hotel Cacts **7**
Hotel Colonial **38**
Hotel Don Carlos **12**

Hotel Grano de Oro **9**
Hôtel Le Bergerac **42**
Hotel Presidente **30**
Hotel Rincón de San José **16**
Hotel Santo Tomás **22**
Kap's Place **15**
Pensión de la Cuesta **32**
Sleep Inn **19**
Tryp Sabana by Windham **5**

shiny, yellow stuff with a smartly curated survey of Pre-Columbian culture, including exhibits on history, metalworking and customs. The Gold Museum is directly underneath the downtown Plaza de la Cultura and is actually one of three housed in this complex (there are numismatic and philatelic museums here, as well). Your admission gets you in to all three. Admission is free every Wednesday.

Calle 5, btw. avs. Central and 2, underneath the Plaza de la Cultura. www.museosdel-bancocentral.org. ✆ **2243-4202.** Admission C5,500 adults, C4,000 students, free for children 11 and under. Free admission Wed. Daily 9:15am–5pm. Closed Jan 1, May 1, Dec 25, Holy Thurs, Good Fri, Easter Sun.

Museo Nacional de Costa Rica (National Museum) ★★

MUSEUM Sitting atop the Plaza de la Democracia, the Museo Nacional provides a solid, all-around sampling of the archaeological, historical, and natural wonders of Costa Rica from pre-Columbian times to the present. That means pre-Columbian art and artifacts, including musical instruments, recreated tombs, pottery and pieces in jade and gold (like those you'd find in either of those two more specifically oriented institutions in this chapter, but obviously not in the same quantities). In the area devoted to the colonial period and onwards, you'll find recreated interiors, paintings, furniture and

A gold artifact at the Museos del Banco Central.

dioramas (with lots of explanations in English). Housed in a large, former army barracks, the building features turrets and outside walls that still bear the bullet marks from fighting in the 1948 civil war. In addition to all the historical exhibits, this place also has a large butterfly garden with more than 25 species fluttering about. I'd plan on around 2 hours to really get a good feel for this museum.

Art displays at Museo de Jade Marco Fidel Tristán.

Calle 17, btw. avs. Central and 2, on Plaza de la Democracia. www.museocostarica. go.cr. © **2257-1433.** Admission $8 adults, $4 students with valid ID; children 12 and under free. Tues–Sat 8:30am–4:30pm; Sun 9am–4:30pm. Closed on national holidays.

BARRIO AMÓN/BARRIO OTOYA

Museo de Jade Marco Fidel Tristán (Jade Museum) ★
MUSEUM   No commodity was more valuable among the pre-Columbian cultures of Central America and Mexico than jade; it was worth more than gold. Set on the western edge of the Plaza de la Democracia, this new five-story building has more than 7,000 sq. m (75,000 sq. ft.) of exhibition space, which for the first time ever, is enough to display the museum's impressive 7,000 piece collection. The museum also houses an extensive collection of pre-Columbian polychrome terra-cotta bowls, vases and figurines, some of which are startlingly modern in design (and exhibit a surprisingly advanced technique). Particularly intriguing is a vase that incorporates actual human teeth, and a display that shows how jade was embedded in human teeth merely for decorative purposes. All of the wall text is translated into English. Allot at least an hour to tour this museum.

Calle 13, btw. avenidas 2 and Central. © **2521-6610.** Admission $15 adults; $5 students with valid ID, free for children 10 and under. Daily 10am–5pm.

LA SABANA/PASEO COLÓN

Museo de Arte Costarricense (Costa Rican Art Museum) ★★
ART MUSEUM   Originally the main terminal and control tower of San José's first international airport, this museum houses the largest and most important collection of works by Costa Rican artists from the colonial time to the present. The museum's permanent collection has over 6,000 pieces, including works by big names like Juan Manuel Sánchez, Max Jiménez, Francisco Amighetti, Lola Fernández, and more. There's a sizeable collection of Amighetti's stark and minimalistic lithographs, and 19th-century oil paintings of classic rural country scene's like "El Porton Rojo (The Red Door)" by Teodorico Quiros. On the back patio—which used to lead to the tarmac—is a sculpture garden. This museum is free, and anchors the eastern edge of La Sabana city

A sculpture at Museo de Arte Costarricense.

A butterfly at the Spirogyra Butterfly Garden.

park, making it easy to combine a visit here, with a stroll through the park.

Calle 42 and Paseo Colón, Parque La Sabana Este. www.musarco.go.cr. ✆ **2256-1281.** Free admission. Tues–Sun 9am–4pm.

ON THE OUTSKIRTS OF DOWNTOWN

Spirogyra Butterfly Garden ★ ZOO   Smaller and less elaborate than the Butterfly Farm, Spirogyra still provides a good introduction to the life cycle of butterflies. First watch the 18-minute video (it runs continuously), then grab the provided butterfly booklet and take a self-guided tour. It's a calm and quiet oasis in a noisy and crowded city, just a short taxi ride to downtown (it's near El Pueblo).

100m (1 block) east and 150m (1½ blocks) south of El Pueblo Shopping Center. www. butterflygardencr.com. ✆ **2222-2937.** Admission $7 adults and students, and $5 children 12 and under. Mon-Fri 9am-Fri 2pm, Sat-Sun 9am–3pm.

Especially for Kids

Museo de Los Niños (Children's Museum) ★ MUSEUM   A massive attraction that's both fun and informative, the Museo del Los Ninos features interactive exhibits and educational displays describing everything from the rainforest, to pre-Columbian village life to the interior of a space ship (in honor of Costa Rican astronaut Franklin Chang). The simulated earthquake exhibit is always a favorite. It's housed in a former prison, so if anyone in your family is acting out, you can actually lock them in an old prison cell to set them straight. The museum is also home to the National Auditorium, and often features temporary exhibitions of contemporary art. You can easily spend 2 to 3 hours here but you'll want to take a taxi for transportation, as the museum sits just in from a rather seedy section of the city's red-light district.

Calle 4 and Av. 9. www.museocr.org. ⓒ **2258-4929.** Admission C2,200 adults, free for children 15 and under. Tues-Fri 8am-4:30pm Sat-Sun 9:30am–5pm.

Outdoor Activities & Spectator Sports

Because of the chaos and pollution, you'll probably want to get out of the city before undertaking anything too strenuous. But if you want to brave the elements, San José does have a few outdoor activities to enjoy. For information on horseback riding, hiking, and white-water rafting trips from San José, see "Side Trips from San José," later in this chapter.

Parque La Sabana ★★ (La Sabana Park, at the western end of Paseo Colón), formerly San José's international airport, is the city's center for active sports and recreation. Here you'll find jogging trails, a banked bicycle track, soccer fields, a roller-rink, a few public tennis courts, and the huge National Stadium. Aside from events at the stadium, all the facilities are free and open to the public. On weekends, you'll usually find free, public aerobic, yoga, or dancercise classes taking place. Families gather for picnics, people fly kites, pony rides are available for the kids, and everyone strolls through the outdoor sculpture garden. If you really want to experience the local culture, try getting into a pickup soccer game. However, be careful in this park, especially at dusk or after dark, when it becomes a favorite haunt for youth gangs and muggers.

BIRD-WATCHING Serious birders will want to head out of San José, but it is still possible to see quite a few species in the metropolitan area. Two of the best spots for urban bird-watching are the campus at the **University of Costa Rica,** in the eastern suburb of San Pedro, and **Parque del Este ★**, located a little farther east on the road to San Ramón de Tres Ríos. You'll see a mix of urban species, and if you're lucky, you might spy a couple of hummingbirds or even a blue-crowned motmot. To get to the university campus, take any San Pedro bus from Avenida Central between calles 9 and 11. To get to Parque del Este, take the San Ramón/ Parque del Este bus from Calle 9 between avenidas Central and 1.

BULLFIGHTING Although I hesitate to call it a sport, **Las Corridas a la Tica (Costa Rican bullfighting)** is a popular and frequently comic stadium event. Instead of the blood-and-gore/life-and-death confrontation of traditional bullfighting, Ticos just like to tease the bull. In a typical *corrida* (bullfight), anywhere from 50 to 150 *toreadores improvisados* (literally, "improvised bullfighters") stand in the ring waiting for the bull. What follows is a slapstick scramble to safety whenever the bull heads toward a crowd of bullfighters. The braver bullfighters try to slap the bull's backside as the beast chases down one of his buddies.

LEFT: **Fountain in La Sabana Park;** RIGHT: **A Costa Rican bullfight.**

You can see a bullfight during the various Festejos Populares (City Fairs) around the country. The country's largest Festejos Populares are in Zapote, a suburb east of San José, during Christmas week and the first week in January. Admission is C5,000 to C10,000. This is a purely seasonal activity and occurs in San José only during the Festejos. However, nearly every little town around the country has yearly *festejos*. These are spread out throughout the year. Ask at your hotel; if your timing's right, you might be able to take in one of these.

JOGGING Try **Parque La Sabana,** mentioned above, or head to **Parque del Este,** east of town in the foothills above San Pedro. Take the San Ramón/Parque del Este bus from Calle 9 between avenidas Central and 1. It's never a good idea to jog at night, on busy streets, or alone, particularly if you're a woman. And remember, Tico drivers are not accustomed to joggers on residential streets, so don't expect drivers to give you much berth.

SOCCER (FÚTBOL) Ticos take their *fútbol* seriously. Costa Rican professional soccer is some of the best in Central America, and the national team, or *Sele (selección nacional),* qualified for the World Cup in 2002 and 2006. Although they failed to qualify for the 2010 World Cup in South Africa, they did qualify for the 2014 in Brazil—and did quite well, considering the odds, losing to the Netherlands on penalty kicks in the quarterfinals.

The local professional soccer season runs from August through June, with a break for Christmas and New Year's, and separate championship playoffs every December and July. The main San José team is

Saprissa (affectionately called El Monstruo, or "The Monster"). **Saprissa's stadium** is in Tibás (www.saprissa.com; ✆ **2240-4034**; take any Tibás bus from Calle 2 and Av. 5). Games are often held on Sunday at 11am, but occasionally are scheduled for Saturday afternoon or Wednesday evening. Check the local newspapers for game times and locations.

International and other important matches are held in the **National Stadium** on the northeastern corner of Parque La Sabana.

Saprissa fans at a *fútbol* match.

Aside from major international matches at the National Stadium, you don't need to buy tickets in advance. Tickets generally run between C1,500 and C8,000. It's worth paying a little extra for *sombra numerado* (reserved seats in the shade). This will protect you from both the sun and the more rowdy aficionados. Costa Rican soccer fans take the sport seriously, and periodic violent incidents, both inside and outside the stadiums, have marred the sport here, so be careful. Other options include *sombra* (general admission in the shade), *palco* and *palco numerado* (general admission and reserved mezzanine), and *sol general* (general admission in full sun).

National Stadium.

It is possible to buy tickets to most sporting events in advance from **E-Ticket** (www.eticket.cr), but the site is entirely in Spanish.

SWIMMING   If you aren't going to get to the beach anytime soon and your hotel doesn't have a pool, you can use the pool at the Multispa facility at the hotel **Crowne Plaza Corobicí** (p. 142) for around $20.

WHERE TO STAY

San José offers up a wide range of hotel choices, from plush boutique hotels to budget pensións and backpacker hangouts. Many downtown hotels and small inns are housed in beautifully converted and restored old mansions. The vast majority of accommodations—and the best deals—are in the moderate range, where you can find everything from elegant little inns to contemporary business class chains. Staying in San José puts you in the center of the action, and close to all of the city's museums, restaurants, and nightlife venues. However, it also exposes you to many urban pitfalls, including noise, traffic, pollution, and street crime.

The prices quoted here are for hotels' rack rates, the maximum that they charge; it is, however, not always necessary to pay that rate. You can typically find discounts of up to 20 percent for rooms when booking directly, or through many websites (see "Tips on Where to Stay," p. 570, for more tips). *Note:* Quoted discount rates almost never include breakfast, local taxes, or other applicable hotel fees.

Downtown San José/Barrio Amón

The urban center of San José is the city's heart and soul, with a wide range of hotels and restaurants and easy access to museums and attractions. It also has several popular public parks and plazas, and the atmospheric Barrio Amón, a charming neighborhood home to the city's greatest concentration of colonial-era architecture. The neighborhood's biggest drawbacks are the street noise, bus fumes, gridlock traffic, and petty crime.

MODERATE

In addition to the hotels listed below, the **Sleep Inn** ★, Av. 3, between calles 9 and 11 (www.sleepinnsanjose.com; ✆ **2521-6500**), is a modern, American-style chain hotel in the heart of downtown, while **Hotel Colonial** ★, Calle 11, between avenidas 4 and 6 (www.hotelcolonialcr.com; ✆ **2223-0109**); and **Hotel Rincón de San José** ★

Barrio Amón, San José.

(www.hotelrincondesanjose.com; ℂ **2221-9702**), on the corner of Avenida 9 and Calle 15, are all solid boutique options.

Aurola Holiday Inn ★   At 17 stories tall, the Aurola Holiday Inn's gleaming glass facade towers over the Parque Morazan and surrounding Barrio Amon neighborhood. This central location provides easy walking access to a host of restaurants, bars, and several of the city's better museums. Despite being one of the older downtown hotels, the rooms and common areas have received regular updating and feel contemporary, with furnishings made from varnished local hardwoods, and firm orthopedic mattresses (now if they'd only swap out the dated tube televisions for some flat screens!). The hotel has a small indoor pool and Jacuzzi, just off its well-equipped gym, however, despite the atrium skylights, I find it a shame to have to use an indoor pool on a sunny day in the tropics. The Holiday Inn was awarded "4 Leaves" by the CST Sustainable Tourism program.

Av. 5 and Calle 5, San José. www.holiday-inn.com. ℂ **800/315-2621** in the U.S. and Canada, or 2523-1000. 195 units. $100–$120 double; $123–$142 suites, $269 presidential suite. Discounts for reservations made online. Free parking. **Amenities:** Restaurant; bar; poolside snack bar; exercise room; pool; room service; free Wi-Fi.

Hotel Presidente ★   The Presidente's setting on a bustling, pedestrian–only street is both its greatest asset and its curse. Shops and restaurants are just steps away for guests, but some rooms can get noisy (try for one higher up if you're a light sleeper). That being said, the rooms are quite attractive: spacious, with white duvets, marble bathrooms, and wire art on the walls that give a taste of local flair. If you fancy spoiling yourself, the spa suites come with a private Jacuzzi for two.

Av. Central and Calle 7, San José. www.hotel-presidente.com. ℂ **877/540-1790** in the U.S. and Canada, or 2010-0000 in Costa Rica. 90 units. $119–$123 double; $152–$189 suite. Rates include breakfast buffet. Free parking. **Amenities:** Restaurant; bar; casino; small gym; spa; room service; free Wi-Fi.

INEXPENSIVE

In addition to the places listed below, **Kap's Place ★** (www.kapsplace. com; ℂ **2221-1169**), across from the Hotel Aranjuez on Calle 19 between avenidas 11 and 13, is another good choice, while real budget hounds might want to try **Hostel Pangea ★** (www.hostelpangea.com; ℂ **2221-1992**), on Avenida 7 and Calle 3, or **Costa Rica Backpackers ★** (www.costaricabackpackers.com; ℂ **2221-6191**), on Avenida 6 between calles 21 and 23.

Gran Hotel Costa Rica ★   Opened in 1930 and set right on the "it doesn't get more central than this" Plaza de la Cultura, catty-corner to the Teatro Nacional, the Gran Hotel's neo-classical building has been declared a National Historic Monument. Alas, the rooms don't have the charm of the facade: Most feel a bit bare and dated, although that may be due to the staff's attempt at historical accuracy. And history has been made here: The JFK Presidential suite is where Kennedy stayed during his 1963 visit. Breakfasts are served on the 5th floor mezzanine; grab a balcony table for a fab view. Meanwhile, down on the ground floor, the hotel's **Cafeteria 1930** is a great place for people-watching.

Av. 2, btw. calles 1 and 3, San José. www. grandhotelcostarica.com. *C* **800/949-0592** in the U.S., or 2221-4000. 107 units. $65–$105 double; $115–$185 suite. Rates include breakfast buffet. Parking nearby. **Amenities:** Restaurant; bar; concierge, small gym; room service; free Wi-Fi.

Patio of Hotel Aranjuez.

Hotel Aranjuez ★★ Set on a quiet side street in the Barrio Amón neighborhood, five adjacent wooden homes have been joined in an intricate maze of hallways and courtyards to create one of the best and most unique budget lodgings in the country. The courtyards and hallways overflow with mature trees, tropical flowers and potted ferns. These lead to quiet nooks for reading and a half-dozen or so common areas where guests gather to trade travel tales and play board games. Rooms vary greatly in size but most feature high ceilings and handsome antique wood or tile floors. A massive buffet breakfast is served each morning and the staff couldn't be more accommodating and helpful. The only downside: Some of the nearly century-old walls in these homes are fairly thin, so noise can be a problem.

Calle 19, btw. avs. 11 and 13. www.hotelaranjuez.com. *C* **2256-1825.** 35 units, 6 with shared bathroom. $38 double with shared bathroom; $53–$69 double with private bathroom. Rates include breakfast buffet. Free parking. **Amenities:** Free Wi-Fi.

Hotel Don Carlos ★★ Brimming with colonial-era charm and an unmistakably Costa Rican ambience, this converted downtown home once belonged to a former Costa Rican president. The rooms and hallways are decorated with a wealth of local art and crafts—large stone sculptures, painted ox cart wheels, wall-mounted mosaics, antique oil paintings and vivid stained glass works, as well as lush potted plants and flowing fountains. Rooms can vary tremendously in size, so ask what you're getting before you book. The restaurant serves local cuisine and has a lovely covered patio. The hotel's Boutique Annemarie gift shop (p. 154) is one of the best stocked in Costa Rica.

779 Calle 9, btw. avs. 7 and 9, San José. www.doncarloshotel.com. ☏ **866/675-9259** in the U.S. and Canada, or 2221-6707 in Costa Rica. 30 units. $85 double, $95-$100 suites. Rates include breakfast. Free parking. **Amenities:** Restaurant; bar; room service; free Wi-Fi.

Hotel Santo Tomás ★★ Built by a coffee baron more than 100 years ago, the house has been lovingly renovated by its owner, Thomas Douglas. Throughout the property you'll enjoy the deep, dark tones of well-aged wood, and various open-air terraces, interior courtyards and garden nooks. Guestrooms vary in size, but most are roomy enough to have, in addition to the bed, a small table and chairs. A newer annex adds even more spacious rooms with balconies. A small outdoor pool with a Jacuzzi is attached to the property; both are solar heated and connected by a tiny water slide. The staff and management are wonderfully gracious, and the restaurant here is topnotch. *Note:* The neighborhood is a tad sketchy after dark, so guests tend to take a taxi to and from then.

Av. 7, btw. calles 3 and 5. www.hotelsantotomas.com. ☏ **2255-0448.** 30 units. $60–$83 double. Rates include breakfast. $12 parking nearby. **Amenities:** Restaurant; bar; lounge; exercise room; Jacuzzi; small outdoor pool; all rooms smoke-free; free Wi-Fi.

Pensión de la Cuesta ★ If you don't mind a shared bathroom down the hall from your room (it's kept sparkling), this little bed-and-breakfast on the hill leading to the Parque Nacional is a genuine bargain (and a few rooms do have private bath). Once the home of Otto Apuy, a well-known Costa Rican artist, it's filled with original artwork from Apuy and others (including Diedre Hyde, and Guillermo Conte). The building itself is a nearly century-old, classic tropical wood-frame home that has been painted an eye-catching pink with blue and white trim. Some rooms are a bit dark and very simply furnished, mostly with one double and a set of bunk beds, so yes, it can feel like a hostel. But there's a lovely sunken courtyard in which to hang, and the owners give guests free run of the kitchen.

1332 Cuesta de Núñez, Av. 1, btw. calles 11 and 15, San José. www.pensiondelacuesta.com. ☏ **2256-7946.** 14 units, 4 with private bathroom. $10–$12 per person in a dorm room; $33 double with shared bath; $43 double with private bath. Rates include breakfast and taxes. Parking nearby. **Amenities:** Free Wi-Fi.

La Sabana/Paseo Colón

Located on the western edge of downtown, La Sabana Park is San José's largest city park, and Paseo Colón is a broad commercial avenue heading straight into the heart of the city. Stay in this neighborhood if you're looking for fast, easy access to the highways heading to Escazú, Santa Ana, the Pacific coast, and the airport and northern zone. Since it's on the edge of town, the area can be pretty dead at night.

The Jacuzzi terrace at the Hotel Grano de Oro.

EXPENSIVE

Hotel Grano de Oro ★★★   This is the standard-bearer for luxury boutique hotels in San José. A combination of restoration and expansion has
transformed this grand colonial-era mansion into a refined refuge in the
center of a busy city. For those that can afford to splurge, the signature suite
is elegantly decorated to evoke a bygone era, with wood-paneled walls, a
carved antique bed and a private Jacuzzi with views of the city skyline
through massive picture windows. But don't worry, if that's beyond your
budget: There are appealing standard rooms too, with such niceties as
wrought iron bed frames, shiny wood floors and plush bedding. The on-site
restaurant is one of the best in the city (p. 147) and the chic rooftop patio
with its two large Jacuzzi spas will almost make you forget you are in bustling
San José. A final reason to visit: Your money will do good. The owners Eldon
and Lori Cook support a range of social and environmental causes.

Calle 30, no. 251, btw. avs. 2 and 4, 150m (1½ blocks) south of Paseo Colón. www.
hotelgranodeoro.com. ✆ **2255-3322.** 40 units. $158–$285 double; $295–$480 suite.
Free parking. **Amenities:** Restaurant; bar; lounge; 2 rooftop Jacuzzis; room service;
spa services; free Wi-Fi.

MODERATE

In addition to the hotel below, **Tryp Sabana by Windham ★** (www.
tryphotels.com; ✆ **800/4683-261** in the U.S. and Canada, or 2547-
2323 in Costa Rica), inside the Centro Colón building on Avenida 3,
between calles 38 and 40, is a well-located business class hotel, with a
very good tapas and small-bite restaurant.

Crowne Plaza Corobicí ★   Set on the northeastern corner of La
Sabana park, this 11-story hotel's odd architecture that makes it look like
a cross between a pyramid, an air-traffic control tower and a Soviet-era

Alternative Accommodations

If you plan to be in town for a while or are traveling with family or several friends, you might want to consider staying in an *apartotel*, a cross between an apartment complex and a hotel. You can rent by the day, week, or month, and you get a furnished apartment with a full kitchen, plus housekeeping. Options include **Apartotel** **El Sesteo** ★ (www.sesteo.com; © **2296-1805**), **Apartotel La Sabana** ★ (www.apartotel-lasabana.com; © **877/722-2621** in the U.S. and Canada, or 2220-2422), and **Apartotel Los Yoses** ★ (www.apartotel.com; © **877/790-5264** in the U.S. and Canada, 2225-0033).

housing block. Don't worry, it's quite handsome inside with a huge lobby and oversized and very comfortable guest rooms. A recent remodel has given most of the rooms happy tangerine-colored walls, fine dark wood furnishings, 37 inch flat screen TV's and luxurious bedding. Typical of a business class hotel there are several dining options plus a casino and well-equipped gym and spa.

Autopista General Cañas, Sabana Norte, San José. www.crowneplaza.com. © **877/834-3613** in the U.S. and Canada, or 2543-6000 in Costa Rica. 213 units. $94–$114 double; $134–$244 suite; $444 presidential suite. Free parking. **Amenities:** 2 restaurants; bar; lounge; casino; extensive health club and spa; Jacuzzi; midsize outdoor pool; room service; sauna; babysitting; free Wi-Fi.

INEXPENSIVE

In addition to the place mentioned below, **Aldea Hostal** ★ (www.aldeahostelcostarica.com; © **2233-6365**) is a solid budget hostel option, with a popular little pizza restaurant attached.

Hotel Cacts ★   This is a solid budget option housed in a converted family home on a side street about 2 blocks in from the busy Paseo Colón. There's a hostel-like vibe to the operation with friendly staff on hand, but you also get a small pool and Jacuzzi. My favorite feature here is the open-air rooftop patio, which has chairs and chaise lounges, and offers up a spectacular view of the city and surrounding mountains.

Av. 3 bis, no. 2845, btw. calles 28 and 30, San José. www.hotelcacts.com. © **2221-2928** or 2221-6546. 25 units. $80 double. Rates include taxes and breakfast buffet. Free parking. **Amenities:** Lounge; Jacuzzi; small outdoor pool; free Wi-Fi.

San Pedro/Los Yoses

Located just east of downtown, Los Yoses is home to numerous foreign embassies and consulates, and was one of the city's early upper-class outposts, while San Pedro is home to the University of Costa Rica, and offers up a distinct college town vibe. Staying here, you'll be close to much of the city's action but still enjoy some peace and quiet. If you've rented a car, be sure your hotel provides secure parking or you'll have to find (and pay for) a nearby lot.

INEXPENSIVE

Hôtel Le Bergerac ★   On a residential side street off the busy Avenida Segunda, about midway between downtown and the university district of San Pedro, the Hôtel Le Bergerac is a delightful boutique hotel with the air of an intimate French inn and an understated elegance. Three contiguous houses have been joined to create this hotel. Rooms are spacious and bright, most with varnished wood floors, and some with French doors opening onto a balcony or patio among the tropical gardens.

Calle 35, avenida 0 y 8, San José. www.bergerachotel.com. ℂ **2234-7850.** 28 units. $87–$157 double. Rates include full breakfast. Free parking. **Amenities:** Restaurant; lounge; free Wi-Fi.

Hotel Milvia ★   Housed in a converted old wooden plantation home, this boutique hotel is the handiwork of Steve Longrigg and Florencia Urbina. Steve has decades in the hospitality industry in Costa Rica, and Florencia is one the country's more prominent artists and the former director of the Costa Rican Art Museum (p. 133). Rooms, hallways and common areas feature a varied and striking collection of contemporary Costa Rican art by Urbina and her friends and cohorts. Guestrooms are also blessed with plenty of natural light and most lead out onto a veranda or common courtyard sitting area. All of these common areas overflow with tropical plants and flowers and striking artworks. This hotel is close to the Universidad Latina and one of the city's few train lines, so street noise can be a problem at times.

1 block north and 2 blocks east of the Muñoz y Nanne Supermarket, San Pedro. www.hotelmilvia.com. ℂ **2225-4543.** 9 units. $69 double. Rates include continental breakfast. **Amenities:** Free Wi-Fi.

WHERE TO DINE

San José has a variety of restaurants serving cuisines from all over the world. You can find superb French, Italian, and contemporary fusion restaurants around the city, as well as Peruvian, Japanese, Swiss, and Spanish spots. The greatest concentration and variety of restaurants is in the downtown area, as well as in the nearby Central Valley suburbs of Escazú and Santa Ana. If you're looking for cheap eats, you'll find them all across the city in little restaurants known as *sodas,* which are the equivalent of diners in the United States.

Fruit vendors stake out spots on almost every street corner in downtown San José. If you're lucky enough to be in town between April and June, you can sample more varieties of mangoes than you ever knew existed. I like buying them already cut up in a little bag; they cost a little more this way, but you don't get nearly as messy. Be sure to try a green mango with salt and chili peppers—it's guaranteed to wake up your taste buds. Another common street food is *pejibaye,* a bright orange palm nut

A vendor selling *pejibaye.*

about the size of a plum. They're boiled in big pots on carts; you eat them in much the same way you eat an avocado, and they taste a bit like squash.

Downtown San José

EXPENSIVE

La Esquina de Buenos Aires ★★ ARGENTINE/STEAKHOUSE Frankly, the Argentines do steak much better than the Ticos, and this Argentine-themed steakhouse is one of the best restaurants in the city. The decor and ambience are pure Porteño, and the extensive menu features a long list of grilled meats, some very good pastas, and various seafood and poultry offerings. Festive and almost always filled to brimming, you'll need reservations to get in.

Calle 11 and Av. 4. Ⓒ **2223-1909** or 2257-9741. Main courses C5,300–C13,800. Mon–Fri 11:30am–3pm and 6–10:30pm; Sat 12:30–11pm; Sun noon–10pm.

MODERATE

Restaurante Nuestra Tierra ★ COSTA RICAN Yes, Nuestra Tierra was built for and is geared towards tourists. But since it brings back the ambiance and food of a bygone era so effectively, I still recommend it. Designed to recreate the feel of an old Costa Rican homestead kitchen, you'll find the wait staff in traditional garb serving traditional Costa Rica fare to crowds sitting at heavy wooden tables on bench seating. Bunches of bananas and onions and scores of painted enamel coffee

145

mugs hang from wooden columns and beams. Hefty portions are served on banana leaves set over large plates. The prices are a bit high for what you get. On the plus side, service is prompt and pleasant, and there are few better selfie spots in town.

Av. 2 and Calle 15. © **2258-6500.** Main courses C6,000–C15,000. Daily 24 hr.

Sapore Trattoria ★★ ITALIAN This traditional trattoria is well located just off the Plaza de la Democracia and a stone's throw from the Jade Museum. The long, narrow dining room features wooden floors, and some exposed brick and stone work. Start things off with a mixed antipasto plate, or some thin-sliced beef *carpaccio,* followed by a perfectly prepared pasta or risotto dish—I especially like the porcini and truffle risotto. For something more filling try the *osso buco* (veal stew). There's a good selection of Italian wines and beers, and sometimes live music in the evenings.

Calle 13 and Avenida 2. © **2222-8906.** Reservations not necessary. Main courses C6,000–C12,000. Mon–Sat 11:30am–2:30pm and 6–10pm (Sat until 11pm); Sun 11:30am–6pm.

Tin Jo ★★★ CHINESE/PAN-ASIAN This has long been one of the best and most popular restaurants in the city. Costa Rica has a long history of Chinese immigration and this family restaurant is on its second generation. The menu here, however, wanders far and wide, with more traditional Szechuan and Cantonese plates sharing the menu with a mix of Thai, Japanese, Indian, and even Malay dishes. There are several dining rooms here each featuring the unique decor from each of the countries or regions. The multiple vegetarian options are all clearly marked as to whether they are vegan and/or gluten free.

Calle 11, btw. avs. 6 and 8. www.tinjo.com. © **2221-7605** or 2257-3622. Reservations recommended. Main courses C6,000–C14,000. Mon–Fri 11:30am–2:30pm and 6–10pm (Fri until 11pm); Sat noon–3pm and 6–11pm; Sun noon–9pm.

INEXPENSIVE

Alma de Café ★ CAFE/COFFEEHOUSE Housed in an anteroom off the main lobby of the neo-baroque National Theater (Teatro Nacional), what should be just a simple coffee shop and restaurant is elevated by its setting—marble tables and floors, as well as elaborate painted ceiling murals, and regularly rotating exhibits of contemporary local artists. The menu features healthful salads, a selection of crepes, sandwiches, and lasagnas. Alma de Cafe often stays open late on theater performance nights.

In the Teatro Nacional, Av. 2, btw. calles 3 and 5. © **2010-1119.** Sandwiches C3,000–C6,200; main courses C4,000–C6,500. Mon–Sat 9am–7pm; Sun 9am–6pm.

Vishnu ★ VEGETARIAN This mini-chain was a pioneer in providing vegetarian cooking to the Costa Rican masses. It doesn't offer the most innovative of menus and the decor resembles that of a run-down diner but it is a safe and popular bet for those looking for vegetarian and vegan options in San José. The fresh fruit juices and smoothies here are the real draw, but they do a decent vegetarian burger, too. A second branch (② **2223-3095**) is on the north side of Avenida 8, between calles 11 and 9, as well as outlets in Heredia and Alajuela.

Av. 1, btw. calles 1 and 3. ② **2256-6063**. Main courses C3,500–C4,500. Mon–Sat 7am–9pm; Sun 9am–7:30pm.

Barrio Amón/Barrio Otoya/Barrio California
MODERATE

Café Mundo ★★ INTERNATIONAL A popular spot with a lively atmosphere and artsy ambience, this restaurant is housed in a remodeled old mansion, with tables and chairs spread through several rooms, hallways, outdoor patios, and terraces. The largest dining room here features floor-to-ceiling over-sized flowers painted by Costa Rican artist Miguel Casafont. Other rooms feature antique wallpaper and painted tile floors. Serving what I'd call bar-food-plus, the menu features a solid selection of salads, thick-crust pizzas, pastas, and a range of main dishes running the gamut from seafood-stuffed tenderloin to chicken in a honey-mustard sauce.

Calle 15 and Av. 9, 200m (2 blocks) east and 100m (1 block) north of the INS Building. ② **2222-6190**. Main courses C4,500–C20,000. Mon–Thurs 11am–10:30pm; Fri 11am–11:30pm; Sat 5–11:30pm.

Kalú ★★★ CAFE/BISTRO Costa Rican-born chef Camille Ratton trained at the Cordon Bleu and has created a wonderfully casual little bistro restaurant and gallery in a converted 1950's-era Art Deco home in a quiet neighborhood. The menu features a range of light and healthful options like salads and lettuce wraps, as well as tacos, panini, burgers, and more. But there are also more sophisticated options like fresh mahi-mahi in a Romesco sauce or risotto with three types of mushrooms. Don't miss out on the desserts, which, to my mind, are Camille's specialty—especially the Tarta Cahuita, an individual tartlette with a caramelized banana filling, grated lime peel, and chocolate ganache. They serve brunch on the weekends, and are renowned for their coffee (they serve 34 different preparations of java!). The attached **Kiosco** (p. 155) is one of San Jose's more creative gift shops.

Calle 31 and Av. 5. www.kalu.co.cr. ② **2253-8426**. Main courses C4,850–C10,500. Tue–Fri noon–10pm; Sat 9am–10pm; Sun 9am–4pm.

La Sabana/Paseo Colón
EXPENSIVE

Grano de Oro Restaurant ★★★ INTERNATIONAL It's no accident that the city's most elegant boutique hotel (p. 142) also has one of its most revered fine dining restaurants. The owners wooed and won

French-born chef Francis Canal, after all, a classically trained chef who has never stopped evolving, combining classic techniques from his homeland with local ingredients, tropical flavors, and contemporary fusion elements. That means a meal here might include appetizer of Costa Rican snails in puff pastry, followed by local pork with tamarind sauce or sea bass crusted with macadamia nuts. Their 200-plus bottle wine list features offerings from 4 continents, nearly a dozen choices daily by the glass. Be sure to leave room for dessert. Their namesake pie is a silky layering of coffee and mocha mousse on a rich cookie crust. The main dining room, a white linen and fine china affair, rings an open-air central courtyard, with a flowing fountain, tall potted trees and large stained glass features.

Calle 30, no. 251, btw. avs. 2 and 4, 150m (1½ blocks) south of Paseo Colón. www. hotelgranodeoro.com. ✆ **2255-3322.** Reservations recommended. Main courses C10,000–30,000. Daily 7am–10pm.

Park Café ★★★ FUSION   While the Grano de Oro (see below) thrives on elegance and consistency, this place has a more "off the cuff" vibe. But the payoff from British chef Richard Neat, who ran a two-star Michelin restaurant in London before moving to Costa Rica, can also be substantial. The menu changes seasonally, but always features creative, contemporary dishes with sometimes dazzling presentations, often in tapa-sized portions to encourage broad samplings. Recent options include prosciutto-wrapped scallops topped with fried onion rings in a Malbec reduction, and a rabbit breast served with confit of rabbit-stuffed ravioli and grilled artichokes. The restaurant is spread throughout the interior courtyard and garden of a stately old home that functions as an antiques and decorative arts shop by day.

Sabana Norte, 1 block north of Rostipollos. www.parkcafecostarica.blogspot.com. ✆ **2290-6324.** Reservations recommended. Main courses C3,900–C7,000. Tues–Sat 5:30–9pm.

MODERATE

Machu Picchu ★★ PERUVIAN/INTERNATIONAL   This long-standing local institution serves up excellent and traditional Peruvian cuisine in a converted old home (exposed brick walls and red tile floors), just off of Paseo Colón. The menu is extensive, with a wide range of ceviches and other cold and hot appetizers. The *parihuela* (a delicious seafood soup almost big and rich enough for a full meal) is a specialty. The house drink is the classic Peruvian pisco sour, made in a blender with pisco, lime juice, ice, and an egg white. A second branch of this restaurant is in San Pedro (✆ **2283-3679**), as well as a sister operation **Pikeo** (✆ **2203-6374**), which serves up a more specialized tapas-style menu, located on the old road between Escazú and Santa Ana.

Calle 32, btw. avs. 1 and 3, 150m (1½ blocks) north of the KFC on Paseo Colón. www. restaurantemachupicchu.com. ✆ **2283-3679.** Reservations recommended. Main courses C7,000–C12,000. Mon–Sat 11am–10pm; Sun 11am–6pm.

INEXPENSIVE

Soda Tapia ★ COSTA RICAN   Dine with the locals at this prototypical Tico *soda* in a retro 1950s-style American diner, complete with bright lights and Formica tables. The food is solid and the service speedy. Its extended hours make it a good choice for a late-night bite. The main branch is just across from the popular La Sabana park and Museo de Arte Costarricense (p. 133). Other branches are around the Central Valley, including ones in Santa Ana (Centro Comercial Vistana Oeste, across from MATRA; *©* **2203-7175**) and Alajuela (Centro Comercial Plaza Real Alajuela; *©* **2441-6033**).

Calle 42 and Av. 2, across from the Museo de Arte Costarricense. www.sodatapia. com. *©* **2222-6734.** Sandwiches C4,000–C4,400; main dishes C3,000–C5,000. Mon–Thurs 6am–2am; Fri–Sun 24 hr.

San Pedro/Los Yoses

In addition to the restaurants listed below, local and visiting vegetarians swear by the little **Comida Para Sentir Restaurante Vegetariano** ★ (*©* **2224-1163**), located 125m (1¼ blocks) north of the San Pedro Church. Despite the massive size and popularity of the nearby **Il Pomodoro** ★ (*©* **2224-0966**), I prefer **Pane E Vino** ★ (www.paneevino. co.cr; *©* **2280-2869**), an excellent pasta-and-pizza joint on the eastern edge of San Pedro, with other outlets around town, as well. If you're hankering for sushi, try **Matsuri** ★★ (www.restaurantematsuri.com; *©* **2280-5522**), which has multiple storefronts around town.

EXPENSIVE

Donde Carlos ★★ ARGENTINE/STEAK   While **La Esquina de Buenos Aires** (p. 145) has a more authentic Argentine vibe, Donde Carlos serves up some seriously mouthwatering traditional Argentine fare. The cuts of meat are thick, tender and perfectly prepared. Sides must be ordered separately and include French fries, mashed potatoes, white rice and grilled eggplant. You'll pass the large, open, charcoal grill just inside the front door of this contemporary converted home in an upscale residential neighborhood. Head upstairs for the better seating, and if it's a nice night try to grab one of the three or four outdoor balcony tables. For dessert, the apple pancake is a well-deserved house specialty, and big enough to be shared.

1 block north of the Fatima Church in Los Yoses. www.dondecarlos.com. *©* **2225-0819.** Main courses C8,000–C21,000. Mon–Thurs noon–3pm and 6:30–10:30pm; Fri noon–3pm and 6:30–11pm; Sat noon–11pm; Sun noon–7pm.

MODERATE

Olio ★★ MEDITERRANEAN   This dimly lit, intimate restaurant has a romantic vibe, with several small rooms and quiet nooks located off the main dining area. A laundry list of classic Greek, Italian, and Spanish dishes is served in tapas-size portions, alongside more hearty pasta and main-course options. The wine list ventures far and wide to include offerings from Chile, Argentina, and even Bulgaria.

Barrio California, 200m (2 blocks) north of Bagelman's. ✆ **2281-0541.** Reservations recommended. Main courses C4,950–C13,750. Mon–Wed noon–11pm; Thurs–Fri noon–midnight; Sat 6pm–midnight.

Whapin' ★ COSTA RICAN/CARIBBEAN It's hard to find authentic Costa Rican Caribbean cooking away from the coast, but this humble place does a good job with a wide range of specialties more commonly served up in Cahuita and Puerto Viejo. They've always got the seafood and root vegetable stew *rondon* on the menu (see "That Run-Down Feeling," on p. 549), as well as rice and beans cooked in coconut milk and served with your choice of chicken, meat or fish. Other specialties: the jerk chicken and the whole fried red snapper. Most dishes come with a side of *patacone* (fried plantain). The decor is Caribbean, too: rustic clapboard wooden walls painted the emblematic reggae colors of red, yellow and green surround rough hewn tables and chairs.

Barrio Escalante, 200m (2 blocks) east of El Farolito. ✆ **2283-1480.** Main courses C5,900–C15,900. Mon–Fri 11am–3pm and 6–10pm, Sat 11am–10pm.

INEXPENSIVE

Mantras Veggie Café and Tea House ★★ VEGETARIAN This is my (mostly) Vegan wife's favorite vegetarian restaurant in the city, and I concur. I especially like the garden seating, under bright red canvas umbrellas. The menu features a broad mix of soups, salads, wraps, sandwiches, and main dishes in both vegan and raw states. Signature dishes here include their raw zucchini "pasta" with pesto and the pad Thai. As the name implies, they serve a broad selection of herbal teas, many grown on site or purchased at local organic markets.

2 blocks east and ¼ block west of El Farolito, in Barrio Escalante. ✆ **2253-6715.** Main courses C3,850–C3,800. Mon–Sat 8:30am–5pm.

Sofía Mediterraneo ★ MIDDLE EASTERN The lure of live music, belly dancers and the fact that several language schools and a University are within easy walking distance help keep this place busy and boisterous most days and nights. As for the fare, I suggest starting off with such Middle Eastern classics as hummus, tabbouleh, and Sofia's delicious stuffed grape leaves. For a main course, I recommend the *Begendili Kuzu,* slow braised lamb shoulder served with an eggplant purée. The grilled squid is also excellent. At around $8, their daily lunch special is a great deal, featuring a main course, soft drink, and dessert.

Calle 33 and Av. 1, 2 blocks north of Bagleman's, in Barrio Escalante. ✆ **2224-5050.** Main courses C6,000–C13,900. Tue–Sat noon–11pm; Sun noon–5pm.

SHOPPING

Serious shoppers will be disappointed in San José. Aside from coffee and oxcarts, there isn't much that's distinctly Costa Rican. To compensate for its own relative lack of goods, San José (and all of Costa Rica) does a brisk business in selling crafts and clothes imported from Guatemala, Panama, and Ecuador.

San José's central shopping corridor is bounded by avenidas 1 and 2, from about Calle 14 in the west to Calle 13 in the east. For several blocks west of the Plaza de la Cultura, **Avenida Central** is a pedestrian-only street mall where you'll find store after store of inexpensive clothes for men, women, and children. Depending on the mood of the police that day, you might find a lot of street vendors as well. Most shops in the downtown district are open Monday through Saturday from about 8am to 6pm. Some shops close for lunch, while others remain open (it's just the luck of the draw for shoppers). You'll be happy to find that sales and import taxes have already been figured into display prices.

Markets

Several markets are near downtown, but by far the largest is the **Mercado Central ★** (p. 155), located between avenidas Central and 1 and calles 6 and 8.

Plaza de la Democracia ★★   Two long rows of outdoor stalls sell T-shirts, Guatemalan and Ecuadorian handicrafts and clothing, small ceramic *ocarinas* (a small musical wind instrument), and handmade jewelry. The atmosphere here is much more open than at the Mercado Central, which I find just a bit too claustrophobic. You might be able to bargain prices down a bit, but bargaining is not a traditional part of the vendor culture here, so you'll have to work hard to save a few colones. On the west side of the Plaza de la Democracia, Calle 13 bis, btw. avs. Central and 2. No phone.

Modern Malls

With globalization taking hold in Costa Rica, much of the local shopping scene has shifted to large megamalls, modern multilevel affairs with cineplexes, food courts, and international brand-name stores. The biggest and most modern of these malls include the **Mall San Pedro, Multiplaza** (one each in Escazú and the eastern suburb of Zapote), and **Terra Mall** (on the outskirts of downtown on the road to Cartago). Although they lack the charm of small shops found around San José, they are a reasonable option for one-stop shopping; most contain at least one or two local galleries and crafts shops, along with a large supermarket, which is always the best place to stock up on local coffee, hot sauces, liquors, and other nonperishable foodstuffs.

Shopping A to Z
ART GALLERIES

Galería Jacobo Karpio ★ This excellent gallery handles some of the more adventurous modern art to be found in Costa Rica. Karpio has a steady stable of prominent Mexican, Cuban, and Argentine artists, as well as some local talent. Av. 1, casa no. 1352, btw. calles 13 and 15. 50m (164 ft.) west of the Legislative Assembly. ✆ **2257-7963.**

Galería Kandinsky ★ Owned by the daughter of one of Costa Rica's most prominent modern painters, Rafa Fernández, this small gallery usually has a good selection of high-end contemporary Costa Rican paintings, be it the house collection or a specific temporary exhibit. Centro Comercial Calle Real, San Pedro. ✆ **2234-0478.**

Galería Valanti ★★ This is a well-lit, and expertly curated gallery. The collection here is ever evolving, but always includes a good mix of contemporary and classic Costa Rican and Latin American artists. Av. 11 #3395, btw. calles 33 and 35, Barrio Escalante. www.galeriavalanti.com ✆ **2253-1659.**

TEORetica ★★ This small downtown gallery was founded by one of the more adventurous and internationally respected collectors and curators in Costa Rica, the late Virginia Pérez-Ratton. It's still one of the best galleries in the country, bringing in guest curators from around the world, and you'll usually find cutting-edge exhibitions and installations here, with everything from sound and light sculptures to contemporary comics on offer. Calle 7, btw. avs. 9 and 11. www.teoretica.org. ✆ **2233-4881.**

A vendor at the Plaza de la Democracia market.

Two words of advice: Buy coffee. Lots of it.

Coffee is the best shopping deal in all of Costa Rica. Although the best Costa Rican coffee is allegedly shipped off to North American and European markets, it's hard to beat the coffee that's roasted right in front of you here. Best of all is the price: 1 pound of coffee sells for around $4 to $7. It makes a great gift and truly is a local product.

Café Britt is the big name in Costa Rican coffee. They have the largest export business in the country, and, although high-priced, their blends are very dependable. Café Britt is widely available at gift shops around the country, and at the souvenir concessions at both international airports. My favorites, however, are the coffees roasted and packaged in Manuel Antonio and Monteverde, by **Café Milagro** and **Café Monteverde,** respectively. If you visit either of these places, definitely pick up their beans.

In general, the best place to buy coffee is in any supermarket. Why pay more at a gift or specialty shop? If you buy prepackaged coffee in a supermarket in Costa Rica, the whole beans will be marked either *grano* (grain) or *grano entero* (whole bean). If you opt for ground varieties *(molido)*, be sure the package is marked *puro*; otherwise, it will likely be mixed with a good amount of sugar, the way Ticos like it.

One good coffee-related gift to bring home is a coffee sock and stand. This is the most common mechanism for brewing coffee beans in Costa Rica. It consists of a simple circular stand, made out of wood or wire, which holds a sock. Put the ground beans in the sock, place a pot or cup below it, and pour boiling water through. You can find the socks and stands at most supermarkets and in the Mercado Central. In fancier crafts shops, you'll find them made out of ceramic. Depending on its construction, a stand will cost you between $1.50 and $15; socks run around 30¢, so buy a few spares.

BOOKS

Librería Internacional ★ This is the closest Costa Rica has to a major book retailer. Most of the books here are in Spanish, but they do have a small-to-modest selection of English-language contemporary fiction, nonfiction, and natural history texts. Librería Internacional has various outlets around San José, including in most of the major modern malls. Av. Central, ¾ block west of the Plaza de la Cultura. www.libreriainternacional.com. ℭ **2257-2563.**

CHOCOLATE

Sibu Chocolate ★★ Building on the success of their organic chocolate production and tour operation in the hills of Heredia (p. 187), the folks from Sibu Chocolate have opened a small storefront in the Sabana Norte neighborhood. This is a great place to pick up a mix of their wonderful truffles and bonbons, as well as cacao powder, chocolate bars, and cacao nibs, which my family loves to sprinkle on cereal and granola in the morning. This is also a great place to grab a cup of hot chocolate (or coffee) and a pastry. 2 blocks north of Rostipollos in Sabana Norte. www.sibuchocolate.com. ✆ **2220-0050.**

HANDICRAFTS

The range and quality of craftworks for sale here has improved greatly in recent years. In addition to the places listed below, you might want to check out the works of Lil Mena, a local artist who specializes in working with and painting on handmade papers and rough fibers, and **Cecilia "Pefi" Figueres** ★★, who specializes in brightly colored abstract and figurative ceramic bowls, pitchers, coffee mugs, and more. Both Mena and Figueres are sold at some of the better gift shops around the city. Another artist to look out for is **Barry Biesanz** ★★, whose bowls and boxes are works of art. Biesanz's works are also carried at fine gift shops around San José, as well as in his workshop and gallery in the hills above Escazú (p. 354). Vendors at the Plaza de la Democracia market (p. 151) also sell handicrafts.

Boutique Annemarie ★★ Occupying two floors at the Hotel Don Carlos (p. 140), this shop has an amazing array of wood products, leather goods, papier-mâché figurines, paintings, books, cards, posters, and jewelry. You'll see most of this merchandise at the city's other shops, but not in such quantities or in such a relaxed and pressure-free environment. At the Hotel Don Carlos, Calle 9, btw. avs. 7 and 9. ✆ **2233-5343.**

Chietón Morén ★★★ "Chietón Morén" means "fair deal" in the Boruca language. This place features arts and craft works from a dozen or so different Costa Rican indigenous communities displayed in a space that is part museum and part showroom and market. Operating as a non-profit and certified "fair trade," all the profits are given directly back to the artisans and their communities. Offerings include a wide range of textiles, carved masks, prints, and jewelry. Calle 1, btw. avs. 10 and 12. www.chietonmoren.org. ✆ **2221-0145.**

Galería Namu ★★★ Galería Namu has some very high-quality arts and crafts, specializing in truly high-end indigenous works, including excellent Boruca and Huetar carved masks and "primitive" paintings. It also carries a good selection of more modern arts and craft pieces, including the ceramic work of Cecilia "Pefi" Figueres. This place organizes tours to visit various indigenous tribes and artisans as well. Av. 7, btw. calles 5 and 7. www.galerianamu.com. ℂ **2256-3412.**

La Casona ★   Just off Avenida Central, in the heart of downtown, La Casona is a 3-story warren of crafts and souvenir stalls. The various stalls sell similar craft and souvenir works imported from Guatemala, Ecuador, Panama, and even China. On a rainy day, this is a great alternative to the outdoor market on the Plaza de la Democracia (p. 151). Calle Central btw. avs. Central and 1. ℂ **2222-7999.**

Mercado Central ★   Although this tight maze of stalls is primarily a food market, vendors also sell souvenirs, leather goods, musical instruments, and many other items. Be especially careful with your wallet, purse, and prominent jewelry, as skilled pickpockets frequent the area. All the streets surrounding the Mercado Central are jammed with produce vendors selling from small carts or loading and unloading trucks. It's always a hive of activity, with crowds of people jostling for space on the streets. Your best bet is to visit on Sunday or a weekday; Saturday is particularly busy. Btw. avs. Central and 1 and calles 6 and 8, San José. No phone.

JEWELRY

Kiosco ★★   Attached to the restaurant Kalú (p. 147), this place features a range of original and one-off pieces of functional, wearable, and practical pieces made by contemporary Costa Rican and regional

Finely crafted artworks form colorful displays at Galería Namu.

A stall at the Mercado Central.

artists and designers. While the offerings are regularly changing, you'll usually find a selection of jewelry, handbags, shoes, dolls, furniture, and knickknacks. Often the pieces are made with recycled or sustainable materials. Calle 31 and Av. 5, Barrio Escalante. www.kioscosjo.com. © **2253-8426.**

Studio Metallo ★★   The outgrowth of a jewelry-making school and studio, this shop has some excellent handcrafted jewelry made in a range of styles, using everything from 18-karat white and yellow gold and pure silver, to some less exotic and expensive alloys. Some works integrate gemstones, while many others focus on the metalwork. 6½ blocks east of the Iglesia Santa Teresita, Barrio Escalante. www.studiometallo.com. © **2281-3207** or 2281-3207.

LEATHER GOODS

Del Río ★   This local leather goods manufacturer has several store-fronts around the city, and in most of the country's modern malls. Works are high quality and fairly priced, and range from wallets and belts to briefcases, boots, and fancy leather jackets and pants. Del Río also has outlets in several of the modern malls around the city. Av. Central, btw. calles 3 and 5, fronting the Plaza de la Cultura. www.delrio.cr. © **2262-1415.**

LIQUOR

The best prices I've seen for liquor are at the city's large supermarkets, such as **Automercado** and **Más × Menos.** A Más × Menos store is on Paseo Colón and Calle 26, and another is on Avenida Central at the east end of town, just below the Museo Nacional de Costa Rica.

ENTERTAINMENT & NIGHTLIFE

Catering to a mix of tourists, college students, and just generally party-loving Ticos, San José has a host of options to meet the nocturnal needs of visitors and residents alike. You'll find plenty of interesting clubs and bars, a wide range of theaters, and some very lively discos and dance salons.

To find out what's going on in San José while you're in town, go to **www.ticotimes.net**, or pick up the *La Nación* (Spanish; www.nacion. com). The former is a good place to find out where local expats are hanging out; the latter's "Viva" and "Tiempo Libre" sections have extensive listings of discos, movie theaters, and live music.

Tip: Several very popular nightlife venues are in the upscale suburbs of Escazú and Santa Ana, as well as in Heredia (a college town) and Alajuela. See "The Central Valley" chapter for more details on nightlife in these areas.

The Performing Arts

Visiting artists stop in Costa Rica on a regular basis. Recent concerts have featured hard rockers Aerosmith, Red Hot Chili Peppers, and Metallica, Mexican crooner Lila Downs, pop legend Elton John, Colombian sensation Shakira, and Latin heartthrob Marc Anthony. These performances take place at one of San José's performing arts theaters or one of the city's large sporting stadiums.

The **National Symphony Orchestra** ✆ **2240-0333** is respectable by regional standards, although its repertoire tends to be rather conservative. Symphony season runs March through November, with concerts roughly every other weekend at the Teatro Nacional. Tickets cost between C4,000 and C7,000 and can be purchased at the box office.

Costa Rica's cultural panorama changes drastically every March when the country hosts large arts festivals. In odd-numbered years, El Festival Nacional de las Artes reigns supreme, featuring purely local talent. In even-numbered years, the month-long fete is **El Festival Internacional de las Artes,** with a nightly smorgasbord of dance, theater, and music from around the world. Most nights of the festival offer between 4 and 10 shows. Many are free, and the most expensive ticket is usually around $6. For exact dates and details, you can contact the **Ministry of Youth and Culture** (www.mcj.go.cr; ✆ **2221-2022**), although information is in Spanish.

It is possible to buy tickets to many cultural events and concerts in advance from **E-Ticket** (www.eticket.cr), however the site is entirely in Spanish.

Interior of the Teatro Nacional.

Auditorio Nacional ★   Housed inside the Museo de Los Niños (p. 134), this is the city's most modern performing arts theater, with the best seats and sound system. However, it gets much less use than the more classic Teatro Nacional and Teatro Melico Salazar. Calle 4 and Av. 9. ✆ **2222-7647.**

Teatro Melico Salazar ★   Built in 1928, this 1,180-seat baroque theater is owned by the Costa Rican Ministry of Culture and houses the National Theater Company and National Dance Company. A regular slate of concerts and dance and theater performances are offered, ranging from productions by the in-house companies to concerts by visiting Latin American pop crooners to full-scale productions of Broadway shows. Av. 2 btw. calles Central and 2. www.teatromelico.go.cr. ✆ **2295-6032** or 2295-6000.

Teatro Nacional (National Theater) ★★   Costa Rica's most elegant and elaborate theater, the Teatro Nacional was opened in 1897. Funded with a special tax on coffee, and modeled on the Paris Opera House, this neo-baroque theater features marble floors and columns, numerous sculptures including busts of Beethoven and Chopin, and a painted fresco on the main auditorium's ceiling meant to suggest the majesty of the Sistine chapel. It is home base for the National Symphony Orchestra, and site of numerous other cultural events. Av. 2 btw. calles 3 and 5. www.teatronacional.go.cr. ✆ **2010-1110.**

The Club, Music & Dance Scene

You'll find plenty of places to hit the dance floor in San José. Salsa and merengue are the main beats that move people here, and many of the city's dance clubs, discos, and salons feature live music on the weekends. You'll find a pretty limited selection, though, if you're looking to catch some small-club jazz, rock, or blues performances.

The daily "Viva" and Friday's "Tiempo Libre" sections of *La Nación* newspaper have weekly performance schedules. Some dance bands to watch for are Gaviota, Chocolate, Son de Tikizia, Taboga Band, and La Orquestra Son Mayor. While Ghandi, Foffo Goddy, Kadeho, Evolucion, and Akasha are popular local rock and pop groups, Marfil is a good cover band, and the Blues Devils, Chepe Blues, and the Las Tortugas are outfits that play American-style hard driving rock and blues. If you're looking for jazz, check out Editus, El Sexteto de Jazz Latino, or pianist and former Minister of Culture Manuel Obregón. Finally, for a taste of something eclectic, look for Santos y Zurdo, Sonámbulo Psicotrópical, or Cocofunka.

Most of the places listed below charge a nominal cover charge; sometimes it includes a drink or two.

Castro's ★   This is a classic Costa Rican dance club. The music varies throughout the night, from salsa and merengue to reggaeton and occasionally electronic trance. It's open daily from noon to anytime between 3 and 6am. Av. 13 and Calle 22, Barrio Mexico. ✆ **2256-8789.**

Salsa dancing at a San José club.

Rapsodia Lounge ★★ Drawing a chic and young crowd of San José's better heeled, this trendy night club and lounge can get loud and rocking. Local and visiting DJs get the massive main dance floor crowded and thumping. This place really only goes off on Friday and Saturday nights, and from around 9pm until near dawn. Paseo Colón and Calle 40. www.rapsodiacr.com. ℂ **2248-1720.**

Vértigo ★★ Tucked inside a nondescript office building and commercial center on Paseo Colón, this club remains one of the more popular places for rave-style late-night dancing and partying. The dance floor is huge and the ceilings are high, and electronic music rules the roost. It's open Friday and Saturday till 6am. Edificio Colón, Paseo Colón. www.vertigocr.com. ℂ **2257-8424.**

The Bar Scene

San José has something for every taste. Lounge lizards will be happy in most hotel bars downtown, while students and the young at heart will have no problem mixing in at the livelier spots around town. Sports fans have plenty of places to catch the most important games of the day, and a couple of brewpubs are drastically improving the quality and selection of the local suds.

The best part of the varied bar scene in San José is something called a *boca,* the equivalent of a tapa in Spain: a little dish of snacks that arrives at your table when you order a drink. Although this is a somewhat dying tradition, especially in the younger, hipper bars, you will still find *bocas* alive and well in the older, more traditional San José drinking establishments. The most traditional of these are known locally as *cantinas.* In most, the *bocas* are free, but in some, where the dishes are more sophisticated, you'll have to pay for the treats. You'll find drinks reasonably priced, with beer costing around $3 to $4 a bottle, and mixed drinks costing $4 to $10.

El Cuartel de la Boca del Monte ★★ This popular bar, one of San José's best, began life as an artist-and-bohemian hangout, and has evolved into a massive melting pot, attracting everyone from the city's young and well-heeled, to foreign exchange students and visitors. Live music is usually Monday, Wednesday, and Friday nights, when the place is packed shoulder to shoulder. From Monday to Friday it's open for lunch and again in the evenings; on weekends it opens at 6pm. On most nights it's open till about 1am, although the revelry might continue till about 3am on Friday or Saturday. Av. 1, btw. calles 21 and 23 (50m/½ block west of the Cine Magaly). ℂ **2221-0327.**

El Observatorio ★★ It's easy to miss the narrow alley-way that leads to the main entrance to this hot spot across from the Cine Magaly. Owned by a local filmmaker, its decor includes a heavy dose of cinema motifs. The main bar and performing space is large, with high ceilings and exposed brick walls on one side. Mondays tend to be for salsa dancing, while Wednesdays often feature stand-up comedy. There's occasional live music and movie screenings, and a decent menu of tapas and assorted appetizers and main dishes drawn from various world cuisines. It's open Mon through Sat 6pm to 2am. Calle 23, btw. avs. Central and 1. www. elobservatorio.tv. © **2223-0725.**

El Sótano ★★★ "El Sótano" translates as "the basement." And that's just where you'll find this tiny bar and performance space. Most nights some of the city's best jazz and blues players hold down the scene, and Tuesdays they host an open jam session. There's a small menu of bar food and sandwiches. When there's no live band, the house music is entirely played from vinyl. Upstairs from El Sótano is a separate bar and lounge space, El Solar. It's open until 2am daily. Calle 3, btw. av 11. © **2221-2302.**

El Steinvorth ★★ This is one of San José's trendiest clubs, and one of the only places you might find a line to get in, or be turned away because the doorman doesn't like how you're dressed or think you're cool enough. Housed in an old brick building with a crumbling facade, inside you'll find a large contemporary space with several rooms, art hanging on the walls and a second-floor balcony area that looks down on one of the main dance spaces. DJs blast their best mixes through a strong sound system, with a heavy emphasis on contemporary electronic dance music. El Steinvorth is open Wednesday through Saturday from 9pm until at least 5am. Calle 1, btw. avs. Central and 1. www.elsteinvorth.com. No phone.

Key Largo ★ Housed in a meticulously restored colonial-era mansion just off Parque Morazán in the heart of downtown, Key Largo is worth a visit if only to admire the dark-stained carved wood. That being said Key Largo is one of San José's top prostitute pickup bars, and there are always working women. Nonetheless, this is still an acceptable place for visiting couples and those not actively "shopping the wares". There are a couple of pool tables and usually a live band. It's open 8pm to 3am daily. Calle 7, btw. avs. 1 and 3. © **2257-7800.**

El Lobo Estepario ★★ Named after Herman Hesse's classic novel, *Steppenwolf,* this popular bohemian hangout is a top place to come for alternative music, poetry or theater, or to just to have a few drinks with friends. There's a dedicated performance space upstairs, and the main room features walls made of blackboard material, with chalk provided for doodles, and tables made from old 55-gallon drums. The simple bar menu features some healthy and vegetarian options. Av. 2 and Calle 13. © **8704-4111.**

HANGING OUT IN SAN PEDRO

The funky 2-block stretch of **San Pedro** ★★ just south of the University of Costa Rica has been dubbed La Calle de Amargura, or the "Street

One of the many bars on La Calle de Amargura in San Pedro.

of Bitterness," and it's the heart and soul of this eastern suburb and college town. Bars and cafes are mixed in with bookstores and copy shops. After dark the streets are packed with teens, punks, students, and professors barhopping and just hanging around. You can walk the strip until someplace strikes your fancy—or you can try one of the places listed below. *Note:* La Calle de Amargura attracts a certain unsavory element. Use caution here. Try to visit with a group, and try not to carry large amounts of cash or wear flashy jewelry.

You can get here by heading out (east) on Avenida 2, and following the flow of traffic. You will first pass through the neighborhood of Los Yoses before you reach a large traffic circle with a big fountain in the center (La Fuente de la Hispanidad). The Mall San Pedro is located on this traffic circle. Heading straight through the circle, you'll come to the Church of San Pedro, about 4 blocks east of the circle. The church is the major landmark in San Pedro. You can also take a bus here from downtown.

Jazz Café ★   The intimate Jazz Café is one of the more happening spots in San Pedro. Jazz buffs will want to test their knowledge by trying to identify the various artists depicted in large sculpted busts behind the main stage. Most nights feature live music. It's open daily till about 2am. Sister club **Jazz Café Escazú** (© **2288-4740**) is on the western end of town. Next to the Banco Popular on Av. Central. www.jazzcafecostarica.com. © **2253-8933.**

Mundoloco El Chante ★★ This club is the brainchild of DJ, radio host, and musician Bernal Monestel. The performance space in the back hosts live music or DJs most nights—usually with a slight cover charge. Bands tend to be eclectic, with a tendency toward electronic and world music, in addition to the homegrown rock and reggae outfits that are popular with the university crowd this place tends to attract. Southeast corner of the Banco Popular on Av. Central. www.facebook.com/MundolocoElChante. © **2253-4125.**

Terra U ★ Set on a busy corner in the heart of the university district, this is one of the most "go-to" bars in the area. Part of this is due to the inviting open-air street-front patio area, and inexpensive drink specials. Although not officially a "sports bar," flat screen televisions are hung all around and crowds are attentive whenever there's a big game or prize fight on. It's open daily 'til 2am. 200m (2 blocks) east and 150m (1½ blocks) north of the church in San Pedro. © **2225-4261.**

The Gay & Lesbian Scene

Because Costa Rica is such a conservative Catholic country, the gay and lesbian communities here are rather discreet. Homosexuality is not generally under attack, but many gay and lesbian organizations guard their privacy, and the club scene is changeable and not well publicized.

The most established and happening gay and lesbian bar and dance club in San José is **La Avispa ★**, Calle 1 between avenidas 8 and 10 (www.laavispa.com; © **2223-5343**). It is popular with both men and women, although it sometimes sets aside certain nights for specific persuasions. There's also **Pucho's Bar ★** (© **2256-1147**), on Calle 11 between Avenida 8 and 10; **El 13** (www.el13cafebar.com; © **2221-3947**) on Calle 9, btw. avs. 12 and 14; and **El Bochinche ★** (© **2221-0500**), on Calle 11 between avenidas 10 and 12.

Casinos

Gambling is legal in Costa Rica, with casinos at virtually every major hotel. However, as with Tico bullfighting, some idiosyncrasies are involved in gambling *a la Tica*. If blackjack is your game, you'll want to play "rummy." The rules are almost identical, except that the house doesn't pay 1½ times on blackjack—instead, it pays double on any three of a kind or three-card straight flush. If you're looking for roulette, what you'll find here is a bingolike spinning cage of numbered balls. The betting is the same, but some of the glamour is lost.

You'll also find a version of five-card-draw poker, but the rule differences are so complex that I advise you to sit down and watch for a while and then ask questions before joining in. That's about all you'll find. There are no craps tables or baccarat.

There's some controversy over slot machines—one-armed bandits are currently outlawed—but you will be able to play electronic slots and poker games. Most casinos here are casual and small by international standards. You may have to dress up slightly at some of the fancier hotels, but most are accustomed to tropical vacation attire.

DAY TRIPS FROM SAN JOSÉ

San José makes an excellent base for exploring the lovely Central Valley. For first-time visitors, the best way to make the most of these excursions is usually to take a guided tour, but if you rent a car, you'll have greater independence. Some day trips also can be done by public bus.

Guided Tours & Adventures

A number of companies offer a wide variety of primarily nature-related day tours out of San José. The most reputable include **Costa Rica Sun Tours ★** (www.crsuntours.com; **℗ 866/271-6263** in the U.S. and Canada, or 2296-7757 in Costa Rica), **Horizontes Nature Tours ★★** (www.horizontes.com; **℗ 888/786-8748** in the U.S. and Canada, or 2222-2022), and **Swiss Travel Service** (www.swisstravelcr.com; **℗ 2282-4898**). Prices range from around $35 to $70 for a half-day trip, and from $70 to $160 for a full-day trip.

Before signing on for a tour of any sort, find out how many fellow travelers will be accompanying you, how much time will be spent in transit and eating lunch, and how much time will actually be spent doing the primary activity. I've had complaints about tours that were rushed, that spent too much time in a bus or on secondary activities, or that had a cattle-car, assembly-line feel to them. You'll find many tours that combine two or three different activities or destinations.

Tip: Virtually every attraction, tour, and activity described in "The Central Valley" chapter makes for an easy day trip out of San José.

In addition, to the tours and attractions offered around the Central Valley, a few other tours and activities just a little bit farther afield are convenient for day trips out of San José. These include the following.

CANOPY TOURS & AERIAL TRAMS

Getting up into the treetops is a big

The Rain Forest Aerial Tram Atlantic.

trend in Costa Rican tourism, and scores of such tours are around the country.

The most popular canopy-style day trip destination from San José is the **Rainforest Aerial Tram Atlantic** ★ (www.rainforesttram.com; © **866/759-8726** in the U.S. and Canada, or 2257-5961 in Costa Rica), built on a private reserve bordering Braulio Carrillo National Park. This pioneering tramway is the brainchild of rainforest researcher Dr. Donald Perry, whose cable-car system through the forest canopy at Rara Avis helped establish him as an early expert on rainforest canopies. On the 90-minute tram ride through the treetops, visitors have the chance to glimpse the complex web of life that makes these forests unique. Additional attractions include a butterfly garden, serpentarium, and frog collection. They also have their own zip-line canopy tour, and the grounds feature well-groomed trails through the rainforest and a restaurant—with all this on offer, a trip here can easily take up a full day. If you want to spend the night, 10 simple but clean and comfortable bungalows cost $125 per person per day (double occupancy), including three meals, a guided hike, taxes, the signature tram ride, and use of the rest of the facilities.

The cost for a full-day tour, including both the aerial tram and canopy tour, as well as all the park's other attractions, is $99 adults; students and anyone under 18 pay $65. Packages, including round-trip transportation and lunch, are also available. Alternatively, you can drive or take one of the frequent Guápiles buses—they leave every half-hour throughout the day and cost C1,405—from the Caribbean bus terminal (Gran Terminal del Caribe) on Calle Central and Avenida 15. Ask the driver to let you off in front of the teleférico. If you're driving, head out on the Guápiles Highway as if driving to the Caribbean coast. Watch for the tram's roadside welcome center—it's hard to miss. Because this is a popular tour for groups, I highly recommend that you get an advance reservation in the high season and, if possible, a ticket; otherwise you could wait a long time for your tram ride or even be shut out. The tram handles only about 80 passengers per hour, so scheduling is tight; the folks here try to schedule as much as possible in advance.

DAY CRUISES Several companies offer cruises to the white sand beaches of the remote and uninhabited Tortuga Island in the Gulf of Nicoya. These full-day tours generally entail an early departure for the 1½-hour chartered bus ride to Puntarenas, where you board your vessel for a 1½-hour cruise to Tortuga Island. Then you get several hours on the uninhabited island, where you can swim, lie on the beach, play volleyball, or try a canopy tour, followed by the return journey.

The original and most dependable company running these trips is **Calypso Tours** ★ (www.calypsocruises.com; © **855/855-1975** in the U.S. and Canada, or 2256-2727 in Costa Rica). The tour costs $145 per

A cruise landing at Tortuga Island.

person and includes round-trip transportation from San José, Jacó, Manuel Antonio or Monteverde, a buffet breakfast before embarking on the boat, all drinks on the cruise, and a buffet lunch on the beach at the island. The Calypso Tours main vessel is a huge motor-powered catamaran. They also run a separate tour to a private nature reserve at **Punta Coral ★**. The beach is much nicer at Tortuga Island, but the tour to Punta Coral is more intimate, and the restaurant, hiking, and kayaking are all superior. Daily pickups are from San José, Manuel Antonio, Jacó, and Monteverde, and you can use the day trip on the boat as your transfer or transportation option between any of these towns and destinations.

HIKING Most of the tour agencies listed above offer 1-day guided hikes to a variety of destinations. In general, I recommend taking guided hikes to really see and learn about the local flora and fauna.

Aerial view of Tortuga Island.

Poás Volcano National Park.

RAFTING, KAYAKING & RIVER TRIPS Cascading down Costa Rica's mountain ranges are dozens of tumultuous rivers, several of which are very popular for white-water rafting and kayaking. If I had to choose just one day-trip out of San José, it would be a white-water rafting trip. For between $99 and $100, you can spend a day rafting through lush tropical forests; multiday trips are also available. Some of the most reliable rafting companies are **Aventuras Naturales** ★★ (www.adventurecostarica. com; ✆ **888/680-9031** in the U.S., or 2225-3939 in Costa Rica), **Exploradores Outdoors** ★ (www.exploradoresoutdoors.com; ✆ **646/205-0828** in the U.S. and Canada, or 2222-6262 in Costa Rica), and **Ríos Tropicales** ★★ (www.riostropicales.com; ✆ **866/722-8273** in the U.S. and Canada, or 2233-6455 in Costa Rica). These companies all ply a number of rivers of varying difficulties, including the popular Pacuare and Reventazón rivers. For details, see "White-Water Rafting, Kayaking & Canoeing," in chapter 5.

VOLCANO VISITS The **Poás, Irazú** (see chapter 7 for more details), and **Arenal** volcanoes are three of Costa Rica's most popular destinations, and the first two are easy day trips from San José. Although numerous companies offer day-trips to Arenal, I don't recommend them because travel time is at least 3½ hours in each direction. For more information on Arenal Volcano, see chapter 10.

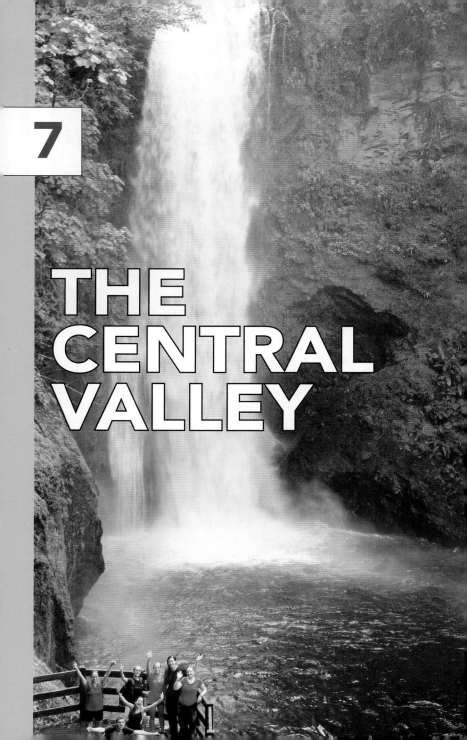

7

THE CENTRAL VALLEY

Known locally as La Meseta Central or El Valle Central, the long, thin, doglegging Central Valley is Costa Rica's most densely populated region. In addition to San José, it is home to both Alajuela and Heredia, numerous smaller cities, suburbs and towns, and the country's principal international airport. Most visitors start and end their vacations in the Central Valley.

The hills, mountains, and volcanoes that ring the Central Valley are an agricultural wonderland, with farms, fields, and plantations growing a wide range of crops, most prominently coffee. These towns, cities, hillsides, and volcanoes are home to a wide range of compelling attractions, from volcanic national parks and La Paz Waterfall Gardens, to pre-Colombian ruins and colonial-era churches. And this is a perfect place to tour a working coffee farm. Although technically one valley over, the colonial-era capital city of Cartago is included in this chapter, because of its general geographic location and proximity to San José. With its ornate and locally revered Basilica, earthquake-damaged Central Park ruins, and the neighboring Orosi Valley, with its rivers and lakes and verdant hillsides, this is an area well worth exploring.

THE best CENTRAL VALLEY EXPERIENCES

- **Dining at a *Mirador*:** Grab a window seat at a *mirador*, and enjoy your meal with the lights of San José at your feet. You'll find *miradores* set up on most of the foothills surrounding the Central Valley. See "Dining Under the Stars," p. 177.

- **Visiting a Volcano:** Several of Costa Rica's most impressive and accessible volcanoes are found in the mountains that define the Central Valley. These include Poás, Irazú, and Turrialba, all active volcanoes with their own namesake national parks. See p. 182, 200, and 206.

- **Visiting La Paz Waterfall Gardens:** This place is akin to a Costa Rican tropical theme park. I enjoy combining a visit here with a stay in their luxurious on-site Peace Lodge (p. 184). Its multiple attractions also make this a great day-trip option. See p. 181.

FACING PAGE: **La Paz Waterfall Gardens and Peace Lodge in Alajuela.**

o **Touring the Orosi Valley:** Arguably one of the most picturesque drives in Costa Rica, a trip around the Orosi Valley offers up stunning vistas, ancient ruins, charming small towns and several top-notch attractions. See p. 201.

o **Getting Wet & Wild in Turrialba:** This small, rural city is Costa Rica's main base for white-water rafting and kayaking. From here, trips leave on both the Pacuare and Reventazón rivers. You'll also find a thrilling canyoning operation, and plenty of opportunities for other adventure activities. See p. 206.

ESCAZÚ & SANTA ANA

Escazú: 5.5km (3½ miles) W of San José; Santa Ana: 13km (8 miles) W of San José

Located just west of San José, these affluent suburbs, which were once comprised almost entirely of farmlands and vacation estates, have boomed as the metropolitan area continues to grow and expand. The two largest cities in this area, Escazú and Santa Ana, are popular with the Costa Rican professional class, as well as North American retirees and expatriates. Quite a few hotels have sprung up to cater to their needs. Both have large modern malls, endless little strip malls, and important business parks. It's easy to commute between Escazú or Santa Ana and downtown San José via car, bus, or taxi. And the area is about the same distance from the airport as downtown San José.

Essentials

GETTING THERE & DEPARTING   By Car: Head west out of San José along Paseo Colón. Turn left when you hit La Sabana Park, and turn right a few blocks later, at the start of the Próspero Fernández Highway (CR27). You will see well-marked exits for both Escazú and Santa Ana.

By Bus: Escazú- and **Santa Ana–bound** buses leave from the Coca-Cola bus station, as well as from Avenida 1 between calles 24 and 28. Alternatively, you can pick up both the Escazú and Santa Ana buses from a busy bus stop at the start of the Próspero Fernández Highway (CR27) on the southeast corner of the Parque La Sabana, next to the Gimnasio Nacional. Buses leave roughly every 5 to 10 minutes from 5am until 8pm, and less frequently during off hours. A bus costs between C295 and C395.

By Taxi: Taxi fare should run around C4,000 to C8,000, each way between San José and Escazú, and another C5,000 to C7,500 or so between Escazú and Santa Ana.

VISITOR INFORMATION   Escazú News ★★ (www.escazunews.com) is an excellent bilingual resource for information on the Escazú and Santa Ana areas. The site has forums, classified ads, maps, restaurant reviews, real estate info, and general advice on the area.

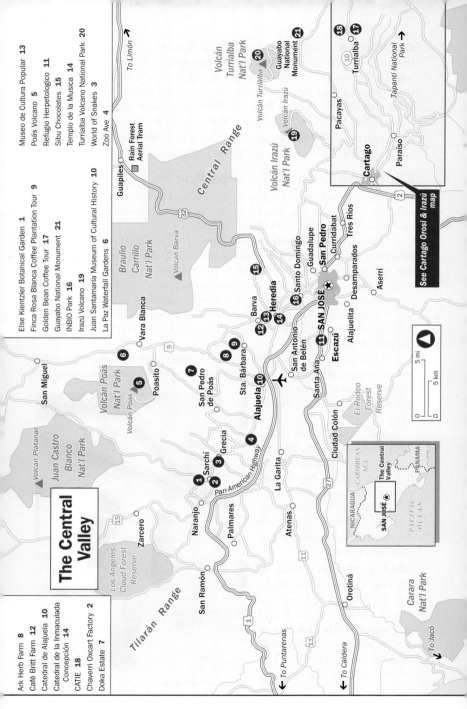

The Central Valley

Ark Herb Farm **8**
Café Britt Farm **12**
Catedral de Alajuela **10**
Catedral de la Inmaculada Concepción **14**
CATIE **18**
Chaverri Oxcart Factory **2**
Doka Estate **7**

Else Kientzler Botanical Garden **1**
Finca Rosa Blanca Coffee Plantation Tour **9**
Golden Bean Coffee Tour **17**
Guayabo National Monument **21**
INBIO Park **16**
Irazú Volcano **19**
Juan Santamaría Museum of Cultural History **10**
La Paz Waterfall Gardens **6**

Museo de Cultura Popular **13**
Poás Volcano **5**
Refugio Herpetologico **11**
Sibu Chocolates **15**
Templo de la Musica **14**
Turrialba Volcano National Park **20**
World of Snakes **3**
Zoo Ave **4**

171

ORIENTATION Both Escazú and Santa Ana are former farming towns that have been swallowed up by metro San José's urban sprawl. Each has a small downtown core built around an old church, with ever-expanding rings of residential and commercial development radiating off this core. Both also have numerous little satellite towns, such as San Antonio de Escazú, San Rafael de Escazú, and Pozos de Santa Ana.

FAST FACTS You'll find banks, ATMs, and Internet cafes all over Escazú and Santa Ana, especially in the many malls.

Exploring Escazú & Santa Ana

Escazú and Santa Ana have few traditional tourism attractions, but both offer easy access to the attractions and activities offered up in San José and elsewhere around the Central Valley.

One of the exceptions to the above rule is the **Refugio Herpetológico** ★ (http://refugioherpetologico.com; © **2282-4614**), a family-run reptile and wildlife exhibition. In addition to a couple of dozen snakes, both venomous and nonvenomous, the center has a few other rehabilitating animals, including a crocodile, iguanas, and a spider monkey. It's open from 9am to 4:30pm, Tuesday to Sunday, and admission is $20 for adults; $10 for students with valid ID; and $10 for seniors and children 3 through 12.

If you are in downtown Santa Ana, do take a few minutes to visit the town's main **cathedral,** a lovely old stone church, with thick wooden beams, colorful stained-glass windows, and a red-clay tile roof.

And while most folks don't come to Costa Rica to see movies, if you do decide to go, head for the **Nova Cinemas** (www.novacinemas.cr; © **2299-7485**) multiplex, with the country's only IMAX theater in the Avenida Escazú shopping complex.

GOLF & TENNIS Some of the best Central Valley facilities for visiting golfers and tennis players can be found at **Parque Valle del Sol** ★ (www.vallesol.com; © **2282-9222**), in Santa Ana. The 18-hole course here is open

Santa Ana's cathedral.

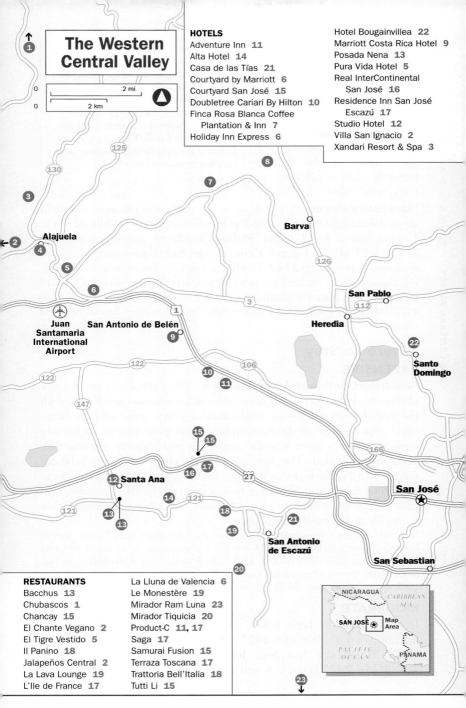

The Western Central Valley

0 [====== 2 mi ======]
0 [====== 2 km ======]

HOTELS
Adventure Inn **11**
Alta Hotel **14**
Casa de las Tías **21**
Courtyard by Marriott **6**
Courtyard San José **15**
Doubletree Cariari By Hilton **10**
Finca Rosa Blanca Coffee
   Plantation & Inn **7**
Holiday Inn Express **6**

Hotel Bougainvillea **22**
Marriott Costa Rica Hotel **9**
Posada Nena **13**
Pura Vida Hotel **5**
Real InterContinental
   San José **16**
Residence Inn San José
   Escazú **17**
Studio Hotel **12**
Villa San Ignacio **2**
Xandari Resort & Spa **3**

Barva

Alajuela

San Pablo

Juan
Santamaria
International
Airport

San Antonio de Belén

Heredia

Santo
Domingo

Santa Ana

San José

San Antonio
de Escazú

San Sebastian

RESTAURANTS
Bacchus **13**
Chubascos **1**
Chancay **15**
El Chante Vegano **2**
El Tigre Vestido **5**
Il Panino **18**
Jalapeños Central **2**
La Lava Lounge **19**
L'Ile de France **17**

La Lluna de Valencia **6**
Le Monestère **19**
Mirador Ram Luna **23**
Mirador Tiquicia **20**
Product-C **11, 17**
Saga **17**
Samurai Fusion **15**
Terraza Toscana **17**
Trattoria Bell'Italia **18**
Tutti Li **15**

NICARAGUA
CARIBBEAN
SEA

SAN JOSÉ Map
Area

PACIFIC
OCEAN

PANAMA

to the general public. Greens fees are $67, including unlimited balls on the driving range. A golf cart will run you an extra $32. The tennis courts here cost $7.50 per hour weekdays and $13 per hour weekends. Reservations are essential. The golf course at the Cariari Country Club is not open to the general public.

HORSEBACK RIDING   Options are nearly endless in the mountains and along the coasts, but it's more difficult to find a place to saddle up in the Central Valley. **La Caraña Riding Academy** (www.lacarana.com; ✆ **2282-6754**) and **Centro Ecuestre del Sol** (Equestrian Sun; www.equestriansun.com; ✆ **2282-1070**) are both in Santa Ana and offer riding classes. But your best bet is to head a little further west to Ciudad Colón, where **Finca Caballo Loco** ★★ (www.fincacaballoloco.com; ✆ **7010-1771**) offers up trail rides through some beautiful rural terrain.

Where to Stay
EXPENSIVE
Real InterContinental San José ★★   All of the ducks are in a row at this swank, business-class hotel. Rooms are spacious and bright, with the type of cushy mattresses, soothing color palette and solid furnishings you'd expect from an Intercontinental. The palm-fringed swimming pools, one with a pretty waterfall, are lovely and large enough that they never feel crowded. The spa and fitness center are state-of-the-art. Guests also like the fact that there are five on-site restaurants and a location that's right across the street from a large mall with a multiplex cinema. But we gotta dock it one star because, well, there's nothing all that Costa Rican feeling about the place.

Autopista Próspero Fernández, across from the Multiplaza mall, Escazú. www.ichotelsgroup.com. ✆ **800/496-7621** in the U.S. and Canada, or 2208-2100 in Costa Rica. 372 units. $300–$308 double; $562 suite. Free parking. **Amenities:** 5 restaurants; 2 bars; concierge; good-size health club and spa; Jacuzzi; pools; room service; outdoor tennis court; free Wi-Fi.

MODERATE
In addition to the hotel below, the **Courtyard San José** ★ (www.marriott.com; ✆ **888/236-2427** in the U.S. and Canada, or 2208-3000), **Residence Inn San José Escazú** ★ (www.marriott.com; ✆ **888/236-2427** in the U.S. and Canada, or 2588-4300), and **Holiday**

Inn Express ★ (www.hiexpress.com; ✆ **800/315-2621** in the U.S. and Canada, or 2506-5000 in Costa Rica) are all modern business-class hotels a few miles from each other, right on the western Próspero Fernández Highway connecting Santa Ana and Escazú with San José.

Alta Hotel ★★ This boutique hotel is blessed with old-world charm. High arches and curves abound. Top touch is the winding interior alleyway that snakes down from the reception through the hotel. Most of the rooms have superb views of the Central Valley from private balconies; the others have pleasant garden patios. Guestrooms are all up to modern resort standards (although some have cramped bathrooms), and are minimalist in style with white-washed walls hung with 1920's black and white photos. The suites are far larger, each with a separate sitting room and big Jacuzzi-style tubs in spacious bathrooms. The hotel's La Luz restaurant is a winner, serving up organic Mediterranean fare.

Alto de las Palomas, old road to Santa Ana. www.thealtahotel.com. ✆ **888/388-2582** in the U.S. and Canada, or 2282-4160. 23 units. $140 double; $170–$280 suite. Rates include continental breakfast. Free parking. **Amenities:** Restaurant; bar; concierge; small exercise room; Jacuzzi; midsize outdoor pool; room service; sauna; free Wi-Fi.

Casa de las Tías ★★ The Escazú and Santa Ana areas are awash in modern, business-class chain hotels and upscale boutique options, but this converted wooden home offers something special for those looking for a real Costa Rican experience at a reasonable price. The charming, detached house features a yellow and blue exterior and offers cozy rooms and a Costa Rican breakfast. Owners Xavier and Pilar live on site and are very hands-on hosts. The hotel is just a block or so away from a bustling Escazú intersection, yet feels a world apart with its large garden and quiet, secure grounds.

San Rafael de Escazú. www.casadelastias.com. ✆ **2289-5517.** 5 units. $100–$110 double. Rates include full breakfast. **Amenities:** Free Wi-Fi.

Studio Hotel ★★ Art lovers will feel right at home in this small contemporary hotel. The lobby, common areas and rooms all feature a wealth of original works by major contemporary and historical Costa Rican artists, including Rafa Fernandez, Isidor Con Wong, and Edgar Zuñiga. The stylish Katowa restaurant here serves up fab Costa Rican fusion cuisine. However, the piece de resistance is the third-floor rooftop pool and lounge area, set under a soaring white canvas tent structure, with mountain and city views. The hotel sits on a busy intersection at the entrance to Santa Ana, with many restaurants and bars a short walk away.

Santa Ana. www.costaricastudiohotel.com. ✆ **866/978-8123** in the U.S. and Canada, or 2282-0505 in Costa Rica. 82 units. $120–$150 double. Rates include full breakfast. **Amenities:** Restaurant; small exercise room; rooftop pool; free Wi-Fi.

INEXPENSIVE

Posada Nena ★ Friendly and helpful service is what sets the Posada Nena apart. Its German owners live on property and make sure that guests are happy and all of the cheerful, bright rooms are kept ship-shape. They're set around a breeze-blessed courtyard garden (with sunken Jacuzzi), shaded by a bamboo canopy. Also on-site is a tiny, rustic restaurant. Posada Nena is booked, often with repeat guests, by folks with friends or family in Santa Ana. Previously called Casa Alegre, the compact residential area hotel is just 2 blocks from the lovely stone church and central park of this once quiet farming town.

Santa Ana. www.posadanena.com. ✆ **2282-1173.** 9 units. $66–$77 double. Rates include breakfast and taxes. **Amenities:** Restaurant; bar; Jacuzzi; free Wi-Fi.

Where to Dine

These two suburbs have the most vibrant restaurant scenes in San José. In addition to the places listed below, **Trattoria Bell'Italia** ★ (✆ **2588-2833**) is primo for Italian cuisine, as is **Il Panino** ★ (www.ilpanino.net; ✆ **2228-3126**), an upscale sandwich shop and cafe. Both are located in the Centro Comercial El Paco.

Good restaurants are also clustered at **Plaza Itskatzú** (just off the highway and sharing a parking lot with the Courtyard San José), and **Avenida Escazú** (which is anchored by the Marriott Residence Inn and is located next to the CIMA Hospital). My favorite options at Plaza Itskatzú include **Chancay** ★ (www.chancay.info; ✆ **2588-2327**), which serves Peruvian and Peruvian/Chinese cuisine; and **Samurai Fusion** ★ (✆ **2288-2240**), a fine sushi and teppanyaki joint. Over on Avenida Escazú, you'll find **Saga** ★ (www.sagarestaurant.com; ✆ **2289-6615**),

A *mirador* **outside San José.**

DINING UNDER THE stars

One of my favorite unique Costa Rican experiences is dining on the side of a volcano with the lights of San José shimmering below. These hanging restaurants, called *miradores*, are a resourceful response to the city's topography. Because San José is set in a broad valley surrounded on all sides by volcanic mountains, people who live in these mountainous areas have no place to go but up—so they do, building roadside cafes vertically up the sides of the volcanoes.

The food at most of these establishments is not spectacular, but the views often are, particularly at night, when the wide valley sparkles in a wash of lights. The town of **Aserrí,** 10km (6¼ miles) south of downtown San José, is the king of *miradores*, and **Mirador Ram Luna** ★ (www.restauranteramluna.com; ✆ **2230-3022**) is the king of Aserrí. Grab a window seat and, if you've got the fortitude, order a plate of *chicharrones* (fried pork rinds). There's often live music. You can hire a cab for around C15,000 or take the Aserrí bus at Avenida 6 between calles Central and 2. Just ask the driver where to get off.

Miradores are also in the hills above Escazú and in San Ramón de Tres Ríos and Heredia. The most popular is **Le Monestère** ★ (www.monastere-restaurant.com; ✆ **2289-4404**; closed Sun), an elegant converted church serving somewhat overrated French and Belgian cuisine in a spectacular setting above the hills of Escazú. I recommend coming here just for the less formal **La Cava Lounge** ★. I also like **Mirador Tiquicia** ★ (www.miradortiquicia.com; ✆ **2289-7330**), which occupies several rooms in a sprawling old Costa Rican home and has live folkloric dance shows on Thursday.

with a contemporary-casual bistro menu; **Terraza Toscana** ★★ (www.terrazzatoscanacr.com; ✆ **4000-2220**) an excellent and elegant Italian restaurant; and **L'Ile de France** ★★ (✆ **2289-7533**), a top-notch, high-end French restaurant.

EXPENSIVE

Bacchus ★★ ITALIAN   Set in an adobe home built in 1870, this elegant restaurant is one of the best Italian options in the city. Paper-thin pizzas come out of the wood-burning oven from the open kitchen. The pastas and raviolis are homemade and all are scrumptious, particularly the pappardelle with white wine, arugula, carrots, and crabmeat. From their selection of creative desserts, the banana and apple croquettes (in phyllo dough and topped with a Gran Marnier sauce) reigns supreme. Regularly rotating art exhibits adorn the walls and there's an ample open-air covered patio.

Downtown Santa Ana. www.bacchus.cr. ✆ **4001-5418.** Reservations required. Main courses C6,500–C14,700. Mon–Fri noon–3pm and 6–11pm; Sat noon–11pm; Sun noon–9pm.

TOP: **Woodwork by Barry Biesanz;**
LEFT: **Musicians at Jazz Café Escazú.**

MODERATE

Product-C ★★ SEAFOOD Although San José is inland, this fish market and restaurant prides itself on daily pre-dawn runs to Puntarenas and other coastal supply points to get the freshest catch possible. They even set up the first and only oyster farm in Costa Rica, producing small, yet very tasty oysters. The daily chalkboard menu features a range of specials that complements the simple menu here. Feel free to check out the display case and choose whatever fish or seafood strikes your fancy, and have it cooked to order in any number of styles.

Av. Escazú. www.product-c.com. © **2288-5570.** Reservations recommended. Main courses C6,500–C13,000. Mon–Sat noon–11pm; Sun noon–6pm.

Shopping

One of the country's best and largest megamalls, **Multiplaza Escazú,** is located along the Próspero Fernández Highway (CR27), just west of downtown Escazú. In the same general area, you'll find two other smaller malls, **Avenida Escazú** and **Plaza Itskatzú,** each of which has an attractive mix of high-end shops, boutiques, restaurants, and art galleries.

Biesanz Woodworks ★★ Biesanz makes a wide range of high-quality wood items, including bowls, jewelry boxes, humidors, and some wonderful sets of chopsticks. The company is actively involved in local reforestation, too. Bello Horizonte, Escazú. www.biesanz.com. ✆ **2289-4337.**

Galería 11–12 ★★★ This outstanding gallery handles high-end Costa Rican art, from neoclassical painters such as Teodorico Quirós to modern masters such as Francisco Amighetti and Paco Zuñiga, as well as current stars such as Rafa Fernández, Rodolfo Stanley, Fernando Carballo, and Fabio Herrera. Plaza Itzkatzú, off the Próspero Fernández Hwy., Escazú. ✆ **2288-1975.**

Entertainment & Nightlife

Escazú has a handful of popular bars and clubs. These are especially popular with the Central Valley's well-heeled urban youth. By far, my favorite is the **Jazz Café Escazú** ★★★ (Próspero Fernández Hwy.; www.jazzcafecostarica.com; ✆ **2288-4740**), a top spot for live music. If a high-level act is visiting from the United States, Europe or South America, they will certainly play here.

ALAJUELA, POÁS ★★ & THE AIRPORT AREA

Airport: 15km (9¼ miles) NW of San José; Alajuela: 18½km (11½ miles) NW of San José; Poás Volcano: 37km (23 miles) northwest of San José

Most folks visiting Costa Rica land at the Juan Santamaría International Airport in Alajuela. The downtown area of Costa Rica's second largest city is just a mile or so north of the airport. The city itself is of little interest to most tourists, although it is the gateway to the Poás Volcano, and several more of the Central Valley's top attractions.

Essentials

GETTING THERE & DEPARTING **By Car:** Head northwest out of San José on the Interamerican Highway (CR1).

By Bus: Two separate lines make the run between San José and Alajuela: **Tuasa** (✆ **2442-6900**) buses are red; **Station Wagon** (✆ **2441-1181**) buses are beige/yellow. Buses leave roughly every 10 minutes between 5am and 11pm, and less frequently in off hours. The fare is C555.

By Train: A commuter train runs between downtown San José and Heredia. This train runs roughly every 10 minutes between 5:30 and 9am, and again between 3:30 and 8:30pm. Fares range from C420 to C460, depending on the length of your ride.

ORIENTATION Downtown Alajuela is a tight jumble of one-way streets, often choked to a standstill with gridlock traffic. Most folks will be heading up into the hills from downtown. The best way to find the route out of town is usually to follow signs for the Poás Volcano, or some other well-known attraction.

FAST FACTS You'll find banks, ATMs, and Internet cafes all over Alajuela, especially in the central downtown area, and nearby malls and shopping centers. The **Hospital San Rafael de Alajuela** (✆ 2436-1001) is large, modern, and well-equipped. If you need a taxi, call **COOTAXA** (✆ 2443-3030) or **Taxi Radio Liga** (✆ 2441-1212).

Exploring Alajuela

Alajuela's main church, the **Catedral de Alajuela** (**Alajuela Cathedral;** ✆ 2441-4665) is a large, relatively ornate Catholic church, with a striking white-washed exterior, ceiling frescos, and a gold-leaf painted interior dome. The cathedral, which fronts the city's central park, received a major renovation in 2010. Mass is held Monday to Friday at 9am and 5pm; Saturday at 9am and 7pm; and Sunday at 9 and 11am and 5 and 7pm.

The **Museo Historico Cultural Juan Santamaría (Juan Santamaría Museum of Cultural History)** ★, Avenida 3 between calles Central and 2 (www.museojuansantamaria.go.cr; ✆ 2441-4775), commemorates Costa Rica's national hero, Juan Santamaría, who gave his life defending the country against a small army led by William Walker, a U.S. citizen who invaded Costa Rica in 1856, attempting to set up a slave state. Housed in a sprawling two-story downtown building with a large open central courtyard, the museum features permanent exhibits about Santamaría and Walker's filibuster exploits, as well as regularly changing temporary expositions, and evening concerts and theater performances. The museum is open Tuesday through Sunday from 10am to 5:30pm; admission is free.

NEARBY ATTRACTIONS

Doka Estate ★ FARM This large and long-standing coffee estate/farm in Alajuela offers a tour that takes you from "seed to cup." Along the way, you'll get a full rundown of the processes involved in the growing, harvesting, curing, packing, and brewing of their award-winning coffee. This coffee tour is similar to that offered at **Café Britt** (p. 188), but is a little more down-home in feel. Also on site: a butterfly garden, Bonsai tree, and orchid exhibit. Allow about 2½ hours.

Sabanilla de Alajuela. www.dokaestate.com. ✆ **888/946-3652** in the U.S. and Canada or 2449-5152 in Costa Rica. Admission $20 adults, $16 students with valid ID, $10 children 6–12, free for children 5 and under. Packages including transportation and breakfast or lunch available. Tours daily at 9, 10, and 11am; 1:30 and 2:30pm. Reservations required.

Catedral de Alajuela.

La Paz Waterfall Gardens ★★ NATURAL ATTRACTION The original attraction here consists of a series of trails through primary and secondary forests alongside La Paz River, with lookouts over a series of powerful falls, including the namesake La Paz Fall. In addition to the orchid garden and a hummingbird garden, you must visit their huge butterfly garden, which is easily the largest in Costa Rica. A small serpentarium, featuring a mix of venomous and nonvenomous native snakes, several terrariums containing various frogs and lizards, and a section of wild cats and local monkey species in large enclosures are added attractions. While the admission fee is a little steep, everything is well done, especially the trails and waterfalls. That said, some find the whole operation a little artificial in feel. I'm of a split mind on this, finding it a great place to get a broad experience in one compact package, and an especially good choice for families with young children. This is also a good stop after a morning visit to the Poás Volcano. Plan to spend 3 to 4 hours here. The hotel rooms here at **Peace Lodge** (p. 184) are some of the nicest in the country.

Doka Coffee Estate.

6km (3¾ miles) north of Varablanca on the road to San Miguel. www.waterfall gardens.com. ℃ **2482-2720.** Admission $40 adults, $24 children 3–12, free for children 2 and under. Daily 8am–5pm. There is no easy or regular bus service here, so you will need to come in a rental car or taxi, or arrange transport with the gardens.

Poás Volcano.

Poás Volcano ★★★ NATURAL ATTRACTION From San José, narrow roads wind through a landscape of fertile farms and dark forests to this active volcano. A paved road leads right to the top, although you'll have to hike in about 1km (.5 mile) to reach the crater. The volcano stands 2,640m (8,659 ft.) tall and is located within a national park, which preserves not only the volcano but also dense stands of virgin forest. The Poás crater, said to be the second largest in the world, is more than a 1.6km (1 mile) across. Geysers in the crater sometimes spew steam and muddy water 180m (590 ft.) into the air, making this the largest geyser in the world.

The information center shows a slideshow about the volcano, and well-groomed and marked hiking trails through the cloud forest ring the crater. About 15 minutes from the parking area, along a forest trail, is an overlook onto beautiful Botos Lake, which has formed in one of the volcano's extinct craters.

Be prepared when you come to Poás: This volcano is often enveloped in dense clouds. If you want to see the crater, it's best to come early and during the dry season. Moreover, it can get cool up here, especially when the sun isn't shining, so dress appropriately.

Poás de Alajuela. 37km (23 miles) from San José. ✆ **2482-1228**. Admission $15. Daily 8:30am–3:30pm.

Zoo Ave ★★ ZOO Dozens of scarlet macaws, reclusive owls, majestic raptors, several different species of toucans, and a host of brilliantly colored birds from Costa Rica and around the world make this one exciting place to visit. In total, over 115 species of birds are on display, including some 80 species found in Costa Rica. Bird-watching enthusiasts will be able to get a closer look at birds they might have seen in the wild. Other critters to observe include iguana, deer, tapir, ocelot, puma, and monkey—and look out for the 3.6m (12-ft.) crocodile. Zoo Ave houses only injured, donated, or confiscated animals. It takes about 2 hours to walk the paths and visit all the exhibits here.

La Garita, Alajuela. www.rescateanimalzooave.org. ☏ **2433-8989.** Admission $20, $15 students with valid ID. Daily 9am–5pm. Catch a bus to Alajuela on Av. 2 btw. calles 12 and 14. In Alajuela, transfer to a bus to Atenas and get off at Zoo Ave before you get to La Garita. Fare is C340.

Where to Stay in & Around Alajuela

Of the following hotels, the **Doubletree Cariari by Hilton, Holiday Inn Express, Marriott Costa Rica Hotel, Courtyard by Marriott Alajuela,** and **Pura Vida Hotel** are the closest to the airport.

EXPENSIVE

Marriott Costa Rica Hotel ★★★   Designed to resemble a colonial-era mansion, the Marriott is close enough to the airport to be considered an "airport hotel," yet feels like an isolated country retreat. The entryway lets out on to a massive central courtyard meant to mimic Havana's Plaza de Armas. The elegant, traditional-style rooms are large and have views to the surrounding hillsides, suburbs and coffee fields. There are several distinct dining choices, and their Casa de Café coffee house and restaurant actually fronts a small working coffee field. With tennis courts, a golf driving range, pools and a top spa, guests rarely run out of amusements here.

San Antonio de Belén. www.marriott.com. ☏ **2298-0000.** 299 units. $199–$249 double; $279–$329 executive level. Valet parking. **Amenities:** 3 restaurants; 2 bars; concierge; golf driving range; spa; Jacuzzi; 2 outdoor pools; room service; sauna; 2 tennis courts; smoke-free rooms; Wi-Fi.

Marriott Costa Rica Hotel.

Peace Lodge ★★★ Part of the popular **La Paz Waterfall Gardens** (p. 181), Peace Lodge is about 45 minutes from the airport, near the Poás Volcano. The rooms and villas are huge and feature faux rustic decor, including massive four-poster log beds and river stone fireplaces. All come with a Jacuzzi on their private balcony, but the deluxe rooms also feature an immense bathroom with a second indoor Jacuzzi backed by a full wall of orchids, flowers, and bromeliads, with a working waterfall. Nightly rates can be steep, but remember: They get you not only these fanciful rooms but also unlimited access to the Waterfall Gardens.

6km (3¾ miles) north of Varablanca on the road to San Miguel. www.waterfall gardens.com. ℂ **954/727-3997** in the U.S., or 2482-2720 in Costa Rica. 17 units. $395–$470 double; $605–$810 villa. Rates include entrance to La Paz Waterfall Gardens. **Amenities:** Restaurant; bar; Jacuzzi; 2 outdoor pools; free Wi-Fi; hiking trails; butterfly exhibits; Frisbee golf.

Xandari Resort & Spa ★★ Set on a hilltop above the city of Alajuela, Xandari commands magnificent views of the surrounding coffee farms and the Central Valley below. The owners Sherrill and Charlene Broudy are artists, and their original works and inventive design touches abound. The villas are huge private affairs with stained-glass windows, high-curved ceilings, living rooms with rattan chairs and sofas, as well as small kitchenettes. All come with both an outdoor patio with a view and a private covered palapa, as well as a smaller interior terrace with seating. The adjacent spa consists of a series of private thatch-roofed treatment rooms; a wide range of fitness classes are offered, too. The hotel grounds contain several miles of trails that pass by jungle waterfalls, fruit orchards and blooming gardens. The restaurant serves excellent spa cuisine, alongside more decadent fare. **GPS:** 10°3'26.87"N; 84°12'43.86"W

Alajuela. www.xandari.com. ℂ **866/363-3212** in the U.S., or 2443-2020. 24 villas. $265–$570 villa for 2. Rates include continental breakfast. $25 for extra person; children 3 and under stay free in parent's room. **Amenities:** Restaurant; bar; lounge; several Jacuzzis; 3 pools; full-service spa; free Wi-Fi.

MODERATE

If you want a classic airport hotel, with regular shuttle service, both the **Courtyard by Marriott** ★ (www.marriott.com; ℂ **888/236-2427** in the U.S. and Canada or 2429-2700 in Costa Rica) and **Holiday Inn Express** ★ (www.hiexpress.com; ℂ **800/439-4745** in the U.S. and Canada, or 2443-0043 in Costa Rica) are solid U.S.-chain hotels located right across from the airport.

Adventure Inn ★ A popular option located right along the main highway between the airport and downtown (it's on the same stretch as the Doubletree Cariari; see above), the Adventure Inn offers up friendly service and good value. Rooms here can feel a bit sparse but, oddly, that's because most of them are quite, quite large; many have murals or painted

The Adventure Inn.

accents on the wall to brighten them up. The common areas are cheery and often filled with fellow travelers, and there's a large central courtyard area with a good-sized pool and Jacuzzi. The management here run a full-service tour operation and generally go out of their way to help guests with onward plans and arrangements.

Autopista General Cañas, Ciudad Cariari, San José. www.adventure-inn.com. *C* **866/258-4740** in the U.S. and Canada, or 2239-2633 in Costa Rica. 34 units. $115–$150 double. Rates include full breakfast and free airport transfers. **Amenities:** Restaurant; bar; pool; Jacuzzi; small gym; free Wi-Fi and international calls.

Doubletree Cariari By Hilton ★★ With its open-air lobby, stone walls and lush garden, the Cariari has a warm tropical feel. The rooms, which feature shiny tile floors and a neutral color scheme enlivened by pops of color, are roomy enough for a king-size bed or two double beds, although I find most of the bathrooms a bit small. The suites are similarly appointed, but are even more spacious and have larger bathrooms. The hotel has a small casino, as well as several restaurants and it's just in front of a small mall with more good dining options.

Autopista General Cañas, Ciudad Cariari, San José. www.cariarisanjose.doubletree. com. *C* **800/222-8733** in the U.S. and Canada, or 2239-0022. 222 units. $139–$179 double; $189–$399 suites. Free parking. **Amenities:** 2 restaurants; 1 bar; casino; concierge; small exercise room; large outdoor pool; Jacuzzi; room service; smoke-free rooms, pets allowed.

Pura Vida Hotel ★★ Located just 10 minutes from the airport, this homey little inn is run by the very genial couple of Bernie Jubb and Nhi Chu. Rooms and private *casitas* (little houses) are spread around a spacious compound and lush gardens of vine-covered arbors, fruit trees and exotic flowers. The two-bedroom *casitas* are perfect for families. Nhi is an expert chef specializing in Asian cuisine. Three-course fixed-menu meals are served around long communal tables and need to be booked in

Villa San Ignacio.

advance. The hotel is located just a kilometer or two north of downtown Alajuela. **GPS:** 10°01'50"N; 84°13'33"W

Tuetal de Alajuela. www.puravidahotel.com. ✆ **2430-2929** or 8878-3899. 6 units. $99–$165 double. Rates include full breakfast and one-way airport transfer. **Amenities:** Restaurant; free Wi-Fi.

INEXPENSIVE

Villa San Ignacio ★★   Formerly the Orquideas Inn, this boutique hotel is only 10 minutes or so from the airport, on the road that leads to the summit of the Poás volcano. After a major remodeling it has emerged as a quietly elegant option, with soft colors, plush appointments and minimalistic decor, all at an amazing price. The hotel sits on 22 acres of land with tall native trees on a sloping hillside and is great for bird watching. There's a refreshing mid-size rectangular pool off the main lobby and restaurant area, with low-lying Balinese-style chaise lounges. Their Pandora restaurant serves excellent creative concoctions rooted in locally grown ingredients, and sometimes has live music on weekends. There are actually several routes to the top of the Poas volcano and this hotel can be a bit hard to find, so be sure you're armed with good directions or a GPS. *Note:* Street noise can be a problem in some rooms.

Poas de Alajuela. www.villasanignacio.com. ✆ **8492-1133.** 12 units. $85 double. Rates include breakfast. Free parking. **Amenities:** Restaurant; bar; pool; free Wi-Fi.

Where to Dine

Vegetarians should definitely head to **El Chante Vegano ★** (www.elchantevegano.com; ✆ **8911-4787**), a tasty and thoughtful vegan restaurant in the heart of downtown, a half-block south of the Post Office.

A longtime favorite up toward the Poás Volcano is **Chubascos ★** (www.chubascos.co.cr; ✆ **2482-2280**), which serves excellent versions of Costa Rican classics in a cozy mountain setting. In addition, the restaurants at **Xandari Resort & Spa and Marriott Costa Rica Hotel** are both excellent.

Jalapeños Central ★ MEXICAN/TEX MEX   Also known as "Norman's Jalapeño" this downtown favorite was opened more than 10 years ago by Norman Flores, a U.S. expat and world traveler. Burritos and chimichangas are the most popular dishes on the menu, but I'm a fan of the tasty sopa Azteca, or tortilla soup. Vegetarians have a number of options on the menu. Jalapenos has a strong local following so it's sometimes hard to get a table in this tiny little spot.

½ block south of the Post Office, downtown Alajuela. ℭ **2430-4027.** Main courses C3,400–C4,500. Mon–Sat 11:30am–9pm; Sun 11:30am–8pm.

HEREDIA

8.8km (5½ miles) north of San José

Founded in 1706 on the flanks of the impressive Barva Volcano, Heredia is affectionately known as "The City of Flowers." Of all the cities in the Central Valley, Heredia has the most colonial feel to it—you'll still see adobe buildings with Spanish tile roofs along narrow streets. Heredia is also the site of the **National University,** and you'll find some nice coffee shops and bookstores near the school.

Surrounding Heredia is an intricate maze of picturesque villages and towns, including Santa Bárbara, Santo Domingo, Barva, and San Joaquín de Flores. The hills and fields surrounding these towns contain some of the best and most fertile coffee plantations in Costa Rica.

Essentials

GETTING THERE & DEPARTING   **By Car:** The road to Heredia turns north off the Interamerican Highway (CR1) between San José and the airport.

By Bus: Buses (ℭ **2261-0506**) leave for Heredia every 10 minutes between 5am and 11pm from Calle 1 between avenidas 7 and 9, or from Avenida 2 between calles 12 and 14. Bus fare is C445.

CITY LAYOUT   Coming from San José, the most common route passes first through Santo Domingo de Heredia, although another popular route leads into downtown Heredia from San Joaquín de los Flores. The **Universidad Nacional Autonoma (National Autonomous University)** sits on the eastern edge of the city.

Exploring Heredia

The colonial **Catedral de la Inmaculada Concepción ★** (Church of the Immaculate Conception; ℭ **2237-0779**), inaugurated in 1763, stands guard over Heredia's central park—the stone facade leaves no questions as to the age of the church. The altar inside is decorated with neon stars and a crescent moon surrounding a statue of the Virgin Mary.

In the middle of the palm-shaded central park is a large gazebo, **El Templo de la Musica (The Music Temple) ★**, where live music is frequently performed. Across the street, beside several red tile-roofed municipal buildings, is **El Fortín ★**, the tower of an old Spanish fort.

Anyone with an interest in medicinal herbs should plan a visit to the **Ark Herb Farm ★★** (www.arkherbfarm.com; ✆ **6253-7655** or 2269-9683). They offer guided tours of their gardens, which feature more than 300 types of medicinal plants, as well as a beekeeping operation. The tour costs $10 per person, and includes a light snack and refreshments. Reservations are required.

A coffee tree at Café Britt.

Chocolate lovers will definitely want to visit **Sibu Chocolates ★★★** (www.sibuchocolate.com; ✆ **2268-1335**). This gourmet organic chocolate maker has a lovely small cafe, gift shop and offers tours of its production facility. Their shop and production facility is open Tuesday through Saturday from 8am to 5pm. The tasting tours are offered on these days at 10:30am. Reservations are essential, and the tour costs $24. The tour includes an informative presentation about the history and techniques of chocolate making, as well as several tempting tastings.

While on the road to Barva, you'll find the small **Museo de Cultura Popular ★** (www.museo.una.ac.cr; ✆ **2260-1619**), which is open Sunday from 10am to 5pm; admission is C500.

TOP ATTRACTIONS

Café Britt Farm ★★ FARM   Café Britt is one of the largest coffee producers in Costa Rica, and the company has put together an interesting and professional tour and stage production at its farm, which is 20 minutes outside of San José. Here, you'll see how coffee is grown. You'll also visit the roasting and processing plant to learn how a coffee "cherry" is turned into a delicious roasted bean. Tasting sessions are offered for visitors to experience the different qualities of coffee. The farm also has a restaurant and a store where you can buy coffee and coffee-related gift items. The entire tour, including transportation, takes about 3 to 4 hours. Allow some extra time and an extra $10 for a visit to their nearby working plantation and mill. You can even strap on a basket and go out coffee picking during harvest time.

North of Heredia on the road to Barva. www.coffeetour.com. ℗ **2277-1600.** Admission $22 adults, $17 children 6–11; $39 adults and $34 children, including transportation from downtown San José. Add $15 for a buffet lunch. Tour daily at 9:30 and 11am and at 1:15 and 3:15pm. Store and restaurant daily 8am–5pm.

Finca Rosa Blanca Coffee Plantation Tour ★★ FARM   This boutique hotel (p. 190) in Heredia also has its own organic coffee plantation, with some 16 hectares (40 acres) of shade-grown Arabica under cultivation. The hotel offers up daily coffee tours led by a very knowledgeable guide. I recommend combining the coffee tour with lunch at the open-air restaurant here; sitting under the shady gazebo, you'll enjoy a wonderful view of the Central Valley along with some fine healthy dining. The good in-house spa offers several treatments featuring homemade, coffee-based products.

Santa Bárbara de Heredia. www.fincarosablanca.com. ℗ **2269-9392.** Admission $35 adults, free for children 10 and under. Reservations required.

INBio Park ★★   Run by the National Biodiversity Institute (Instituto Nacional de Biodiversidad, or INBio), this place is part museum, part educational center, and part nature park. In addition to watching a

INBio Park.

15-minute informational video, visitors can tour two large pavilions explaining Costa Rica's biodiversity and natural wonders, and hike on trails that re-create the ecosystems of a tropical rainforest, dry forest, and premontane forest. A 2-hour guided hike is included in the entrance fee, and self-guided-tour booklets are also available. There's a good-size butterfly garden, as well as a Plexiglas viewing window into the small lagoon. One of my favorite attractions is the series of animal sculptures donated by one of Costa Rica's premiere artists, José Sancho. A simple cafeteria-style restaurant is on-site for lunch, as well as a coffee shop and gift shop. You can easily spend 2 to 3 hours here.

400m (4 blocks) north and 250m (2½ blocks) west of the Shell station in Santo Domingo de Heredia. www.inbioparque.com. 𝄐 **2507-8107.** Admission $25 adults, $19 students, $15 children 12 and under. Fri 9am–3pm (admission closes at 2pm); Sat–Sun 9am–4pm.

Where to Stay

While I don't recommend any hotels right in the city center, the small towns and agricultural villages surrounding Heredia are home to one of the country's finest boutique inns.

EXPENSIVE

Finca Rosa Blanca Coffee Plantation & Inn ★★★   Finca Rosa Blanca is an eccentric architectural gem set amid the green, lush hillsides of a coffee plantation. A turret tops the main building, and arched

Finca Rosa Blanca Coffee Plantation & Inn.

windows, walls of glass, and curves instead of corners are at almost every turn. Throughout, the glow of polished hardwood blends with white stucco walls and brightly colored murals. If breathtaking bathrooms are your idea of luxury, splurge on the Rosa Blanca suite, which has a stone waterfall that cascades into a tub in front of a huge picture window, and a spiral staircase that leads to the top of the turret. All of the suites and villas have the same sense of creative luxury, with lovely tile work, fab views, and other design touches. The restaurant and spa here are top-notch, and the owners have a real dedication to sustainable practices. The hotel has 14 hectares (35 acres) of organic coffee under cultivation, and their in-house coffee tour is terrific. **GPS:** 10°02'44.91"N; 84°09'03.86"W

Santa Bárbara de Heredia. www.fincarosablanca.com. ✆ **305/395-3042** in the U.S., or 2269-9392 in Costa Rica. 15 units. $320–$565 double. Rates include breakfast. Free parking. **Amenities:** Restaurant; bar; lounge; concierge; small free-form pool set in the hillside; room service; full-service spa; all rooms smoke-free; free Wi-Fi.

MODERATE

Hotel Bougainvillea ★★ Tennis courts, a large pool, a bar and business center—for those hankering for a real resort experience, this three-story property is the ticket. It's not fancy by any means, with endless corridors and spacious but faceless rooms. But the lovely landscaping of the grounds, the unusually attentive service and the fact that there's a darn good restaurant on site make up for a lot. Each of the rooms has a balcony; ask for one overlooking of the gardens, as they're much quieter and sport nicer views.

In Santo Tomás de Santo Domingo de Heredia, 100m (1 block) west of the Escuela de Santo Tomás, San José. www.hb.co.cr. ✆ **866/880-5441** in the U.S. and Canada, or 2244-1414 in Costa Rica. 81 units. $119–$129 double; $135–$145 suites. Rates include breakfast buffet. Free parking. **Amenities:** Restaurant; bar; pool; 2 lighted tennis courts; free Wi-Fi.

Where to Dine

It's also worth making the winding drive to San Pedro de Barva de Heredia to stop in at **La Lluna de Valencia ★★** (www.lallunadevalencia.com; ✆ **2269-6665**), a delightful rustic Spanish restaurant with amazing paella, sangria, and a very colorful and amiable host.

El Tigre Vestido ★★ INTERNATIONAL/VEGETARIAN This is the in-house restaurant for the artsy Finca Rosa Blanca Coffee Plantation & Inn (p. 190). Owners Glenn and Teri Jampol are hard-core foodies and environmentalists, meaning much of the produce used is grown on site (you'll also find their homegrown coffee making its way into rubs, sauces, and desserts). The menu here seeks to jazz up traditional Costa Rican classics and to create new dishes out of local ingredients. M favorite seats are on the deck, which is set under tall trees overlooking the city lights of the Central Valley below.

At Finca Rosa Blanca, Santa Bárbara de Heredia. http://eltigrevestido.com. ℭ **305/395-3042** in the U.S., or 2269-9392 in Costa Rica. Main courses $16–$22. Daily 7am–10pm.

Entertainment & Nightlife

Home to the National Autonomous University, the center of Heredia is chock-full of bars and clubs frequented by college kids. Of these, **Bulevar Relax** (ℭ **2237-1832**), **Fresas** (ℭ **2262-5555**), and **La Choza** (ℭ **2238-3495**), all right near each other on Avenida Central, are my favorites, with lively, fun-loving crowds.

GRECIA, SARCHÍ & ZARCERO

All these towns are northwest of San José and can be combined into a long day trip (if you have a car), perhaps in conjunction with a visit to Poás Volcano and/or the Waterfall Gardens. The scenery here is rich and verdant, and the small towns and scattered farming communities are truly representative of Costa Rica's agricultural heartland and *campesino* (rural farmer) tradition. This is a great area to explore on your own in a rental car, if you don't mind getting lost a bit (roads are narrow, winding, and poorly marked). If you're relying on buses, you'll be able to visit any of the towns listed below, but probably just one or two per day.

Grecia

9km (12 miles) NW of Alajuela; 37km (23 miles) NW of San José

The picturesque little town of Grecia is noteworthy for its unusual **metal church,** which is painted a deep red with white gingerbread trim, and is just off the town's central park. About 1km (½ mile) outside of Grecia, on the old road to Alajuela, you will find the **World of Snakes** (www.theworldofsnakes.com; ℭ **2494-3700**). Open daily from 8am to 5pm, this serpentarium has more than 150 snakes representing more than 50 species. Admission, which includes a guided tour, is $12 for adults and $6 for children 7 to 14.

GETTING THERE   By Car: Grecia is located just off the Interamerican Highway (CR1), on the way from San José to Puntarenas.

   By Bus: Tuan (ℭ **2494-2139**) buses leave San José half-hour for Grecia from Calle 18 between avenidas 3 and 5 (on the east side of the Abonos Agros building). The fare is C1,095.

Sarchí ★

7km (4 miles) NW of Grecia; 44km (27 miles) NW of San José

Sarchí is Costa Rica's main artisan town. The colorfully painted miniature **oxcarts** that you see all over the country are made here. Oxcarts such as these were once used to haul coffee beans to market. Today,

An oxcart factory in Sarchí.

although you might occasionally see oxcarts in use, most are purely decorative. However, they remain a well-known symbol of Costa Rica. In addition to miniature oxcarts, many carved wooden souvenirs are made here with rare hardwoods from the nation's forests. The town has dozens of shops, and all have similar prices. Perhaps your best one-stop shop in Sarchí is the large and long-standing **Chaverri Oxcart Factory** ★★ (www. sarchicostarica.net; ℂ **2454-4411**), which is right in the center of things, but it never hurts to shop around and visit several of the stores. The **Fabrica de Carretas Eloy Alfaro** ★ (www. fabricadecarretaseloyalfaro.com; ℂ **2454-4131**) is another good option, offering up a small factory tour, and meals at a cafeteria-style restaurant.

Close-up of a typical Costa Rican oxcart.

Built between 1950 and 1958, the town's main **church** ★ is painted pink with aquamarine trim and looks strangely like a child's birthday cake. It's definitely worth a quick visit.

GETTING THERE **By Car:** If you're going to Sarchí from San José, head north on the Interamerican Highway (CR1), and take the exit for Grecia. From Grecia, the road to Sarchí heads off to the left as you face the main church, but because of all the one-way streets, you'll have to drive around the church. Rural roads connect Sarchí to Naranjo, San Ramón, and Zarcero.

By Bus: Tuan (© 2494-2139) buses leave San José for Grecia, with connections to Sarchí from Calle 18 between avenidas 3 and 5. Fare is C985. Or you can take one of the Alajuela-Sarchí buses, leaving every 30 minutes from Calle 8 between avenidas Central and 1 in Alajuela.

Else Kientzler Botanical Garden ★★ GARDEN   Located on the grounds of an ornamental flower farm, on the outskirts of the tourist town Sarchí, these are extensive, impressive, and lovingly laid-out botanical gardens. Over 2.5km (1.5 miles) of trails run through a collection of more than 2,000 species of flora. All the plants are labeled with their Latin names, with some further explanations around the grounds in both English and Spanish. On the grounds are a topiary labyrinth, as well as a variety of lookouts, gazebos, and shady benches. A children's play area features some water games, jungle gym setups, and a child-friendly, little zip-line canopy tour. Over 40 percent of the gardens are wheelchair accessible.

About 6 blocks north of the central football (soccer) stadium in the town of Sarchí, Alajuela. www.elsegarden.com. © **2454-2070.** Admission $12 adults, $9 students with valid ID and children 5–12. Entrance includes a 1-hr. guided tour. Reservations recommended. Daily 8am–4pm.

Where to Stay & Dine

Very few folks stay in Sarchí itself, and there are few noteworthy options. The best by far is **Hotel Paraíso Río Verde** ★ (© 2454-3003), located just 2 blocks from the San Pedro de Sarchi church.

El Silencio Lodge & Spa ★★★   This isolated luxury lodge, a member of the swank Relais & Châteaux, features large, individual bungalows scattered over a forested hillside with idyllic views over primary rain forests. The bungalow suites each offer a King bed (with luscious bedding), a large sitting area with built-in couches that convert to two twin beds, a spacious balcony and an outdoor Jacuzzi (with privacy provided by artistic bamboo screening). The two-bedroom family suites are the only units here that come with televisions. There are trails around the grounds and private reserve, as well as a top-notch spa and open-air yoga studio; classes and hikes are often included in nightly costs. They also run their

The topiary gardens in Zarcero.

own waterfall rappel canyoning and zip-line canopy tour operations. On-site organic gardens supply the kitchen, which specializes in spa cuisine. El Silencio has earned "5 Leaves" in the CST Sustainable Tourism program, the highest rating.

To get here, you must first drive to the town of Sarchí. From the Pali supermarket in the center of town, head north and follow the signs. El Silencio is some 22km (13 miles) outside of Sarchí.

Bajos del Toro, Alajuela. www.elsilenciolodge.com. ✆ **2231-6122** reservations office in San José, or 2476-0303 at the hotel. 20 units. $342–$392 suites; $688 2-bedroom villas. Rates include breakfast. **Amenities:** Restaurant; bar; small spa; Wi-Fi.

Zarcero

60km (38 miles) NW of San José

Beyond Sarchí, on picturesque roads lined with cedar trees, is the town of Zarcero. In a small park in the middle of town is a **menagerie of sculpted shrubs** that includes a monkey on a motorcycle, people and animals dancing, an ox pulling a cart, a man wearing a top hat, and an elephant. Behind all the topiary is a wonderful rural **church.** It's not worth the drive just to see this park, but it's a good idea to take a break in Zarcero to walk the gardens, on the way to La Fortuna and Arenal.

GETTING THERE   By Car: Zarcero is located along the popular route from San José to La Fortuna. Take the Interamerican Highway (CR1) north to Naranjo, and follow signs to Ciudad Quesada and Zarcero.

By Bus: Daily buses (© **2255-0567**) for Zarcero leave from San José hourly from the Atlántico del Norte bus station at Calle 12, Avenidas 14 and 18. This is actually the Ciudad Quesada–San Carlos bus. Just tell the driver that you want to get off in Zarcero, and keep an eye out for the topiary. The ride takes around 1½ hours, and the fare is C1,870.

CARTAGO ★

24km (15 miles) SE of San José

Cartago is the original capital of Costa Rica. Founded in 1563, it was Costa Rica's first city—and was, in fact, the *only* city for almost 150 years. Irazú Volcano rises up from the edge of town, and although it's quiet these days, it has not always been so peaceful. Earthquakes have damaged Cartago repeatedly over the years, so today few of the old colonial buildings are left standing. In the center of the city, a public park winds through the ruins of a large church that was destroyed in 1910 before it could be finished.

Essentials

GETTING THERE & DEPARTING   By Car: Head east out of San José on Avenida 2, toward the suburbs of Los Yoses and San Pedro, continuing on through Curridabat. As you exit Curridabat, you will see signs to Cartago, putting you on the Interamerican Highway (CR2) to Cartago. This section of the highway is also known locally as the Florencio del Castillo Highway. There's a C75 toll charged in one direction, as you leave Curridabat heading toward Cartago.

By Bus: Lumaca buses (© **2537-2320**) for Cartago leave San José every 3 to 5 minutes between 4:30am and 9pm, with slightly less frequent service until midnight, from Avenida 5, between Calle 4 and 6. You can also pick up one en route at any of the little covered bus stops along Avenida Central in Los Yoses and San Pedro. The length of the trip is 45 minutes; the fare is C570.

By Train: San José's scenic, but sporadic main train line **INCOFER** (www.incofer.go.cr; © **2542-5800**) runs all the way from downtown San Jose to downtown Cartago, with no stops. The train runs during commuter hours roughly every ½ hour between 5:30 and 9:30am and again between 3:30 and 8pm. One-way fare is C550.

**ORIENTATION   ** The main route into town from the highway, Avenida 2, enters downtown Cartago from the west and leads right to the center of town, and the central park and ruins. The Basilica is 6 blocks farther east, near where you pick up the road out to Paraiso and the Orosi Valley.

Exploring Cartago

Cartago is a quiet city, with little going on or of interest to tourists, aside from the Basilica (p. 199). If you spend time in the city, head to the

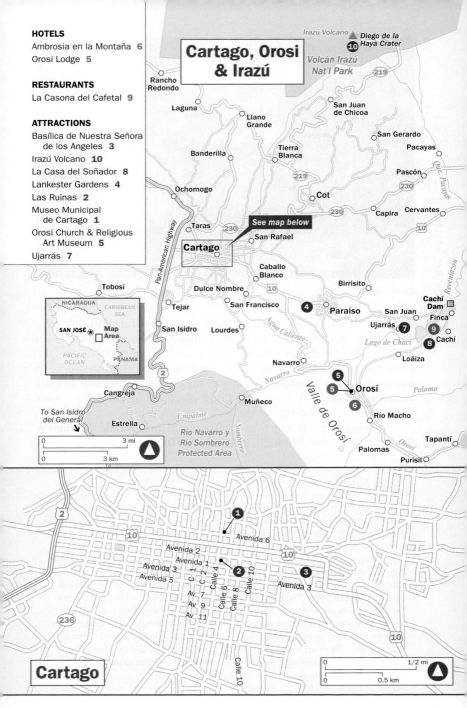

HOTELS
Ambrosia en la Montaña **6**
Orosi Lodge **5**

RESTAURANTS
La Casona del Cafetal **9**

ATTRACTIONS
Basílica de Nuestra Señora
de los Angeles **3**
Irazú Volcano **10**
La Casa del Soñador **8**
Lankester Gardens **4**
Las Ruinas **2**
Museo Municipal
de Cartago **1**
Orosi Church & Religious
Art Museum **5**
Ujarrás **7**

Cartago, Orosi & Irazú

Irazú Volcano
Diego de la
Haya Crater **10**
Volcán Irazú
Nat'l Park
219

Rancho
Redondo

Laguna
Llano
Grande
San Juan
de Chicoa

San Gerardo
Pacayas

Tierra
Blanca
Banderilla
Pascón
219
230

Ochomogo
Cot
Capira
Cervantes
230
10

Taras
230
San Rafael
See map below

Cartago

Caballo
Blanco

Tobosí
Dulce Nombre
10
Birrisito
Cachí
Dam

NICARAGUA
CARIBBEAN
SEA
Tejar
San Francisco
Paraíso
San Juan
Finca
SAN JOSÉ
Map
Area
San Isidro
Lourdes
Ujarrás **7**
9
Cachí
Lago de Chací
8

PACIFIC
OCEAN
PANAMA
Navarro
Loáiza

5
Orosí
Paloma

Cangreja
5
6
Río Macho

To San Isidro
del General
Estrella
Muñeco

Empalme
Río Navarro y
Río Sombrero
Protected Area
Valle de Orosí
Orosí
Tapantí
Palomas
Purisil

0   3 mi
0   3 km
2

Cartago

1
Avenida 6
2
10
Avenida 2
Avenida 1
2
3
10
Avenida 3
Avenida 5
Avenida 3
Av 7
Av 9
Av 11

236
Calle 10

0   1/2 mi
0   0.5 km

Las Ruinas.

Parque Central (Central Park), also known as **Las Ruinas (the Ruins)** ★. This is the site of the city's ill-fated original cathedral. Begun in 1575, the church was devastated by a series of earthquakes. Despite several attempts, construction was abandoned after the massive 1910 quake, and today the stone and mortar ruins sit at the heart of a neatly manicured park, with quiet paths and plenty of benches. The ruins themselves are closed off, but the park itself is lovely.

You might want to stop in at the **Museo Municipal de Cartago** ★ (Cartago Municipal Museum; ☎ **2591-1050**), on Avenida 6 between

---

La Negrita

Legend has it that Juana Pereira stumbled upon the statue of La Negrita sitting atop a rock, while gathering wood. Juana took it home, but the next morning it was gone. She went back to the rock, and there it was again. This was repeated three times, until Juana took her find to a local priest. The priest took the statue to his church for safekeeping, but the next morning it was gone, only to be found sitting upon the same rock later that day. The priest eventually decided that the strange occurrences were a sign that the Virgin wanted a temple or shrine built to her upon the spot. And so work was begun on what would eventually become today's impressive Basilica.

Miraculous healing powers have been attributed to La Negrita, and, over the years, parades of pilgrims have come to the shrine seeking cures for their illnesses and difficulties. August 2 is her patron saint's day. Each year, on this date, tens of thousands of Costa Ricans and foreign pilgrims walk to Cartago from San José and elsewhere in the country in devotion to this powerful statue.

The cathedral Basílica de Nuestra Señora de los Angeles in Cartago.

calles 2 and 4. Located in a former, and wonderfully restored military barracks, the museum houses a series of local historical displays, as well as a range of changing exhibits, including some featuring local artists. The museum is open Tuesday to Saturday, 9am to 4pm and Sunday till 3pm, free admission.

Cartago (and the Orosi Valley) is also a good stop along the way to visit one of the quetzal-viewing lodges in the Dota and Cerro de la Muerte region (p. 459).

Since there's no real reason to stay in Cartago, and no highly recommendable hotels right in the city, I suggest picking a hotel in the Orosi Valley or Turrialba region if you're looking to stay in the area.

Basílica de Nuestra Señora de los Angeles ★★★ CHURCH
Dedicated to the patron saint of Costa Rica, the impressive Basilica of Our Lady of the Angels anchors the east side of the city. Within the walls of this Byzantine-style church is a shrine containing the tiny carved figure of **La Negrita,** the Black Virgin, which is nearly lost amid its ornate altar. The walls of the shrine are covered with a fascinating array of tiny silver images left in thanks for cures affected by La Negrita. Amid the plethora of diminutive silver arms and legs, are also hands, feet, hearts, lungs, kidneys, eyes, torsos, breasts, and—peculiarly—guns, trucks, beds, and planes. Outside the church, vendors sell a wide selection of these trinkets, as well as little candle replicas of La Negrita.
Calle 16, btw. avs. 2 and 4. ✆ **2551-0465.** Free admission. Daily 5:30am–6:30pm.

Irazú Volcano.

Attractions Around Cartago

Irazú Volcano ★★ NATURAL ATTRACTION The 3,378m (11,080-ft.) Irazú Volcano is historically one of Costa Rica's more active volcanoes, although it's relatively quiet these days. It last erupted on March 19, 1963, the day that President John F. Kennedy arrived in Costa Rica. The landscape here is often compared to that of the moon. A good paved road leads right to the rim of the crater, where a desolate expanse of gray sand nurtures few plants and the air smells of sulfur. The drive up from Cartago has magnificent views of the fertile Meseta Central and Orosi Valley, and if you're very lucky, you might be able to see both the Pacific Ocean and the Caribbean Sea. Clouds usually descend by noon, so get here as early in the day as possible. Dress in

---

DIY: Irazú Volcano

If you don't have a rental car and don't want to sign on for an organized tour, buses leave San José for Irazú Volcano daily at 8am from Avenida 2 between calles 1 and 3 (across the street from the entrance to the Gran Hotel Costa Rica). The fare is C4,500 round-trip, with the bus leaving the volcano at 12:30pm. This company is particularly fickle. To make sure that the buses are running, call ☎ **2530-1064,** although that might not help much, since they often don't answer their phone, and speak only Spanish.

An orchid in bloom at Lankester Gardens.

layers; this might be the Tropics, but it can be cold up at the top if the sun's not out.

A short trail leads to the rim of the volcano's two craters, their walls a maze of eroded gullies feeding onto the flat floor far below. A 2km (1.25-mile) trail loops around the rim of the Playa Hermosa Crater. The visitor center up here has information on the volcano and natural history. The park restaurant, at an elevation of 3,022m (9,912 ft.), with walls of windows looking out over the valley far below, claims to be the highest restaurant in Central America.

Irazú de Cartago, 52km (32 miles) east of San José. (©) **2200-4222** or 2220-2025. Admission $15 adults, $15 children. Daily 8am–3:30pm.

Lankester Gardens ★★ GARDEN   Costa Rica has more than 1,400 varieties of orchids, and almost 800 species are cultivated and on display at this botanical garden. Created in the 1940s by English naturalist Charles Lankester, the gardens are now administered by the University of Costa Rica. The primary goal is to preserve the local flora, with an emphasis on orchids and bromeliads. Paved, well-marked trails meander from open, sunny gardens into shady forests. In each environment different species of orchids are in bloom. An information center and a gift shop are also on site. Plan to spend between 1 and 3 hours here if you're interested in flowers and gardening; you could run through it more quickly if you're not. You can easily combine a visit here with a tour at Cartago and/or the Orosi Valley and Irazú Volcano.

1km (½ mile) east of Cartago, on the road to Paraíso de Cartago. www.jbl.ucr.ac.cr. (©) **2511-7949.** Admission $8 adults, $5 students and children 6–16. Daily 8:30am–4:30pm.

THE OROSI VALLEY ★★

The Orosi Valley, southeast of Cartago, is generally considered one of the most beautiful valleys in Costa Rica. The Reventazón River meanders through this steep-sided valley until it collects in the lake formed by the Cachí Dam. A well-paved road winds a near-perfect loop around the lake, allowing for easy access to all of the attractions listed below. Scenic

The Orosi Valley.

The Ujarrás ruins.

overlooks are near the town of Orosi, at the head of the valley, and in Ujarrás, on the banks of the lake.

GETTING THERE & DEPARTING

If you're driving, take the road to Paraíso from Cartago, head toward Ujarrás, continue around the lake, and then pass through Cachí and on to Orosi. From Orosi, the road leads back to Paraíso. It is difficult to explore this whole area by public bus because this is not a densely populated region and connections are often infrequent or unreliable. However, regular buses do run from Cartago to the town of Orosi and around the entire loop. These buses run roughly every half-hour and leave the main bus terminal in Cartago. The trip takes 30 minutes, and the fare runs between C250 to C500, depending upon where you get off the bus.

Exploring the Orosi Valley

Near **Ujarrás** are the ruins of Costa Rica's oldest church, which was built in 1693. Little remains beyond the worn brick and adobe facade of

Sculptures at La Casa del Soñador.

the church, but the gardens are a great place to sit and gaze at the surrounding mountains.

Along the main road around the valley, especially near the town of Orosi, are several **scenic overlooks;** take the time to pull over and admire the views and snap a photo or two. In the town of **Orosi** itself is yet another **colonial church** (see below) and convent worth visiting.

From the Orosi Valley, it's a quick shot to the entrance to the **Tapantí National Park ★** (⊘ **2571-1781** or 2206-5615), where you'll find some gentle and beautiful hiking trails, as well as riverside picnic areas. The park is open daily from 8am to 4pm; admission is $10.

TOP ATTRACTIONS

La Casa del Soñador ★ COMMERCIAL ART GALLERY The "House of the Dreamer" is the home and gallery of the late sculptor Macedonio Quesada. Quesada earned fame with his primitive sculptures of La Negrita (see "La Negrita," p. 198) and other religious and secular characters carved on coffee tree roots and trunks. You can see some of Macedonio's original work here, including his version of "The Last Supper" carved onto one of the walls of the main building. Today, his sons carry on the family tradition, making small sculptures, carved religious icons, and ornate walking sticks.

1km (½ mile) south of Cachí. ⊘ **8955-7779.** Daily 9am–5:50pm.

Orosi Church & Religious Art Museum ★ CHURCH/ART MUSEUM The beautiful Orosi river valley is home to Costa Rica's oldest still-functioning church. The church, which was first built by Franciscan monks in the mid–18th century, features well-maintained traditional adobe walls that have weathered centuries, and several major earthquakes. Off to the side you'll find a small museum with a collection of religious paintings and artifacts, as well as original antique furniture and period clothing exhibits.

West side of the soccer field, Orosi. ℂ **2533-3051.** Admission C500 adults, C250 children. Daily 9am–noon; 1–5pm.

Iglesia de San José de Orosi.

Where to Stay & Eat

If you're interested in staying out here, check out the charming little **Orosi Lodge** ★ (www.orosilodge. com; ℂ **2533-3578**), on the south side of the tiny town of Orosi, right next to some simple hot-spring pools. A little farther out of town is **Ambrosia en la Montaña** ★ (www. ambrosiaenlamontana.com; ℂ **2533-2336** or 8385-7609), a pretty little inn, with two individual wooden cabins, great views, and an excellent restaurant.

La Casona del Cafetal ★ COSTA RICAN A dependable lunch stop for your drive around the Orosi Valley, this long-standing institution is set on expansive grounds overlooking Lake Cachí. Tables are spread around patios and verandas designed to take in the view, and a few heavy concrete tables are around the lawn. The restaurant serves up hearty, authentic traditional Costa Rican cuisine. Local ladies are always on hand forming and cooking up fresh corn tortillas. They also offer an all-you-can eat Sunday buffet for around $22, including tax and tip.

Cachí. www.lacasonadelcafetal.com. ℂ **2577-1414.** Main courses C6,500–C15,500 taxes included. Daily 11am–4pm.

TURRIALBA ★★

53km (33 miles) E of San José

This attractive little town was, until recently, best known as the starting point and home base for many popular white-water rafting trips. But the city's increasingly active namesake volcano has brought it another kind of fame in recent years. In March of 2015, a series of ash eruptions closed the San Jose International Airport for almost 2 days. Despite all the volcanic activity, Turrialba is considered safe, as the eruption patterns head away from the town.

Turrialba is situated in the heart of a rich agricultural region with coffee and sugar cane are the principal crops. Along with rafters, many come to explore the area's pre-Columbian history and tropical botany.

The area is lower in elevation than San José and much of the rest of the Central Valley, and for visitors (and the happy crops) this translates into generally higher temperatures. See "The Central Valley" map on p. 171.

Turrialba sits on the old transit route between San José and the Caribbean port city Limón. This makes Turrialba an excellent stop as part of an itinerary taking you to or from the Caribbean coast.

Essentials

GETTING THERE & DEPARTING **By Car:** If you're driving, follow the directions to Cartago (p. 196), and then take the road from Cartago to Paraíso, through Juan Viñas, and on to Turrialba. It's pretty well marked. (Alternatively you can head toward the small town of Cot, on the road to Irazú Volcano, and then through the town of Pacayas on to Turrialba, another well-marked route.)

By Bus: Transtusa buses (www.transtusacr.com; ✆ **2222-4464** or 2557-5050; fare C1,455) leave San José at least once every hour for Turrialba between 5:15am and 10pm from Calle 13 between avenidas 6 and 8. Around three buses also head to Guayabo daily from the main bus terminal in Turrialba. The fare is C545.

Turrialba Valley.

CITY LAYOUT Turrialba itself is a bit of a jumble, and you will probably have to ask directions to get to locations in, around, and outside of town. Guayabo is about 20km (12 miles) beyond Turrialba on a road that is paved the entire way except for the last 3km (1¾ miles).

Exploring Turrialba

Most of the white-water rafting companies in Costa Rica have an operational base in Turrialba, and the put-in points for several of the more popular river trips are nearby. See p. 110 for more info on rafting.

In addition to rafting and kayaking, **Explornatura** ★★ (www.explornatura.com; 𝒞 **866/571-2443** in the U.S. and Canada, or 2556-0111 in Costa Rica) is an excellent local adventure tour operator that offers up a range of trips and activities, including canopy and canyoning tours, horseback riding, hiking, and mountain biking. Their **canyoning tour** ★★ is a wet adventure that includes several rappels down the face of rainforest waterfalls.

Guayabo National Monument ★ (𝒞 **2559-1220**) is one of Costa Rica's only pre-Columbian sites open to the public. It's 19km (12 miles) northeast of Turrialba and preserves a town site that dates from between 1000 b.c. and a.d. 1400. Archaeologists believe that Guayabo might have supported a population of as many as 10,000 people, but no clues yet explain why the city was abandoned only shortly before the Spanish arrived in the New World. Excavated ruins consist of paved roads, aqueducts, stone bridges, and house and temple foundations. The site also has gravesites and petroglyphs. The monument is open daily from 8am to 3:30pm. This is a national park, and admission is $5 at the gate.

Hovering over the town, the **Turrialba Volcano National Park** ★★ boasts nearly 1,600 hectares (3,950 acres) of lush rainforest, as well as its namesake 3,340m (10,955-ft.) volcano. The volcano is in a fairly active phase, and the park trails are sometimes closed to the public. When it's open, it is possible to hike to the volcano's summit, which offers fantastic views. It's best to visit as part of a tour, since the final 8km (5 miles) to the park entrance is on a rough gravel road.

Botanists and gardeners will want to pay a visit to the **Center for Agronomy Research and Development** ★ (**CATIE;** www.catie.ac.cr; 𝒞 **2556-2700**), which is located 5km (3 miles) southeast of Turrialba on the road to Siquirres. This center is one of the world's foremost facilities for research into tropical agriculture. Among the plants on CATIE's 810 hectares (2,000 acres) are hundreds of varieties of cacao and thousands of varieties of coffee. The plants here have been collected from all over the world. In addition to trees used for food and other purposes, other plants grown here are strictly for ornamental purposes. CATIE is open Monday through Friday from 7am to 3pm. Guided tours are available with advance notice for $15 per person.

If you're a java junkie, you'll want to take the **Golden Bean Coffee Tour** ★ (*℃ **2251-0853** or 8701-2637; $22/person), a comprehensive and informative tour of a working coffee plantation. The mill and processing facilities here have been in operation for almost a century. The tour takes around 2 hours, and operates daily at 9am and 2pm.

Where to Stay & Eat

In addition to the places listed below, check out **Turrialtico** ★ (www. turrialtico.com; *℃ **2538-1111**), a simple hotel with an open-air restaurant on a hill overlooking the Turrialba Valley. The view here is one of the finest in the area, with volcanoes in the distance. The Costa Rican food is good and reasonably priced, and a double room in the rambling old wooden building will cost $64 to $75, including breakfast and taxes. Turrialtico is popular with rafting companies that bring groups for meals and overnights before, during, and after multiday rafting trips.

Casa Turire ★★   This lakefront boutique hotel was built to resemble a majestic old plantation home, replete with a long entrance driveway lined with tall Royal palms. The large rooms have painted tiles or varnished wood floors and colonial-style furnishings that evoke a bygone era. Casa Turire was actually built before the nearby hydroelectric dam created Lake Angostura, which now laps gently just below the hotels well-tended gardens. The hotel has earned "4 Leaves" in the CST Sustainable Tourism program.

1.5km (1 mile) from the Cruce de Atirro, Turrialba. www.hotelcasaturire.com. *℃ **2531-1111** in Costa Rica. 16 units. $186 double; $288 suite; $452 master suite. Rates include full breakfast. **Amenities:** Restaurant; bar; Jacuzzi; outdoor pool; small spa; smoke-free rooms; free Wi-Fi.

Pacuare Lodge ★★★   Set on the edge of the roaring Pacuare river, this luxurious raft in–raft out jungle lodge is a marvel. The first time I rafted the Pacuare River more than 20 years ago, it was with Aventuras Naturales (p. 167), the owners of this lodge. We camped in tents on this very spot. Today the individual bungalows and private suites are some of the most plush nature lodge digs you'll find anywhere in the country. A few even come with private plunge pools. Of these, the remote honeymoon suite is the real star, reached by a long private suspension bridge. For a really unique experience, be sure to reserve *El Nido* or "The Nest," located 40 feet or so above the ground on a treetop platform that is reached by zip-lining in. The Pacuare Lodge has received the highest "5 Leaves" rating from the CST Sustainable Tourism program.

On the banks of the Pacuare River. www.pacuarelodge.com. *℃ **800/963-1195** in the U.S. and Canada, or 2225-3939 in Costa Rica. 19 units. Rates begin at $360 per person for a 2-day/1-night package, including 3 meals, transportation to and from San José and 2 days on the river. **Amenities:** Restaurant; bar; outdoor solar-heated pool; spa; all rooms smoke-free.

GUANACASTE:
THE GOLD COAST

8

Guanacaste is known as Costa Rica's "Gold Coast"— and not because this is where the Spanish Conquistadors found vast quantities of the precious metal ore. Instead, it's because more and more visitors to Costa Rica are choosing Guanacaste as their first—and often only—stop. Beautiful beaches abound along this coastline. Several are packed with a mix of hotels and resorts, some are still pristine and deserted, and others are backed by small fishing villages. Choices range from long, broad sections of sand stretching on for miles, to tiny pocket coves bordered by rocky headlands. There are several famous surf breaks and beaches, and other protected spots perfect for a mellow swim or snorkel.

This is Costa Rica's most coveted vacation destination and the site of its greatest tourism development. The international airport in Liberia receives daily direct flights from a host of major U.S. and Canadian hub cities, allowing tourists to visit some of Costa Rica's prime destinations without having to go through San José.

This is also Costa Rica's driest region. The rainy season starts later and ends earlier, and overall it's more dependably sunny here than in other parts of the country. Combine this climate with a coastline that stretches south for hundreds of miles, from the Nicaraguan border, all the way to the Nicoya Peninsula, and you have an equation that yields beach bliss.

One caveat: During the dry season (mid-Nov to Apr), when sunshine is most reliable, the hillsides in Guanacaste turn browner than the chaparral of Southern California. Dust from dirt roads blankets the trees in many areas, and the vistas are far from tropical, and you might think you were at Burning Man at times. Driving these dirt roads without air-conditioning and the windows rolled up tight can be extremely unpleasant, and walking along them can be awful.

On the other hand, if you happen to visit this area in the rainy season (particularly from May–Aug), the hillsides are a beautiful, rich green, and the sun usually shines all morning, giving way to an afternoon shower— just in time for a nice siesta.

FACING PAGE: **Peninsula Papagayo in Guanacaste.**

Playa Virador in Guanacaste.

Inland from the beaches, Guanacaste remains Costa Rica's "Wild West," a land of dry plains populated with cattle ranches and cowboys, who are known here as *sabaneros,* a name that derives from the Spanish word for "savanna" or "grassland." If it weren't for those rainforest-clad volcanoes in the distance, you might swear you were in Texas.

Guanacaste is home to several active volcanoes and some beautiful national parks, including **Santa Rosa National Park ★**, the site of massive sea turtle nestings and of a major battle to maintain independence; **Rincón de la Vieja National Park ★★**, which features hot springs and bubbling mud pots, pristine waterfalls, and an active volcanic crater; and **Palo Verde National Park ★**, a beautiful expanse of mangroves, wetlands, and savanna.

THE best GUANACASTE EXPERIENCES

- **Barefoot Dining with Your Feet in the Sand:** Beachfront dining options range from the fine seared tuna and Belgian fries found at **Lola's** (p. 278) to the just-grilled daily catch at a simple Costa Rican *soda.* See the "Where to Dine" sections of the various destinations below for recommendations.

- **Catching Your First Wave:** All up and down the Guanacaste coast are excellent breaks, and many are perfect for beginners. See the "Exploring" sections of the various destinations below for surf school recommendations.

- **Taking a Sailboat Cruise:** Most of the beach towns and destinations in Guanacaste boast a small fleet of charter boats. Trips often include lunch and a snorkel stop or two. Some stop at deserted beaches, or linger at sea for the sunset. See the "Exploring" sections of the destinations below for boat recommendations.

- **Taking a Sunset Stroll on the Beach:** What could be more peaceful or romantic than a leisurely stroll on a Guanacaste beach in the late afternoon, as the sun sets into the Pacific? I prefer more isolated stretches of sand, like Playa Avellanas or Playa Grande, but it's hard to go wrong almost anywhere along this coastline.

- **Checking Out Rincón de la Vieja's Hot Springs, Hiking & Adventures:** Even if you're staying at one of the region's beach resorts, Rincón de la Vieja National Park's namesake volcano and fabulous trails are definitely worth a visit. Also worth seeing are the hot springs just outside the park and the amazing Hacienda Guachipelín's adventure tours. See "Rincón de la Vieja National Park" below.

LIBERIA

217km (135 miles) NW of San José; 132km (82 miles) NW of Puntarenas

Founded in 1769, Liberia is the capital of Guanacaste province, and although it can hardly be considered a bustling metropolis, it's growing rapidly, in large part as a business center to feed the coastal boom. The city serves as a housing hub for the many workers needed to man the tourist hotspots along the coast here.

That said, Liberia offers up more colonial atmosphere than almost any other city in the country. Its streets are lined with charming old adobe homes, many of which have ornate stone accents on their facades, carved wooden doors, and aged red-tile roofs above shuttered windows (some don't even have iron bars for protection) opening onto the narrow streets. The central plaza, which occupies 2 square blocks in front of the church, remains the city's social hub and principal gathering spot.

Liberia can serve as a base for exploring this region or as an overnight stop in a longer itinerary. You'll find several moderately priced hotels in the city and its outskirts. Still, all things considered, it's usually preferable to base yourself either at the beach or at a mountain lodge, and to visit the city on a day trip.

Essentials

GETTING THERE & DEPARTING By Plane: The **Daniel Oduber International Airport** (airport code LIR) in Liberia receives a steady stream of scheduled commercial and charter flights throughout the year.

Liberia's central park.

Major North American airlines have direct links to Liberia; check p. 563. In addition, numerous commercial charter flights from various North American cities fly in throughout the high season. **Nature Air** (www. natureair.com; ✆ **800/235-9272** in the U.S. and Canada, or 2668-1106 in Liberia) and **Sansa** (www.flysansa.com; ✆ **877/767-2672** in the U.S. and Canada, or 2290-4100 in Costa Rica) both have several flights daily to Liberia. Fares run between $105 and $155 each way. Flight duration is around 50 minutes.

Along with the multinational chains, the following local companies rent cars from the airport: **Adobe** (✆ **2667-0608**) and **Toyota** (✆ **2668-1212**). You can reserve with these and most major international car rental companies via their San José and international offices (see "Getting Around," in chapter 6).

The airport is 13km (8 miles) from downtown Liberia. Taxis await all incoming flights; a taxi into town should cost around $10. The ride takes around 10 minutes.

By Car: From San José, you can either take the Interamerican Highway (CR1) north all the way to Liberia from downtown San José, or first head west out of the city on the San José–Caldera Highway (CR27). When you reach Caldera, follow the signs to Puntarenas, Liberia, and the Interamerican Highway (CR1). This will lead you to the unmarked entrance to CR1. You'll want to pass under the bridge and follow the on-ramp, which will put you on the highway heading north. This latter route is a faster and flatter drive. Depending upon which route you take and traffic conditions, it's a 3- to 4-hour drive.

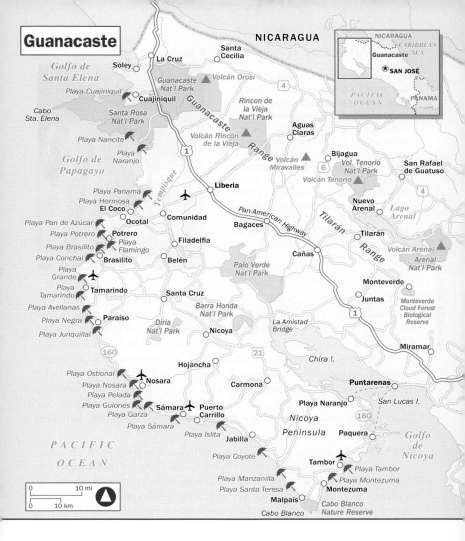

Guanacaste

NICARAGUA

Golfo de Santa Elena

Soley
La Cruz
Santa Cecilia
Volcán Orosí

Playa Cuajiniquil
Cuajiniquil
Guanacaste Nat'l Park
Rincon de la Vieja Nat'l Park
4

Cabo Sta. Elena
Santa Rosa Nat'l Park
Volcán Rincón de la Vieja
Aguas Claras

Playa Nancite
Volcán Miravalles
Bijagua
Vol. Tenorio Nat'l Park
San Rafael de Guatuso

Golfo de Papagayo
Playa Naranjo
Volcán Tenorio

Liberia
6
4

Playa Panamá
Playa Hermosa
El Coco
Comunidad
Nuevo Arenal
Lago Arenal

Playa Pan de Azúcar
Ocotal
Bagaces
Pan-American Highway
Tilarán

Playa Potrero
Potrero
Filadelfia
Cañas
Volcán Arenal

Playa Brasilito
Playa Flamingo
Belén
Arenal Nat'l Park

Playa Conchal
Brasilito
Palo Verde Nat'l Park

Playa Grande
Tamarindo
Santa Cruz
Monteverde

Playa Tamarindo
Juntas
Monteverde Cloud Forest Biological Reserve

Playa Avellanas
Barra Honda Nat'l Park

Playa Negra
Paraíso
Diria Nat'l Park
Nicoya
La Amistad Bridge

Playa Junquillal
160
Chira I.
Miramar

Hojancha
21
Puntarenas

Playa Ostional
Nosara
Carmona
San Lucas I.

Playa Nosara
Playa Pelada
Playa Naranjo
160

Playa Guiones
Sámara
Puerto Carrillo
Nicoya

Playa Garza
Paquera
Golfo de Nicoya

Playa Sámara
Playa Islita
Jabilla
Peninsula

PACIFIC
Playa Coyote
Tambor
Playa Tambor

OCEAN
Playa Manzanilla
Playa Montezuma

Playa Santa Teresa
Montezuma

Malpaís
Cabo Blanco Nature Reserve

Cabo Blanco

0   10 mi
0   10 km

NICARAGUA
CARIBBEAN SEA
Guanacaste
SAN JOSÉ
PACIFIC OCEAN
PANAMA

By Bus: Pulmitan express buses (📞 **2222-1650** in San José, or 2666-0458 in Liberia) leave San José roughly every hour between 6am and 8pm from Calle 24 between avenidas 5 and 7. The ride to Liberia takes around 4 hours. A one-way fare costs C4,005. As we went to press, a new terminal for Guanacaste busses called **Terminal Central 7-10** was scheduled to open; check www.terminal7-10.com to see if it's open when you arrive. It will likely serve most of the bus lines mentioned in this chapter and will be located at Avenida 7 and Calle 10 in Barrio Mexico. However your best bet will probably be to tell your taxi driver "diagonal al antiguo Cine Libano (diagonal to the old Cine Libano)."

An Artful Stop on Your Way to Liberia

If you're driving to or from Guanacaste, be sure to take a brief break to check out the **Iglesia de Cañas (Cañas Church) ★★** in Cañas. Well-known painter, installation artist, and local prodigal son Otto Apuy has designed and directed the envelopment of the entire church in colorful mosaic. The work uses whole and broken tiles in glossy, vibrant colors to depict both religious and abstract themes. The church's nearly 30m-tall (100-ft.) central tower is entirely covered in mosaics. It is estimated that more than a million pieces of ceramic were used in the work. The church is located in the center of town, just a few blocks off the highway.

Gray Line (www.graylinecostarica.com; ℂ **800/719-3905** in the U.S. and Canada, or 2220-2126 in Costa Rica) and **Interbus** (www.interbusonline.com; ℂ **4100-0888**) both have two daily buses leaving San José for Liberia and all beaches in this area, one in the morning and one in the afternoon. The fare is around $50. The morning bus (for either company) makes connections to Rincón de la Vieja and Santa Rosa national parks. Both companies will pick you up at most San José–area hotels, and provide connections to and from most other destinations in Costa Rica. Express buses for San José leave roughly every hour between 3am and 8pm.

CITY LAYOUT　Liberia's small city center lies just to the east of the main intersection of the Interamerican Highway and the road to the beaches. On the southern outskirts of the city is a modern shopping mall, the place to come for a food court fix or to catch a semi-late-run movie. Smaller, contemporary strip malls and shopping centers can be found near the airport, and right at the major intersection near the entrance to town.

FAST FACTS　Several bank offices are clustered in downtown Liberia, as well as a branch of the **Banco de Costa Rica** inside the airport. The local **police** number is ℂ **2690-0129,** and the **Liberia Hospital** number is ℂ **2690-2300.** If you need a taxi, dial ℂ **2666-3330.**

Exploring the Town

The central plaza in Liberia is a great place to people-watch, especially in the early evenings and on weekends. Grab a seat on one of the many concrete benches, or join the families and young lovers as they leisurely stroll around.

A colonial-era building in Liberia.

Just off the northwest corner of the main central plaza, the **Museo de Guanacaste** (Guanacaste Museum; ✆ **2665-7114**) occupies the city's former military barracks and prison. There's no permanent collection, but the space is often used for traveling exhibits and cultural events—concerts, lectures, recitals. Inaugurated in 1940, the building is known locally as either the Comandancia de Plaza de Liberia, or El Cuartel.

If you venture for a few blocks down **Calle Real ★**, you'll see fine examples of the classic Spanish colonial adobe buildings with ornate wooden doors, heavy beams, central courtyards, and faded, sagging, red-tile roofs.

While the Catholic church that anchors the central plaza is unspectacular, if you head several blocks east of the plaza, you will come to **Iglesia La Ermita de la Agonía ★** (✆ **2666-0518**). Built in 1865, this whitewashed stone church is in surprisingly good shape. Inside it is plain and bare, but it is the only remaining colonial-era church to be found in Guanacaste. The visiting hours are seriously limited (daily 2:30–3:30pm), but not to worry: Local tour agencies can sometimes arrange visits during off hours. Even if you can't enter, you'll still get a good feel for the place by checking out its whitewashed stucco exterior.

Outdoor Adventures Near Liberia

In addition to the activities listed below, Liberia is a major jumping-off point for Rincón de la Vieja National Park (p. 221).

LLANO DE CORTES WATERFALL ★★

Located about 25km (16 miles) south of Liberia, the **Llanos del Cortés Waterfall ★★** is a jungle waterfall with an excellent pool at the base for cooling off and swimming. At roughly 12m (40 ft.) wide, the falls are actually slightly wider than they are tall. This is a good spot for a picnic. The turnoff for the dirt road to the falls is well marked and about 3km (1¾ miles) north of the crossroads for Bagaces. From the turnoff, you must drive a rough dirt road to the parking area and then hike down a short steep trail to the falls. Admission is C1,000 and goes to support the local school. Even though guards are on duty, be careful about leaving anything of value in your car.

8

GUANACASTE

Liberia

215

Llanos de Cortes Waterfall.

BIRDING

The **Río Tempisque Basin ★**, southwest of town, is one of the best places in the country to spot marsh and stream birds by the hundreds. This area is an important breeding ground for gallinules, jacanas, and limpkins, as well as numerous heron and kingfisher species and the roseate spoonbill. Several tour operators offer excursions the region. **Swiss Travel Services** (www. swisstravelcr.com; ✆ **2282-4898**) is the largest and most reliable of the major operators here.

One of the most popular tours is a boat tour down the Bebedero River to **Palo Verde National Park ★**, which is south of Cañas and is best known for its migratory bird populations. Some of the best bird-watching requires little more than walking around the park's Biological Station.

You can get a similar taste of these waterways and bird-watching opportunities at **El Viejo Wetlands** (p. 253) and **Rancho Humo** (p. 319).

RAFTING TRIPS

Leisurely raft trips (with little white water) are offered by **Ríos Tropicales ★★** (www.riostropicales.com; ✆ **2233-6455**), about 40km (25 miles) south of Liberia. Its 2-hour ($110) float trips are great for families and bird-watchers. Along the way you may see many of the area's more exotic critters: howler monkeys, iguanas, caimans, coatimundis, otters, toucans, parrots, motmots, trogons, and many other species of birds. Aside from your binoculars and camera, a bathing suit and sunscreen are the only things you'll need. Ríos Tropicales is based out of the Restaurant Rincón Corobicí, which is located right on the Interamerican Highway (CR1).

Shady Business

This province gets its name from the abundant Guanacaste (*Enterolobium cyclocarpum*), Costa Rica's national tree. This distinctive tree is known for its broad, full crown, which provides welcome shade on the Guanacaste's hot plains and savannas. The Guanacaste is also known as the elephant-ear tree, because of the distinctive shape of its large seedpods. Its fragrant white flowers bloom between February and April.

Africa Safari Adventure Park.

For a much wetter and wilder ride, the folks at **Hacienda Guachipelín** (see below) offer white-water inner-tube trips on the narrow Río Negro.

ESPECIALLY FOR KIDS

Believe it or not, antelopes, zebras, giraffes, and elands roam the grassy plains of Guanacaste. **Africa Safari Adventure Park** (www. africasafaricostarica.com; ✆ **2288-1000**) offers safari-style open-jeep tours through its 100-hectare (247-acre) private reserve populated with a wide range of nonnative (predominantly African) species. All the animals are herbivores, so don't expect to see any lions, hyenas, or cheetahs. The trip does provide some sense of being on the Serengeti and the animals have plenty of room to roam. Be sure to buy a bag or two of carrots for feeding the giraffe before heading out. The tours here visit two local waterfalls, so bring a bathing suit as it gets hot, so you'll want to take a quick dip or shower. Admission, which is $100 for adults, and $50 for children 11 and under, includes a 90-minute guided tour and safari style tractor ride through the park. These folks also offer a separate ATV tour, and full day passes are available. Africa Safari Adventure Park is located just off the Interamerican Highway, 8km (5 miles) south of Liberia. The park is open daily from 9am to 5pm.

Where to Stay

MODERATE

Hilton Garden Inn Liberia Airport ★   Located directly across the two-lane Highway 21 from the Daniel Oduber International Airport (LIR), this five-story contemporary chain hotel is a good choice for folks with late arrivals or early departures. Still, with drive times of between 30 minutes to an hour to most nearby beach hotels, I debate how useful staying this close to the airport really is. Still should your needs dictate an airport stay, you'll get everything that you'd expect from a Hilton Garden Inn, with a free airport shuttle, as well as a small shopping mall adjacent to the hotel with a few restaurant options.

Across from the airport, Liberia, Guanacaste. www.hilton.com. ℂ **800/445-7444** in the U.S. and Canada, or 2690-8888 in Costa Rica. 169 units. $129–$149 double; $159–$229 suite. Rates include taxes. **Amenities:** Restaurant; bar; exercise room; Jacuzzi; outdoor pool; room service; all rooms smoke-free; free Wi-Fi.

INEXPENSIVE

Hotel Liberia ★   A colonial-era adobe home on the historic Calle Real, the Hotel Liberia was first pressed into service as a hotel back in 1918. Ornate painted tile floors in the lobby and main dining room date back to the colonial period. All of the rooms are spacious and kept meticulously clean, with locally built hardwood beds and crisp linens. I recommend the La Casona rooms off the main central hallway, which open on to a broad shady shared veranda. The restaurant here serves up fairly priced local cuisine, with both indoor and outdoor seating.

Calle Real, ¾ block south of the old Government building, Liberia, Guanacaste. www.hotelliberiacr.com. ℂ **2666-0161.** 18 units. $13 per person, dorm room; $35–$40 double. Rates include taxes. **Amenities:** Restaurant; bar; free Wi-Fi.

Where to Dine

Liberia has plenty of dining choices. For local flavor, choose one of the *sodas* around the central park. The best of these is **Restaurante Paseo Real** ★ (ℂ **2666-3455**). Another option for Costa Rican cuisine is **La Choza de Laurel** (www.lachozadelaurel.com; ℂ **2668-1019**), located along the main highway, about 800m (2,624 ft.) east of the Liberia airport entrance. It serves good authentic Costa Rican food, but has a more touristy feel than the simple places you'll find in town. For a slightly more upscale option, head along Avenida Central, a block beyond the central park to **Toro Negro Steakhouse** ★★ (ℂ **2666-2456**), which offers thick-cut steaks, wood-oven fired pizzas and sushi. Another popular alternative is **Pizzería Pronto** (ℂ **2666-2098**), which for wood-oven pizzas and assorted pasta dishes, in a restored colonial home.

    For seafood and a good bar scene, try **LIB** (ℂ **2665-0741**), which sometimes features live music and dancing at night, and is in the Centro Comercial Santa Rosa, at the main highway crossroads.

INEXPENSIVE

El Café Liberia ★★ INTERNATIONAL/COSTA RICAN   Set in an atmospheric colonial-era home, with a sagging clay tile roof that shows its age, El Café Liberia is *the* place to eat in Liberia. Helmed by a chef from Luxembourg who has made the cuisine of the Americas his own, its specialties are superb ceviche, chicken *casado* (a rice and chicken dish), a rich spinach dip, grilled steaks and fresh seafood in many preparations. All are served on large white plates, with colorful patterns made from sauces and reductions. One warning though: I'm a bit doubtful that the $8 hamburger is really made from imported "wagu" beef as advertised. Dessert lovers will want to save room for their decadent "lava flow" molten chocolate cake.

Calle Real. 1⅕ blocks south of the Central Plaza. © **2665-1660.** Main courses $7–$17. Mon 3–9pm and Tue-Sat 9am–9pm.

Shopping

On the road to the beaches, just west of the airport, are several large souvenir shops. The best of the bunch for a one-stop shop is **La Gran Nicoya** (www.lagrannicoya-cr.com; © **2667-0062**). However, you might find better selections and prices, especially for Guaitíl pottery, at some of the smaller makeshift roadside kiosks that line the road between Liberia and the Guanacaste beaches.

For something different, check out the **Hidden Garden Art Gallery** ★★ (http://hiddengarden.thevanstonegroup.com; © **8386-6872**), a well-stocked contemporary art gallery, with a large stable of prominent Costa Rican and expatriate artists, and regularly changing special exhibitions. It's located 5km (3 miles) west of the Liberia airport, on the road to the beaches.

RINCÓN DE LA VIEJA NATIONAL PARK

242km (151 miles) NW of San José; 25km (16 miles) NW of Liberia

This sprawling national park begins on the flanks of the Rincón de la Vieja Volcano and includes this volcano's namesake active crater. Down lower is an area of geothermal activity similar to that of Yellowstone National Park in the United States. Fumaroles, geysers, and hot pools cover this small area, creating a bizarre, otherworldly landscape. In addition to hot springs and mud pots, you can explore waterfalls, a lake, and volcanic craters. Bird-watching here is rewarding, as the sparse foliage of the dry forest makes spotting easier, and from the high volcanic slopes here you can enjoy sweeping views all the way to the ocean.

Rincón de la Vieja National Park mud pots.

Essentials

GETTING THERE   By Car: Follow the directions to Liberia (p. 212). When you reach Liberia, head straight through the major intersection, following signs to Peñas Blancas and the Nicaraguan border.

To reach the **Las Pailas (Las Espuelas) entrance,** drive about 5km (3 miles) north of Liberia and turn right on the dirt road to the park. The turnoff is well marked. In about 12km (7½ miles), you'll pass through the small village of Curubandé. Continue on this road for another 6km (3¾ miles) until you reach the Hacienda Guachipelín. The lodge is private property, and the owners charge vehicles a C700 toll to pass through their gate and continue on to the park. I'm not sure if this is legal or mandatory, but it's not worth the hassle to protest. Pay the toll, pass through the gate, and continue for another 4km (2½ miles) until you reach the park entrance.

Two routes lead to the **Santa María entrance.** The principal route heads out of the northeastern end of Liberia toward the small village of San Jorge. This route is about 25km (16 miles) long and takes about 45 minutes. A four-wheel-drive

What's in a Name?

Rincón de la Vieja translates literally as "the old lady's corner." In this case, "la vieja" has the connotation of a witch or hag, while "rincón" is better interpreted as a "lair" or "hangout." The smoking, belching volcanic crater and mud pots gave rise to this name.

vehicle is required. Alternatively, you can reach the entrance on a turnoff from the Interamerican Highway at Bagaces. From here, head north through Guayabo, Aguas Claras, and Colonia Blanca. Though the road is paved up to Colonia Blanca, a four-wheel-drive vehicle is required for the final, very rough 10km (6¼ miles) of gravel road.

Exploring Rincón de la Vieja National Park ★★

Rincón de la Vieja National Park has several excellent trails. The easiest hiking is the gentle **Las Pailas loop ★**. This 3km (1.75-mile) trail is just off the Las Espuelas park entrance and passes by several bubbling mud pots and steaming fumaroles. Don't get too close, or you could get scalded. Happily, the strong sulfur smell given off by these formations works well as a natural deterrent. This gentle trail crosses a river, so you'll have to either take off your shoes or get them wet. The whole loop is 3.2km (2 miles) and takes around 2 hours at a leisurely pace.

My favorite hike here is to the **Blue Lake** and **La Cangreja Waterfall ★★★**. Along this well-marked 9.6km (6-mile) round-trip trail, you will pass through several different ecosystems, including tropical dry

forest, transitional moist forest, and open savanna. You are likely to spot a variety of birds and mammals and have a good chance of coming across a group of coatimundi—a raccoonlike local mammal. While not requiring any great climbs or descents, the hike is nonetheless long, and that makes it arduous. Still, every time I do it, I swear it's worth it. At the end of your 2-hour hike in, you'll come to the aptly named Blue Lake, where a 30m (98-ft.) waterfall empties into a small crystal blue pond. This is one of my favorite spots for a swim. Pack in a lunch and have a picnic before attempting the hike back out.

Due to volcanic activity and the extreme nature of the hike, the summit trail has been closed to visitors since late 2013. If it's reopened, energetic hikers can tackle the **summit ★** and explore

La Cangrejo Waterfall.

the several craters and beautiful lakes up here. On a clear day, you'll be rewarded with a fabulous view of the plains of Guanacaste and the Pacific Ocean below. The trail is 16.6km (10.3 miles) round-trip and should take about 7 hours (the trail head is at the ranger station). It heads pretty much straight up the volcano and is pretty steep in places. Along the way, you'll pass through several different ecosystems, including sections of tropical moist and tropical cloud forests, while climbing some 1,000m (3,280 ft.) in altitude. After about 6km (3.7 miles), the trail splits. Take the right-hand fork to the Crater Activo (Active Crater). Filled with rainwater, this crater is some 700m (2,300 ft.) in diameter and still active. Off to the side is the massive Laguna Jigueros. Because this crater emits large amounts of sulfur and acid gases, it's not recommended that you linger here long. If you have the energy, a side trail leads to the Von Seebach Crater.

The park entrance fee is $15 per person per day, and the park is open Tuesday to Sunday from 8am to 4pm.

Camping will cost you an extra $2 per person per day. There are actually two entrances and camping areas here: **Santa María** and **Las Pailas** (also called Las Espuelas; © **2666-5051**) ranger stations. Las Pailas is by far the more popular and accessible, and it's closer to the action. These small camping areas are near each other. I recommend the one closer to the river, although the restroom and shower facilities are about 90m (295 ft.) away, at the other site. For those seeking a less rugged tour of the park, several lodges are around the park perimeter and offer guided hikes and horseback rides into the park.

Other Adventures Around Rincón de la Vieja

ONE-STOP ADVENTURE SHOP

Hacienda Guachipelín (p. 224) offers up a range of adventure tour options, including horseback riding, hiking, white-water river inner-tubing, a waterfall canyoning and rappel tour, and a more traditional zip-line canopy tour. The most popular is the hacienda's **1-Day Adventure pass ★★**, which allows you to choose as many of the hotel's different tour options as you want and fit them into 1 adventure-packed day. The price for this is $85, including a buffet lunch. Almost all Guanacaste beach hotels and resorts offer day trips here, or you can book directly with the lodge. **Be forewarned:** During high season, the operation has a cattle-car feel, with busloads of day-trippers coming in from the beach.

HOT SPRINGS & MUD BATHS

The active Rincón de la Vieja Volcano has blessed this area with several fine hot springs and mud baths. Even if you're not staying at the **Hacienda Guachipelín** (p. 224) or the **Hotel Borinquen Mountain Resort** (p. 224), you can take advantage of their hot spring pools and hot mud baths. Both have on-site spas offering massages, facials, and other treatments.

Horseback riding at Hacienda Guachipelín.

Up the road from their lodge, Hacienda Guachipelín has opened the **Río Negro Hot Springs ★★** (*©* **2666-8075**). A $15 entrance fee gets you access to the pools and an application of the hot volcanic mud. For $62 you can do a horseback ride from the main lodge to the springs. A wide range of massages, mud wraps, facials, and other treatments are available at reasonable prices.

At the **Hotel Borinquen Mountain Resort,** a $25 entrance fee allows you access to their range of **hot spring–fed pools ★**, which vary from tepid to very hot, as well as their fresh volcanic mud bath area, and large freshwater pool.

Finally, **Vandara Hotsprings ★★** (www.vandarahotsprings.com; *©* **4000-0660**) is an excellent spa and adventure center run by the staff of Buena Vista Lodge, with a lovely manmade pool fed by natural hot springs. Unlike many of the other pools mentioned above, this one has no sulfuric smell. Entrance to the pool runs $30, but various packages, with a canopy tour, horseback ride, water slide, hanging bridges, and other adventure activities, are available. Meals and spa treatments also on offer.

Where to Stay & Dine Around the Rincón de la Vieja National Park

In addition to the hotels listed below, a couple of other good choices are by the park. On the Cañas Dulces road, **Buena Vista Lodge ★** (www.buenavistalodgecr.com; *©* **2690-1414**) is set on the edge of the national park and offers a wide range of activities and attractions, including its own water slide and canopy tour.

Over in the area around Aguas Claras, **Finca La Anita ★★** (www.laanitarainforestranch.com; *©* **8388-1775** or 2466-0228) is a remote and rustic, yet very cozy lodge, with a series of wooden cabins set on a working farm, on the edge of lush rain and cloud forests. The area around the lodge is home to several hot springs, and this area also provides easy access to the seldom-used Santa Maria sector of Rincón de la Vieja National Park.

EXPENSIVE

Hotel Borinquen Mountain Resort ★★   This is the swankiest resort in the Rincón de la Vieja area. Individual and duplex bungalows are set on a hillside above the main lodge, restaurants, and hot springs. Rooms feature heavy wooden beds and armoires, high ceilings and plush decor. All include a spacious wooden deck with a view over the valley and surrounding forests. At the foot of the valley are a natural sauna, several hot-spring pools of varying temperatures, and an area for full-body mud baths given with hot volcanic mud. The hotel also boasts a lovely, free-form outdoor pool and full-service spa, set beside a rushing creek in the middle of dense forest. Hiking and horseback riding trails, ATV adventures, zip-lining and nice waterfalls nearby add to the fun here. Golf carts are available to shuttle you around.

Cañas Dulces, Guanacaste. www.borinquenresort.com. ℂ **2690-1900.** 39 units. $194 double villa; $216–$286 double bungalow; $323 junior suite. Rates include breakfast and unlimited use of the hot springs, sauna, and mud baths. Drive 12km (7½ miles) north of Liberia along the Interamerican Hwy. (CR1), take the turnoff toward Cañas Dulces, and follow the signs. The hotel is approximately 21km (13 miles) from the highway, along a mostly rugged dirt road. **Amenities:** 2 restaurants; bar; large outdoor pool; small spa; all rooms smoke-free; Wi-Fi.

MODERATE

Hacienda Guachipelín ★★   Cows' moos and horses neighing provide an early wake-up call most mornings at this working ranch. To really get the feel for the life here, join the daily, hands-on milking of the cows, which begins at 6am. You'll want to get an early start anyway to take advantage of all those hiking and adventure options—see "One-Stop Adventure Shop". The hotel operates a free shuttle several times a day to the national park entrance, as well as to its own, riverside hot springs in the middle of a pristine forest. Most of the rooms are housed in a large horseshoe around an ample garden area a short walk from the main lodge and restaurants. The rooms themselves are spacious and airy, with heavy wood and iron framed beds and lots of natural light. A few standard rooms are still housed in some of the ranch's older buildings, and while they offer up a certain sense of historic charm, they are more rustic than the newer rooms. Sustainable tourism is practiced here.

Rincón de la Vieja (23km/14 miles northeast of Liberia). www.guachipelin.com. ℂ **888/730-3840** in the U.S. and Canada, or 2690-2900 for reservations in Costa Rica, or 2666-8075 at the lodge. 54 units. $102 double; $121 superior double; $189 suite. Rates include taxes and breakfast. Rates higher during peak periods. Follow the directions/signs to Curubandé and Rincón de la Vieja National Park. **Amenities:** Restaurant; outdoor pool; small spa; Wi-Fi.

Río Celeste & the Tenorio Volcano

Offering similar attractions and activities to Rincón de la Vieja, this is a much less visited and more remote-feeling area. At the heart of its offerings is a crystalline turquoise pool at the foot of a forest waterfall, with nearby hot springs and volcanic mud. These make the **Río Celeste ★★** a must-see. Río Celeste, which means "Blue River," is inside the **Parque Nacional Volcán Tenorio** (Tenorio Volcano National Park; © **2206-5369;** daily 8am–4pm; admission $12). The hike there takes about 2 hours each way, and is steep in places. Above the main pool and waterfall, a loop trail will take you along the river to a few spots where underground hot springs bubble up into the blue waters. Locals have made well-worn pools at the spots best for soaking. Along the riverbanks you can find volcanic mud deposits perfect for a free, mid-hike facial.

If you want easy access to the Tenorio Volcano and Río Celeste, I recommend the humble, yet delightful, **La Carolina Lodge ★** (www.lacarolinalodge.com; © **843/343-4201** in the U.S. and Canada, or 2466-6393), which is on a working farm, next to a clear flowing river. Another solid option is the **Celeste Mountain Lodge ★** (www.celestemountainlodge.com; © **2278-6628**), a handsome property boasting swell views of the surrounding volcanoes. The most luxurious option in these parts is the **Río Celeste Hideaway ★★** (www.riocelestehideaway.com; © **800/320-3541** in the U.S. and Canada, or 2206-5114 in Costa Rica), which is actually located on the "back side" of the Tenorio National Park, and reached via the road connecting Upala to the small town of Guatuso.

Getting There: Tenorio National Park is located near the small town of Bijagua. The road to Bijagua (CR6) heads north off of the Interamerican Highway about 5km (3 miles) northwest of Cañas. From here, it's another 30km (18½ miles) to Bijagua, and another 12km (7½ miles) to the park entrance. The last part of this is on rough dirt roads, and even though it's a short distance as the crow flies, it can often take 30 to 40 minutes. There are also other accesses to the area if coming from the La Forutna area.

Río Celeste Hideaway ★★   This remote lodge sits in a patch of dense tropical rainforest and alongside the area's namesake river. The lodge is one of the closest to the national park, and also has its own well-kept trail system along the Rio Celeste. All of the lodgings are individual *casitas* (little houses), with varnished wood floors, high peaked ceilings made from locally cut cane and either four-poster King-bed or two queens with hand-carved headboards. The rooms are very similar to those found at Arenal Nayara (p. 349), as they have same owners. All of the *casitas* are virtually identical in terms of size and layout, but the Suite units have forest-view balconies and Jacuzzi tubs (I'm not sure these amenities merit the price difference). This is by far the best lodge to choose to visit Rio

Walking across Rio Celeste.

Celeste and Tenorio National Park, but be aware this is a cool and moist region, and some folks can find that those two elements make sleeping here a bit of a challenge.

Rio Celeste. www.riocelestehideaway.com. ☏ **800/320-3541** in the U.S. and Canada, or 2206-5114 in Costa Rica. 26 units. $190 double Casita Forest; $259 double Casita Suite. Rates include breakfast. Follow the directions/signs to Rio Celeste and Tenorio National Park. **Amenities:** Restaurant; outdoor pool; Jacuzzi; small spa; Wi-Fi.

Near the Miravalles Volcano

Part of a string of active volcanoes running down the spine of the country, the **Miravalles Volcano** is a major energy supplier for the country's electric grid, but a rather undiscovered area for tourism. **Río Perdido** ★★ (www. rioperdido.com; ☏ **888/326-5070** in the U.S. and Canada, or 2673-3600) aims to change all that. With a setting among rolling hills and striking rock formations, this hotel, spa and adventure center features lovely rooms, and a gorgeous hot spring complex. The hot springs here range from a modern pool structure fed by warm mineral waters up near the main lodge, to a natural river with pools of clear water and varied temperatures. The lodge also has a zip-line canyon tour, an extensive mountain bike park, and white water river tubing.

LA CRUZ & BAHÍA SALINAS

277km (172 miles) NW of San José; 59km (37 miles) NW of Liberia; 20km (12 miles) S of Peñas Blancas

Near the Nicaraguan border, La Cruz is a tiny hilltop town that has little to offer beyond a fabulous view of Bahía Salinas (Salinas Bay), but it does serve as a gateway to the nearly deserted beaches down below, a few mountain lodges bordering the nearby Santa Rosa and Guanacaste national parks, and the Nicaraguan border crossing at Peñas Blancas.

Essentials

GETTING THERE & DEPARTING   **By Plane:** The nearest airport with regular service is in Liberia (see "Liberia," earlier in this chapter).

By Car: Follow the directions for driving to Liberia (p. 212). When you reach Liberia, head straight through the major intersection, following signs to Peñas Blancas and the Nicaraguan border. Allow approximately 5 hours to get from San José to La Cruz.

By Bus: Transportes Deldú buses (www.transportesdeldu.com; ☎ **2256-9072** in San José, or 2679-9323 in La Cruz) leave San José roughly every 2 hours (more frequently during the middle of the day) between 3:30am and 7pm for **Peñas Blancas** from Calle 10 and 12, Avenida 9. These buses stop in La Cruz and will also let you off at the entrance to Santa Rosa National Park if you ask. The ride to La Cruz takes 5½ hours; a one-way fare costs between C4,565 and C5,000. Additional buses are often added on weekends and holidays.

Grupo Transbasa (☎ **2666-0517**) leave Liberia for Peñas Blancas periodically throughout the day. The ride to La Cruz takes about 1 hour and costs C1,670. Buses depart for San José from Peñas Blancas daily between 3:30am and 5:30pm, passing through La Cruz about 20 minutes later. Daily buses leave Liberia for San José roughly every hour between 3am and 8pm.

CITY LAYOUT   The highway passes slightly to the east of town. You'll pass the turnoffs to Santa Rosa National Park and Playa Caujiniquil before you reach town. For the Bahía Salinas beaches, head into La Cruz and take the road that runs along the north side of the small central park and then follow the signs down to the water.

Exploring Santa Rosa National Park

Known for its remote, pristine beaches (reached by several kilometers of hiking trails or a 4WD vehicle), **Santa Rosa National Park ★** (www.acguanacaste.ac.cr; ☎ **2666-5051;** entrance $15; day visits 8am–3:30pm) is a swell place to camp on the beach, surf, bird-watch, or (if you're lucky) watch sea turtles nest. Located 30km (19 miles) north of Liberia and 21km (13 miles) south of La Cruz on the Interamerican Highway, Costa Rica's first national park blankets the Santa Elena Peninsula. Unlike other national parks, it was founded not to preserve the land but to save a building, known as **La Casona,** which played an important role in Costa Rican independence. It was here, in 1856, that Costa Rican forces fought the decisive Battle of Santa Rosa, forcing the U.S.-backed soldier of fortune William Walker and his men to flee into Nicaragua. La Casona was completely destroyed by arson in 2001, but it has been rebuilt, very accurately mimicking the original building, and now houses a small museum, detailing the political history of the ranch house and housing rotating temporary art exhibits. The museum descriptions, however, are in Spanish only.

On to Nicaragua

Guanacaste is a popular starting point for trips into Nicaragua. The main border point is at Peñas Blancas, Costa Rica. Several tour agencies and hotel desks arrange day trips to Nicaragua from resorts and hotels around Guanacaste.

Costa Rica charges $7 to exit or enter the country by land, while Nicaragua charges $13 to enter and $3 to leave. Though it's by no means necessary, it's somewhat common to hire a helper or *gavilán* (literally, seagull), to expedite the process. These locals can occasionally cut lines, alleviate confusion, and speed up the process slightly. However, their main mission in life is to make money off of you, so be careful. On the Costa Rican side, expect to spend about $5 for a bilingual *gavilán*, whereas on the Nicaraguan side, the cost should be around $3.

La Casona has few nearby hiking trails. The best for most visitors is the **Indio Desnudo (Naked Indian) trail.** This 2.6km (1.5-mile) loop trail should take you about 45 minutes. It leads through a small patch of tropical dry forest and into overgrown former pastureland. If you're lucky, you might spot a white-tailed deer, coatimundi, black guan, or mantled howler monkey along the way.

Camping is allowed at several sites within the park. A campsite costs $19 per person per day. Camping is near the entrance, the principal ranger station, La Casona, and down by playas Naranjo and Nancite.

THE BEACHES ★★ Eight kilometers (5 miles) west of La Casona, down a rugged road that's impassable during the rainy season (it's rough on 4WD vehicles even in the dry season), is **Playa Naranjo.** Four kilometers (2½ miles) north of Playa Naranjo, along a hiking trail that follows the beach, you'll find **Playa Nancite. Playa Blanca** is 21km (13 miles) down a dirt road from Caujiniquil, which itself is 20km (12 miles) north of the park entrance. None of these three beaches has shower or restroom facilities. (Playa Nancite does have some facilities, but they're in a reservation-only camping area.) Bring along your own water, food, and anything else you'll need, and expect to find things relatively quiet and deserted.

La Casona at Santa Rosa National Park.

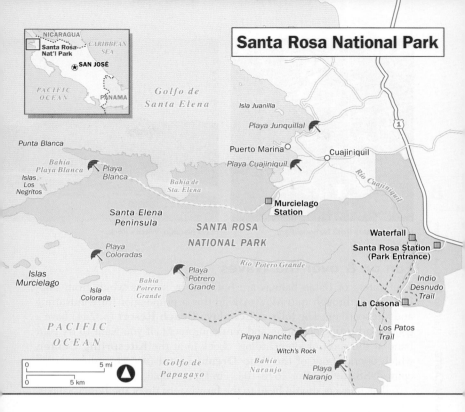

Playa Nancite is known for its *arribadas* ("arrivals," grouped egg-layings) of olive ridley sea turtles, which come ashore to nest by the tens of thousands each year in October. Playa Naranjo is legendary for its perfect surfing waves. In fact, this spot is quite popular with day-trippers who come in by boat from the Playa del Coco area to ride the waves that break around **Witch's Rock,** which lies just offshore.

On the northern side of the peninsula is **Playa Blanca,** a lovely, remote white sand beach with calm waters. It is reached by way of the small village of Caujiniquil and is accessible only during the dry season.

If you reach Caujiniquil and then head north on a rugged dirt road for a few kilometers, you'll come to a small annex to the national park system at **Playa Junquillal ★ (© 2666-5051)**, not to be confused with the more-developed beach of the same name farther south in Guanacaste. This is a handsome little beach that is also often good for swimming. You'll have to pay the park entrance fee ($10) to use the beach, and $2 more to camp here. There are basic restroom and shower facilities.

Hiking in Santa Rosa National Park.

Playa Naranjo, Witch's Rock.

Fun on & over the Waves

The waters of Bahía Salinas are buffeted by serious winds from mid-November through mid-May, making this a prime spot for windsurfing and kiteboarding. The folks at **Ecoplaya Beach Resort** (p. 231) have a good windsurfing operation and rent equipment. If you want to try your hand at the sport of kiteboarding, check in at the **Kitesurfing Center,** which operates out of the **Blue Dream Hotel** (www.bluedreamhotel. com; ✆ **8826-5221** or 2676-1042) in Playa Copal.

Beach lovers should head to the far western tip of the Bahía Salinas, where you will find **Playa Rajada ★★**, a beautiful little white sand beach, with gentle surf and plenty of shade trees.

Note: If you're coming to this area and aren't interested in windsurfing or kitesurfing, the winds can make your beach time rather unpleasant during the peak wind months. If you're just looking for a beach vacation, I recommend heading to one of the towns farther south in Guanacaste.

Where to Stay & Dine near La Cruz

To get to either of these hotels from La Cruz, take the dirt road that heads toward Bahía Salinas and Playa Soley, and then follow signs to the hotels. This is a very rough, washboard dirt road most of the year.

In addition to the places listed below, the **Dreams Las Mareas** (www.dreamsresorts.com/las-mareas; ✆ **866/2DREAMS** in the U.S. and Canada, or 2690-2400 in Costa Rica) is a 447-room luxury all-inclusive resort on remote Playa Jobo.

EXPENSIVE

Recreo ★   More a pool of vacation rentals than a true resort, Recreo is popular for family vacations, organized yoga retreats and basically anyone else who needs a multi-room villa with cooking facilities (one- to five-bedroom units are available; all come with a private pool or plunge pool).

The houses are individually decorated and part of a remote gated development, spread over rolling hills. The property lacks a restaurant, but you can arrange to have a private chef cook for you in your villa, for a fee, of course. The resort itself is not right on the water, but is just a few minutes away from the gorgeous and almost always semi-deserted Playa Rajada. A rental car is a necessity here.

El Jobo Beach, Salinas Bay. www.recreocostarica.com. ☎ **877/268-2911** in the U.S. and Canada, or 2676-1230 in Costa Rica. 5 units. $330–$795 villa. **Amenities:** Bar; small, well-equipped exercise room; outdoor pools; tennis court; free Wi-Fi.

MODERATE

Ecoplaya Beach Resort ★   Ecoplaya primarily caters to windsurfers especially between December and March when the winds up here really howl. Rentals and lessons are available for those who'd like to try the sport. The resort itself has two distinct sections. The standard hotel rooms are very standard, set in a two-story concrete building. Each boasts floor-to-ceiling glass walls, with sliding doors that open out on to a private balcony or patio. But I prefer the fully equipped villas, where you can read a book in a wood and leather rocking chair on a much more spacious front porch. The hotel is fairly isolated and there's not much else going on in this area.

La Coyotera Beach, Salinas Bay. www.ecoplaya.com. ☎ **2676-1010.** 44 units. $115–$220 double; $140–$280 villa. Rates include taxes. From La Cruz, take the dirt road that heads toward Bahía Salinas and Playa Soley, and then follow signs to the hotel. **Amenities:** Restaurant; bar; 2 Jacuzzis; midsize outdoor pool; kayak rental.

Junior suite at Dreams Las Mareas.

PLAYA HERMOSA, PLAYA PANAMÁ & PAPAGAYO ★

258km (160 miles) NW of San José; 40km (25 miles) SW of Liberia

While most of Costa Rica's coast is highly coveted by surfers, the beaches here tend to be protected and calm, making them good destinations for families. **Playa Hermosa ★** means "beautiful beach," which is an apt moniker for this pretty crescent of sand. Surrounded by steep forested hills, this curving gray sand beach is long and wide and the surf is usually quite gentle. Fringing the beach is a swath of trees that stays surprisingly green even during the dry season. The shade provided by these trees, along with the calm protected waters, is a big part of the site's appeal. Rocky headlands jut out into the surf at both ends of the beach, and at the base of these rocks are fun tide pools to explore.

Beyond Playa Hermosa, you'll find **Playa Panamá ★** and, farther on, the calm waters of **Bahía Culebra ★**, a large protected bay dotted with small, private patches of beach and ringed with mostly intact dry forest. Around the north end of Bahía Culebra is the **Papagayo Peninsula ★**, home to two large all-inclusive resorts and one championship golf course. This peninsula has a half-dozen or so small to midsize beaches, the nicest of which might just be **Playa Nacascolo ★★★**, which is inside the domain of the Four Seasons Resort here—but all beaches in Costa Rica are public, so you can still visit, albeit after passing through security and parking at the public parking lot.

Essentials

GETTING THERE & DEPARTING   By Plane: The nearest airport with regularly scheduled service is in Liberia (p. 211). From there, a taxi ride takes about 25 minutes and should cost $40 to $60.

By Car: Follow the directions for getting to Liberia (p. 212). When you reach the main intersection in Liberia, take a left onto CR21, which heads toward Santa Cruz and the beaches of Guanacaste. The turnoff for the Papagayo Peninsula is prominently marked 8km (5 miles) south of the Liberia airport. At the corner here, you'll see a massive Do It Center hardware store and lumberyard.

If you are going to a hotel along the Papagayo Peninsula, turn at the Do It Center and follow the paved road out and around the peninsula. If you are going to Playa Panamá or Playa Hermosa, you should also turn here and take the access road shortcut that leads from a turnoff on the Papagayo Peninsula road, just beyond the Do It Center, directly to Playa Panamá. When you reach Playa Panamá, turn left for Playa Hermosa.

To get to Playa Hermosa, you can also continue on a bit farther west on CR21, and, just past the village of Comunidad, turn right. In about 11km (6¾ miles) you'll come to a fork in the road; take the right fork.

Sunset on Playa Hermosa.

These roads are all relatively well marked, and a host of prominent hotel billboards should make it easy enough to find the beach or resort you're looking for. The drive takes about 4 to 4½ hours from San José.

By Bus: A **Tralapa** express bus (© **2221-7202**) leaves San José daily at 3:30pm from Calle 20 and Avenida 3, stopping at Playa Hermosa and Playa Panamá, 3km (1¾ miles) farther north. One-way fare for the 5-hour trip is around C5,500.

Gray Line (www.graylinecostarica.com; © **800/719-3105** in the U.S. and Canada, or 2220-2126 in Costa Rica) and **Interbus** (www. interbusonline.com; © **4100-0888**) both have two daily buses leaving San José for all beaches in this area, one in the morning and one in the afternoon. The fare is around $50. Both companies will pick you up at most San José-area hotels, and offer connections to most other major tourist destinations in Costa Rica.

You can take a bus from San José to Liberia (see "Essentials," earlier in this chapter), and then take a bus from Liberia to Playa Hermosa and Playa Panamá. **Transportes La Pampa** buses (© **2665-7530**) leave Liberia for Playa Hermosa and Playa Panamá at least a half-dozen times daily between 4:30am and 5:30pm. The trip lasts 40 minutes because the bus stops frequently to drop off and pick up passengers. The one-way fare costs C750. These bus schedules change from time to time, so it's best to

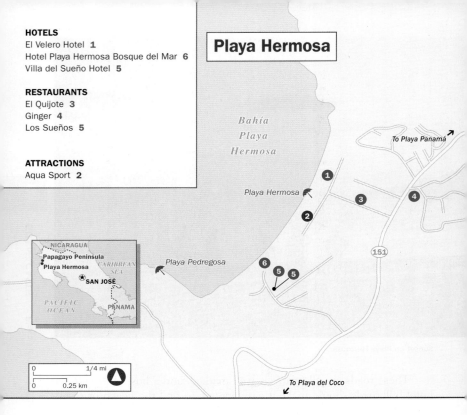

Playa Hermosa

HOTELS
El Velero Hotel **1**
Hotel Playa Hermosa Bosque del Mar **6**
Villa del Sueño Hotel **5**

RESTAURANTS
El Quijote **3**
Ginger **4**
Los Sueños **5**

ATTRACTIONS
Aqua Sport **2**

Bahía
Playa
Hermosa

To Playa Panamá

Playa Hermosa

NICARAGUA
Papagayo Peninsula
Playa Hermosa
CARIBBEAN SEA
SAN JOSÉ
PACIFIC OCEAN
PANAMA

Playa Pedregosa

151

To Playa del Coco

0   1/4 mi
0   0.25 km

check in advance. During the high season and on weekends, extra buses from Liberia are sometimes added. You can also take a bus to Playa del Coco, from which playas Hermosa and Panamá are a relatively quick taxi ride away. Taxi fare should run C8,000–C10,000.

One direct bus departs for San José daily at 5am from Playa Panamá, with a stop in Playa Hermosa along the way. Buses to Liberia leave Playa Panamá regularly between 6am and 7pm, stopping in Playa Hermosa a few minutes later. Ask at your hotel about current schedules, and where to catch the bus.

AREA LAYOUT   From the well-marked turnoff for the Papagayo Peninsula (near the prominent Do It Center hardware store), a paved road leads around to the Allegro Papagayo and Four Seasons resorts. If you are heading to the beaches a little farther south, continue on to the well-marked turnoff for Playa del Coco and Playa Hermosa. This road forks before reaching Playa del Coco. You'll come to the turnoff for Playa Hermosa first. Playa Panamá is a few kilometers farther along the same road. A road connects the Papagayo Peninsula road and Playa Panamá. This 11km (6¾-mile) shortcut is definitely your quickest route to Playa Panamá.

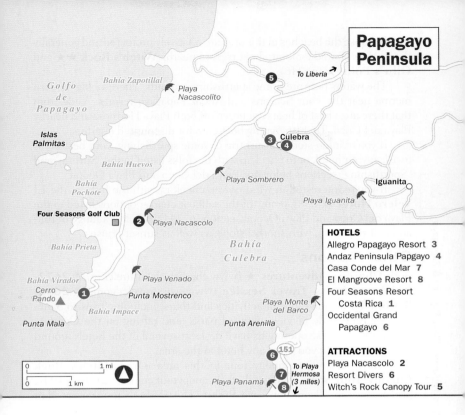

Golfo de Papagayo

Bahía Zapotillal

Playa Nacascolito

To Liberia

Islas Palmitas

Culebra

Bahía Huevos

Playa Sombrero

Iguanita

Bahía Pochote

Playa Iguanita

Four Seasons Golf Club

Playa Nacascolo

Bahía Culebra

Bahía Prieta

Bahía Virador

Cerro Pando

Playa Venado

Punta Mostrenco

Bahía Impace

Playa Monte del Barco

Punta Mala

Punta Arenilla

151

To Playa Hermosa (3 miles)

Playa Panamá

0   1 mi

0   1 km

HOTELS
Allegro Papagayo Resort **3**
Andaz Peninsula Papgayo **4**
Casa Conde del Mar **7**
El Mangroove Resort **8**
Four Seasons Resort
    Costa Rica **1**
Occidental Grand
    Papagayo **6**

ATTRACTIONS
Playa Nacascolo **2**
Resort Divers **6**
Witch's Rock Canopy Tour **5**

Playa Hermosa is about a 450m (1,476-ft.) stretch of beach, with all the hotels laid out along this stretch. From the main road, which continues on to Playa Panamá, three access roads head off toward the beach. All the hotels are well marked, with signs pointing guests down the right access road. Playa Panamá is the least developed of the beaches out here. Somewhat longer than Playa Hermosa, it also has several access roads heading in toward the beach from the main road, which is slightly inland.

Exploring Playa Hermosa, Playa Panamá & Papagayo

Most of the beaches up here are usually quite calm and good for swimming. If you want to do some diving, check any of the dive operations listed in the Playa del Coco and Playa Ocotal section.

In the middle of Playa Hermosa, **Aqua Sport** (© **2672-0051**) is where to go for watersports equipment rental. Kayaks, sailboards, canoes, bicycles, beach umbrellas, snorkel gear, and parasails are available at fairly reasonable rates. You'll also find a small supermarket, public phones, and a restaurant.

Because the beaches in this area are relatively protected and generally flat, surfers should look into boat trips to nearby **Witch's Rock ★★** and **Ollie's Point ★** (p. 246).

The waters here are prime sportfishing grounds. There's a big modern marina near the Four Seasons and Andaz Papagayo resorts. Aside from that there are a host of boats anchored off both Playa Hermosa and nearby Playa del Coco. Try http://getmyboat.com for discounted charters.

If you're interested in a surf trip or some sportfishing, your best bet is to ask at your hotel, or to check in with the folks listed in the "Surfing" and "Sportfishing" sections below for Playa del Coco and Playa Ocotal.

If you're interested in wind power, check in with the folks at the **El Velero Hotel** (p. 238), or any of the sailboat charter options listed in the Playa del Coco and Playa Ocotal section (p. 244). All offer a range of full- and half-day tours, with snorkel stops, as well as sunset cruises.

Other Options

Both **Charlie's Adventures ★** (www.charliesadventure.com; ☏ **2672-0317**) and **Swiss Travel Service** (www.swisstravelcr.com; ☏ **2666-0606**) offer a wide range of activities and tours, including trips to Santa Rosa or Rincón de la Vieja national parks, and rafting on the Corobicí River. Both of these operations have desks at several of the hotels around here and will pick you up at any hotel in the area.

The best zip-line canopy tour in this area is the **Witch's Rock Canopy Tour ★★** (www.witchsrockcanopytour.com; ☏ **2696-7101**), just before the Allegro Papagayo Resort. The 1½-hour tour covers 3km (1¾ miles) of cables touching down on 24 platforms and crossing three suspension bridges. The tour costs $75.

Finally, the Arnold Palmer–designed course at the Four Seasons Resort (see below) is hands-down the most scenic and challenging **golf course** in the country. Alas, it is open only to Four Seasons' guests.

Where to Stay
EXPENSIVE

In addition to the Four Seasons, **El Mangroove Resort ★** (www.elmangroove.net; ☏ **2291-7750**) and the **Andaz Peninsula Papagayo Resort ★★★** (http://papagayo.andaz.hyatt.com; ☏ **800/233-1234** in the U.S. and Canada, or 2690-1234 in Costa Rica) are two more luxury resorts on the Papagayo Peninsula.

Over on Playa Panamá, **Casa Conde del Mar ★** (www.grupocasaconde.com; ☏ **2227-4232** or 2227-4232) is a pretty, boutique resort, with plush rooms and lush grounds.

Four Seasons Resort Costa Rica ★★★ Set near the narrowest point along a long peninsula with pristine, white sand beaches on either side, this is hands-down Costa Rica's premier luxury resort hotel. Its look,

Four Seasons Resort Costa Rica.

by architect Ronald Zucher's architecture, is quite unique, featuring roof lines and building shapes that are meant to evoke turtles and armadillos. Rooms are as creative: large, plush and graced with colorful patterned throw pillows and rattan and/or fine wood furnishings. Suites and villas are downright dazzling, with multiple rooms, full kitchens and private infinity pools. Four restaurants offer up the top-notch dining experience you'd expect from the Four Seasons—and the hotel's famed service remains peerless. The Arnold Palmer-designed golf course is my fave in the country, with ocean views from the tees, greens and fairways of 15 of its 18 holes. In addition to providing all this luxury, the resort has been awarded "4 Leaves" by the CST Sustainable Tourism program.

Papagayo Peninsula, Guanacaste. www.fourseasons.com/costarica. © **800/332-3442** in the U.S., or 2696-0000. 154 units. $475–$900 double; $800 and up suites and villas. Children stay free in parent's room. **Amenities:** 4 restaurants; 2 bars; lounge; babysitting; children's programs; championship 18-hole golf course; 3 free-form outdoor pools; room service; smoke-free rooms; full-service spa; 5 tennis courts; watersports equipment; Wi-Fi.

Hotel Playa Hermosa Bosque del Mar ★★★ Steps away from the sands on the quiet southern end of Playa Hermosa, this is my favorite beachfront boutique hotel in the area. Rooms and suites are spread around a free-form pool amid the shade of tall, lovingly preserved old-growth trees (which are inhabited by iguanas and troops of monkeys). In fact, those gorgeous trees are everywhere, popping up through decking and roofs in the main lobby and even passing right through the center of a balcony of one of the junior suites. The oceanfront suites—colorful, comfortable and practical (with tile floors for sandy feet) come with a Jacuzzi on their private balcony where you can soak as you listen to the sounds of the waves, or watch the sun set through coconut palms.

Playa Hermosa, Guanacaste. www.hotelplayahermosa.com. © **2672-0046.** 32 units. $226–$339 suite; $678 and up penthouse suites. **Amenities:** Restaurant; bar; Jacuzzi; pretty outdoor pool w/sculpted waterfall; free Wi-Fi.

Occidental Grand Papagayo ★ This sprawling, adults-only all-inclusive is set on a hilly point of land overlooking the Papagayo Peninsula and Pacific Ocean, although not all rooms here boast sea views. Wildlife abounds in the trees spread around the property, and you're almost guaranteed to spot monkeys right on the hotel grounds. At the base of the hotel's property you'll find a beach that is broad and calm at low tide, but recedes up to the tree line at high tide. The rooms won't take your breath away, but they are a cozy enough home for a few days, and feature red or white tile floors, bright white linens and a small private balcony. *Note:* Although an all-inclusive, they only restock the in-room minibar every other day, unless you upgrade to the Royal level.

Papagayo Peninsula, Guanacaste. www.occidentalhotels.com. **℃ 855/565-5147** in the U.S. or 2672-0191 in Costa Rica. 169 units. $250–$340 double occupancy; $350–$450 Royal Club room double, $500–$640 Suites. Rates include food, drinks, a range of activities, and taxes. **Amenities:** 4 restaurants; 4 bars; large health club and spa; 2 free-form outdoor pools; lighted tennis court; watersports equipment; free Wi-Fi.

MODERATE

Allegro Papagayo Resort ★ It comes down to value. The Allegro is significantly cheaper than other all-inclusives in this area, and it does offer a dark sand beach right on property (which stays shallow waaaay out, which is great for families), numerous organized activities, and a massive pool area with popular swim-up bar. A free shuttle also takes guests to a more picturesque, nearby white sand beach. So those are the positives. But value here comes with some downsides: The food is just passable, housekeeping can be lax, and the rooms and facilities show wear and tear. Should you decide to book, know that all rooms are exactly the same size, and come with either one king or two twin beds, and a small private balcony. You'll pay extra for the "premium" rooms but the only difference with those is a better view.

Playa Manzanillo, Guanacaste www.occidentalhotels.com. **℃ 855/565-5147** in the U.S. and Canada, or 2690-9900 at the resort. 300 units. $165–$220 double occupancy. Rates include food, drinks, a range of activities, and taxes. **Amenities:** 3 restaurants; 3 bars; babysitting; children's programs; small fitness center; 2 Jacuzzis; outdoor pool; watersports equipment; free Wi-Fi.

INEXPENSIVE

El Velero Hotel ★ This longstanding hotel is a solid option just steps from the sand on Playa Hermosa. The design motif here is Mediterranean, with whitewashed walls, tile floors and interior archways. Rooms are all very spacious, if somewhat spartan, with plain, at times worn, bed linens, and simple Rattan headboards and nightstands. I recommend those on the second floor, which have higher ceilings. There's a small plunge pool and a popular restaurant and bar. El Velero means "the sailboat" and these folks do, indeed, have a sailboat bobbing just offshore and available for charter.

Playa Hermosa, Guanacaste. www.costaricahotel.net. © **2672-1017.** 22 units. $79–$89 double. **Amenities:** Restaurant; bar; small outdoor pool; free Wi-Fi.

Villa del Sueño Hotel ★★   Tall trees and mature gardens give this slightly sprawling complex of hotel rooms and condo units a cool and refreshing feel, even on the hottest of Guanacaste's summer days. A thatch roof tiki bar just off the main pool also helps beat the heat. There are actually several pools here, including one with a little island sporting 3 palm trees, and the beach is just a block away. As soon as you arrive, French-Canadian owners Claude and Sylvia make you feel part of the family. Red tile floors, bright tropical paintings and wall hangings give the rooms a cheery feel, and those on the second floor enjoy higher ceilings. The in-house restaurant is one of the best in town.

Playa Hermosa, Guanacaste. www.villadelsueno.com. © **800/378-8599** in the U.S., or 2672-0026 in Costa Rica. 43 units. $89–$149 double; $159–$289 suite. Free for children 12 and under. Rates included taxes. **Amenities:** Restaurant; bar; room service; 2 outdoor pools; free Wi-Fi.

Where to Dine

In addition to the places listed below, you'll find good restaurants at both the **El Velero Hotel** (p. 238) and the **Hotel Playa Hermosa Bosque del Mar** (p. 237). I also like the fresh seafood, sushi and relaxed yet lively ambiance at **El Quijote** (© **2672-0176**) located along the second entrance road towards the beach.

Abbocato ★★★   FUSION/BISTRO   Husband-wife chefs Andrea and Paola create two distinct nightly tasting menus. One typically features Asian-inspired flavors and preparations, and the other is Mediterranean in style. It's anybody's guess which of the two is behind any one dish. No matter, everything is sublime. On the Asian side, you might get home-smoked fresh tuna in a light ginger dressing with homemade pickles; on the Mediterranean side, it could be mushroom sausage in a phyllo quiche shell with pesto and Fontina cheese. As for the ambiance: The dining room features Travertine tile floors, heavy wooden tables, walls of glass, and high peaked ceilings with exposed wood beams. The whole shebang opens onto a broad patio that overlooks the Pacific Ocean and provides great sunset views. An excellent wine list and cellar complete the experience. Abbocato is also open for lunch and tapas.

Inside Hacienda del Mar, 1km (½ mile) inland from Playa Panamá. www.abbocatocr. com. © **2672-0073** or 8820-2576. Reservations necessary for dinner. Main courses $10–$35. 4-course prix-fixe dinner $45. Tues–Sat noon–9pm.

Ginger ★★   INTERNATIONAL/TAPAS   With a design by famed Costa Rican architect Víctor Cañas, creative cocktails and wide-ranging tapas menu, this is easily the hippest place to drink and dine in the Papagayo area. The entire restaurant is open air, on a raised deck under tall trees, with angled steel supports and slanted rooflines. The menu ranges the globe from to Thailand to Spain, and Italy. I especially like the firecracker shrimp and the shredded pork lettuce wraps in a mango-tamarind sauce. For tipples, there are a more than a dozen options amongst the specialty martinis, margaritas and mojitos. Friday night is "Martini Night," featuring $3 martinis.

On the main road, Playa Hermosa. www.gingercostarica.com. ☏ **2672-0041.** Tapas $5–$13. Tues–Sun 5–10pm.

Los Sueños ★ INTERNATIONAL   You get dinner and a show at the in-house restaurant of the Villa del Sueño Hotel and condo complex (p. 239). Throughout the high season, a house band, which features one of the owners, usually plays (I've heard that Celine Dion once joined in). But even if there's no music, this open-air restaurant is wonderfully pleasant with a dimly lit, covered dining room (its tables set with linens), and outdoor tables and chairs spread around the lush gardens. The kitchen serves up local ingredients used in contemporary Continental recipes, like steak with pepper sauce, or fresh red snapper topped with locally caught shrimp in a cream sauce.

At the Villa del Sueño Hotel. ☏ **2672-0026.** Main courses $20–$27. Daily 7am–9:30pm.

Entertainment & Nightlife

Most of the large resorts here have bars, and a few feature nightly entertainment revues or live bands. In general, Playa Hermosa, Playa Panama and the Papagyo peninsula are very laid back, and fairly spread out. For a mellow cocktail scene on an open-air deck, head for **Ginger** (p. 239) or **Los Sueños** restaurant (see above) on a night the band is playing (ask). For a livelier bar and club scene many visitors here head to Playa del Coco (see below).

PLAYA DEL COCO & PLAYA OCOTAL

253km (157 miles) NW of San José; 35km (22 miles) W of Liberia

Playa del Coco is one of Costa Rica's busiest and most developed beach destinations. A large modern mall and shopping center anchor the eastern edge of town. You'll pass through a tight jumble of restaurants, hotels, and souvenir shops for several blocks before you hit the sand and sea; homes, condos, and hotels are strung along the access roads that parallel the beach in either direction. This has long been, and remains, a popular destination with middle-class Ticos and weekend revelers from San José. It's also a prime base for some of Costa Rica's best scuba diving. The beach, which has grayish-brown sand and gentle surf, is quite wide at low tide and almost nonexistent at high tide. The crowds that come here like their music loud and late, so if you're in search of a quiet retreat, stay away from the center of town. Still, if you're looking for a beach with a wide

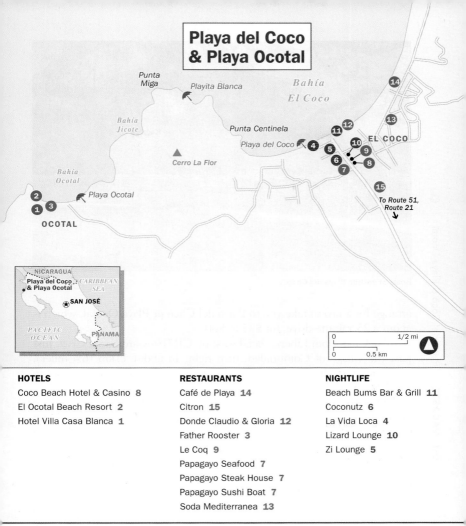

Playa del Coco & Playa Ocotal

Punta Miga

Playita Blanca

Bahía El Coco

Bahía Jicote

Punta Centinela

Playa del Coco

EL COCO

Cerro La Flor

Bahía Ocotal

Playa Ocotal

OCOTAL

To Route 51, Route 21

NICARAGUA

CARIBBEAN SEA

Playa del Coco & Playa Ocotal

SAN JOSÉ

PACIFIC OCEAN

PANAMA

0   1/2 mi
0   0.5 km

HOTELS

Coco Beach Hotel & Casino **8**
El Ocotal Beach Resort **2**
Hotel Villa Casa Blanca **1**

RESTAURANTS

Café de Playa **14**
Citron **15**
Donde Claudio & Gloria **12**
Father Rooster **3**
Le Coq **9**
Papagayo Seafood **7**
Papagayo Steak House **7**
Papagayo Sushi Boat **7**
Soda Mediterranea **13**

NIGHTLIFE

Beach Bums Bar & Grill **11**
Coconutz **6**
La Vida Loca **4**
Lizard Lounge **10**
Zi Lounge **5**

range of hotels, lively nightlife, and plenty of cheap food and beer close at hand, you'll enjoy Playa del Coco.

More interesting still, in my opinion, is **Playa Ocotal ★**, which is a few miles to the south. This tiny pocket cove features a small salt-and-pepper beach bordered by high bluffs that's quite beautiful. When it's calm, good snorkeling can be had around rocky islands close to shore.

Essentials

GETTING THERE & DEPARTING   **By Plane:** The nearest airport with regularly scheduled flights is in Liberia (p. 211). From there, you can

Boats at anchor, Playa del Coco.

arrange for a taxi to take you to Playa del Coco or Playa Ocotal, which is about a 25-minute drive, for $35 to $60.

By Car: From Liberia, head west on CR21 toward Santa Cruz. Just past the village of Comunidad, turn right. In about 11km (6¾ miles), you'll come to a fork in the road. Take the left fork. The right fork goes to Playa Hermosa. The drive takes about 4 hours from San José.

By Bus: Pulmitan express buses (✆ **2222-1650** in San José, or 2670-0095 in Playa del Coco) leave San José for Playa del Coco at 8am and 2 and 4pm daily from Calle 24 between avenidas 5 and 7. Allow 5 hours for the trip. A one-way ticket is C4,350. From Liberia, buses (✆ **2666-0458**) to Playa del Coco leave regularly throughout the day between 5am and 7pm. A one-way ticket for the 40-minute trip costs around C850. These bus schedules change frequently, so it's always best to check in advance. During the high season and on weekends, extra buses from Liberia are sometimes added. The direct bus for San José leaves Playa del Coco daily at 4 and 8am and 2pm. Local buses for Liberia leave daily between 5am and 7pm.

Depending on demand, the Playa del Coco buses sometimes go as far as Playa Ocotal; it's worth checking beforehand. Otherwise, a taxi should cost around C3,000 to C5,000.

Gray Line (www.graylinecostarica.com; ✆ **800/719-3105** in the U.S. and Canada, or 2220-2126 in Costa Rica) and **Interbus** (www.interbusonline.com; ✆ **4031-0888**) both have two daily buses leaving San José for the beaches in this area, one in the morning and one in the afternoon. The fare is $50. Both companies will pick you up at most San José-area hotels, and have connections to most other tourist destinations around Costa Rica.

GETTING AROUND   You can rent cars from any number of rental companies. Most are based in Liberia, or at the airport. See p. 211. If you can't flag down a **taxi** on the street, call ✆ **2670-0408.**

CITY LAYOUT   Playa del Coco is a compact and busy beach town. At the center of town, running for a few hundred meters in either direction is a seafront walkway, or *malecón*. You'll find benches spread along this walkway, as well as patches of grass and a basketball court. Most of its hotels and restaurants are either on the water, on the road leading into town, or on the road that heads north, about 100m (328 ft.) inland from and parallel to the beach.

Playa Ocotal is south of Playa del Coco on a paved road that leaves the main road about 183m (600 ft.) before the beach. It's a small collection of vacation condos and hotels with one bar and a restaurant on the beach.

FAST FACTS   The nearest major hospital is in Liberia (✆ **2690-2300**). For the local **health clinic,** call ✆ **2670-1717;** for the local **pharmacy,** call ✆ **2670-2050.** For the local **police,** dial ✆ **2670-0258.** You'll find several banks and ATMs around town.

Exploring Playa del Coco & Playa Ocotal

Plenty of boats are anchored at Playa del Coco, and that means plenty of opportunities to go fishing, diving, or sailing. Still, the most popular activities, especially among the hordes of Ticos who come here, are lounging on the beach, walking along the *malecón* (seafront walkways), hanging out in the *sodas,* cruising the bars and discos at night and playing pick-up soccer. (The soccer field is in the middle of town.) You can also arrange horseback rides; ask at your hotel.

BEACH CLUB   If you're staying at a hotel without a pool, or just want a sense of exclusivity on the beach, you might check out **Café de Playa Beach & Dining Club** (www.cafedeplaya.com; ✆ **2670-1621**). In addition to having an excellent restaurant (p. 246), it offers day passes for $15 allowing access to their pool and a private grassy lawn fronting the beach, which is filled with comfortable teak chaise lounges. They also have watersports equipment rental and tour options, and a small spa.

CANOPY TOUR   The **Congo Trail Canopy Tour** ★ (✆ **2666-4422** or 2697-1801) is set in a stand of thick, tropical dry forest on the outskirts of Playa del Coco, along a dirt road that leads to Playa Pan de Azúcar. In addition to a zip-line, there's a small butterfly farm, and a few zoo-enclosures, with monkeys and reptiles. The tour runs every day from 8am to 5pm, and costs $35 for the canopy tour, plus $5 to see the animals.

GOLF   Located about 10km (6¼ miles) outside Playa del Coco, the **Papagayo Golf & Country Club** ★ (www.costaricagolf.com/courses/papagayo; ✆ **2697-0169**) is a full 18-hole course, with a pro shop, driving range, and rental equipment. It costs $100 in greens fees, including a cart, and access to the pool area before or after your round. Tee time

The Congo Trail Canopy Tour.

reservations are necessary on weekends. It's closed on Mondays during the off season.

GYM If you want to work out while in town, head to the **Coco Gym** (🕿 **2670-2129**; $5/day), which is on the road between Playa del Coco and Ocotal. Weights, cardio machines, and a range of classes are offered.

HORSEBACK RIDING You can't ride on the beaches here, but the folks at **Haras del Mar** (https://harasdelmar.wordpress.com; 🕿 **2707-2121**) offer great trail and country riding on well-tended, trained horses about 20 minutes outside of Playas del Coco.

SAILING Several cruising sailboats and longtime local salts offer daily sailing excursions. The 47-foot ketch-rigged **"Kuna Vela"** (www.kunavela.com; 🕿 **8301-3030**) and the 45-foot ketch **"Seabird"** (www.seabirdsailingexcursions.com; 🕿 **8880-6393**) both ply the waters off Playa del Coco. They also offer half- and full-day and sunset sailing options, with snorkel stops and an open bar.

SCUBA DIVING Scuba diving is the most popular watersport in the area, and dive shops abound. **Sirenas Diving Costa Rica** ★★ (www.costaricadiving.net; 🕿 **2670-0603**), **Summer Salt** ★ (www.summer-salt.com; 🕿 **2670-0308**), and **Rich Coast Diving** ★★ (www.richcoastdiving.com; 🕿 **2670-0176**) are the most established and offer equipment rentals and dive trips. A two-tank dive, with equipment, should cost between $85 and $150 per person, depending on the distance to the dive site. The more distant dive sites visited include the Catalina Islands and Bat Island. All also offer PADI certification courses.

SPORTFISHING Full- and half-day sportfishing excursions can be arranged through any of the hotel tour desks, or with **Dream On Sportfishing** ★★ (www.dreamonsportfishing.com; 🕿 **8735-3121**) or **North Pacific Tours** ★ (www.northpacifictours.com; 🕿 **2670-1564**).

A half-day of fishing, including the boat, captain, food, and tackle, should cost $800 to $1150 for two to four passengers; a full day $700 to $1200.

SURFING Playa del Coco has no rideable surf to speak of, but is a popular jumping-off point for daily boat trips to Witch's Rock or Roca Bruja, and Ollie's Point up in Santa Rosa National Park (p. 227). Most of the above-mentioned sportfishing and dive operations also ferry surfers to these isolated surf breaks. A boat that carries five surfers for a full day, including lunch and beer, should run $350 to $600. ***Note:*** Both Witch's Rock and Ollie's Point are technically within Santa Rosa National Park. Permits are required, and boats without permits are sometimes turned away. If you decide to go, be sure your boat captain is licensed and has cleared access to the park. You will also have to pay the park's $15 fee. **Single Fin Surf Charters** (www.singlefinsurfcharters.com; ✆ **8935-2583**) offers a plush trip out to these surf spots at $235 per person for a full day trip. But if you ask around town, you should be able to find one of the local skippers, who tend to offer trips for up to six surfers for much less. Alternatively, check the website www.getmyboat.com.

Pacific Coast Stand Up Paddle & Surf Trips (www.pacific coastsuptours.com; ✆ **8359-8115**) offer lessons and guided outings for both traditional surfing, and for those looking to try out stand up paddling (a sport that can be done without traveling to another beach area).

Where to Stay

MODERATE

Coco Beach Hotel & Casino ★ If you want to be in the center of the action this is the place for you. Set right in the heart of Playa del Coco's busiest restaurant, bar and commercial strip, the hotel offers clean if fairly plain rooms that get a shot of life from the bright, multicolor paintings based on local indigenous designs that grace the walls. The staff is friendly and helpful. Thatch roof structures ring the pool area and separate the rooms from the street (they also help block the blazing Guanacaste sun and street noise). The beach is 2 blocks away.

Playa del Coco, Guanacaste. www.cocobeachhotelandcasinocr.com. ✆ **2670-0494.** 32 units. $145–$186 double. Rates include full breakfast. **Amenities:** Restaurant; bar; small casino; small outdoor pool; free Wi-Fi.

El Ocotal Beach Resort ★ This small resort has an enviable location, perched on a steep hillside overlooking the Pacific Ocean. Most rooms enjoy these wonderful views, which is their biggest selling point. The rooms and facilities themselves are a mixed bag (some just fine, some showing their age), and service and upkeep can be lax at times. El Ocotal operates one of the best dive operations in the area.

Playa del Coco, Guanacaste. www.ocotalresort.com. ✆ **2670-0321.** 42 units. 12 bungalows, 3 suites. $99–$220 double; $110–$265 bungalow and suite. Rates include full breakfast. Free for kids under 12. **Amenities:** Restaurant; Jacuzzi; 3 outdoor pools and 3 plunge pools; lighted tennis court; free Wi-Fi.

Hotel Villa Casa Blanca ★ A friendly staff, serene setting (it's slightly uphill from Playa Ocotal), and nice pool area are the reasons you pick the Casa Blanca, along with the reasonable nightly rate. But this is not the place for those who hanker for swank, or even new, furnishings (it doesn't get more basic than this and some of the bathrooms are in lousy shape, with chipped and stained tiles). For budgeteers only.

Playa Ocotal, Guanacaste. www.villacasablancahotel.com. © **2670-0448.** 11 units. $110–$125 double; $55–$155 double suite. Rates include taxes and breakfast. **Amenities:** Outdoor lounge and bar; Jacuzzi; small outdoor pool; free Wi-Fi.

Where to Dine

A clutch of basic open-air *sodas* is at the traffic circle in the center of El Coco village, serving Tico standards, with an emphasis on fried fish. Prices are quite low—and so is the quality, for the most part.

You can get excellent Italian food, however, at **Soda Mediterránea** ★ (© **8742-6553**), in the little El Pueblito strip mall on the road running north and parallel to the beach, and a good mix of Mediterranean and Peruvian cuisine at the beachfront **Donde Claudio & Gloria** ★ (www. dondeclaudioygloria.com; © **2670-1514**). For a quick or light meal, try **Le Coq** (© 2670-0608), an open-air Lebanese restaurant on the main drag in the center of town.

Right on the main strip, you'll also find the various Papagayo operations. Building on the success of their seafood restaurant, **Papagayo Seafood** ★ (© **2670-0298**), **Papagayo Steak House** ★ (© **2670-0605**), and **Papagayo Sushi Boat** ★ (© **2670-0298**) attempt to cover all possible bases.

Café de Playa ★ FUSION/INTERNATIONAL Eat, drink, swim, repeat. That's the appeal of this casually chic beach resto, where many guests spend the entire day lounging, drinking well-mixed cocktails and dipping in both the ocean and the pool. Meals (breakfast, lunch, and dinner) are served on heavy teak tables and chairs spread on a large, open-air wooden deck and out onto the grassy lawn. Food ranges from burgers and fish-and-chips to more upscale fare like Thai beef salad or fresh sea bass in a coconut-milk sauce.

Charlie Don't Surf, but Ollie Does

Ollie's Point is named after Oliver North, the famous and felonious former lieutenant colonel at the center of the Iran-Contra scandal. The beaches and ports of northern Guanacaste were a staging ground for supplying the Nicaraguan Contra rebels. Legend has it that during a news broadcast of an interview with North, some surfers noticed a fabulous point break going off in the background. Hence, the discovery and naming of Ollie's Point.

On the beach, Playa del Coco. www.cafedeplaya.com. *C* **2670-1621**. Reservations recommended. Main courses C7,500–C20,000. Sun–Fri 8am–9:30pm; 8am–10pm

Citron ★★★ FUSION/INTERNATIONAL   Even though it's set in a small strip mall, this is easily the town's most elegant and creative restaurant. The service is topnotch, the setting romantic (local cane ceiling, soft lighting, neutral colors) and the food is leaps and bounds better than what you'll get elsewhere in the area. Though I've yet to find a loser on the menu, Citron does particularly well by sea bass, usually served with orzo and a Catalan sauce. Other star dishes include the tenderloin and portobello risotto in red-wine reduction and the vanilla crème brûlée, which is made with local organic vanilla. There's outdoor seating on a broad, open deck, but frankly I find that the daytime heat and nighttime bugs make this a less than ideal option.

In the Pacífico mall, on the main road into town. Playa del Coco. www.citroncoco. com. *C* **2670-0942.** Main courses $12–$19. Mon–Sat 5:30–10pm.

Father Rooster ★ SEAFOOD/BAR   A casual, open-air beachfront bar, Father Rooster is just steps from the water on tiny Playa Ocotal. Burgers, tacos, beer-battered fish or shrimp, nachos and other typical bar fare are on offer. The building itself is a rustic wood affair painted in haphazard primary colors with a pool table is in one room. Most try to get seats at the tables on the sand; all are shaded by canvas umbrellas and a tall mango tree. On the weekends, you'll sometimes catch a live band here.

On the beach, Playa Ocotal. www.fatherrooster.com. *C* **2670-1246**. Main courses C6,500–C9,000. Daily 11:30am–10pm.

The Lookout ★ SEAFOOD/BAR   It's worth the short drive or taxi ride to this rooftop bar restaurant on the outskirts of Playas del Coco, for the outstanding sunsets and upscale pub food. Menu standouts include their tuna poke nachos and the lobster grilled cheese, both created from locally sourced seafood. A wide-ranging selection of Costa Rican craft beers are on offer as well as fresh, locally farmed oysters.

On the outskirts of Playas del Coco, inside the Hotel Chantel. www.thelookoutcoco. com. *C* **8755-7246.** Main courses C3,000–C8,500. Tue–Sun 3–10pm.

En Route: Playas del Coco & Playa Flamingo

Hotel Sugar Beach ★★   Spread over a gently curved, forested hillside that cradles Playa Pan de Azúcar (Sugar Beach), this isolated hotel's lovely grounds are rich in wildlife (it's not uncommon to find troops of howler monkeys in the trees here, so be prepared for some unrequested early wake-up calls). While there are no private beaches in Costa Rica, for all intents and purposes the beach here is the exclusive playground of the hotel guests. (The rocky outcroppings just off and around this beach are very good for snorkelling.) Rooms are all spacious, spotless and comfortable, some with romantic four-poster beds.

Playa Pan de Azúcar, Guanacaste. www.sugar-beach.com. © **2654-4242.** 32 units. $158–$198 double; $277–$280 suite; $575–$667 3-bedroom villa. Rates include breakfast and taxes. **Amenities:** Restaurant; bar; small pool; free Wi-Fi.

RIU Guanacaste ★   With some 700 hundred rooms this massive all-inclusive resort (it does a brisk business with charter companies) is not the place for getting away from it all. Throughout the high season, the bars, buffets and pool are brimming with sunburned revelers looking to take as much advantage as they can of all the free flowing food, booze and activities. That's not to say RIU doesn't do a good job at this type of travel. The rooms are large and well equipped and most offer at least some sea view from their private balcony. Activities are non-stop, the food is palatable (if not great) and the casino is always bustling with optimists. Next door is the 538-room, all suite **RIU Palace Guanacaste,** a sister resort with more upscale rooms, more a la carte restaurants, and more attentive service. The dark sand beach they share is rocky in places.

Playa Matapalo, Guanacaste. www.riu.com. © **800/748-4990** in the U.S. and Canada, or 2681-2300 at the hotel. 701 units. $199–$450 double RIU Guanacaste; $350–$600 RIU Palace. Rates include all meals, drinks, taxes, a wide range of activities, and use of non-motorized land and watersports equipment. Spa services extra. **Amenities:** 8 restaurants; 7 bars; 2 lounges; casino; discotheque; babysitting; free bike usage; children's programs; exercise facilities and spa; large outdoor pool w/several Jacuzzis; lighted tennis court; watersports equipment rental; Wi-Fi.

Entertainment & Nightlife

Playa del Coco is one of Costa Rica's liveliest beach towns after dark. Most of the action is centered along a 2-block section of the main road into town, just before you hit the beach. Here you'll find the **Lizard Lounge ★** (© **2670-0307**), which has a raucous party vibe. Just across the street is the large, open-air **Zi Lounge ★★** (www.zilounge.com; © **2670-1978**). For a gringo-influenced sports bar try **Coconutz ★** (www.coconutz-costarica.com; © **2670-1982**). Just off the beach, at the center of town you'll find **Beach Bums Bar & Grill ★** (© **2671-0110**). This is a very popular spot, with frequent live bands and DJs. On the south end of the beach, reached via a rickety footbridge over the estuary, you'll find **La Vida Loca ★** (www.lavidalocabeachbar.com; © **2670-0181**), a lively beachfront bar with a pool table, Ping-Pong table, foosball table, and live bands.

PLAYAS CONCHAL & BRASILITO

280km (174 miles) NW of San José; 67km (42 miles) SW of Liberia

Playa Conchal ★★ is the first in a string of beaches stretching north along this coast. It's almost entirely backed by the massive Westin Playa Conchal resort and Reserva Conchal condominium complex. The unique beach here was once made up primarily of soft crushed shells—a

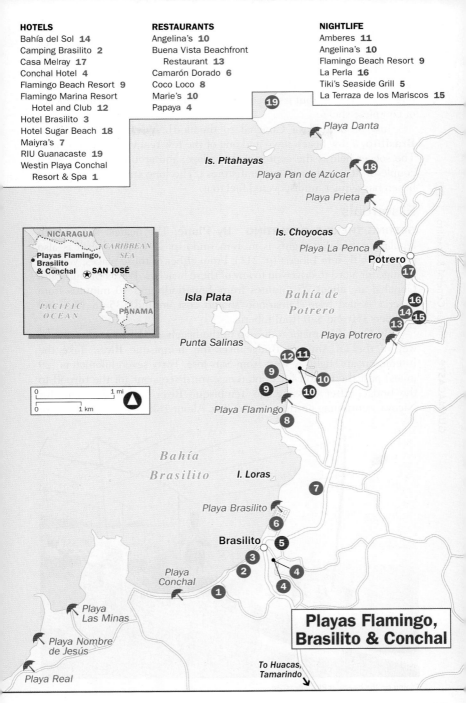

HOTELS
Bahía del Sol **14**
Camping Brasilito **2**
Casa Melray **17**
Conchal Hotel **4**
Flamingo Beach Resort **9**
Flamingo Marina Resort
  Hotel and Club **12**
Hotel Brasilito **3**
Hotel Sugar Beach **18**
Maiyra's **7**
RIU Guanacaste **19**
Westin Playa Conchal
  Resort & Spa **1**

RESTAURANTS
Angelina's **10**
Buena Vista Beachfront
  Restaurant **13**
Camarón Dorado **6**
Coco Loco **8**
Marie's **10**
Papaya **4**

NIGHTLIFE
Amberes **11**
Angelina's **10**
Flamingo Beach Resort **9**
La Perla **16**
Tiki's Seaside Grill **5**
La Terraza de los Mariscos **15**

Playa Danta

Is. Pitahayas

Playa Pan de Azúcar **18**

Playa Prieta

Is. Choyocas

Playa La Penca

Potrero **17**

NICARAGUA

CARIBBEAN
SEA

Playas Flamingo,
Brasilito
& Conchal   SAN JOSÉ

PACIFIC
OCEAN   PANAMA

Isla Plata

Bahía de
Potrero

16

14 **15**
13

Punta Salinas

Playa Potrero

12 **11**

9

9   **10**

10

0   1 mi
0   1 km

Playa Flamingo

8

Bahía
Brasilito   I. Loras

7

Playa Brasilito

6

Brasilito **5**

3
2

Playa
Conchal   **4**

1   **4**

Playa
Las Minas

Playa Nombre
de Jesús

Playa Real

To Huacas,
Tamarindo

**Playas Flamingo,
Brasilito & Conchal**

19

shell-collectors' heaven. Unfortunately, as Conchal's popularity spread, unscrupulous builders brought in dump trucks to haul away the namesake seashells for landscaping and construction, and the impact is, sadly, quite noticeable. The beach is still primarily comprised of crushed bits of polished sea shells, but it's become increasingly hard to find larger pieces or complete shells.

Just beyond Playa Conchal to the north, you'll come to **Playa Brasilito,** a tiny beach town and one of the few real villages in the area. The soccer field is the center of the village, and around its edges are a couple of little *pulperías* (general stores). The long stretch of gray sand beach has a quiet, undiscovered feel to it.

Essentials

GETTING THERE & DEPARTING   By Plane: The nearest airport with regularly scheduled flights is in Tamarindo (p. 264) although it is also possible to fly into Liberia (p. 211). From either of these places, you can arrange for a taxi to drive you to any of these beaches. Playas Brasilito and Conchal are about 25 minutes from Tamarindo and 40 minutes from Liberia. A taxi from Tamarindo should cost around $35 to $50, and between $50 and $70 from Liberia.

By Car: Two major routes go to the beaches. The most direct is by way of the La Amistad Bridge over the Tempisque River. Take the Interamerican Highway west from San José. Forty-seven kilometers (29 miles) past the turnoff for Puntarenas, you'll see signs for the turnoff to the bridge. After crossing the Tempisque River, follow the signs for Nicoya, continuing north to Santa Cruz. About 16km (10 miles) north of

Dining on the beach at Playa Brasilito.

Playa Conchal.

Santa Cruz, just before the village of Belén, take the turnoff for playas Conchal, Brasilito, Flamingo, and Potrero. After another 20km (12 miles), at the town of Huacas, take the right fork to reach these beaches. The drive takes about 4½ hours.

Alternatively, you can drive here via Liberia. When you reach Liberia, turn west and follow the signs for Santa Cruz and the various beaches. Just beyond the town of Belén, take the turnoff for playas Flamingo, Brasilito, and Potrero, and continue following the directions given above. This route takes around 5 hours.

By Bus: Tralapa express buses (© **2221-7202** in San José, or 2654-4203 in Flamingo) leave San José daily at 8 and 10:30am and 3pm from Calle 20 between avenidas 3 and 5, stopping at playas Brasilito, Flamingo, and Potrero, in that order. The ride takes around 5 hours. A one-way ticket costs C6,290.

Alternatively, the same company's buses to Santa Cruz (© **2680-0392**) connect with one of the several buses from Santa Cruz to Playa Potrero. Buses depart San José for Santa Cruz roughly every 2 hours daily between 7:15am and 6pm from Calle 20 between avenidas 3 and 5. The trip duration is around 4 hours; the fare is C5,425. From Santa Cruz, the ride is about 90 minutes; the fare is C1,500.

Gray Line (www.graylinecostarica.com; © **800/719-3105** in the U.S. and Canada, or 2220-2126 in Costa Rica) and **Interbus** (www.interbusonline.com; © **4031-0888**) both have two daily buses leaving San José for the beaches in this area, one in the morning and one in the afternoon. The fare is $50. Both companies will pick you up at most San José–area hotels, and offer connections to most other tourist destinations in the country.

Express buses depart **Playa Potrero** for San José at 3 and 9am and 2pm, stopping a few minutes later in playas Flamingo and Brasilito. Ask

The village of Playa Brasilito.

at your hotel where to catch the bus. Buses to **Santa Cruz** leave Potrero at regular intervals throughout the day and take about 90 minutes. If you're heading north toward Liberia, get off the bus at Belén and wait for a bus going north. Buses leave Santa Cruz for San José roughly every other hour between 6am and 6pm.

ORIENTATION The pavement ends just beyond Playa Conchal as you leave the small village of Brasilito.

Exploring Playas Conchal & Brasilito

Playa Conchal ★★, which is most famous for its crushed seashells, is also stunningly beautiful, but the drop-off is quite steep, making it notorious for strong riptides. The water at **Playa Brasilito** is often fairly calm, which makes it a good swimming choice. This is also a great base for visiting other nearby and less popular beaches, like **Playa La Penca ★★** and **Playa Pan de Azúcar ★★**, both of which are north of here.

All of the hotels here have tour desks offering a range of tour and activity options, including those available in the Flamingo and Potrero area (p. 258).

Tip: All beaches in Costa Rica are public property. But the land behind the beaches is not, and the Westin hotel and Reserva Conchal condo development own almost all of it in Playa Conchal, so the only public access is along the soft-sand road that follows the beach south from Brasilito. Before the road reaches Conchal, you'll have to ford a small river and then climb a steep, rocky hill, so four-wheel-drive is recommended.

GOLF The **Westin Playa Conchal Resort & Spa ★★** (© 2654-4123) is home to the excellent **Reserva Conchal Golf Course.** Robert Trent Jones II designed the course, which features broad open fairways, fast greens, and a few wonderful views of the ocean. It costs $150 in

A Day Trip Destination: El Viejo Wetlands

Located a bit inland from the Guanacaste agricultural town of Filadelfia and bordering the Palo Verde National Park, **El Viejo Wildlife Refuge & Wetlands** ★★ (www.elviejowetlands.com; ✆ **2296-0966**) is a unique and intriguing option for a day tour. The principal attraction here is the wildlife, which is abundant, and viewed both from open-air safari-style vehicles and small boats on the Tempisque River. You'll certainly see scores of water birds, and most probably a crocodile or two. The main hacienda-style building at the heart of this operation dates to 1870, and is where they serve up excellent Costa Rican lunches. Additional tour options here include a zip-line canopy tour, and a tour of the on-site organic farm and sugar cane processing mill or *trapiche*. Rates run from $60 to $130, depending upon how many activities or tours you take, and whether or not you want lunch.

Crocodile in Palo Verde National Park.

greens fees for 18 holes and $95 for 9 holes. If you tee off after 1pm, the price drops to $95 for all the rounds you can squeeze in.

WATERSPORTS You can rent jet skis and Wave Runners on the beach in Playa Conchal, from **Dorado Jet Ski Tours** (✆ **8824-4293**). These folks also offer guided snorkel tours out to the Catalina Islands, as well as wet and wild "Banana Boat" rides, where a group of friends and family get pulled behind a speed boat on a giant, inflatable banana boat.

Where to Stay

EXPENSIVE

Westin Playa Conchal Resort & Spa ★★★   This has long been my favorite large-scale, all-inclusive resort in Costa Rica, for good reason. Make that reasons, the first of which has to do with water: Not only does it sit on one of the country's prettiest beaches, its massive, amoeba-like free-form swimming pool is a marvel, meant to mimic a tropical lagoon. (Parents might want to tag their kids with GPS chips in order not to lose them in one of the many interconnected sections of water.) Guests are treated to numerous eating options, all topnotch. And every one of the handsome rooms here is rightly considered a suite and comes with either one king-size or two double beds, set in a raised sleeping room. All have either a private patio or balcony in front of the sliding door entrance. For golfers there's a wide, open resort-style course with trees and water features that attract a range of local wildlife. One of the lakes is even home to a resident caiman. And golf is just one of the many, many activities guests can take part in each day.

Playa Conchal, Guanacaste. www.westinplayaconchal.com. ℭ **800/937-8461** in the U.S., or 2654-3442. 406 units. $415 and up double; $850 and up suite double; children 3–12 add $160–$185 per child per day; kids 13 and up charged as adults; kids under 3 free. Rates include all meals, drinks, taxes, a wide range of activities, and use of non-motorized watersports equipment. Golf and spa services extra. **Amenities:** 6 restaurants; 5 bars; casino; babysitting; bike rental; children's programs; Robert Trent Jones II–designed 18-hole golf course and pro shop; modest exercise facilities and spa; massive 2 outdoor pools w/several Jacuzzis; room service; 4 lighted tennis courts; watersports equipment rental; free Wi-Fi.

INEXPENSIVE

A string of inexpensive *cabinas* line the main road leading into Brasilito, just before you hit the beach. It's also possible to camp on playas Potrero and Brasilito. At the former, contact **Mayra Camping** (ℭ **2654-4213**); at the latter, try **Camping Brasilito** (ℭ **2654-4452**). Both of these places offer some budget rooms as well. Each charges around C4,000 per person to make camp and use the basic restroom facilities or around C15,000 to C30,000 per person to stay in a rustic room.

Conchal Hotel ★★   Burned to the ground in early 2013, the Conchal was quickly rebuilt and is better than ever. Rooms are spacious and feature sturdy steel bed frames, white linens and whitewashed walls offset with bright primary accents. Superior rooms come with large, flat-screen televisions and more space. Most rooms open on to a private or shared balcony or veranda fronting the small central pool and gardens. Despite its name, this hotel really should be considered part of Playa Brasilito, which is about a 2 block walk away. Owners Simon and Hilda are delightful and very hands-on. The hotel's tropical fusion Papaya restaurant (p. 255) is one of the best in the area.

Playa Brasilito, Guanacaste. www.conchalcr.com. ℭ **2654-9125.** 13 units. $96 double; $238 family suite. Rates include continental breakfast and taxes. Seriously reduced rates available in the off season. **Amenities:** Restaurant; bar; pool; free Wi-Fi.

Hotel Brasilito ★   This longstanding budget hotel offers clean, well-kept rooms in a pair of two-story wood buildings just a stone's throw from the water right. Snag a room with a balcony and you'll be in budget heaven. These owners offer excellent in-house tour operation and their open-air restaurant, El Oasis, is equally recommendable.

Playa Brasilito, Guanacaste. www.hotelbrasilito.com. ℭ **2654-4237.** 15 units. $44–$84 double. **Amenities:** Restaurant; free Wi-Fi.

Where to Dine

Camarón Dorado ★ SEAFOOD The quintessential beach restaurant, complete with plastic lawn furniture set in the sand and Tiki torches, Camaron Dorado offers a seafood-centric menu featuring a half dozen different preparations of fresh local fish, lobster, shrimp and shellfish (there are fried chicken, steaks, and burgers for the carnivores). Everything is very well prepared, although the success this place enjoys has led them to jack up the prices a bit above what you should be paying in what is really a simple, beachfront fish shack.

Playa Brasilito. ✆ **2654-4028.** Reservations recommended in high season. Main courses C5,000–C17,000. Daily 11am–10pm.

Papaya ★★★ INTERNATIONAL/SEAFOOD Easily the finest restaurant in the Brasilito/Conchal area, Papaya specializes in Pacific Rim fusion and Nuevo Latino fare. Occupying a large, open-air second-floor space overlooking the pool and gardens of the Conchal Hotel, it's also date night central thanks to its dim lighting and table top candles. As for what to order: Either go with a special from the chalkboard or try their fresh mahi-mahi in a coconut crust and local lobster tails seasoned with Chinese five spice. A winner!

Playa Brasilito. ✆ **2654-9125.** Main courses C8,750–C11,400. Thurs–Tues 7am–8:30pm.

Entertainment & Nightlife

Pretty much all of the nightlife in Playa Conchal happens at the large Westin resort (p. 253), which has a range of bars, nightly entertainment, and a casino. Over in Brasilito, there might be live music or sporting events on the TVs at **Tiki's Seaside Grille** (✆ **2654-9028**).

PLAYAS FLAMINGO ★★ & POTRERO

285km (176 miles) NW of San José; 71km (44 miles) SW of Liberia

Playa Flamingo is one of the prettiest beaches in the region. A long, broad stretch of pinkish white sand, it is on a long spit of land that forms part of Potrero Bay. At the northern end of the beach is a high rock outcropping upon which most of Playa Flamingo's hotels and vacation homes are built. This rocky hill has great views.

If you continue along the road from Brasilito without taking the turn for Playa Flamingo, you'll come to **Playa Potrero,** which sits in a broadly curving bay, protected by the Flamingo headlands. The sand here is a brownish gray, but the beach is long, clean, deserted, and very calm for swimming. You can see the hotels of Playa Flamingo across the bay. Drive a little farther north and you'll find the still-underdeveloped beaches of **Playa Prieta ★**, **Playa La Penca ★** and, finally, **Playa Pan de Azúcar ★★**, or Sugar Beach.

Essentials

GETTING THERE & DEPARTING   By Plane: The nearest airport with regularly scheduled flights is in Tamarindo (p. 264), although it is also possible to fly into Liberia (p. 211). From either, you can arrange for a taxi

Playa Flamingo.

to drive you to any of these beaches. Playas Flamingo and Potrero are about 30 minutes from Tamarindo and 45 minutes from Liberia. A taxi from Tamarindo should cost around $35 to $55, and between $60 and $80 from Liberia.

By Bus: For information on reaching these beaches by bus, see p. 251.

By Car: See the information for driving to Playas Conchal and Brasilito, p. 250. Playa Flamingo is the first beach you'll come to beyond Playa Brasilito. Two prominent turnoffs on your left will take you to the beach, whereas if you continue straight, and follow signs bearing right, you'll soon come to Playa Potrero.

GETTING AROUND   Economy Rent A Car (② **2654-4152**) has an office in Playa Flamingo.

Exploring Playas Flamingo & Potrero

Playa Flamingo ★★ is a long and beautiful stretch of soft white sand, although the surf can sometimes get a bit rough. The beach doesn't have much shade, so be sure to use plenty of sunscreen and bring an umbrella if you can. If you're not staying here, parking spots are available all along the beach road—although do not leave anything of value inside the car. **Playa Potrero** has much gentler surf and, therefore, is the better swimming beach. However, the beach is made up of hard-packed dark sand that is much less appealing than Playa Flamingo.

A BEACH CLUB If your hotel doesn't have a pool or beach access, you can always head to **El Coconut Beach Club** (www.elcoconut-tamarindo.com; ☏ **2654-4300**), which has both. It's located right on Playa Potrero. You can enjoy the facilities, as long as you eat and drink at their excellent **Buena Vista Beachfront** restaurant, a sister to **El Coconut** in Tamarindo (p. 274).

HORSEBACK RIDING You can arrange a horseback ride with **Casagua Horses** (www.paintedponyguestranch.com; ☏ **2653-8041**). Depending on the size of your group, it should cost between $25 and $50 per person per hour.

LANGUAGE LEARNING The **Centro Panamericano de Idiomas** (www. cpi-edu.com; ☏ **2265-6306**), which

Playa Pan de Azúcar.

has schools in San José and Monteverde, has a branch in Flamingo, across from the Flamingo Marina, facing Potrero Bay. A 1-week program with 4 hours of class per day and a homestay with a Costa Rican family costs $730.

SCUBA DIVING Scuba diving is quite popular here. **Costa Rica Diving** (www.costarica-diving.com; ☏ **2654-4148**) has a shop in Flamingo and offers trips to the Catalina Island for around $85. Alternatively, you can check in at the **Flamingo Marina Resort Hotel and Club** (p. 259).

WATERSPORTS You can rent jet skis, boogie boards, skim boards, and stand up paddle boards on Playa Flamingo from **Playa Vida** (☏ **2654-4444**). These folks are on the south side of the Flamingo Beach resort (p. 259) and offer guided snorkel tours out to the Catalina Islands.

If you're interested in stand up paddling, surfing or surf lessons, check in at **Point Break Surf School** (www.pointbreaksurf.com; ☏ **8866-4413**).

SPORTFISHING & SAILBOAT CHARTERS Although the Flamingo Marina is currently closed, you still have plenty of sportfishing and sailboat charter options here. Jim McKee, the former force behind the Flamingo Marina, manages a fleet of boats. Contact him via his company, **Oso Viejo** (www.flamingobeachcr.com; ☏ **8827-5533** or 2653-8437). A full-day fishing excursion costs between $700 and $2,200, depending on the size and quality of the boat, and distance traveled to the fishing grounds. Half-day trips cost between $500 and $700.

A sailboat cruise near Tamarindo.

If you're looking for a full- or half-day sail or sunset cruise, check in with Oso Viejo to see what boats are available, or ask about the 52-foot cutter **Shannon.** Prices range from around $50 to $120 per person, depending on the length of the cruise. Multiday trips are also available.

Alternatively, you can ask at the **Flamingo Marina Resort Hotel and Club** (p. 259).

Another option is to head down the beach at Playa Potrero to the **Costa Rica Sailing Center** (www.learntosailcr.com; ✆ **8699-7289**), which offers sailing lessons and rentals, with a wide range of small sailcraft to choose from. They also rent out stand up paddle boards, kayaks, fishing gear and snorkel equipment.

Where to Stay

Along with the places mentioned below, **Casa Melray** ★ (www.casa melray.com; ✆ **2654-4316**) is a swank, beachfront B&B in Playa Potrero.

If you plan to be here for a while or are coming down with friends or a large family, you might consider renting a condo or house. For info and reservations, contact the folks at **ETS Costa Rica** (www.etscr.net; ✆ **888/215-3657** in U.S. and Canada, 2653-7444 in Costa Rica).

MODERATE

Bahía del Sol Beachfront & Boutique Hotel ★★ Mother Nature rules at this small resort, a place beloved by both humans and other critters for its handsome, lush landscaping (I'm particularly fond of the flowering ginger that overflows in the tropical gardens). The hotel is set on a grassy patch of land just in from the center of Playa Potrero, a calm and protected beach with hard-packed, dark gray sand. Inside isn't quite as spectacular: Rooms are simple and plain, with high ceilings and beds that can be too hard. That said, the housekeeping staff is diligent and rooms are fairly priced, particularly the studio apartments with kitchenettes (they're good for families or for longer stays). A very good restaurant is also on the property, as is a small spa. Daily yoga and Pilates classes are included in the rate. This hotel has received "4 Leaves" in the CST Sustainable Tourism program.

Playa Potrero, Guanacaste. www.bahiadelsolhotel.com. © **866/223-2463** in the U.S. and Canada, or 2654-4671 in Costa Rica. 28 units. $120–$225 double; $240–$410 suite. Rates include breakfast. **Amenities:** Restaurant; bar; Jacuzzi; outdoor pool; room service; spa; free Wi-Fi.

Flamingo Beach Resort ★

This is the only true beachfront hotel in Playa Flamingo. And what it lacks in style and pizzazz, it makes up for in location. You can enjoy sunsets from their second-floor beachfront restaurant, and spend the day between body surfing sessions off Playa Flamingo and lounging in the large resort pool. The ocean front rooms here are my favorites, though all the digs are large, with tile floors, modern furnishings, and a splash of color provided by locally produced paintings. Some of the suites and family rooms come with kitchenettes, although these are some of the more dated units in the resort, with appliances and furnishings that could use some refreshing. The resort offers an "all-inclusive" option, but I highly advise against it.

Playa Flamingo, Guanacaste. www.resortflamingobeach.com. © **877/856-5519** in the U.S. and Canada, or 2654-4444 in Costa Rica. 120 units. $145–$280 double; $290–$455 suite. **Amenities:** Restaurant; 2 bars; casino; exercise room; large outdoor pool; room service; small spa; lighted tennis court; watersports equipment rental; free Wi-Fi.

Flamingo Marina Resort Hotel and Club ★

This is one of the older resorts in the area, and despite periodic updates and renovations, many of the rooms feel a bit worn and tired. Still, I find the black-and-white checkered tiles found in some units charming, and most of the rooms have excellent views, from private balconies. The resort is set on a steep hillside overlooking Flamingo Bay and Playa Potrero, and features a mix of hotel rooms and condo units plus a popular bar and restaurant. It's a bit of a walk, or short car ride, to the Flamingo or Potrero beaches.

Playa Flamingo, Guanacaste. www.flamingomarina.com. © **940/440-8310** in the U.S., or 2654-4141 in Costa Rica. 30 units, 15 condo units. $159 double; $189–$219 suite; $309–$329 condo. **Amenities:** Restaurant; bar; Jacuzzi; 2 small outdoor pools; tennis court; watersports equipment rental; Wi-Fi.

Where to Dine

You also can't go wrong with the California-style and Asian fusion cuisine and fresh baked pizzas at **Angelina's** ★★ (www.angelinasplayaflamingo. com; ☎ **2654-4839**), on the second floor of La Plaza shopping center, or at **Buena Vista Beachfront Restaurant** (www.elcoconut-tamarindo. com; ☎ **2654-4300;** see "A Beach Club," p. 257).

Coco Loco ★★★ COSTA RICAN/SEAFOOD While many still bemoan the closing of Mar y Sol restaurant, there's plenty of reason to rejoice, now that its former owner, chef Jean-Luc Taulere has opened up this casual beachfront bar and restaurant. It has, after all, a lovely setting, with teak wood tables under white canvas umbrellas spread out on the sand at the far southern end of Playa Flamingo. The menu features such items as blackened swordfish wrap, fresh yellow fin tuna tacos and slow-cooked pork ribs in a pineapple barbeque sauce. I'm partial to the dishes served inside a hollowed out half-coconuts like the fresh ceviche, homemade coconut ice cream, and house specialty Loco Coco, a coconut rice dish featuring mussels, octopus and fresh caught snapper, with a Thai-inspired basil, ginger and lime sauce. Come for a drink at sunset (there's an extensive cocktail menu) and stay through the evening as they often host live music or DJs after sundown.

South end of Playa Flamingo. www.cocolococostarica.com. ☎ **2654-6242.** Main courses C3,400–C5,700. Daily 11am–9pm.

Marie's ★★ COSTA RICAN/SEAFOOD Marie has been serving up fresh, fairly priced food here for decades, and her restaurant is justifiably popular. She's still running the show, which means the menu thankfully hasn't changed from burritos and quesadillas, plus simply grilled fish or chicken. The large, open-air restaurant features extremely high thatch ceilings with slow-turning ceiling fans.

Playa Flamingo. www.mariesrestaurantincostarica.com. ☎ **2654-4136.** Main courses C3,800–C13,000. Daily 6:30am–9:30pm.

Entertainment & Nightlife

With both a disco and casino, **Amberes** (☎ **2654-4001**), just slightly up the hill at the north end of town, is the undisputed hot spot in this area; however, **Flamingo Beach Resort** (p. 259) also has a casino. You'll find a mellower bar and lounge scene at the bar of **Angelina's** ★ (see above), or on the beach at **Coco Loco** (see above).

Over in Potrero, the rooftop bar at **La Terraza de los Mariscos** (☎ **2654-4379**) sometimes has live music. However, my favorite bar here is **Bar La Perla** ★ (☎ **2654-4500**), a simple concrete slab construction with corrugated zinc roof and mostly open walls using chain link fencing for window screens. Located on a dusty corner, this is a very typical Costa Rican style cantina, but it draws a good mixed crowd of locals, expats and tourists alike.

PLAYA GRANDE ★★

295km (183 miles) NW of San José; 70km (43 miles) SW of Liberia

Playa Grande is one of the principal nesting sites for the giant leatherback turtle, the largest turtle in the world. The beach is a long, straight stretch of soft, golden sand that boasts a well-formed and consistent beach break with surfable waves along its entire length. When the surf is up, the beach can be a bit rough for casual swimming. Playa Grande has very little development at the moment. I almost hate to mention places to stay in Playa Grande because the steady influx of tourists and development is severely threatening it as a turtle-nesting site. For help locating the following hotels, restaurants, and attractions, see the map "Around Tamarindo," on p. 267.

Essentials

GETTING THERE & DEPARTING By Plane: The nearest airport with regularly scheduled flights is in Tamarindo (p. 264), although it is also possible to fly into Liberia (p. 211). From either of these places, you can arrange for a taxi to drive you to Playa Grande. Playa Grande is about 15 minutes from Tamarindo and 45 minutes from Liberia. A taxi from Tamarindo should cost $30 to $40; between $60 and $80 from Liberia.

By Car: See the information for driving to Tamarindo on p. 264. The dirt and gravel entrance roads to Playa Grande are located along CR155 between Tamarindo and Huacas.

Exploring Playa Grande

Leatherback sea turtles nest on Playa Grande between early October and mid-February. The turtles come ashore to lay their eggs only at night. During the nesting season, you'll be inundated with opportunities to sign up for nightly tours, which usually cost $35 to $50 per person. No flash photography or flashlights are allowed because any sort of light can confuse the turtles and prevent them from laying their eggs; guides must use red-tinted flashlights.

Note: Turtle nesting is a natural, unpredictable, and increasingly rare event. Sadly, things have gotten worse here over

Leatherback turtle hatchlings on Playa Grande.

the years. All indications are that excessive building and lighting close to the beach are the culprits. With a limited nesting season, the annual numbers of nesting turtles fluctuates wildly. There are good years and bad years. Even during heavy nesting years, you sometimes have to wait your turn for hours, hike quite a way, and accept the possibility that no nesting mothers will be spotted that evening.

If your hotel can't set a tour up for you, you'll see signs all over town offering tours. Make sure you go with someone licensed and reputable. Do-it-yourselfers can drive over to Playa Grande and book a $30 tour directly with the **National Parks Service** (✆ **2653-0470**). The Parks Service operates out of a small shack just before the beach, across from the Hotel Las Tortugas (p. 262). It opens each evening at around 6pm to begin taking reservations. They sometimes answer their phone during the day, and it's best to make a reservation in advance because only a limited number of people are allowed on the beach at one time. Spots fill up fast, and if you don't have a reservation, you may have to wait until really late, or you may not be able to go out onto the beach.

Where to Stay

In addition to the places listed below, **Hotel Bula Bula** ★ (www.hotelbulabula.com; ✆ **877/658-2880** in the U.S. and Canada, or 2653-0975 in Costa Rica) is an excellent inland option, while the **Playa Grande Surf Camp** (www.playagrandesurfcamp.com; ✆ **2653-1074**) is geared toward surfers and budget travelers.

Hotel Las Tortugas ★   Owner and local surf legend Louis Wilson came to Costa Rica decades ago for the waves. He's stayed and still surfs, but has also been a leading figure in creating a protected habitat for the nesting sea turtles. The hotel sits right at the center of Playa Grande, near some of the best breaks, and is quite popular with surfers. Some guests complain about the lack of ocean view at this beachfront hotel; however, the reason is simple, a natural barrier of trees and shrubs is a deliberate measure to block manmade lighting from reaching the beach, as it confuses and scares off potential nesting turtles. Rooms here vary greatly in size and comfort level. All have A/C, and the main lodge rooms boast cool, local smooth stone floors and interesting accents like clear glass blocks used in walls. Economy rancho rooms, on the other hand, feel a little small, and dormlike, with bunk beds and limited natural light. The hotel also rents and manages fully equipped apartments and condos.

Playa Grande, Guanacaste. www.lastortugashotel.com. ✆ **2653-0423** or 2653-0458. 11 units. $25–$45 economy room double; $50–$90 double; $120 suite. **Amenities:** Restaurant; bar; Jacuzzi; small outdoor pool; free Wi-Fi.

Rip Jack Inn ★★   I find these to be the most comfortable and best equipped rooms in Playa Grande, particularly the deluxe rooms and suites, with their wall-mounted A/C units, hardwood beds, and wall hangings imported from Bali, Indonesia and India. The hotel itself is about a block or so in from the beach. Daily yoga and Pilates classes are offered in the large yoga space here. There's a refreshing but very small pool, and the hotel's second-floor restaurant is one of the better dining options in town, serving fresh healthy fare and sushi.

Playa Grande, Guanacaste. www.ripjackinn.com. ℂ **800/808-4605** in the U.S. and Canada, or 2653-1636 in Costa Rica. 20 units. $90–$140 double; $165–$240 suite. **Amenities:** Restaurant; bar; lap pool; Wi-Fi.

Where to Dine

Dining options are pretty limited in Playa Grande. I like **Upstairs ★**, the restaurant at the Rip Jack Inn (p. 262), or the **Great Waltini's ★**, at the Hotel Bula Bula (p. 262). Both serve fresh seafood and prime meats, cooked with care. You might also try the **Taco Star** (no phone) a simple open-air beachfront joint serving up fresh fish tacos and other Mexican favorites. For breakfasts, head to **Mamasa** (www.mamasarestaurant.com; ℂ **8445-1797**) for its eggs Benedict with a jalapeño Hollandaise, filling breakfast burritos, and homemade bagels.

PLAYA TAMARINDO ★ & PLAYA LANGOSTA ★★

295km (183 miles) NW of San José; 73km (45 miles) SW of Liberia

Tamarindo is the biggest boomtown in Guanacaste—and in some ways, I think the boom has gone a bit too far, a bit too fast. The main road into Tamarindo is a helter-skelter jumble of strip malls, surf shops, hotels, and restaurants. This two-lane road is the only way in and out of town, and often features bumper-to-bumper traffic. Ongoing development is spreading up the hills inland from the beach and south to Playa Langosta. None of it is regulated or particularly well planned out.

Still, the wide range of accommodations, abundant restaurants, and active nightlife, along with very dependable surf, have established Tamarindo as one of the most popular beaches on this coast. The beautiful beach here is a long, wide swath of white sand that curves gently from one rocky headland to another. Fishing boats bob at their moorings and brown pelicans skim the water's surface just beyond the breakers. A sandy islet off the southern end of the beach makes a fun destination if you're a strong swimmer; if you're not, it makes a scenic foreground for sunsets. Tamarindo is very popular with surfers, who ply the break right here or use the town as a jumping-off place for beach and point breaks at playas Grande, Langosta, Avellanas, and Negra.

Essentials

GETTING THERE & DEPARTING   **By Plane:** Both **Nature Air** (www. natureair.com; ℂ **800/235-9272** in the U.S. and Canada, or 2299-6000)

and **Sansa** (www.flysansa.com; ☏ **877/767-2672** in the U.S. and Canada, or 2290-4100 in Costa Rica) have several daily direct flights throughout the day to the small airstrip on the outskirts of Tamarindo. Fares run $141 to $158. During the high season, additional flights are sometimes added. Nature Air also connects Tamarindo and Arenal, Liberia, and Quepos.

Whether you arrive on Sansa or Nature Air, a couple of cabs or minivans are always waiting for arriving flights. It costs C8,000 to C10,000 for the ride into town.

If you're flying into Liberia, a taxi should cost around $120. Alternatively, you can use **Tamarindo Transfers & Tours** (www.tamarindoshuttle.com; ☏ **929/800-4621** in the U.S., or 2653-4444 in Costa Rica), which charges $20 per person, one-way for a shared shuttle, with a three-person minimum. These folks also offer a variety of tours and transfer services.

By Car: The most direct route is by way of the La Amistad bridge. From San José, you can either take the Interamerican Highway (CR1) north from downtown San José, or first head west out of the city on the San José–Caldera Highway (CR27). This latter route is a faster and flatter drive. When you reach Caldera on this route, follow the signs to Puntarenas, Liberia, and the Interamerican Highway (CR1). This will lead you to the unmarked entrance to CR1. You'll want to pass under the bridge and follow the on-ramp, which will put you on the highway heading north. Forty-seven kilometers (29 miles) north of the Puntarenas exit on the Interamerican Highway, you'll see signs for the turnoff to the bridge. After crossing the river, follow the signs for Nicoya and Santa Cruz. Continue north out of Santa Cruz, until just before the village of Belén, where you will find the turnoff for Tamarindo. In another 20km (12 miles), take the left fork for Playa Tamarindo at Huacas and continue on

Surfing in Tamarindo.

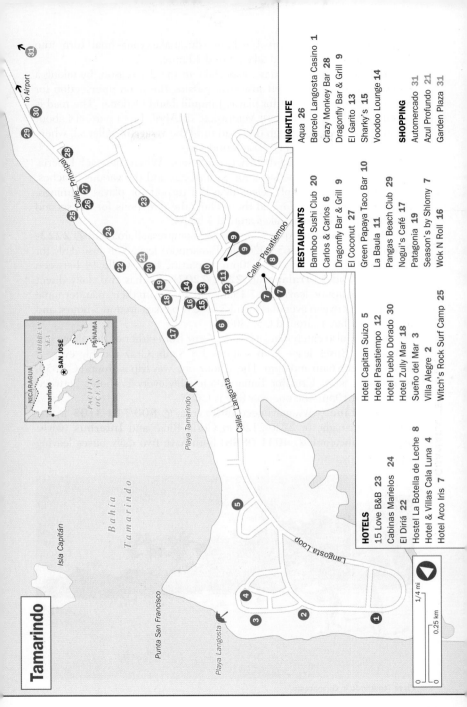

Tamarindo

HOTELS
15 Love B&B **23**
Cabinas Marielos **24**
El Diriá **22**
Hostel La Botella de Leche **8**
Hotel & Villas Cala Luna **4**
Hotel Arco Iris **7**
Hotel Capitan Suizo **5**
Hotel Pasatiempo **12**
Hotel Pueblo Dorado **30**
Hotel Zully Mar **18**
Sueño del Mar **3**
Villa Alegre **2**
Witch's Rock Surf Camp **25**

RESTAURANTS
Bamboo Sushi Club **20**
Carlos & Carlos **6**
Dragonfly Bar & Grill **9**
El Coconut **27**
Green Papaya Taco Bar **10**
La Baula **11**
Pangas Beach Club **29**
Nogui's Café **17**
Patagonia **19**
Season's by Shlomy **7**
Wok N Roll **16**

NIGHTLIFE
Aqua **26**
Barcelo Langosta Casino **1**
Crazy Monkey Bar **28**
Dragonfly Bar & Grill **9**
El Garito **13**
Sharky's **15**
Voodoo Lounge **14**

SHOPPING
Automercado **31**
Azul Profundo **21**
Garden Plaza **31**

265

until the village of Villareal, where you make your final turn into Tamarindo. The trip should take around 4 hours.

You can save a little time, especially in the dry season, by taking a rougher route: You turn left just after passing the main intersection for Santa Cruz at the turnoff for playas Junquillal and Ostional. The road is paved until the tiny village of Veintesiete de Abril. From here, it's about 20km (12 miles) on a rough dirt road until the village of Villareal, where you make your final turn into Tamarindo.

Alternatively, you can drive here via Liberia. When you reach Liberia, turn west and follow the signs for Santa Cruz and the various beaches. Just beyond the town of Belén, take the turnoff for playas Flamingo, Brasilito, and Tamarindo, and then follow the directions for the second option above. This route takes around 5 hours.

By Bus: Alfaro express buses (www.empresaalfaro.com; ✆ **2222-2666** in San José, or 2653-0268 in Tamarindo) leave San José daily for Tamarindo at 11:30am and 3:30pm, departing from Calle 14 between avenidas 3 and 5. **Tralapa** (✆ **2221-7202**) also has two daily direct buses to Tamarindo leaving at 7:15am and 4pm from their main terminal at Calle 20 between avenidas 3 and 5. The trip takes around 5 hours, and the one-way fare is around C5,7300.

You can also catch a bus to Santa Cruz from either of the above bus companies. Buses leave both stations for Santa Cruz roughly every 2 hours between 6am and 6pm. The 4-hour, one-way trip is around C5,650. Buses leave Santa Cruz for Tamarindo roughly every 1½ hours between 5:45am and 10pm; the one-way fare is C685.

Gray Line (www.graylinecostarica.com; ✆ **800/719-3105** in the U.S. and Canada, or 2220-2126 in Costa Rica) and **Interbus** (www.interbusonline.com; ✆ **4031-0888**) both have two daily buses leaving

Playa Tamarindo in Guanacaste.

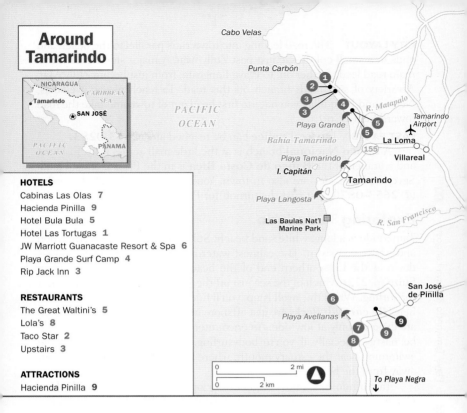

Around Tamarindo

HOTELS

Cabinas Las Olas **7**
Hacienda Pinilla **9**
Hotel Bula Bula **5**
Hotel Las Tortugas **1**
JW Marriott Guanacaste Resort & Spa **6**
Playa Grande Surf Camp **4**
Rip Jack Inn **3**

RESTAURANTS

The Great Waltini's **5**
Lola's **8**
Taco Star **2**
Upstairs **3**

ATTRACTIONS

Hacienda Pinilla **9**

San José for Tamarindo (one in the morning, one in the afternoon); the fare is $50. Both companies will pick you up at most San José-area hotels, and offer connections to most other major tourist destinations in Costa Rica.

Direct buses leave Tamarindo for San José daily at 3:30 and 5:30am (except on Sun) and 2 and 4pm. Buses to Santa Cruz leave roughly every 2 hours between 4:30am and 8:30pm. In Santa Cruz, you can transfer to one of the frequent San José buses.

GETTING AROUND   **Adobe** (✆ **2542-4800**), plus all the multinational chains have rental car offices in Tamarindo.

The town itself is very compact and you should be able to walk most places. Heck, it's not even that far a walk from Playa Langosta. Still, a large fleet of taxis are usually cruising around town, or hanging out at principal intersections and meeting points. If you need to, you can contact **PDQ Taxi** (www.tamarindo-taxi.com; ✆ **8918-3710**).

If you need a ride to either the Tamarindo airstrip or Liberia international airport, contact **Tamarindo Transfers & Tours ★** (www.tamarindoshuttle.com; ✆ **2653-4444**).

CITY LAYOUT The road leading into town runs parallel to the beach and ends in a small cul-de-sac just past Zully Mar. A major side road off this main road leads farther on, to Playa Langosta, from just before Zully Mar. A variety of side roads branch off this road. To reach playas Avellanas, Negra, and Junquillal, you have to first head out of town and take the road toward Santa Cruz.

FAST FACTS The local **police** can be reached at ℭ **2653-0283.**

A **Banco Nacional** branch is at the little mall across from El Diria, and a branch of the **Banco de Costa Rica** is in the Plaza Conchal mall. Several pharmacies are also in town. You'll find **Back Wash Laundry** (ℭ **2653-0870**) just past the turnoff for Playa Langosta.

Exploring Tamarindo

Tamarindo is a long, white sand beach. Still, you have to be careful when and where you swim. The calmest water and best swimming are always down at the far southern end of the beach, toward the Hotel Capitan Suizo (p. 272). Much of the sea just off the busiest part of the town is best for surfing. When the swell is up, you'll find scores of surfers in the water here. **Be careful:** Rocks are just offshore in several places, some of which are exposed only at low tide. An encounter with one of these rocks could be nasty, especially if you're bodysurfing. I also advise that you avoid swimming near the estuary mouth, where the currents can carry you out away from the beach.

Tamarindo has a host of good tour operators. The best are **Xplore CR ★** (www.xplorecostarica.com; ℭ **844/278-6877** in U.S. and Canada; 2653-4130 in Costa Rica), **Tamarindo Transfers & Tours ★** (www.tamarindoshuttle.com; ℭ **2653-4444**), and **Iguana Surf** (ℭ www.iguanasurf.net; ℭ **2653-0613**). All offer a range of half- and full-day trips, including outboard or kayak tours through the nearby estuary and mangroves, excursions to Santa Cruz and Guaitíl, raft floats on the Corobicí River, and tours to Palo Verde and Rincón de la Vieja national parks. Rates run between $50 and $185, varying by the length of the tour and group size. All of the hotel desks and tour operators here offer **turtle nesting tours** to Playa Grande (p. 261), in season, or you can contact **ACOTAM** (ℭ **2653-1687**), a specialized local operator.

CANOPY TOURS No canopy tour is available right in Tamarindo, but the **Monkey Jungle Canopy Tour** (www.canopymonkeyjungle.com;

Yo Quiero Hablar Español

If you want to try an intensive immersion program or just brush up on your rusty high school Spanish, check in with the folks at **Wayra Instituto de Español** (www.spanish-wayra.co.cr; ℭ **2653-0359**). The school is located up a side street from the dirt road that connects Tamarindo to Playa Langosta.

The Hacienda Pinilla golf course.

© 2653-1172) and **Cartagena Canopy Tour** ★ (*©* 2675-0801) are nearby. Both charge $50 per person and include transportation from Tamarindo. Of these two, the Monkey Jungle operation is much closer, but I prefer the Cartagena tour, which has a much more lush forest setting. Still, I think your best bet is to take a day trip to Hacienda Guachipelín (p. 224) and do the zip-line and canyoning tours there.

FOUR-WHEELING **Arenas Adventure Tours** (www.tamarindoaventuras. com; *©* 2653-0108) offers a variety of guided ATV tours from 1 to 3 hours from $45 to $130/person. The company also rents dirt bikes, snorkel equipment, surf and boogie boards, and jet skis and offers a full menu of other guided tours around the region.

GOLF **Hacienda Pinilla** ★★ (www.haciendapinilla.com; *©* 2681-4500) is an eye-candy 18-hole links-style course located south of Tamarindo. Greens fees run around $150 for 18 holes, including a cart, with discounts for guests staying at Hacienda Pinilla or the JW Marriott resort. Many folks staying in Tamarindo also play at the **Westin Playa Conchal Resort & Spa** ★★, an excellent resort course (p. 253).

HORSEBACK RIDING Although some will be disappointed, I think it's a very good thing that horses are no longer allowed on the beach. Fortunately, you'll find plenty of opportunities to ride in the hills and forests around Tamarindo. Most local tour operators offer horseback riding options, but I recommend you go riding with **Casagua Horses** ★ (www.paintedponyguestranch.com; *©* 2653-8041 or 8871-9266). Rates for horse rental, with a guide, are around $25 and $40 per hour.

SAILBOAT CHARTERS Several boats offer cruises from Tamarindo; the 40-foot catamaran **"Blue Dolphin"** ★ (www.bluedolphinsailing.com; *©* 855/842-3204 in the U.S., or 8842-3204 in Costa Rica) and 66-foot catamaran **"Marlin del Rey"** (www.marlindelrey.com; *©* 877/827-8275 in the U.S., or 2653-1212 in Costa Rica) are both solid choices. A half-day snorkel or shorter sunset cruise should cost $70 to $85 per person, and a full day should run between $100 and $150. This usually includes an open bar and snacks on the half-day and sunset cruises, and all of that plus lunch on the full-day trip.

SCUBA DIVING   For scuba diving or snorkeling, check in with **Agua Rica Diving Center ★** (www.aguarica.net; © **2653-0094**), the best and longest running operator in Tamarindo. This is a full-service dive shop offering day trips, multiday dive cruises, and standard resort and full-certification courses.

SPORTFISHING   A host of captains offer anglers a chance to go after the "big ones" that abound in the offshore waters. From the Tamarindo estuary, it takes only 20 minutes to reach the edge of the continental shelf, where the waters are filled with mostly marlin and sailfish. Although fishing is good all year, the peak season for billfish is between mid-April and August. Contact **Tamarindo Sportfishing** (www.tamarindosport fishing.com; © **2653-0090**), **Capullo Sportfishing ★** (www.capullo. com; © **2653-0048**), or **Osprey Sportfishing** (www.osprey-sportfishing. com; © **8754-9292**).

TENNIS   You can rent court time and equipment at the **Tamarindo Tennis Club** (© **2653-0898**), which features two lighted outdoor courts on the back road on the way to the Hotel El Jardín del Edén. It is open daily from 7:30am to 8pm, and court time runs $10 per day. You can also play at Hacienda Pinilla (see "Golf," p. 269) for $5 per hour during the day, and $10 per hour at night.

WATERSPORTS   If you want to try snorkeling, surfing, or sea kayaking in Tamarindo, **Agua Rica Diving Center, Iguana Surf,** and **Arenas Adventure Tours** (p. 269) rent all the necessary equipment. They have half-day and hourly rates for many of these items.

Tamarindo has a host of surf shops and surf schools, if you want to learn to catch a wave while in town. Tamarindo's got a great wave to learn on, although it can get very crowded at the popular beginners' breaks. For gear and lessons, try **Tamarindo Surf School** (www.tamarindosurfschool. com; © **2653-0923**), **Kelly's Surf Shop ★** (www.kellyssurfshop.com; © **888/710-4746** in the U.S. and Canada, or 2653-1355 in Costa Rica), or **Witch's Rock Surf Camp ★** (www.witchsrocksurfcamp.com; © **888/318-7873** in the U.S. and Canada, or 2653-1262 in Costa Rica).

WELLNESS CENTERS   Most of the higher-end hotels have their own spas, and most hotels can call you a massage therapist. But if you're looking for a local day spa experience, try **Cocó Day Spa** (www. cocobeautyspa.com; © **2653-2562**), which has a wide range of treatments and packages, from facials and pedicures to hot stone massages. Alternately, you can head about 15 to 20 minutes inland to **Los**

Altos de Eros ★ (www.losaltosdeeros.com; © **800/391-1944** in the U.S. and Canada or 8850-4222 in Costa Rica) for one of their signature, full-day spa experiences.

For a good yoga session, contact **Ser Om Shanti Yoga Studio** (www.seryogastudio.com; © **8951-6236**).

Especially For Kids

Bolas Locas Mini Golf (www.bolaslocas.com; © **2653-1178;** daily 9am–11pm), located next to Dragonfly Bar & Grill (p. 275), is a nice change from the beach and pool. This 18-hole course features a wave wall, a waterfall and a traditional Costa Rican ox cart as obstacles. A round of golf costs $7 for adults, and $5 for children under 10.

Where to Stay

In addition to the hotels listed below, Tamarindo, Playa Langosta, and Playa Grande have a wide range of beach houses and condos for rent by the night, the week, or the month. For more information on this option, check out **RE/MAX Tamarindo** (www.remax-oceansurf-cr.com; © **866/976-8898** in the U.S. and Canada, or 2653-0073 in Costa Rica) or **RPM Vacation Rentals** ★ (www.rpmvacationrentals.com; © **2653-0738**). You'll also find many options on VRBO.com and FlipKey.com.

EXPENSIVE

Cala Luna Boutique Hotel & Villas ★★   By far the most luxurious option in Tamarindo, the guestrooms at Cala Luna are beauts, done in warm tones with a stone-wash effect on the walls. Sawed off tree trunks are used as nightstands, and sea shells and driftwood are incorporated into the decor. However, the real draw here are the two- and three-bedroom villas, each with its own private kidney-shaped swimming pool, a large and fully equipped kitchen, ample living and dining areas, and a washer and dryer. Playa Langosta is reached via a short private path across a dirt road, and Tamarindo beach is a short taxi ride, or 15-minute walk away. The hotel's grounds and gardens are lushly landscaped, and it's not uncommon to spot a howler monkey in the trees.

Playa Langosta, Guanacaste. www.calaluna.com. © **800/774-7729** in the U.S. and Canada, or 2653-0214 in Costa Rica. 20 units, 16 villas. $210–$450 double; $350–$750 villa. Rates for rooms, but not villas, include breakfast. **Amenities:** 2 restaurants; bar; babysitting; pool w/poolside bar; room service; watersports equipment rental; free Wi-Fi.

El Diriá ★   Frankly, I find this resort has grown a bit too big and service and upkeep can suffer at times. Many of the beds are too hard, the Wi-Fi is spotty and some of the rooms need updating. Still, El Diria has arguably the best location of any hotel in Tamarindo, a short walk to all of the town's restaurants and shops in one direction, a hop to the beach in the other. The landscaping is still lovely with tall sea grape trees and coconut palms providing shade and the thatch roofs over the restaurant and bar areas giving the resort tropical feel. The original hotel rooms are beachfront, and are my favorites, as they are just steps away from the waves. I especially like the third-floor sunset rooms, which offer up sensational ocean and sunset views from their private balconies. However, most of the rooms and suites, as well as several other pools, are located just inland in a series of faceless high-rise.

Playa Tamarindo, Guanacaste. www.tamarindodiria.com. © **866/603-4742** in the U.S. and Canada, or 4032-0032 in Costa Rica. 240 units. $156–$294 double. Rates include breakfast buffet. **Amenities:** 2 restaurants; 2 bars; 4 outdoor pools; free Wi-Fi.

Hotel Capitán Suizo ★★★   It doesn't get much better than this. Right on the beach at the quieter far southern end, the service is top-notch, and the rooms are large, well kept, and thoroughly inviting. Most feature colonial-style terra cotta floors and four-poster canopy beds. Private balconies and patios open on to exuberant tropical gardens, where squirrels, monkeys and magpie jays are common. The hotel's free-form pool is one of the largest and best in town, with a slowly sloping shallow entrance that mimics the beach, a rope swing for a touch of playfulness and a large children's section. This hotel is great for families and honeymooners alike. Rooms don't have TVs, if that matters, and about half are cooled simply by fans and well-designed cross-ventilation.

Playa Tamarindo, Guanacaste. www.hotelcapitansuizo.com. © **2653-0075** or 2653-0075. 28 units and 6 bungalows. $199–$280 double; $360–$440 bungalow; $440–$680 suite. Rates include breakfast buffet. **Amenities:** Restaurant; bar; midsize outdoor pool and children's pool; spa; Wi-Fi.

MODERATE

In addition to the places listed here, **Hotel Pueblo Dorado** (www.pueblodorado.com; © **2653-0008**) is a well-located option just across from the beach, while tennis lovers (and anyone else) might want to check out the **15 Love Bed & Breakfast** (www.15lovebedandbreakfast.com; © **2653-0898**), attached to the Tamarindo Tennis Club (p. 270).

Hotel Arco Iris ★★   The charm quotient is high at this little complex of rooms and bungalows located about a 5-minute walk from the beach. Much of that has to do with the attentiveness of Richard, the American owner and his staff; they make all the guests feel like VIP's. But the rooms are sweet, too, immaculate and featuring white travertine tile floors and pure white linens and bedcovers on excellent beds with hardwood and woven bamboo headboards. There's a small pool, and the restaurant here, **Season's By Shlomy** (p. 276), is excellent.

Playa Tamarindo, Guanacaste. www.hotelarcoiris.com. © **2653-0330**. 13 units. $160–$210 double, $130 bungalows. Rates include breakfast. **Amenities:** Restaurant; bar; small outdoor pool; free Wi-Fi.

Sueño del Mar ★★   This intimate bed-and-breakfast has built a loyal following who come back year after year for the personalized service, gorgeous sunsets, and spectacular breakfasts. A quiet setting on Playa Langosta doesn't hurt, either. The Luna Suite is the prime room in the house (the only one with an ocean view) and is worth the splurge if it's available—it's a second floor affair with wrap-around windows facing the sea, and an open-air shower that also shares the view. The standard rooms have hand-painted linens and also have cute open-air showers with small gardens and plantings providing privacy (although they all open on to the hotel's main walkway, so that privacy is somewhat limited). Hammocks are strung under shade trees, and wooden chairs in the sand set to face the waves are where guests gather every evening to toast the sunset.

Playa Langosta, Guanacaste. www.sueno-del-mar.com. © **2653-0284.** 4 units, 2 casitas. $155-$204 double; $185–$310 suite or casita. Rates include full breakfast. No children 12 and under. **Amenities:** Small outdoor pool; free use of snorkel equipment and boogie boards; free Wi-Fi.

Villa Alegre ★★   In a converted home bordering a small private reserve, this intimate bed-and-breakfast is an excellent, friendly option. The rooms and small villas are all decorated in a distinct country theme, adorned with items gathered over the years by the owners during their own globetrotting adventures. The villas feature small kitchenettes and private balconies. The "Mexico" room, with its large outdoor shower, is considered the top honeymoon choice. Copious and varied breakfasts are served family-style on a shaded patio that fronts the pool. A short path leads to a lookout point and rugged wooden bench set on a small bluff over Playa Langosta, just a few steps above the beach is one of the best sunset spots in the area.

Playa Langosta, Guanacaste. www.villaalegrecostarica.com. © **2653-0270.** 5 units, 2 villas. $170–$185 double; $230 villa. Rates include breakfast. **Amenities:** Midsize outdoor pool; free Wi-Fi.

INEXPENSIVE

In addition to the hotels listed below, **Hostel La Botella de Leche** ★ (www.labotelladeleche.com; © **2653-0189**) bills itself as a "5 star" hostel and is a popular backpacker option. The beachfront **Witch's Rock Surf Camp** ★ (www.witchsrocksurfcamp.com; © **888/318-7873** in the U.S. and Canada, or 2653-1262 in Costa Rica) caters to young, budget-minded surfers.

Cabinas Marielos ★   This longstanding, family-run budget hotel is located right across from the beach near the entrance to town. Owner Maria de los Angeles ("Marielos") Gonzalez and her children run a tight ship, meaning rooms are neat as a pin. They come either with fans or air-conditioning and a few even have kitchenettes. The best rooms here are the second-floor units with private balconies. Although right near the center of all the action and just steps from the sand, the gardens and grounds here create a quiet oasis amid all the tumult of Tamarindo.

Playa Tamarindo, Guanacaste. www.cabinasmarieloscr.com. © **2653-0141** or 2653-0954. 24 units. $50–$60 double. Rates include taxes. **Amenities:** Surfboard and boogies rentals.

Hotel Pasatiempo ★★ This lovely small resort, located a few blocks inland from the water, offers rooms that are spacious and well maintained, with cool tile floors and a relaxed, tropical decor. Each room is named after a distinct and different local beach, and comes with a hammock, chaise lounge or wooden Adirondack chairs on a private patio perfect for reading a good book. The large central pool is quite inviting, with a broad natural stone and wooden deck area encircling it and tall shade trees all around. The hotel's bar and restaurant is one of the livelier spots in town (Wed is open-mic night).

Playa Tamarindo, Guanacaste. www.hotelpasatiempo.com. © **2653-0096**. 22 units. $89–$99 double; $129 suite. Rates include breakfast. **Amenities:** Restaurant; bar; pool; free Wi-Fi.

Mar Rey Hotel ★ For more than 40 years, the Martinez and Reyes families have run this budget favorite under the name Zully Mar, but have recently decided on a rebranding. But though the name has changed, the ambiance and prices, thankfully haven't. The two-story building is still painted a blinding white and features heavy concrete arches, balcony railings and bannisters. The rooms continue on with the all-white theme, getting their only splash of color from a vibrant print bedspread. The individually carved hardwood doors, featuring animal and native life motifs are perhaps the most striking design element here. It's worth the small splurge for a room with air-conditioning and television. You can enjoy a small, free-form pool for cooling off, but the beach is literally just steps away, across the street. Still, be forewarned, this hotel is located right on the busiest corner of Tamarindo, so this is not a good choice for those seeking a quiet getaway or a peaceful retreat.

Playa Tamarindo, Guanacaste. www.hotelmarrey.com. © **2653-0028**. 22 units. $61–$69 double. **Amenities:** Small outdoor pool, small spa, free Wi-Fi.

Where to Dine

Tamarindo has a glut of darn good restaurants. **El Coconut ★** (www.elcoconut-tamarindo.com; © **2653-0086**), right on the main road, is an institution, specializing in fresh seafood, with a European flair. **Nogui's Café ★** (www.noguistamarindo.com; © **2653-0029**) is one of the more popular places in town—and rightly so. This simple open-air cafe just off the beach on the small traffic circle serves hearty breakfasts and well-prepared salads, sandwiches, burgers, and casual meals. They even have a few tables and chairs on the beach.

Wok N Roll ★ (www.woknrollonline.com; ☏ **2653-0156**), a half-block inland from Zully Mar along the road that leads to Playa Langosta, is a lively, open-air affair, with a big menu of Asian cuisine. For pizzas, I recommend **La Baula ★** (☏ **2653-1450**), another open-air place, on the road to Dragonfly (see below), and for Mexican fare and good breakfast burritos, try **Green Papaya Taco Bar** (☏ **2653-0863**), just across the street. If you want sushi, head to the **Bamboo Sushi Club ★** (☏ **2653-4519**), on the main road, near the turnoff for Langosta. And, for hearty steaks and Argentinean fare, try **Patagonia** (☏ **2653-0612**), located right across from the Tamarindo Diria Hotel.

Finally, if you're staying in a condo, or just too lazy to head out for a meal, **Tico To Go** (http://ticotogo.com; ☏ **800/8426-8646**) offers up delivery service from a wide range of local restaurants.

Carlos & Carlos ★ ITALIAN The sister restaurant to a Chicago area staple of the same name, Carlos & Carlos is Northern Italian specialist, which means the pastas are primo. The black Angel Hair pasta with shrimp and lobster is one of the most popular items on the menu, as is the fresh mahi-mahi. For meat lovers, the filet mignon with porcini mushrooms is excellent. And for dessert try their take on the local favorite Tres Leches ("Three Milks"), a sweet cake soaked in plain milk, condensed milk and caramelized *dulce de leche*. The restaurant is one of the few enclosed and air-conditioned options in town.

On the road to Playa Langosta. ☏ **2653-0862.** Reservations recommended during the high season. Main courses $14–$26. Daily 5–10pm

Dragonfly Bar & Grill ★★ INTERNATIONAL/FUSION New Canadian owners bought Dragonfly in April 2015, but say they plan to keep the current chef, good news since he's quite accomplished. His menu features spices and flavors from around the world with prominent influences from the Pacific Rim and southwestern United States. So you might find yourself dining on thick-cut pork loin crusted in panko and served with a brandy-Dijon cream sauce or a similarly creative fish dish. Portions are large, so don't be afraid to share. The look of the place is as fun as the food: A zinc roof is held high by columns made from locally farmed tree trunks, and finished underneath with woven mats and thin bamboo. The bar serves up fab cocktails, sometimes to live music.

Down a dirt road behind the Hotel Pasatiempo. www.dragonflybarandgrill.com. ☏ **2653-1506.** Reservations recommended. Main courses C5,500–C9,500. Mon–Sat 6–9:30pm.

Pangas Beach Club ★★★ SEAFOOD/INTERNATIONAL Chef Jean-Luc Taulere had a very successful run at Mar y Sol restaurant in Playa Flamingo, but real estate issues forced him to close up shop there—much to the betterment of the dining scene in Tamarindo. Located on the main road near the northern end of town, his current resto lets out on to the beach, right about where the ocean meets the estuary, a scenic spot. Heavy wooden tables are spread on hard-packed sand under tall coconut trees, which are strung with rope lighting and bare bulbs giving this place a rustically romantic feel by night. While fresh seafood is the specialty here, the steak tenderloin cooked at the table on a hot volcanic stone is the sleeper hit here. Breakfast and lunch are also served.

On the waterfront, north end of Tamarindo. www.lasmareas.com/pangas-beach-club. © **2653-0024.** Reservations recommended. Main courses C7,500–C18,000. Mon–Thurs noon–10pm and Sun 9am–10pm.

Season's by Shlomy ★★ INTERNATIONAL   Cordon Bleu–trained chef and owner Shlomy Koren began his time in Tamarindo at Pachangas. But for the past 5 years or so he's been serving up his tasty Mediterranean-inspired cuisine out of a small kitchen at the Hotel Arco Iris (p. 272). Not exactly a show kitchen, but there is a small service window and the door is always open, so it is possible and fun to watch Shlomy and crew at work. I recommend pretty much anything and everything on the menu, but find myself going back for the rice-paper-wrapped red snapper with a sun-dried-tomato tapenade and lemon-chili sauce. Still, it's hard to get too attached to any one dish, as the menu changes regularly, with daily specials and seasonal variations.

Inside the Hotel Arco Iris. www.seasonstamarindo.com. © **8368-6983.** Reservations recommended. Main courses $18–$19. No credit cards. Mon–Sat 6–10pm.

Shopping

Tamarindo's main boulevard is awash in souvenir stands, art galleries, jewelry stores, and clothing boutiques. For original beachwear and jewelry, try **Azul Profundo** ★ (www.azulprofundoboutique.com; © **2653-0395**), in the Plaza Tamarindo shopping center. The modern **Garden Plaza** shopping center, near the entrance to town, has several high-end shops, as well as a massive **Automercado** (supermarket).

Pretty Pots

The lack of any longstanding local arts and crafts tradition across Costa Rica is often lamented. One of the outstanding exceptions to this rule is the small village of Guaitíl, located on the outskirts of the provincial capital of Santa Cruz. The small central plaza—actually a soccer field—of this village is ringed with craft shops and artisan stands selling a wide range of ceramic wares. Most are low-fired relatively soft clay pieces, with traditional Chorotega indigenous design motifs. All of the local tour agencies offer day trips to Guaitíl, or you can drive there yourself, by heading first to Santa Cruz, and then taking the well-marked turnoff for Guaitíl, just south of the city, on the road to Nicoya.

Entertainment & Nightlife

As a popular surfer destination, Tamarindo has a raging nightlife scene. The most happening bars in town are **El Garito** ★★ (© **2653-2017**), located about a block inland, on the road leading toward Playa Langosta, and **Aqua** ★ (© **8934-2896**), on the main road through town. Other popular spots throughout the week include the **Crazy Monkey Bar** at the Best Western Tamarindo Vista Villas (© **2653-0114**), and the **Dragonfly Bar & Grill** (p. 275). For a chill-out dance party, try the **Voodoo Lounge** (© **2653-0100**); those looking for a rocking sports bar can head to **Sharky's** ★★ (© **8918-4968**). These latter two places are just across from each other, a little up the road that heads to Playa Langosta. The best casino in town is at the **Barceló Playa Langosta** (© **2653-0363**) resort down in Playa Langosta.

En Route South: Playa Avellanas & Playa Negra

Heading south from Tamarindo are several as-yet-undeveloped beaches, most of which are quite popular with surfers. Beyond Tamarindo and Playa Langosta are **Playa Avellanas** and **Playa Negra,** both with a few basic surfer cabinas, and little else. To locate the hotels and restaurants listed below, see the map "Around Tamarindo," on p. 267.

WHERE TO STAY

The **Mono Congo Lodge** (www.monocongolodge.com; © **2652-9261**), just outside of Playa Negra, is a rustic but plush option in a forested setting a few hundred yards from the water. About a 15- to 20-minute drive inland is **Los Altos de Eros** ★ (www.losaltosdeeros.com; © **8850-4222**), a small, adults-only, luxury hotel and spa.

In addition to the JW Marriott (see below), the large golf, residential, and vacation resort complex of **Hacienda Pinilla** (www.haciendapinilla.com; © **2681-4318**) features a couple of small hotels and condo rental units.

Expensive

JW Marriott Guanacaste Resort & Spa ★★★   This handsome, resort is built around a massive pool (claimed to be the largest in Central America) and fronts a gorgeous, but decidedly small patch of soft white sand beach. The rooms are ample and well equipped, with fine dark wood furnishings and red tile floors set in a herringbone pattern. Guests get some of the plushest bathrobes I've ever fondled. Every room has a large balcony or patio though some of the patios, open on to heavily trafficked walkways (potted plants, palms, and bamboo have been placed to try to provide some privacy). The best rooms have ocean and sunset views. The various dining options include a semi-formal steakhouse and contemporary Asian Fusion restaurant. The hotel runs a regular shuttle to nearby Playa

Langosta, where guests have access to a small beach club, with a pool, showers, bathrooms, restaurant, and bar, as well as boogie and surf board rental.

Hacienda Pinilla, Guanacaste. www.marriott.com. ✆ **888/236-2427** in the U.S. and Canada, or 2681-2000. 310 units. $289–$635 double; $483 and up suite. **Amenities:** 4 restaurants; bar; babysitting; children's programs; championship 18-hole golf course nearby; large health club and spa; massive outdoor pool; room service; smoke-free rooms; tennis courts nearby; watersports equipment; Wi-Fi for a fee.

Moderate

In addition to the places listed below, **Villa Deevena** (www.villadeevena. com; ✆ **2653-2328**) offers up six cool, comfortable and well-appointed rooms in a quiet setting, a few hundred yards from the beach at Playa Negra.

Cabinas Las Olas ★ This is the only hotel in Playa Avellanas with direct beach access, making it surfers' fave, as a range of gnarly breaks stretch up and down the white sand beach in each direction. The five duplex buildings that house the rooms are actually located a hundred yards or so inland under tall native trees and reached via a raised walkway through a mangrove reserve. The rooms themselves are fairly plain and basic, but they are very spacious, and feature a private little veranda with hammock that is perfect for an afternoon siesta.

Playa Avellanas, Guanacaste. www.cabinaslasolas.co.cr. ✆ **2652-9315.** 10 units. $100 double. Taxes an breakfast included. **Amenities:** Restaurant; bar; bike rentals; limited watersports equipment rentals; free Wi-Fi.

Hotel Playa Negra ★ This small collection of hexagonal thatch-roofed concrete bungalows is just steps away from Playa Negra, a legendary right-handed point break that was made famous in the surf film classic "Endless Summer II." As with Cabinas Las Olas (above), Hotel Playa Negra caters to surfers, and the rooms and services offered are rather basic. Most of the beds are built-in concrete affairs, although the mattresses are comfortable. The tables at the simple seafood and Costa Rican-style restaurant and bar have prime views of the wave and action.

Playa Negra, Guanacaste. www.playanegra.com. ✆ **2652-9134.** 17 units. $100 bungalow; $150 bungalow suite. Rates higher during peak periods. **Amenities:** Restaurant; bar; midsize outdoor pool; Wi-Fi.

WHERE TO DINE

In addition to those listed below, the restaurants inside the **JW Marriott** resort (p. 277) are excellent, and open to the general public, while the restaurant at **Villa Deevena** (see above), in Playa Negra, is also first rate.

Lola's ★★★ INTERNATIONAL/SEAFOOD Named for the owner's pet pig (who sometimes frolics in the waves as diners watch), this quintessential beach bar and restaurant sits on a patch of land and sand fronting the quiet and underdeveloped Playa Avellanas beach. The

Belgian and American owners serve up hearty, fresh food (like seared tuna atop salad with an Asian dressing) on homemade heavy wooden tables and chairs underneath the shade of palm trees and large linen umbrellas. Lola's is extremely popular, especially on weekends, so be prepared to wait occasionally for food or a table (sorry, no reservations). When you're finished, and if you're really lucky, you might snag a siesta in one of the hammocks strung between the many coconut palms.

On the beach, Playa Avellanas. ℂ **2652-9097.** Main courses $12–$18. Tues–Sun 9am–sunset.

PLAYA JUNQUILLAL ★

30km (19 miles) W of Santa Cruz; 20km (12 miles) S of Tamarindo

A long, windswept beach that, for most of its length, is backed by grasslands, Playa Junquillal remains mostly undiscovered on an increasingly crowded coast. With no village to speak of here and a rough road, this is a good place to get away from it all and enjoy some unfettered time on a nearly deserted beach. The long stretch of white sand is great for strolling, and the sunsets are superb. When the waves are big, this beach is great for surfing, but can be a little dangerous for swimming. When it's calm, jump right in.

Essentials

GETTING THERE & DEPARTING **By Plane:** The nearest airport with regularly scheduled flights is in Tamarindo (p. 263). You can arrange a taxi from the airport to Playa Junquillal. The ride should take around 40 minutes and cost about $50 to $70.

By Car: From San José, you can either take the Interamerican Highway (CR1) north from downtown San José, or first head west out of the city on the San José–Caldera Highway (CR27). This latter route is a faster and flatter drive. When you reach Caldera on this route, follow the signs to Puntarenas, Liberia, and the Interamerican Highway (CR1). This will lead you to the unmarked entrance to CR1. You'll want to pass under the bridge and follow the on-ramp, which will put you on the highway heading north. Forty-seven kilometers (29 miles) past the Puntarenas on-ramp, you'll see signs and the turnoff for the La Amistad Bridge. After crossing the river, follow the signs for Nicoya and Santa Cruz. Just after leaving the main intersection for Santa Cruz, you'll see a marked turnoff for Playa Junquillal, Ostional, and Tamarindo. The road is paved for 14km (8½ miles), until the tiny village of Veintesiete de Abril. From here, it's another rough 18km (11 miles) to Playa Junquillal.

From Liberia, head south to Santa Cruz on the main road to all the beach towns, passing through Filadelfia and Belén. Then follow the directions above from Santa Cruz.

By Bus: To get here by bus, you must first head to Santa Cruz and, from there, take another bus to Playa Junquillal. Buses depart San José for Santa Cruz roughly every 2 hours between 7:15am and 6pm from the **Tralapa** bus station (✆ **2221-7202**) at Calle 20 between avenidas 3 and 5, and from the **Alfaro** bus station (www.empresaalfaro.com; ✆ **2222-2666**) at Calle 14 between avenidas 3 and 5. The 4-hour trip is C5,425.

Buses leave Santa Cruz for Junquillal about 6 times daily, roughly every 2 hours between 5am and 6pm from the town's central plaza. The ride takes about 1 hour, and the one-way fare is C1,100. Buses depart Playa Junquillal for Santa Cruz daily pretty much just after they arrive.

Always check with your hotel in advance as the schedule of buses between Junquillal and

Playa Junquillal.

Santa Cruz is notoriously fickle. If you miss the connection, or there's no bus running, you can hire a taxi for the trip to Junquillal for $90 to $100. From Tamarindo, a taxi should cost $55 to $70.

Exploring Playa Junquillal

Other than walking on the beach, surfing, swimming when the surf isn't too strong, and exploring tide pools, there isn't much to do here—which is just fine with me. This beach is ideal for anyone who wants to relax without any distractions. Bring a few good books. If you have a car, you can explore the coastline just north and south of here.

Junquillal is a nesting site for both olive ridley and leatherback turtles, although conservation efforts and organized turtle watching tours are both in their infancy here.

For surfers, the Junquillal beach break is often pretty good. I've also heard that if you look hard enough, a few hidden reef and point breaks are around. However, be careful here, as the beach and rip currents are often a bit rough for casual swimming.

Several sportfishing boats operate out of Playa Junquillal. Inquire at your hotel or ask at the Iguanazul Hotel. To rent a mountain bike, you can also check in at the Iguanazul.

Where to Stay & Dine

In addition to the two hotels mentioned below, **Hotel & Pizzería Tatanka** (www.hoteltatanka.com; © **866/498-0824** in the U.S. and Canada, or 2658-8426 in Costa Rica) offers up well-designed rooms at very reasonable rates as well as excellent wood-oven pizzas and fresh seafood. It's near the Iguanazul Hotel on your left as you come into Junquillal, and also has good ocean and sunset views. Budgeteers might consider **Camping Los Malinches** (© **8981-5773**), which has wonderful campsites on fluffy grass amid manicured gardens set on a bluff above the beach. Camping costs C3,500 per person, and includes restroom and shower privileges. You'll see a sign on the right as you drive toward Playa Junquillal, a little bit beyond the Iguanazul Hotel. The campground is about 1km (½ mile) down this dirt road. These folks also have some simple, rustic rooms.

Hotel Hibiscus ★   This long-established, German-owned hotel is located just a few hundred feet or so from the beach at Playa Junquillal. The shady grounds, tropical gardens and cozy rooms are all immaculately maintained. The rooms themselves feature bright white walls and polished red-tile floors. They all have air-conditioning, but it will cost you an extra $8 daily to use it. The good on-site restaurant offers a range of international and local fare, and serves up the best Wiener Schnitzel and Spatzle in Guanacaste.

Playa Junquillal, Guanacaste. www.hibiscus-info.com. © **2658-8437.** 5 units. $40–$60 double. Rates include taxes. **Amenities:** Restaurant.

Iguanazul Hotel ★   This intimate and isolated hotel has an idyllic settings, on a high, flat bluff and steep grassy cliff overlooking the Pacific Ocean at the north end of Playa Junquillal. It's under new management as of January 2015, and all indications are that the owners are making a serious effort to update the worn and outdated furnishings and decor, and improve the overall food and service. Hopefully the work will be done by the time you arrive as this is a charming spot, with a free-form pool that has a coconut palm growing from a tiny island at its center.

Playa Junquillal, Guanacaste. www.hoteliguanazul.com. © **2658-8124.** 24 units. $99–$139 double. **Amenities:** Restaurant; bar; outdoor pool; small spa; free Wi-Fi.

9

PUNTARENAS & THE NICOYA PENINSULA

The beaches of the Nicoya Peninsula don't get nearly as much attention or traffic as those to the north in Guanacaste. However, they are just as stunning, varied, and rewarding. Montezuma, with its jungle waterfalls and gentle surf, was the first beach destination out this way to capture any attention. However, it's been eclipsed by the increasingly trendy hot spots of Malpaís and Santa Teresa.

Farther up the peninsula lie the beaches of **Playa Sámara** and **Playa Nosara.** With easy access via paved roads and the time-saving La Amistad Bridge, Playa Sámara is one of the coastline's more popular destinations, especially with Ticos looking for an easy weekend getaway. Just north of Sámara, Nosara and its neighboring beaches remain remote and sparsely visited, thanks in large part to the horrendous dirt road that separates these distinctly different destinations. However, Nosara is widely known and coveted as one of the country's top **surf spots,** with a host of different beach and point breaks from which to choose.

Nearby **Puntarenas** was once Costa Rica's principal Pacific port. The town bustled and hummed with commerce, fishermen, coffee brokers, and a weekend rush of urban dwellers enjoying some sun and fun at one of the closest beaches to San José. Today, Puntarenas is a run-down shell of its former self. Still, it remains a major fishing port, and the main gateway to the isolated and coveted beaches of the Nicoya Peninsula.

THE best PUNTARENAS & THE NICOYA PENINSULA TRAVEL EXPERIENCES

o **Taking a Dip in the Pool at the Foot of Montezuma Waterfall:** Nestled in thick forest, the Montezuma waterfall features a large, deep, and cool pool at its base—perfect for swimming. The hike in is pretty awesome as well. See p. 299.

o **Getting Your Yoga On:** The Nicoya Peninsula is home to several of the country's top yoga retreat centers. **Pranamar Villas & Yoga Retreat** (p. 311) in Santa Teresa, **Anamaya Resort** (p. 302) in Montezuma, and the **Nosara Yoga Institute** (p. 326) are all top-notch choices. See below for even more options.

FACING PAGE: **Sunset over Manuel Antonio Public Beach in Puntarenas.**

- **Having Playa Barrigona (Almost) to Yourself:** Access is a bit rough, especially in the rainy season, but if you're feeling adventurous, head to Playa Barrigona, a largely undiscovered gem of white sand and clear waters. You'll probably need local help in finding the unmarked entrance, but it's worth it. See p. 318.

- **Going Deep (Underground) at Barra Honda:** Strap on a headlamp and some climbing gear and descend into the underworld at **Barra Honda National Park.** After exploring the nooks and crannies of Terciopelo Cave, take a refreshing dip in La Cascada. See p. 319.

- **Mingling with the Hip & Famous in Malpaís & Santa Teresa:** Arguably the most happening of Costa Rica's beach hot spots, **Malpaís and Santa Teresa** are the country's best destinations for celebrity sightings. Even if you don't bump into Leo DiCaprio, Flea, or Tom & Giselle, you can wander the miles of nearly deserted beaches and enjoy the beautiful sunsets. See p. 306.

PUNTARENAS

115km (71 miles) W of San José; 191km (118 miles) S of Liberia; 75km (47 miles) N of Playa de Jacó

They say you can't put lipstick on a pig, and this has proven true for Puntarenas. Despite serious investment and the steady influx of cruise ship passengers, Puntarenas can't seem to shed its image as a rough-and-tumble, perennially run-down port town. While the seafront **Paseo de los Turistas (Tourist Walk)** has a string of restaurants and souvenir

Puntarenas's Catholic church.

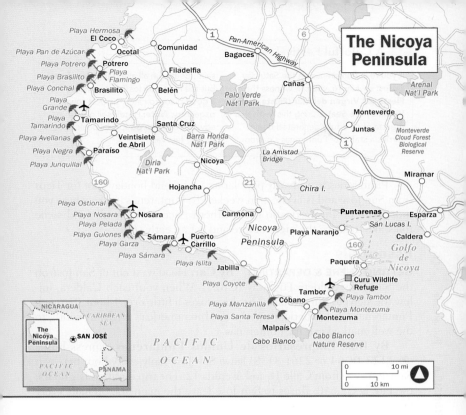

stands, this town has little to interest visitors, and the beach here pales in comparison to almost any other beach destination in the country.

A 16km (10-mile) spit of land jutting into the Gulf of Nicoya, Puntarenas was once Costa Rica's busiest port, but that changed drastically when the government inaugurated nearby Puerto Caldera, a modern container port facility. After losing its shipping business, the city has survived primarily on commercial fishing.

You can reach Puntarenas (on a good day, with little traffic) in little more than an hour by car from San José, which makes it one of the closest beaches to the capital. A long, straight stretch of sand with gentle surf, the beach is backed for most of its length by the Paseo de los Turistas. Across a wide boulevard from the Paseo de los Turistas are hotels, restaurants, bars, discos, and shops. The sunsets and the views across the Gulf of Nicoya are quite beautiful, and a cooling breeze usually blows in off the water. All around town, you'll find unusual old buildings, reminders of the important role that Puntarenas once played in Costa Rican history. It was from here that much of the Central Valley's coffee crop was once shipped, and while the coffee barons in the highlands were getting rich, so were the merchants of Puntarenas.

Puntarenas is primarily popular as a weekend holiday spot for Ticos from San José and is liveliest on weekends. Puntarenas is also where you must pick up the ferries to the southern Nicoya Peninsula, and some folks like to arrive the night before and get an early start.

Essentials

GETTING THERE & DEPARTING **By Car:** Head west out of San José on the San José–Caldera Highway (CR27). When you reach Caldera, follow the signs to Puntarenas. The drive takes a little over 1 hour. To reach Puntarenas from Liberia, just take the Interamerican Highway south, to the well-marked exit for Puntarenas.

By Bus: Empresarios de Unidos Puntarenas express buses (© **2222-0064** or 2261-3138) leave San José daily every hour between 6am and 7pm from Calle 16 and Avenida 12. The trip duration is 2 hours; the fare is C2,640. Buses to San José leave the main station daily every hour between 6am and 7pm.

The main Puntarenas bus station is cater-cornered to the main pier on the Paseo de los Turistas. Buses to Quepos and Manuel Antonio leave the main station daily at 5, 7, 9, and 10:30am and 1, 2:30, and 4:30pm. The trip's duration is 1 hour; the fare is C2,430. There are also about three daily buses between Puntarenas and Monteverde and Santa Elena.

By Ferry: See "Playa Tambor" or "Playa Montezuma," below, for information on crossing to and returning from Puntarenas from Paquera or Naranjo on the Nicoya Peninsula.

GETTING AROUND If you need a taxi, call **Coopetico** (© **2663-2020**).

CITY LAYOUT Puntarenas is built on a long, narrow sand spit that stretches 16km (10 miles) out into the Gulf of Nicoya and is marked by only five streets at its widest. The north side of town faces an estuary, and the south side faces the mouth of the gulf. The Paseo de los Turistas is on the south side of town, beginning at the pier and extending out to the point. The ferry docks for the Nicoya Peninsula are near the far end of town, as are the bus station and market.

FAST FACTS   Several banks and general markets are all within a 2-block radius of the town's small church and central park. The town's main post office can be found here as well.

The **Hospital Monseñor Sanabria** (© **2663-0033**), on the outskirts of downtown, is the largest and best-equipped hospital in this region. However, it was severely damaged in a 2013 earthquake, and reparations are slow going. Still, the hospital is up and running.

Exploring Puntarenas

Many folks are spooked by Puntarenas's image as a rough and dangerous port town, but the city's biggest challenge to tourists is probably the stifling midday heat. If the heat's not too bad, take a walk along the ocean-facing **Paseo de los Turistas,** which feels a bit like a Florida beach town from the 1950s. The hotels here range in style from converted old wooden homes with bright gingerbread trim to modern concrete monstrosities to tasteful Art Deco relics that need a new coat of paint.

If you venture into the center of the city, be sure to check out the **central plaza around the Catholic Church.** The large, stone church itself is interesting because it has portholes for windows, reflecting the city's maritime tradition. In addition, it's one of the few churches in the country with a front entry facing east (most face west). Here you'll also find the city's cultural center, **La Casa de la Cultura** (© **2661-1394**). In addition to rotating exhibits and the occasional theater performance or poetry reading, this place houses the **Museo Histórico** (© **2661-1394**), a small museum on the city's history, especially its maritime history, with exhibits in both English and Spanish. Admission is free, and it's open Monday to Saturday from 8am to 4pm. If you're looking for a shady spot some inviting benches are in a little park off the north side of the church.

The largest attraction in town is the **Parque Marino del Pacífico** (**Pacific Marine Park;** www.parquemarino.org; © **2661-5272**), a collection of saltwater aquariums highlighting the sea life of Costa Rica. Of the 23 separate tanks, the largest re-creates the undersea environment of Isla del Coco. Still, this park has a neglected and run-down feel to it. It's 2 blocks east of the main cruise ship terminal and is open Tuesday through Sunday from 9am to 4:30pm. Admission is $10 for adults and $5 for children 11 and under.

If you want to go swimming, the gulf waters in front of Puntarenas are perfectly safe (pollution had been a problem for many years), although the beach is not very attractive. Some folks choose to head a few kilometers south of town, to **Playa Doña Aña,** a popular local beach with picnic tables, roadside vendors, and a couple of *sodas* (diners). If you head a little farther south, you will come to **Playa Tivives,** which is virtually unvisited by tourists, but quite popular with Ticos, many of whom have beach houses up and down this long, brown-sand beach. Surfers should check out the beach break here or head to the mouth of the Barranca River, which boasts an amazingly long left break. Still, surfers and swimmers should be careful; crocodiles live in both the Barranca and Tivives river mouths, and I'd be wary of pollution in the waters emptying out of the rivers here.

If you don't want to swim in the gulf and your hotel doesn't have a pool, head to the **San Lucas Beach Club** (www.sanlucasbeachclub. com; ✆ **2661-3881**; daily 9am–5pm; C2,750). This misleadingly named attraction is actually a landlocked recreation complex with a large free-form pool and small snack bar. It's set at the end of the peninsula, with a view of the gulf.

Puntarenas isn't known as one of Costa Rica's prime sportfishing ports, but a few charter boats are usually available. Head to the docks and ask around or go to GetMyBoat.com. Rates (for up to six) are between $400 and $600 for a half-day and between $800 and $1,800 for a full day.

You can also take a yacht cruise through the tiny, uninhabited islands of the Guayabo, Negritos, and Pájaros Islands Biological Reserve. These cruises include a lunch buffet and a relaxing stop on beautiful and undeveloped **Tortuga Island ★**, where you can swim, snorkel, and sunbathe. The water is clear blue, and the sand is bright white. However, this trip has surged in popularity, and many cruises have a cattle-car feel.

Calypso Tours ★ (www.calypsocruises.com; ✆ **855/855-1975** in the U.S. and Canada, or 2256-2727 in Costa Rica) is the most reputable company that cruises out of Puntarenas. In addition to **Tortuga Island** trips, Calypso Tours takes folks to its own private nature reserve at **Punta Coral** or on a sunset dinner cruise with stargazing. Either cruise will run you $145 per person, $135 students with valid ID. The company provides daily pickups from San José, Manuel Antonio, Jacó, and Monteverde, and you can use the day trip on the boat as your transfer or transportation option between any of these towns and destinations.

Where to Stay

In addition to the places mentioned below, the **Double Tree Resort by Hilton Puntarenas** (www.puntarenas.doubletree.com; ✆ **800/445-8667** in the U.S. and Canada, or 2663-0808 in Costa Rica) is an all-inclusive resort set on a decidedly unspectacular patch of sand. While the accommodations and service are certainly acceptable, it's still not a top beach resort pick in my book.

MODERATE

Hotel Las Brisas ★   There's a touch of a Greek theme to some of the design elements and menu items here, thanks to the charming owner's mix of American and Greek heritage. The rooms are simple, but very

DIVING TRIPS TO isla del coco

This little speck of land located some 480km (300 miles) off the Pacific coast was a prime pirate hide-out and refueling station. Robert Louis Stevenson most likely modeled "Treasure Island" on Cocos. Sir Francis Drake, Captain Edward Davis, William Dampier, and Mary Welch are just some of the famous corsairs who dropped anchor in the calm harbors of this Pacific pearl. They allegedly left troves of buried loot, although scores of treasure hunters over several centuries have failed to unearth more than a smattering of the purported bounty. The Costa Rican flag was first raised here on September 15, 1869. Throughout its history, Isla del Coco has provided anchorage and fresh water to hundreds of ships and has entertained divers and dignitaries. (Franklin Delano Roosevelt visited it three times.) In 1978 it was declared a national park and protected area.

The clear, warm waters around Cocos are widely regarded as one of the most rewarding **dive destinations** ★★★ on the planet. This is a prime place to see schooling herds of scalloped hammerhead sharks. On my shallow-water checkout dive—normally, a perfunctory and uninspiring affair—I spotted my first hammerhead lurking just 4.5m (15 ft.) below me within 15 seconds after flipping into the water. Soon there were more, and soon they came much, much closer.

Other denizens of the waters around Isla del Coco include white- and silver-tipped reef sharks; marbled, manta, eagle, and mobula rays; moray and spotted eels; octopi; spiny and slipper lobsters; hawksbill turtles; squirrel fish, trigger fish, and angelfish; surgeon fish, trumpet fish, grouper, grunts, snapper, jack, and tangs; and more. Two of the more spectacular underwater residents here include the red-lipped batfish and the frogfish.

Most diving at Cocos is relatively deep (26–35m/85–115 ft.), often with strong currents and choppy swells to deal with—not to mention all those sharks. This is not a trip for novice divers.

The perimeter of Isla del Coco is ringed by steep, forested cliffs punctuated by dozens of majestic waterfalls cascading down in stages or steady streams for hundreds of feet. The island itself has a series of trails that climb its steep hills and wind through its rainforest interior. Several endemic bird, reptile, and plant species here include the ubiquitous Cocos finch, which I spotted soon after landing onshore, and the wild Isla del Coco pig.

With just a small ranger station housing a handful of national park guards, Isla del Coco is essentially uninhabited. Visitors come on a variety of boats. It's a long trip: Most vessels take 30 to 36 hours to reach Cocos.

Both **Aggressor Fleet Limited** (www.aggressor.com; ☎ **800/348-2628**) and **Undersea Hunter** (www.underseahunter.com; ☎ **800/203-2120** in the U.S., or 2228-6613 in Costa Rica) regularly run dive trips to Isla del Coco from Puntarenas.

spacious and clean. The hotel has plenty of secure parking, if you're waiting for the next day's ferry, as well as a refreshing small pool.

Paseo de los Turistas, Puntarenas. www.lasbrisashotelcr.com. ☎ **2661-4040.** 30 units. C59,500–C79,500 double. Rates include taxes and breakfast. **Amenities:** Restaurant; bar; small outdoor pool; free Wi-Fi.

INEXPENSIVE

Apartotel Alamar ★★ If you need to spend a night or more in Puntarenas, this should be your top choice. The staff is friendly and helpful, the property is extremely well-maintained and, along with the standard hotel rooms (modest-looking, but spotless and comfortable), are one- and two-bedroom condo-style units with full kitchens. The hotel is located right on the Paseo de los Turistas, out toward the western end of the peninsula, directly across the street from the beach, and walking distance to several good restaurants. It boasts small, rectangular pool and unheated Jacuzzi.

Paseo de los Turistas, Puntarenas. www.alamarcr.com. ℃ **2661-4343.** 34 units. C45,000–C54,000 double, C61,000-C83,000 suite. Rates include taxes and breakfast buffet. **Amenities:** Restaurant; bar; Jacuzzi; small outdoor pool; free Wi-Fi.

Hotel La Punta ★ Another solid budget option, Hotel La Punta is one of the closest hotels to the ferry docks (on the downside, that means it's on the estuary side of the peninsula, so has no sea views and is a longer walk to the beach). Rooms feature wooden beds and red tile floors giving them a hint of colonial era charm. A small kidney-shaped pool with a broad surrounding deck and tall palm trees for shade, offers some cooling respite from the grueling midday heat.

Puntarenas (½ block south of the ferry terminal). www.hotellapunta.net. ℃ **2661-0696.** 8 units. C42,500 double. **Amenities:** Small outdoor pool.

Where to Dine

You're in a seaport, so try some of the local catch. Corvina (sea bass) is the most popular offering, and it's served in various forms and preparations. My favorite dish on a hot afternoon is *ceviche,* and you'll find that just about every restaurant in town serves it.

The most economical option is to pull up a table at one of the many open-air *sodas* along the Paseo de los Turistas (sandwiches for around $2, a fish filet with rice and beans for about $4, plus ice cream, snacks, and more). If you want seafood in a slightly more formal atmosphere, try the **Jardín Cervecero, Capitán Moreno, Casa de los Mariscos,** or the open-air **Delicias del Puerto,** all located on the Paseo de los Turistas.

Also check out **Shrimp Shack** (℃ **2661-0585;** Tues–Thurs 11am–5pm, Fri–Sat 11am–8pm) run by the staff of Calypso Tours out of their offices on the water on the mangrove side of the peninsula, a half-block west of the BAC San Jose bank in downtown. They offer a wide range of shrimp dishes, plus burgers, salads and wraps.

Casa Almendro ★★ STEAK/SEAFOOD Occupying the former home of La Yunta (see below), this converted residence has been given a major makeover. Today, you'll climb wide varnished wood entrance steps and grab a varnished wood table along the (you know what's coming)

A Frosty Churchill

No one should leave Puntarenas without trying a "Churchill." Sold by scores of vendors out of makeshift carts, food trucks and kiosks all along the Paseo de los Turistas, these concoctions are made from freshly shaved ice smothered with a wide range of toppings—usually sweet syrup, condensed milk, or fruit salad. Some also come with ice cream and some sort of sweet cookie or cracker. Most of the sellers serve them in plastic cups, but if you look around, you might find them in large soda fountain style glasses, which I prefer. Dating to at least the 1940s, the local legend claims that the original creator of these refreshing sweet treats bore a striking resemblance to the then British Prime Minister.

varnished wood railing fronting the beach to enjoy excellent views of the water with your meal. It's all quite nice as is the food: *arroz con mariscos* (fish with seafood) loaded with fresh local catch, or the *filete al diablo* (Devil's fish filet), a boneless fillet of corvina in a well-seasoned tomato sauce, with jalapeños for kick. There are also excellent grilled steak and chicken options, as well as a small children's menu.
Corner of Avenida 4 and Calle 21, Paseo de los Turistas. © **2661-0900.** Main courses C4,300–C11,000. Daily 10am–11pm.

La Yunta Steakhouse ★ STEAK/SEAFOOD   For decades now, this has been my go-to restaurant in Puntarenas, but most of that was due to the lovely ambience of its former home, now occupied by the Casa Almendro (see above). Its new location, a single story, street-level affair, lacks the charm and view that it once had. Still, it's a solid operation serving up good fare. Despite the name, there's probably more seafood than meat on the menu here, and both are good choices. The more traditional standards are now accompanied by contemporary choices like wraps and tempura fried shrimp.
Avenida 4, btw. calles 19 and 21, Paseo de los Turistas. © **2661-3216.** Main courses C3,500–C15,000. Daily 10am–midnight.

PLAYA TAMBOR
150–168km (93–104 miles) W of San José (not including ferry ride); 20km (12 miles) S of Paquera; 38km (24 miles) S of Naranjo

Playa Tambor was the site of Costa Rica's first large-scale all-inclusive resort, the Barceló Playa Tambor Beach Resort. Despite big plans, the resort and surrounding area have never really taken off. Today, Tambor has a forgotten, isolated feel to it. Part of the blame lies with the beach itself. Playa Tambor is a long, gently curving stretch of beach protected on either end by rocky headlands (making this a good beach for swimming). However, the sand is an unattractive dull gray-brown color, and often receives large amounts of flotsam and jetsam from the sea. Playa Tambor pales in comparison to the beaches located farther south along the Nicoya Peninsula.

However, Tambor is the site of the only major commuter airport on the southern Nicoya Peninsula, and you'll be arriving and departing here if you choose to visit Montezuma, Malpaís, or Santa Teresa by air.

Essentials

GETTING THERE & DEPARTING

By Plane: Sansa (www.flysansa. com; ✆ **877/767-2672** in the U.S. and Canada, or 2290-4100 in Costa Rica) and **Nature Air** (www. natureair.com; ✆ **800/235-9272** in the U.S. and Canada, or 2299- 6000 in Costa Rica) both have several flights daily to a small airstrip in **Tambor airport** (airport code: TMU; no phone). The flight is about 30 minutes, and fares range from $99 to $115, one-way.

Playa Tambor.

By Car: The traditional route here is to drive to Puntarenas and catch the ferry to either Naranjo or Paquera. Tambor is about 30 minutes south of Paquera and about an hour and 20 minutes south of Naranjo. The road from Paquera to Tambor is paved and taking the Paquera ferry will save you time and some rough, dusty driving. The road from Naranjo to Paquera is all dirt and gravel and often in very bad shape. For directions on driving to Puntarenas, see p. 286.

Naviera Tambor (www.navieratambor.com; ✆ **2661-2084**) car ferries to Paquera leave Puntarenas at 5, 9 and 11am and 2, 5, and 8:30pm. The trip takes 1½ hours. The fare is C11,400 per car, including the driver; C810 for each additional adult, and C485 for children. I recommend arriving early during the peak season and on weekends because lines can be long; if you miss the ferry, you'll have to wait 2 hours or more for the next one. Moreover, the ferry schedule changes frequently, with fewer ferries during the low season, and the occasional extra ferry added during the high season to meet demand. It's always best to check in advance.

The car ferry from Paquera to Puntarenas leaves at 5:30, 9 and 11am and 2, 5, and 8pm. *Note:* If you have to wait for the ferry, try not to leave your car unattended, since break-ins are common.

The **Naranjo ferry** (www.coonatramar.com; © **2661-1069**) leaves daily at 6:30 and 10am and 2:30 and 7:30pm. The trip takes 1½ hours. Return ferries leave Naranjo for Puntarenas daily at 8am and 12:30, 5:30, and 9pm. The fare is C9,000 per car, including the driver; C1,005 for each additional adult; and C600 for children.

Another option is to drive via La Amistad Bridge over the Tempisque River. I recommend this route only when the ferries are on the fritz, or when the wait for the next car ferry is over 3 hours. (When the lines are long, you may not find room on the next departing ferry.) Although heading farther north and crossing the bridge is more circuitous, you'll be driving the whole time, which beats waiting around in the midday heat. To go this route, take the Interamerican Highway west from San José. Forty-seven kilometers (29 miles) past the turnoff for Puntarenas, turn left for La Amistad Bridge. After you cross the Tempisque River, head to Quebrada Honda and then south to Route 21, following signs for San Pablo, Jicaral, Lepanto, Playa Naranjo, and Paquera.

To drive to Tambor from Liberia, head out of town on the main road to the Guanacaste beaches, passing through Filadelfia, Santa Cruz, and Nicoya on your way toward the turnoff for La Amistad Bridge. Continue straight at this turnoff, and follow the directions for this route as listed above.

By Bus & Ferry: Transportes Cobano (© **2642-1112**) runs two daily direct buses between San José and Cóbano, dropping passengers off in Tambor en route. The buses leave from the Coca-Cola bus terminal at Calle 12 and Avenida 5 at 6am and 2pm. The fare is C6,900, including the ferry ride, and the trip takes a little over 4 hours.

Alternatively, it takes two buses and a ferry to get to Tambor. **Empresarios Unidos de Puntarenas** express buses (© **222-8321**) leave San José daily every hour between 6am and 7pm from Calle 16 and Avenida 12. Trip duration is 2 hours; the fare is C2,640. From Puntarenas, take the car ferry to Paquera mentioned above. A bus south to Montezuma (this will drop you off in Tambor) will be waiting to meet the ferry when it arrives in Paquera. The bus ride takes about 40 minutes; the fare is C1,195. Be careful not to take the Naranjo ferry because it does not meet with regular onward bus transportation to Tambor.

When you're ready to head back, buses originating in Montezuma, Cóbano, or Malpaís pass through Tambor roughly every 2 hours between 6am and 4:30pm. Theoretically, these should connect with a waiting ferry in Paquera. Total trip duration is 3½ hours. Buses to San José leave Puntarenas daily every hour between 5am and 8pm.

ORIENTATION Although there's a tiny village of Tambor, through which the main road passes, the hotels themselves are scattered along several kilometers, with Tango Mar (p. 296) definitely outside Tambor proper. You'll see signs for all these hotels as the road passes through and beyond Playa Tambor. If you need a bank, pharmacy, or post office, you'll have to head to nearby Cóbano.

A woodpecker at Curú Wildlife Refuge.

Exploring Tambor

Curú Wildlife Refuge ★★ (www.curuwildliferefuge.com; © **2641-0100;** $10/person per day admission), 16km (10 miles) north of Tambor, is this private reserve of (several) pretty, secluded beaches, as well as forests and mangrove swamps. This area is extremely rich in wildlife. Mantled howler and white-faced monkeys are often spotted here, and quite a few species of birds, including scarlet macaws (the refuge is actively involved in a macaw protection and repopulation effort). Horses are available to rent for $10 per hour. Typically, you'll ride, with a guide, for about an hour to a lovely beach, hang out on the sand for about an hour, and then ride back. Happily, you only get charged for the time you're actually on horseback, so trips run about $20. Some very rustic cabins are available with advance notice for $30 per person per day. Meals are $10. If you

Getting ready for bioluminescence kayak tours out of Curú.

Kayaking through the mangroves with Tambor Adventure.

don't have a car, you should arrange pickup with the staff who manage this refuge. Or you can contact **Turismo Curú** (www.curutourism.com; ℂ **2641-0004**), which specializes in guided tours to the refuge, as well as kayaking trips and other area adventures.

Both the hotels listed below offer horseback riding and various tours around this part of the peninsula and can arrange fishing and dive trips.

Where to Stay & Dine

Aside from the hotels listed here, a few inexpensive cabinas are available near the town of Tambor, at the southern end of the beach. Most are very rustic and basic, and charge around $10 per person. Another option is **Costa Coral** (www.hotelcostacoral.com; ℂ **2683-0105**), an attractive place with a good restaurant. *Downside:* It's set right off the busy main road, several hundred meters from the beach.

Paddle After Dark

The waters off of the Curú Wildlife Refuge are ripe with **bioluminescent dinoflagellates,** a plankton that emits light when moved or agitated. This creates an effect commonly known as bioluminescence. The phenomenon exists year-round here although it varies in intensity. The best timing for a visit is around a new moon in the dry season. Strong moonlight and muddy waters from runoff both diminish the effect. If interested in doing a nighttime kayak tour here contact **Bahia Rica Tours** (www.bahiarica.com; ℂ **2641-8111**). The tour costs $35 per person, or $25 per person for groups of 4 or more.

The **Barceló Playa Tambor Beach Resort** was Costa Rica's first all-inclusive resort, but its beach is mediocre, and the Barceló company has been accused of violating Costa Rica's environmental laws and mistreating workers. Although the resort is a major presence, I don't recommend it; better all-inclusives are available in Guanacaste.

Tambor Tropical ★   This is easily the best beach hotel in Playa Tambor, although there's really not much competition. Lodgings are in individual and two-story bungalows, huge octagonal affairs, with walls, floors, ceilings, and furnishings of brightly varnished local hardwoods. I don't know how they do it, but every time I visit it looks as if they just laid on a fresh coat. They also come with full kitchens. I prefer the second-floor rooms which feature huge wrap-around verandas facing the sea and offering up inspiring morning sunrise views. A small free-form pool is set under tall coconut palms and the beach is just a stone's throw away. The restaurant and bar are housed under a soaring thatch roof and serve up excellent fresh seafood, continental cuisine, and cocktails.

Tambor, Puntarenas. www.tambortropical.com. ℂ **866/890-2537** in the U.S., or 2683-0011 in Costa Rica. 14 units. $192–$260 double. Rates include continental breakfast. No children 16 and under. **Amenities:** Restaurant; bar; room service; small free-form outdoor pool and Jacuzzi; small spa; Wi-Fi.

Tango Mar Resort ★★   Very popular with honeymooners, Tango Mar fronts a beautiful white-sand beach, and is a short hike from a jungle waterfall that empties into a pool formed by a rock formation adjacent to the sea. Because of its extremely isolated location the beach feels like the private domain of the resort. Of the several pools here, one particularly gorgeous one is set just a few steps away from the surf. As for the colorful and well-appointed rooms and suites, those are honeymoon-worthy, too, set in several distinct buildings the sprawling grounds. Deluxe beachfront room have private ocean view balconies but for panoramic views, you can't beat the Tropical Suites, which are set on a high bluff and come with Jacuzzi tubs. The resort also has a 9-hole, par-3 golf course and two tennis courts. Villas around the grounds also for rent.

Playa Tambor, Puntarenas. www.tangomar.com. ℂ **800/297-4420** in the U.S., or 2683-0001 in Costa Rica. 45 units. 17 tropical suites, 6 deluxe, 5 bungalows, and 2 villas. $195–$250 double; $295 suite; $500–$1,150 villa. Rates include breakfast. **Amenities:** 2 Restaurants; 2 bars; bike rental; 9-hole par-3 and 4 golf course ($40 full-day greens fee); 4 outdoor pools; room service; small spa; 2 lighted tennis courts.

PLAYA MONTEZUMA ★★

166–184km (103–114 miles) W of San José (not including the ferry ride); 36km (22 miles) SE of Paquera; 54km (33 miles) S of Naranjo

For decades, this remote village and its surrounding beaches, forests, and waterfalls have enjoyed near-legendary status among backpackers, UFO seekers, hippie expatriates, natural healers, and European budget

Sunset at Playa Montezuma.

travelers. Although it maintains its alternative vibe, Montezuma is a great destination for all manner of travelers looking for a beach retreat surrounded by some stunning scenery and lush forests. Active pursuits abound, from hiking in the Cabo Blanco Absolute Nature Reserve to horseback riding to visiting a beachside waterfall. The natural beauty, miles of almost abandoned beaches, rich wildlife, and jungle waterfalls here are what first made Montezuma famous, and they continue to make this one of my favorite beach towns in Costa Rica.

Essentials

GETTING THERE & DEPARTING   By Plane: The nearest airport is in Tambor, 17km (11 miles) away (p. 292). Some of the hotels listed below might pick you up in Tambor for a reasonable fee. If not, you'll have to hire a taxi, which could cost anywhere between $40 and $50. **Taxis** are generally waiting to meet regularly scheduled planes, but if they aren't, call **Gilberto Rodríguez** (© **8826-9055;** gilbertotaxi@gmail.com).

By Car: The traditional route here is to first drive to Puntarenas and catch the ferry to either Naranjo or Paquera. Montezuma is about 30 minutes south of Tambor, 1 hour south of Paquera, and 2 hours south of Naranjo. The road from Paquera to Tambor is paved, and taking the Paquera ferry will save you time and some rough, dusty driving. The road from Naranjo to Paquera is all dirt and gravel and often in bad shape. For info on car ferries, see p. 292. For driving directions to Puntarenas, see p. 286.

To drive to Montezuma from Liberia, head out of town on the main road to the Guanacaste beaches, passing through Filadelfia, Santa Cruz, and Nicoya on your way toward the turnoff for La Amistad Bridge. Continue straight at this turnoff, and follow the directions for this route as listed above.

By Bus & Ferry: Transportes Cóbano (ℂ **2642-1112**) runs two daily direct buses between San José and Montezuma. The buses leave from the Coca-Cola bus terminal at Calle 12 and Avenida 5 at 6am and 2pm. Fare is C7,500, including the ferry. The trip takes a bit over 5 hours.

Alternatively, it takes two buses and a ferry ride to get to Montezuma. **Empresarios Unidos de Puntarenas** express buses (ℂ **2222-0064**) to Puntarenas leave San José daily every hour between 6am and 7pm from Calle 16 and Avenida 12. The trip takes 2 hours; the fare is C2,640. From Puntarenas, you can take the ferry to Paquera, mentioned on p. 292. A bus south to Montezuma will be waiting to meet the ferry when it arrives in Paquera. The bus ride takes about 1½ hours; the fare is C1,800. Be careful not to take the Naranjo ferry because it does not meet with regular onward bus transportation to Montezuma.

Buses are met by hordes of locals trying to corral you to one of the many budget hotels. Remember, they are getting a commission, so their information is biased. Not only that, they are often flat-out lying when they tell you the hotel you wanted to stay in is full.

When you're ready to head back, direct buses leave Montezuma daily at 6:30am and 2:30pm. Regular local buses to Paquera leave Cóbano roughly every 2 hours throughout the day starting around 4am. Buses to San José leave Puntarenas daily every hour between 6am and 7pm.

Buses Montezuma-Paquera: roughly every 2 hours starting between 5:30am and 5pm.

CITY LAYOUT As the winding mountain road that descends into Montezuma bottoms out, you turn left onto a small dirt road that defines the village proper. On this 1-block road, you will find El Sano Banano Village Cafe and, across from it, a small shaded park with plenty of tall trees, as well as a basketball court and children's playground. The bus stops at the end of this road. From here, hotels are scattered up and down the beach and around the village's few sand streets. Around the center of town are several tour agencies among the restaurants and souvenir stores.

Exploring Montezuma

The ocean here is a gorgeous royal blue, and idyllic beaches stretch out along the coast on either side of town. Be careful, though: The waves can occasionally be too rough for casual swimming, and you need to be aware of stray rocks at your feet. Be sure you know where the rocks and tide are before doing any bodysurfing. Given the prevailing currents and winds here, Montezuma also has experienced several severe and long-lasting red tide episodes at different times over the years. During these periods of massive algae bloom, the ocean is reddish-brown in color and not recommended for swimming. The best places to swim are a couple of hundred meters north of town in front of **El Rincón de los Monos,** or several kilometers farther north at Playa Grande.

If you're interested in more than simple beach time, head for the **Montezuma waterfall ★★** just south of town—it's one of those tropical fantasies where water comes pouring down into a deep pool. It's a popular spot, and it's a bit of a hike up the stream. Along this stream are a couple of waterfalls, but the upper falls are by far the most spectacular. You'll find the trail to the falls just over the bridge south of the village (on your right just past Las Cascadas restaurant). At the first major outcropping of rocks, the trail disappears and you have to scramble up the rocks and river for a bit. A trail occasionally reappears for short stretches. Just stick close to the stream and you'll eventually hit the falls. **Note:** Be very careful when climbing close to the rushing water, and also if you plan on taking any dives into the pools below. The rocks are quite slippery, and several people each year get very scraped up, break bones, and otherwise hurt themselves here.

Another popular local waterfall is **El Chorro ★**, located 8km (5 miles) north of Montezuma. It cascades down into a tide pool at the edge of the ocean, making it a delightful mix of fresh- and seawater. You can bathe while gazing out over the sea and rocky coastline. When the water is clear and calm, this is one of my favorite swimming holes in all of Costa Rica. However, a massive landslide in 2004 filled in much of this pool and also somewhat lessened the drama and beauty of the falls. Moreover, the pool here is dependent upon the tides—it disappears entirely at very high tide. It's about a 2-hour hike along the beach to reach El Chorro. Alternatively, you can take a horseback tour here with any of the tour operators or horseback riding companies in town.

Buy the Book . . . or Just Borrow It

If you came unprepared or ran out of reading material, check in at **Librería Topsy** (☏ **2642-1187**), which, in addition to selling books, runs a lending library and serves as the local post office. They also have a branch up in Cabuya.

BUTTERFLY GARDEN For an intimate look at the life cycle and acrobatic flights-of-fancy of butterflies, head to the **Mariposario Montezuma Gardens** (www.montezumagardens.com; © **2642-1317** or 8888-4200; daily 8am–4pm; $8 entry). This is perhaps the most wild and natural feeling of all the butterfly gardens in Costa Rica. Wooden walkways wind through thick vegetation under black screen meshing. Most of the butterflies in the enclosure are self-reproducing. You can also see butterflies and other wildlife on trails through open forested areas outside the enclosure. It's set along the dirt road heading up the hill just beyond the entrance to the waterfall trail. These folks also rent out a few pretty rooms.

A UNIQUE CANOPY TOUR The **Waterfall Canopy Tour** ★ (www.montezumatraveladventures.com; © **2642-0808**; daily at 9am, 1pm and 3pm; $45) is built right alongside Montezuma's famous falls. The tour, which features nine cables connecting 13 platforms, includes a swim at the foot of the falls.

HORSEBACK RIDING Several people around the village rent horses for around $10 to $20 an hour, although most people choose to do a guided 4-hour horseback tour for $30 to $50. Any of the hotels or tour agencies in town can arrange this, or you can contact Marvin at **El Pinto Expeditions** (www.elpintoexpeditions.com; © **8492-3249**).

OTHER ACTIVITIES Some shops in the center of the village rent bicycles by the hour or day, as well as boogie boards and snorkeling equipment (although the water must be very calm for snorkeling).

A range of guided tour and adventure options is available in Montezuma. **CocoZuma Traveller** (www.cocozuma.com; © **2642-0911**) and **Sun Trails** (www.montezumatraveladventures.com; © **2642-0808**) can both arrange horseback riding, boat excursions, scuba-dive and snorkel tours, ATV outings, and rafting trips; car and motorcycle rentals; airport transfers; and currency exchange.

An Excursion to Cabo Blanco Absolute Nature Reserve

As beautiful as the beaches around Montezuma are, the beaches at **Cabo Blanco Absolute Nature Reserve** ★★ (© **2642-0093**), 11km (6¾ miles) south of the village, are even more stunning. At the southernmost tip of the Nicoya Peninsula, Cabo Blanco is a national park that preserves a nesting site for brown pelicans, magnificent frigate birds, and brown boobies. The beaches are backed by a lush tropical forest that is home to howler monkeys. The main trail here, Sendero Sueco (Swiss Trail), is a rugged and sometimes steep hike through thick rainforest. The trail leads to the beautiful Playa Balsita and Playa Cabo Blanco, two white-sand stretches that straddle either side of the namesake Cabo

Cabo Blanco Absolute Nature Reserve.

Blanco point. The beaches are connected by a short trail. It's 4km (2.5 miles) to Playa Balsita. Alternately, you can take a shorter 2km (1.25-mile) loop trail through the primary forest here. This is Costa Rica's oldest official bioreserve and was set up thanks to the pioneering efforts of conservationists Karen Mogensen and Nicholas Wessberg. Admission is $10; the reserve is open Wednesday through Sunday from 8am to 4pm.

On your way out to Cabo Blanco, you'll pass through the tiny village of **Cabuya.** There are a couple of private patches of beach to discover in this area, off deserted dirt roads. A small offshore island serves as the town's picturesque cemetery; snorkel and kayak trips to this island are offered out of Montezuma.

Shuttle buses head from Montezuma to Cabo Blanco roughly every 2 hours beginning at 8am, and then turn around and bring folks from Cabo Blanco to Montezuma; the last one leaves Cabo Blanco around 5pm. The fare is $3 each way. These shuttles often don't run during the off season. Alternatively, you can share a taxi: The fare is around $15 to

Backroads Exploring & Beach Hopping

This is a great area to explore by 4X4 or ATV. A single coastal road heads up the coast to Cabuya and Cabo Blanco, with a half-dozen or more spots to pull over for a swim at a semi-private beach.

Moreover, several dirt roads head into the hills here connecting Montezuma with Cabuya, Delicias, Malpaís and Santa Teresa.

$20 per taxi, which can hold four or five passengers. Taxis tend to hang around Montezuma center. One dependable *taxista* is **Gilberto Rodríguez** (📞 8826-9055; gilbertotaxi@gmail.com).

Where to Stay

EXPENSIVE

In addition to the places mentioned below, the **Anamaya Resort ★** (www.anamayaresort.com; 📞 866/412-5350 in the U.S. or 2642-1289 in Costa Rica) is a lovely and luxe option on a high hillside above Montezuma. Anamaya specializes in yoga and wellness retreats.

Ylang Ylang Beach Resort ★★★   This pioneering rainforest resort does an excellent job of blending tropical fantasy with hints of luxury. The whole complex is set just off the beach in a dense patch of forest and flowering gardens. Lodging options range from glamping-style tent cabins (slat wood floors, private porches, indoor plumbing, batik window coverings) to individual bungalows and geodesic domes. All are comfortable and quite pretty. The on-site restaurant serves some of the tastiest fare on this stretch of coastline. There are no roads or regular vehicular access to the resort, so check-in is at El Sano Banano Village Cafe (p. 305) in town; you and your bags are shuttled in via Jeep or dune buggy. The owners, Lenny and Patricia, have been here for decades and have done much to promote and protect the area.

Montezuma, Cóbano de Puntarenas. www.ylangylangbeachresort.com. 📞 **888/795-8494** in the U.S. and Canada, or 2642-0636 in Costa Rica. 22 units. $190–$360 tent cabin, $220–$360 double. Rates include breakfast and dinner. **Amenities:** Restaurant; bar; midsize outdoor pool; spa; free Wi-Fi.

MODERATE

Amor de Mar ★★★   A little slice of paradise, Amor de Mar is a large house perched on a high spot of land that runs down to a rocky outcropping that hides a lovely, small natural swimming pool carved into the coral stones. You can't see the pool or folks swimming in it from the house or grounds, which makes it a good spot for a quick romantic smooch. Between this pool and the rooms is more loveliness: a broad lawn and a small grove of mango trees and coconut palms strung with hammocks. The rooms themselves are comfortable and pretty, awash in varnished hardwoods, with large windows (though they vary greatly in size and location; the prized choices are those on the second floor, especially those with oceanview balconies). Beside and behind the main hotel building lie Casa Luna and Casa Sol, two separate two-story fully equipped villas perfect for families and small groups. The entrance to the trail for Montezuma's famous waterfall is directly across the dirt street from Amor de Mar, and it's a short walk into town. The in-house restaurant is only open for breakfast and lunch.

Montezuma, Cóbano de Puntarenas. www.amordemar.com. 📞 **2642-0262.** 11 units. $120–$150 double; $250–$270 villa. **Amenities:** Restaurant; Wi-Fi.

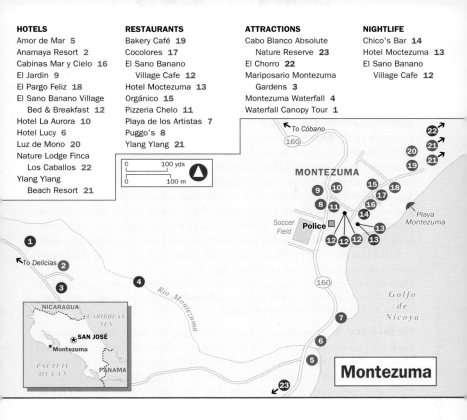

HOTELS	RESTAURANTS	ATTRACTIONS	NIGHTLIFE
Amor de Mar **5**	Bakery Café **19**	Cabo Blanco Absolute	Chico's Bar **14**
Anamaya Resort **2**	Cocolores **17**	Nature Reserve **23**	Hotel Moctezuma **13**
Cabinas Mar y Cielo **16**	El Sano Banano	El Chorro **22**	El Sano Banano
El Jardin **9**	Village Cafe **12**	Mariposario Montezuma	Village Cafe **12**
El Pargo Feliz **18**	Hotel Moctezuma **13**	Gardens **3**	
El Sano Banano Village	Orgánico **15**	Montezuma Waterfall **4**	
Bed & Breakfast **12**	Pizzeria Chelo **11**	Waterfall Canopy Tour **1**	
Hotel La Aurora **10**	Playa de los Artistas **7**		
Hotel Lucy **6**	Puggo's **8**		
Luz de Mono **20**	Ylang Ylang **21**		
Nature Lodge Finca			
Los Caballos **22**			
Ylang Ylang			
Beach Resort **21**			

Montezuma

INEXPENSIVE

In addition to the places mentioned below, **El Pargo Feliz** (© 2642-0064) and **Cabinas Mar y Cielo** (© 2642-0261) are two recommended budget options right in the center of town. I should also note that the owners of Ylang Ylang (p. 306) also run the in-town **El Sano Banano B&B** (www.elbanano.com; © 866/795-8494 in the U.S. and Canada, or 2642-0636 in Costa Rica), just off their popular restaurant. Double rooms are $75 to $95. Rates include breakfast.

El Jardín ★★   As you descend the steep hill that leads into Montezuma, you'll find this place on your right, just before the main crossroads of the village. Rooms here are clean and tidy, and feature Guatemalan woven bedspreads and either varnished wood or cool concrete block walls. A couple have smooth locally collected river stones integrated into the masonry. They are spread up the hillside and some offer up excellent views over the town and out to the ocean. Rooms furthest from the road and reception require a bit of a steep hike, but the higher vantage point and better views are definitely worth it. The hotel's pool and Jacuzzi area is its best feature, built in two-distinct tiers connected by a sculpted waterfall. I also enjoy the location, which provides easy access to the town, yet feels a bit removed.

Montezuma, Cóbano de Puntarenas. www.hoteleljardin.com. © **2642-0074.** 17 units. $75–$195 double; $100 villa. Prices include taxes. **Amenities:** Jacuzzi; small outdoor pool; Wi-Fi.

Hotel La Aurora ★   You'll see the stone columns and yellow archway entrance to this intimate budget option on your left as soon as you hit the town's main crossroad. Spread over three floors, the rooms are not as comfortable as they could be, with low wooden beds and rather thin mattresses. Still the German owner Angela Kock runs a tight ship, so rooms and common areas (including a much-used communal kitchen for the guests) are immaculate. On the top floor, you'll find a two-bedroom apartment that enjoys just a hint of a sea view through the thick trees. Guests tend to gather in the several common areas, including the well-stocked lending library. Or you can grab a siesta in one of the shade covered hammocks hung around the hotel.

Montezuma, Cóbano de Puntarenas. www.hotelaurora-montezuma.com. © **2642-0051.** 20 units. $40 double; $50–$60 suites. **Amenities:** Lounge; communal kitchen; free Wi-Fi in the lobby and common areas.

Hotel Lucy ★   For a budget hotel, this place has some serious location cache, as it's set right on the beach a short walk south of the village and close to the Montezuma Waterfall trail entrance. However, the rooms here are incredibly basic and only sporadically maintained, and the service and personal attention provided are minimal. Guests choose between rooms with private bathrooms or shared dorm-style affairs.

Montezuma, Cóbano de Puntarenas. © **2642-0273.** 17 units, 6 with bathroom. $24 double with shared bathroom; $28 double with private bathroom. Rates include taxes. **Amenities:** Free Wi-Fi.

Luz de Mono ★   Set in the middle of thick forest at the northern edge of Montezuma, Luz de Mono feels very remote, despite being walking distance to the beach and all of Montezuma's shops and restaurants. Most guestrooms are housed in an unpainted, grey concrete, two-story building. The individual casitas are more inviting, with much more space, high peaked ceilings, private Jacuzzi tubs, and ocean view patio decks in front. The hotel's best feature is its small pool, which is set on a high spot of the property surrounded by tall shade trees and flowering gardens, yet also boasting a straight view out to the sea.

Montezuma, Cóbano de Puntarenas. www.luzdemono.com. © **2642-0090.** 18 units. $75–$95 double; $150 casita. Rates include breakfast. **Amenities:** Restaurant; bar; free Wi-Fi.

Nature Lodge ★★   An oasis of serenity set in the heart of the forest (you'll need a car if you stay here), Nature Lodge was originally a ranch. Today it's delighting tourists with better-than-usual food, excellent service, and rooms that are on the verge of being stylish (white walls with an occasional splash of color from a painting or wall hanging, low-lying beds made of varnished bamboo or local hardwoods). Some have ocean views, most look out into the jungle or garden.

3km (1¾ miles) outside of Montezuma, on the way to Cóbano de Puntarenas. www. naturelodge.net. © **2642-0124.** 12 units. $86–$146 double. Rates include breakfast buffet. **Amenities:** Restaurant; small outdoor pool; spa; free Wi-Fi.

Where to Dine

You'll find several basic *sodas* and casual restaurants right in the village. My favorite is the **Pizzería Chelo Pizzeria** (© **2642-1430**), which is at the crossroads into town and serves thin-crust pizzas, calzones, and pastas. You might also want to check out the Spanish cuisine and fabulous setting at the downtown **Hotel Moctezuma** (© **2642-0058**), or the varied international fare at **Cocolores** (© **2642-0348**). Just outside of downtown proper, the Israeli-owned **Puggo's ★** (© **2642-0325**) serves up an eclectic menu that ranges from falafel to *ceviche* to focaccia and beyond.

For breakfast, coffee, and light meals, **Orgánico ★** (© **2642-1322**) is the pick, with a range of healthy sandwiches, daily specials, and freshly baked goods. The **Bakery Café** (© **2642-0458**) is another option, serving everything from gourmet coffee drinks to full meals.

El Sano Banano Village Cafe ★★ INTERNATIONAL/VEGETARIAN El Sano Banano has always been the heart and soul and social center of Montezuma. It doesn't hurt matters that it's also located at the rough geographic center of town as well, just across from the small central park. The menu is focused on vegetarian and market-fresh cooking, with a long list of vegan, gluten-free and raw food choices. The salads are huge and plentiful and the sandwiches are served on home baked whole wheat bread and buns. No red meat is offered, but seafood and poultry make their way into a range of dishes, from Thai-style spring rolls, to burritos and pasta dishes. Every evening at 7:30pm, recent releases and classic movies are shown on a large screen. *Tip:* There are lot of seating options, but the prized tables are located in the back patio garden, under the tall shade trees.

On the main road into the village. © **2642-0944.** Main courses C4,000–C8,500. Daily 7am–10pm.

Playa de los Artistas ★★★ ITALIAN/MEDITERRANEAN For a special occasion meal or a date night, head here. Dim lighting, soft electronic music and large wooden tables spread around the covered patio and open garden area (just a few steps from the ocean) make this a wonderfully romantic place to dine. And the food is superb. It arrives from two distinct places: a small kitchen in the owners' home behind the dining area, and a large outdoor grill and wood burning oven. The menu is handwritten every day and varies according to what's fresh and available. You might find some fresh caught octopus grilled and served over crostini, or slow cooked pork ribs in a rum and honey glaze. Still, seafood is the main draw here, and I often simply ask for the whole grilled fresh catch of the day in whatever sauce the chef feels like whipping up at the moment.

Across from Hotel Los Mangos. ℂ **2642-0920.** Reservations recommended. No credit cards. Main courses C6,000–C10,000. Mon–Fri 5–9:30pm, Sat noon–9:30pm. **Note:** Lunch is sometimes served during the high season.

Ylang Ylang ★★ INTERNATIONAL/VEGETARIAN The main restaurant at the wonderful Ylang Ylang Beach Resort (see above) tries to please all its guests (and usually succeeds) by offering quite a few vegan, gluten-free, and raw options, as well as sushi and a range of Asian-inspired dishes. Presentations are artistic, and there are plenty of meat, chicken and seafood dishes for those seeking to indulge those guilty pleasures. The setting is also pleasing: an open-air but covered patio, where you'll be able to see the beach and the ocean beyond.

At the Ylang Ylang Beach Resort. ℂ **2642-0402.** Reservations recommended. Main courses $12–$26, including tax and tip. Daily 7am–9pm.

Entertainment & Nightlife

Montezuma has had a tough time coming to terms with its nightlife. For years, local businesses banded together to force most of the loud, late-night activity out of town. This has eased somewhat, allowing for quite an active nightlife in Montezuma proper. The local action seems to base itself either at **Chico's Bar** ★ (no phone) or at the bar at the **Hotel Moctezuma** (ℂ **2642-0058**). Both are located on the main strip in town facing the water. If your evening tastes are mellower, **El Sano Banano Village Cafe** (p. 305) doubles as the local movie house, with nightly late-run features projected on a large screen.

MALPAÍS & SANTA TERESA ★★

150km (93 miles) W of San José; 12km (7½ miles) S of Cóbano

Malpaís (or Mal País) translates as "badlands," and, while this may have been an apt moniker years ago, it no longer accurately describes this booming beach area. Malpaís is also a bucket term often used to refer to a string of neighboring beaches running from south to north, and including Malpaís, Playa Carmen, Santa Teresa, Playa Hermosa, and Playa Manzanillo. To a fault, these beaches are long, wide expanses of light sand dotted with rocky outcroppings. This is one of Costa Rica's hottest spots, and development rages on at a dizzying pace, especially in Santa Teresa. Still, it will take some time before this place is anything like more developed destinations Tamarindo or Manuel Antonio. In Malpaís and Santa Teresa today, you'll find a mix of beach hotels and resorts, restaurants, shops, and private houses, as well as miles of often deserted beach, and easy access to some nice jungle and the nearby **Cabo Blanco Absolute Nature Reserve** (p. 300).

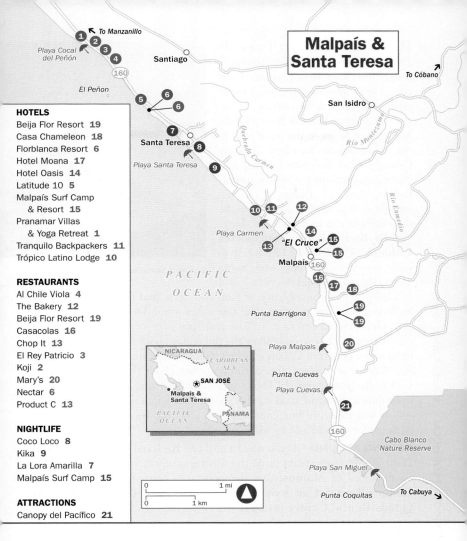

Malpaís & Santa Teresa

To Manzanillo

Playa Cocal del Peñón

Santiago

(160)

El Peñon

San Isidro

Río Montezuma

Quebrada Carmen

Santa Teresa

Playa Santa Teresa

Río Enmedio

Playa Carmen

"El Cruce"

Malpaís (160)

PACIFIC OCEAN

Punta Barrigona

Playa Malpaís

NICARAGUA

CARIBBEAN SEA

SAN JOSÉ

Malpaís & Santa Teresa

PACIFIC OCEAN

PANAMA

Punta Cuevas

Playa Cuevas

(160)

Cabo Blanco Nature Reserve

Playa San Miguel

0   1 mi
0   1 km

Punta Coquitas

To Cabuya

To Cóbano

HOTELS

Beija Flor Resort **19**
Casa Chameleon **18**
Florblanca Resort **6**
Hotel Moana **17**
Hotel Oasis **14**
Latitude 10 **5**
Malpaís Surf Camp
    & Resort **15**
Pranamar Villas
    & Yoga Retreat **1**
Tranquilo Backpackers **11**
Trópico Latino Lodge **10**

RESTAURANTS

Al Chile Viola **4**
The Bakery **12**
Beija Flor Resort **19**
Casacolas **16**
Chop It **13**
El Rey Patricio **3**
Koji **2**
Mary's **20**
Nectar **6**
Product C **13**

NIGHTLIFE

Coco Loco **8**
Kika **9**
La Lora Amarilla **7**
Malpaís Surf Camp **15**

ATTRACTIONS

Canopy del Pacífico **21**

Essentials

GETTING THERE & DEPARTING   By Plane: The nearest airport is in Tambor (p. 292), about 22km (14 miles) from Malpaís; the ride takes around 20 to 25 minutes. Some of the hotels listed below might be willing to pick you up in Tambor for a reasonable fee. If not, you'll have to hire a taxi, which could cost anywhere between $60 and $70. **Taxis** are generally waiting to meet most regularly scheduled planes, but if they aren't, you can call **Richard** (© **8360-8166** or 2640-0099) for a cab.

By Car: Follow the directions above to Montezuma (see "Playa Montezuma," earlier in this chapter). At Cóbano, follow the signs to

Malpaís and Playa Santa Teresa. It's another 12km (7½ miles) down a rough dirt road that requires four-wheel-drive much of the year, especially during the rainy season.

To drive to Malpaís from Liberia, head out of town on the main road to the Guanacaste beaches, passing through Filadelfia, Santa Cruz, and Nicoya on your way toward the turnoff for La Amistad Bridge. Continue straight at this turnoff, and follow the directions for this route as listed above.

By Bus & Ferry: Transportes Cóbano (© **2642-1112**) has two daily buses to Malpaís and Santa Teresa departing from Avenida 7 and

Surfing in Santa Teresa.

9, Calle 12. The buses leave at 6am and 2pm, and the fare is C7,535, including the ferry passage. The ride takes around 6 hours. The return buses leave Santa Teresa at 5:15am and 2pm.

Alternatively, you can follow the directions above for getting to Montezuma, but get off in Cóbano. From Cóbano, there are several daily buses for Malpaís and Santa Teresa running throughout the day. The fare is C950. **Be forewarned:** These bus schedules are subject to change according to demand, road conditions, and the whim of the bus company.

If you miss the bus connection in Cóbano, you can hire a cab to Malpaís for around $25 to $30.

GETTING AROUND If you need a taxi, call **Richard** (© **8317-7614** or 2640-0099). If you want to do the driving yourself, you can contact the local offices of **Alamo** (www.alamocostarica.com; © **2640-0526**) or **Budget Rent A Car** (www.budget.co.cr; © **2640-0500**). Or head to **Quads Rental Center** (© **2640-0178**), which stocks ATVs.

VILLAGE LAYOUTS Malpaís and Santa Teresa are two tiny beach villages. As you reach the ocean, the road forks; Playa Carmen is straight ahead, Malpaís is to your left, and Santa Teresa is to your right. If you continue beyond Santa Teresa, you'll come to the even-more-deserted beaches of playas Hermosa and Manzanillo (not to be confused with beaches of the same names to be found elsewhere in the country). To get to playas Hermosa and Manzanillo, you have to ford a couple of rivers, which can be tricky during parts of the rainy season.

Exploring Malpaís & Santa Teresa

If you decide to do anything here besides sunbathe on the beach and play in the waves, your options include nature hikes, horseback riding,

ATV tours, scuba diving, and snorkeling, which most hotels can help arrange. Surfing is a major draw, with miles of beach breaks to choose from and a few points to boot. If you want to rent a board or take a lesson, I recommend **Costa Rica Surf & SUP** (www.costaricasurfandsup. com; ✆ **2640-0328**), **Surfing Costa Rica Pura Vida** (www.surfing costaricapuravida.com; ✆ **8333-7825**), and **Del Soul Surf School** (www.surfvacationcostarica.com; ✆ **8878-0880**).

If you've gotten beat up by the waves, or are sore from paddling out, you'll find several excellent spas in town. The best and most extensive (and most expensive) of these is at the **Florblanca Resort** (p. 309). But you might also check in to the **Pranamar Villas & Yoga Retreat** (p. 311), located on the beach, at the northern end of Santa Teresa.

For canopy adventures, head to **Canopy del Pacífico** (www.cano pyMalpaís.com; ✆ **2640-0360;** $45), which is toward the southern end of Malpaís and just slightly inland. A 2-hour tour over the nearly 2km (1 mile) of cables touches down on 11 platforms, features two rappels, and offers good views of both the forest and the ocean below. Round-trip transportation from an area hotel is $5 per person.

For fishing, wildlife viewing and birdwatching, I highly recommend **Sapao Adventures** ★★ (www.sapoaadventures.com; ✆ **8996-9000**).

Where to Stay
EXPENSIVE
Florblanca Resort ★★★ This is the premier boutique luxury beach resort in this area, which is saying a lot. The resort consists of a collection of massive, elegant private villas spread around exuberant gardens. The

Santa Teresa.

Florblanca Resort.

foliage is so thick and abundant that I often get lost on the stone walkways that weave through the resort connecting everything. About half of the villas are designed for couples, and the rest feature a separate upstairs bedroom with two twins perfect for families—although no children under 6 are allowed. All feature a humongous living room that lets out on to an equally spacious private patio area, as well as large, open-air bathrooms with outdoor rain showers and separate free-standing tubs set in a small private garden. Enjoy a morning Pilates or Ashtanga yoga class in the ocean-view open-air Dojo, and follow it up with a cool dip the large two-tiered pool. The spa is superb and the on-site Nectar restaurant (see below) is one of the best in the area.

Playa Santa Teresa. www.florblanca.com. © **800/683-1031** in the U.S. and Canada, or 2640-0232 in Costa Rica. 11 units. $380–$500 double; $550–$675 1-bedroom villa; $725–$925 2-bedroom villa for 4; $775–$925 honeymoon house. No children under 6. **Amenities:** Restaurant; bar; small gym; outdoor pool; room service; spa; watersports equipment rental; free Wi-Fi.

Casa Chameleon ★★   Don't let the steep narrow driveway scare you off. Once you make it to the top, you'll find a collection of refined, fully equipped bungalows at this couples-only retreat. Every bungalow is different, but all feature airy layouts, large kitchenettes or full kitchens and French doors that open on to a private plunge pool with panoramic ocean and jungle views. Antique dressers and nightstands, four-poster beds and Balinese lamps are all part of the swank decor. The bungalows are spread over a steep hillside and those furthest from the main lodge and restaurant are a bit of exercise on the way up. The food here is standout, with chef Pabro Sanchez preparing a set menu with a few unique options every night, usually involving the fusion of local ingredients with recipes from around the globe. On my last visit, the owners of Casa Chameleon were discussing opening of their restaurant to outside guests, with reservations.

Malpaís. www.hotelcasachameleon.com. © **888/705-0274** in the U.S. and Canada, or 2288-2879 in Costa Rica. 6 units. $245–$645 double. No children allowed. **Amenities:** Restaurant; bar; small outdoor pool; Wi-Fi.

Latitude 10 ★★ If you're looking for an intimate and exclusive beachfront getaway it's hard to beat this fine-looking little resort. With only five independent bungalows and one main lodge room, Latitude 10 never gets crowded, and quite often is rented out entirely by a family or group. The bungalows are built from local hardwoods and show heavy Indonesian and Balinese influences in both the design and decor. With sliding wooden doors and slatted windows they are designed to be entirely open (there's no A/C or locks on the doors), especially during the day. This may be a bit too open and close to nature for some folks, so there's a prominent "Is Latitude 10 for Me" tab on their website. The resort sits on the far northern end Santa Teresa beach, with just a pool, a patch of well-manicured lawn and a string of coconut palms separating it from the sand and sea.

Playa Santa Teresa, Cóbano de Puntarenas. www.latitude10resort.com. © **8309-2943.** 6 units. $210–$250 double; $270–$430 junior suite; $490–$610 master suite. Rates include breakfast. **Amenities:** Restaurant, bar; outdoor pool; Wi-Fi.

Pranamar Villas & Yoga Retreat ★★ Pranamar place feels like a small village, with tight windy paths overflowing with tropical foliage weaving between thatch-roofed buildings, with wood and bamboo walls. As is common on this coast, there's a heavy dose of Balinese, Thai and Indonesian artwork, crafts and furnishings to the decor, but here that's mixed in with elements from Mexico, Guatemala, and Ecuador. The mélange is a lovely one. As the name suggests, yoga is an integral part of the program here, with regular daily classes, a steady stream of visiting workshops and a large and lovely yoga studio. The hotel's Buddha Eyes restaurant specializes in healthy and vegetarian cuisine, without skimping on flavor. This hotel is located on the far northern edge of Santa Teresa, right where it becomes Playa Hermosa.

Playa Santa Teresa, Cóbano de Puntarenas. www.pranamarvillas.com. © **2640-0852.** 10 units. $242–$425 double, $370 house. Rates include breakfast and daily yoga class. **Amenities:** Restaurant; bar; saltwater pool; spa treatments; free Wi-Fi.

MODERATE

Beija Flor Resort ★ (www.beijaflorresort.com; © **2640-1007**) is a cozy little resort with an excellent restaurant in Malpaís. Look at it if the ones below are full.

Hotel Moana ★ Spread over a steep mountainside towards the northern end of Malpaís, just a little inland from the beach, the Hotel Moana has an African theme, which makes for a fun change. Many of the rooms are decorated with tribal masks, shields, spears and even a zebra skin hung on the walls. The best rooms and the hotel's Papaya restaurant are on the highest points of the property. And though it requires a bit of energy to climb the steps, it's definitely worth the effort to soak in the unobstructed views of the Pacific Ocean and rugged coastline. Hotel Moana also rents out a spectacular 5-bedroom independent house, Casa Moana, located above the hotel, perfect for larger groups or families.

Malpaís, Cóbano de Puntarenas. www.moanacostarica.com. ℂ **888/865-8032** in the U.S. and Canada, or 2640-0230 in Costa Rica. 10 units. $95–$145 double; $220–$280 suite; $600–$950 house. Rates include breakfast and taxes. Closed Sept–Oct. **Amenities:** Restaurant, bar; Jacuzzi; outdoor pool; free Wi-Fi.

Trópico Latino Lodge ★★ This small beachfront resort is set on a large, mostly forested piece of land fronting a prime patch of sand in the center of Santa Teresa. You can opt for the older, spacious and economical garden units, or splurge for a newer beachfront room or bungalow. These latter bungalows feature roughhewn wood planks for walls and peaked wood ceilings; it's a handsome look. The expansive grounds here are covered with tall pochote trees that are often frequented by roaming bands of howler monkeys. The hotel has a small pool and lovely yoga studio and spa, all with ocean views, and their Shambala restaurant is excellent. Some of the most coveted surf spots in Santa Teresa are directly in front of this resort.

Playa Santa Teresa, Cóbano, Puntarenas. www.hoteltropicolatino.com. ℂ **800/724-1235** in the U.S. and Canada, or 2640-0062 in Costa Rica. 21 units. $135–$260 double; $730 suite. **Amenities:** Restaurant; bar; Jacuzzi; pool; small spa; free Wi-Fi.

INEXPENSIVE

Hardcore budget travelers should check out **Tranquilo Backpackers** ★ (www.tranquilobackpackers.com; ℂ **2640-0589**), a bit inland off the road to Santa Teresa. It has a mix of dorm-style and private rooms.

Hotel Oasis ★★ This hotel is aptly named. Individual bungalows and studio apartments are quite as they're spread around shady grounds, just a short walk from the beach and some of Malpaís's most popular surf breaks. The rooms themselves are simple in decor, but well-maintained, and very fairly priced. Most feature exposed beam ceilings and varnished wood lattice work over the windows. All have a usable kitchenette (three-burner stove, toaster, minifridge, rice cooker and coffeemaker), and those in the studios are outdoors, which I find a nice touch. The bungalows are fab for families, with separate master and kids rooms. However, only the two studios have air conditioning. There's a small pool, and the owners are very hands-on and attentive.

Malpaís, Cóbano de Puntarenas. www.oasis.cr. ✆ **2640-0259.** 8 units. $75–$140 double. **Amenities:** Small outdoor pool; Wi-Fi.

Malpaís Surf Camp & Resort ★   This multifaceted, budget-conscious resort offers a wide range of rooms and price points. You can opt for everything from bunk-bed rooms with shared bathrooms to private poolside villas. You can also pitch a tent here, if you so desire. Budget conscious surfers tend to fill the garden ranchos which have crushed stone floors, and tree trunk columns supporting corrugated plastic roofs. This same green roofing material is used as half-walls to divide up the ranchos into separate sleeping areas. On the other end of the spectrum there are fully equipped villas with air-conditioning and contemporary appointments. You'll usually find older, better off surfers staying in these. A good-size, free-form pool sits at the center of the complex, which itself is about a 5-minute walk from the waves.

Malpaís, Cóbano de Puntarenas. www.Malpaíssurfcamp.com. ✆ **2640-0031.** 16 units, 8 with shared bathroom. $10 per person, camping; $25 double with shared bathroom; $35 double with private bathroom; $65 villa. **Amenities:** Restaurant; bar; small exercise room; midsize outdoor pool; surf board rental; free Wi-Fi.

Where to Dine

Mary's (www.maryscostarica.com; ✆ **2640-0153**) is a very popular open-air joint that features wood-oven baked pizzas and fresh seafood. It's toward the northern end of Malpaís. The fresh creative cooking at the **Beija Flor Resort** (www.beijaflorresort.com; ✆ **2640-1007**) is another good option in Malpaís.

Right at the Playa Carmen Commercial Center, at the crossroads at the entrance to town, you'll find a small food court with a wide range of options, including the bistro-style **Chop It—Holy Cow Burger** ★★ (✆ **2640-0000**). Open just for lunch, it serves a range of salads, wraps and justifiably popular burgers. Gluten free buns are even offered. My favorite option here, however, is **Product C** ★★ (www.product-c.com; ✆ **2640-1026**), a seafood retail outlet that also cooks up the daily catch, makes fresh *ceviche,* and serves fresh, farm-grown, local oysters. Just across the street you'll find **The Bakery** ★★ (✆ **2640-0560**), which serves an amazing array of fresh pastries and baked goods, along with sandwiches and pizzas.

On the far northern end of Playa Santa Teresa, **El Rey Patricio** ★★ (www.elreypatricio.com; ✆ **2640-0248**) has tasty tapas, drinks, and a sunset view, and **Al Chile Viola** ★ (✆ **2640-0433**) is my go-to Italian restaurant in town. Even farther, near the start of Playa Hermosa, **Koji** ★★ (✆ **2640-0815**) is the area's most popular sushi joint.

EXPENSIVE

Nectar ★★★ FUSION   The flagship restaurant at Florblanca Resort (p. 309) is consistently one of the top fine dining experiences in the country. Chef Norman Roqhuett Mata has built upon a long tradition of fine chefs at the helm of the kitchen here. Start things off with a tuna tartar tower featuring mango and avocado. Main courses run the gamut from a fresh-caught jumbo shrimp risotto to perfectly grilled steaks. Those looking for lighter fare can peruse the sushi and tapas menus. Meals are served at heavy Teak tables in an elegant open-air dining area overlooking the pool and beach. At night, dim lighting and candles create a romantic vibe.

At Florblanca Resort in Santa Teresa. ✆ **2640-0232.** Reservations recommended. Main courses $11–$30. Daily 7am–9pm.

INEXPENSIVE

Caracolas ★★ SEAFOOD/COSTA RICAN/MEXICAN   This place would win major points for the view and ambiance alone, but the food, too, is super fresh, tasty and a great value. The ceviche here is made daily with locally caught fish and seafood, and you can't go wrong with a grilled filet of dorado in garlic sauce. And while I really like the fish tacos, they might not be exactly what you'd expect, and come served in a crispy fried flour tortilla, more like what I'd call a *flauta*. As for the ambiance, patrons dine at large communal tables under trees close to the water, or in a series of more intimate pop up shade structures and rustic thatch roof palapas spread around the sloping grounds. When you're finished with your meal, feel free to stretch out in one of the hammocks hung between the coconut palms. Caracolas is also a perfect choice for sunset cocktails and appetizers.

On the beach, about 1km south of the main crossroads in Malpaís. ✆ **2291-1470.** Main courses C4950–C9500. Daily 7am–10pm.

Entertainment & Nightlife

The most popular bar in the area is **Coco Loco ★** (no phone), right on the beach in Malpaís. It features a mix of live bands and DJs, with weekly reggae and Latin nights, as well as a monthly full moon party. Thursday nights in Santa Teresa belong to the punk-ska-reggae band that hold forth at **Kika** (✆ **2640-0408**). Also in Santa Teresa, **La Lora Amarilla** (✆ **2640-0134**) is a classic local nightspot which heats up on Saturday night when the locals come to salsa and merengue dance.

A Truly Remote Beach: Undiscovered, for Now

The Nicoya Peninsula coastline between Santa Teresa and Playa Sámara is perhaps the last, long undeveloped stretch of Costa Rican coastline. The following hotel is roughly midway between Santa Teresa and Playa

Sámara. It can be reached year round by rough, mostly unmarked dirt roads, so it's best to coordinate your transportation with the hotel.

Cristal Azul ★   You'll need a four-wheel-drive vehicle to reach this isolated hilltop hotel and its four individual cabins. They are simple, almost to the point of austere, but they all offer up 180 degree views out over a patch of flat farmland and out to the sea. At the beach, Playa San Miguel is a virtually undiscovered piece of Pacific coast sand. The hotel operates a small beachfront bar and restaurant during the day. Hosts Zene and Henner Morales are very personable and attentive and pretty much always on site. Their commitment to conservation has helped earn the hotel "4 Leaves" from the CST Sustainable Tourism program.

Playa San Miguel, Guanacaste. www.cristalazul.com. © **888/822-7369** in the U.S. and Canada, or 2655-8135 in Costa Rica. 4 units. $190–$220 double. Rates include full breakfast. **Amenities:** Restaurant; bar; midsize outdoor pool; Wi-Fi.

PLAYA SÁMARA ★

35km (22 miles) S of Nicoya; 245km (152 miles) W of San José

Playa Sámara is a long, broad beach on a gently curved horseshoe-shape bay. Unlike most of the other beaches along this stretch of the Pacific coast, the water here is usually relatively calm and safe for swimming because an offshore island and rocky headlands break up most of the surf. That said, there are often gentle rollers, and you'll find plenty of surf schools and lessons perfect for beginners. Playa Sámara is popular both with Tico families seeking a quick and inexpensive getaway and with young Ticos looking to do some serious beach partying. On weekends, in particular, Sámara can get crowded and rowdy. Still, the calm waters and steep cliffs on the far side of the bay make this a very attractive spot, and the beach is so long that the crowds are usually well dispersed. Moreover, if you drive along the rugged coastal road in either direction, you'll discover some truly spectacular and isolated beaches.

Essentials

GETTING THERE & DEPARTING   By Car: Head west out of San José on the San José–Caldera Highway (CR27). When you reach Caldera, follow the signs to Puntarenas and the Interamerican Highway (CR1). You will actually follow signs for Liberia and San José, which are, in fact, leading you to the unmarked entrance to CR1. This road (CR23) ends when it hits the Interamerican Highway. You'll want to pass under the bridge and follow the on-ramp, which will put you on the highway heading north. Forty-seven kilometers (29 miles) after you get on the Interamerican Highway heading north, you'll see signs and the turnoff for La Amistad Bridge (CR18). After crossing the bridge, continue on CR18 until it hits CR21. Take this road north to Nicoya. Turn in to the town of

Playa Sámara.

Nicoya, and head more or less straight through town until you see signs for Playa Sámara. From here, it's a well-marked and paved road (CR150) all the way to the beach.

To drive to Sámara from Liberia, head out of town on the main road to the Guanacaste beaches, passing through Filadelfia, Santa Cruz, and Nicoya. Once you reach Nicoya, follow the directions outlined above.

By Bus: Alfaro express buses (www.empresaalfaro.com; © **2222-2666**) leave San José daily at noon and 5pm from Avenida 5 between calles 14 and 16. The trip lasts 5 hours; the one-way fare is C4,620. Extra buses are sometimes added on weekends and during peak periods.

Alternatively, you can take a bus from this same station to Nicoya and then catch a second bus from Nicoya to Sámara. **Alfaro** buses leave San José nearly every hour between 5:30am and 5pm. The fare is C4,045. The trip can take between 4 and 5½ hours, depending if the bus goes via Liberia or La Amistad Bridge. The latter route is much faster and much more frequent. **Empresa Rojas Castro** (© **2685-5032**) buses leave Nicoya for Sámara and Carrillo regularly throughout the day, between 5am and 9pm. The trip's duration is 1½ hours. The fare to Sámara is C1,135; the fare to Carrillo is C1,300.

Express buses to San José leave daily at 10am and noon. Buses for Nicoya leave throughout the day between 5am and 6pm. Buses leave Nicoya for San José nearly every hour between 3am and 5pm.

Interbus (www.interbusonline.com; © **4100-0888**) has a daily bus that leaves San José for Playa Sámara at 8am. The fare is $50, and they will pick you up at most San José-area hotels.

GETTING AROUND   If you need a ride around Sámara, or to one of the nearby beaches, have your hotel call you a taxi. Rides in town should cost $2 to $5; rides to nearby beaches might run $10 to $25, depending upon the distance.

VISITOR INFORMATION   The website **www.samarabeach.com** is an excellent, all-around resource for info on Playa Sámara and the vicinity.

CITY LAYOUT   Sámara is a busy little town at the bottom of a steep hill. The main road heads straight into town, passing the soccer field before coming to an end at the beach. Just before the beach is a road to the left that leads to most of the hotels listed below. This road also leads to Playa Carrillo (see below) and the **Hotel Punta Islita** (p. 322). If you turn right 3 blocks before hitting the beach, you'll hit the coastal road that goes to playas Buena Vista, Barrigona, and eventually Nosara.

FAST FACTS   To reach the local police, dial © **2656-0436.** Sámara has a small **medical clinic** (© **2656-0166**). A branch of **Banco Nacional** (© **2656-0089**) is on the road to Playa Buena Vista, just as you head out of town. For full-service laundry, head to **Green Life Laundry** (© **2656-1051**), about 3 blocks west of the Banco Nacional.

Exploring Playa Sámara

Playa Sámara is a somewhat quiet and underdeveloped beach town, and most folks are content to simply hang on the beach and swim in the gentle waves. But if you're looking for something more, there's horseback riding either on the beach or through the bordering pastureland and forests. Other options include sea kayaking in the calm waters off Playa Sámara, sportfishing, snorkeling, scuba diving, boat tours, mountain biking, and tours to Playa Ostional to see the mass nesting of olive ridley sea turtles. You can book any of these tours at your hotel or through **Carrillo Adventures** (www.carrilloadventures.com; © **2656-0606**), an excellent all-around local tour company.

You'll find that the beach is nicer and cleaner down at the south end. Better yet, head about 8km (5 miles) south to **Playa Carrillo ★★**, a long crescent of soft, white sand. With almost no development here, the beach is nearly always deserted. Loads of palm trees provide shade. If you've got a good four-wheel-drive vehicle, ask for directions at your

Playa Carrillo.

Scuba diving.

hotel and set off in search of the hidden gems of **Playa Buena Vista** and **Playa Barrigona ★★**, which are north of Sámara, less than a half-hour drive.

CANOPY TOURS **Wingnuts Canopy Tours** (www.wingnutscanopy. com; ✆ **2656-0153**) offer zip-line and harness "canopy tours". The 2-hour outing costs $60 per person or $45 for those under 12. If you want to repeat the adventure, Wingnuts offers a 50-percent discount on your second tour. You'll find their office by the giant strangler fig tree, or matapalo, toward the southern end of the beach.

SPORTFISHING Almost every hotel in the area can arrange sportfishing trips, or you can contact **Kingfisher ★** (www.costaricabillfishing.com; ✆ **800/783-3817** in U.S or 8358-9561 in Costa Rica). Rates run from $850 for a half-day and $1,250 for a full day outing.

SURFING The waves hitting Playa Sámara are somewhat muffled by an offshore reef and headlands on each side. For some this makes it a great wave to learn on. For lessons or to rent a board, check in with **C&C Surf Shop and School** (www.cncsurfsamara.webs.com; ✆ **5006-0369**) or **Choco's Surf School** (www.chocossurfschool.com; ✆ **8937-5246**). Surfboard rentals run around $10 per day. Private lessons cost $30 to $50 per hour.

ULTRALIGHT FLYING For a bird's-eye view of the area, head over to the **Flying Crocodile ★★** (www.flying-crocodile.com; ✆ **2656-8048** or 8330-3923) in Playa Buena Vista. It offers flights in a two-seat (one for you, one for the pilot) Gyrocopter, the ultralight equivalent of a helicopter. Although it might feel like little more than a modified tricycle with a nylon wing and lawnmower motor, these winged wonders are very safe. A 20-minute flight runs $110, while an hour-long tour costs $230.

WILDLIFE VIEWING Located near Barra Honda National Park (see below), **Rancho Humo ★★** (www.ranchohumo.com; ℂ **2233-2233**) is a private wildlife reserve that offers fabulous bird-watching and wildlife viewing opportunities along the Tempisque River basin and surrounding wetlands. The area is rich in waterbird species, shore lizards, and crocodiles. A full-day tour ($95) includes a river boat trip, a tour of the reeds and lowland forest in a motorized safari-style vehicle, and a tour of the neighboring cattle ranching operations, as well as lunch. Transportation can be provided, and you can choose a half-day tour that takes in only one or two of the elements of the full-day tour.

Learn the Language

Sámara Language School (www.samaralanguageschool.com; ℂ **866/978-6668** in the U.S. and Canada, or 2656-3000 in Sámara) offers a range of programs and private lessons and can arrange for a homestay with a local family. The facility even features classes with ocean views, although that might be a detriment to your language learning.

Going Down Under

Barra Honda National Park ★ (ℂ **2659-1551**; daily 8am–4pm; $12 admission) is an extensive system of caves, some of which reach more than 200m (656 ft.) in depth. Human remains and indigenous relics have been found in other caves, but those are not open to the public. The last tour into the caves starts at 1pm.

If you plan to descend the one publicly accessible cave, you'll need to hire a local guide at the park entrance station. These guides are always available, and will provide harnesses, helmets, and flashlights. Depending upon your group size and bargaining abilities, expect to pay between $30 to $40 per person for a visit to the **Terciopelo Cave. *Note:*** The cave is open only during the dry season (mid-Nov to Apr). You begin the roughly 3-hour tour with a descent of 19m (62 ft.) straight down a wooden ladder with a safety rope attached. Inside you'll see plenty of impressive stalactites and stalagmites while visiting several chambers of varying sizes. Even if you don't descend, the trails around Barra Honda and its prominent limestone plateau are great for hiking and bird-watching. Be sure to make a stop at **La Cascada,** a gentle waterfall that fills and passes through a series of calcium and limestone pools, some of them large enough to bathe in. The entire operation is slightly reminiscent of Ocho Rios in Jamaica. **Getting there:** Spelunkers will want to head 62km (38 miles) northeast of Playa Sámara on the road to La Amistad Bridge. If you don't have a car, your best bet is to get to Nicoya, which is about a half-hour away by bus, and then take a taxi to the park, which should cost about $24.

Where to Stay

MODERATE

Fenix Hotel ★   These beachfront studio apartments are a real value. Set towards the middle section of the long, gentle Playa Sámara, they have a primo location—just a short walk from most of the restaurants, clubs, and downtown activity—and yet quiet and slightly removed. Rooms are in a tight ring around the hotel's small pool, each unit featuring tropical rattan furnishings, and a fully equipped kitchen. Boogie boards are offered free for guest use, and there's a series of hammocks strung from coconut palms perfectly positioned right between the pool and sea. The owners are very hands-on, friendly and helpful.

Playa Sámara, Nicoya, Guanacaste. www.fenixhotel.com. ℂ **2656-0158.** 6 units. $114–$145 double. Children 17 and under stay free in parent's room. **Amenities:** Small outdoor pool; free Wi-Fi.

The Hideaway Hotel ★★   This two-story boutique hotel has the feel of a converted home, due in no small part to the warm welcome owner Martina and her staff give the guests. Rooms are oversized, with really handsome blue, green and white comforters and curtains (the exact pattern varies from room to room). The color theme continues outside where bright blue chairs and lounges ring a crescent shaped pool. The hotel is set about a block or so inland from the far southern end of Playa Sámara, so a rental car is helpful to get to and from the many restaurants, bars and shops in town.

Playa Sámara, Nicoya, Guanacaste. www.thehideawayplayasamara.com. ℂ **2656-1145.** 12 units. $99–$139 double. Rates include full breakfast. **Amenities:** Restaurant; bar; outdoor pool; free Wi-Fi.

Hotel Guanamar ★   Guests spend a lot of time in and around the pool here. It's right next to the restaurant and bar, has a broad wooden deck on all sides, and boasts captivating views of Carillo Bay, offshore islands and shimmering seas. As for the rooms: They tend to be spare looking but those that are set into the hillside have those same spectacular views from their balconies, so you likely won't mind much. The Bay Front rooms are located on the lowest point of the property, so you'll be getting a workout going to and from meals, although you are also much closer to the beach. As at The Hideaway Hotel (see above), it helps to have a rental car here

Puerto Carrillo. www.guanamarhotel.com. ℂ **2282-8700.** 37 units. $110–$160 double $280 suite. Rates include breakfast. **Amenities:** Restaurant; bar; large outdoor pool; room service; free Wi-Fi.

INEXPENSIVE

In addition to the hotels listed below, **Tico Adventure Lodge ★** (www.ticoadventurelodge.com; ℂ **2656-0628**) is another good option, about 2 blocks from the beach, in the heart of town. A slew of very inexpensive places to stay are along the road into town and around the soccer field but most of these joints are less attractive than your average jail cell.

Casa del Mar ★★ You enter under a shower of flowering bougainvillea and immediately are enveloped by the calm, cool and relaxed atmosphere that pervades the Casa del Mar, my favorite budget option in Playa Sámara. Rooms are spacious, clean and comfortable, and most come with A/C and private bathrooms (a few of the very cheap ones here have neither). The beach is just a few steps away across the street. The pool is just a hair bigger and no deeper than a fountain, but it will cool you off on a hot day.

Playa Sámara, Nicoya, Guanacaste. www.casadelmarsamara.net. ℂ **2656-0264.** 17 units, 11 with private bathroom. $45 double with shared bathroom; $85–$95 double with private bathroom and A/C. Rates include taxes. Breakfast included for private bathroom rates year round. Breakfast included for shared bathroom rates in off season. **Amenities:** Unheated outdoor pool/Jacuzzi; free Wi-Fi.

Hotel Belvedere ★ German emigrants Manfred and Michaela Landwehr opened the Belvedere more than two decades ago, and it was the first place I ever stayed in Playa Samara. It's grown over the years, but always kept to its mission of providing clean, cozy rooms at a reasonable price. Despite minor pangs of nostalgia, I prefer the newer rooms in the annex a bit uphill from the original hotel, where you'll find a larger pool and more exuberant gardens. These gardens in fact join wild forest and are occasionally visited by troops of howler and spider monkeys. No matter the location, rooms are well-kept and many feature a yellow hand painted wash effect meant to work as wainscoting. Large, filling breakfasts are served at the main lodge, where you'll also find a second, smaller pool. It's just a 1-block walk down into the heart of town, and 2 blocks to the beach.

Playa Sámara. www.belvederesamara.net. ℂ **2656-0213.** 24 units. $75–$90 double, $80–$120 apartment. Rates include taxes. **Amenities:** Lounge; Jacuzzi; 2 outdoor pools; free Wi-Fi.

Sámara Tree House Inn ★★ It's not possible to find a room closer to the waves in Playa Sámara. While not true tree houses, four raised-stilt wooden cabins are supported by columns made from whole tree trunks set in a tight line facing the ocean. They have prized ocean views from the elevated perch of their large sitting rooms, although the bedrooms do feel a bit small and spartan, and there's no air-conditioning. However, every unit here does come with a full kitchenette, as well as a large area underneath the living area equipped with a varnished wood table and chairs, as well as a couple of woven hammocks. There's a postage stamp–size round pool at the center of the complex, and a few chaise lounges on a patch of well-tended grass facing the beach.

Playa Sámara, Guanacaste. www.samaratreehouse.com. ℂ **2656-0733.** 6 units. $89–$145 double. Rates include breakfast. **Amenities:** Jacuzzi; small outdoor pool; free Wi-Fi.

A NEARBY LUXURY HOTEL

Hotel Punta Islita ★★★ This exclusive and remote luxury resort sits on a hilltop above the beach. Most of the rooms are private bungalows or villas, adorned with terracotta floor tiles, thatch and antique clay tile roofs which given them a tropical feel. White muslin is hung from the driftwood log used to fashion the locally produced four-poster beds— very romantic! And many come with either a private Jacuzzi or plunge pool. The larger villas are appropriate for families and small groups. The beach is a 10-minute or so hike away, but the hotel runs regular shuttle services and has a canopy tour that ends at the beach (the last is the most fun way to get to the sands). The resort's fab infinity pool is up on the hillside; another pool and bar and grill are down by the beach. Punta Islita actively supports a range of local social, artistic, and conservation projects. In 2014, Punta Islita was added to the Marriott hotel chain's exclusive Autograph Collection.

Playa Islita. www.hotelpuntaislita.com. ✆ **866/446-4053** in the U.S. and Canada, or 2231-6122 in Costa Rica. 58 units, 10 villas. $210–$330 double; $476 suite; $528 casita; $613–$723 villas 4 people. Rates include breakfast. **Amenities:** 2 restaurants; 2 bars; 9-hole par 3 golf course and driving range; small exercise room and spa; Jacuzzi; outdoor pool and lap pool; room service; 2 lit tennis courts; free Wi-Fi.

Where to Dine

Sámara has numerous inexpensive *sodas* (diners), and most of the hotels have their own restaurants. In addition to the places mentioned below, **El Ancla** (www.isamara.co/ancla.htm; ✆ **2656-0716**), located a bit south of downtown, serves up good, simple meals, with an excellent view of the beach and waves.

Hotel Punta Islita.

El Lagarto ★ STEAK/GRILL   Here's the butch way to dine! A massive fire churns out a stream of hot wood-burning coals to feed the large, long barbeque grill stations at this restaurant and bar. Tables are made from massive heavy planks and the food is served on huge, crosscut blocks of wood, which adds to the rustic vibe. Grilled grass-fed and aged meats, seafood, and organic veggies are the heart of the long menu here. North end of Playa Sámara. www.ellagartobbq.com. ℭ **2656-0750.** Reservations recommended. Main courses $8–$32. Daily 3–11pm.

Gusto Beach ★★ ITALIAN/BISTRO   This simple, Italian-run restaurant is basically a beachfront trattoria—and then some. It's also a beach club, where people rent chaise lounges to hang for the day, playing volleyball and catching rays. And the food goes well beyond pastas, panini, and thin-crust pizzas to take in sushi, sashimi, and curries. Presentations can be creative, like the side of crisp pan-fried potatoes served in the cooking pan, or the fresh gelato made and served in a mason jar and topped with shaved chocolate. At night, this become nightlife central with live music or DJs. On the beach, north end of Playa Sámara. ℭ **2656-0252.** Reservations recommended. Main courses C4,900–C14,000. Daily 9am–11pm.

Entertainment & Nightlife

After dark the most happening place in town is **Bar Arriba** ★ (no phone), a second-floor affair with a contemporary vibe a couple of blocks inland from the beach on the main road into town. You might also check out what's going on at **Gusto Beach** ★ (see above), **La Vela Latina** (ℭ **2656-2286**), or **Tabanuco** (ℭ **2656-1056**), all on the beach or fronting the water, right near the center of the action, on the main road running parallel to the beach off the center of town.

PLAYA NOSARA ★★

55km (34 miles) SW of Nicoya; 266km (165 miles) W of San José

As is the case in Malpaís, **Playa Nosara** is a bucket term used to refer to several neighboring beaches, spread along an isolated stretch of coast. In addition to the namesake beach, **Playa Guiones, Playa Pelada, Playa Garza,** and (sometimes) **Playa Ostional** are also lumped into this area. In fact, the village of Nosara itself is several kilometers inland from the beach. Playa Nosara marks the northern limit of the Nicoya Peninsula.

Playa Guiones is one of Costa Rica's most dependable beach breaks, and surfers come here in good numbers throughout the year. Happily, the waves are much less crowded than you would find in Tamarindo.

The best way to get to Nosara is to fly, but, with everything so spread out, that makes getting around difficult after you've arrived. The roads to, in, and around Nosara are almost always in very rough shape, with little sign that this will improve anytime soon.

Essentials

Playa Guiones.

GETTING THERE & DEPARTING By Plane: Nature Air (www.natureair.com; ✆ **800/235-9272** in the U.S. and Canada, or 2299-6000 in Costa Rica) has several flights daily to **Nosara airport** (airport code: NOB). Fares run between $110 and $160 each way.

It's usually about a 5- to 10-minute drive from the airport to most hotels. Taxis wait for every arrival, and fares range between C3,000 and C6,000 to most hotels in Nosara.

By Car: Follow the directions for getting to Playa Sámara (p. 315), but watch for a well-marked fork in the road a few kilometers before you reach that beach. The right-hand fork leads to Nosara over another 22km (14 miles) of rough dirt road.

By Bus: An **Alfaro** express bus (www.empresaalfaro.com; ✆ **2222-2666** in San José, or 2682-0064 in Nosara) leaves San José daily at 5:30am from Avenida 5 between calles 14 and 16. The trip's duration is 5½ hours; the one-way fare is C4,805.

You can also take an Alfaro bus from San José to Nicoya and then catch a second bus from Nicoya to Nosara. **Alfaro** buses leave San José nearly every hour between 7:30am and 5pm. The fare is C3,950. The trip can take between 4 and 5½ hours, depending on whether the bus goes via Liberia or La Amistad Bridge. The latter route is much faster and much more frequent. **Empresa Rojas** buses (✆ **2685-5352**) leave Nicoya for Nosara daily at 4:45 and 10am, 12:30pm, and 3:30 and 5:30pm. The trip is about 2 hours, and the one-way fare is C1,870. Return buses leave Nosara for Nicoya at 5, 6, and 7am, noon and 3:30pm. A direct Alfaro bus from Nosara to San José leaves daily at 12:30pm. Buses to Nicoya leave Nosara daily at 4:45 and 10am, noon, and 3 and 5:30pm. Buses leave Nicoya for San José nearly every hour 3am to 5pm.

GETTING AROUND If you want to rent a car, both **Economy** (www.economyrentacar.com; ✆ **877/326-7368** in the U.S. and Canada, or 2582-1246 in Costa Rica) and **National** (www.natcar.com; ✆ **2242-7878**) have offices here. Because demand often outstrips supply, I recommend you reserve a car in advance. Alternatively, you can rent an ATV from several operators around town, including **Iguana Expeditions** and **Boca Nosara Tours** (p. 326). If you need a taxi, call **Taxi Freddy** (✆ **8662-6080**) or **Gypsy Cab Company** (www.gypsycabnosara.com; ✆ **8302-1903**).

VILLAGE LAYOUT The village of Nosara is about 5km (3 miles) inland from the beach. The small airstrip runs pretty much through the center of town; however, most hotels listed here are on or near the beach itself.

This area was originally conceived and zoned as a primarily residential community. The maze of dirt roads and lack of any single defining thoroughfare can be confusing for first-time visitors. Luckily, a host of hotel and restaurant signs spread around the area help point lost travelers in the direction of their final destination.

FAST FACTS You'll find the post office and police station (✆ **2682-1130**) right at the end of the airstrip. An EBAIS medical clinic (✆ **2682-0266**) and a couple of pharmacies are in the village as well. Both Banco Popular and Banco de Costa Rica have offices in Nosara with ATMs. There's even a tiny strip mall at the crossroads to Playa Guiones.

Exploring Playa Nosara

Among the several beaches at Nosara are the long, curving **Playa Guiones ★★**, **Playa Nosara ★**, and the diminutive **Playa Pelada ★**. Because the village of Nosara is several miles inland, these beaches tend to be clean, secluded, and quiet. Surfing and bodysurfing are good here, particularly at Playa Guiones, which is garnering quite a reputation as a consistent and rideable beach break. Pelada is a short white-sand beach with three deep scallops, backed by sea grasses and mangroves. There isn't too much sand at high tide, so you'll want to hit the beach when the tide's out. At either end of the beach, rocky outcroppings reveal tide pools at low tide.

When the seas are calm, you can do some decent snorkeling around the rocks and reefs just offshore. Masks, snorkels, and fins can be rented at **Café de Paris** (p. 329) or **Coconut Harry's** (p. 326). Bird-watchers should explore the mangrove swamps around the estuary mouth of the Río Nosara. Just walk north from Playa Pelada and follow the riverbank; then take the paths into the mangroves. In addition to numerous water, shore, and sea bird species, you're apt to spot a range of hawks and other raptors, as well as toucans and several parrot species.

FISHING All the hotels in the area can arrange fishing charters for $200 to $500 for a half-day, or $400 to $1,200 for a full day. These rates are for one to four people and vary according to boat size and accouterments.

HIKING & WILDLIFE VIEWING Located on land surrounding the Nosara river mouth, the **Nosara Biological Reserve** (www.lagarta. com; ✆ **2682-0035**) features a network of trails and raised walkways through tropical transitional forests and mangrove swamps. More than 270 species of birds have been spotted here. This private reserve is owned and managed by the folks at the **Lagarta Lodge** (p. 328), and the trails start right at the hotel. Admission is $6. Guided tours and guided boat tours are also available.

HORSEBACK RIDING & QUAD TOURS   The folks at **Boca Nosara Tours** (www.bocanosaratours.com; ✆ **2682-0280**) have a large stable of well-cared-for horses and a range of beach, jungle, and waterfall rides to choose from. They also run similar tours on motorized off-road quads. Rates run between $40 and $70 per person, depending on the size of your group and the length of the tour. Another good option for ATV tours and rentals, is **iQuad** (www.iquadnosara.com; ✆ **8629-8349**).

SEA TURTLE–WATCHING   If you time your trip right, you can do a night tour to nearby **Playa Ostional** to watch nesting olive ridley sea turtles. These turtles come ashore by the thousands in a mass egg-laying phenomenon known as an *arribada*. The *arribadas* are so difficult to predict that no one runs regularly scheduled turtle-viewing trips, but when the *arribada* is in full swing, several local guides and agencies offer tours. These *arribadas* take place 4 to 10 times between July and December; each occurrence lasts between 3 and 10 days. Consider yourself very lucky if you happen to be around during one of these fascinating natural phenomena. Your best bet is to ask the staff at your hotel or check in with the **Associacion de Guias de Ostional ★** (Ostional Local Guide Association; ✆ **2682-0428;** asoc.guiasostional@hotmail.com). Tours are generally run at night, but because the turtles come ashore in such numbers, you can sometimes catch them in the early morning light as well. Even if it's not turtle-nesting season, you might want to look into visiting Playa Ostional just to have a long, wide expanse of beach to yourself. However, be careful swimming here because the surf and riptides can be formidable. During the dry season (mid-Nov to Apr), you can usually get here in a regular car, but during the rainy season you'll need four-wheel-drive. This beach is part of **Ostional National Wildlife Refuge** (✆ **2682-0428**). At the northwest end of the refuge is **India Point,** which is known for its tide pools and rocky outcrops.

SURFING   With miles of excellent beach breaks and relatively few crowds, this is a great place to surf or learn how to surf. If you want to try to stand up for your first time, check in with the folks at **Coconut Harry's Surf Shop** (www.coconutharrys.com; ✆ **2682-0574**), **Del Mar Surf Camp** (www.delmarsurfcamp.com; ✆ **855/833-5627** in the U.S. and Canada, or 2682-1433 in Costa Rica), or **Safari Surf School** (www.safarisurfschool.com; ✆ **866/433-3355** in the U.S. and Canada, or 2682-0113 in Costa Rica). All of the above offer hourly solo or group lessons, multiday packages with accommodations and meals included, and board rental.

YOGA & MORE   **Nosara Yoga Institute ★★** (www.nosarayoga.com; ✆ **866/439-4704** in the U.S. and Canada, or 2682-0071 in Costa Rica) offers daily yoga classes, and a host of custom-designed "retreat" options. This is an internationally recognized institute. Their daily 90-minute classes are open to the public and cost just $15; they even provide a mat.

You might also check in to see if anything is being offered up at the Harmony Hotel & Spa (see below).

Where to Stay

In addition to the places listed below, the **Nosara Beach House ★** (www.thenosarabeachhouse.com; ✆ **2682-0019**), on Playa Guiones, has clean, comfortable rooms and a swimming pool—and it's right on the beach, to boot. For an intimate option that's also a very good deal, check out the **Nosara B&B Retreat ★** (www.nosararetreat.com; ✆ **2682-0209**).

EXPENSIVE

The Harmony Hotel & Spa ★★★   With an enviable setting right on Playa Guiones, this is by far the best hotel option in Nosara. Well-heeled surfers and yogis flock here, and it's often hard to get a room, their occupancy is so high. Even the entry level "Coco" rooms are quite spacious, with high peaked wood paneled ceilings, queen-size beds and a private, enclosed garden deck area featuring an outdoor shower with massive rainwater-style shower head. The bungalows are even larger, with king beds; there are two-bedroom suites for families or small groups of friends. A short path through thick foliage leads to the waves, and the hotel has a shower and fresh towels waiting for guests right where the property lets out on to the beach. There's an excellent onsite spa and yoga facility, and the restaurant serves top-notch locally sourced spa cuisine. This hotel was awarded "5 Leaves" from the CST Sustainable Tourism program, thanks to a comprehensive commitment to environmental protection.
Playa Guiones. www.harmonynosara.com. ✆ **2682-4114.** 25 units. $210–$330 double; $280–$380 bungalow; $560–$690 2-bedroom suite. Rates include breakfast and 1 yoga class. **Amenities:** Restaurant; bar; complimentary use of bikes; midsize outdoor pool; spa; surfboard rental; free Wi-Fi.

L'Acqua Viva ★   L'Acqua Viva features some unique and beautiful architectural touches, including soaring thatch roofs and exposed bamboo walls. Rooms feature bamboo floors, high bamboo headboards backing the beds, and balconies with bamboo railings. Bamboo's a locally grown renewable resource, so its use here is commendable. The hotel also has a wide range of pools and water features, both functional for swimming and decorative for admiring—thus the name, which is Italian for "Living Water." Downside? The L'Acqua Viva is located a good deal inland from the beach and getting to and from the sands make having a rental car almost a necessity. Moreover, Nosara's main road, a dusty unpaved thoroughfare, wraps around the property, blanketing the rooms and buildings closest to the road in thick dust throughout most of the high season.

Playa Guiones. www.lacquaviva.com. ✆ **888/273-1977** in the U.S., or 2682-1087 in Costa Rica. 35 units. $180 double; $270–$300 suite; $450–$625 villa. Rates include continental breakfast. **Amenities:** Restaurant; bar; Jacuzzi; 2 large outdoor pools; room service; full-service spa; Wi-Fi.

MODERATE

Harbor Reef Surf Resort ★   This sprawling miniresort features a mix of rooms and suites at excellent prices, and is quite popular with the surf crowd. All of the rooms are spacious and clean, although a bit bare, with very few decorative touches. Some of the suites come with full kitchens; the staff also rent out several fully equipped houses. The grounds feature tall trees, pretty gardens and two swimming pools—one with a swim up bar and the other with a stone waterfall that forms a small private grottolike area underneath. The beach and popular surf break at Playa Guiones is about a 3-minute walk away. Attached to the resort is a well-stocked convenience store that rents bicycles, ATVs and golf carts.

Playa Guiones. www.harborreef.com. ✆ **2682-5049.** 23 units. $120–$165 double; $175–$280 suite. Rates include continental breakfast. **Amenities:** Restaurant; bar; 2 small outdoor pools; free Wi-Fi.

INEXPENSIVE

In addition to the places mentioned below, **Kaya Sol ★** (www.nosara hotelkayasol.com; ✆ **2682-1459**) is a popular budget option and surfer hangout.

The Gilded Iguana ★   Located in the heart of Playa Guiones, about 200m (600 ft.) inland from the beach, the Iguana features a mix of rooms, a mid-size kidney-shaped pool, and one of the best restaurant and bar scenes in the area (p. 329). The downside to the restaurant and bar's popularity is that it can be noisy here, especially when there's a live band or major sporting event going on. The most economical rooms are simple and road-worn, with low wooden beds and colorful Guatemalan textile bedspreads. I think it's worth a splurge for the newer rooms, which not only feature air-conditioning, but are located behind the pool and away from the restaurant and its hubbub.

Playa Guiones. www.thegildediguana.com. ✆ 2682-0450. 12 units. $60–$65 double; $85–$110 suite. **Amenities:** Restaurant; bar; midsize outdoor pool; free Wi-Fi.

Lagarta Lodge ★★   Geared more to nature lovers than surfers, this small lodge sits on a high hilltop overlooking the Nosara River. Standard rooms are simple, but clean and cozy, with red tile floors and textured concrete walls meant to look like painted river stones. The superior rooms or suites (they use both terms interchangeably), have a more contemporary feel and offer up the lodge's signature view over the river and rainforests and beyond to the long stretch of Ostional Beach in the distance. It's only a 10- to 15-minute jaunt down to the beach, but it's a pretty steep and strenuous hike back up to the hotel. The owners of this hotel own 35 hectares (86 acres) of land bordering the Nosara River, which they've converted into a private reserve. Guests here get unlimited access to the trails of the reserve, which pass through tropical lowland rainforests and mangrove forests.

Playa Nosara. www.lagarta.com. © **2682-0035.** 12 units. $80–$125 double. **Amenities:** Restaurant; bar; midsize outdoor pool; Wi-Fi.

Where to Dine

In addition to the places mentioned below, **Marlin Bill's** (© 2682-0458) is a popular and massive open-air haunt on the hillside on the main road, just across from **Café de París** (see below). You can expect to get good, fresh seafood and American classics here. **La Dolce Vita ★★** (© 2682-0107), on the outskirts of town on the road to Playa Sámara, serves up Italian fare nightly. **Robin's Ice Cream ★** (www.robinsicecream.com; © 2682-0617) makes homemade ice cream and also serves breakfast, lunch, and dinner. Finally, **Go Juice ★** (© 8682-4692) is a semipermanent "food truck" dishing out fresh juices, iced coffee drinks, and tuna *poki* bowls. Their signature frozen banana coffee drink has won over more than a few skeptics, myself included. For local flavor, **Doña Olga's** (no phone) is a simple Costa Rican *soda* right on the beach in Playa Pelada.

Café de Paris ★ BAKERY/BISTRO   I like to stop here for a freshly baked croissant and cup of coffee before an early morning surf session—and I often return for a full breakfast afterwards. But it's also worthwhile for lunch (think burgers, nachos, or wraps) or dinner—both the steak au poivre and fish curry are excellent. A pool, minigolf course and children's play set just off the main dining area make this a good choice for families with young kids. Café de Paris is located right at the main crossroads for access to Playa Guiones.

On the main road into Nosara. www.cafedeparis.net. © **2682-1036.** Main courses C6,500–C9,900. Daily 7am–5pm.

The Gilded Iguana ★★ SEAFOOD/GRILL   The food here is bar-food-plus, with all the staples you'd expect—burgers, nachos, quesadillas, fajitas, and wings—as well as more substantial (chicken Parmesan) or eclectic (Thai shrimp) fare. The menu also features vegetarian, gluten-free, and low-calorie options. I highly recommend the fresh fish dishes, as they're provided daily by Chiqui, the owner's husband, a Nosara-born fisherman and tour guide. There's live music here Tuesdays and Fridays; sporting events are shown on the TV's daily.

About 90m (295 ft.) inland from the beach at Playa Guiones. www.thegildediguana. com. © **2682-0259.** Main courses C4,000–C9,000. Daily 7am–10pm.

La Luna ★★ INTERNATIONAL   This funky, oceanfront bistro enjoys the best setting of any restaurant in Nosara. From its sand and grass perch right above Playa Pelada, you can watch surfers just below from one of the outdoor tables or long couches with overstuffed pillows. This is also a great place to catch the sunset. As darkness sets in, candlelight and strings of bare bulbs running between the trees and main building are lit to create a romantic atmosphere. Wood oven–fired pizzas and Mediterranean fare are the specialties here, but nightly chalkboard specials might feature anything from pad Thai to chicken curry. For lunch, I really like their fish tacos. Service can be slow and a bit gruff.

Playa Pelada. ✆ **2682-0122.** Main courses C6,700–C11,200. Daily Noon–9pm.

Entertainment & Nightlife

When evening rolls around, don't expect a major party scene. **Kaya Sol** (✆ **2682-1459**) has a lounge that's popular with surfers, and the **Gilded Iguana** (p. 329) often has live music. In "downtown" Nosara, you'll probably want to check out either the **Tropicana** (✆ **2682-0140**), the town's long-standing local disco, or the **Legends Bar** (✆ **2682-0184**), an American-style bar with big-screen TVs and pool and foosball tables.

North of Nosara

Just north of Nosara lies Playa Ostional, famous for its massive nestings of olive ridley sea turtles (p. 326). This is a very underdeveloped beach village with only a few hotels, the best of which is **Hotel Luna Azul ★** (www.hotellunaazul.com; ✆ **2682-1400**), which features nice individual bungalows and a great view of the ocean—although the beach is a good distance away. If you come to Ostional to surf, try the **Ostional Turtle Lodge** (www.surfingostional.com; ✆ **2682-0131**), a basic hostel-type affair right on the beach near the center of the village.

Playa Ostional.

THE NORTHERN ZONE:

MOUNTAIN LAKES, CLOUD FORESTS & A VOLCANO

C osta Rica's northern zone is a fabulous destination for all manner of adventurers, naturalists, and down-to-earth travelers. The region is home to several prime ecotourist destinations, including the majestic **Arenal Volcano ★★** and the misty **Monteverde Cloud Forest Biological Reserve ★★★**. Changes in elevation create unique microclimates and ecosystems throughout the region. You'll find rainforests and cloud forests, jungle rivers and waterfalls, mountain lakes, lowland marshes, and an unbelievable wealth of birds and other wildlife. In addition to these natural wonders, this region also provides an intimate glimpse into the rural heart and soul of Costa Rica. Small, isolated lodges flourish, and the region's many towns and villages remain predominantly small agricultural communities.

This area is also a must for adventure travelers. The northern zone has one of the best windsurfing spots in the world, on **Lake Arenal ★**, as well as excellent opportunities for mountain biking, hiking, canyoning, and river rafting. Zip-line canopy tours and suspended forest bridges abound. And after you partake these adventure activities, you'll find soothing natural hot springs in the area where you can soak your tired muscles. Most travelers would do well to include some time spent in the Northern Zone on any trip to Costa Rica.

THE best NORTHERN ZONE TRAVEL EXPERIENCES

- o **Soaking in a Hot Spring at the Foot of Arenal Volcano:** Although the eruptions have subsided, Arenal Volcano remains the source of several natural hot springs, ranging from the over-the-top splendor of Tabacón Grand Spa Thermal Resort, to the simple forest enshrouded pools at the family-run Eco Termales. See p. 348.

- o **Rappelling Down the Face of a Rainforest Waterfall:** Canyoning is a wet and wild adventure sport that is thriving in the northern zone. A mix of hiking, river wading, and rappelling, these tours are offered in La Fortuna and Monteverde. See p. 342 and 374.

PREVIOUS PAGE: **Arenal Volcano.**

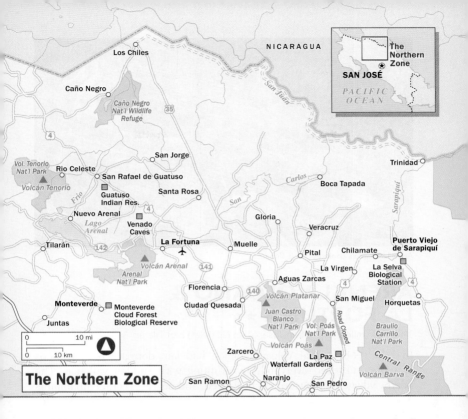

The Northern Zone

- **Hiking the Trails of a Cloud Forest:** The well-groomed network of trails at the Monteverde Cloud Forest Biological Reserve reveals its rich mysteries with stunning regularity. Walk through gray mist and peer up at the dense tangle of epiphytes and vines, looking for exotic birds and troops of monkeys. See p. 371.

- **Climbing Over Cooled-Off Lava at Arenal National Park:** This area has tons of great hiking, but I especially like scrambling over the volcano's old lava flows. Most are on the relatively flat flanks of the volcano, so there's not too much climbing involved. See p. 339.

- **Riding a Horse or Mountain Bike Along a Rural Back Road:** The dirt roads and ox-trails of this rural zone provide a wealth of great opportunities for mountain biking and horseback riding. See the "Exploring" sections of individual destinations throughout this chapter.

Arenal Volcano's cooled-off lava flows.

ARENAL VOLCANO & LA FORTUNA ★★

140km (87 miles) NW of San José; 61km (38 miles) E of Tilarán

In July 1968, Arenal Volcano, which had lain dormant for hundreds of years, surprised everybody by erupting with sudden violence. The nearby village of Tabacón was destroyed, and nearly 80 of its inhabitants were killed. At 1,607m (5,271 ft.) high, Arenal was for many decades afterward one of the world's most regularly active volcanoes. Sometime around December 2010, it entered into a relatively quiet phase. No one knows how long this may last. Still, rising to a near-perfect cone, the volcano itself remains majestic to gaze upon. And the area offers up a rich variety of primary rainforests, rushing jungle rivers and waterfalls, lush natural hot springs, and a wide range of adventure activities.

Lying at the eastern foot of this natural spectacle is the town of **La Fortuna.** Once a humble little farming village, La Fortuna has become a magnet for travelers from around the world.

La Fortuna Waterfall.

Essentials

GETTING THERE & DEPARTING **Nature Air** (www.natureair.com; © **800/235-9272** in the U.S. and Canada, or 2299-6000 in Costa Rica) and **Sansa** (www.flysansa.com; © **877/767-2672** in the U.S. and Canada, or 2290-4100 in Costa Rica) each have one daily flight to Arenal/La Fortuna (airport code: FOR) from Juan Santamaría International Airport in San José (airport code: SJO). Fares range from $80–$110 one-way. Nature Air also sometimes has direct flights between La Fortuna and Tortuguero, which are incredibly convenient and eliminate a lot of driving, and potentially long layovers.

The La Fortuna airstrip is actually in the small village of El Tanque, about a 15 minute drive from La Fortuna, and anywhere from 20 to 40 minutes from most of the popular area hotels. **Taxis** are sometimes waiting for arriving flights. If not, you can call one at © **2479-9605.** The fare to La Fortuna runs around C8,000–C15,000. Alternatively, Nature Air can arrange to have a van waiting for you, for $62 to $130 for up to six people depending upon the location of your hotel.

By Car: Several routes connect La Fortuna and San José. The most popular is to head west on the Interamerican Highway (CR1) from San José and then turn north at Naranjo, continuing north through Zarcero to Ciudad Quesada on CR141. From Ciudad Quesada, CR141 passes through Florencia, Jabillos, and Tanque on its way to La Fortuna. This route offers fab views of the San Carlos valley as you come down from Ciudad Quesada; Zarcero, with its topiary gardens and quaint church, makes a good place to stop, and snap a few photos (see chapter 7).

You can also stay on the Interamerican Highway (CR1) until San Ramón (west of Naranjo) and then head north through La Tigra on CR142. This route is very scenic and passes the Villa Blanca Cloud Forest & Spa (p. 356). The travel time on any of the above routes is roughly 3 to 3½ hours.

A new highway connecting San Ramon with Ciudad Quesada/San Carlos is expected to open in mid-2016. However, if history is any indication, I'd expect it to be delayed by at least a year.

By Bus: Buses (© **2255-0567** or 2255-4318) leave San José for La Fortuna at 6:30, 8:40, and 12:30am from the **Atlántico del Norte** bus station at Avenida 7 and 9 and Calle 12. The trip lasts 4 hours; the fare is C2,575. The bus you take might be labeled tilarán. Make sure it passes through Ciudad Quesada (also known as San Carlos). If so, it passes through La Fortuna; if not, you'll end up in Tilarán via the Interamerican Highway, passing through the Guanacaste town of Cañas, a long way from La Fortuna.

Alternatively, you can take a bus from the same station to Ciudad Quesada (San Carlos) and transfer there to another bus to La Fortuna. These buses depart roughly every 40 minutes between 5am and 7:30pm. The fare for the 3 hours trip is C1,860. Local buses between Ciudad Quesada and La Fortuna run regularly through the day, although the schedule changes frequently, depending on demand. The trip lasts an hour; the fare is C1,300.

Buses depart **Monteverde/Santa Elena** for Tilarán every day at 7am. This is a journey of only 35km (22 miles), but the trip lasts 2½ hours because the road is in rough shape. People with bad backs should think twice about making the trip, especially by bus. The return bus from Tilarán to Santa Elena leaves at 12:30pm. The fare is C1,250. Buses from Tilarán to La Fortuna depart daily at 7am and 12:20 and 4:30pm,

boats, HORSES & TAXIS

You can travel between La Fortuna and Monteverde by boat and taxi, or on a combination of boat, horseback, and taxi. A 10- to 20-minute boat ride across Lake Arenal cuts out hours of driving around its shores. From La Fortuna to the put-in point is about a 25-minute taxi ride. It's about a 1½-hour four-wheel-drive taxi ride between the Río Chiquito dock on the other side of Lake Arenal and Santa Elena. These trips can be arranged in either direction for between $30 and $50 per person, all-inclusive.

You can also add on a horseback ride on the Santa Elena/Monteverde side of the lake. Several routes and rides are on offer. The steepest heads up the mountains and through the forest to the town of San Gerardo, only a 30-minute car ride from Santa Elena. Other routes throw in shorter sections of horseback riding along the lakeside lowlands. With the horseback ride, this trip runs around $85 per person.

Warning: The riding is often rainy, muddy, and steep. Many find it much more arduous than awe-inspiring. Moreover, I've received complaints about the condition of the trails and the treatment of the horses, so do your research before signing on. Find out what route you'll be taking, as well as the condition of the

horses. **Desafío Expeditions** ★★ (www.desafiocostarica.com; ✆ 855/818-0020 in the U.S. and Canada, or 2479-0020 in Costa Rica) is one of the more reputable operators. They will even drive your car around for you while you take the scenic route.

If you're looking to make the ride just by taxi and boat, check in with **Jeep Boat Jeep** (www.jeepboatjeep.com; ✆ 8305-0113), which has daily fixed departures in each direction at 8am and 2pm for $25 per person. *Note:* This is a very popular service and it is booked by almost all of the hotels and tour operators in town. However, it's also very hit-or-miss in terms of customer service. Travelers often have to carry their own luggage from the van or jeep to the boat (or vice versa), sometimes over rough, muddy terrain, and there's often confusion during the transitions between boat and van or jeep. For their part, **Desafío Expeditions** has begun their own **Monteverde Express** van-boat-van shuttle between Arenal and Monteverde. It's a little more expensive, but much better in terms of service and ease of use. Moreover, it can also be combined with a stop at the Don Juan Coffee Farm (p. 377) and lunch.

and make the return trip at 8am and 12:15 and 5:30pm. The trip is 2 to 3 hours; the fare is C1,600.

Buses depart La Fortuna for San José roughly every 2 hours between 5am and 6pm; in most instances, you will have to transfer in Ciudad Quesada to one of the frequent buses to San José.

Gray Line (www.graylinecostarica.com; ✆ 800/719-3105 in the U.S. and Canada, or 2220-2126 in Costa Rica) and **Interbus** (www.interbusonline.com; ✆ 4031-0888) both have two buses daily leaving San José for La Fortuna. The fare is around $50. Both companies will pick you up at most San José-area hotels. And both companies also run routes from La Fortuna with connections to most other major destinations in Costa Rica.

CITY LAYOUT   As you enter La Fortuna from the east, you'll see the massive volcano directly in front of you. The main road into town, CR142, passes through the center of the La Fortuna and then out toward Tabacón and the volcano. La Fortuna is only a few streets wide, with almost all the hotels, restaurants, and shops clustered along the main street and around the small central park.

VISITOR INFORMATION   **Desafío Expeditions ★★** (www.desafio costarica.com; ℂ **855/818-0020** in the U.S. and Canada, or 2479-0020 in Costa Rica), **Jacamar Tours** (www.arenaltours.com; ℂ **888/719-6377** in the U.S. and Canada, or **2479-9767**), and **Pure Trek Canyoning ★★** (www.puretrek.com; ℂ **866/569-5723** in the U.S. and Canada, or 2479-1313 in Costa Rica) are the main tour operators in the area. All of these companies offer most of the tours listed in this section, as well as fishing and sightseeing excursions on the lake, and transfers to and from other destinations around Costa Rica.

GETTING AROUND   If you don't have a car, you'll need to either take a cab or go on an organized tour if you want to visit the hot springs or view the volcano. La Fortuna has tons of taxis (you can flag one down practically anywhere, or dial ℂ **2479-9605**), and a line of them is always ready and waiting along the main road beside the central park. Another alternative is to rent a car when you get here. **Alamo** (www.alamo costarica.com; ℂ **2479-9090**) has an office in downtown La Fortuna.

SPECIAL EVENTS   Each year, starting around February 1, La Fortuna pulls out all the stops for a 2-week celebration of the town's *Fiestas Civicas,* or Civic Celebrations. There are horse parades, bull fights, mechanical rides, food stands, and concerts.

FAST FACTS   You'll find several information and tour-booking offices, as well as a couple of pharmacies, general stores, banks, and laundromats within a few blocks' radius of the town's central park and church. If you need assistance, call the Tourist Police at ℂ **2479-7257.**

Exploring Arenal Volcano & La Fortuna

It's worth a quick visit to tour the town's **Catholic Church,** a contemporary church designed by famous Costa Rican artist Teodorico Quirós. It features a soaring concrete front steeple and clock tower.

EXPERIENCING THE VOLCANO ★★★

As I mention earlier, since December 2010, the Arenal Volcano has been very quiet, with no loud eruptions or pyroclastic blasts. Still, the actual volcano remains a stunning sight and the natural park, and surrounding trails and activities make this a fabulous destination. That said, Arenal is surrounded by cloud forests and rainforests, and the volcano's cone is often socked in by clouds and fog. Many people come to Arenal and never see the exposed cone. ***Note:*** Although it's counterintuitive, the rainy season is often a better time to see the exposed cone of Arenal Volcano. I don't know why this is, but I've had excellent volcano-viewing sessions at various points during the rainy season; during the dry season, the volcano can often be shrouded for days at a time. The bottom line is that catching a glimpse of the volcano's cone is never a sure thing.

Despite its current state of dormancy, climbing Arenal Volcano is neither common nor recommended. Over the years, many daredevil climbers have lost their lives, and others have been severely injured. This is still a very "alive" volcano, with steam vents and a molten core.

Arenal National Park

Arenal National Park ★★ (© **2461-8499;** daily 8am–3pm; $15/person) constitutes an area of more than 2,880 hectares (7,114 acres), which includes the viewing and parking areas closest to the volcano. The trails through forest and over old lava flows inside the park are gorgeous and fun. (Be careful climbing on those volcanic boulders, though.)

The principal trail inside the park, **Sendero Coladas (Lava Flow Trail) ★★**, is just under 2km (1.25 miles) long and passes through secondary forest and open savanna. At the end of the trail, a short natural stairway takes you to a broad, open lava field left in the wake of a massive 1992 eruption. Scrambling over the cooled lava is a real treat, but be careful, as the rocks can be sharp in places. Many spots throughout the park offer great views of the volcano, but the closest view can be found at **El Mirador (The Lookout) ★**, where you not only can see the volcano better, but also can hear it rumble and roar on occasion. From the parking lot near the trailhead for the Lava Flow Trail, you have the option of hiking or driving the 1km (.6 mile) to El Mirador.

Arenal Volcano looms over La Fortuna church.

NEARBY ATTRACTIONS

BUTTERFLY GARDEN   Located 2km (a little over a mile) beyond the Arenal dam out beyond the Mistico Arenal Hanging Bridges Park, the **Mot Mot Jungle** (☎ **2479-1170;** daily 7:30am–4pm; $10 admission) has a large enclosure where a wide variety of local butterfly species are bred and displayed. The attraction also has gentle paths planted with local flowers that attract a number of free flying butterflies and hummingbirds. A tour here includes an exhibit on the insect's life cycle.

COOKING CLASSES   **Tropical Cooking Class** ★ (www.costarica cooking.com; ☎ **2479-1569;** $125/person; advance reservations required), offered by the Lava Lounge, is a 3½-hour class on Costa Rican cuisine. It's held at a beautiful lookout and open-air kitchen near the **Río Fortuna waterfall.**

ESPECIALLY FOR KIDS

Located a couple of miles outside of La Fortuna, the **Ecocentro Danaus** ★ (www.ecocentrodanaus.com; ☎ **2479-7019;** daily 8am–4pm; admission $17 with tour, $12 for self-guided visit) is a private biological reserve and sustainable tourism project, which offers educational and engaging tours. Among the attractions here are a butterfly garden and reproduction center, botanical and medicinal plant gardens, and a small museum honoring the local Maleku indigenous culture. Night tours ($37) are offered by reservation. Children 5 to 10 get a 50-percent discount, and children 4 and under are free.

Those looking for close and intimate animal encounters might want to head to **Proyecto Asis** ★ (www.institutoasis.com; ☎ **2475-9121**), a wildlife rescue center and volunteer project. These folks offer two types of daily tours twice daily (once in the morning and once in the afternoon). The standard tour is informative and comprehensive and takes you through the facility and introduces you to their charges and mission. This tour lasts 1½ hours and costs $29 for adult and $17 for children 4 through 9. However, if you sign up for the "volunteering" addition, you get to stay on for another 2 hours and help around the center, nursing an injured animal or cleaning cages. This option costs $51 for adults and $29 for children 4 through 9. They also offer longer term volunteer residencies and language classes. Proyecto Asis is located about 30 to 40 minutes outside of La Fortuna, on the way to Ciudad Quesada.

Set along the banks of the Arenal River, **Club Río** ★★ (www.thespringscostarica.com; ☎ **954/727-8333** in the U.S., or 2401-3313 in Costa Rica; 2-day pass $99 adults, $75 for kids 12 and under) is a wonderful playground for parents and kids alike. You can go inner tubing on the river, ride a horse through the forest trails, visit their midsize zoo, and take a shot at their three-story climbing wall. There's also a series of naturally fed hot springs sculpted alongside the river, as well as a restaurant. It's part of the **Springs Resort and Spa** (p. 350), but you don't have to be staying at the resort to enjoy the activities and facilities here. The pass gets you access to the facilities and two of the above-mentioned adventure activities, as well as a full lunch and free run of all the pools and waterslides at the resort itself.

Finally, the newest attraction on the block is the **Kalambu Hot Springs & Water Park** ★ (www.kalambu.com; ✆ **2479-0170;** daily 9am–10pm; $32 adults, $16 children). While most of the other hot springs in the area might have a water slide or two, this place is a true water park, with several large waterslides and a massive and very entertaining children's play area and pools. The latter includes a giant bucket that is constantly filled and then dumped on everyone below. There are also a few quieter pool and hot spring areas. If you enter after 5pm, the entrance is $20 adult and $10 children.

OUTDOOR ACTIVITIES

ATV   Best of the area's operators is **Original Arenal ATV** (www.origin alarenalatv.com; ✆ **2479-7522**), which offers a 2½-hour ATV tour along the area around the lake and National Park. The cost is $99 per person, or $130 for two people riding tandem. Another option is **La Pradera** (www.lapraderadelarenal.com; ✆ **2479-9597**), which offers a 3-hour adventure through the forests and farmlands around La Fortuna. The cost is $85 per ATV.

Sky Adventures in Monteverde.

CANOPY TOURS & HANGING BRIDGES You have numerous ways to get up into the forest canopy here. Perhaps the simplest is to hike the trails and bridges of **Mistico Arenal Hanging Bridges** ★ (www.misticopark.com; ✆ **2479-1170;** daily 7:30am–4pm; $36 admission). Located just over the Lake Arenal dam, this attraction is a complex of gentle trails and suspension bridges through a beautiful tract of primary forest. Night tours depart at 5:30pm every evening.

Another option is the **Sky Tram** ★★ (www.skyadventures. travel; ✆ **844/468-6759** in the U.S., or 2479-4100), an open gondola-style ride that begins near the shores of Lake Arenal and rises up, providing excellent views of the lake and volcano. From here, you hike a series of trails and suspended bridges. In the end, you can hike down, take the gondola, or strap on a harness and ride their zip-line

A canyoning tour.

down to the bottom. The zip-line tour features several very long and very fast sections, with impressive views of the lake and volcano. The cost is $93 for the combined tram ride up, a guided hike to the trails and hanging bridges, and the zip-line tour back down. It's $44 to ride the tram round-trip. The tram runs daily from 7:30am to 3pm. Also on site: a butterfly and orchid garden.

Ecoglide ★ (www.arenalecoglide.com; ✆ **2479-7120**) and **Athica Canopy** (www.athicacanopy.com; ✆ **2479-1405**) are two other good zip-line canopy tour operations close to La Fortuna.

CANYONING This adventure sport is a mix of hiking through and alongside a jungle river, punctuated with periodic rappels through and alongside the faces of rushing waterfalls. **Pure Trek Canyoning** ★★★ (www.puretrek.com; ✆ **866/569-5723** in the U.S. and Canada, or 2479-1313 in Costa Rica; $101/person) and **Desafío Adventure Company** ★★★ (www.desafiocostarica.com; ✆ **855/818-0020** in the U.S. and Canada, or 2479-0020 in Costa Rica; $99/person) are the primary operators in this area. Pure Trek's trip is probably better for first-timers and families with kids, while Desafío's tour is just a bit more rugged and adventurous. Both of these companies offer various combination full-day excursions, mixing canyoning with other adventure tours, and tend to have two to three daily departures.

In 2015, Desafío added a new, more extreme canyoning option that they call **Gravity Falls ★★★**. Although it only features one major rappel, this tour consists of a series of leaps off of high rocks into river pools below. The cost of this tour is $125. I've done it and it's a lot of fun. However, I'm a bit torn about which I'd recommend for first timers, and in the end think that the "traditional" canyoning tour might be a better fit for most travelers.

FISHING   With Lake Arenal just around the corner, fishing is a popular activity here. The big fish to catch is *guapote,* a Central American species of rainbow bass. However, you can also book fishing trips to Caño Negro, where snook, tarpon, and other game fish can be stalked. Most hotels and adventure-tour companies can arrange fishing excursions. Or try GetMyBoat.com. Costs run around $150 to $250 per boat, and a full day goes for around $250 to $500.

HIKING & HORSEBACK RIDING   Horseback riding is a popular activity in this area, with scores of good rides on dirt backroads and through open fields and dense rainforest. Volcano and lake views come with the terrain on most rides. Horseback trips to the Río Fortuna waterfall are perhaps the most popular, but remember, the horse will get you only to the entrance; from there, you'll have to hike a bit. A horseback ride to the falls should cost between $30 and $45, including the entrance fee. Alternately, you can book with **Cabalgata Don Tobías** (www.cabalgatadontobias.com; ✆ **2479-1780**), which runs a 2½-hour tour on their private land—a mix of farmland and forest, with terrific views of the volcano. Two tours leave daily at 8:30am and 1:30pm, cost is $65/person.

El Silencio Mirador y Senderos ★ (www.miradorelsilencio.com; ✆ **2479-9900;** daily 7am–7pm; $8) is a great place for hiking outside of the national park. This private reserve has four well-marked and well-groomed trails, one of which takes you to a patch of the 1968 lava flow. There's a pretty pond, and excellent views of the volcano.

If you're looking for a more strenuous hike, sign up to climb **Cerro Chato ★★**, a dormant volcanic cone on the flank of Arenal with a beautiful little crater lake. **Desafío Adventures Company ★★** (www.desafiocostarica.com; ✆ **855/818-0020** in the U.S. and Canada, or 2479-0020 in Costa Rica) leads a 5- to 6-hour hike for $85, including lunch.

LA FORTUNA FALLS   Leading the list of side attractions in the area is the impressive **Río Fortuna Waterfall ★★** (www.arenaladifort.com; ✆ **2479-8338;** daily 8am–5pm; $10 entrance), about 5.5km (3½ miles) outside of town in a dense jungle setting. A sign in town points the way to the road out to the falls. You can drive or hike to just within viewing distance. It's another 15- to 20-minute hike down a steep and often

Horseback riding in the Arenal area.

muddy path to the pool formed by the waterfall. The hike back up will take slightly longer. You can swim, but stay away from the turbulent water at the base of the falls—several people have drowned here. Instead, check out and enjoy the calm pool just around the bend, or join the locals at the popular swimming hole under the bridge on the paved road, just after the turnoff for the road up to the falls.

It's also possible to reach the falls by horseback. Most tour operators in town, as well as the waterfall folks themselves, offer this option for around $45. The tour generally lasts around 3 to 4 hours.

MOUNTAIN BIKING This region is very well suited for mountain biking. Rides range in difficulty from moderate to extremely challenging. You can combine a day on a mountain bike with a visit to one or more of the popular attractions here. **Bike Arenal ★** (www.bikearenal.com; © **866/465-4114** in the U.S. and Canada, or 2479-9020 in Costa Rica) offers top-notch bikes and equipment and a wide range of tour possibilities.

Hardcore bikers come in March for the **Vuelta al Lago ★** (www.vueltaallago.net; © **2695-5297**), a 2-day race around the lake.

WHITE-WATER RAFTING, CANOEING & KAYAKING For adventurous tours of the area, check out **Desafío Expeditions ★★** (www.desafiocostarica.com; © **855/818-0020** in the U.S. and Canada, or 2479-0020 in Costa Rica) or **Wave Expeditions ★★** (www.waveexpeditions.com; © **888/224-6105** in the U.S. and Canada, or 2479-7262 in Costa Rica). Both companies offer daily raft rides of Class I to II, III, and IV to V on different sections of the Toro, Peñas Blancas, and Sarapiquí rivers. If you want a wet and personal ride, try Desafío's tour in inflatable kayaks, or "duckies." For families, a gentle safari float on the Peñas Blancas

White-water rafting the Río Toro.

is probably the best bet. A half-day float trip on a nearby river costs around $70 per person; a full day of rafting on some rougher water costs around $89 per person, depending on what section of river you ride. Both companies also offer mountain biking and local guided trips.

A more laid-back alternative is to take a canoe tour with **Canoa Aventura** (www.canoa-aventura.com; © **2479-8200**), which offers half-, full-, and multiday excursions on a variety of rivers in the region, which range from $49 to $155 per person.

DAY TRIPS

Caño Negro National Wildlife Refuge ★ is a vast network of marshes and rivers (particularly the Río Frío) 100km (62 miles) north of La Fortuna near the town of Los Chiles. The refuge is best known for its abundance of bird life, including roseate spoonbills, jabiru storks, herons, and egrets, but you can also see caimans and crocodiles. Bird watchers should not miss this refuge, although keep in mind that the main lake dries up in the dry season (mid-Apr to Nov), which reduces the number of wading birds. Full-day tours to Caño Negro average between $70 and $80 per person. However, most of the tours run out of La Fortuna that are billed as Caño Negro never really enter the refuge but instead ply sections of the nearby Río Frío, which features similar wildlife and ecosystems. If you're interested in staying in this area and really visiting the refuge, head to **Caño Negro Natural Lodge** (p. 357).

You can also visit the **Venado Caverns** ★★, a 45-minute drive away. In addition to plenty of stalactites, stalagmites, and other limestone formations, you'll see bats and unique cave fish and crabs. This tour is not for the claustrophobic, and includes wading through a river and scrambling over rocks and passing through a few semi-tight squeezes. This cave system is quite extensive, although tourists only have access to around 10 chambers. Still these are quite striking, with impressive stone formations and ceilings over 100-foot high in places. Tours here cost between $65 and $80, including the guide and headlamps. Be prepared to get wet and muddy.

Watch for spider monkeys in Caño Negro National Wildlife Refuge.

All of the tour agencies and hotel tour desks can arrange or directly offer trips to Caño Negro and Venado Caverns.

Where to Stay in La Fortuna

MODERATE

Hotel Magic Mountain ★ You can enjoy a postcard perfect view of Arenal volcano's perfect cone while lying in bed in most of the rooms at Magic Mountain. But even if you can't see it from your bed, every room comes with a private balcony or patio with a volcano view (junior suites have the view from a private Jacuzzi!). I'd try to land a room on the second or third floor if possible, and the end units are especially well-placed. As for the grounds, they feature flowering gardens that let out onto a large free-form pool with a swim-up bar, and a couple of Jacuzzis. Magic Mountain is located at the far end of town so a rental car come in handy, though one could conceivably walk into the town of La Fortuna. "Lina's" restaurant here is quite good; there's also a separate sports bar.

La Fortuna, San Carlos. www.hotelmagicmountain.com. ✆ **2479-7246.** 42 units. $135 double; $185 junior suite. Rates include buffet breakfast. **Amenities:** Restaurant; bar; 2 Jacuzzis; outdoor pool; spa; free Wi-Fi.

INEXPENSIVE

Right in La Fortuna you'll find a score of budget options. One of the better options is **Arenal Backpackers Resort** ★ (www.arenalbackpackers resort.com; ✆ **2479-7000**), which bills itself as a "five-star hostel" for its large pool, Wi-Fi, and volcano views. It has both shared-bathroom dorm rooms, and more upscale private rooms.

A couple of places both in town and right on the outskirts of La Fortuna allow camping, with access to basic bathroom facilities, for around $5 to $10 per person per night. If you have a car, drive a bit out of town toward Tabacón and you'll find several more basic cabins and camping sites, some that even offer views of the volcano.

Hotel Las Colinas ★ This centrally located three-story hotel is a great value. The less expensive rooms here are all clean and cozy, while for a bit more you can upgrade and get a private volcano-view balcony and in-room Jacuzzi. Even if you don't, there's a gorgeous, large open-air second-floor terrace with perfect views of the Arenal Volcano. This common area, with its potted palms, Chinese lanterns and tables, loaner board games, and chairs and couches under atrium-style open-air roofs really is the highlight and social center of the hotel. The service at this family-run operation is friendly, attentive and knowledgeable.

La Fortuna, San Carlos. www.lascolinasarenal.com. ℭ **2479-9305.** 21 units. $65 budget room double; $80–$85 double; $98–$103 suite. Rates include breakfast and taxes. **Amenities:** Restaurant, free Wi-Fi.

Hotel La Fortuna ★ I've been around long enough to remember when this simple, two-story, wood-and-zinc hostel was one of the few, and always most popular hotels in town. But a fire changed all of that, and now it's a modern, five-story affair. The best rooms are West-facing and have volcano-view balconies. Of these, those on the top two floors are the best, as their views aren't blocked by Las Colinas (see above) and other nearby buildings. Inside, the rooms are fairly plain, with white tile floors and locally made furnishings that show a hint of Japanese aesthetics, with their smooth, square lines. The restaurant here is only open for breakfast, but you're right in the heart of downtown and close to all of the restaurants and shops of La Fortuna.

1 block south of the gas station, downtown La Fortuna, San Carlos. www.fortunainn. com. ℭ **415/315-9595** in the U.S. and Canada or 2479-9197 in Costa Rica. 40 units. $80–$92 double. Rates include continental breakfast and taxes. **Amenities:** Restaurant; free Wi-Fi.

Where to Stay near the Volcano

While La Fortuna is the major gateway town to Arenal Volcano, for my money, the best places to stay are on the road between La Fortuna and the National Park. One other very unique alternative is to stay aboard the *Rain Goddess* (www.bluwing.com; ℭ **866/593-3168** in the U.S., or 2231-4299), a luxurious houseboat with four staterooms, ample lounge and dining areas, and cruises around Lake Arenal.

TAKING A SOOTHING SOAK IN hot springs

Tabacón Grand Spa Thermal Resort ★★★ (www.tabacon.com; ℂ **2479-2099;** daily 10am–10pm) is the most luxurious, extensive, and expensive spot in the area to soak your tired bones. A series of variously sized pools, fed by natural springs, are spread out among sumptuous gardens. One of the stronger streams flows over a sculpted waterfall, with a rock ledge underneath that provides a perfect place to sit and receive a free hydraulic shoulder massage. The extensive grounds are worth exploring, but the pools and springs closest to the volcano are the hottest— makes sense, doesn't it? The resort also has an excellent, offering professional massages, mud masks, and other treatments, as well as yoga classes (appointments required). Most of the treatments are conducted in lovely open-air gazebos. The spa here even has several permanent sweat lodges, based on a Native American traditional design. A full-service restaurant, garden grill, and several bars round out the offerings here.

Admission is $60 for adults and $10 for children 11 and under. A range of packages, including meals, are available. The pools are busiest between 2 and 6pm. After 6pm, you can enter for $45, not including meals. Management enforces a policy of limiting visitors, so reservations are recommended.

Baldi Hot Springs (www.baldihot springs.cr; ℂ **2479-2190;** $34 admission) are the first hot springs you'll come to as you drive from La Fortuna toward Tabacón. This place has grown substantially over the years, with many different

EXPENSIVE

Arenal Kioro ★   You'll feel like you're right on top of the volcano here, and that, along with the superbly landscaped grounds, are the main draw. As for the rooms they're very large, with extremely high ceilings and a wall of windows with a sliding glass door that lets out onto a private balcony or patio with a perfect volcano view. But sadly, they're a tad dated, with ugly floral bedspreads and a free-standing, large in-room spa Jacuzzi, which I find to be unnecessary—the outdoor hot springs and pool here are much more appealing. (Also the Jacuzzis give off an odor from the water's treatment system.) I'm not a fan of the on-site restaurant (disappointing food, though the view is good). Arenal Kioro has "4 Leaves" in the CST Sustainable Tourism program.

picturesque and luxurious, although it has far fewer pools, lacks a view of the volcano, and the spa services are much less extensive. There's a restaurant serving basic local fare, but I recommend just coming for the springs. They run three distinct time periods daily, 10am to 1pm, 1pm to 5pm, and 5pm to 9pm, and advance reservations are highly recommended as admissions are limited to make sure the pools don't get crowded.

Termales Los Laureles (www. termalesloslaureles.com; ☏ **2479-1395**) is located between Baldi and Eco Termales and Tabacón. This is the area's most local feeling spot, and by far the most economical, charging just C6,000 for adults.

Finally, you can also enjoy the hot springs, pools, and facilities at the **Springs Resort & Spa ★★** (p. 350). In addition to the main pools by the hotel, they have a few more at a beautiful riverfront area about 1km away. The Springs is open to day visitors from 8:30am to 10pm, and admission is $60 per person.

pools, slides, and bars and restaurants spread around the expansive grounds. They have even added rooms. However, I find Baldi far less attractive than the other options. Baldi has much more of a party vibe, with loud music blaring at some of the swim-up bars.

Just across the street from Baldi Hot Springs is the unmarked entrance of my current favorite local hot spring, **Eco Termales ★★★** (www.ecotermales fortuna.cr; ☏ **2479-8787;** $34 admission). Smaller and more intimate than Tabacón, this series of pools set amid dense forest and gardens is almost as

On the main road btw. La Fortuna and Lake Arenal, 10km (6 miles) from La Fortuna. www.hotelarenalkioro.com. ☏ **2479-1700.** 53 units. $334 double. Rates include taxes and buffet breakfast. **Amenities:** 2 restaurants; 2 bars; exercise room; Jacuzzi; small hot spring complex; large outdoor pool; small spa; free Wi-Fi.

Nayara Hotel, Spa & Gardens ★★★   Intimate, romantic, and pampering: Those are the words that come to mind when describing Nayara. It's a special place, with lodgings in large and luxurious private bungalows, with wide volcano-facing balconies, each with a large, two-person Jacuzzi, and both an indoor and garden shower. Units 1 through 5 are closest to the restaurants and pool and thus the least isolated and private. Around the bungalows are well-tended tropical gardens (wonderful for bird-watching); trails lead through the property and down to a river. The dining options are varied and all well executed, from the classy

Spring Villa plunge pool at Nayara Hotel, Spa & Gardens.

wine and tapas bar to the Peruvian-influenced sushi bar. However, unlike most of the other offerings in this price category, the hotel does not have a natural hot springs on site. In their adjoining property, **Nayara Springs Resort** (www.nayarasprings.com), there is a natural spring-fed hot pool. It's reached via a long and high suspension bridge, and populated with even larger villas, decorated with lovely Balinese-style pieces. Each comes with a hot, natural spring-fed private pool.

On the main road btw. La Fortuna and Lake Arenal. www.arenalnayara.com. ℭ **888/332-2961** in the U.S. and Canada, or 2479-1600 in Costa Rica. 66 units. $285 deluxe; $395 suite, $590 Springs villas. Rates includes buffet breakfast. **Amenities:** 4 restaurants; 2 bars; small spa; exercise room; 2 large outdoor pools; 3 Jacuzzis; room service; free Wi-Fi.

The Springs Resort & Spa ★★★ In contrast to the intimate Arenal Nayara (see above), the Springs Resort & Spa is built on a grand scale. This massive complex features huge, comfortable rooms (great beds!), but the key here is the wide range of on-site attractions and activity options, including an extensive collection of hot and temperate pools (the largest has a swim-up sushi bar), a jungle waterslide, free yoga classes and a separate "Club Rio" adventure park (p. 340) a short shuttle ride away on the banks of the Arenal River. This also is the only lodge in the area with its own heliport, if that's important to you. All rooms are oriented to offer views of the Arenal Volcano. And local cane (caña brava) is used extensively as paneling and wall ornamentation. This is a smart option for families, thanks to all of activities, as well as the family suites and private villas that have either kitchenettes or full kitchens. The restaurants, spa, and overall service here are top notch.

Off the main road btw. La Fortuna and Lake Arenal, 10km (6 miles) from La Fortuna. www.thespringscostarica.com. © **954/727-8333** in the U.S. or 2401-3313 in Costa Rica. 45 units. $205–$625 double, $325–$595 suite; $750–$880 2-bedroom suite; $990 and up villa for 4–6 people. **Amenities:** 4 restaurants; 4 bars; spa and exercise room; outdoor pools and hot springs; room service; free Wi-Fi.

Hotel Royal Corin ★★   The pool, sauna, steam, and hot spring complex at this contemporary resort are first rate, and include such fun touches lounge chairs submerged in some of the pools. Around this "main attraction" are the five-story buildings that house the guestrooms, each of which has a private balconies overlooking the pools and Arenal Volcano. The rooms themselves are cheerily decorated—white tile floors, white walls and ceilings, with splashes of color provided by artwork, patterned linens and throw pillows—spacious and immaculately clean. An excellent little spa is attached to the hotel, and the restaurant here is quite good.

On the main road btw. La Fortuna and Lake Arenal, 4km (2½ miles) from La Fortuna. www.royalcorin.com. © **800/6459-7826** in the U.S. and Canada, or 2479-2201 in Costa Rica. 54 units. $195-$255 double; $379–$408 suite. Rates include buffet breakfast. **Amenities:** Restaurant; 2 bars; babysitting; exercise room; 6 Jacuzzis; pools and hot springs; room service; small spa; sauna, free W-Fi.

Tabacón Grand Spa Thermal Resort ★★   I'd stay here for the fab hot springs, even if the rooms were dark, dank and dingy—but they're not. Far from it. Guestooms are large and well-maintained with heavy, dark stained wood furnishings and at least one wall of windows or sliding glass doors. Not all of the rooms have volcano views, and they maddeningly won't guarantee a volcano-view room, no matter how hard you beg. On the plus side, management has a deep commitment to locally sustainable development and environmental conservation. Plus, staying at the resort gets you unlimited access to the impressive Tabacón hot spring complex, as well as slightly extended hours and access to a private, hotel-guests-only section of the hot springs dubbed Shangri-La. If you take into account the hefty entrance fee to the springs, this place is practically a bargain.

On the main road btw. La Fortuna and Lake Arenal, Tabacón. www.tabacon.com. © **855/822-2266** in the U.S. and Canada, 2479-2099 for reservations in San José, or 2479-2000 at the resort. 102 units. $240–$370 double; $375–$850 suite. **Amenities:** 2 restaurants; 3 bars; exercise room; Jacuzzi; pool w/swim-up bar; room service; all rooms smoke-free; hot springs and spa facilities across the street; free Wi-Fi.

MODERATE

Arenal Kokoro ★★   This place gets my vote for best bang for your buck in this area. The individual Eco-Cabinas are spacious and free-each with volcano views and a small private balcony. The more economical Casona rooms are a tad more rustic and housed in two-story blocks of four rooms. Inside you'll find a mix of locally milled wood-plank paneling and painted concrete walls—some with handpainted murals of birds, butterflies and fanciful trees. The hotel has a pool, a small, natural hot springs complex and spa, as well as extensive and lush gardens and grounds. The staff is very friendly and helpful.

On the main road btw. La Fortuna and Lake Arenal. www.arenalkokoro.com. © **800/649-5913** in the U.S. and Canada, or 2479-1222 in Costa Rica. 30 units. $115–$140 double. Rates include breakfast. **Amenities:** Restaurant; bar; outdoor pool; small hot springs complex and spa; free Wi-Fi.

Arenal Observatory Lodge ★★

Originally a scientific observatory associated with the Smithsonian to monitor volcanic activity, this is one of the closest hotels to the Arenal Volcano. The views from the rooms, restaurant and common areas are simply spectacular. The main dining room, in particular features a massive wall of glass, with a "V"-shaped peak that perfectly frames the Arenal volcano. The lodge is a bit isolated from the rest of the hustle and bustle of this busy region, and is graced with a large, private reserve and an excellent network of trails, that directly border the National Park. The best rooms and views are found in the suites and private villas set below the main lodge building. Given the remote location, you need a rental car to stay here.

On the flanks of Arenal Volcano. To get here, head to the national park entrance, stay on the dirt road past the entrance, and follow the signs to the Observatory Lodge. A 4WD vehicle is not essential, although you'll always be better off with the clearance afforded by one. www.arenalobservatorylodge.com. © **877/804-7732** in the U.S. and Canada or 2290-7011 for reservations in San José, or 2479-1070 at the lodge. 48 units. $97 La Casona double; $133 standard double; $171 Smithsonian; $195 junior suite. Rates include taxes and breakfast buffet; rates reduction in off-season. **Amenities:** Restaurant; bar; Jacuzzi; midsize outdoor pool; small spa; free Wi-Fi.

Hotel Silencio del Campo ★★

This friendly, family-run resort features a small collection of individual cabins oriented to take in the volcano view. All are quite spacious, with red tile floors, wooden walls, a/c, TV's and minifridges. They are a little bit close together for my taste, but large tropical flowers and palms planted all around give them some sense of privacy. Still try for one farthest from the main road and parking area. The best feature here is the lovely pool and hot spring complex. This is by far the best hotel hot spring complex in this price range. Service is extremely personalized and attentive.

On the main road btw. La Fortuna and Lake Arenal. www.hotelsilenciodelcampo. com. © **2479-7055.** 23 units. $173–$182 double. Rates include full breakfast. **Amenities:** Restaurant; bar; pool and hot spring complex; free Wi-Fi.

Volcano Lodge and Springs ★★

Most of the rooms at this sprawling midsize resort offer unobstructed views of the Arenal Volcano from a private patio with locally crafted leather rocking chairs. Masonry halfwalls of smooth river stones give the lodge a rustic feel, but inside you'll find a flat screen TVs and quiet A/C units. Volcano Lodge has steadily grown over the years, and now features two pool areas and two separate restaurants, as well as its own little hot spring complex, hiking trails and children's playground. The gardens here are handsomely landscaped, and the service is very attentive, despite the fact that they often cater to large tour groups.

On the main road btw. La Fortuna and Lake Arenal. www.volcanolodge.com. © **800/649-5913** in the U.S. or 2479-1717. 62 units. $160–$215 double, $295 suites. Rates include taxes and buffet breakfast. **Amenities:** Restaurant; 2 bars; 2 Jacuzzis; 2 outdoor pools; small spa; free Wi-Fi.

INEXPENSIVE

While the hotels along the road between La Fortuna and the National Park tend to be geared toward higher-end travelers, more budget-conscious travelers do have a few choices, the best of which is **Cabinas Los Guayabos** (www.cabinaslosguayabos.com; © **2479-1444**), with views and a location that rival the more expensive lodgings listed above.

Where to Dine in & Around La Fortuna

Dining in La Fortuna is nowhere near as inspiring as the area's natural attractions, but, given the town's booming tourist business, options abound. For a casual breakfast or lunch, I like **Gecko Gourmet ★** (www.geckogourmet.com; © **2479-8905**), located behind the church. Other options include **Rancho La Cascada** (© **2479-8790**), **La Choza de Laurel** (www.lachozadelaurel.com; © **2479-7063**), and **Restaurante Nene's** (© **2479-9192**) for Tico fare, and **Las Brasitas** (© **2479-9819**) for Mexican. For good pizza and Italian cuisine, try either **Café Mediterranea** (© **2479-7497**), just outside of town on the road to the La Fortuna waterfall, or **Anch'io** (© **2479-7560**), just beyond Las Brasitas, on the road towards Tabacón. Both are quite good. For fancy dining, **Los Tucanes ★★** (© **2479-2020**) at the Tabacón Grand Spa resort (p. 351) is a solid choice.

Don Rufino ★★ COSTA RICAN Don Rufino is the semi-official social center of town, with a popular open-air bar overlooking the main street. The decor has rustic touches, but the menu takes Costa Rican fare and adds a lot fusion flourishes. In addition to juicy steaks and local staples, the large array of offerings range from Szechuan chicken to Cajun shrimp pasta. Prices are on the high end but worth it.

Main road through downtown La Fortuna, 2 blocks east of the church. www.don rufino.com. © **2479-9997.** Main courses $10–$50. Daily 11am–10:30pm. Reservations recommended during the high season.

El Novillo del Arenal ★ COSTA RICAN/STEAKHOUSE If you want local steaks or grilled chicken, but don't need the fancier ambience or accouterments of the other places listed here, this is your spot.

Portions are hearty and the price is right. The restaurant is a simple affair set on a plain concrete slab under a very high, open-air, corrugated-zinc-roof structure. When it's clear, you get an excellent view of the volcano.

On the road to Tabacón, 10km (6¼ miles) outside of La Fortuna. ✆ **2479-1910.** Main courses C4,000–C12,000. Daily 11am–10pm.

Lava Lounge ★ INTERNATIONAL   California meets Costa Rica at this popular downtown restaurant. Lava Lounge's menu ranges from glorified bar food—think nachos, quesadillas, wings, and wraps—to a hearty Costa Rican blue-plate special, or *casado,* with dishes such as a thick-cut grilled pork chop or coconut shrimp with spicy mango salsa quite well done. Chef and owner Scott Bradley is often on hand, and also runs the **Tropical Cooking Class** (p. 340) cooking school. Note: Wooden picnic tables with bench seating fill the main dining room. If you're just two, you might have to share the table.

Downtown La Fortuna, on the main road. www.lavaloungecostarica.com. ✆ **2479-7365.** Main courses $11–$25. Daily 11am–11pm.

Shopping

La Fortuna is chock-full of souvenir shops selling standard tourist fare. However, the town also has an authentic craft shop, **Original Grand Gallery** (✆ **8946-0928**). This local artisan and his family produce sculptures in a variety of styles, specializing in faces, many of them larger than a typical home's front door. You can also find a host of animal figures, ranging in style from purely representational to rather abstract.

To get there: As you leave the town of La Fortuna toward Tabacón, keep your eye on the right-hand side of the road. When you see a massive collection of wood sculptures slow down. **Art Shop Onirica** (www.galeriaoniricacr.com; ✆ **2479-7589**), located next to La Fortuna's post office, is another good shop, featuring original oil paintings and acrylics, as well as one-off jewelry and jade pieces.

Entertainment & Nightlife

Now that the volcano is not throwing up lava with any real frequency, the after-dark activities around La Fortuna and the Arenal Volcano have cooled off as well. In town, the folks at Luigi's Hotel have a midsize **casino** (✆ **2479-9898**) next door to their hotel and restaurant, while the open-to-the-street bar at **Don Rufino** (p. 353) is a popular spot for a drink. Finally, a cozy sports bar with a pool table and flatscreen televisions is on the second floor at the **Hotel Magic Mountain** (p. 346).

Where to Stay & Dine Farther Afield

All the hotels listed in the following four sections are at least a half-hour drive from La Fortuna and the volcano. Most, if not all, offer both night and day tours to Arenal and Tabacón, but they also attract guests with their own natural charms.

EAST OF LA FORTUNA

The broad, flat San Carlos valley spreads out to the east of La Fortuna. This is agricultural heartland, with large plantations of yuca, papaya, and other cash crops. The popular Ciudad Quesada route to, or from, La Fortuna will take you through this area.

In addition to the places listed below, **Leaves & Lizards** (www.leavesandlizards.com; © **888/828-9245** in the U.S. and Canada, or 2478-0023 in Costa Rica), near El Muelle, wins high praise as an intimate, isolated getaway.

Termales del Bosque ★   The name of this place translates to "Hot Springs in the Forest," and that's exactly what you'll find at this simple collection of rooms and bungalows housed in single story concrete block buildings spread around the open grounds of a large former farm. The rooms themselves are unadorned, with plain white walls, red tile floors and minimal furnishings, but do have A/C and TVs. The bungalows are two-bedroom units with full kitchens. The namesake hot springs are the real draw, though, featuring a series of pools built alongside a rushing creek in the midst of dense rainforest. There's a rustic, natural steam room and pools in a range of temperatures. A host of tours and activities are offered. If you're not staying at the hotel, you can visit the hot springs with a $12 admission.

On the road from San Carlos to Aguas Zarcas, just before El Tucano. Ciudad Quesada, San Carlos. www.termalesdelbosque.com. © **2460-1356** or 2640-4748. 48 units. $112 double; $150 bungalow. Rates include full breakfast, unlimited use of the hot springs, and taxes. **Amenities:** 2 restaurant; bar, several hot springs pools set beside a forest river; limited spa services; free Wi-Fi.

Tilajari Resort Hotel ★   A low-key small resort and nature lodge Tilajari is set on the banks of the San Carlos River, making it a wonderful place for bird-watching and wildlife viewing. The river is home to crocodiles, lizards, turtles and perfect habitat for a great variety of bird species. Oversized rooms, with forest green walls, tile floors and wood ceilings are found in a row of two-story buildings that run parallel to the water, and most have a private patio or balcony with a river view. Popular with tour groups and Costa Rican families, Tilajari has extensive facilities, including tennis courts, soccer fields, game rooms, an orchid garden, a butterfly garden and a medicinal herb garden. The hotel lies about 35 minutes from La Fortuna and the Arenal Volcano, but also provides good access to attractions in Aguas Zarcas.

Muelle, San Carlos. www.tilajari.com. © **2462-1212.** 76 units. $113–$124 double; $130–$136 suite. Rates include full breakfast and taxes. **Amenities:** Restaurant; bar; exercise room; Jacuzzi; pool; spa; 5 lighted tennis courts (2 indoors); free Wi-Fi.

SOUTH OF LA FORTUNA

In addition to the places listed below, **Finca Luna Nueva Lodge** ★★ (www.fincalunanuevalodge.com; © **800/903-3470** in the U.S. and Canada, or 2468-4006 in Costa Rica) is a fascinating sustainable farm and tourism project, and proud advocate for the international "Slow Foods" movement.

Chachagua Rainforest Hotel & Hacienda ★★   This boutique rainforest lodge is set on 100 hectares (247 acres) of land, much of which is primary rainforest. While the rooms are certainly comfortable and cozy, I recommend splurging for one of the individual wooden bungalows, which are much roomier, have TVs and Jacuzzi tubs and come with their own large, covered-deck area. Throughout you'll find lots of varnished hardwood, and handsome headboards on the beds studded with sections of hardwood tree trunks. The large central pool here is fed by a natural spring and kept chemical-free. The lodge has opened miles of excellent trails, leading through thick wildlife-rich rainforest, with waterfalls, rivers and jungle lagoons to explore. They also offer a host of adventure tours and guided activities.

The small village of Chachagua sits 10km (6 miles) south of La Fortuna, on the road to San Ramón. The lodge itself is another 2km (1¼ miles) along a dirt road from the village. The entrance is well-marked and easy to spot.

Chachagua, Alajuela. www.chachaguarainforesthotel.com. © **2468-1011.** 28 units. $179 double, $229–$259 bungalows. Rates include breakfast. **Amenities:** Restaurant; bar; concierge, lounge area, large outdoor pool; mountain bike rental, free Wi-Fi.

Villa Blanca Cloud Forest & Spa ★★   Once the country retreat and family-run hotel of former Costa Rican President Rodrigo Carazo Odio, this lovely little mountain lodge features a series of individual little houses, or *casitas,* with clay-tile roofs, whitewashed stucco walls, rustic tile floors, and open-beam and cane ceilings. Each *casita* has a working wood-burning fireplace, which comes in handy in the cool, moist climate. The deluxe *casitas* and suites come with their own Jacuzzi tubs. The hotel's private reserve borders the Los Angeles Cloud Forest Reserve, a fascinating area and ecosystem, very similar to that found in Monteverde. In fact, lucky visitors even have spotted the elusive Resplendent Quetzal here. A member of the "Green Hotels of Costa Rica," this lodge has earned "5 Leaves" in the CST Sustainable Tourism program.

To reach the hotel, you must first drive to the mountain city of San Ramón, which sits on the Interamerican Highway (CR1), northwest of San José. From here, you'll drive north on CR142 towards Los Angeles, following signs to Villa Blanca.

San Ramón, Alajuela. www.villablanca-costarica.com. © **877/256-8399** in the U.S. and Canada, or 2461-0300 in Costa Rica. 35 units. $205 double; $255 superior; $230 deluxe. Rates include full breakfast. **Amenities:** Restaurant; bar; small spa; free Wi-Fi.

NORTH OF LA FORTUNA

Caño Negro Natural Lodge ★ Serious bird watchers, nature lovers, and fishermen should consider this very remote lodging, in the tiny lagoon-side village of Caño Negro. Bordering the area's namesake Caño Negro Wildlife Refuge, this simple place offers easy access to the lakes, lagoons, and waterways of this beautiful, low-lying wetlands area (one of the best places in the region to spot a Jaibiru stork). The rooms themselves are roomy, clean, and cool, with large sliding glass doors opening on to a small patio overlooking the well-tended gardens. To get there, drive towards Los Chiles, and just before reaching the town of Los Chiles, follow the well-marked signs for Caño Negro Natural Lodge and the wildlife refuge. The final 18km (11 miles) is on a rugged, dirt road.

Caño Negro. www.canonegrolodge.com. © **2471-1426** in Costa Rica. 42 units. $125 double. Rates include continental breakfast. **Amenities:** Restaurant; bar; midsize outdoor pool; free Wi-Fi.

REALLY REMOTE NATURE LODGES

This little visited region, right along the San Carlos River, near the Nicaraguan border is hard to get to: Roads up here are rough and poorly maintained. But those who go, get right into the heart of nature, particularly at the **Manquenque Ecolodge ★** (www.maquenqueecolodge.com; © **2479-8200**), where birders have been known to spot green macaws in the wild. *Tip:* To get here, you head first to Pital and then continue on dirt roads to the town of Boca Tapada. It's also possible, albeit difficult, to get here on public transportation (ask your lodge for directions), or you can arrange for the lodge to handle your transportation from San José or La Fortuna (for a cost). Since anyone with four-wheel-drive can make the trip here independently, though, you're best off driving on your own.

La Laguna del Lagarto Lodge ★ Though it's not exactly at the end of the road, La Laguna del Lagarto Lodge certainly feels like it. Tucked into a far northern section of Costa Rica, close to the Nicaraguan border, this is rustic lodge carters primarily to bird watchers (the bird count here tops 390 species, including the rare Green Macaw). Rooms are adequate and little more, with low-lying wooden bedframes sporting thin mattresses, and little else in the way of furnishings, decor and amenities. The lodge features two man-made lakes and keeps a fleet of canoes. They also have an extensive network of hiking trails and offer a range of active adventure tours and guided hikes.

7km (3¾ miles) north of Boca Tapada. www.lagarto-lodge-costa-rica.com. © **2289-8163.** 20 units. $75 double. **Amenities:** Restaurant; bar, free Wi-Fi.

ALONG THE SHORES OF LAKE ARENAL ★

200km (124 miles) NW of San José; 20km (12 miles) NW of Monteverde; 70km (43 miles) SE of Liberia

Despite its many charms, this remains one of the least-developed tourism regions in Costa Rica. Lake Arenal, the largest lake in Costa Rica, is the centerpiece here. A long, beautiful lake, it is surrounded by rolling hills that are partly pastured and partly forested. Loads of adventures are available both on the lake and in the surrounding hills and forests. While the towns of Tilarán and Nuevo Arenal remain quiet rural communities, several excellent hotels spread out along the shores of the lake.

Locals here used to curse the winds, which often come blasting across this end of the lake at 60 knots or greater. However, since the first sailboarders caught wind of Lake Arenal's combination of warm, fresh water, steady blows, and spectacular scenery, that's changed. Even if you aren't a fanatical sailboarder, you might enjoy hanging out by the lake, hiking in the nearby forests, riding a mountain bike on dirt farm roads and one-track trails, and catching glimpses of Arenal Volcano.

The lake's other claim to fame is its rainbow-bass fishing. These fighting fish are known in Central America as *guapote* and are large members of the cichlid family. Their sharp teeth and bellicose nature make them a real challenge.

Lake Arenal and Arenal Volcano.

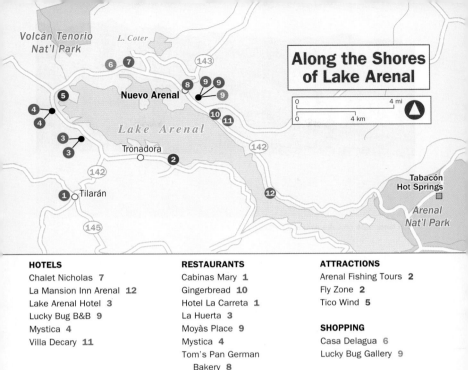

Along the Shores of Lake Arenal

0		4 mi
0	4 km	

Volcán Tenorio Nat'l Park

L. Coter

143

Nuevo Arenal

Lake Arenal

Tronadora

142

Tilarán

145

142

Tabacón Hot Springs

Arenal Nat'l Park

HOTELS
Chalet Nicholas 7
La Mansion Inn Arenal 12
Lake Arenal Hotel 3
Lucky Bug B&B 9
Mystica 4
Villa Decary 11

RESTAURANTS
Cabinas Mary 1
Gingerbread 10
Hotel La Carreta 1
La Huerta 3
Moyàs Place 9
Mystica 4
Tom's Pan German
   Bakery 8
Willy's Caballo Negro 9

ATTRACTIONS
Arenal Fishing Tours 2
Fly Zone 2
Tico Wind 5

SHOPPING
Casa Delagua 6
Lucky Bug Gallery 9

Essentials

GETTING THERE & DEPARTING   By Car: From San José, you can either take the Interamerican Highway (CR1) north all the way from San José to Cañas, or first head west out of San José on the San José–Caldera Highway (CR27). When you reach Caldera, follow the signs to Puntarenas and the Interamerican Highway (CR1). You will actually follow signs for Liberia and San José, which are, in fact, leading you to the unmarked entrance to CR1. This road (CR23) ends when it hits the Interamerican Highway. You'll want to pass under the bridge and follow the on-ramp, which will put you on the highway heading north. This latter route is a faster and flatter drive, with no windy mountain switchbacks to contend with. In Cañas, turn east on CR142 toward Tilarán. The drive takes 3 to 4 hours. If you're continuing on to Nuevo Arenal, follow the signs in town, which will put you on the road that skirts the shore of the lake. Nuevo Arenal is about a half-hour drive from Tilarán. You can also drive here from La Fortuna, along a scenic road that winds around the lake. From La Fortuna, it's approximately 1 hour to Nuevo Arenal and 1½ hours to Tilarán.

Lush landscape on Lake Arenal.

By Bus: Transportes Tilarán buses (✆ **2222-3854**) leave San José for Tilarán roughly five times throughout the day between 7:30am and 6:30pm from Calle 20 and Avenida 3. The trip lasts from 4 to 5½ hours, depending on road conditions; the fare is C4,400.

Morning and afternoon buses connect **Puntarenas** to Tilarán. The ride takes about 3 hours; the fare is C1,300. (For details on getting to Puntarenas, see "Puntarenas," in chapter 9.)

The daily bus from **Monteverde** (Santa Elena) leaves at 7am. The fare for the 2½-hour trip is C1,150.

Buses from **La Fortuna** leave for Tilarán daily at 8am and 12:15 and 5:30pm, returning at 7am and 12:20 and 4:30pm. The trip takes around 2 to 3 hours; the fare is C2,300.

Direct buses to San José leave from Tilarán beginning at 5am. Buses to Puntarenas leave at 6am and 1pm daily. The bus to Santa Elena (Monteverde) leaves daily at 12:30pm. Buses also leave regularly for Cañas, and can be caught heading north or south along the Interamerican Highway.

GETTING AROUND   Both Tilarán and Nuevo Arenal are very small towns, and you can easily walk most places in the compact city centers. If you need a taxi to get to a lodge on Lake Arenal, call **Taxis Unidos Tilarán** (✆ **2695-5324**) in Tilarán, or either **Taxis Nuevo Arenal** (✆ **8388-3015**) or **Pencho** (✆ **8817-6375**) in Nuevo Arenal.

Exploring Along the Shores of Lake Arenal

ARTS, CRAFTS & DOWN-HOME COOKING   About halfway between Nuevo Arenal and Tilarán is **Casa Delagua** ★ (✆ **2692-1324**), the studio, gallery, and coffee shop of Costa Rican artist Juan Carlos Ruiz. Onsite is also a good used book and DVD collection on sale.

Windsurfing on Lake Arenal.

The **Lucky Bug Gallery ★★** (www.luckybugcr.net; ✆ **2695-4515**) is an excellent roadside arts-and-crafts and souvenir shop, selling locally produced functional and decorative pieces. It's attached to the Lucky Bug Bed & Breakfast (p. 363).

FISHING   Ask at your hotel if you want to try your hand at fishing for *guapote*. A half-day fishing trip should cost around $150 to $300 per boat, and a full day goes for around $300 to $500. The boats will usually accommodate up to three people. I personally recommend **Captain Ron** at **Arenal Fishing Tours** (www.arenalfishing.com; ✆ **2694-4678**).

HORSEBACK RIDING   Any of the hotels in the area can hook you up with a horseback-riding tour for around $10 to $20 per hour.

SWIMMING   You can certainly swim in Lake Arenal, although it can get a bit rough in places, especially during peak windsurfing season. Up above Lake Arenal on the far side of the lake from Tilarán, you'll find the little heart-shaped **Lake Coter.** This lake is surrounded by forest and has good, protected swimming. (UFO watchers also claim that this is a popular pit stop for extraterrestrials.) A taxi to Lake Coter costs around C15,000.

WINDSURFING & KITEBOARDING   If you want to try windsurfing or kiteboarding, check in with the folks at **Tico Wind ★** (www.ticowind.com; ✆ **2692-2002**), which sets up shop on the shores of the lake each year from December 1 to the end of April. Rates run $88 per day, including lunch; multiday and lesson packages also available. This is also the place to rent standup paddle boards and equipment.

WAKEBOARDING   Lake Arenal is a big lake with plenty of calm quiet corners to practice wakeboarding. If you're interested in lessons, or just a reliable pull on a wakeboard or water skis, contact **Fly Zone** (www.flyzone-cr.com; ✆ **8339-5876**). Simple pulls behind their specialized boat run around $125 per hour, including boards, skis, and any other necessary gear.

Where to Stay

In addition to the places listed below, **La Mansion Inn Arenal** (www. lamansionarenal.com; ☎ **877/660-3830** in U.S. and Canada, or 2692-8018 in Costa Rica) is an upscale option with an excellent setting and cozy cabins.

MODERATE

Mystica ★★　This Italian-owned hilltop retreat is a primo place to unwind. Rooms are simple, but immaculate, with wood or tile floors, large windows, and a shared common lake-view veranda, with brightly varnished decking and columns made from whole tree trunks. Settle into one of the cushioned Adirondack chairs here to soak in the view or read a book. The best rooms are the private villa and the individual cabin, which offer more space and a greater sense of privacy. Families or small groups can book the two-bedroom Ra Ma Da Sa house, with a full kitchen. It's set on the highest spot on the property and features an outdoor bathroom with a mosaic-tiled hot tub and waterfall shower. The expansive grounds and gardens include a lovely river-stone pool and open-air yoga platform, as well as a massage room in a tree house. The hotel's in-house restaurant (p. 364) is a real plus, as well.

On the road btw. Tilarán and Nuevo Arenal. www.mysticacostarica.com. ☎ **2692-1001.** 9 units. $120 double; $140-$165 villa or cabin; $275 2-bedroom house. Rates include breakfast, except for the house. **Amenities:** Restaurant; outdoor pool; yoga center and small spa; free Wi-Fi.

Villa Decary ★★　The original owners of Villa Decary were hardcore palm enthusiasts, so the grounds and gardens are planted with scores of unique species, including the Madagascar three-sided palm, or dypsis decaryi, named for the French botanist Raymond Decary, who is also the namesake of this B&B. So yes, you're going to love the grounds but I think you'll also enjoy the cozy rooms here, which are decorated with panache (bright Guatemalan bedspreads and walls are adorned with wildlife photos and primitive-style nature paintings). Rooms in the main building feature picture windows and private balconies with wonderful views of Lake Arenal; there are also three private casitas with full kitchens and more space.

Nuevo Arenal. www.villadecary.com. ☎ **800/556-0505** in the U.S and Canada, or 2694-4330 in Costa Rica. 5 units, 3 casitas. $109 double; $142–$164 casita for 2. Rates include full breakfast. **Amenities:** Free Wi-Fi.

INEXPENSIVE

Chalet Nicholas ★　You'll be made to feel right at home by John and Catherine Nicholas, who have owned this intimate, 3-room bed-and-breakfast for some 25 years. The owners' three Great Danes, will also give you a warm welcome, which will be a plus for some visitors, a turn-off for others. All of the rooms are in the main house, feature volcano views and are quite cozy and comfy. The hotel has some 6 hectares (15 acres) of land, with trails and hiking opportunities right on site along with lovely gardens with extensive orchid and heliconia collections.

2.5km (1½ miles) west of Nuevo Arenal. www.chaletnicholas.com. © **2694-4041.** 3 units. $87 double. Rates include full breakfast. No children under 10 allowed. No credit cards.

Lake Arenal Hotel ★ This place has changed hands a couple of times over the years. Originally it was the Greek-themed Hotel Tilawa, and its most recent incarnation was as the Volcano Brewing Company. Despite the new and more generic name, large Greek columns are still a major architectural detail here and there's a happening microbrewery and brewpub still on site. Beyond those oddities (and actually the beer and pub grub is quite good), you won't find much charm in the nothing special but adequate and clean rooms. And the current management seems to be the most attentive in quite some time. Set on a high hillside overlooking Lake Arenal, the hotel caters primarily to the windsurf and kitesurf crowds.

On the road btw. Tilarán and Nuevo Arenal. www.lakearenalhotel.com. © **2695-5050.** 21 units. $88–$118 double. Rates include continental breakfast. **Amenities:** Restaurant; bar; outdoor pool; Jacuzzi; tennis court; free Wi-Fi.

Lucky Bug Bed & Breakfast ★★ Set back from the road, on a small hill above a small lake, this intimate bed-and-breakfast is a swell pick. Though rooms don't have any view to speak of, they are spacious, cheery, and creative, featuring handmade furniture, hand-painted tiles, and unique artwork. All of this handiwork was done by the owner and her triplet daughters. The handcrafted iron and steel headboards are particularly captivating, and that in the Flower room is filled in with colored stained glass. Still, the Butterfly and Frog rooms are my favorites, each with small private balconies. There's a lovely restaurant attached to the place, as well.

Nuevo Arenal. www.luckybugcr.net. © **2694-4515.** 5 units. $89–$109 double. Rates include full breakfast. **Amenities:** Restaurant; free Wi-Fi.

Where to Dine

Tilarán has numerous inexpensive places to eat, including the restaurant at **Hotel La Carreta** (© **2695-6593**) and **Cabinas Mary** (www. hotelmarytilaran.com; © **2695-5479**). Another couple of good options are the brew pub and **La Huerta** restaurant at the **Lake Arenal Hotel** (see above).

In Nuevo Arenal, **Tom's Pan German Bakery** (www.tomspan. com; © **6694-4547**) is a popular spot for breakfast, snacks, and lunch.

Caballo Negro ★ INTERNATIONAL/VEGETARIAN This popular spot is part of the Lucky Bug Bed & Breakfast and their inventive gift shop and art gallery. The Krauskopf family bring their German heritage to the table here, offering up *Jaeger Schnitzel* (cutlet with cream sauce),

Zigeuner Scnitzel (cutlet with tomato/paprika sauce), homemade *Spaetzle* (noodles), and bratwursts. I especially like the corned beef hash for breakfast. The menu also has some non-German dishes and a host of vegetarian items. The eggplant parmesan is a perennial favorite.

Nuevo Arenal (about 3km/1¾ miles out of town on the road to Tilarán). ℂ **2694-4715.** Main courses $8–$16. Daily 7am–5pm.

Gingerbread ★★★ MEDITERRANEAN/INTERNATIONAL   Israeli-born chef Eyal Ben-Menachem is a loud, gregarious, gracious host who he keeps the needs of his guests foremost. Therefor the menu changes regularly, based on which local ingredients are at their peak though the duck quesadillas, seared tuna salad, and shrimp risotto are a few regularly occurring specials. Portions are large, often big enough to share. In fact, depending upon your group size, you may just be served a family-style meal, with no menu or selections offered—although the food will be abundant, with plenty of variety and pizzazz. If you want a touch of romance and privacy, choose patio seating. Most guests, however, prefer to be close to Eyal's amusing banter, and grab seats at one of the heavy wooden tables inside. The large U-shape bar stays open long after the kitchen has closed.

On the road btw. Tilarán and Nuevo Arenal. www.gingerbreadarenal.com. ℂ **2694-0039.** Main courses $27–$32. No credit cards. Reservations recommended. Tues–Sat 5–8pm.

Moya's Place ★★ INTERNATIONAL/VEGETARIAN/PIZZA   This cozy spot is the top pick right in the town of Nuevo Arenal for their delicious wood-oven pizzas. I also really enjoy the hearty and healthy wraps and meal-sized fresh salads. And who wouldn't like a place that's covered with kooky hand-painted murals of Mayan temples and a giant Aztec calendar? On-site is lending/exchange library, and if there's any live music happening in Nuevo Arenal, it's most likely to be happening here.

Downtown Nuevo Arenal. ℂ **2694-4001.** Main courses $5–$12. Daily 6:30am–9pm.

Mystica ★★ ITALIAN/PIZZA   The owners of this hotel restaurant are Italian, so they ensure the food is both authentic and excellent. The menu changes daily based on what's fresh and available, and many of the ingredients in their sauces, salads, and sides come straight from the hotel's organic gardens. Top picks are the brick-oven pizzas and the delicious Italian pastas and main dishes. Most also enjoy the ambiance here: The chairs are painted a rainbow of bright primary colors and no two at any table match at any one time. A fireplace is lit every night, making things cozy and romantic.

In the Mystica hotel. On the road btw. Tilarán and Nuevo Arenal. www.mysticacosta rica.com. ℂ **2692-1001.** Main courses C4,500–C7,500. Dinner by reservation only. Daily 7–9pm.

MONTEVERDE ★★

167km (104 miles) NW of San José; 82km (51 miles) NW of Puntarenas

Monteverde, which translates to "Green Mountain," is one of world's first and finest ecotourism destinations. The mist-enshrouded and marvelous Monteverde Cloud Forest Biological Reserve and extensive network of neighboring private reserves are both rich and rewarding. Bird watchers flock here for a chance to spot the myth-inspiring Resplendent Quetzal, scientists come to study the bountiful biodiversity, and a bevy of attractions and adventures await everyone else.

Cloud forests are a mountaintop phenomenon. Moist, warm air sweeping in off the ocean is forced upward by mountain slopes, and as this moist air rises, it cools, forming clouds. The mountaintops around Monteverde are blanketed almost daily in dense clouds, and as the clouds cling to the slopes, moisture condenses on forest trees. This

> ### Today's Forecast . . .
> ### Misty & Cool
>
> The climatic conditions that make Monteverde such a biological hot spot can leave many tourists feeling chilled to the bone. More than a few visitors are unprepared for a cool, windy, and wet stay in the middle of their tropical vacation, and can find Monteverde a bit inhospitable, especially from August through November.

constant level of moisture has given rise to an incredible diversity of innovative life forms and a forest in which nearly every square inch of space has some sort of plant growing. Within the cloud forest, the branches of huge trees are draped with epiphytic plants: orchids, ferns, and bromeliads. This intense botanical competition has created an

Monteverde Cloud Forest Biological Reserve.

Cloud forest in Monteverde National Park.

almost equally diverse population of insects, birds, and other wildlife. Beyond the **Resplendent Quetzal,** the Monteverde area boasts more than 2,500 species of plants, 450 types of orchids, 400 species of birds, and 100 species of mammals.

Essentials

GETTING THERE & DEPARTING   By Car: The principal access road to Monteverde is located along the Interamerican Highway (CR1); about 20km (12 miles) north of the exit for Puntarenas is a marked turnoff for Sardinal, Santa Elena, and Monteverde. From this turnoff, the road is

Yellow flowers in the rainforest, Monteverde.

Forest canopy walk in Monteverde.

Monteverde

See Inset

To San José

SANTA ELENA

Post Office

Gas Station

CERRO PLANO

CASEM

Quebrada Máquina

Río Guacimal

Bus Terminal

Santa Elena

NICARAGUA

CARIBBEAN SEA

SAN JOSÉ

Monteverde

PANAMA

PACIFIC OCEAN

MONTEVERDE

MONTEVERDE CLOUD FOREST BIOLOGICAL RESERVE

Park Entrance

0   1/2 mi
0   0.5 km

NIGHTLIFE
Bar Amigos **7**
La Taberna **14**

RESTAURANTS
Café Caburé **28**
Choco Café
  Don Juan **13**
Las Orquideas
  Café **12**
Morpho's Café **10**
Sabor Español **3**
Sabor Tico **2**
Sofia **23**
Stella's Bakery **30**
Tramonti **29**

HOTELS
Arco Iris Lodge **9**
El Establo Mountain
  Hotel **22**
El Sol **1**
Hidden Canopy
  Treehouses **4**
Hotel Fonda Vela **36**
Hotel Heliconia **21**
Hotel Poco a Poco **17**
La Colina Lodge **35**
Monteverde Country
  Lodge **19**
Monteverde Lodge
  & Gardens **18**
Pensión Santa Elena **8**

SHOPPING
CASEM **31**
Casa de Arte **20**

ATTRACTIONS
Bajo del Tigre Trail **26**
Bat Jungle **28**
Centro Panamericano de Idiomas **27**
Chocolate Tour **28**
Curicancha Reserve **32**
Don Juan Coffee Tour **3**
Ecological Sanctuary **25**
El Trapiche Tour **3**
Finca Modelo Canyoning Tour **37**
Frog Pond of Monteverde **16**
Monteverde Butterfly Garden **24**
Monteverde Cheese Factory **33**
Monteverde Cloud Forest Biological
  Reserve **38**
Monteverde Coffee Tour **37**
Monteverde Serpentarium **15**
Orchid Garden **11**
Original Canopy Tour **6**
Rio Shanti **34**
Santa Elena Cloud Forest Reserve **5**
Selvatura Park **5**
Sky Trek **4**
Sky Walk **4**

367

paved for 15km (9½ miles), to just beyond the tiny town of Guacimal. From here, it's another 20km (12 miles) to Santa Elena, the gateway town to Monteverde.

From San José, you can either take the Interamerican Highway (CR1) north all the way to the turnoff, or first head west out of San José on the San José–Caldera Highway (CR27). When you reach Caldera, follow the signs to Puntarenas and the Interamerican Highway (CR1). You will actually follow signs for Liberia and San José, which are, in fact, leading you to the unmarked entrance to CR1. This road (CR23) ends when it hits the Interamerican Highway. You'll want to pass under the bridge and follow the on-ramp, which will put you on the highway heading north. This latter route is a faster and flatter drive.

Another access road to Santa Elena is found just south of the Río Lagarto Bridge. This turnoff is the first you will come to if driving from Liberia. From the Río Lagarto turnoff, it's 38km (24 miles) to Santa Elena, and the road is unpaved the entire way.

Once you arrive, the roads in and around Santa Elena are paved, including all the way to Cerro Plano, and about halfway to the Cloud Forest Preserve.

To drive from Monteverde to La Fortuna, head out of Santa Elena toward Sky Trek and the Santa Elena Cloud Forest Reserve. Follow signs for Tilarán, which are posted at most of the critical intersections. If there's no sign, stick to the most well-worn road. This is a rough dirt road, all the way to Tilarán. From Tilarán, you have mostly well-marked and paved roads around the lake, passing first through Nuevo Arenal, and then over the dam and through Tabacón, before reaching La Fortuna.

By Bus: Transportes Monteverde express buses (© **2256-7710** in San José, or 2645-7447 in Santa Elena) leave San José daily at 6:30am and 2:30pm from Calle 12 between avenidas 7 and 9. The trip takes around 4 hours; the fare is C2,905. Buses arrive at and depart from Santa Elena. If you're staying at one of the hotels or lodges near the reserve, arrange pickup if possible, or take a taxi or local bus. Return buses for San José also depart daily at 6:30am and 2:30pm.

Three daily **Transportes Monteverde** buses depart Puntarenas for Santa Elena at 7:50am, and 1:50 and 2:15pm. The bus stop in Puntarenas is across the street from the main bus station. The fare for the 2½-hour trip is C1,565. A daily bus from Tilarán (Lake Arenal) leaves at 12:30pm. Trip duration, believe it or not, is 2 hours (for a 40km/25-mile trip); the fare is C1,150. The express bus departs for San José daily at 6:30am and 2:30pm. The buses from Santa Elena to Puntarenas leave daily at 6:30 and 2:30pm.

Gray Line (www.graylinecostarica.com; © **800/719-3105** in the U.S. and Canada, or 2220-2126 in Costa Rica) and **Interbus** (www.interbusonline.com; © **4031-0888**) both offer two daily buses that leave San José for Monteverde, one in the morning and one in the afternoon. The fare is around $50. Both of the above companies will pick you up and drop you off at most San José and Monteverde area hotels. Both Gray Line and Interbus offer routes with connections to most major destinations in Costa Rica.

If you're heading to Manuel Antonio, take the Santa Elena/Puntarenas bus and transfer in Puntarenas. To reach Liberia, take any bus down the mountain and get off as soon as you hit the Interamerican Highway. You can then flag down a bus bound for Liberia (almost any bus heading north). The Santa Elena/Tilarán bus leaves daily at 7am.

GETTING AROUND   Five or so daily buses connect the town of Santa Elena and the Monteverde Cloud Forest Biological Reserve. The first bus leaves Santa Elena for the reserve at 6:15am and the last bus from the reserve leaves at 4pm. The fare is C500. Periodic van transportation also runs between the town of Santa Elena and the Santa Elena Cloud Forest Reserve. Ask around town and you should be able to find the current schedule and book a ride for around C1,000 per person. A **taxi** (© **2645-6969** or 2645-6666) between Santa Elena and either the Monteverde Reserve or the Santa Elena Cloud Forest Reserve costs around C5,500 for up to four people. Count on paying between C5,000 and C5,500 for the ride from Santa Elena to your lodge in Monteverde. Finally, several places around town rent **ATVs,** or all-terrain vehicles, for around $60 to $90 per day.

CITY LAYOUT   The tiny town of **Santa Elena** is the gateway to Monteverde and the Monteverde Cloud Forest Biological Reserve, 6km (3¾ miles) outside of town along a windy road that dead-ends at the reserve entrance. As you approach Santa Elena, take the right fork in the road if you're heading directly to Monteverde. If you continue straight, you'll come into the little town center of tiny **Santa Elena,** which has a bus stop, a health clinic, a bank, a supermarket, and a few general stores, and a collection of simple restaurants, budget hotels, souvenir shops,

---

Alternative Transport

You can travel between Monteverde and La Fortuna by boat and taxi, or on a combination boat, horseback, and taxi trip. See "Boats, Horses & Taxis," on p. 337, for details. Any of the trips described there can be done in the reverse direction departing from Monteverde. Most hotels and **Desafío Expeditions** ★★ (www.desafiocostarica.com; © **855/818-0020** in the U.S. and Canada, or 2479-0020 in Costa Rica) can arrange this trip for you. Desafío offers multiday hikes from Monteverde to Arenal; you spend the night in rustic research facilities inside the Bosque Eterno de Los Niños. They also offer transfers to Pacific coast beach towns combined with a day rafting on the Tenorio River.

An ATV ride off road.

and tour offices. Heading just out of town, toward Monteverde, is a small strip mall with a large and prominent Megasuper supermarket. **Monteverde,** on the other hand, is not a village in the traditional sense of the word. There's no center of town—only dirt lanes leading off from the main road to various farms. This main road has signs for all the hotels and restaurants mentioned here, and it dead-ends at the reserve entrance.

For a map of Monteverde Cloud Forest Reserve, see the inside front cover of this book.

FAST FACTS The telephone number for the **local clinic** is ✆ **2645-5076;** for the **Red Cross,** ✆ **2645-6128;** and for the **local police,** ✆ **911** or 2645-6248. The **Farmacia Monteverde** (✆ **2449-5495**) is right downtown. A **Banco Nacional** (✆ **2645-5027**) is located on a prominent corner in downtown Santa Elena, and has a 24-hour ATM.

Peace, Love & Ecotourism

Monteverde was settled in 1951 by Quakers from the United States who wanted to leave behind the fear of war, as well as their obligation to support continued militarism through paying U.S. taxes. They chose Costa Rica, a country that had abolished its army in 1948. Although Monteverde's founders came here to farm, they wisely recognized the need to preserve the rare cloud forest that covered the mountain slopes above their fields, and to that end, they dedicated the largest adjacent tract of cloud forest as the Monteverde Cloud Forest Biological Reserve.

If you want an in-depth look into the lives and history of the local Quaker community, pick up a copy of the "Monteverde Jubilee Family Album." Published in 2001 by the Monteverde Association of Friends, this collection of oral histories and photographs is 260 pages of local lore and memoirs. It's very simply bound and printed but well worth the $20 price.

Because the entrance fee to Monteverde
is valid for a full day, I recommend taking
an early-morning walk with a guide and
then heading off on your own either
directly after that hike or after lunch. A
guide will certainly point out and explain
a lot, but there's also much to be said for
walking quietly through the forest on
your own or in very small groups. This
will also allow you to stray from the well-
traveled paths in the park.

Birds at the Hummingbird Gallery.

Exploring the Monteverde Cloud Forest Biological Reserve ★★★

The **Monteverde Cloud Forest Biological Reserve** (www.reserva monteverde.com; © **2645-5122**) is one of the most developed and well-maintained natural attractions in Costa Rica. The trails are clearly marked, regularly traveled, and generally gentle in terms of ascents and descents. The cloud forest here is lush and largely untouched. Still, keep in mind that most of the birds and mammals are rare, elusive, and nocturnal. Moreover, to all but the most trained of eyes, those thousands of exotic ferns, orchids, and bromeliads tend to blend into one large mass of indistinguishable green. However, with a guide hired through your hotel, or on one of the reserve's official guided 2- to 3-hour hikes, you can see and learn far more than you could on your own. At $18 per person, the reserve's tours might seem like a splurge, especially after you pay the entrance fee, but I strongly recommend that you go with a guide.

Perhaps the most famous resident of the cloud forests of Costa Rica is the quetzal, a robin-size bird with iridescent green wings and a ruby-red breast, which has become extremely rare due to habitat destruction. The male quetzal also has two long tail feathers that can reach nearly.6m (2 ft.) in length, making it one of the most spectacular birds on earth. The best time to see quetzals is early morning to midmorning, and the best months are February through April (mating season).

Other animals that have been seen in Monteverde, although sightings are extremely rare, include jaguars, ocelots, and tapirs. After the quetzal, Monteverde's most famous resident used to be the golden toad (*sapo dorado*), a rare native species. However, the golden toad has disappeared from the forest and is feared extinct. Competing theories of the toad's demise include adverse effects of a natural drought cycle, the disappearing ozone layer, pesticides, and acid rain.

ADMISSION, HOURS & TOURS   The reserve is open daily from 7am to 4pm, and the entrance fee is $20 for adults and $10 for students and children. Because only 220 people are allowed into the reserve at any one time, you might be forced to wait. Most hotels can reserve a guided walk and entrance to the reserve for the following day for you, or you can get tickets in advance directly at the reserve entrance.

Some of the trails can be very muddy, depending on the season, so ask about current conditions. Before venturing into the forest, have a look around the info center. Several guidebooks are available, as well as postcards of some of the reserve's more famous animal inhabitants.

Night tours of the reserve leave every evening at 6:15pm. The cost is $17, including admission to the reserve, a 2-hour hike, and, most important, a guide with a high-powered searchlight. For an extra $5, they'll throw in round-trip transportation to and from your area hotel.

Exploring Outside the Reserve

In addition to everything mentioned below, all of the area hotels can arrange a wide variety of other tours and activities, including guided night tours of the cloud forest and night trips to the Arenal Volcano (a tedious 4-hr. ride each way).

BIRD-WATCHING & HIKING

You'll find ample bird-watching and hiking opportunities outside the reserve boundaries. Avoid the crowds at Monteverde by heading 5km (3 miles) north from the village of Santa Elena to the **Santa Elena Cloud Forest Reserve ★★** (www.reservasantaelena.org; ✆ **2645-5390;** daily 7am–4pm). This 310-hectare (765-acre) reserve has a maximum elevation of 1,680m (5,510 ft.), making it the highest cloud forest in the Monteverde area. The reserve has 13km (8 miles) of hiking trails, as well as an info center. Because it borders the Monteverde Reserve, a similar richness of flora and fauna is found here, although quetzals are not nearly as common. The $14 entry fee at this reserve goes directly to support a variety of good causes, including conservation and improving the local schools. Three-hour guided tours are $15 per person, not including the entrance fee. (Call the number above to make a reservation for the tour.)

Located just before the Monteverde Cloud Forest Reserve, and sharing many of the same ecosystems and habitats, the **Curicancha Reserve ★★★** (www.reservacuricancha.com; ✆ **2645-6915;** daily 7am–3pm and 5:30–7:30pm) is an excellent alternative, especially for folks looking to avoid some of the crowds and confusion that can sometimes be found at the area's namesake attraction. The reserve covers some 86 hectares (240 acres), of which almost half is primary cloud forest. The trails here are rich in flora and fauna, and quetzals are frequently

A SELF-GUIDED hike THROUGH THE RESERVE

I know I strongly recommend going on a guided tour, but if you're intent on exploring the reserve on your own, or heading back for more, I suggest starting off on the **Sendero El Río (River Trail) ★ ★**. This trail, which heads north from the reserve office, puts you immediately in the midst of dense primary cloud forest, where heavy layers of mosses, bromeliads, and epiphytes cover every branch and trunk. This very first section of trail is a prime location for spotting a Resplendent Quetzal.

After 15 or 20 minutes, you'll come to a little marked spur leading down to a *catarata,* or waterfall. This diminutive fall fills a small, pristine pond and is quite picturesque, but if you fail in your attempts to capture its beauty, look for its image emblazoned on postcards at souvenir stores all around the area. The entire trek to the waterfall should take you an hour or so.

From the waterfall, turn around and retrace your steps along the River Trail until you come to a fork and the **Sendero Tosi (Tosi Trail).** Follow this shortcut, which leads through varied terrain, back to the reserve entrance.

Once you've got the River Trail and waterfall under your belt, I recommend a slightly more strenuous hike to a lookout atop the Continental Divide. **Sendero Bosque Nuboso (Cloud Forest Trail) ★** heads east from the reserve entrance. As its name implies, the trail leads through thick, virgin cloud forest. Keep your eyes open for any number of bird and mammal species, including toucans, trogans, honeycreepers, and howler monkeys. Some great specimens of massive strangler fig trees are on the trail. These trees start as parasitic vines and eventually engulf their host tree. After 1.9km (1.2 miles), you will reach the Continental Divide. Despite the sound of this, there's only a modest elevation gain of some 65m (213 ft.).

A couple of lookout points on the Divide are through clearings in the forest, but the best is **La Ventana (The Window) ★**, just beyond the end of this trail and reached via a short spur trail. Here you'll find a broad, elevated wooden deck with panoramic views. Be forewarned: It's often misty and quite windy up here.

On the way back, take the 2km (1.2-mile) **Sendero Camino (Road Trail).** As its name implies, much of this trail was once used as a rough all-terrain road. Since it is wide and open in many places, this trail is particularly good for birdwatching. About halfway along, you'll want to take a brief detour to a **suspended bridge ★**. Some 100m (330-ft.) long, this midforest bridge gives you a bird's-eye view of the forest canopy. The entire loop should take around 3 hours.

spotted here. Entrance is $14, and a 3- to 4-hour guided hike can be arranged for an additional $15 per person.

Sky Walk ★★ (www.skyadventures.travel; © **2479-4100;** daily 7am–4pm) is a network of forest paths and suspension bridges that provides visitors with a view previously reserved for birds, monkeys, and the much more adventurous traveler. The bridges reach 39m (128 ft.) above the ground at their highest point, so acrophobia could be an issue. The Sky Walk and its sister attraction, **Sky Trek** (see "Canopy & Canyoning

Tours," below), are about 3.5km (2¼ miles) outside the town of Santa Elena, on the road to the Santa Elena Cloud Forest Reserve. Admission is $35, which includes a knowledgeable guide. For $71/person, you can do the Sky Trek canopy tour and Sky Tram, and then walk the trails and bridges of the Sky Walk. Reservations recommended; round-trip transportation from Santa Elena is just $7 per person.

To learn even more about Monteverde, stop in at the **Monteverde Conservation League** (www.acmcr.org; © **2645-5003**), which administers the 22,000-hectare (54,000-acre) private reserve **Bosque Eterno de Los Niños (Children's Eternal Forest)** as well as the Bajo del Tigre Trail. The Conservation League has an info center and small gift shop at the trail head/entrance to the Bajo del Tigre Trail. In addition to being a good source for information, it also sells books, T-shirts, and cards, and all proceeds go to purchase more land for the Bosque Eterno de Los Niños. The **Bajo del Tigre Trail ★** is a 3.5km (2.3-mile) trail that's home to several different bird species not usually found within the reserve. You can take several different loops, lasting anywhere from 1 hour to several hours. The trail starts a little past the CASEM artisans' shop (see "Shopping," below) and is open daily from 8am to 4pm. Admission is $12 for adults and $10 for students and children under 12. These folks also do a 2-hour night hike that departs at 5:30pm, and costs $22 per adult, and $19 per student. All of this is free for kids 6 and under.

Finally, you can walk the trails and grounds of the **Ecological Sanctuary ★★** (www.santuarioecologico.com; © **2645-5869**; daily 7am–5pm), a family-run wildlife refuge and private reserve located down the Cerro Plano road. This place has four main trails through a variety of ecosystems, and wildlife-viewing is often quite good. A couple of pretty waterfalls are off the trails. Admission is $17 for self-guided hiking on the trails, $35 adults, $31 students and $29 children during the day for a 2-hour guided tour, and $30 adults, $25 students and $23 children for the 2-hour guided night tour at 5:30pm.

> ### If Not Here, Where?
>
> For many, the primary goal in visiting Monteverde is to glimpse the rare and elusive **quetzal**, a bird once revered by the pre-Columbian peoples of the Americas. However, if you just care about seeing a quetzal, you should also consider visiting other cloud forest areas. In particular, San Gerardo de Dota and Cerro de la Muerte areas are home to several specialty lodges (see "Where to See Quetzals in the Wild: Cerro de la Muerte & San Gerardo de Dota," in chapter 11), where you'll find far fewer crowds and often will have better chances of seeing the famed quetzal.

CANOPY & CANYONING TOURS

Selvatura Park ★★ (www.selvatura.com; © **2645-5929**; daily 7am–4:30pm), located close to the Santa Elena Cloud Forest Reserve, is the best one-stop shop for various adventures and attractions in the area. In addition to an extensive canopy tour, with 13 cables connecting 15 platforms, they also have a network of trails and suspended bridges, a huge butterfly garden, a hummingbird garden, a snake exhibit, and a wonderful insect display and museum. Prices vary depending upon how much you want to see and do. Individually, the canopy tour costs $45; the walkways and bridges $30; the snake and reptile exhibit, the butterfly garden, and the insect museum, $15 each. Packages to combine the various exhibits are available, although it's definitely confusing, and somewhat annoying, to pick the perfect package. For $132, you get the run of the entire joint, including the tours, lunch, and round-trip transportation from your Monteverde hotel.

Another popular option is offered by **Sky Adventures ★★** (www.skyadventures.travel; ☎ **2479-4100**), which is part of a large complex of aerial adventures and hiking trails. This is one of the most extensive canopy tours in the country, and begins with a cable car ride (or **Sky Tram**) up into the cloud forest, where their zip-line canopy tour commences and features 10 cables. The longest of these stretches some 770m (2,525 ft.), high above the forest floor. There are no rappel descents, and you brake using the pulley system for friction. Nearby, their **Sky Walk ★★** (p. 373) is a network of forest paths and suspension bridges that can easily be combined with this adventure tour. Also here: a serpentarium and hummingbird garden. This place is about 3.5km (2¼ miles) outside the town of Santa Elena, on the road to the Santa Elena Cloud Forest Reserve. The Sky Walk is open daily from 7am to 1pm; admission is $35, which includes a knowledgeable guide. For $89 per person, you can do the Sky Trek canopy tour and Sky Tram, and then walk the trails and bridges of the Sky Walk. Reservations recommended; round-trip transportation from Santa Elena is $7.50 per person.

One of the oldest canopy tours in the country is run by the **Original Canopy Tour ★** (www.canopytour.com; ☎ **305/433-3341** in U.S or 2291-4465 in Costa Rica). Its highlight is the initial ascent which is made by climbing up the hollowed-out interior of a giant strangler fig. The tour has 13 platforms and one rappel. The 2- to 2½-hour tours run tree times daily and cost $45/adults, $35/students, and $25/children 12 and under.

Finally, if you want to add a bit more excitement to your adventure, and definitely more water, try the **Finca Modelo Canyoning Tour ★★** (www.familiabrenestours.com; ☎ **2645-5581**). This tour involves a mix of hiking and then rappelling down the face of a series of forest waterfalls. The tallest of these waterfalls is around 40m (132 ft.). You will get wet on this tour. The cost is $70.

Anybody in average physical condition can do any of the adventure tours in Monteverde, but they're not for the fainthearted or acrophobic. Try to book directly with the companies listed above. Beware of touts on the streets of Monteverde, who make a small commission and frequently try to steer tourists to the operator paying the highest percentage.

HORSEBACK RIDING

Monteverde has excellent terrain for horseback riding. **Horse Trek Monteverde★** (www.costaricahorsebackridingvacations.com;✆**866/811-0522** in U.S and Canada or 2645-5874 in Costa Rica) and **Sabine's Smiling Horses** ★ (www.smilinghorses.com; ✆ **2645-6894**) are the most established operators, offering guided rides for around $20 to $23 per hour. Horseback/boat trips link Monteverde/Santa Elena with La Fortuna (p. 343).

OTHER ATTRACTIONS IN MONTEVERDE

It seems as if Monteverde has an exhibit or attraction dedicated to almost every type of tropical fauna. It's a pet peeve of mine, but I really wish these folks would band together and offer some sort of general pass. However, as it stands, you'll have to shell out for each individual attraction.

Butterflies abound here, and the long-established **Monteverde Butterfly Garden** ★ (www.monteverdebutterflygarden.com; ✆ **2645-5512;** daily 8:30am–4pm), located near the Pensión Monteverde Inn, displays many of Costa Rica's most beautiful species. Aside from seeing the hundreds of preserved and mounted butterflies, you can watch live butterflies in the garden and greenhouse. Admission, including a guided tour, is $15/adults, $10/students, and $5 for kids ages 4 to 6. If you can, visit between 9 and 11am, when the butterflies tend to be most active.

If your taste runs toward the slithery, you can check out the informative displays at the **Monteverde Serpentarium** ★ (✆ **2645-6002;** daily 9am–8pm), on the road to the reserve. It charges $13 for adults, $11 for students and $8 for children for admission.

Monteverde Theme Park ★ (www.ranariomonteverde.com; ✆ **2645-6320;** daily 9:30am–8pm), a couple of hundred meters north of the Monteverde Lodge, has several attractions. A variety of amphibians populates a series of glass terrariums; nearby is a butterfly garden and on-site canopy tour. The entrance fee ($14 for adults and $12 for students) gets you a 45-minute guided tour, and your ticket is good for 1 week, allowing for multiple visits. I especially recommend that you stop by at least once after dark, when the tree frogs are active.

The **Bat Jungle ★★★** (www.batjungle.com; ✆ **2645-7701;** daily 9am–7:30pm) provides an in-depth look into the life and habits of these odd flying

A tree frog at the Monteverde Serpentarium.

mammals. A visit here includes several different types of exhibits, from skeletal remains to a large enclosure where you get to see various live species in action—the enclosure and room are kept dark, and the bats have had their biological clocks tricked into thinking that it's night. It's quite an interesting experience. The last tour starts at 6:45pm. Admission is $13/adults and $11/students. Children under 6 are free.

If you've had your fill of critters, you might want to stop at the **Orchid Garden ★★** (www.monteverdeorchidgarden.net; ℂ **2645-5308;** daily 8am–5pm), in Santa Elena across from the Pensión El Tucano. This botanical garden has more than 425 species of orchids. The tour is fascinating, especially given the fact that you need (and are given) a magnifying glass to see some of the flowers in bloom. Admission is $10 for adults, $7 for students and free for children under 12.

AGRICULTURAL & CULINARY TOURISM

If you're looking for a glimpse into the practices and processes of daily life in this region, **Don Juan Coffee Tour ★★** (www.donjuancoffeetour.

A sugar cane field.

com; ℂ **2645-7100**) is a local, family-farm operation that offers a 2-hour tour on their sprawling farm. Coffee is the primary crop and focus of the tour, although these folks also have a range of crops, including macadamia; a trapiche, or sugar cane mill; and small boutique-chocolate production area. As a bonus, you get a snack and coffee tasting, and you may even get to meet the farm's namesake septuagenarian, Don Juan. The tour costs $35/adults and $15/children.

El Trapiche Tour ★★ (www.eltrapichetour.com; ℂ **2645-7780** or 2645-7650) is another family-run tour, which gives you insight into the traditional means of harvesting and processing sugar cane, as well as the general life on a farm that includes bananas, macadamia, and citrus groves. Back at the farmhouse, you get to see how the raw materials are turned into cane liquor, raw sugar, and local sweets. The 2-hour tour includes a ride in an ox-drawn cart, and a visit to the family's coffee farm and roasting facility. Depending upon the season, you may even get to pick a bushel of raw coffee beans. Tours run daily at 10am and 3pm, and cost $32 for adults, and $12 for children 10 through 12, and include transportation.

Finally, if you want a detailed explanation of the processes involved in growing, harvesting, processing, and producing chocolate, be sure to stop by Café Caburé (p. 382) for their **Chocolate Tour.** You'll take some chocolate beans right through the roasting, grinding, and tempering processes, in the 45-minute tour. The tour is offered most days at 1:30pm, and by appointment. The cost is $10.

LEARN THE LANGUAGE

The **Centro Panamericano de Idiomas** ★ (www.cpi-edu.com; ☎ **2645-5441**) offers immersion language classes in a wonderful setting. A 1-week program with 4 hours of class per day and a homestay with a Costa Rican family costs $730. They offer language seminars on topics such as social work, medicine, and security. Be sure to check their website for the dates the seminars are taking place.

LOOSE & LIMBER

If you're interested in a massage treatment or yoga class, head to **Río Shanti** (www.rioshanti.com; ☎ **2645-6121**). This delightful spot offers regular, open yoga classes, private lessons, and various massage treatments. Their little boutique sells handmade jewelry, clothing, and a range of oils and lotions, most made with organic local ingredients.

Where to Stay

When choosing a place to stay in Monteverde, be sure to check whether the rates include a meal plan. In the past, almost all the lodges included three meals a day in their prices, but this practice is waning. Check before you assume anything.

EXPENSIVE

El Establo Mountain Hotel ★ I remember when the Beeche family transformed their old horse stable (hence, *el establo*) into a simple roadside budget lodging. Today that original hostel is gone, and in its place is arguably the biggest and most conventionally swank hotel in Monteverde. Large rooms are spread around sprawling grounds that rise up a steep hillside from the main road between Santa Elena and the Monteverde Cloud Forest Reserve. The hotel provides a shuttle service to help you get around the hilly property, but it's not the most convenient arrangement and often makes for some unwanted waiting at times. All rooms have a private balcony or patio, and those on the higher floors of the buildings highest up the hillside have some amazing views out to the Gulf of Nicoya, which you can enjoy from the comfort of the provided wooden rocking chairs. Rooms have a contemporary vibe with crisp coverlets, angular wooden furniture and TV's (this is one of the few hotels in Monteverde to have that latter amenity). There are two covered pools, two good restaurants, a small spa, an outdoor, lighted tennis court, and an on-site zip-line canopy tour.

Monteverde. www.hotelelestablo.com. ☎ **855/353-7822** in the U.S. and Canada or 2645-5110 in Costa Rica. 155 units. $195–$216 double; $295–$325 suite. Rates include taxes. **Amenities:** 2 restaurants; bar; 2 covered pools; tennis court; room service; small spa.

Hidden Canopy Treehouses ★★★ If you're looking for an intimate, unique, in-touch-with-nature experience in the Monteverde area, you can't beat this place. While a couple of perfectly lovely rooms are off the main lodge building, you'll definitely want one of the individual "tree houses." Set amid the forest canopy these are all ample, individual bungalows built on raised stilts, awash in polished hardwoods, slate bathrooms with waterfall showers, canopied beds and featuring large picture windows and a balcony or outdoor deck. I especially like the wrap-around floor-to ceiling windows in Glade, and the private Jacuzzi nook, also with floor to ceiling windows, in Eden. You can take in superb sunset views from the main lodge, where afternoon tea is served daily. Owner Jennifer King is almost always onsite and really pays attention to the fine details. These folks have excellent in-house guides and provide very personalized service.

On the road to the Santa Elena Cloud Forest Reserve. www.hiddencanopy.com. ⓒ **2645-5447.** 7 units. $225 double; $285–$445 double tree house. Rates include breakfast and afternoon happy hour. No children 14 or under. 2-night minimum. **Amenities:** Afternoon tea; free Wi-Fi.

MODERATE

Hotel Fonda Vela ★★ This longstanding hotel is one of the closest you'll find to the Monteverde Cloud Forest Reserve, just a 15-minute or so walk away. But we'd recommend it even if it weren't for its unique and pretty look. Owner Paul Smith's paintings, stained-glass works, and large sculptures are scattered throughout the hotel and grounds. Rooms, in several separate blocks of buildings, have views over the forests to the Gulf of Nicoya. Locally milled tongue-and groove wood planking is used for their walls, floors, ceilings and wainscoting. The junior suites are especially spacious. A short walk from the restaurant and rooms is a pool, a couple of Jacuzzis, pool and Ping-Pong tables, board games, and a casual bar, all housed under a high, curving atrium roof.

On the road to the Monteverde Cloud Forest Reserve. www.fondavela.com. ⓒ **2645-5125.** 40 units. $142–$177 double; $244 junior suite. Extra person $17. Rates include taxes. **Amenities:** 2 restaurants; 2 bars; Jacuzzi; pool; free Wi-Fi

Hotel Heliconia ★ Located right at the Cerro Plano intersection along the road between Santa Elena and the Monteverde Cloud Forest Reserve, this is another local lodging that has steadily grown and expanded over the years. The largest building (which is set on the highest part of the property) is where you'll find the rooms with the best views. Personally, I think the wood paneled walls and carpeted floors give the decor a very dated, motel-like feel, but it's clean and the staff are friendly. Five different hot tubs and Jacuzzis are spread around the lush grounds between the hotels several buildings. There's a large private cloud forest preserve behind the hotel; the owners also run the Selvatura canopy tour and adventure center (p. 374).

Monteverde. www.hotelheliconia.com. ☎ **2645-6616.** 55 units. $92 double; $125-$175 suite. **Amenities:** Restaurant; bar.

Hotel Poco a Poco ★★ A good choice for families with kids, Hotel Poco a Poco is a hive of activity, with a pool, small playhouse and nice grounds (there's also a restaurant, heated Jacuzzi, and small spa). Located on the outskirts of Santa Elena, Poco a Poco has clean, comfortable rooms (cream tiled floors, quality beds) with all the modern amenities, including TV/DVD systems and access to their massive DVD library. Some are a bit tight in terms of size, so ask to move if you're not happy. The restaurant is excellent and features live music nightly. These folks take sustainable tourism seriously and have earned "4 Leaves" in the CST Sustainable Tourism program.

Santa Elena. www.hotelpocoapoco.com. ☎ **855/557-7262** in U.S. and Canada, or 2645-6000 in Costa Rica. 32 units. $134–$154 double. **Amenities:** Restaurant; bar; Jacuzzi; small indoor pool; spa; sauna; Jacuzzi; free Wi-Fi.

Monteverde Lodge & Gardens ★★★ Some things do get better with age, and that's certainly true of this pioneering ecolodge, which is run by Michael Kaye and Costa Rica Expeditions (p. 80). Rooms are large and cozy, and all of the furnishings, appointments, are what I'd call rustic yet elegant. They feature hard wood floors, orthopedic beds and a wall of windows or French doors opening out to views of the gardens and surrounding forests. Meals are served in a large central dining room, with walls of windows all around and a large, open fire burning under a suspended conical steel chimney. There are well-marked trails onsite through the lush and beautiful gardens, and there's a mid-size heated outdoor pool with slate decking all around, as well as butterfly, orchid and hummingbird attractions. These folks also operate one of the best guide and tour operations in the area.

Santa Elena. www.monteverdelodge.com. ☎ **2257-0766** San José office, or 2645-5057 at the lodge. 27 units. $99–$228 double. Rates include full breakfast. **Amenities:** Restaurant; bar; swimming pool; free Wi-Fi.

INEXPENSIVE

In addition to the hotels listed below, **El Sol ★** (www.elsolnuestro.com; ☎ **2645-5838**) is a unique little boutique option, on the road to the Interamerican Highway, about 10 minutes south of Santa Elena. Also consider **Monteverde Country Lodge** (www.monteverdecountrylodge.com; ☎ **888/936-5696** in U.S and Canada, or 2645-7600 in Costa Rica), a homey, simple hotel run by the folks at Hotel Poco a Poco (see above).

For real budgeteers, there are quite a few backpacker havens in Santa Elena and spread along the road to the reserve. The best of these is the **Pensión Santa Elena** (www.pensionsantaelena.com; ☎ **2645-5051**).

Finally, it's possible to stay in a room right at the **Monteverde Cloud Forest Biological Reserve** (www.cct.or.cr; ☎ **2645-5122**). A bunk bed, shared bathroom, and three meals per day here run $70 per person. For an extra $11, you can get a room with a private bathroom. Admission to the reserve is included in the price.

Arco Iris Lodge ★★   This small boutique hotel is actually right in the town of Santa Elena, but you'd never know it. The expansive grounds and gardens give it a great sense of isolation and privacy (though you can still walk to shops and restaurants). The rooms come in a variety of shapes and sizes from simple standards, some with bunk beds, to individual cabins and Superior rooms with a kitchenette and sleeping loft. All feature shiny varnished wood and local stonework, as well as low lying beds with colorful Guatemalan bedspreads. German owner Susanna and her engaged staff make sure service is always top notch.

Santa Elena. www.arcoirislodge.com. ✆ **2645-5067.** 24 units. $42–$50 budget rooms; $88–$145 double; $195 honeymoon cabin. Rates include taxes. **Amenities:** Lounge; free Wi-Fi.

La Colina Lodge ★   This rustic old lodge (originally the Pensión Flor Mar) is fairly close to the Monteverde Cloud Forest Reserve, and it radiates a friendly, homey vibe. Guests from all over the world gather in the common lounge area, or cook together in the communal kitchen. The walls, tables and chairs here are painted bright colors, with fanciful hand painted patterns and designs. Rooms are basic, but well-kept and cozy. You have a choice of shared bathroom dorm accommodations or rooms with their own private bath. You can even pitch a tent on their grounds, while enjoying kitchen and bathroom privileges. Yoga and art classes are offered in a big open room, with one whole wall of windows.

Monteverde. www.lacolinalodge.com. ✆ **2645-5009.** 11 units, 6 with private bathroom. $25 double with shared bathroom; $35 double with private bathroom; $8 per person camping. Rates include taxes. **Amenities:** Restaurant, free Wi-Fi.

Where to Dine

Because most visitors want to get an early start, they usually grab a quick breakfast at their hotel. It's also common for people to have their lodge pack them a bag lunch to take to the reserve, although a decent little *soda* is at the reserve entrance.

In addition to the places listed below, you can get good pizzas and pastas at **Tramonti ★** (www.tramonticr.com; ✆ **2645-6120**), along the road to the reserve, and great paella and other Spanish specialties at **Sabor Español ★** (✆ **2645-5387**), a few miles outside of Santa Elena on the road to Tilarán. Also, the restaurant at the **Hotel Poco a Poco** (✆ **2645-6000**) gets high marks for its wide range of international dishes.

A popular choice for lunch is **Stella's Bakery** (✆ **2645-5560**), across from the CASEM gift shop. Bright and inviting, its selection changes regularly but might include vegetarian quiche, eggplant *parmigiana,* and different salads. Stella's also features a number of decadent baked goods.

EXPENSIVE

Sofia ★★ COSTA RICAN/FUSION   Here's your splurge choice, a happy change from the simple, typical Costa Rican cooking you might be getting your fill of. The Nuevo Latino cuisine here is still based on classic Tico dishes and local ingredients, but with intriguing twists, like tenderloin in chipotle butter salsa or guava-glazed chicken. Owner and restauranteur Karen Nielsen has created a sophisticated and romantic ambiance here, with solid wooden tables and chairs, soft lighting and cool jazz in the background. Try to grab a seat in front of one of the large arched picture windows overlooking cloud forest foliage.

Cerro Plano, just past the turnoff to the Butterfly Farm, on your left. ℂ **2645-7017.** Reservations recommended during high season. Main courses $14–$20. Daily 11:30am–9:30pm.

MODERATE

Café Caburé ★★★ INTERNATIONAL/CHOCOLATES   Set on the second floor of a small complex also housing the Bat Jungle (p. 376), with open-air seating on a broad wooden veranda we recommend this place for a decadent dessert break (though lunches and dinners here are also solid). The homemade chocolates and fancy, flavored truffles here are truly scrumptious. (And if you want to learn more about the chocolate-making and -tempering process, be sure to take their Chocolate Tour; see p. 377). On the savory side, the main menu features a wide range of international dishes, with everything from chicken mole to shrimp curry to more straightforward but very tasty sandwiches, wraps, and fresh empanadas (one of the owners is Argentinian).

On the road btw. Santa Elena and the reserve, at the Bat Jungle. www.cabure.net. ℂ **2645-5020.** Reservations recommended during high season. Main courses C2,900–C9,500. Mon–Sat 9am–9pm.

INEXPENSIVE

Morpho's Restaurant ★ COSTA RICAN/VEGETARIAN   Although it's moved around over the years, Morpho's is a local institution, serving up hearty meals at reasonable prices. The large and varied *casado* (a local blue-plate special) is quite popular, as are the fresh fruit smoothies and home-baked desserts. For something a bit fancier, try the thick pork chop in a plum/cherry sauce. There are also a host of excellent vegetarian selections. You can't miss this place, with its painted exterior covered with oversize, fluttering blue morpho butterflies. The hand-painted murals continue inside where they're

---

Take a Break

If all the activities in Monteverde have worn you out, stop in at **Las Orquídeas Café** (ℂ **2645-6850**) or the **Choco Café Don Juan** ★ (ℂ **2645-7444**), two excellent local coffee shops just off the main drag in Santa Elena. The latter is connected to the Don Juan Coffee Farm (p. 377) and has a small gift shop attached.

joined by rustic furnishings including chairs made from whole tree branches and trunks.

In downtown Santa Elena, next to the Orchid Garden. www.morphosrestaurant.com. ℂ **2645-5607.** Main courses C2,500–C9,200. Daily 11am–9pm.

Sabor Tico ★★ COSTA RICAN   The name of this place translates as "Tico Flavor," and that's what you get at this family-run, traditional joint. The portions are huge, and everything is extremely tasty and well pre-pared, although service can be slow (but friendly) when they are busy. The *casados, arroz con pollo,* and fresh fruit juices are all excellent. I always try to snag one of the few tables on the front veranda overlooking the town's soccer field. These folks have opened a second location (ℂ **2645-5968**) in the Centro Comercial Monteverde shopping plaza, but I much prefer the more casual and authentic vibe of the original location.

In downtown Santa Elena, across from the soccer field. ℂ **2645-5827.** Main courses C2,700–C4,900. Daily 7am–9pm.

Shopping

The **Monteverde Cloud Forest Biological Reserve** has a well-stocked gift shop, just off their entrance. You'll find plenty of T-shirts, postcards, and assorted crafts here, as well as science and natural history books.

Shopping in Monteverde.

Another top shop is **CASEM COOP** ★ (http://casemcoop.blog spot.com; ℂ **2645-5190;** daily 7am–5pm), on the right side of the main road, just across from Stella's Bakery. This crafts cooperative sells embroidered clothing, T-shirts, posters, and postcards, Boruca weavings, locally grown and roasted coffee, and many other items to remind you of your visit to Monteverde. CASEM COOP is open daily 7am to 5pm.

Over the years, Monteverde has developed a nice little community of artists. Around town, you'll see paintings by local artists Paul Smith and Meg Wallace, whose works are displayed at Hotel Fonda Vela and Stella's Bakery, respectively. You should also check out **Casa de Arte** ★★ (www.monteverdearthouse.com; ℂ **2645-5275**), which has a mix of arts and crafts in many mediums.

Finally, it's worth stopping by the **Monteverde Cheese Factory** (www.monteverde.net; ✆ **2645-5150**) to pick up some of the best cheese in Costa Rica. You can even watch cheese being processed and get homemade ice cream. The cheese factory is right on the main road about midway between Santa Elena and the reserve. They offer 1-hour tours at 9am and 2pm, at a cost of $12.

Entertainment & Nightlife

Perhaps the most popular after-dark activities in Monteverde are night hikes in one of the reserves. However, if you want a taste of the local party scene, head to **Bar Amigos** (www.baramigos.com; ✆ **2645-5071**), a large and often loud bar in the heart of Santa Elena. You'll find a bunch of flatscreen TVs showing sporting events, a couple of pool tables, and occasional live bands. I prefer **La Taberna** ★ (✆ **8839-5569**), on the edge of Santa Elena town, below the Serpentarium. With a more contemporary club vibe, this place attracts a mix of locals and tourists, cranks its music loud, often gets people dancing.

PUERTO VIEJO DE SARAPIQUÍ ★

82km (51 miles) N of San José; 102km (63 miles) E of La Fortuna

The Sarapiquí region, named for the principal river that runs through this area, lies at the foot of the Cordillera Central mountain range. To the west is the rainforest of **Braulio Carrillo National Park,** and to the east are **Tortuguero National Park ★★** and **Barra del Colorado National Wildlife Refuge ★**. In between these protected areas lay thousands of acres of banana, pineapple, and palm plantations. Here you see the great contradiction of Costa Rica: On the one hand, the country is known for its national parks, which preserve some of the largest tracts of rainforest left in Central America; on the other hand, nearly every acre of land outside of these parks, save a few private reserves, has been clearcut and converted into plantations—and the cutting continues.

Within the remaining rainforest are several lodges that attract naturalists (both amateur and professional). Two of these lodges, **La Selva** and **Rara Avis,** are famous for the research that's conducted on their surrounding reserves. Birdwatching and rainforest hikes are the primary attractions, but more

Howler monkey at La Selva Biological Station.

adventure-oriented travelers will find plenty of other available activities, including canopy tours and boating and rafting trips along the Sarapiquí River.

Essentials

GETTING THERE & DEPARTING   By Car: The Guápiles Highway (CR32), which leads to the Caribbean coast, heads north out of downtown San José on Calle 3. Turn north before reaching Guápiles on the road to Río Frío (CR4), and continue north through Las Horquetas, passing the turnoffs for Rara Avis, La Selva, and El Gavilán lodges before reaching Puerto Viejo.

A more scenic route goes through Heredia, Barva, Varablanca, and San Miguel before reaching Puerto Viejo. This route passes very close to the Poás Volcano and directly in front of La Paz waterfall. If you want to take this route, head west out of San José, then turn north to Heredia and follow the signs for Varablanca and La Paz Waterfall Gardens.

Tip: If you plan to stop on the way to see **La Paz Waterfall Gardens** (p. 181) or ride the **Rain Forest Aerial Tram** (p. 388), budget at least 2 hours to visit either attraction.

By Bus: Empresarios Guapileños buses (© **2222-0610** in San José, or 2710-7780 in Puerto Viejo) leave San José roughly every hour between 6:30am and 6pm from the **Gran Terminal del Caribe,** on Calle Central, 1 block north of Avenida 11. The trip takes around 2 hours; the fare is C2,580. Buses for San José leave Puerto Viejo roughly every hour between 5:30am and 5:30pm.

CITY LAYOUT   Puerto Viejo is a very small town, with a soccer field at its center. If you continue past the soccer field on the main road and stay on the paved road, and then turn right at the Banco Nacional, you'll come to the Río Sarapiquí and the dock, where you can look into arranging a boat trip.

Exploring Puerto Viejo de Sarapiquí

BOAT TRIPS   The Río Sarapiquí was originally this region's major transportation thoroughfare, connecting the town of Puerto Viejo with the Caribbean coast. For the adventurous, Puerto Viejo is a jumping-off point for trips down the Río Sarapiquí to Barra del Colorado National Wildlife Refuge and Tortuguero National Park on the Caribbean coast. A

10

THE NORTHERN ZONE

Puerto Viejo de Sarapiquí

boat for up to 10 people will cost you around $400 to $600 to Barra del Colorado or $500 to $700 to Tortuguero.

In addition to the longer trips, you can take shorter trips on the river for between $10 and $20 per person per hour. A trip down the Sarapiquí, even if it's for only an hour or two, provides opportunities to spot crocodiles, caimans, monkeys, sloths, and dozens of bird species.

If you're interested in any of the boat trips on the river, you are best off checking at your hotel, or with **Oasis Nature Tours** (www.oasis naturetours.com; ✆ **2766-6108**). Alternatively, you can head down to the town dock on the bank of the Sarapiquí and see if you can arrange a boat trip on your own by tagging along with another group or, better yet, with a bunch of locals.

CANOPY TOUR & MORE   Hacienda Pozo Azul ★ (www.pozoazul. com; ✆ **877/810-6903** in the U.S. and Canada, or 2438-2616 in Costa Rica; daily 8am to 6pm) is a working cattle farm and extensive zip-line canopy tour operation, with 13 platforms connected by 9 different cable runs. In addition, Hacienda Pozo Azul offers white-water rafting, horseback riding, and guided hikes. They even run a tent-camp and separate rustic lodge at a deep rainforest. Several differently priced combo packages are offered.

HIKING & GUIDED TOURS   Anyone can take advantage of the 56km (35 miles) of well-maintained **trails at La Selva** ★★ (p. 391). If you're not staying there, however, you'll have to take a guided hike, led by experienced and well-informed naturalists. Half- and full-day hikes ($35 and $45, respectively) are offered daily, but you must reserve in advance (www.threepaths.co.cr; ✆ **2524-0607**). Tours at 8am and 1:30pm daily.

My favorite hike starts off with the Cantarrana ("singing frog") trail, which includes a section of low bridges over a rainforest swamp. From here, you can join up with either the near or far circular loop trails—**CCC** and **CCL.** Another good hiking option is the trails and suspended bridges at the **Centro Neotrópico SarapiquíS.**

For a more orderly introduction to the local flora, head to a botanical garden, like the **Chester Field Biological Gardens** (p. 387) or the nearby **Heliconia Island** (www.heliconiaisland.com; ✆ **2764-5220**), an interesting garden with more than 70 varieties of heliconia on a small island. This place is open daily from 8am to 5pm. Admission is $12 for a self-guided walk, or $18 for a guided tour.

A NATURAL-HISTORY THEME PARK   The **Alma Ata Archaeological Park** is a small ongoing dig of a modest pre-Columbian gravesite, that is attached to a local hotel, **SarapiquíS Rainforest Lodge** (www.sarapiquis.com; ✆ **2761-1004**). So far, 12 graves, some petroglyphs, and numerous pieces of ceramic and jewelry have been unearthed. The hotel has a small museum that displays examples of the ceramics, tools, clothing, and carvings found here, as well as other natural-history exhibits.

Just across the hotel's driveway, you'll find the Chester Field Biological Gardens, with its well-tended displays of local medicinal and ornamental plants and herbs, as well as food crops. Admission to the archaeological park and gardens costs $25, and includes lunch. If you just want to visit the museum, the cost is $15/adults, $10/students. Open daily, 6am to 5pm.

Across the river from the SarapiquíS Rainforest Lodge is the 300-hectare (741-acre) private **Tirimbina Rainforest Center ★** (www. tirimbina.org; ✆ **2761-0333**), with a small network of trails and several impressive suspension bridges, both over the river and through the forest canopy. A self-guided walk of the reserve's bridges and trails costs $17 per person, and a 2-hour guided tour costs $28 per person—definitely worth the extra few bucks. The center is open daily from 7:30am to 5pm, and from 7:30 to 9:30pm for night tours; specialized early morning bird-watching tours are also available.

RAFTING & KAYAKING **Aguas Bravas** (www.costaricaraftingvacation. com; ✆ **2292-2072**) and **Aventuras del Sarapiquí ★** (www.sarapiqui. com; ✆ **2766-6768**) both companies offer wet and wild rides on a variety of sections of the Sarapiquí and Puerto Viejo rivers, ranging from Class I to Class IV. Trips cost between $56 and $110 per person. Aventuras del Sarapiquí also operates mountain-biking and horseback-riding tours in the area. They rent kayaks, give kayaking classes, and offer kayak trips for more experienced and/or daring river rats, and offer inner-tube floats for those with lesser skill.

SNAKES UNDER GLASS Just a few blocks west of the Centro Neo-trópico SarapiquíS, you'll find **Jardín de Serpientes** (**Snake Garden;** snakegarden@hotmail.com; ✆ **2761-1059;** daily 9am–5pm), a collection of over 50 snakes, both venomous and nonvenomous, and other reptiles and amphibians. Two of the prize attractions here, although not native, are a massive, yellow Burmese python and similarly impressive anaconda. There are also caiman and crocodiles. All are kept in clean, well-lit displays. Admission is $30/adults for a guided tour, or $15/adult

Eyelash vipers are one of the many reptiles that you'll see at Jardín de Serpientes.

Rafting on Sarapiquí River.

for self-guided entrance. Children 4–12 years of age are $24 for the guided tour and $12 for self-guided. Night tours offered with advance reservations.

PINEAPPLE PRODUCTION   If you want a peak into the world of pineapple production, I recommend a visit to the **Organic Paradise Tour** (© **2761-0706**) in Chilamate. The farm has 33 hectares under cultivation. The 2-hour tour includes a trip through the plantation, explanations and demonstrations of the processes involved, and a sampling of the fruit. Mass pineapple production is notorious for its negative impact on the environment and workers' rights, and these folks are an important model of a sustainable alternative. The cost is $40 per person for the tour.

ONE MAJOR ATTRACTION EN ROUTE   If you're driving to Puerto Viejo de Sarapiquí via the Guápiles Highway, stop in at the **Rain Forest Aerial Tram ★**. You'll see the entrance on your right shortly after the Zurquí tunnel. For more info, see "Side Trips from San José," in chapter 6.

Where to Stay & Dine

All the lodges listed below arrange excursions throughout the region, including boat trips on the Sarapiquí, guided hikes in the rainforest, and horseback or mountain bike rides.

MODERATE

Hacienda La Isla ★ (www.haciendalaisla.com; © **2764-2576**) is an intimate boutique hotel near the small town of Las Horquetas. As well as

A bungalow at Selva Verde Lodge.

the places outside town that are reviewed below, the **Tirimbina Rain-forest Center ★** (p. 387) also has rooms.

Hotel Hacienda Sueño Azul ★   This hotel is located fairly close to the Highway 32 which connects San José to the Caribbean coast, on the outskirts of the tiny village of Las Horquetas. You reach the property by crossing a couple of hammock bridges that appear too narrow for most vehicles, but seem to do the job. The rooms are large and feature rustic four-poster wooden beds and private verandas. The best of these are close to and overlooking a river or lagoon. The hotel sits at the meeting point of two rivers, and water features prominently. One of the property's two pools is a very large, river-fed, semi-natural pool. This place often hosts yoga or wellness retreats, but horseback riding, hiking and other active adventures are also offered.

Las Horquetas de Sarapiquí. www.suenoazulresort.com. ✆ **2253-2020** reservation number in San José, 2764-1000 at the lodge. 64 units. $150–$180 double; $220 suite. **Amenities:** Restaurant; bar, Jacuzzi; 2 outdoor pools; small spa, free Wi-Fi.

La Quinta de Sarapiquí Country Inn ★★   Leo and Beatriz run a cozy, laid-back little lodge on the edge of the Sardinal River. Rooms are found in a series of buildings spread around the ample grounds and gardens. The rooms are feature blindingly white tile floors and painted walls, with splashes of color provided by small framed paintings hung over the bed and brightly colored bedspreads. They're kept immaculately maintained, have lots of natural light and a cheery feel. The hotel has two separate swimming pools, as well as a butterfly garden, poison dart frog garden and a riverside trail through a reclaimed forest area. They also operate a separate six-room lodge next door, Kinkajou Town, geared more towards researchers and itinerant NGO workers. La Quinta was awarded "5 Leaves" by the CST Sustainable Tourism program.

Chilamate, Sarapiquí. www.laquintasarapiqui.com. © **2222-3344** reservations office in San José, or 2761-1052 at the lodge. 40 units. $110 double; $140 suite. Children 11 and under stay free in parent's room. **Amenities:** Restaurant; bar; 2 outdoor pools.

Selva Verde Lodge ★★   Begun in 1982 by Giovanna Holbrook and Holbrook Travel, this was one of the first ecotourist lodges in Costa Rica and is still running strong. Set in a patch of thick forest on the banks of the Sarapiquí River, the property includes a large private reserve on the other side of the river. A series of raised wooden buildings connected by a maze of covered walkways house the main river lodge rooms, which are rather bare bones. The decor consists of varnished wood floors, screen and lathe windows, beds with plain white linens, a fan and a rather smallish bathroom. A few bungalows are a bit larger and have air-conditioning, but these are located across the street and a nice walk away from the main lodge, restaurant and river. My favorite feature here is the large, open-air main dining room that overlooks the river. In addition to a more typical lodge menu, they also offer buffet dining (aimed primarily at tour groups), as well as pizzas from a wood-burning brick oven. There's a lovely pool area, as well as several swimming holes along the river. A bridge leads across the river to a network of trails through the rainforest, and they also have their own little zip-line.

Chilamate, Sarapiquí. www.selvaverde.com. © **800/451-7111** in the U.S. and Canada, or 2761-1800 in Costa Rica. 40 units, 8 bungalows. $141 double, $170 bungalows. Rates include breakfast and taxes. **Amenities:** 2 restaurants; bar; outdoor pool.

INEXPENSIVE

The **Posada Andrea Cristina** (www.andreacristina.com; © **2766-6265**), just on the outskirts of Puerto Viejo, is run by Alex Martínez, an excellent local guide and pioneering conservationist in the region. You may also consider staying at the jungle tent-camp or isolated Magsasay Lodge at **Hacienda Pozo Azul ★** (www.pozoazul.com; © **877/810-6903** in the U.S. and Canada, or 2438-2616).

Gavilán Sarapiquí River Lodge ★   This long-established local lodge is fairly basic, but well-run, friendly and relaxed. Most of the rooms are quite large, although some show their age, especially in the bathrooms, where hot water is provided by electric shower head units affectionately known in Costa Rica as "suicide showers." The expansive grounds have beautiful gardens, as well as an unheated sunken Jacuzzi fed by a natural spring. The hotel is set right on a high bank of the Sarapiquí River, but on the other side of the river from town, so it's quiet and feels remote. These owners control a 49-hectare (120-acre) private reserve, and more than 450 bird species have been spotted in the area.

Puerto Viejo de Sarapiquí. www.gavilanlodge.com. © **2234-9507** reservation office in San José, 2766-7131 or 8343-9480 at the lodge. 20 units. $60 double; $75 superior double. **Amenities:** Restaurant; bar; Jacuzzi, free Wi-Fi.

La Selva Biological Station ★   The name says it all, this is no prissy upscale ecolodge. Built primarily to accommodate biologists, researchers and student groups, La Selva also accepts everyday tourists. That said, don't expect fine linens, pampering service or memorable meals. There are very basic bunk bed and dorm-style rooms, as well as a few more plush rooms geared towards tourists more than scientists. The better rooms are a good 15- to 20-minute hike from the main lodge, restaurant and research facilities. La Selva, is operated by the Organization for Tropical Studies (OTS) and has more than 1,614 hectares (3,656 acres) of private reserve, and this borders the even larger Braulio Carrillo National Park. On-site are a very extensive, well-marked and well-maintained trail system through these forests, and the wildlife viewing and flora here are some of the best in Costa Rica.

Puerto Viejo. www.threepaths.co.cr. © **2524-0607** reservations office in San José, or 2766-6565 at the lodge. 24 units, 16 with shared bathroom. $93 double. Rates include all meals, 1 guided walk and taxes. Rates lower for researchers and student groups. **Amenities:** Restaurant.

Rara Avis ★   Owner Amos Bien is a pioneer in sustainable tourism in Costa Rica. That means that Rara Avis is quite rustic and rough around the edges (see below), but those looking for a real nature lodge in the middle of some of Costa Rica's richest rainforests will be greatly rewarded. Electricity—provided by a small hydro plant—is only available a few hours a day, and only at the main lodge and restaurant. Rooms feature rough-hewn wooden beds and built-in bunk beds, thin foam mattresses and no modern amenities. Only those in the Waterfall Lodge have private bathrooms and a private balcony. On every visit here I've encountered serious naturalists and working biologists among the other guests. Aside from the amazing wildlife and lush fauna, the star attraction here is a nearby swimming hole fed by a beautiful two-tiered waterfall. Meals are standard Tico fare and forgettable, although the service and guides are top notch.

If you plan to stay here, prior reservations are essential. Be sure to get very specific directions and coordinate your arrival time closely with the staff, as the lodge is 15km (10 miles) up a very rugged dirt road and can only be reached via horse, tractor or a very long strenuous hike.

15km (9⅓ miles) from Las Horquetas. www.rara-avis.com. © **2764-1111.** 11 units. 8 with private bathroom. $65 per person with shared bathroom; $84 per person with private bathroom. Rates include all meals and 2 guided tours per day. **Amenities:** Restaurant.

THE CENTRAL PACIFIC COAST:

WHERE THE MOUNTAINS MEET THE SEA

After Guanacaste, the beaches of Costa Rica's central Pacific coast are the country's most popular. Options here range from the surfer and snowbird hangout of Jacó, to the ecotourist mecca of Manuel Antonio, to remote and largely undeveloped Dominical and Uvita, with their jungle-clad hillsides and rainforest waterfalls. With a dependable highway connecting San José to the coast, and improvements along the Costanera Sur highway heading south, this region has gotten even easier to visit.

Jacó and Playa Herradura are the closest major beach destinations to San José. They have historically been the first choice for young surfers and city-dwelling Costa Ricans. Just north of Playa Herradura sits **Carara National Park ★★**, one of the few places in Costa Rica where you can see the disappearing dry forest join the damp, humid forests that extend south down the coast. It's also a place to see scarlet macaws in the wild.

Just a little farther south, Manuel Antonio is one of the country's foremost ecotourist destinations, with a host of hotel and lodging options and an easily accessible national park that combines the exuberant lushness of a lowland tropical rainforest with several gorgeous beaches. **Manuel Antonio National Park ★★** is home to all four of Costa Rica's monkey species, as well as a wealth of other easily viewed flora and fauna. This is one of the country's most visited destinations, and for good reason. The wildlife is fabulous, and there are a wide range of tour and activity options open to all styles and ages of travelers.

If you're looking to get away from it all, **Dominical** and the **beaches south of Dominical ★** should be your top destination on this coast. Still a small village, the beach town of Dominical is flanked by even more remote and undeveloped beaches, including those found inside **Ballena Marine National Park ★★**.

Finally, if you can tear yourself away from the beaches and coastline here, and head slightly inland, you'll find **Chirripó National Park ★★**, a misty cloud forest that becomes a barren *páramo* (a region above 3,000m/9,840 ft.) at the peak of its namesake, Mount Chirripó—the tallest peak in Costa Rica.

The climate here is considerably more humid than that farther north in Guanacaste, but it's not nearly as hot and steamy as along the southern Pacific or Caribbean coasts.

PREVIOUS PAGE: **Manuel Antonio National Park.**

THE best CENTRAL PACIFIC TRAVEL EXPERIENCES

○ **Having Miles of Pacific Beach Practically to Yourself:** While Jacó, Manuel Antonio, and Dominical are all bustling tourist beaches, the rest of the long, Central Pacific coastline is almost entirely deserted. Rent a car or hire a taxi to visit any number of isolated and virtually undiscovered beaches.

○ **Visiting Carara National Park:** The Tárcoles River crocodiles are best viewed from a boat, or by simply standing on the bridge just outside the park entrance. And the resident scarlet macaws can often be seen outside the park as well. Yet, I still highly recommend hiking the lush and varied trails inside Carara National Park. You'll be rewarded with rich foliage and the chance to see much more wildlife. See p. 399.

○ **Hiking the Trails in Manuel Antonio National Park:** The trails here wind through thick tropical rainforest and periodically offer beautiful ocean views as well as opportunities to spot wildlife—all four of Costa Rica's monkey species call this national park home. You may not knock all four species off your life list, but a visit here almost—I said almost—guarantees you'll see these primates darting around the tropical treetops. See p. 423.

○ **Visiting the Nauyaca Waterfalls Outside of Dominical:** Nestled in a patch of thick tropical rainforest, the Nauyaca Waterfalls are gorgeous, and feature an inviting pool at its base. See p. 444.

○ **Climbing Mount Chirripó:** The highest mountain in Costa Rica, Mount Chirripó is a challenging, but accessible peak whose summit sometimes offers simultaneous views of the Pacific Ocean and Caribbean Sea. Most folks come to Costa Rica for the tropical climate and fauna, but the summit here is above tree line, and sometimes gets frost and even a dusting of snow. See p. 453.

En Route to Jacó: An Isolated Boutique Beauty

If you're planning on heading to the beaches of the central Pacific coast via Ciudad Colón and Puriscal, you might consider a stop at **Ama Tierra Retreat & Wellness Center** ★ (www.amatierra. com; ℂ **866/659-3805** in the U.S. and Canada, or 2419-0110 in Costa Rica), a lovely little boutique hotel and retreat center about 1½ hours outside of San José along this route, and approximately 1 hour from Jacó.

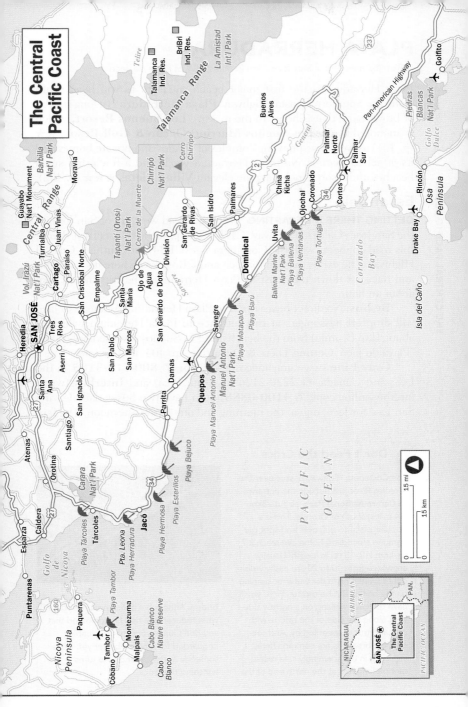

PLAYA HERRADURA

11

108km (67 miles) W of San José; 9km (6 miles) NW of Playa de Jacó

Playa Herradura is the first major beach you'll hit as you head south along the Southern Coastal Highway. **Playa Herradura** is a long stretch of brown sand that is home to the massive **Los Sueños Resort,** which is anchored by the **Los Sueños Marriott Ocean & Golf Resort ★★** (p. 401) as well as a sprawling complex of condos and private homes and its attached marina. North of Herradura you'll find a few other small beaches and resorts, including the elegant **Villa Caletas ★★★** (p. 402).

Essentials

GETTING THERE & DEPARTING   By Car: Head west out of San José on the San José–Caldera Highway (CR27). Just past the toll booth at Pavón, this road connects with the Costanera Sur (CR34), or Southern Coastal Highway. The exit is marked for Jacó and CR34. From here it's a straight and flat shot down the coast to Playa Herradura. The trip should take about an hour.

    By Bus: No direct buses run into Playa Herradura. All buses to Jacó will drop off passengers at the entrance to Playa Herradura, which is about 1km (½ mile) from the beach and Los Sueños resort complex. See "Playa de Jacó: Getting There & Departing," p. 405, for bus info.

    Gray Line (www.graylinecostarica.com; © **800/719-3105** in the U.S. and Canada, or 2220-2126 in Costa Rica) and **Interbus** (www.interbusonline.com; © **4100-0888**) both have two buses daily leaving San José for Jacó, one in the morning and one in the afternoon. The fare

---

Don't Feed the Crocs

The Costanera Highway passes over the Tárcoles River just outside the entrance to **Carara National Park,** about 23km (14 miles) south of Orotina. This is a popular place to pull over and spot gargantuan crocodiles. Some can reach 3.7 to 4.6m (12–15 ft.) in length. Usually anywhere from 10 to 20 are easily visible, either swimming in the water or sunning on the banks. But be careful. First, you'll have to brave walking on a narrow sidewalk along the side of the bridge with cars and trucks speeding by. And second, car break-ins are common here, including in the seemingly safe restaurant parking lots at the north end of the

bridge. Although a police post has somewhat reduced the risk, I recommend that you don't leave your car or valuables unguarded for long, or better yet, leave someone at the car and take turns watching the crocs.

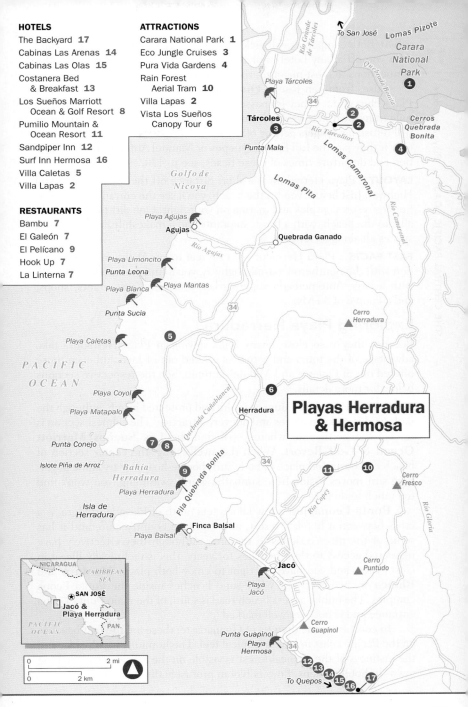

HOTELS

The Backyard **17**
Cabinas Las Arenas **14**
Cabinas Las Olas **15**
Costanera Bed
& Breakfast **13**
Los Sueños Marriott
Ocean & Golf Resort **8**
Pumilio Mountain &
Ocean Resort **11**
Sandpiper Inn **12**
Surf Inn Hermosa **16**
Villa Caletas **5**
Villa Lapas **2**

RESTAURANTS

Bambu **7**
El Galeón **7**
El Pelícano **9**
Hook Up **7**
La Linterna **7**

ATTRACTIONS

Carara National Park **1**
Eco Jungle Cruises **3**
Pura Vida Gardens **4**
Rain Forest
Aerial Tram **10**
Villa Lapas **2**
Vista Los Sueños
Canopy Tour **6**

Playas Herradura & Hermosa

is $40. Both companies will pick you up at most San José-area hotels and drop you off at any hotel in or around Playa Herradura. Both also offer connections to most major tourist destinations in the country.

Buses from San José to **Quepos** and Manuel Antonio also pass by Playa Herradura. (They let passengers off on the highway about 1km/½ mile from town.) However, during the busy months, some of these buses will refuse passengers getting off in Playa Herradura or will accept them only if they pay the full fare to Quepos or Manuel Antonio. For information and departure times of these buses, see p. 420.

LAYOUT   Playa Herradura is a short distance off the Southern Coastal Highway. Just before you hit the beach, you'll see the entrance to the Los Sueños resort complex and marina on your right. One dirt road runs parallel to the beach, with a few restaurants and a makeshift line of parking spaces all along its length.

FAST FACTS   Playa Herradura has no real town. At the main intersection with the Southern Coastal Highway, you'll find a modern strip mall, with a large Automercado supermarket, and some restaurants, shops, and a couple of ATMs.

Exploring Playa Herradura

Because they're so close, many folks staying in Playa Herradura take advantage of the tours and activities offered out of Jacó and even those offered out of Quepos and Manuel Antonio. See the respective sections below for more details.

BEACHES   Playa Herradura is a calm and protected beach, although the dark sand is rocky in places and not very attractive. The calmest section is toward the north end, where you'll find the **Los Sueños Marriott Ocean & Golf Resort.** When the swell is big, the center section of beach can be a good place to body surf, boogie-board, or try some beginning surf moves. Aside from sunbathing and swimming, you won't find too much to do here.

Punta Leona, just a few kilometers north of Playa Herradura, is a cross between a hotel, a resort, and a private country club, and it has some of the nicer beaches in the area. Although they effectively have restricted access to their beaches for years, this is technically illegal in Costa Rica, and you have the right to enjoy both playas **Manta** ★ and **Blanca** ★, two very nice white-sand beaches inside the Punta Leona complex. The public access beach road is south of the main Punta Leona entrance and is not very well marked.

In contrast to the dryness of Guanacaste, these are the first beaches on the Pacific coast to have a tropical feel. The humidity is palpable, and the lushness of the tropical forest is visible on the hillsides surrounding town. In hotel gardens, flowers bloom profusely throughout the year.

CANOPY TOURS Vista Los Sueños Rainforest Tours ★ (www. canopyvistalossuenos.com; ☎ 321/220-9631 in the U.S. or 2637-6020 in Costa Rica; $60) is set in the hills above Playa Herradura. This tour features 12 zip-lines, excellent views, and the longest cable in the area, at nearly a kilometer (almost a half-mile) in length. Round-trip transportation can be added on. The company also offers horseback riding and ATV tours to a nearby waterfall.

CROCODILE TOURS Several companies offer boat tours of the river and mangroves, and every hotel and tour agency in the area can make arrangements for you. Nearly all the operators bring along plenty of freshly killed chickens to attract the crocs—a practice I cannot endorse. That's why I suggest going with the more responsible tour operator, **Eco Jungle Cruises** ★ (www.ecojunglecruisescom; ☎ 2582-0181; 2-hr. tour $72 adults, $36 kids 4–10); its staff doesn't believe in feeding the crocs or altering their behaviors. There are plenty (hundreds, in fact) of crocodiles to be seen along the stretch of river and mangrove they tour, and plenty of photo opportunities. Transportation from Jacó, Playa Herradura, Manuel Antonio, or San José is available.

GOLF The excellent **La Iguana,** an 18-hole golf course at the Los Sueños Marriott Ocean & Golf Resort (www.golflaiguana.com; ☎ 2630-9028), is open to non-guests. Greens fees are $150. Club and shoe rentals are available. Marriott guests pay slightly less to play here.

PURA VIDA GARDENS & WATERFALLS Just beyond Carara National Park on the Costanera Sur in the direction of Jacó, you'll find the **Pura Vida Gardens and Waterfalls** ★ (www.puravidagarden.com; ☎ 2645-1001; $20 adults, $10 those under 10; daily 8am–5pm). Admission covers free run of the gardens and trails (which lead to a couple of small waterfalls). To get here, turn off at the signs for Villa Lapas (p. 403). From there, it's a rough 8km (5 miles) up to the gardens.

SPORTFISHING, SCUBA DIVING & SEABORNE FUN Since the Los Sueños Marriott Resort (p. 401) and its adjacent 250-slip marina opened, most local maritime activity has shifted over here. If you're interested in doing sportfishing, scuba diving, or any other waterborne activity, I recommend that you check with your hotel or at the marina. Dependable operators include **Maverick Sportfishing Tours** (www.mavericksportfish. com; ☎ 800/405-8206 in the U.S., or 8712-9683 in Costa Rica) and **Costa Rica Dreams** (www.costaricadreams.com; ☎ 337/205-0665 in the U.S., or 2637-8942 in Costa Rica). A half-day fishing trip for four costs around $800 to $1,500, and a full day costs between $1,000 and $2,000.

Carara National Park ★★

A little more than 17.5km (11 miles) north of Playa Herradura is **Carara National Park** (☎ 2637-1054; daily 7am–4:30pm; $10/person), a world-renowned nesting ground for **scarlet macaws.** It has a few kilometers of trails open to visitors. The **Sendero Accesso Universal (Universal Access Trail),** which heads out from the national park office, is broad, flat, and wheelchair-accessible (hence the trail name). The first half of this 1km (.7-mile) stretch leads into the forest and features various informative plaques, in both English and Spanish, pointing out prominent flora. About 10 or 15 minutes into your hike, you'll see that the trail splits, forming a loop (you can go in either direction). The entire loop trail should take you about an hour. The macaws migrate daily, spending their days in the park and their nights among the coastal mangroves. It's best to view them in the early morning when they arrive, or around sunset when they head back to the coast for the evening, but a good guide can usually find them for you during the day. Whether or not you see them, you should hear their loud squawks. Among the other wildlife that you might see are caimans, coatimundis, armadillos, pacas, peccaries, and, of course, hundreds of species of birds.

Bring along insect repellent or, better yet, wear light cotton long sleeves and pants. (I was once foolish enough to attempt a hike while returning from Manuel Antonio, still in beach clothes and flip-flops.)

Although you can certainly hike the gentle and well-marked trails of Carara independently, my advice is to take a guided tour; you'll learn a lot more about your surroundings. Most hotel desks can arrange for a guided hike to Carara National Park, or you can contact **Vic Tours** (www.victourscostarica.com; © **8723-3008**) for one. Also, there are always bilingual naturalist guides available to hire at the park entrance.

A scarlet macaw, one of the many birds you might spot in Carara National Park.

Where to Stay

EXPENSIVE

In addition to its hotel rooms, the Los Sueños resort has scores of condominium units for rent. All come with kitchens, access to swimming pools, and rights to use the golf course here. These are excellent options for families who want to do some cooking, and for longer stays. If you want to rent a condo here, contact **Stay in Costa Rica** (www.stayin costarica.com; ✆ **866/439-5922** in the U.S. and Canada, or 2637-2661 in Costa Rica). Rates begin around $210 to $280 nightly for one- and two-bedroom units, to well over $1,000 for some of the more luxurious three-bedroom and larger units.

For something a little farther from the beach, **Pumilio Mountain & Ocean Hotel** (www.hotelpumilio.com; ✆ **800/410/8018** in U.S. and 2643-5678 in Costa Rica) is a boutique hotel and spa, located on a hillside a bit inland, between Playa Herradura and Jacó.

Los Sueños Marriott Ocean & Golf Resort ★★   This is the largest resort hotel on the Central Pacific coast, and also the best of the biggies. In fact, I'd say it revels in its size, offering up niceties that a smaller hotel couldn't match, like an 18-hole regulation golf course and a massive maze of pools that are designed to bring to mind the canals of Venice. (They really are a wonder, featuring a host of small bridges connecting islands of chaise lounges and lush gardens, interspersed with secret grottoes and quiet corners.) It's a good thing that the pool is so fabulous, as the beach in front of the resort is unappealing hard-packed dark sand.

Los Sueños Marriott Ocean & Golf Resort.

But the rooms are quite swank, harkening back to the Spanish Colonial era with stucco walls, heavy wooden doors and furnishings, pale yellow Spanish tile floors and a wrought iron railing on the (usually) tiny balcony. Buffet breakfasts are massive. And a host of good dining options are available on site and in the nearby marina, everything from a poolside grill to an elegant Nuevo Latino eatery.

Playa Herradura www.lossuenosmarriott.com. ✆ **888/236-2427** in the U.S. and Canada, 2298-000 or 2630-9000 in Costa Rica. 201 units. $192–$509 double; $419–$559 suite; $700 and up presidential suite. **Amenities:** 4 restaurants; coffee shop; bar; children's program; golf course and pro shop; miniature golf course; health club and spa; outdoor pool; room service; 4 outdoor lit tennis courts; Wi-Fi in most public areas.

Villa Caletas ★★★ Whimsy and luxury don't always go hand in hand, but they do at this cliff-top hideaway which has given decor themes to each suite (from Egyptian to Imperial Rome) and scattered "follies" (charming but out-of-place buildings) around the grounds. So guests sip cocktails and watch the sunset from a recreated Greek amphitheater . . . and it's delightful (you'll know the sun is about to set when you hear the opening notes of Strauss's "Thus Spoke Zarathustra" blaring over the outdoor speakers). The resort itself, which includes a main house with rooms, suites and a number of sniffy villas, is done in a pert "tropical Victorian" style. Suites and junior suites come with private outdoor Jacuzzis or plunge pools; most provide jaw-dropping views of the Pacific Ocean. On-site are several pools; a decent beach is in walking distance. The service is top notch throughout, but particularly in the "Zephyr Palace" part of the hotel, where guests get a private concierge.

Infinity pool at Villa Caletas.

Btw. Punta Leona and Playa Herradura. www.hotelvillacaletas.com. ✆ **2630-3000.** 54 units. $175–$226 double; $268 villa; $352–$657 suite; $347–$1,586 Zephyr Palace suites. Extra person $42 at Villa Caletas; $85 at Zephyr Palace. **Amenities:** 3 restaurants; 2 bars; concierge; 4 midsize outdoor pools; Jacuzzi; spa; free Wi-Fi.

Villa Lapas ★ This small, locally owned resort hotel on the banks of the Tarcolitos River provides an intriguing alternative to the beach resorts that typically define this region. The lodge is set right on the border of Carara National Park, which means superb bird watching and wildlife viewing. It's not uncommon to see some namesake *lapas,* or Scarlet Macaws, flying right overhead. The hotel has its own trails and hanging bridges plus a recreated rural Costa Rican village, complete with a wedding chapel based on the old colonial-era church in Ujarrás (p. 202). Rooms are housed in a series of single-story concrete block buildings and feature red tile floors, whitewashed stucco walls and red clay tile roofs. They are plenty spacious, but feel a bit worn. From here it's 15–25 minutes by car to Jacó, Play Hermosa, and Herradura.

Tárcoles. www.villalapas.com. ✆ **2439-1816.** 58 units. $123 per person. Rates include 3 meals daily, and drinks. **Amenities:** 2 restaurants; 2 bars; small outdoor pool; free Wi-Fi.

Where to Dine

At the Los Sueños Marina you'll find several other options, including **Bambu,** a sushi bar and Pan-Asian restaurant; **La Linterna,** a fancy Italian restaurant; and **Hook Up,** an excellent American-style grill, serving primo lunch and light fare, with a second-floor perch and good views. You can make reservations at any of the marina restaurants by calling ✆ **2630-4050.**

EXPENSIVE

El Galeón ★★ FUSION Although pricey, this is easily the best restaurant at the Los Sueños Marina. The menu is broad and creative, and the presentations are artful. On my last visit, I enjoyed a slider appetizer, small buns sporting a mix of thin-sliced prime rib, barbeque pork and beef short ribs, served with Cajun spiced sweet potato fries. For a main dish, you can't go wrong with the Moroccan-style lamb tangine, or the whole fried red snapper with a black bean and garlic sauce. El Galeon has the best-curated wine list in the area. The setting here is lovely too: a large, open-air dining room that overlooks the marina and Herradura Bay. Whole tree trunks support a huge and soaring thatch roof, from which slow turning ceiling fans hang.

At the marina of the Los Sueños Marriott Resort (p. 401). www.lsrestaurants.com. ✆ **2630-4254.** Reservations recommended. Main courses $15–$60. Daily 5:30–10pm.

MODERATE

El Pelícano ★ SEAFOOD/COSTA RICAN   Set just across the single-lane dirt road that runs along the beach, this simple, open-air spot serves up fresh ceviche, fish, and seafood, and other Tico standards. You can also get steak and chicken, but I recommend the seafood as that's caught and brought in daily. Most meals come with a visit to their small salad bar. They sometimes have live music at night.

On the beach in Playa Herradura. www.elpelicanorestaurante.com. © **2637-8910.** Reservations recommended during high season. Main courses C6,500–C38,000. Daily noon–10pm.

PLAYA DE JACÓ

Jacó: 117km (73 miles) W of San José; 75km (47 miles) S of Puntarenas

Playa de Jacó is a long stretch of beach backed by a dense hodgepodge of hotels in all price categories, souvenir shops, seafood restaurants, pizza joints, and rowdy bars. The main strip, running parallel to the shoreline, is an overcrowded and congested collection of restaurants, shops, and small strip malls, where pedestrians, bicycles, scooters, cars, and ATVs vie for right of way both day and night.

Surfers are the largest group of vacationers here, drawn by the consistent beach break. Sadly, the beach itself is not particularly appealing, consisting of dark-gray sand with lots of little rocks. The surf is often too rough for swimming. Still, given its proximity to San José, Jacó is almost always packed with a mix of foreign and Tico vacationers.

A Jacó surf shop.

Mercado des Frutas in Jacó.

Beyond the surf, Jacó is also known for its nightlife. The raging bars here offer everything from live music venues to chill lounge environments to beachfront sports bars with pool and foosball tables.

Essentials

GETTING THERE & DEPARTING   By Car: Head west out of San José on the San José–Caldera Highway (CR27). Just past the toll booth at Pavón, this road connects with the Costanera Sur (CR34), or Southern Coastal Highway. The exit is marked for Jacó and CR34. From here, it's a straight and flat shot down the coast to Jacó. The trip should take a little over an hour.

By Bus: Transportes Jacó express buses (www.transportesjacoruta655.com; ✆ **2290-2922**) leave San José daily every 2 hours between 7am and 7pm from the Coca-Cola bus terminal at Calle 16 between avenidas 1 and 3. The trip takes between 2½ and 3 hours; the fare is C2,445. On weekends and holidays, extra buses are sometimes added, so it's worth calling to check.

Gray Line (www.graylinecostarica.com; ✆ **800/719-3105** in the U.S. and Canada, or 2220-2126 in Costa Rica) and **Interbus** (www.interbusonline.com; ✆ **4031-0888**) both have two buses daily leaving San José to Jacó, one in the morning and one in the afternoon. The fare is around $38. Both companies will pick you up at most San José-area hotels. Both also offer connections to most major tourist destinations in the country.

Buses from San José to **Quepos** and Manuel Antonio also pass by Jacó. (They let passengers off on the highway about 1km/½ mile from town.) However, during the busy months, some of these buses will refuse passengers getting off in Jacó or will accept them only if they pay the full fare to Quepos or Manuel Antonio. For information and departure times of these buses, see p. 420.

From **Puntarenas,** you can catch daily **Transportes Quepos Puntarenas** (✆ **2777-1617**) Quepos-bound buses at 5, 7, 9, 10:30 and 11am and 1, 2:30, 4, 4:30 and 5:30pm. The buses drop you off on the highway outside of town. The trip's duration is 3 hour; the fare is C2,430.

The Jacó bus station is at the north end of town, at a small mall across from the Jacó Fiesta Hotel. Buses for San José leave daily every 2 hours between 5am and 5pm. Buses returning to San José from Quepos pass periodically and pick up passengers on the highway. Because schedules can change, it's best to ask at your hotel about current departure times.

CITY LAYOUT   Playa de Jacó is a short distance off the southern highway. One main road runs parallel to the beach, with a host of arteries heading toward the water; you'll find most of the town's hotels and restaurants off these roads.

GETTING AROUND   Almost everything is within walking distance in Jacó, but you can call **Asotaxi** (✆ **2643-2020** or 2643-1919) for a cab.

You can also rent a bicycle or scooter from a variety of different shops and stands along the main street. A bike rental should run you around $10 to $15 per day, and a scooter should cost between $40 and $70 per day. Shop around, and make sure you get a bike that is in good condition.

For longer excursions, you can rent a car from **Budget** (✆ **2643-2665**), **Economy** (✆ **2643-1719**), **National** (✆ **2643-3224**), or **Zuma** (✆ **2643-1528**). Expect to pay approximately $50 to $120 for a 1-day rental. You might also consider talking to a local taxi driver, who'd probably take you wherever you want to go for about the same price, saving you some hassle and headache.

FAST FACTS   A handful of state-run and private banks have branches in town on the main road. The **health center** (✆ **2643-3667**) and **post office** (✆ **2643-2175**) are at the Municipal Center at the south end of town. However, the best-equipped medical center is the **ProSalud** (✆ **2643-5059**), located 4 blocks inland from the Pop's ice-cream shop. You'll find a half-dozen or so pharmacies along the town's main drag.

A gas station is on the main highway, between Playa Herradura and Jacó, and another station, **El Arroyo,** on the highway on the southern edge of Jacó. Both are open 24 hours.

Exploring Jacó

ATV TOURS   Several operations run ATV tours through the surrounding countryside. Tours range in length from 2 to 4 hours up to a full day, and cost between $70 and $175 per person. Contact **Adventure Tours Costa Rica** (www.adventuretourscostarica.com; ✆ **2643-5720**).

BEACHES   Jacó's beach has a reputation for dangerous riptides (as does most of Costa Rica's Pacific coast). Even strong swimmers have been known to drown in the powerful rips. In general, the far southern end of the beach is the calmest and safest place to swim.

As an alternative to Playa de Jacó, you may want to visit other nearby beaches, like **Playa Manta, Playa Blanca, Playa Hermosa, Esterillos,** and **Playa Bejuco.** These beaches are just south of Jacó and easily reached by car or even bicycle—if you've got a lot of energy. All are signposted, so you'll have no trouble finding them.

CANOPY TOURS The easiest way to get up into the canopy here is on the **Rain Forest Aerial Tram Pacific ★** (www.rfat.com; © **866/759-8726;** in the U.S. and Canada, or 2257-5961 in Costa Rica; see map "Playas Herradura & Hermosa"). A sister project to the original Rain Forest Aerial Tram (p. 165), this attraction features modified ski-lift type gondolas that take you through and above the transitional forests bordering Carara National Park. The $60 entrance fee includes the guided 50-minute tram ride, and a guided 45-minute hike on a network of trails, which feature an orchid garden and serpentarium. You can also hike the company's trails for as long as you like. There's a zip-line canopy tour on the same grounds. The Aerial Tram is a few kilometers inland from an exit just north of the first entrance into Jacó.

Another notable zip-line tour is available at **Chiclets Tree Tour** (© **2643-1880**) in nearby Playa Hermosa. This is an adventurous tour, with 16 platforms set in transitional forest, and sweeping views of the Pacific.

GOLF The excellent **La Iguana,** an 18-hole golf course at the **Los Sueños Marriott Ocean & Golf Resort** (www.golflaiguana.com; © **2630-9028**), is open to non-guests. See p. 401 for details.

HORSEBACK RIDING Horseback riding tours take travelers away from all the development in Jacó so they can see a bit of nature. The best operator in the area, with the best horses, is **Discovery Horseback** (www.horseridecostarica.com; © **8838-7550**) in Playa Hermosa. It's $75 per person for a 2½-hour tour. Options range from beach riding to trails through the rainforest with stops at a jungle waterfall.

KAYAKING **Kayak Jacó** (www.kayakjaco.com; © **2643-1233**) operates several different trips with guests in either single or tandem sea kayaks, as well as eight-person outrigger canoes. They allow participant to admire the beautiful coastline, and—when conditions permit—take a snorkel break. Kayak fishing tours and sailing trips aboard 25-foot Trimarans are also available. Most tours run around 4 hours and include transportation to and from the put-in, as well as fresh fruit and soft drinks during the trip. The tours cost between $55 and $140 per person, depending on the particular trip and group size.

ORGANIZED TOURS FARTHER AFIELD If you're spending your entire Costa Rican visit in Jacó but would like to see other parts of the country, you can arrange tours with **Piko Travel** (www.pikotravel.com; © **8833-1772**) or through the local offices of **Gray Line Tours** (© **2643-3231**), which operates out of the Best Western Jacó Beach Resort (p. 409). Both offer a wide range of day trips, including jaunts to Arenal and Poás volcanoes; white-water rafting trips; and cruises to Tortuga Island. Rates range from $55 to $160 for day trips. Overnight trips are also available. In addition to the above-mentioned companies, many local operators offer tour

Fishing vessels at Los Sueños Marina.

options in **Manuel Antonio,** including trips to the national park, the Rainmaker Nature Refuge, and the Damas Island estuary. See the "Manuel Antonio National Park" section (p. 417) for more details on the types of tours and activities available there. Thanks to improvements to the road, you can reach Manuel Antonio in about 1 hour from Jacó.

SPA   Catleya ★ (☏ **2643-1624**) offers massages, as well as mud packs, face and body treatments, and manicures and pedicures. The spa's Jacó branch is on the first floor, among a tiny little cul-de-sac of shops next to Zuma Rent-A-Car.

SPORTFISHING, SCUBA DIVING & SEABORNE FUN   Since the Los Sueños Marriott Resort (p. 401) and its adjacent 250-slip marina opened, most local maritime activity has shifted over there. See p. 399 for info.

SURFING   The same waves that often make Playa de Jacó a bit rough for swimmers make it one of the most popular beaches in the country with surfers. Nearby **Playa Hermosa, Playa Tulin,** and **Playa Escondida** are also excellent surfing beaches. Those who want to challenge the waves can rent surfboards and boogie boards, for around $3 an hour or $10 to $20 per day, from any one of the numerous surf shops along the main road. If you want to learn how to surf, try the **Del Mar Surf Camp ★★** (www.delmarsurfcamp.com; ☏ **855/833-5627** in the U.S or 2643-3197 in Costa Rica) or **Jacó Surf School** (www.jacosurfschool.com; ☏ **8829-4697**).

Where to Stay

Because Playa Herradura, Playa Hermosa de Jacó (not to be confused with either Playa Hermosa in Guanacaste or Playa Hermosa on the Nicoya Peninsula), Playa Esterillos, and Playa Bejuco are close, many people choose accommodations in these beach towns as well.

Playa de Jacó

EXPENSIVE

In addition to the place mentioned below, early 2015 saw the opening of **Croc's Casino & Resort** (www.crocscasinoresort.com; ✆ **800/809-5506** in the U.S. and Canada, or 4001-5398 in Costa Rica), a massive high-rise resort on the southern end of Jacó, with 150 hotel rooms, 3 restaurants, a large casino and condo and fractional ownership units.

Best Western Jacó Beach Resort ★ A no-frills all-inclusive, the Best Western feels a bit dated, and is a too popular with large charter groups for my taste. The midsize round main pool is not quite big enough for the resort when it's full, and features an odd waterfall sculpture at its center that just gets in the way. Still, room upkeep has been good over the years, and the Best Western offers decent value for those looking for an affordable all-inclusive option in Jacó. And its location, right on the beach on the southern end of Jacó, just a short walk to all of the town's best bars, restaurants, and shops, is tops.

Playa de Jacó, Puntarenas. www.bestwesternjacobeach.com. ✆ **800/780-7234** U.S. and Canada, or 2643-1000 in Costa Rica. 125 units. $190–$280 double. Rates are all-inclusive, covering meals, drinks, and taxes. **Amenities:** Restaurant; 2 bars; well-equipped gym; 2 pools; tennis and volleyball courts; free calls to U.S. and Canada.

Playa de Jacó.

MODERATE

In addition to the places listed below, the oceanfront **Apartotel Girasol** ★ (www.girasol.com; ✆ **800/923-2779** in U.S or 2643-1591), with 16 fully equipped one-bedroom apartments, is a smart option for longer stays. **Hotel Poseidon** (www.hotel-poseidon.com; ✆ **2643-1642**) is a pretty boutique hotel in the heart of downtown, while **Canciones del Mar** (www.cancionesdelmar.com; ✆ **888/260-1523** in the U.S. and Canada, or 2643-3273 in Costa Rica) and **Hotel Catalina** (www.hotel catalinacr.com; ✆ **2643-1237**) are two more good beachfront choices.

Club del Mar ★★★   My favorite hotel in Playa de Jacó, Club del Mar is located at the far southern end of the beach, so it feels far removed from the crowds and craziness that can sometimes plague Jacó. This is also the safest part of the beach to swim, as it's somewhat protected by the rocky headlands. So families tend to flock here, drawn both by the calmer waters and the fact that all of the comfortable, well-maintained one- and two-bedroom condos here come with fully equipped kitchens, and large living rooms. These, and the regular rooms, are housed in a series of two-story buildings spread around gardens that are chock full of flowering heliconia and ginger. There's also a midsize pool with a volley-ball net (it often attracts a casual pick-up game), and a very good on-site restaurant.

Playa de Jacó. www.clubdelmarcostarica.com. ✆ **866/978-5669** in the U.S. and Canada, or 2643-3194 in Costa Rica. 27 units. $138–$167 double; $199–$335 condo; $395 penthouse. **Amenities:** Restaurant; bar; babysitting; outdoor pool; room ser-vice; small spa; free Wi-Fi.

Hotel Nine ★★★   Though it's called the Hotel Nine, I'd rank this place a 10 our 10. The staff are incredibly efficient and friendly, the hotel is on the serene and (usually) swimmable southern end of the beach and the place has happy dose of "South Beach Miami" style in the architectural details and decor. That means guestrooms with handsome rattan and wood furnishings, and colorful throws on the beds. A small multi-tiered pool with a swim up bar, waterfall and Jacuzzi is at the center of the complex and ocean views can be had from the narrow shared veranda that fronts most rooms. The on-site restaurant is terrific.

Playa de Jacó, Puntarenas. www.hotelnine.com. © **800/477-2486** in U.S. and Canada or 2643-5335 in Costa Rica. 14 units. $118–$143 double; $273–$398 suite. Rates include breakfast. No children under 6. **Amenities:** Restaurant; bar; Jacuzzi; midsize outdoor pool; room service; surfboards; free Wi-Fi.

Pochote Grande ★ Named for a native tree, this tidy German-run hotel, towards the northern end of the beach, used to be in an isolated and quiet spot. Sadly, high-rise condos and hotels have risen all around, robbing it of its serenity. Still, this remains a very well-kept option, with lush gardens in the immediate vicinity, and a beachfront location. Rooms feature white washed walls, low lying beds, and tie-dyed curtains and bed throws (which are either groovy or weird, depending on your point of view). A wall of windows and (mostly) glass doors in each open on to a shared veranda. A nice pool is at the center of the compound, and a good little restaurant is on site.

Playa de Jacó, Puntarenas. www.hotelpochotegrande.net. © **2643-3236.** 24 units. $120 double. **Amenities:** Restaurant; bar; outdoor pool; free Wi-Fi.

INEXPENSIVE

In addition to the hotels reviewed below, quite a few backpacker hotels are around town. If you're looking to stay on the cheap, your best bet is to simply walk the strip and see who's got the best room at the best price.

Hotel Mar de Luz ★★ Just 1 block inland from the main drag, all the rooms at this small hotel are comfortable and immaculate. Some feature small sitting areas, masonry walls of smooth river stones and beds placed in a raised sleeping nook. All have at least a microwave and mini-fridge, and others have complete kitchens. The hotel itself has two pools, a children's playground, and a small garden area, with a couple of grills for guests' use. The Dutch owner, Victor Keulen is a good host and works hard to ensure that all guests receive top service. The hotel's sister property, **Hotel Playa Bejuco** (p. 417), is 20 minutes down the road.

Playa de Jacó. www.mardeluz.com. © **2643-3000.** 29 units. $100 standard; $100 bungalow; $135 family room. Rates include breakfast. **Amenities:** Restaurant; Jacuzzi; 2 outdoor small-to-midsize adult pools and children's pool; free Wi-Fi.

Hotel Perico Azul ★★ Located a couple blocks inland from the water, on the south end of Jacó, this hotel is a favorite of surfers, backpackers, and budget travelers of all stripes. Clean, well-kept rooms surround a central courtyard with an often crowded—it is quite small—plunge pool. Rooms are adorned with local paintings and Indonesian wooden geckos, and many feature a wall, or two, painted sea blue or lavender. A couple come with own kitchenette, but there's also a communal kitchen for guests. The best room here is the second-floor one-bedroom studio, with its own private veranda. Owners Mike and Celine are very hands-on, and also run a surf school, Tortuga Surf.

Playa de Jacó, Puntarenas. www.hotelpericoazuljaco.com. © **2643-1341.** 6 units. $60–$70 double. Rates include taxes. **Amenities:** Small pool; free Wi-Fi.

Where to Dine

Playa de Jacó has a wide range of restaurants, many catering to surfers and budget travelers. In addition to the places listed below, if you're looking for simply prepared fresh seafood, **El Barco de Mariscos** (© 2643-2831) and **El Recreo** (© 2643-1172) are both good bets. Sushi lovers should head to **Tsunami Sushi** (© 2643-3678), inside the El Galeone strip mall. For a coffee break and freshly baked pastries, head to **Café del M@r** (© 2643-1250) or the **Pachi's Pan** (© 2643-6068).

EXPENSIVE

El Hicaco ★ COSTA RICAN/SEAFOOD   I still remember when this was a very humble fish shack. A remodeling changed all that and now it's not uncommon to see tour buses parked out front and a line to be seated. Personally, I think success has gone to the owner's heads; prices have skyrocketed and service has suffered. Still El Hicaco serves very fresh seafood, and its beachfront setting is stellar.

On the beach in downtown Jacó. www.elhicaco.net. © **2643-3226.** Reservations recommended during high season. Main courses C6,500–C19,750. Daily 11am–11pm.

Graffiti Resto Café & Wine Bar ★★★ FUSION   It's a little hard to find Graffiti Resto as it's wedged in the far back corner of a nondescript strip mall near the center of town. But it's worth the search for food that's at the apex of what you'll find in Costa Rica. Each night a short selection of specials is written on a chalkboard, based on the chef's whims and what's fresh. I almost always order one of the specials, though main menu is also excellent, featuring Graffiti's signature cacao- and coffee-crusted tenderloin and Asian-spiced seared tuna. Occasionally live music is on the menu, and it's worth perusing the attached gift shop, which features hand-carved wooden surfboards and unique body surfing paddles. As you might expect, it's a hip-looking place with graffiti art covering the walls. Along with the interior dining rooms, there's limited outdoor seating in the front of the restaurant, abutting the parking lot.

Centro Comercial Pacific Center, downtown Jacó. www.graffiticr.com. © **2643-1708.** Reservations recommended during high season. Main courses C5,000–C18,500. Mon–Sat 5–10pm.

Green Room Café ★★ BISTRO/SEAFOOD   This is yet another excellent little restaurant whipping up tasty dishes from fresh local ingredients. Green Room Cafe sources as much as it can from organic producers and local fisherman. The menu staples feature a range of breakfast and brunch items, plus sandwiches, wraps, tacos and burgers. Nightly specials are where you'll find the most creativity; recently they've included excellent mango-shrimp tartar and thick-cut rib eye steak with gorgonzola butter. While the food borders on fine dining at night, the atmosphere is decidedly casual and very cheery with colored cloths draped from the ceiling and wooden chairs painted bright pastel colors. On weekend nights there's often live music or a DJ.

On the Cocal Casino road in Jacó. ✆ **2643-4425.** Reservations recommended during high season. Main courses C3,000–C13,000. Tues–Sat 10am–11pm and Sun 8:30am–3pm. No credit cards accepted.

Lemon Zest ★★ SEAFOOD/FUSION   Chef/owner Richard Lemon left a teaching gig at the famed Le Cordon Bleu culinary school to open this superb eatery. His food, not surprisingly, is complex and sophisticated, ranging over a number of world influences. Among the many excellent appetizers, I'm partial to the Buffalo Lobster Bites with blue cheese dipping sauce and the Korean style beef skewers with a homemade banana ketchup. Main courses are as impressive, especially the green curry shrimp and the Jerk pork chop with pineapple-chipotle sauce. I have to dock Lemon Zest one star for the terrible dining room acoustics. Be sure to grab one of the few wooden tables on the outdoor balcony so you can converse comfortably with your dining companion.

Downtown Jacó, second floor. www.lemonzestjaco.com. ✆ **2643-2591.** Reservations recommended during high season. Main courses $11–$29. Daily 5–10pm; closed Monday in the off season. Closed mid-Sept through Oct 31.

INEXPENSIVE

Caliche's Wishbone ★ SEAFOOD/MEXICAN   A local landmark, Caliche's Wishbone was the brainchild and baby of a local surfing legend, Caliche. It serves up hearty fare, everything from pizzas, burritos, and stuffed potatoes to fresh, seared tuna in a soy-wasabi sauce (my favorite). Surf videos play on TVs in the main dining room, but I prefer the tables closest to the busy sidewalk, on the covered veranda.

On the main road in Jacó. ✆ **2643-3406.** Main courses C3,500–C13,000. Thurs–Tues noon–10pm.

Los Amigos ★ INTERNATIONAL/SEAFOOD   Occupying a prime location on one of the busiest corners in downtown Jacó, this casual spot feels like a mix between a sports bar and a college town club. The menu features a mix of typical American-style bar food, fresh seafood, Tex-Mex favorites, and Thai curries, rice bowls and noodle dishes. There's outdoor seating under broad canvas umbrellas, but on hot days, you'll want to opt for the indoor air-conditioned dining room. Live sporting events and surf videos are shown on seven flatscreen TVs and broadcast onto the flat wall of a large neighboring building.

On the main road in Jacó. www.losamigosjaco.com. ✆ **2643-2961.** Main courses C3,600–C8,000. Sun–Thurs noon–11pm; Fri–Sat noon–1am

Taco Bar ★ MEXICAN/INTERNATIONAL   Taco Bar is so popular that it's opened several branches in San José, and is looking to expand elsewhere around the country. This is the original, an open-air joint featuring two long, wooden bars with seating on "swings" supported by heavy ropes (you can also choose from more traditional tables and picnic tables). It serves up a wide range of tacos, burritos, and pizzas; seafood varieties are prepared using freshly caught fish. After choosing the main plate, you also have ample choices at their well-stocked and inventive salad bar. Also open for breakfast. *Note:* Don't confuse this place with Jacó Taco, which is located on the main strip and doesn't have nearly as good quality grub.

½ block inland from Pop's, central Jacó. www.tacobar.info. ℂ **2643-0222.** Main courses C3,675–C7,000. Mon 11am–10pm; Tues–Sun 7am–10pm.

Shopping

If you try to do any shopping in Jacó, you'll be overrun with shops selling T-shirts, cut-rate souvenirs, and handmade jewelry and trinkets. Most of the offerings are of pretty poor quality.

Entertainment & Nightlife

Playa de Jacó is the central Pacific's party town, with tons of bars and several discos. For a casual atmosphere, head to either **Los Amigos** or **Tabacón** ★ on the main street, near the center of town. Tabacón has pool and foosball tables, and often has live music. **Jacó Blu,** located right on the beach near the center of town, is a mellow beach club, with a pool, cabanas and restaurant service, by day, but at night becomes a fairly raucous bar and dance spot.

Other popular bars in town include **Monkey Bar,** with DJs and a large dance floor, and **Jacó Taco,** a two-story affair with regular live bands that is open 24 hours every day of the year. Both of the aforementioned bars are along the main strip through town.

Morada Haze (which is Spanglish for Purple Haze) and **Le Loft** ★, both on the main street and near the center of town, attract a more sophisticated and chic clubbing crowd.

Sports freaks can catch the latest games at **Clarita's Beach Bar & Grill, Hotel Copacabana** (both are right on the beach toward the north end of town), or **Hotel Poseidon** (on a side street near the town center).

If you're into casino games, head to the **Casino Amapola** (ℂ **2643-2255**) at the Hotel Amapola. The latter is a modest casino situated toward the southern end of the main road through Jacó (Av. Pastor Díaz), about a block beyond where it takes a sharp turn inland toward the Costanera Sur.

Note: Jacó has a good amount of prostitution and it's not uncommon to find working women at any of the bars around town. That's not necessarily a knock against the bar.

Side Trips from Playa de Jacó: Playas Hermosa, Esterillos & Bejuco

South of Jacó, Costa Rica's coastline is a long, almost entirely straight stretch of largely undeveloped beach backed by thick forests and low-lying rice and African palm plantations.

Playa Hermosa ★, 10km (6¼ miles) southeast of Jacó, is the first beach you'll hit as you head down the Southern Coastal Highway. This is primarily a surfers' choice, but it is still a lovely spot to spend some beach time. In fact, even though the surf conditions here can be rather rough and unprotected, and the beach is made of dark volcanic sand, I find Playa Hermosa and the beaches south of it much more attractive than Jacó. Aside from a small grouping of hotels and restaurants, most of Playa Hermosa is protected, as **olive ridley sea turtles** lay eggs here from July to December. During turtle nesting season, all of the hotel tour desks and local tour agencies can help you arrange a nighttime turtle nesting tour, for around $40 to $50 per person.

Playa Hermosa is the only beach in this section located right along the Southern Coastal Highway; all of the rest are a kilometer or so in from the road and reached by a series of dirt access roads. If you exit the highway in Playa Hermosa, you can follow a dirt-and-sand access road that runs parallel to the shore along several miles of deserted, protected beach, as Playa Hermosa eventually becomes **Playa Tulin,** near the Tulin River mouth. This is another popular surf spot, but be careful—crocodiles live in the Tulin River.

As you continue down the coastal highway from Playa Hermosa, you will hit Esterillos. **Playa Esterillos,** 22km (14 miles) south of Jacó, is long and wide and almost always nearly deserted. Playa Esterillos is so long, in fact, that it has three separate entrances and sections, Esterillos Oeste, Centro, and Este—West, Center, and East, in order as you head away from Jacó.

If you keep heading south (really southeast), you next come to **Playa Bejuco,** another long, wide, nearly deserted stretch of sand. Playa Bejuco, which features a very narrow strip of land fronting the beach, with mangroves and swampland behind, has very little development.

Safety notes: While beautiful, isolated, and expansive, the beaches of Hermosa, Esterillos, and Bejuco can be quite rough at times and dangerous for swimming. Caution is highly advised here. Also be careful on Playa Hermosa, as the fine dark sand can get extremely hot in the tropical sun; be sure to have adequate footwear and a large towel or mat to lay out on the sand.

WHERE TO STAY IN PLAYA HERMOSA
Moderate

Beyond those listed below, check out **Surf Inn Hermosa** (www.surf innhermosa.com; ℂ **2643-7184**), which offers one-bedroom studios

Playa Esterillos.

with a kitchenette, and two-bedroom fully equipped condo units, or the **Sandpiper Inn** ★ (www.sandpipercostarica.com; ✆ **2643-7042**), a cozy surfer joint. Both are right on the beach.

The Backyard ★ The Backyard is run by and for surfers, so service and attention to detail can be a bit lax. Rooms are simple and unadorned, aside from framed photos of tropical beach scenes. The Backyard's restaurant and bar are pretty much the only game in town, and are jam packed most nights, with noise from the bar wafting up to the rooms—another strike against staying here. Still, right out in front is one of the best surf breaks on this coastline, and that's enough for many.

Playa Hermosa de Jacó, Puntarenas. www.backyardhotel.com. ✆ **2643-7011.** 8 units. $110–$133 double; $200–$230 suite. Breakfast included. **Amenities:** Restaurant; bar; small outdoor pool; free Wi-Fi.

Inexpensive

Playa Hermosa has a host of simple hotels and *cabinas* catering to surfers. Prices, conditions, and upkeep can vary greatly. If you've got the time, your best bet is to visit a few until you find the best deal on the cleanest room. **Costanera Bed & Breakfast** (www.costaneraplaya hermosa.com; ✆ **2643-7044**), **Cabinas Las Arenas** (www.cabinas lasarenas.com; ✆ **8729-4532**), and **Cabinas Las Olas** (www.lasolas hotel.com; ✆ **2643-7021**) are three good options.

WHERE TO STAY IN PLAYA ESTERILLOS

If you're looking for something even more remote and undeveloped than the hotel listed below, head to Playa Esterillos Este and the **Pelican Hotel** (www.pelicanbeachfronthotel.com; ✆ **2778-8105**), a homey beachfront bed-and-breakfast.

   Note: Playa Esterillos and Playa Bejuco are about midway between Jacó and Manuel Antonio, and it's very useful to have a rental car if staying here.

Expensive

Alma del Pacífico Hotel ★★   This upscale boutique hotel is a hidden gem on a very undiscovered patch of sand. Originally built as a sister resort to Xandari (p. 184), it now has separate owners and management. Still, the individual villas here feature the same artsy sensibility, which means they're oversized, with white tile floors, white walls, white bed linens and loads of natural light, all accented with bold splashes of primary colors found in paintings, mosaic tile works, curtains, and more. The arched wood planked ceilings remind me of the hulls of wooden boats. The best villas feature ocean views and private plunge pools. The open-air ocean-view restaurant is top notch.

Playa Esterillos Centro, Puntarenas. www.almadelpacifico.com. © **888/960-2562** in the U.S. and Canada, or 2778-7070 in Costa Rica. 20 units. $188–$289 double bungalow, $345–$413 villa. Rates include Alma breakfast. **Amenities:** Restaurant; bar; concierge; Jacuzzi; 2 outdoor lap pools; room service; full-service spa; free Wi-Fi.

WHERE TO STAY IN PLAYA BEJUCO
Moderate

Hotel Playa Bejuco ★   The sister hotel of the Mar de Luz hotel in Playa de Jacó (p. 411), Hotel Playa Bejuco is a throwback to another era. Some of the rooms look like they could have been decorated in the 1970s (though they're immaculate and quite spacious), and the area has yet to be touched by the rampant development of Jacó, a blessing. If you come here knowing those two things, and knowing that, beside the on-site restaurant and bar, there's no nightlife at all, you'll enjoy yourself. Though the hotel's not right on the beach, it's quite close and you'll likely have the sands all to yourself. On-site is a small pool.

Playa Bejuco, Puntarenas. www.hotelplayabejuco.com. © **2779-2000.** 20 units. $129 double. Rate include breakfast and taxes. Lower rates in off season. **Amenities:** Restaurant; bar; outdoor pool, Jacuzzi; and free Wi-Fi

MANUEL ANTONIO NATIONAL PARK ★★

140km (87 miles) SW of San José; 69km (43 miles) S of Playa de Jacó

Manuel Antonio was Costa Rica's first major ecotourist destination and remains one of its most popular. The views from the hills overlooking Manuel Antonio are spectacular, the beaches (especially those inside the national park) are idyllic, and its rainforests are crawling with howler, white-faced, spider and squirrel monkeys, among other forms of exotic wildlife. The downside is that you'll have to share it with more fellow travelers than you would at other rainforest destinations around the country. Moreover, booming tourism and development have begun to destroy what makes this place so special. What was once a smattering of small hotels tucked into the forested hillside has become a string of lodgings along the 7km (4⅓ miles) of road between Quepos and the national park entrance. Hotel roofs now regularly break the tree line, and there seems to be no control over zoning and unchecked ongoing construction. A jumble of snack shacks, souvenir stands, and make-shift parking lots choke the beach road just outside the park, making the entrance road look more like a shanty town than a national park.

An easy trail through Manuel Antonio National Park.

Still, this remains a beautiful destination, with a wide range of attractions and activities that make it perfect for all sorts of travelers. Gazing down on the blue Pacific from high on the hillsides of Manuel Antonio, it's almost impossible to hold back a gasp of delight. Offshore, rocky islands dot the vast expanse of blue, and in the foreground, the rich, deep green of the rainforest sweeps down to the water. Even cheap cell phone cameras regularly produce postcard-perfect snapshots.

One of the most popular national parks in the country, Manuel Antonio is also one of the smallest, covering fewer than 680 hectares (1,680 acres). Its several nearly perfect small beaches are connected by trails that meander through the rainforest. The mountains surrounding the beaches quickly rise as you head inland from the water; however, the

View towards Manuel Antonio National Park and Cathedral Point.

park was created to preserve not its beautiful beaches but its forests, home to endangered squirrel monkeys, three-toed sloths, purple-and-orange crabs, and hundreds of other species of birds, mammals, and plants. Once, this entire stretch of coast was a rainforest teeming with wildlife, but now only this small rocky outcrop of forest remains.

Those views that are so bewitching also have their own set of drawbacks. If you want a great view, you aren't going to be staying on the beach—in fact, you probably won't be able to walk to the beach. This means that you'll be driving back and forth, taking taxis, or riding the public bus. Also keep in mind that it's hot and humid here, and it rains a lot. However, the rain is what keeps Manuel Antonio lush and green, and this wouldn't be the Tropics if things were otherwise.

If you're traveling on a rock-bottom budget or are mainly interested in sportfishing, you might end up staying in the nearby town of **Quepos,** which was once a quiet banana port and now features a wide variety of restaurants, shops, and lively bars; the land to the north was used by Chiquita to grow its bananas. Disease wiped out most of the banana plantations, and now the land is planted primarily with African oil-palm trees. To reach Quepos by road, you pass through miles of these **oil-palm plantations;** see the box "Profitable Palms," p. 421, for info.

Essentials

GETTING THERE & DEPARTING   By Plane: Both **Nature Air** (www.natureair.com; ⓒ **800/235-9272** in the U.S. and Canada, or 2299-6000) and **Sansa** (www.flysansa.com; ⓒ **877/767-2672** in the U.S. and Canada, or 2290-4100 in Costa Rica) offer several daily direct flights to the **Quepos airport** (airport code: XQP). The flight is 30 minutes long; the fare is $60 to $90 each way.

Both **Sansa** (ⓒ **2777-1912** in Quepos) and **Nature Air** (ⓒ **2777-2548** in Quepos) provide minivan airport-transfer service coordinated with their arriving and departing flights. The service costs around $8 per person each way. Taxis meet incoming flights and may be more economical. Expect to be charged between $10 and $20 per car for up to four people, depending on the distance to your hotel.

A tractor on a palm plantation near Quepos.

When you're ready to depart, **Sansa** (℘ **2777-1912** in Quepos) flights begin departing at 8:45am, with the final flight leaving at 4pm. **Nature Air** (℘ **2777-2548** in Quepos) flights leave for San José daily at 7:35am and 3:20pm.

By Car: From San José, take the San José–Caldera Highway (CR27) west to Orotina. Just past the toll booth at Pavón, this road connects with the Costanera Sur (CR34), or Southern Coastal Highway. The exit is marked for Jacó and CR34. From here, it's a straight and flat shot down the coast to Quepos and Manuel Antonio.

If you're coming from Guanacaste or any point north, take the Interamerican Highway to the Puntarenas turnoff and follow signs to the San José–Caldera Highway (CR27). Take this east toward Orotina, where it connects with the Costanera Sur (CR34). It's about a 4½-hour drive from Liberia to Quepos and Manuel Antonio.

By Bus: Tracopa buses (www.tracopacr.com; ℘ **2221-4214** or 2290-1308) to Manuel Antonio leave San José regularly throughout the day between 6am and 7:30pm from Calle 5 between avenidas 18 and 20. Trip duration is around 3 hours; the fare is C4,675. These buses go to the park entrance and will drop you off at any of the hotels along the way.

For your return trip, the **Quepos bus station** (℘ **2777-0263**) is next to the market, 3 blocks east of the water and 2 blocks north of the road to Manuel Antonio. Buses depart for San José daily between 4am and 5pm.

Gray Line (www.graylinecostarica.com; ℘ **800/719-3105** in the U.S. and Canada, or 2220-2222 in Costa Rica) and **Interbus** (www.interbusonline.com; ℘ **4031-0888**) both have two buses daily leaving San José for Quepos and Manuel Antonio, one in the morning and one in the afternoon. The fare is around $50. Both companies will pick up at most San José-area hotels. Both also offer connections to most major tourist destinations in the country.

Many of the buses for Quepos stop to unload and pick up passengers in **Playa de Jacó.** If you're in Jacó heading toward Manuel Antonio, you can try your luck at one of the covered bus stops on the Interamerican Highway.

Timing Tips

Despite the above caveats, Manuel Antonio is still a fabulous destination with a wealth of activities and attractions for all types and all ages. If you steer clear of the peak months (Dec–Mar), you'll miss most of the crowds. If you must come during the peak months, try to avoid weekends, when the beach is packed with families and young Ticos from San José. If you visit the park early in the morning, you can leave when the crowds begin to show up at midday. In the afternoon, you can lounge by your pool or on your patio.

Profitable Palms

On any drive to or from Quepos and Manuel Antonio, you'll pass through miles and miles of African palm plantations. Native to West Africa, *Elaeis guineensis* was planted along this stretch in the 1940s by United Fruit, in response to a blight that was attacking their banana crops. The palms took hold and soon proved quite profitable, being blessed with copious bunches of plum-size nuts that are rich in oil. This oil is extracted and processed in plantations that dot the road between Jacó and Quepos. The smoke and distinct smell of this processing is easily noticed. The processed oil is eventually shipped overseas and used in a wide range of products, including soaps, cosmetics, lubricants, and food products.

These plantations are a major source of employment in the area—note the small, orderly "company towns" built for workers—but their presence is controversial. The palm trees aren't native, and the farming practices are thought by some to threaten Costa Rica's biodiversity.

In the busy winter months, tickets sell out well in advance, especially on weekends; if you can, purchase your ticket several days in advance. However, you must buy your Quepos-bound tickets in San José and your San José return tickets in Quepos. If you're staying in Manuel Antonio, you can buy your return ticket for a direct bus in advance in Quepos, and then wait along the road to be picked up. There is no particular bus stop; just make sure you are out to flag down the bus and give it time to stop—you don't want to be standing in a blind spot when the bus comes flying around a tight corner.

Buses leave **Puntarenas** for Quepos daily at 5, 8, and 11am and 12:30, 2:30, and 4:30pm. The ride takes 2 hours; the fare is C1,100. Buses for **Puntarenas** leave daily at 4:30, 7:30, and 10:30am and 12:30, 3, and 5:30pm. Any bus headed for San José or Puntarenas will let you off in Playa de Jacó.

GETTING AROUND A taxi between Quepos and Manuel Antonio (or any hotel along the road toward the park) costs between C4,000 and C5,000, depending upon the distance. At night or if the taxi must leave the main road (for hotels such as La Mariposa, Parador, Makanda, and Arenas del Mar), the charge is a little higher. If you need to call a taxi, dial © **2777-0425** or 2777-1207. Taxis are supposed to use meters, although they don't always. If your taxi doesn't have a meter, or the driver won't use it, try to negotiate in advance. Ask your hotel desk what a specific ride should cost, and use that as your guide.

The bus between Quepos and Manuel Antonio (© **2777-0318**) takes 15 minutes each way and runs roughly every half-hour from 5:30am to 9:30pm daily. The buses, which leave from the main bus terminal in Quepos, near the market, go all the way to the national park entrance before turning around and returning. You can flag down these buses from any point on the side of the road. The fare is C250.

You can also rent a car from **Adobe** (℡ **2777-4242**), **National/ Alamo** (℡ **2777-3344**), **Economy** (℡ **2777-5260**), or **Hertz** (℡ **2777-3365**) for between $53 and $150 a day. All have offices in downtown Quepos or Manuel Antonio, but with advance notice, someone will meet you at the airport with your car for no extra charge.

If you rent a car, never leave anything of value in it. Car break-ins are common here. A couple of parking lots just outside the park entrance cost around $3 for the entire day. You should definitely keep your car in one of these while exploring the park or soaking up sun on the beach. And although these lots do offer a modicum of protection, you still should not leave anything of value exposed in the car. The trunk is probably safe.

CITY LAYOUT   Quepos is a small port city at the mouth of the Boca Vieja Estuary. If you're heading to Manuel Antonio National Park, or any hotel on the way to the park, after crossing the bridge into town, take the lower road (to the left of the high road). In 4 blocks, turn left, and you'll be on the road to Manuel Antonio. This road winds through town a bit before starting over the hill to all the hotels and the national park.

FAST FACTS   The telephone number of the **Quepos Hospital** is ℡ **2777-0922.** In the event of an emergency, you can also call the **Cruz Roja** (Red Cross; ℡ **2777-0116**). For the **local police,** call ℡ **2777-3608.** The **post office** (℡ **2777-1471**) is in downtown Quepos. Several pharmacies are in Quepos, as well as a pharmacy at the hospital, and another close to the park entrance. A half-dozen or so laundromats and laundry services are in town.

Several major Costa Rican banks have branches and ATMs in downtown Quepos, and a couple of ATMs have sprung up along the road to the national park.

Exploring the National Park

Manuel Antonio is a small park with three major trails. Most visitors come primarily to lie on a beach and check out the white-faced monkeys, which sometimes are as common as tourists. A guide is not essential here, but unless you're experienced in rainforest hiking, you'll see and learn a lot more with one. You can always stay on inside the park after your guided tour is over. A 2- or 3-hour guided hike should cost between $40 and $75 per person. Almost any of the hotels in town can help you set up a tour of the park, if not, contact **Manuel Antonio Expeditions** (www.manuelantonioexpeditions.blogspot.com; ℡ **8365-1057**), run by Juan Brenes, who does a wonderful job. Avoid touts dressed as guides stopping you on the street and doing a hard sell. If you decide to explore the park solo, see the trail map on the inside front cover of this book.

ENTRY POINT, FEES & REGULATIONS In 2015, the park (© **2777-5185**) was open every day of the week during the high season, but it's not clear if that will continue. Usually the park is open Tuesday through Sunday from 7am to 4pm. The entrance fee is $16 per person. The **main park entrance** is located almost about 1.5km (almost a mile) inland, at the end of the road that leads off perpendicular to Playa Espadilla at the corner featuring the popular Marlin Restaurant.

Another ranger station and exit point is at the end of the road from Quepos. This ranger station is located across a small stream that's little more than ankle-deep at low tide but that can be knee- or even waist-deep at high tide. It's even reputed to be home to a crocodile or two. For years there has been talk of building a bridge over this stream; in the meantime access to or from the park via this point is prohibited.

MINAE, the national ministry that oversees the park, has been frustratingly inconsistent about which entrance visitors may use. However, for the past several years, tickets have been sold and entry allowed only at the inland entrance. This requires about 20 to 30 minutes of hiking along an often muddy access road before you get to the beach and principal park trails. *Note:* The Parks Service allows only 800 visitors to enter each day, which could mean that you won't get in if you arrive in mid-afternoon during the high season. Camping is not allowed.

The combined problem of people feeding monkeys, and monkeys robbing food, has become serious. The park service no longer allows visitors to bring in unprepared foods. Gone are the days where folks would bring in a portable Hibachi and large cooler. You can still pack in snacks and sandwiches and soft drinks.

THE BEACHES   **Playa Espadilla Sur** (as opposed to Playa Espadilla, which is just outside the park; see "Hitting the Water," p. 424) is the first beach within the actual park boundaries. It's usually the least crowded and one of the best places to find a quiet shade tree to plant yourself under. However, if there's any surf, this is also the roughest beach in the park. If you want to explore further, you can walk along this soft-sand beach or follow a trail through the rainforest parallel to the beach. **Playa Manuel Antonio,** which is the most popular beach inside the park, is a short, deep crescent of white sand backed by lush rainforest. The water here is sometimes clear enough to offer good snorkeling along the rocks at either end, and it's usually fairly calm. At low tide, Playa Manuel Antonio shows a very interesting relic: a circular stone turtle trap left by its pre-Columbian residents. From Playa Manuel Antonio, another slightly longer trail leads to **Puerto Escondido,** where a blowhole sends up plumes of spray at high tide.

THE HIKING TRAILS   From either Playa Espadilla Sur or Playa Manuel Antonio, you can take a circular loop trail (1.4km/.9 mile) around a high promontory bluff. The highest point on this hike, which takes about 25

Playa Espadilla.

to 30 minutes round-trip, is **Punta Catedral ★★**, where the view is spectacular. The trail is a little steep in places, but anybody in average shape can do it. I have done it in sturdy sandals, but you might want to wear good hiking shoes. This is a good place to spot monkeys, although you're more likely to see a white-faced monkey than a rare squirrel monkey. Another good place to see monkeys is the **trail inland** from Playa Manuel Antonio. A linear trail it's mostly uphill, but it's not too taxing. It's great to spend hours exploring the steamy jungle and then take a refreshing dip in the ocean.

Finally, a trail connects Puerto Escondido (p. 423) and **Punta Serrucho,** which has some sea caves. Be careful when hiking beyond Puerto Escondido: What seems like easy beach hiking at low tide becomes treacherous to impassable at high tide. Don't get trapped.

Hitting the Water

BEACHES OUTSIDE THE PARK   **Playa Espadilla,** the gray-sand beach just outside the park boundary, is often perfect for board surfing and bodysurfing. At times it's a bit rough for casual swimming, but with no entrance fee, it's the most popular beach with locals and visiting Ticos. Some shops by the water rent boogie boards, beach chairs and umbrellas. A full-day rental of a beach umbrella and two chaise lounges costs around $10. (These are not available

> ### Helping Out
>
> If you want to help in efforts protecting the local environment and the endangered squirrel monkey (*mono tití*), make a donation to the **Titi Conservation Alliance** (www.monotiti.org; ✆ **2777-2306**), an organization supported by local businesses, or to **Kids Saving the Rainforest** (www.kidssavingtherainforest.org; ✆ **2777-2592**), which was started in 1999 by local children.

inside the park.) This beach is actually a great spot to learn how to surf, because several open-air shops renting surfboards and boogie boards are along the beachfront road. Rates run $5 to $10 per hour, and around $20 to $30 per day. If you want a lesson, I recommend the **Blue Horizon Surf School** (www.bluehorizonsurfschool.com; ✆ **8994-1424**), which provides excellent attention for individuals, small groups and families.

BOATING, KAYAKING, RAFTING & SPORTFISHING TOURS Iguana **Tours** (www.iguanatours.com; ✆ **2777-2052**) is the most established tour operator in the area, offering river rafting, sea kayaking, mangrove tours, and guided hikes.

The above company as well as **Amigos del Río** (www.amigosdelrio. net; ✆ **877/393-8332** in the U.S or 2777-0082 in Costa Rica) offer full-day rafting trips for around $90 to $95. Large multiperson rafts are used during the rainy season, and single-person "duckies" are broken out when the water levels drop. Both companies also offer half-day rafting adventures and sea-kayaking trips for around $65 to $90. Depending on rainfall and demand, they will run either the Naranjo or Savegre rivers. I very much prefer the **Savegre River** ★★ for its stunning scenery.

Another of my favorite tours in the area is the mangrove tour of the **Damas Island estuary.** These trips generally include lunch, a stop on Damas Island, and roughly 3 to 4 hours of cruising the waterways. You'll see loads of wildlife. The cost is usually $65 to $70. **Manuel Antonio Expeditions** (www.manuelantonioexpeditions.blogspot.com; ✆ **8365-1057**) is my choice operator for this tour.

Among the other boating options around Quepos/Manuel Antonio are excursions in search of dolphins and sunset cruises. **Iguana Tours** (see above) and **Planet Dolphin** ★ (www.planetdolphin.com; ✆ **800/943-9161** in the U.S or 2777-1647 in Costa Rica) offer these tours

LEFT: **A Damas Island boat tour.**
RIGHT: **White-water rafting the Savegre River.**

A Planet Dolphin sailing tour.

for around $80 per person, depending upon the size of the group and the length of the cruise. Most tours include a snorkel break and, if lucky, dolphin sightings. For more of a booze cruise experience, you could try the 100' long **Ocean King** (www.catamaranadventurescr.com; ☎ **4000-5740**).

Quepos is one of Costa Rica's sportfishing centers, and sailfish, marlin, and tuna are all common in these waters. In recent years, fresh- and brackish water fishing in the mangroves and estuaries has also become popular. If you're into sportfishing, try hooking up with **Blue Fin Sportfishing** (www.bluefinsportfishing.com; ☎ **2777-0000**) or **Luna Tours Sportfishing** (www.lunatours.net; ☎ **272/242-5982** in U.S or 2777-0725 in Costa Rica). A full day of fishing should cost between $600 and $1,900, depending on the size of the boat, distance traveled, tackle provided, and amenities. With so much competition here, it pays to stop by the marina and shop around.

SCUBA DIVING & SNORKELING   Oceans Unlimited ★ (www.scubadivingcostarica.com; ☎ **401/385-6598** in the U.S or 2777-0114 in Costa Rica) offers both scuba diving and snorkel outings, as well as certification and resort courses. Because of river run-off and often less-than-stellar visibility close to Quepos, the best trips involve some travel time. Tours around Manuel Antonio run $99 per person for a two-tank scuba dive. However, **Isla del Caño** (p. 442) is only about a 90-minute ride each way. This is one of the best dive sites in Costa Rica, and I highly recommend it. Trips to Isla del Caño are $125 for snorkeling and $165 for two-tank scuba diving.

Other Activities in the Area

ATV   Midworld ★★ (www.midworldcostarica.com; ☎ **2777-7181**) offer a range of tours through forests and farmlands at their center on the outskirts of Quepos and Manuel Antonio.

BUTTERFLY GARDEN Manuel Antonio Nature Park ★★ (www.manuel antonionaturepark.com; ℗ **888/742-6667** in U.S. and Canada or 2777-0850 in Costa Rica) is just across from (and run by) Hotel Sí Como No (p. 432). A lovely bi-level **butterfly garden ★** is the centerpiece attraction here, but there is also a private reserve and a small network of well-groomed trails through the forest. A 1-hour guided tour of the butterfly garden costs $15 per person. This is also a good place for a night tour ($39).

A butterfly at Fincas Naturales.

CANOPY ADVENTURES The most exciting local canopy tour is **Midworld ★★** (www.midworldcostarica.com; ℗ **2777-7181**). Their main zip-line tour features 10 cables, including the longest cables in the area. However they also have a "Superman" cable, which is very long, very fast, and ridden in a prone position, as well as a ropes course. Their ATV tours through the surrounding rainforest stop at a waterfall pool for a dip. **Canopy Safari ★** (www.canopysafari.com; ℗ **888/765-8475** in the U.S. and Canada, or 2777-0100 in Costa Rica) is another good option, featuring 18 treetop platforms connected by a series of cables and suspension bridges; the tour also features a Tarzan-type swing and two rappels. The on-site butterfly garden and serpentarium are an added bonus. A canopy tour should cost around $85 per person, and up to $125 for a combo package that includes various adventures and lunch.

About 20 minutes outside of Quepos is **Rainmaker Park** (www.rainmakercostarica.org; ℗ **540/349-9848** in the U.S or 2777-3565 in Costa Rica; daily 7:30am–4:30pm). Its main attraction is a system of connected suspension bridges strung through the forest canopy, crisscrossing a deep ravine. Of the six bridges, the longest is 90m (295 ft.) across. The refuge also has a small network of trails and some great swimming holes. Entrance fee is $20, $15 additional for a guided tour.

FOR KIDS For a taste of local Tico rural culture, mixed in with fabulous scenery and adventure, sign up for the **Santa Juana Mountain Tour & Canopy Safari ★★** (www.sicomono.com; ℗ **888/742-6667** in the U.S. and Canada, or 2777-0777 in Costa Rica). This full-day tour starts off with a visit to the Canopy Safari (see above) and then takes you to a local farming village in the mountains outside of Quepos. Depending upon your interests once you arrive in the village, you can tour coffee and citrus farms, go for a horseback ride, hike trails, swim in rainforest pools, fish for tilapia, or see how sugar cane is processed. A typical Tico lunch is included. Rates are $129 to $155 per person, depending upon the size of your group, and $89 for kids under 12.

HORSEBACK RIDING While you can still sometimes find locals renting horses on the beaches outside the national park, I discourage this, as there are just too many crowds, the beach is too short, and the horse droppings are problematic. Better yet, head back into the hills and forests. Both **Finca Valmy** (www.toemmers.com; ✆ **2779-1118**) and **Brisas del Nara** (www.horsebacktour.com; ✆ **2779-1235**) offer horseback excursions that pass through both primary and secondary forest and feature a swimming stop or two at a jungle waterfall. Full-day tours, including breakfast and lunch, cost between $70 and $75 per person. Finca Valmy also offers an overnight tour for serious riders, with accommodations in rustic cabins in the Santa María de Dota mountains.

PARASAILING **Aguas Azules** (www.costaricaparasailing.com; ✆ **2777-9192**) sets up shop every morning on Playa Espadilla right in front of the souvenir store Caycosta, and offer parasailing rides behind a speedboat. Prices start at $75 for a single ride, which lasts around 15-minutes.

ONE-STOP ADVENTURE HOT SPOT The **ADR Adventure Park** ★★ (www.adradventurepark.com; ✆ **877/393-8332** in the U.S and Canada or 2777-0082 in Costa Rica) is an excellent one-stop spot for thrill seekers. Billing itself as a 10-in-1 adventure tour, its 7-hour full-day tour includes a zip-line, waterfall rappels, a high plunge into a jungle river pool, horseback riding, and more. The cost is $130, and includes transportation and lunch.

SOOTHE YOUR BODY & SOUL The best of the local day spas is **Raindrop Spa** (www.raindropspa.com; ✆ **800/381-3770** in the U.S. and Canada, or 2777-2880 in Costa Rica) offering a wide range of treatments, wraps, and facials. **Holis Spa** (www.spaholis.com; ✆ **2777-0939**) has open yoga classes ($15) daily at 8am in the event center at Hotel Costa Verde and also offers private classes.

SPICE UP YOUR LIFE Located 16km (10 miles) outside of Quepos, **Villa Vanilla** ★★ (www.rainforestspices.com; ✆ **2779-1155** or 8839-2721) offers an informative and tasty tour of their open-air botanical

---

Yo Quiero Hablar Español

Academia de Español D'Amore (www.academiadamore.com; ✆ **877/434-7290** in the U.S. and Canada, or 2777-0233 in Costa Rica) offers language-immersion programs out of a former hotel with a fabulous view on the road to Manuel Antonio. A 2-week conversational Spanish course, including a homestay and two meals daily, costs $1100. Or you can try the **Costa Rica Spanish Institute** (COSI; www.cosi.co.cr; ✆ **2234-1001** or 2777-0021), which charges $1,180 for a similar 2-week program with a homestay.

gardens and spice farm. The on-site commercial vanilla operation is the centerpiece, but you'll also learn about a host of other tropical spices and assorted flora. You'll even sample some sweet and savory treats and drinks made with the on-site bounty. The half-day guided tour runs daily at 9am and 1pm, and costs $50, which includes round-trip transportation from any area hotel. Be sure to stock up at their small shop, which offers pure vanilla, cinnamon, and locally grown pepper.

Where to Stay

Take care when choosing your accommodations in Quepos/Manuel Antonio. You won't have much luck finding a hotel where you can walk directly out of your room and onto the beach, since Manuel Antonio has very few true beachfront hotels. In fact, most of the nicer hotels here are 1km (½ mile) or so away from the beach, high on the hill overlooking the ocean.

If you're traveling on a rock-bottom budget, you'll get more for your money by staying in Quepos and taking the bus to the beaches at Manuel Antonio. The rooms in Quepos might be small, but they're generally cleaner and more appealing than those available in the same price category closer to the park.

EXPENSIVE

Buena Vista Luxury Villas ★★ (www.buenavistaluxuryvillas.com; ℂ **866/569-6241** in the U.S. and Canada, or 2777-0580 in Costa Rica) is the current incarnation of the former Tulemar Resort. It features a wide range of private villas and bungalows in a gated community; each unit has access to Buena Vista's own secluded and protected bit of beach.

Arenas del Mar, Manuel Antonio.

If you're coming for an extended stay with the family or a large group, consider **Escape Villas ★★★** (www.escapevillas.com; © 888/771-2976 in the U.S., or 2203-4401 in Costa Rica) or **Manuel Antonio Rentals ★★** (www.manuelantoniovacationrentals.com; © 985/247-4558 in the U.S., or 8913-9415 in Costa Rica). Both outfits rent a broad selection of large and luxurious private villas and homes, with all the amenities and some of the best views in Manuel Antonio.

In addition to the place listed below, you might check out **Byblos Resort ★** (www.bybloshotelcostarica.com; © 888/929-2567 in the U.S. and Canada, or 2777-0411 in Costa Rica), which features a mix of rooms, suites, and jungle bungalows. Although they're the oldest and simplest units on the property, I really like the individual bungalows set in deep forest.

Arenas del Mar ★★★ This beachfront resort is in a league of its own in Manuel Antonio, with handsome rooms, fabulous views, great dining, and direct access to not one, but two, beaches. On the lodging front first, all of the rooms are wonderfully spacious featuring pale yellow antique-style tile floors, cushy beds complete with leaf-print headboards and sleek, minimalist decor. Many rooms come with a private outdoor Jacuzzi tub on a private balcony. There are two main centers of operation here—one near the highest point of the property, the other down by one of the beaches—and each has its own pool, restaurant, and bar. This property is a leader in sustainable tourism and conservation, and all stays here include a guided tour on sustainable living. Tortilla making classes are also free and very popular with guests.

Manuel Antonio. www.arenasdelmar.com. © **2777-2777.** 38 units. $350–$470 double; $590–$780 suite. Additional person $70. Rates include full breakfast and free local and international calls. **Amenities:** 2 restaurants; 2 bars; babysitting; concierge; 2 small outdoor pools; room service; spa; free Wi-Fi.

Gaia Hotel & Reserve ★★ Set on a series of rolling hills amidst its own private reserve, this ultra-hip hotel offers up the most luxury and pampering in the Manuel Antonio area. Every guest enjoys personal concierge services, as well as a complimentary 20-minute spa treatment. Rooms come in a range of sizes and categories, although you'll need to opt for a suite if you want a private balcony (deluxe suites get both a balcony and private rooftop terrace). All have shiny hardwood floors, a living area with rattan sofa and chairs, and cloudlike mattresses. On-site is a three-tiered pool with connecting waterfalls carved into the hillside; the hotel also provide shuttle service to the beach. The hotel's Luna restaurant is terrific. Gaia is a proudly "green" resort and has been awarded "4 Leaves" by the CST Sustainable Tourism program.

Manuel Antonio. www.gaiahr.com. © **800/226-2515** in the U.S., or 2777-9797 in Costa Rica. 20 units. $207–$435 studio; $350–$665 suite; $520–$715 family suite. No children 13 and under. **Amenities:** Restaurant; bar; concierge; small gym; multilevel outdoor pool; room service; extensive spa; free Wi-Fi.

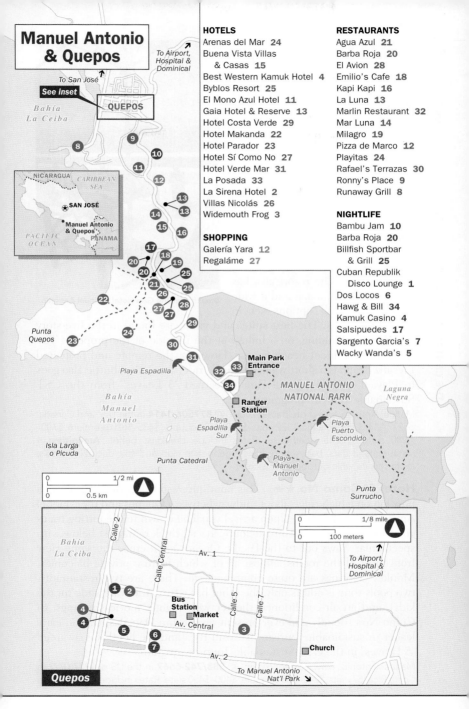

Manuel Antonio & Quepos

To Airport, Hospital & Dominical

To San José

See inset

QUEPOS

Bahía La Ceiba

NICARAGUA
CARIBBEAN SEA
SAN JOSÉ
Manuel Antonio & Quepos
PACIFIC OCEAN
PANAMA

HOTELS
Arenas del Mar 24
Buena Vista Villas
  & Casas 15
Best Western Kamuk Hotel 4
Byblos Resort 25
El Mono Azul Hotel 11
Gaia Hotel & Reserve 13
Hotel Costa Verde 29
Hotel Makanda 22
Hotel Parador 23
Hotel Sí Como No 27
Hotel Verde Mar 31
La Posada 33
La Sirena Hotel 2
Villas Nicolás 26
Widemouth Frog 3

SHOPPING
Galería Yara 12
Regaláme 27

RESTAURANTS
Agua Azul 21
Barba Roja 20
El Avion 28
Emilio's Cafe 18
Kapi Kapi 16
La Luna 13
Marlin Restaurant 32
Mar Luna 14
Milagro 19
Pizza de Marco 12
Playitas 24
Rafael's Terrazas 30
Ronny's Place 9
Runaway Grill 8

NIGHTLIFE
Bambu Jam 10
Barba Roja 20
Billfish Sportbar
  & Grill 25
Cuban Republik
  Disco Lounge 1
Dos Locos 6
Hawg & Bill 34
Kamuk Casino 4
Salsipuedes 17
Sargento Garcia's 7
Wacky Wanda's 5

Bahía La Ceiba

Punta Quepos

Playa Espadilla

Main Park Entrance

Ranger Station

MANUEL ANTONIO NATIONAL PARK

Laguna Negra

Bahía Manuel Antonio

Isla Larga o Picuda

Playa Espadilla Sur

Playa Puerto Escondido

Punta Catedral

Playa Manuel Antonio

Punta Surrucho

0 1/2 mi
0 0.5 km

Bahía La Ceiba

Calle 2
Calle Central
Av. 1
Calle 5
Calle 7

Bus Station
Market
Av. Central

Church

Av. 2

To Airport, Hospital & Dominical

0 1/8 mile
0 100 meters

To Manuel Antonio Nat'l Park

Quepos

Hotel Parador ★★ Located at the end of the road, with more than 4.8 hectares (12 acres) of land, and a private reserve that takes up most of a sizeable peninsula, this resort-style hotel covers some serious ground. Some seriously lovely ground, actually, inhabited by as many animals as you'll see in the national park, beautifully landscaped, laced with trails and dotted with swimming pools (including a fabulous, large two-tiered family pool with a concrete crocodile in the shallow end as well as a central fountain and a swim-up bar). The resort also has four restaurants, a spa and a wide range of lodging options set in

Breakfast at the Gaia Hotel, Manuel Antionio.

several buildings. The best suites and views are found in the five-story "Las Suites" building, on a hilltop at the far side of the property. The resort has no direct beach access. However, the remote and protected Biesanz beach is a short walk, or shuttle ride, away (the shuttle also goes to Playa Espadilla). Hotel Parador earned "5 Leaves" from the CST Sustainable Tourism program.

Manuel Antonio. www.hotelparador.com. ℂ **877506-1414** in the U.S. and Canada, or 2777-1411 in Costa Rica. 122 units. $250–$430 double; $435–$520 premium; $730–1,280 suite, $1,645 penthouse. Rates include breakfast buffet. **Amenities:** 4 restaurants; 2 bars; babysitting; concierge; health club and spa; Jacuzzi; 3 pools; room service; unlit outdoor tennis court.

Hotel Sí Como No ★★ This boutique resort occupies a privileged position on a high ridge about midway between Quepos and the Manuel Antonio National Park. Upon arrival you'll be drawn to the jutting triangular lookout point just off the lobby. It's all thick rainforest below with spectacular views out to the Pacific Ocean. You'll enjoy the same view from most of the rooms, almost all of which feature private balconies. Monkey sightings are quite common here. There are two restaurants, two pools (one is adults only, the other has a fun little waterslide for the kids), and an air-conditioned theater with nightly movie showings. Sí Como No's friendly and ever-present owner, Jim Damalas, was an early leader in sustainable tourism in Costa Rica and the hotel was awarded "5 Leaves" in the CST Sustainable Tourism program.

Manuel Antonio. www.sicomono.com. ℂ **888/742-6667** in the US or 2777-0777 in Costa Rica. 57 units. $242–$350 double; $400–$450 suite. Rates include full breakfast.

Extra person $30. Children 5 and under stay free in parent's room. **Amenities:** 2 restaurants; 2 bars; babysitting; concierge; 1 Jacuzzi; 2 midsize outdoor pools, including 1 w/small water slide; modest spa; free Wi-Fi.

Hotel Makanda ★★   The original owners sold Makanda in 2014, and the hotel was in the midst of a major overhaul as we went to press. The changes will include the addition of some private plunge pools, as well as a shift towards a more contemporary and edgy design aesthetic. But we don't expect massive changes, as the new owners have great original materials to work with. This adults-only resort, set on over 11 acres of rainforest hillside sloping down to the sea, has long been one of the most scenic in the Manuel Antonio area. The lodgings, a mix of one-bedroom studio units and larger villas, are spread around the grounds (each with full kitchen or kitchenette), and were already darn nice, with hardwood walls, stone floors, and in some, vaulted ceilings. All are large and open. Breakfast is delivered to the villas. The hotel's poolside restaurant is excellent.

Manuel Antonio. www.makanda.com. ✆ **888/625-2632** in the U.S., or 2777-0442 in Costa Rica. 12 units. $265–$315 studio; $400–$700 villa. Rates include full breakfast. Children 16 and under are not allowed, unless booking the entire resort. **Amenities:** Restaurant; bar; concierge; Jacuzzi; midsize outdoor pool; room service; free Wi-Fi.

MODERATE

Hotel Costa Verde ★   This sprawling complex features everything from cheery, clean rooms and cottages to a converted Boeing 727 that serves as a two-bedroom suite, with the cockpit and nose appearing to be flying straight out of the rain forest. Most of the rooms, however, are found in two tall buildings (one for families, one adults only), featuring large balconies with wonderful rainforest and ocean views. The studio and studio-plus rooms all have kitchenettes and flatscreen TVs. Not all of the rooms have air-conditioning or televisions and some can be quite a hike to the main restaurant, so be sure to check before making your final choice. The hotel has a series of trails, one of which leads to the beach. It's about a 10-minute walk down, but since the complex is located on a steep hillside, the return trip from the beach and to some of the rooms can be strenuous. Breakfast is served at the main hotel complex; three additional restaurants are across the street.

Manuel Antonio. www.costaverde.com. ✆ **866/854-7958** in the U.S. and Canada, or 2777-0584 in Costa Rica. 70 units. $79–$200 double; $180–$350 bungalows. **Amenities:** 4 restaurants; 4 bars; 3 small outdoor pools; free Wi-Fi.

Villas Nicolás ★★   Located right next to Sí Como No (p. 432), this collection of spacious condo units offers up the very same classic Manuel Antonio views, but at near bargain prices. Virtually all of the rooms here come with large balconies, reached via arched wooden French doors. Every balcony comes equipped with a sleep-inducing rope hammock.

And as at Si Como No, monkey sightings are common. Some units have full kitchens, and many can be combined to accommodate families or groups. All have different owners, so interior decor can vary from tropical casual to contemporary chic. The lovely pool is set amidst blooming gardens, and the service is friendly and personal.

Manuel Antonio. www.villasnicolas.com. © **2777-0481.** 19 units. $125–$160 double; $180–$230 suite; $305-$340 villa. Rates include full breakfast. **Amenities:** Restaurant; bar; small outdoor pool; free Wi-Fi.

INEXPENSIVE

In addition to the hotels mentioned below, the **Best Western Kamuk Hotel** (www.kamuk.co.cr; © **2777-0811**) and **La Sirena Hotel** (www. lasirenahotel.com; © **954/493-5144** in U.S and Canada **or 2777-0572 in Costa Rica**) are two dependable options right in downtown Quepos. Both are popular with sportfishing enthusiasts, while **La Posada Private Jungle Bungalows** (www.laposadajungle.com;©2777-1446) is a clean option a few blocks inland from the beach, right near the main entrance to the National Park.

True budget hotels are hard to come by in and around Quepos and Manuel Antonio. Those on a tight budget should look at **Widemouth Frog** ★ (www.widemouthfrog.org; © **2777-2798**), a hostel right in downtown Quepos, which offers everything from bunk-bed dorm rooms with shared bathrooms to cozy double rooms with a private facilities. It even has its own swimming pool.

El Mono Azul Hotel ★ "The Blue Monkey" has a hostel-like feel and very social vibe, with slightly more upscale accommodations that you'd find in a typical hostel. Rooms, which can be dated, are on both sides of the main road that runs from Quepos to the national park entrance, and vary quite a bit in size and amenities. The several pool areas are quite nice, with overgrown gardens and plenty of shade. The little restaurant here is a hub of activity and great place to meet fellow travelers. Final reason to stay here? The owners were instrumental in founding Kids Saving the Rainforests, a non-profit conservation and art program, and part of all of their proceeds goes to support the project.

Manuel Antonio. www.monoazul.com. © **2777-1548.** 20 units. $65–$95 double. **Amenities:** Restaurant; bar; lounge; 2 small outdoor pools; free Wi-Fi.

Hotel Verde Mar ★ Just a short walk on a raised walkway through shady trees to Playa Espadilla, this two-story hotel has a to-die-for location, and remains the best budget beachfront hotel in Manuel Antonio. The rooms are all of good size, most come with a kitchenette, and while the linens and some of the furnishings could use an update, all is kept clean. They're also prettier than they need to be with pale yellow or green walls, and a hand-carved wooden door with a local animal and nature scene. Given that there's a small free-form pool and overall the staff is friendly and helpful, the hotel provides solid value.

Manuel Antonio. www.verdemar.com. ℂ **877/872-0459** in the U.S. and Canada or 2777-2122 in Costa Rica. 30 units. $95–$105 double. $115–$125 suites. Amenities: Small outdoor pool; free Wi-Fi.

Where to Dine

Scores of dining options are available around Manuel Antonio and Quepos, and almost every hotel has some sort of restaurant. For the cheapest meals around, try a simple *soda* in Quepos, or head to one of the open-air joints on the beach road before the national park entrance. Here, the standard Tico menu prevails, with prices in the C3,500-to-C6,500 range. Of these, **Marlin Restaurant ★** (ℂ **2777-1134**), right in front of Playa Espadilla, is your best bet. **Mi Lugar,** or **"Ronny's Place" ★** (www.ronnysplace.com; ℂ **2777-5120**), on the outskirts of Quepos, is another fine option. **Mar Luna** (ℂ **2777-5107**), on the main road as you climb the hill from Quepos toward Manuel Antonio, would be a fourth choice, a Tico-owned spot specializing in seafood.

For lunch, try the beachfront **Playitas ★★** at Arenas del Mar (p. 430); in addition to its great location and secure parking, you get pool privileges for the price of an excellent meal.

For a taste of the high life, head to the **La Luna ★** restaurant at Gaia Hotel & Reserve (p. 430) for their sunset tapas menu. The views are stellar and the creative tapas very reasonably priced.

EXPENSIVE

Kapi Kapi ★★★ FUSION/NUEVO LATINO   Wanna propose? Kapi Kapi is the place to pick. Dim lighting, an elegant, almost Asian decor and generous space between tables make tables make Kapi Kapi romantic and very private. The food won't break the spell. It's very fresh, making use of local produce and seafood whenever possible, and highly inventive. Favorites on the menu include local shrimp skewered on spikes of sugar cane, grilled, and then bathed in a glaze of rum, tamarind, and coconut; and the mahi-mahi crusted in macadamia nuts, and served with a sweet plum-chili sauce and Jasmine rice. The wide-ranging wine list includes selections from Italy, France, Argentina, and Chile.

On the road btw. Quepos and Manuel Antonio. www.restaurantekapikapi.com. ℂ **2777-5049.** Main courses C8,500–C14,500. Daily 4–10pm.

MODERATE

Agua Azul ★★ INTERNATIONAL   Sitting high above the rainforest with sweeping views over the trees to the Pacific Ocean below, this corrugated zinc-roofed, open-air restaurants has one of the best settings in town. There's little in the way of decor, but there really doesn't need to be when the sunsets are this lovely (grab a table at the railing if you can for an unobstructed vista). Agua Azul's menu seems, at first glance, to be heavy in bar food standards, but dishes often have a creative twist (like their signature Tuna Margarita, seared tuna over a cucumber salad with a lime vinaigrette, all served in a salt-rimmed margarita glass). You can also get burgers, burritos, nachos, chicken fingers, and a few more substantial plates, like whole snapper in a tamarind sauce, and the chef's nightly pasta special.

Manuel Antonio, near Villas del Parque. www.cafeaguaazul.com. © **2777-5280.** Main courses C4,500–C10,500. Tues–Mon 11am–9:30pm.

Barba Roja ★ SEAFOOD/INTERNATIONAL This is a prime sunset-admiring spot, so on clear nights, you'll want to grab one of the lounge-style low tables on the broad wooden deck. The food isn't as exciting as the show in the sky, but it's usually tasty, ranging from Tex-Mex to Asian fusion. They also serve Tico standards, and traditional bar food, and have a pretty good sushi bar to boot.

Manuel Antonio. www.barbarojarestaurant.com. © **2777-0331.** Reservations recommended in high season. Main courses C4,200–C9,700. Tues–Sun 1–10pm.

El Avión ★ SEAFOOD/INTERNATIONAL El Avión, or "the plane," is a former CIA C-123 supply plane that was shot down by the Sandinistas during the Contra War. It now provides shade and cover for outdoor dining on this large wooden deck built under the plane's wings and an even more expansive open-air roof structure above. The food is the usual: fresh seafood, steaks, burgers, and sandwiches. But the fresh caught seared tuna is particularly well done here, as is the *arroz con pollo* (rice with chicken). Portions are generous. The sunset view here is sought after so you should reserve in advance if you want a table with a view. The restaurant's bar is inside the old cargo plane's fuselage.

Manuel Antonio. www.elavion.net. © **2777-3378.** Reservations recommended. Main courses C5,000–C11,000. Daily noon–11pm.

Emilio's Café ★★ INTERNATIONAL/BAKERY There's no better place to start the day than Emilio's Café, as it's a bakery, too, with fabulous bagels and a range of pastries. But you might also want to stop here for lunch, as the salads are bursting with flavor as are the sandwiches made on house-baked ciabatta bread. And then there's dinner when fresh fish, thick steaks and nightly specials are snapped up by Emilio's grateful diners. Let's just say it straight out: You could dine here for every meal and come away satisfied—Emilio's is that good (the view is pretty swell, too). And in the evenings, you may get live music.

On the Mariposa road, ½ block from the intersection with the road btw. Quepos and Manuel Antonio. © **2777-6807.** Reservations recommended. Main courses C4,500–C12,500. Daily 7am–9pm.

Milagro ★★★ NUEVO LATINO/FUSION A local institution, this off-shoot of the coffee roasting operation offers a full range of barista-brewed concoctions. But the appeal here goes well beyond java—breakfast, lunch, and dinner are served in the crayon-colored dining room and patios here, and they're all top-notch. For lunch I like their take on a traditional Cuban sandwich, replacing the pork with fresh, local mahi-mahi. The dinner menu features fusion-inspired Latin fare with everything from jerk chicken to shrimp in a coconut-rum sauce served over mango-infused rice. Creative, contemporary cocktails, as well as excellent South American wines, can be ordered at the bar or at the tables. There's often live music in the evening.

On the road btw. Quepos and Manuel Antonio. www.cafemilagro.com. © **2777-2272.** Reservations recommended. Main courses C6,300–C13,000. Daily 7am–10pm.

Rafael's Terrazas ★★ SEAFOOD/COSTA RICAN This simple open-air restaurant has a stunning location, clinging to a steep hillside with a perfect view of the Pacific over zinc roofs and a small patch of thick rain forest. The hillside is so steep the dining rooms are terraced (hence the name) and spread over three floors connected by steep steps. The menu features a host of Tico classics and is heavy on fresh seafood. I recommend the excellent ceviche as a starter, followed by a *casado* of fish, chicken or beef for the entree. They also have more worldly options, including seared tuna with a ginger, soy, and wasabi sauce. Meat lovers should try the bacon-wrapped tenderloin in a fresh mushroom sauce.

On the road btw. Quepos and Manuel Antonio. © **2777-6310.** Reservations recommended. Main courses C5,300–C15,000. Tues–Sun 11am–11pm.

Runaway Grill ★★ SEAFOOD Housed on the open second floor above and overlooking the Pez Vela Marina, Runaway Grill has kept most of the menu, vibe and management of the old El Gran Escape. Which is a smart move, because El Gran always had a wonderful way with seafood (including a "you hook 'em, we cook 'em" policy for anyone heading out fishing) and that tradition continues today. Start things off with the fresh tuna sashimi, and then go for the catch of the day, simply grilled—you won't be disappointed. Chicken, beef, and vegetarian fare are also available. The attached bar is lively, and they usually have any important sports event on the flat screen televisions.

At the Pez Vela Marina. © **2519-9095.** Reservations recommended in high season. Main courses C8,500–C20,000. Daily 11:30am–10pm.

Shopping

If you're looking for souvenirs, you'll find plenty of beach towels, beachwear, and handmade jewelry in a variety of small shops in Quepos and at the rows of open-air shops and impromptu stalls down near the national park. My favorite gift shop is the one found inside **Milagro** ★★ (p. 436), which features a host of excellent, locally sourced craft items, as well as their top-notch freshly roasted coffee. For higher-end gifts, check out Hotel Sí Como No's **Regálame** (www.regalameart.com; © **2777-0777**) gift shop, which has a wide variety of craft works, clothing, and original paintings and prints, or **Galería Yara** (© **2777-4846**), a contemporary art gallery in the Plaza Yara shopping center.

Manuel Antonio Nightlife & Entertainment

The bars at the **Barba Roja** restaurant, about midway along the road between Quepos and Manuel Antonio, and the **Hotel Sí Como No** (p. 432) are good places to hang out and meet people in the evenings. To shoot some pool, I head to the **Billfish Sportbar & Grill ★** at the Byblos Resort (on the main road btw. Quepos and the park entrance). For tapas and local *bocas,* try **Salsipuedes** (roughly midway along the road btw. Quepos and the National Park entrance), which translates as "get out if you can." If you want live music, **Bambu Jam ★** (along the road btw. Quepos and the park entrance) and **Dos Locos** (in the heart of downtown) are your best bets. You might also try **Hawg & Bill,** which fronts the beach down in Playa Espadilla. In downtown Quepos, **Sargento Garcia's, Wacky Wanda's,** and the **Fish Head Bar** at El Gran Escape are all popular hangouts.

Night owls and dancing fools have several choices here, although the bulldozing of Mar y Sombra down by the beach has really hurt the scene. The live music at **Bambu Jam** is often salsa and merengue, perfect for dancing. For real late-night action, the hottest club in town is the **Cuban Republik Disco Lounge**, in the heart of downtown Quepos.

The **Best Western Kamuk Hotel** in Quepos and the **Byblos Resort** (p. 430) both have small casinos and will even foot your cab bill if you try your luck gaming. If you want to see a flick, check what's playing at **Hotel Sí Como No**'s (p. 432) little theater, although you have to eat at the restaurant or spend a minimum at the bar to earn admission.

Side Trip from Manuel Antonio: Playa Matapalo

Playa Matapalo is a long expanse of flat beach that's about midway between Quepos and Dominical. It's an easy but bumpy 26km (16 miles) south of Quepos on the Costanera Sur. It's nowhere near as developed as either of those two beaches, but that's part of its charm. The beach here seems to stretch on forever, and it's usually deserted. The surf and strong riptides frequently make Matapalo too rough for swimming, although surfing and boogie-boarding can be good. Foremost among this beach's charms are peace and quiet.

WHERE TO STAY

Matapalo is a tiny coastal village, although the actual beach is about 1km (½ mile) away. A few very small and intimate lodges are located right on the beach. One of the more unusual is **Bahari Beach Bungalows** (www.baharibeach.com; © **2787-5014**), which offers deluxe tents with private bathrooms, and more standard rooms, right on the beach. **Dreamy Contentment** (www.dreamycontentment.com; © **2787-5223**) is a more traditional beachfront hotel. **El Coquito del Pacifico** hotel (www.elcoquito.com; © **855/765-9642** in the U.S or 2787-5031 in Costa Rica) has a restaurant popular with tourists and locals alike.

For something completely different, you can head into the hills alongside the Savegre River to **Rafiki Safari Lodge ★** (www.rafiki safari.com; *©* **2777-2250**), which features a collection of large safari tents on elevated platforms in a rich forest setting.

DOMINICAL ★

29km (18 miles) SW of San Isidro; 42km (26 miles) S of Quepos; 160km (99 miles) S of San José

With a stunning setting, and miles of nearly deserted beaches backed by rainforest-covered mountains, Dominical and the coastline south of it well repay a visit. They boast spectacular views, remote jungle waterfalls, and everything from abundant budget lodgings to luxurious rainforest villas. The beach at Dominical is one of the prime surf destinations in Costa Rica, with both right and left beach breaks. When the swell is big, the wave here is a powerful and hollow tube, and the town is often packed with surfers. It is often too rough for casual bathers. However, you will find excellent swimming, sunbathing, and strolling beaches just a little farther south at **Dominicalito, Playa Hermosa,** and inside **Ballena Marine National Park ★★**.

Leaving Manuel Antonio, the road south to Dominical runs by mile after mile of oil-palm plantations. However, just before Dominical, the mountains again meet the sea. From Dominical south, the coastline is dotted with tide pools, tiny coves, and cliff-side vistas. Dominical is the largest village in the area and has several small lodges both in town and along the beach to the south. The village enjoys an enviable location on

Dominicalito.

the banks of Río Barú, right where it widens considerably before emptying into the ocean. The banks of the river and throughout the surrounding forests offer good birding (numerous shore and sea birds, including herons, egrets, and kingfishers, and colorful tanagers, toucans, and trogons in the forested areas).

Essentials

GETTING THERE & DEPARTING **By Plane:** The nearest airport with regular service is in Quepos (p. 419). From there you can hire a taxi, rent a car, or take the bus.

By Car: The traditional route from San José involves heading east out of town (toward Cartago), and then south on the Interamerican Highway (CR2) to the city of San Isidro de El General. From San Isidro, a well-marked and well-traveled route (CR243) leads to Dominical and the coast. The entire drive takes about 4 hours.

However, it's faster and easier to take the San José–Caldera Highway (CR27) west to Orotina. Just past the toll booth at Pavón, this road connects with the Costanera Sur (CR34), or Southern Coastal Highway. The exit is marked for Jacó and CR34. From here, it's a straight and flat shot down the coast. When you reach Quepos, follow the signs for Dominical This route should take you just over 3 hours.

The Costanera Sur (CR34) heading south from Dominical to Palmar Norte, passing all the beaches mentioned below, is in excellent shape.

By Bus: To reach Dominical, you must first go to San Isidro de El General or Quepos. Buses leave San José for San Isidro roughly every hour between 4:30am and 5:30pm. See "Getting There & Departing" in "San Isidro de El General: A Base for Exploring Chirripó National Park," p. 452. The trip takes 3 hours; the fare is C3,500. The main bus stop in Dominical is near the soccer field and San Clemente restaurant.

From Quepos, **Transportes Blanco** buses (© **2771-4744**) leave daily at 7, 9, and 11:30am and 3:30 and 4pm. The trip takes about an 1½ hours and costs C2,540.

From San Isidro de El General, **Transportes Blanco** buses (© **2771-4744**) leave for Dominical at 7, 9, and 11:30am, and 3:30pm. The bus station in San Isidro for rides to Dominical is 1 block south of the main bus station and 2 blocks west of the church. The trip duration is 1½ hours; the fare is C1,540.

When you're ready to leave, buses depart Dominical for San Isidro at 6am and 1, 2, and 4pm. Buses leave San Isidro for San José roughly every hour between 4:30am and 5:30pm. Buses to Quepos leave Dominical at 8am and 12:30 and 4:30pm.

GETTING AROUND Taxis tend to congregate in front of the soccer field. If you need a car, **Solid Rental Car** (© **2787-0111**) will arrange drop-off and pickup at any area hotel.

SPECIAL EVENTS Each year, this area hosts the **Envision Festival ★★★** (www.envisionfestival.com), a 3-day celebration of art, music, and dance, that's a little bit like Burning Man in the Tropics. The festival usually takes place in late-February or early March.

VILLAGE LAYOUT Dominical is a small village on the banks of the Río Barú. The village is to the right after you cross the bridge (heading south) and stretches out along the main road parallel to the beach. As you first come into town, you'll see the small Pueblo del Río shopping center dead ahead of you, where the road hits a "T" intersection. On your left is the soccer field and the heart of the village. To the right, a rough road heads to the river and up along the riverbank. If you stay on the Costanera Highway heading south, just beyond the turnoff into town is a little strip mall, **Plaza Pacífica,** with a couple of restaurants, a pharmacy, bank, and a grocery store.

FAST FACTS A branch of the **Banco de Costa Rica,** with an ATM, is located in the Plaza Pacifica.

Exploring the Beaches South of Dominical & Ballena Marine National Park

The open ocean waters just in front of town and toward the river mouth are often too rough for swimming. However, you can swim in the calm waters of the Río Barú, just in from the river mouth, or head down the beach a few kilometers to the little sheltered cove at **Roca Verde.**

If you have a car, you should continue driving south, exploring beaches as you go. You will first come to **Dominicalito,** a small beach and cove that shelters the local fishing fleet and that can be a decent place to swim, but continue on a bit. You'll soon hit **Playa Hermosa,** a long stretch of desolate beach with fine sand. As in Dominical, this beach is unprotected and can be rough, but it's a nicer place to sunbathe and swim than Dominical.

At the village of Uvita, 16km (10 miles) south of Dominical, you'll reach the northern end of the **Ballena Marine National Park ★★**, which protects a coral reef that stretches from Uvita south to Playa Piñuela and includes the little Isla Ballena, just offshore. To get to **Playa Uvita** (which is inside the park), turn in at the village of Bahía and continue until you hit the ocean. The beach here is actually well protected and good for swimming. At low tide, an exposed sandbar allows you to walk about and explore another tiny island. This park is named for the whales that are sometimes sighted close to shore in the winter months. If you ever fly over this area, you'll notice that this little island and the spit of land that's formed at low tide compose the perfect outline of a whale's tail. An office at the entrance here regulates the park's use and even runs a small turtle-hatching shelter and program. Entrance to the

Ballena Marine National Park.

national park is $10 per person. Camping is allowed here for $2 per person per day, including access to a public restroom and shower.

Dominical is a major surf destination. Its long and varied beach break is justifiably popular. In general, the beach's powerful waves are best suited to experienced surfers but beginners can do so with the instructors at the **Green Iguana Surf Camp ★** (www.greeniguanasurfcamp.com; ✆ **8855-5866**), who offer lessons and comprehensive "surf camps." Rates run around $835 to $1,375 per person, based on double occupancy, for a 1-week program including accommodations, lessons, unlimited surfboard use, transportation to various surf breaks, and a T-shirt.

Outdoor & Wellness Activities in the Area

In addition to the activities mentioned below, other adventure activities offered in Dominical include kayak tours of the mangroves, river floats in inner tubes, and day tours to Caño Island and Corcovado National Park. To arrange any of these activities, contact **Dominical Adventures** (www.dominicalsurfadventures.com; ✆ **2787-0431**) or the staff at the **Hotel Roca Verde** (www.rocaverde.net; ✆ **2787-0036**).

DIVING For diving the rocky sites off Ballena National Park or all the way out to Isla del Caño, call **Mystic Dive Center** (www.mysticdive. com; ✆ **2786-5217;** Dec 1–Apr 15 only), which has its main office in a small roadside strip mall down toward Playa Tortuga and Ojochal. Prices for Ballena National Park are $80 for snorkeling and $100 for a two-tank dive; rates for Isla del Caño are $130 for snorkeling and $170 for a two-tank dive.

FISHING   For sportfishing, I recommend **Sportfishing Dominical** (www.sportfishingdominical.co.cr; © **2787-8012**), which is based out of the hotel Cuna del Angel (p. 449).

FLYING   **Fly Adventure CR** (www.flyadventurecr.com; © **8318-9685**) offers a variety of airborne tours of the area. Near the beach in Uvita, these folks offer everything from 30-minute introductory flights for $140 to a roughly hour-long circuit exploring the Ballena Marine National Park and neighboring mangrove forests for $235.

HIKING & HORSEBACK RIDING   Several local farms offer horseback tours through forests and orchards, and some of these farms provide overnight accommodations. **Hacienda Barú ★** (www.haciendabaru.com; © **2787-0003**) offers several different hikes and tours, including a walk through mangroves and along the riverbank (for some good bird-watching), a rainforest hike through 80 hectares (198 acres) of virgin jungle, an all-day trek from beach to mangrove to jungle that includes a visit to some Indian petroglyphs, an overnight camping trip, and a combination horseback-and-hiking tour. The operation, which is dedicated to conservation and reforestation, even has tree-climbing tours and a small canopy platform 30m (98 ft.) above the ground, as well as one of the more common zip-line canopy tours. Tour prices range from $25 for the mangrove hike to $125 to overnight in the jungle. If you're traveling with a group, you'll be charged a lower per-person rate, depending on the number of people. In addition to its eco- and adventure tourism activities, Hacienda Barú also has six comfortable cabins with two bedrooms each, full kitchens, and even a living room (prices range from $80–$90 for a double, including breakfast). Hacienda Barú is about 1.5km (1 mile) north of Dominical on the road to Manuel Antonio.

Slithery Fun

In my opinion, **Parque Reptilandia ★★** (www.crreptiles.com; © **2787-0343**; daily 9am–4pm; $12 adult, $6 children 14 and under) is the best snake and reptile attraction in Costa Rica. With more than 70 well-designed and spacious terrariums and enclosed areas, the collection includes a wide range of snakes, frogs, turtles, and lizards, as well as crocodiles and caimans. Both native and imported species are on display, including the only Komodo dragon in Central America; and the brilliant eyelash pit viper and sleek golden vine snake. For those looking to spice up their visit, Fridays are feeding days. The park is few miles outside Dominical on the road to San Isidro.

Nauyaca Waterfalls.

WATERFALLS The jungles just outside of Dominical are home to two spectacular waterfalls. The most popular and impressive is the **Santo Cristo** or **Nauyaca Waterfalls ★**, a two-tiered beauty with an excellent swimming hole. Most of the hotels in town can arrange for the horseback ride up here, or you can contact operator **Don Lulo** (www.cataratas nauyaca.com; ℂ **2787-0541**) directly. A full-day tour, with both breakfast and lunch, should cost around $70–$90 per person, including transportation to and from Dominical. The tour is a mix of hiking, horseback riding, and hanging out at the falls. It is also possible to reach these falls by horseback from an entrance near the small village of Tinamaste. (You will see signs on the road.) Similar tours (at similar prices) are offered to the **Diamante Waterfalls,** which are a three-tiered set of falls with a 360m (1,180-ft.) drop, but not quite as spacious and inviting a pool as the one at Santo Cristo.

YOGA **Danyasa Eco-Retreat ★★** (www.danyasa.com; ℂ **2787-0229**) offers a wide range of regular yoga and surf classes, as well as private instruction and longer retreats. A drop-in class costs $15, and weeklong or multi-class deals are offered.

Where to Stay

In addition to the places listed below, a host of beautiful private homes on the hillsides above Dominical regularly rent out rooms. Most come with several bedrooms and full kitchens, and quite a few have private pools. If you're here for an extended stay and have a four-wheel-drive vehicle (a must for most of these), check in with the folks

Spanish Classes

Adventure Education Center (www.adventurespanishschool.com; ✆ **800/237-2730** in the U.S. and Canada, or 2787-0023 in Costa Rica), right in the heart of town, offers a variety of immersion-style language programs. A standard, 1-week program including 16 hours of class, homestay, and breakfasts and dinners costs $420. These folks also offer specialized family and medical language courses, and can throw some surf lessons into the package, if you're interested.

at **Villas Alturas** ★★ (www.villasalturas.com; ✆ **760/560-3903** in the U.S. or 2200-5440 in Costa Rica).

MODERATE

Cascadas Farallas Waterfall Villas ★★   In a category all their own, these handsome villas are set in the midst of thick forest and on the edge of a gorgeous stepped waterfall. Decor is Balinese-inspired and features four-poster beds decked out in white muslin mosquito netting. All of the villas open on to patios or balconies with views of the rainforest or waterfalls. Specializing in unplugged, vegan yoga retreats and general mind-body rejuvenation, this boutique hotel and wellness retreat center is about 8km (5 miles) outside of Dominical proper. An accomplished on-site kitchen puts out predominantly vegetarian, vegan and raw foods. Sorry, no Wi-Fi.

8km (5 miles) northeast of Dominical, on the road to San Isidro www.waterfallvillas. com. ✆ **2787-4137.** 9 units. $165–$300 double, $190–$430 suites. Rates include breakfast. **Amenities:** Restaurant; spa.

Hotel Diuwak ★   This surfer-friendly mini-resort is just a half-block away from the waves. Rooms are in need of some upkeep and remodeling, and the service can be slack. But most folks don't seem to care, seeing that as a fair trade off for easy access to the waves and town. The hotel has a very good sized pool area, as well as a restaurant, bar, surf shop and well-stocked convenience store.

Dominical. www.diuwak.com. ✆ **2787-0087.** 36 units. $100–$105 double; $115–$125 deluxe; $170–$180 suites. Rates include full breakfast and taxes. **Amenities:** Restaurant; bar; midsize outdoor pool, free Wi-Fi.

Hotel Roca Verde ★★   Located a bit south of town, the setting at the Hotel Roca Verde is fantastic—on a protected little cove with rocks and tide pools. Rooms are in a two-story building beside the swimming pool and they're spacious with polished cement floors and lovely hand-painted murals. Each comes with one queen-size and one single bed, and either a balcony or a patio (but you'll want to try for a second-floor unit if possible, as the balconies are a bit nicer to have). The massive open-air restaurant and bar here are quite popular, serving up delicious thin crust pizza, and featuring live music on Friday nights.

1km (½ mile) south of Barú River Bridge in Dominical, just off the coastal hwy. www. rocaverde.net. ✆ **2787-0036.** 10 units. $99 double. Rate include breakfast and taxes. **Amenities:** Restaurant; bar; small outdoor pool; free Wi-Fi.

INEXPENSIVE

As a popular surfer destination, budget lodgings abound in Dominical. I try to list the best below, but if you're really counting pennies, it's always a good idea to walk around and check out what's currently available. You might find deals at the **Montanas de Agua** (www.montanasdeagua. com; ✆ **2787-0200**), about a block and a half inland from the beach, across from Domilocos. There are plenty of camping options as well. I recommend **Piramys** (✆ **2787-0196**; piramys@hotmail.com) or **Camping Antorchas** (✆ **2787-0307**; pablo0462@yahoo.es), both of which offer basic rooms very close to the beach.

Cabinas San Clemente ★   Owner Mike McGigginis is an old-school surfer and pioneer in these parts, who settled this spot after falling in love with the deep barrels that form just in front. The best rooms here are the second-floor units with private bathrooms. These have wood floors, wicker furnishings, low lying beds with thin mattresses and a pretty, hand painted wash effects on the walls. If budget's tight, you can opt for dorm rooms with bunk beds, shared bath and access to a communal kitchen. The hotel's small Surf Shak restaurant serves breakfast and lunch.

Dominical. ✆ **2787-0026** or 2787-0055. 18 units, 12 with private bathroom. $10 per person with shared bathroom; $35–$70 double with private bathroom. **Amenities:** Restaurant; free Wi-Fi.

Tortilla Flats ★   If your ideal vacation is mainly about surfing on the cheap, you'll fit right in at Tortilla Flats. The unbeatable right-on-the-sand location pulls in surfers, and its wood-paneled *cabinas* create a cozy cabin-in-the-woods feel, though rooms are pretty bare bones (think: thin mattresses). Rooms vary in size, amenities, and the number and style of beds. There are twin beds, Queen beds and even bunk beds on offer here. Also here: a cute beach bar-restaurant and a small, covered half-pipe for skateboarders.

Dominical. ✆ **2787-0033.** 16 units. C15,000 double. **Amenities:** Restaurant; bar.

Where to Dine

On the beach, **Tortilla Flats** (see above) is the best and most happening spot, and their menu features excellent fresh-fish dishes and a touch of fusion cuisine. Nearby, **Surf Shak** (✆ 2787-0026), at Cabinas San Clemente, serves up hearty breakfasts, smoothies and lunch fare. For sushi, look no further than the aptly named **Domincal Sushi** (✆ **8826-7946**) in the Rio Mar commercial center. If you head a bit south of town, you can check out the restaurant at the **Hotel Roca Verde** (p. 445), which is usually pretty good for grilled fish, steaks, and burgers.

Soda Nanyoa (✆ **2787-0164**) is a basic Tico restaurant on the main road, just down a bit from the soccer field, serving local food and fresh seafood at good prices.

If you're staying in Dominical and have a car, it's probably worthwhile to head south and sample some of the options mentioned in the next section below.

Maracatú ★ INTERNATIONAL/VEGETARIAN   Located in the heart of Dominical village, right across from the soccer field, this local hotspot specializes in healthy cuisine, particularly vegetarian and vegan fare, although you can also get fresh seafood. Choose from vegetarian fajitas, veggie burgers, a range of pasta dishes, and Middle Eastern classics, like falafel and tabbouleh. All of the produce and seafood is locally sourced, and much of it comes from their own organic farm Selva Armonia in the nearby hills. Maracatu also has a vibrant lounge and bar scene and often features live music or DJs.

Across from the soccer field, Dominical. www.maracatucostarica.com. ✆ **2787-0091.** Main courses C4,000–C8,000. Daily noon–9:30pm.

Patron's Bar & Grill ★ INTERNATIONAL/STEAKHOUSE   Patron's is impossible to miss, with its full-sized Volkswagen bus mounted on a concrete pillar acting as billboard. The menu and vibe here is that of a casual steakhouse though, along with thick cuts of beef, you can also get ribs, burgers, entrée-sized salads and pasta dishes. Patron's features a good and varied wine list, as well as an excellent selection of local Costa Rican craft beers. A separate lounge area has live music and a relaxed vibe, with patrons lolling on long wicker couches.

Next to the soccer field, Dominical. www.patronscostarica.com. ✆ **2787-8010.** Main courses C6,800–C9,800. Daily 6am–2am.

Dominical Nightlife & Entertainment

The big party scenes shift from night to night. **Maracatú** (see above) hosts an open jam session every Sunday and a ladies' night every Wednesday, while **Tortilla Flats** (p. 446) holds regular sunset jam sessions and a big disco night on Saturday. There's usually live music on Friday nights at **Roca Verde** (p. 445). In addition, **Patron's Bar & Grill** (see above) in the center of town is a great place to hang, with a relaxed contemporary feel, and live music every Friday, Saturday and Sunday.

South of Dominical

The beaches south of Dominical are some of the nicest and most unexplored in Costa Rica. With the paving of the Costanera Sur, hotels and *cabinas* have begun popping up all along this route. This is a great area to roam in a rental car—it's a beautiful **drive** ★★. I especially recommend making a loop from San Isidro to Dominical, down the Costanera Sur, hitting several deserted beaches, and then returning along the Interamerican Highway.

Dominical's coastline.

Among the beaches you'll find are **Playa Ballena, Playa Uvita, Playa Piñuela, Playa Ventanas,** and **Playa Tortuga.** *Tip:* Most of these beaches are considered part of **Ballena Marine National Park** (p. 441) and are subject to the national park entrance fee of $6 per person. If you're visiting several of these beaches in 1 day, save your ticket—it's good at all of them.

WHERE TO STAY

Just south of Dominical, on a point over Dominicalito beach, **La Parcela** (www.laparcelacr. com; ✆ **2787-0016**) rents four simple, but ideally located individual cabins that sleep up to four people, for $75 per night, while the nearby **Coconut Grove** (www.coconut grovecr.com; ✆ **2787-0130**) offers a mix of cottages and guesthouses with direct access to Dominicalito, for between $85 and $150 per double. If you're looking for luxury, I'd recommend **Kura Design Villas ★★★** (www.kuracostarica.com; ✆ **8848-5744**), an all-villa, boutique hotel overlooking Ballena National Park.

> ### Get the Scoop
>
> The staff at the **Uvita Tourist Information Center** (www.uvita.info; ✆ **2743-8072**) offers a wealth of knowledge, has a tour booking agency and rental car operation, and even functions as the local branch of the Costa Rican post office, DHL, and UPS. You'll find them right on the Costanera Sur, at the main intersection in Uvita.

Moderate

Costa Paraiso Lodge ★   With lush gardens and tall palm trees, this friendly small boutique hotel sits just above a series of rocky outcroppings and tide pools at the northern end of Dominicalito beach. The rooms are mostly fully equipped studio apartments. All feature cool tile floors, peaked exposed beam ceilings and loads of ambient light streaming in through large windows and French doors. The Toucan Nest is the prized room here, a private bungalow in a prime location overlooking the sea. The other units are all part of two separate duplex buildings that primarily overlook the hotel's gardens and parking area. The lodge has a small swimming pool. Perhaps the best feature here is their excellent Por Que No? restaurant (p. 451).

2km (1¼ miles) south of Dominical, just off the coastal hwy., Dominicalito. www. costa-paraiso.com. ✆ **2787-0025.** 5 units. $140–$150 double. **Amenities:** Restaurant; small outdoor pool; free Wi-Fi.

Cuna del Angel ★★   This boutique-cum-country club hotel has a look that's part Boruca indigenous ceremonial dwellings (love the palapa roof over the restaurant) but inside feels more like an Italian villa. In the airy, amenity-laden "deluxe" rooms, walls are painted a warm ochre, beds have brocaded comforters and there are floor-to-ceiling windows and balustrade balconies. The standard "Jungle" rooms are going for a more Caribbean "shabby chic" look, with purposefully distressed armoires, and a simpler, woodsy decor. The grounds are lush (you'll spot monkeys and toucans) and there's a good-sized pool, a spa and a dining room specializing in healthy cuisine with numerous vegetarian and vegan choices, most of the produce coming from the hotel's own organic farm. The hotel earned "4 Leaves" in the CST Sustainable Tourism program.

9km (5½ miles) south of Dominical, just off the coastal hwy. www.cunadelangel.com. ✆ **2787-4343.** 22 units. $94–$250 double. Rates include buffet breakfast. **Amenities:** Restaurant; bar; Jacuzzi; outdoor pool; sauna; small spa, free Wi-Fi.

Inexpensive

In addition to the place listed below, you'll find a campground at Playa Ballena and a couple of basic *cabinas* in Bahía and Uvita. The best of these is the **Tucan Hotel** (www.tucanhotel.com; ✆ **2743-8140**), with a mix of private rooms and dorm accommodations and a friendly hostel-like vibe.

However, if you want to be closer to the beach, check out **Canto de Ballenas** (www.hotelcantoballenas.com; ✆ **2743-8085**), an interesting local cooperative with neat rooms located about .7km (a little less than a half-mile) from the national park entrance at Playa Uvita.

Hotel Villas Gaia ★   Down towards the end of the Costanera Sur highway, this quiet nature lodge offers up a handful of individual bungalows scattered through dense forests. Each of the bungalows comes with wooden walls, polished concrete floors, a private veranda and one twin and one queen bed. Most, but not all, have air-conditioning. The land here heads up a modest hill from the highway. At the top of the property, you'll find the pool and pool bar, as well as my favorite bungalows, which have great views over rain forests to the Pacific Ocean. The rest of the bungalows are surrounded by and look out into the lush forests. Whatever you do, do try to get one as far from the roadside and parking area as possible.

Playa Tortuga. www.villasgaia.com. © **2786-5044** reservations in San José, or 2786-5044 at the lodge. 14 units. $75–$90 double, rates includes breakfast. **Amenities:** Restaurant; bar; small outdoor pool, free Wi-Fi.

La Cusinga Lodge ★★   This is a small, sustainable ecolodge set on a lovely hillside with a view to Ballena National Park. Accommodations range from dorm rooms to private cabins, all of them charmingly rustic. Locally produced reforested lumber and river stones were used extensively throughout for the walls, floors, ceilings, bathrooms, walkways and pillars. Folks gather every afternoon in the beautiful open-air common area to take in the spectacular sunsets, while a handsome, large, open-air yoga center hosts regular classes and visiting retreat groups. A rugged trail leads down to a secluded beach, about a 10 to 15 minute walk away. The food is tops, mostly vegetarian and organic.

Bahía Ballena. www.lacusingalodge.com. © **2770-2549.** 10 units. $95–$172 double; $204 suite. Rates include breakfast. **Amenities:** Restaurant; small spa.

Pacific Edge ★   If "away from it all with drop dead ocean and valley views" sounds like just the ticket, this cabin compound is for you. Lots of guests spend lots of time just drinking in the vistas (like the sunsets from your hammock or one of the oversize balcony/deck areas). You can go birding (more than 800 species have been logged on property), take a swim in the pool or spot howler monkeys from the observation deck. As a place to stay, it has a homier vibe than most, thanks to the chatty owners George and Susie Atkisson, who love trading tales with guests over breakfast or dinner in the open-air bamboo dining room. The four cabins are rustic but appealing, their all-wood interiors livened up by bright Guatemalan fabrics on the beds and curtains. Solar panels provide hot water and power the cabins' reading lights.

Dominical. www.pacificedge.info. © **2200-5428.** 4 units. $70–$110 double. Rates include taxes. No children under 13. **Amenities:** Midsize outdoor pool; free Wi-Fi.

WHERE TO DINE

In addition to the places mentioned below, in Ojochal you'll also find the charming **Ylang-Ylang ★★** (© **2786-5054**), which serves up Indonesian fare Wednesday through Saturday, for dinner only.

Citrus Restaurante ★★ BISTRO/FUSION   This popular local spot mixes culinary influences from far and wide. You can start things off with a Caribbean inspired seafood soup with coconut milk and thyme, or fried calamari with a spicy Asian mayonnaise. For a main course, I recommend the yellow fin tuna with a Panko and wasabi crust served over organic soba noodles, with house-made tamarind-Siracha. There are also daily specials and a great range of cocktails and fresh fruit drinks. Whatever you do, be sure to save room for their basil and orange blossom crème brûlée and their Belgian chocolate and brandy mousse. The large main dining room features a high peaked ceiling with exposed wooden beams and a massive ironwork chandelier. But I prefer the sometimes breezy seating on the open-air garden facing patio. Weekend nights during the high season often feature live music, a DJ, or a belly dancer or fire performance troupe.

On the main road in Plaza Filibustero. ℂ **2786-5175** or 8304-1717. restocitrus@yahoo.ca. Reservations recommended. Main courses $10–$21 Mon–Sat noon–9:30pm. Reduced hours in the off season.

Exotica ★★★ FRENCH/INTERNATIONAL Robert and Lucy's roadside restaurant is the grand dame of Ojochal's unexpectedly vibrant fine dining scene. Only a handful of tables are found under the open-air thatch roof that houses this place and you'll definitely want to have a reservation. Although rooted in classic French cuisine, the menu shows a wide range of worldly influences especially from Thailand, Africa, and Costa Rica. There are daily specials, as well as longstanding favorites, like the namesake Chicken Exotica, which comes in a red pepper sauce and is stuffed with bacon, prunes, and blue cheese. *Note:* Exotica is the farthest of the bunch from the main road, and you may think you're lost before finding your way here.

1km (½ mile) inland from the turnoff for Ojochal. ℂ **2786-5050.** Reservations required. Main courses $10–$41. Tues–Sat 4–9pm.

Por Que No? ★★★ FUSION This casual, open-air spot serves up some excellent grub in a striking tropical setting. The best tables have ocean and coastline views. I especially like the tables in the separate little gazebo furthest away from the main building and closest to the water. From here it's a short walk to some ocean-fed tide pools. This is one of the best breakfast spots in the area, and as the day heats up, they also fire up their outdoor wood-burning brick pizza oven and serve gourmet pizzas for lunch and dinner. Sandwiches (really full meals on buns) range from jerk chicken to a veggie burger to the house special: slow pulled pork with a pineapple barbeque sauce. You can also get a refreshing cold Asian noodle salad, or some blackened mahi-mahi with a coffee and chipotle rub.

At Costa Paraiso Lodge. 2km (1¼ miles) south of Dominical, just off the coastal hwy., Dominicalito. www.cpporqueno.com. ℂ **2787-0025.** Main courses $7–$14; pizzas $16–$24. Tues–Sun 7am–1:30pm and 5–10pm.

SAN ISIDRO DE EL GENERAL: A BASE FOR EXPLORING CHIRRIPÓ NATIONAL PARK

120km (74 miles) SE of San José; 123km (76 miles) NW of Palmar Norte; 29km (18 miles) NE of Dominical

San Isidro de El General is just off the Interamerican Highway in the foothills of the Talamanca Mountains and is the largest town in this region. Although there isn't much to do right in town, this is the jumping-off point for trips to **Chirripó National Park.**

Essentials

GETTING THERE & DEPARTING   By Car: The long and winding stretch of the Interamerican Highway between San José and San Isidro is one of the most difficult sections of road in the country. Not only are there the usual car-eating potholes and periodic landslides, but you must also contend with driving over the 3,300m (10,824-ft.) **Cerro de la Muerte (Mountain of Death).** This aptly named mountain pass is legendary for its dense afternoon fogs, blinding torrential downpours, steep drop-offs, severe switchbacks, and unexpectedly breathtaking views. (Well, you wanted adventure travel, so here you go!) Drive with extreme caution, and bring a sweater or sweatshirt—it's cold up at the top. It'll take you about 3 hours to get to San Isidro.

Tip: If you want a break from the road, stop for a coffee or meal at **Mirador Valle del General** (www.valledelgeneral.com; ✆ **8384-4685** or 2200-5465; at Km 119), a rustic roadside joint with a great view, gift shop, hiking trails, and orchid collection. These folks also have a few rustic cabins, as well as a zip-line canopy tour.

By Bus: Musoc buses (✆ **2222-2422** in San José, or 2771-0414 in San Isidro) leave from their terminal at Calle Central and Avenida 22 roughly hourly between 5:30am and 6:30pm.

Tracopa (www.tracopacr.com; ✆ **2221-4214** or 2771-0468) also runs express buses between San José and San Isidro that leave at 6 and 8:30am and 12:30, 2:30, 4, and 6:30pm from Calle 5, between avenidas 18 and 20.

Whichever company you choose, the trip takes a little over 3 hours, and the fare is roughly C3,500. Return buses depart San Isidro for **San José** roughly every hour between 4:30am and 6:30pm. Buses from **Quepos** to San Isidro leave daily at 5:30 and 11:30am and 3pm. The trip duration is 3 hours; the fare is C2,500. Buses to or from **Golfito** and **Puerto Jiménez** will also drop you off in San Isidro.

CITY LAYOUT   Downtown San Isidro is just off the Interamerican Highway. A large church fronts the central park, and you'll find several banks,

Little Devils

If you're visiting the San Isidro area in February, head out to the nearby **Rey Curré** village for the **Fiesta of the Diablitos,** where costumed Boruca Indians perform dances representative of the Spanish conquest of Central America. The 3-day event also includes fireworks and an Indian handicraft market—this is *the* best place in Costa Rica to buy hand-carved Boruca masks. The date varies, so it's best to contact the **Costa Rica Tourist Board** (http://visitcostarica.com) for more information.

and a host of restaurants, shops, and hotels within a 2-block radius of the park. The main bus station is 2 blocks west of the north end of the central park.

Exploring Chirripó National Park ★★

At 3,819m (12,526 ft.) in elevation, Mount Chirripó is the tallest mountain in Costa Rica. If you're headed up this way, come prepared for chilly weather. Actually, dress in layers and come prepared for all sorts of weather: Because of the great elevations, temperatures frequently dip below freezing, especially at night. However, during the day, temperatures can soar—remember, you're still only 9 degrees from the equator. The elevation and radical temperatures have produced an environment here that's very different from the Costa Rican norm. Above 3,000m (9,840 ft.), only stunted trees and shrubs survive in páramos. If you're driving the Interamerican Highway between San Isidro and San José, you'll pass through a páramo on the Cerro de la Muerte.

Hiking up to the top of Mount Chirripó is one of Costa Rica's best adventures. On a clear day (usually in the morning), an unforgettable **view ★★★** is your reward: You can see both the Pacific Ocean and the Caribbean Sea from the summit. Although it's possible to hike from the park entrance to the summit and back down in 2 days (in fact, some daredevils even do it in 1 day), it's best to allow 3 to 4 days for the trip in order to give yourself time to enjoy your hike fully and spend some time on top, because that's where the glacier lakes and páramos are. For much of the way, you'll be hiking through cloud forests that are home to abundant tropical fauna, including the spectacular **quetzal,** Costa Rica's most beautiful bird. However, quetzal sightings on summit climbs are rare. If you really want to see one of these birds, head to one of the specialized lodges listed below.

Mount Chirripó.

Several routes lead to the top of Mount Chirripó. The most popular, by far, leaves from **San Gerardo de Rivas.** However, it's also possible to start your hike from the nearby towns of **Herradura** or **Canaan.** All these places are within less than 2km (a mile) or so of each other, reached by the same major road out of San Isidro. San Gerardo is the most popular because it's the easiest route to the top and has the greatest collection of small hotels and lodges, as well as the National Parks office. Information on all of these routes is available at the parks office.

When you're at the summit lodge, you have a number of hiking options. Just in front of the lodge are Los Crestones (the Crests), an impressive rock formation, with trails leading up and around them. The most popular, however, is to the actual summit (the lodge itself is a bit below the summit itself), which is about a 2-hour hike that passes through the Valle de los Conejos (Rabbit Valley) and the Valle de los Lagos (Valley of Lakes). Other hikes and trails lead off from the summit lodge, and it's easy to spend a couple of days hiking around here. A few trails will take you to the summits of several neighboring peaks. These hikes should be undertaken only after carefully studying an accurate map and talking to park rangers and other hikers.

Warning: It can be dangerous for more inexperienced or out-of-shape hikers to climb Chirripó, especially by themselves. It's not very technical climbing, but it is a long, arduous hike. If you're not sure you're up for it, you can just take day hikes out of San Isidro and/or San Gerardo de Rivas, or ask at your hotel about guides.

ENTRY POINT, FEES & REGULATIONS   Although it's not that difficult to get to Chirripó National Park from nearby San Isidro, it's still rather remote. Moreover, the most difficult part of hiking Chirripo just might be the arcane reservation system. Before climbing Mount Chirripó, you must make a reservation with the local office of **SINAC,** basically the National Parks Service (© **2742-5083**). This office is officially open from 8am to noon and 1pm to 4pm, Monday through Friday for reservations, although they begin taking reservations on the first Monday of every fourth month for the subsequent next 4 months in the future. Slots sell out fast—often on the first day. In the past, walk-in hikers were usually allowed to climb up the following day, but this practice has been cut off and advanced reservations are required now.

Once you have a slot you must then check in with **Aguas Eternas Chirripo** (© **2742-5097;** infochirriposervicios@gmail.com) in San Gerardo de Rivas. This is a consortium of local businesses that handles the specific reservations for room and board up at the summit lodge. Without excellent Spanish skills and persistence, it's very hard to reserve a slot in advance. Many folks rely on their local hotel or an agency to do so. The park service only allows a maximum of 3 nights at the lodge.

Once you have a reservations all ironed out you will need to get to the trail head. You have three choices: car, taxi, or bus. If you choose to drive, take the road out of San Isidro, heading north toward San Gerardo de Rivas, which is some 20km (12 miles) down the road. Otherwise, you can catch a bus in San Isidro that will take you directly to the trail head in San Gerardo de Rivas. Buses (© **2771-2314**) leave about a half-dozen times daily from the bus station beside the central market, a block or so south of San Isidro's central park, beginning around 5:45am. It costs C1,010 one-way and takes 1½ hours. Buses return to San Isidro daily at roughly the same frequency every day. A taxi from town should cost around C15,000 to C20,000.

Because the hike to the summit of Mount Chirripó can take between 6 and 12 hours, depending on your physical condition, I recommend taking a taxi, so that you can start hiking when the day is still young. Better

Movin' On Up

From San Gerardo de Rivas, the 14.5km (9-mile) trail to the summit lodge is well marked and well maintained. The early parts of the trail are pretty steep and will take you through thick cloud forests and rainforests. After about 7.5km (4.7 miles), you will reach the "Water Ridge," a flat ridge that features a small shelter and water spigot. This is roughly the midway point to the lodge and a great place to take a break.

From Water Ridge, three steep uphill sections remain: Cuesta de Agua (Water Hill), Monte Sin Fe (Mountain Without Hope), and La Cuesta de los Arrepentidos (The Hill of Regret). As you continue to climb, you will notice the flora changing. The entire elevation gain for this hike is 2,200m (7,215 ft.). La Cuesta de los Arrepentidos, your final ascent, brings you to a broad flat valley, where you'll find the summit lodge. This hike can take anywhere from 6 to 10 hours, depending on how long you linger along the way.

still, you should arrive the day before and spend the night in San Gerardo de Rivas (there are several inexpensive *cabinas,* a couple of mid-range options, and one very nice hotel there) before setting out early the following morning.

Note that camping is not allowed in the park. It's possible to have your gear carried up to the summit by horseback during the dry season (Dec–Apr). Independent guides and porters can always be found outside the park entrance in San Gerardo de Rivas. They charge between $30 and $40 per pack, depending on size and weight. In the rainy season, the same guides work, but they take packs up by themselves, not by horseback. The guides like to take up the packs well before dawn, so arrangements are best made the day before. The entrance fee to the national park is $18 per day.

STAYING AT THE SUMMIT LODGE   Once you get to the lodge, you'll find various rooms with bunk beds, several bathrooms and showers, and a common kitchen area, as well as a simple restaurant. It has good drinking water. **Note:** It gets cold up here at night, and the lodge seems to have been designed to be as cold, dark, and cavernous as possible. The showers are freezing. It costs $35 per person per night to stay here, and this includes a sheet, blanket and sleeping bag. Buffet meals at the restaurant run around $10 for breakfast, and $14 for lunch or dinner.

Other Adventures in & Around San Isidro

If you want to undertake any other adventures while in San Isidro, contact **Costa Rica Trekking Adventures** (www.chirripo.com; ✆ **2771-4582**), which offers organized treks through Chirripó National Park, as well as white-water rafting trips and other adventure tours.

Just 7km (4⅓ miles) from San Isidro is **Las Quebradas Biological Center** (✆ **2771-4131**), a community-run private reserve with 2.7km (1.75 miles) of trails through primary rainforest. The rustic lodge for visitors and researchers is $8 per person (C25,000 per person, if part of a group, including three meals and entrance to the center), and camping is also permitted. You can hike the trails and visit the small information center on site for $4. From San Isidro, you can take a local bus to Quebradas, but you'll have to walk the last mile to the entrance. You can also take a taxi for around C7,000. If you're driving, take the road to Morazán and Quebradas.

Alternative Booking Options

Since the reservation process is so complex and difficult for foreign tourists, your best bet is to coordinate your climb with a local hotel or tour operator.

Ocarina Expeditions (www.ocarina expeditions.com; ✆ **2269-6074**) is one of the best and most experienced local operators to use for Chirripo climbs.

Race to the Top

If simply climbing the tallest peak in Costa Rica is a bit too mundane for you, why not join the annual **Carrera Campo Traviesa Al Cerro Chirripó** (www.carrera chirripo.com). Held the third or fourth Saturday of February, this is a grueling 34km (21-mile) race from the base to the summit and back. The record time, to date, is 3 hours, 15 minutes, and 3 seconds.

Where to Stay & Dine in San Isidro

San Isidro doesn't have much of a dining scene. Sure, the town has its fair share of local joints and simple *sodas*, but most visitors are content at their hotel restaurant. If you do venture beyond your hotel, I recommend stopping in at **Delicias Cafe ★★** (© 2770-2421), a lively and inviting coffee shop and simple restaurant, just across from the central park. Another good option for a coffee break or light meal is **Kafe de la Casa ★** (© 2770-4816), which offers up free Wi-Fi, along with its regular breakfast, lunch, and dinner menu, and is located next to the **Thunderbird Hotel & Casino** (www.tbrcr.com; © 2770-9100).

INEXPENSIVE

Hotel Los Crestones ★ Central San Isidro doesn't have a lot of great hotel choices, but this downtown option is the best of the bunch. A complex of two- and three-story pale yellow buildings, it offers basic rooms with tile floors and bare walls. A small television is hung in the corner. The hotel has a swimming pool and outdoor Jacuzzi for guests to use. Secure parking is provided in the central area between the buildings. Los Crestones is on the main road heading out to Dominical, on the south side of the city, across from the main soccer stadium.

San Isidro de El General (southwest side of the stadium). www.hotelloscrestones. com. © **908/751-3602** in the U.S or 2770-1200 in Costa Rica. 27 units. $50–$60 double. **Amenities:** Restaurant; outdoor pool; room service.

Where to Stay & Dine Closer to the Trail Head

If you're climbing Mount Chirripó, you'll want to spend the night as close to the trail head as possible. As I mention above, several basic *cabinas* right in San Gerardo de Rivas charge between $10 and $30 per person. The best of these are **El Descanso** (www.hoteldescansocr. com;©2742-5061), **CasaMariposa** (www.hotelcasamariposa.net;©2742-5037), and **Roca Dura** (© 2742-5071; rocadurareservations@gmail. com). If you're looking for a little more comfort and a swimming pool, check out **El Pelicano** (www.hotelpelicano.net; © 2742-5050), the **Río Chirripó Retreat** (www.riochirripo.com; © 2742-5109), or the hotels listed below.

Rest Your Weary Muscles Here

If you're tired and sore from so much hiking, be sure to check out the small **Aguas Termales Gevi** (☏ **2742-5210**), located off the road between San Gerardo de Rivas and Herradura. The entrance to these humble hot springs is 1km (½ mile) beyond San Gerardo de Rivas. There are two small pools here, as well as showers and changing rooms. The entrance fee is C3,500.

For good general information on the tiny village and its surrounding area, check out www.sangerardocostarica.com.

EXPENSIVE

Monte Azul ★★★   This boutique hotel is chic, artsy and luxurious. Set among lush gardens, the casitas are spacious and brimming with contemporary art, part of the owners' collection (they have a huge studio space on the grounds and often host visiting artists). All lodgings feature a queen-size bed, kitchenette, and a private garden patio. Spa treatments are offered in the comfort of your room, and meals at the hotel's Café Blue restaurant are terrific, using only organic and locally produced fruits, vegetables, coffees, meats, and cheeses. Various arts, crafts, cooking and mixology classes are regularly held, and the hotel has an extensive network of trails, as well as good access to the relatively nearby Chirripó National Park.

Rivas, San Isidro. www.monteazulcr.com. ☏ **415/967-4300** in the U.S. or 2742-5222 in Costa Rica. 4 casitas. $498 double. Rates include 3 daily meals. **Amenities:** Restaurant; bar; concierge; free Wi-Fi

INEXPENSIVE

Talari Mountain Lodge ★   This lodge offers up more comfortable rooms and better grounds at nearly the same low price as the cluster of backpacker hotels near the Chirripó National Park entrance. It's set on the banks of the Río General, some 8km (5 miles) outside of San Isidro. Rooms are housed in a simple buildings set on plain concrete blocks, with clay tile roofs, and whole tree trunks used as columns to hold up that roof. These tree trunks also come in handy for supporting the hammocks that are generously hung around. While cozy, the rooms certainly feel as if they could use a little modernization.

Rivas, San Isidro. www.talari.co.cr. ☏ **2771-0341.** 14 units. $84 double. Rates include full breakfast. **Amenities:** Restaurant; bar; Jacuzzi; small outdoor pool and separate children's pool; indoor lit tennis court.

A Luxury Hacienda

Set on an expansive piece of land on the outskirts of San Isidro, **Alta Gracia ★★** (www.altagracia.cr; ☏ **2105-3000**) is a collection of 50 individual *casitas*, or little houses, three restaurants, boutique spa and equestrian center. This very exclusive and expensive retreat features its own private airstrip accepting charter and private flights in, and offering up ultralight flights around the region.

Where to See Quetzals in the Wild: Cerro de la Muerte & San Gerardo de Dota ★★

Between San José and San Isidro de El General, the Interamerican Highway climbs to its highest point in Costa Rica and crosses over the **Cerro de la Muerte (the Mountain of Death).** About midway between San Isidro and Cartago, a deep valley descends toward the Pacific coast and the tiny town of San Gerardo de Dota. This area is one of the best places in Costa Rica to see quetzals. March through May is nesting season for these birds, and this is usually the best time to see them. However, it's often possible to spot them year round. On my first visit here, during a 2-hour hike without a guide, my small group spotted eight of these amazing birds. I was hooked.

If you plan on spending any time in the region and want to take an organized tour, contact **Santos Tours ★** (www.santostour.net; © **8855-9386**), a local, community tourism project that offers a range of active adventures, including waterfall hikes, coffee plantation tours, and even a canopy tour.

In addition to the places listed below, **Dantica Cloud Forest Lodge ★** (www.dantica.com; © **2740-1067**) is a small collection of lovely, private bungalows in a forested setting near San Gerardo de Dota.

MODERATE

Savegre Hotel ★   Also known as Finca Chacón, this hotel is owned by the local Chacón family, who were pioneers in converting this remote rural farming area into a mecca for bird watchers and ecotourists. The small resort is spread around a working apple and pear farm. These fruit trees, as well as the surrounding cloud and rain forests, attract more than 180 species of birds, including the prized Resplendent Quetzal. Rooms are very clean and spacious, with tile floors and wood paneling on the walls. Each comes with a little space heater or fireplace, which is often necessary. The lodge is 9km (5½ miles) down a rugged dirt road off the Interamerican Highway. Four-wheel-drive is recommended, although not absolutely necessary. GPS: Latitude: 9°33[sp]2.46"N; Longitude: 83°48[sp]27.66"O

Carretera Interamericana Sur Km 80, San Gerardo de Dota. www.savegre.com. © **866/549-1178** in the U.S. and Canada or 2740-1028 in Costa Rica. 50 units. $110–$150 double. Rates include breakfast, entrance to their reserve, and taxes. **Amenities:** Restaurant; bar; spa; free Wi-Fi.

Trogón Lodge ★   This is a pretty little nature lodge in a splendid setting. The rooms are in individual and duplex buildings scattered over rolling hillsides and well-tended gardens. At the center, there's a mid-size pond stocked with local trout and featuring a deck out into its center, which you can use for sightseeing or a fishing perch. Even if you don't fish for the trout yourself, you'll often find it on the menu here. The varnished wood rooms are homey and enlivened by a simple photo or flower print framed and hung above the beds. They could use a little more light, but they do have gas heaters and plenty of room, and most have a very pleasant little porch or veranda. There is also a zip line on site here. This is a sister lodge to Mawamba Lodge (p. 522) in Tortuguero.

Carretera Interamericana Sur Km 80, San Gerardo de Dota. www.trogonlodge.com. ℂ **2293-8181** in San José, or 2740-1051 at the lodge. 23 units. $106 double; $162 junior suite with Jacuzzi. Rates include breakfast. A full meal package runs $30–$39 per person. **Amenities:** Restaurant; bar; lounge.

INEXPENSIVE

Albergue Mirador de Quetzales ★   This is one of the more rustic of the quetzal viewing lodges in this area. It's also the closest to the main highway. Also, known as Finca Eddie Serrano, it is run by the friendly local Serrano family. Choose from a series of small wooden cabins and A-frame log cabins, as well as dormitory rooms in the main lodge building. Inside you'll find low-lying beds and exposed log or varnished wood walls. Many have low ceilings, thanks to the pitch of the A-frame roofs. Meals are served family style and both breakfast and dinner are included in the rates, as is a 2-hour guided tour of trails through the lodge's private reserve. The quetzal viewing at this place is as good as it gets, especially between December and May, although they can often be spotted year round.

Carretera Interamericana Sur Km 70, about 1km (½ mile) down a dirt road from the hwy. www.elmiradordequetzales.com. ℂ **8381-8456** or 2200-4185. 15 units. $70 per person. Rate includes breakfast and dinner, a 2-hr. tour, and taxes. **Amenities:** Restaurant.

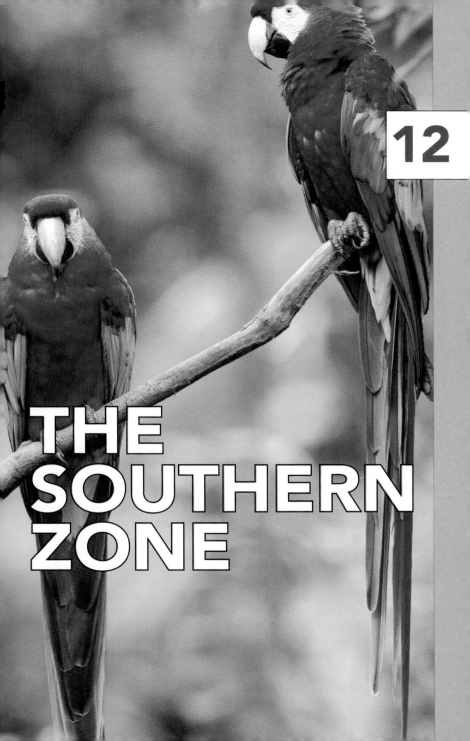

12

THE SOUTHERN ZONE

Costa Rica's southern zone is an area of jaw-dropping beauty, with vast expanses of virgin lowland rainforest, loads of wildlife, tons of adventure opportunities, and few cities, towns, or settlements. When people ask, I invariably answer that this is my favorite part of Costa Rica. Lushly forested mountains tumble into the sea, streams still run clear and clean, scarlet macaws squawk raucously in the treetops, and dolphins and whales frolic in the Golfo Dulce. The Osa Peninsula is the most popular attraction in this region and one of the premier ecotourism destinations in the world. It's home to **Corcovado National Park ★★★**, the largest single expanse of lowland tropical rainforest in Central America, and its sister, **Piedras Blancas National Park ★★**. Scattered around the edges of these national parks and along the shores of the Golfo Dulce are some of the country's finest nature lodges. These lodges, in general, offer comfortable to nearly luxurious accommodations, attentive service, knowledgeable guides, and a wide range of activities and tours, all close to the area's many natural wonders.

But this beauty doesn't come easy. If you want to visit the Southern zone properly, you should have plenty of time (or plenty of money—or, preferably, both) and a desire for adventure. It's a long way from San José, and many of the most fascinating spots can be reached only by small plane or boat—although hiking and four-wheeling will get you into some memorable surroundings as well. And take into consideration, most of the most famous and "luxurious" of the nature lodges in this area have no televisions, telephones, Wi-Fi or other modern amenities. In many cases, they boast outdoor bathrooms and large windows and doors that are meant to be kept wide open in order to better commune with nature.

In many ways, this is Costa Rica's final frontier, and the cities of Golfito and Puerto Jiménez are nearly as wild as the jungles that surround them. Tourism is still underdeveloped here, with no large resorts in this neck of the woods. Moreover, the heat and humidity are more

PREVIOUS PAGE: **Scarlet Macaws in Corcovado.**

than some people can stand. It's best to put some forethought into a vacation down here, and wise to book your rooms and transportation in advance.

THE best SOUTHERN ZONE TRAVEL EXPERIENCES

- **Hiking in Corcovado National Park:** The Neotropic's largest single tract of lowland rainforest provides fabulous hiking opportunities, with beautiful forest trails, isolated jungle waterfalls, and a bounty of wildlife spotting opportunities. See p. 480.

- **Paddling a Kayak on the Golfo Dulce:** The calm, protected waters of the "Sweet Gulf" are perfect for kayaking. Gorgeous sunsets and dolphin or whale sightings are additional perks that sometimes come with the territory. See p. 479.

- **Landing a Billfish:** The waters of southern Costa Rica are some of the country's richest fishing grounds, with a long list of world record catches. Hook a blue marlin or sailfish for some serious deep sea adventure. See p. 494.

- **Scuba Diving or Snorkeling at Caño Island:** The clear waters around this isolated Pacific island consistently offer up Costa Rica's best snorkeling and scuba diving. You're almost guaranteed to see white tip reef sharks. See p. 469.

- **Riding a Seemingly Endless Wave in Pavones:** This legendary left is well known and probably best left to serious surfers. However, even if this is beyond your ken, a host of other point breaks around the southern zone are perfect for more intermediate surfers, and even rank beginners. See p. 502.

DRAKE BAY ★★

145km (90 miles) S of San José; 32km (20 miles) SW of Palmar

While Drake Bay remains one of the more isolated spots in Costa Rica, the small town located at the mouth of the **Río Agujitas** has boomed over the years. Most of that is due to the year-round operation of the small airstrip here, and the sometimes passable condition of the rough dirt road connecting Drake Bay to the coastal highway—just a decade or so ago there was no road, and the nearest regularly functioning airstrip was in Palmar Sur. That said, the village of Drake Bay is still tiny, and the lodges listed here remain quiet and remote getaways catering to naturalists, anglers, and scuba divers. Tucked away on the northern edge of the Osa Peninsula, Drake Bay is a great place to get away from it all.

The bay is named after Sir Francis Drake, who is believed to have anchored here in 1579. Emptying into a broad bay, the tiny Río Agujitas

Flock of wild Scarlet Macaws flying near Drake Bay, Corcovado National Park.

acts as a protected harbor for small boats and is a great place to do a bit of canoeing or swimming. Many of the local lodges dock their boats and many **dolphin- and whale-watching tours** leave from here. Stretching south from Drake Bay are miles of deserted beaches and dense primary tropical rainforest. Adventurous explorers will find tide pools, spring-fed rivers, waterfalls, forest trails, and some of the best birdwatching in all of Costa Rica. If a paradise such as this appeals to you, Drake Bay makes a good base for exploring the peninsula.

South of Drake Bay are the wilds of the **Osa Península,** including **Corcovado National Park.** This is one of Costa Rica's most beautiful regions, yet it's also one of its least accessible. Corcovado National Park covers about half of the peninsula and contains the largest single expanse of virgin lowland rainforest in Central America. For this reason, Corcovado is well known among naturalists and researchers studying rainforest ecology. If you come here, you'll learn firsthand why they call them rainforests: Some parts of the peninsula receive more than 635cm (250 in.) of rain per year.

Puerto Jiménez (p. 474) is the best base if you want to spend a lot of time hiking in and camping inside Corcovado National Park. Drake Bay is primarily a collection of mostly high-end hotels, very isolated and mostly accessible by boat. Travelers using these hotels can have great day hikes and guided tours into Corcovado Park, but Puerto Jiménez is the

---

Helping Out

If you want to help local efforts in protecting the fragile rainforests and wild areas of the Osa Peninsula, contact the **Corcovado Foundation** (www.corcovado foundation.org; ⓒ **2297-3013**) or **Osa Conservation** (www.osaconservation. org; ⓒ **2735-5756**). Moreover, if you're looking to really lend a hand, both of the aforementioned groups have volunteer programs ranging from trail maintenance to environmental and English-language education to sea-turtle-nesting protection programs.

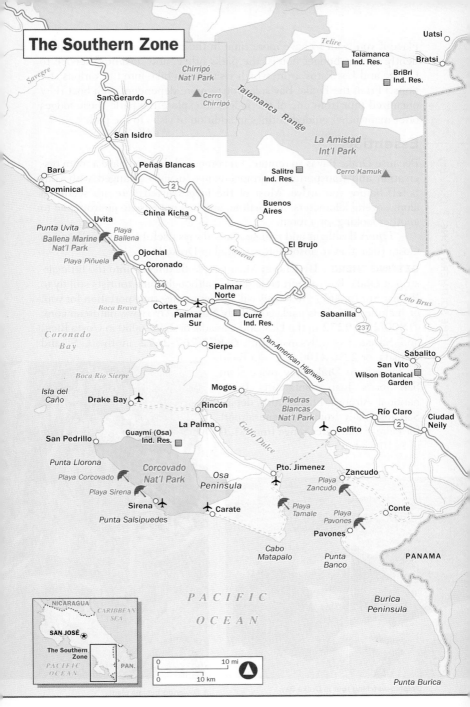

The Southern Zone

Uatsi

Telire

Bratsi

Talamanca
Ind. Res.

BriBri
Ind. Res.

Savegre

Chirripó
Nat'l Park

Cerro
Chirripó

Talamanca Range

La Amistad
Int'l Park

San Gerardo

San Isidro

Cerro Kamuk

Barú

Peñas Blancas

Salitre
Ind. Res.

Dominical

2

Uvita

China Kicha

Buenos
Aires

Punta Uvita

Playa
Ballena

Ballena Marine
Nat'l Park

El Brujo

Playa Piñuela

Ojochal

General

Coronado

34

Boca Brava

Cortes

Palmar
Norte

Palmar
Sur

Currě
Ind. Res.

Sabanilla

Coto Brus

237

Coronado
Bay

Sierpe

Pan-American Highway

Sabalito

Boca Río Sierpe

Mogos

San Vito

Sabanilla

Wilson Botanical
Garden

Isla del
Caño

Drake Bay

Rincón

Piedras
Blancas
Nat'l Park

Río Claro

Ciudad
Neily

San Pedrillo

La Palma

Golfo Dulce

Golfito

2

Guaymí (Osa)
Ind. Res.

Punta Llorona

Corcovado
Nat'l Park

Osa
Peninsula

Pto. Jimenez

Zancudo

Playa Corcovado

Playa
Zancudo

Conte

Playa Sirena

Sirena

Carate

Playa
Tamale

Playa
Pavones

Punta Salsipuedes

Cabo
Matapalo

Punta
Banco

Pavones

PANAMA

PACIFIC

Burica
Peninsula

OCEAN

NICARAGUA

CARIBBEAN
SEA

SAN JOSÉ

The Southern
Zone

PACIFIC
OCEAN

PAN.

0   10 mi

0   10 km

Punta Burica

place if you want to have more time in the park or to explore independently. (It has budget hotels, the parks office, and "taxi/bus" service to Carate and Los Patos, from which visitors can hike into the various stations.) From the Drake Bay side, you're more dependent on a boat ride/organized tour from one of the lodges to explore the park; these lodges offer many other guided outings in addition to visits to the park.

Essentials

Because Drake Bay is so remote, I recommend that you have a room reservation and transportation arrangements (usually arranged with your hotel) before you arrive. Most of the lodges listed here are scattered along several kilometers of coastline, and it is not easy to go from one to another looking for a room.

Tip: A flashlight and rain gear are always useful to have on hand in Costa Rica; they're absolutely essential in Drake Bay.

GETTING THERE   By Plane: Most people fly directly into the little airstrip at Drake Bay (airport code: DRK), although some tourists still fly to Palmar Sur (p. 467). All lodges will either arrange transportation for you, or include it in their packages. Both **Nature Air** (www.natureair.com; ✆ **800/235-9272** in the U.S. and Canada, or 2299-6000 in Costa Rica) and **Sansa** (www.flysansa.com; ✆ **877/767-2672** in the U.S. and Canada, or 2290-4100 in Costa Rica) fly directly to Drake Bay twice from San José's Juan Santamaría International Airport. Flights also depart San José daily from the same airport for Palmar Sur. Fares range from $120 to $210 each way.

A flowering banana plant.

Dolphin-watching tour in Drake Bay.

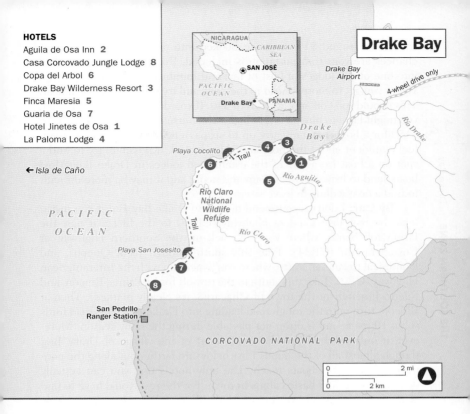

HOTELS

Aguila de Osa Inn **2**
Casa Corcovado Jungle Lodge **8**
Copa del Arbol **6**
Drake Bay Wilderness Resort **3**
Finca Maresia **5**
Guaria de Osa **7**
Hotel Jinetes de Osa **1**
La Paloma Lodge **4**

← Isla de Caño

If your travels take you to Drake Bay via Palmar Sur, you must then take a 15-minute bus or taxi ride over dirt roads to the small town of **Sierpe.** This bumpy route runs through several **banana plantations** and quickly past some important archaeological sites. In Sierpe, you board a small boat for a 40km (25-mile) ride to Drake Bay; see "By Taxi & Boat from Sierpe," below. The first half of this trip snakes through a maze of mangrove canals and rivers before heading out to sea for the final leg to the bay. *Warning:* Entering and exiting the Sierpe River mouth is often treacherous; I've had several white-knuckle moments here.

By Bus: Tracopa buses (www.tracopacr.com; ✆ **2221-4214** or 2290-1308) leave San José daily for the southern zone throughout the day, between 5am and 6:30pm from Calle 9 and avenida 18. Almost all stop in Palmar Norte, but make sure to ask. The ride takes around 6 hours; fares range from C7,590 to C7,970.

Once in Palmar Norte, ask when the next bus goes out to Sierpe. If it doesn't leave for a while (buses aren't frequent), consider taking a taxi.

By Taxi & Boat from Sierpe: When you arrive at either the Palmar Norte bus station or the Palmar Sur airstrip (airport code: PMZ), you'll most likely first need to take a taxi to the village of Sierpe. The fare should be around $15. If you're booked into one of the main lodges, chances are your transportation is included. Even if you're not booked into one of the lodges, a host of taxi and minibus drivers offer the trip. When you get to Sierpe, head to the dock and try to find space on a boat. This should run you another $20 to $40. If you don't arrive early enough, you might have to hire an entire boat, which usually runs around $100 to $150 for a boat that can carry up to six passengers. Make sure that you feel confident about the boat and skipper, and, if possible, try to find a spot on a boat from one of the established lodges in Drake Bay. Most boats tend to leave between 9am and noon, and it may be more difficult to find a boat willing to leave later.

By Car: I don't recommend driving to Drake Bay. But if you insist, take the San José–Caldera Highway (CR27) to the first exit past the Pozón toll booth, where you will pick up the Southern Highway, or Costanera Sur (CR34). Take this south through Jacó, Quepos, and Dominical to Palmar Norte, where you'll meet up with the Interamerican Highway (CR2). Take this south to the turnoff for La Palma, Rincón, and Puerto Jiménez (at the town of Chacarita; it's clearly marked). Then at Rincón, turn onto the rough road leading into Drake Bay. This road fords some 10 rivers and is often not passable during the rainy season. Moreover, it only reaches into the small heart of the village of Drake Bay, though almost all of the hotels I list below are farther out along the peninsula, where only boats reach. The only hotels that you can actually drive up to are very basic cabins in town. For the rest, you'd have to find someplace secure to leave your car and either haul your bags quite a way or get picked up in a boat.

DEPARTING   If you're not flying directly out of Drake Bay, have your lodge arrange a boat trip back to Sierpe for you. Be sure that the lodge also arranges for a taxi to meet you in Sierpe for the trip to Palmar Sur or Palmar Norte. (If you're on a budget, you can ask around to see whether a late-morning public bus is still running from Sierpe to Palmar Norte.) In the two Palmars, you can make onward plane and bus connections. At the Palmar Norte bus terminal, almost any bus heading north will take you to San José, and almost any bus heading south will take you to Golfito.

Exploring Drake Bay

Beaches, forests, wildlife, and solitude are the main attractions of Drake Bay. Although Corcovado National Park (see "Puerto Jiménez: Gateway to Corcovado National Park," p. 474) is the area's star attraction, plenty of other attractions are in and around Drake Bay. The Osa Peninsula is home to an unbelievable variety of plants and animals: more than 140 species of mammals, some 400 species of birds, and 130 species of amphibians and reptiles. You aren't likely to see anywhere near all of these animals, but you can expect to see quite a few, including several

A Baird's tapir.

types of monkeys, coatimundis, scarlet macaws, parrots, and humming-birds. Other park inhabitants include jaguars, tapirs, sloths, and croco-diles. If you're lucky, you might even see one of the region's namesake *osas,* or giant anteaters.

Around Drake Bay and within the national park are many miles of trails through rainforests and swamps, down beaches, and around rock headlands. All of the lodges listed offer guided excursions into the park. It's also possible to begin a hike around the peninsula from Drake Bay.

All lodges in the area have their own in-house tour operations and offer a host of half- and full-day tours and activities, including hikes in Corcovado National Park, trips to Caño Island, horseback rides, and sportfishing. In some cases, tours are included in your room rate or pack-age; in others, they must be bought a la carte. Other options include mountain biking and sea kayaking. Most of these tours run between $60 and $120, depending on the activity, with scuba diving ($100–$140 for a two-tank dive) and sportfishing ($900–$1,800, depending on the size of the boat and other amenities) costing a bit more.

CANOPY TOUR   If you want to try a zip-line canopy adventure, the **Drake Bay Canopy Tour** (www.canopytourdrakebay.com; ✆ **8314-5454** or 2231-5806) has six cable runs, several "Tarzan swings," and a hanging bridge, all set in lush forests just outside of Drake Bay. The 2-hour tour costs $35 taxes included.

ISLA DEL CAÑO   One of the most popular excursions from Drake Bay is a trip out to **Isla del Caño** and the **Caño Island Biological Reserve** ★★ for a bit of exploring and snorkeling or scuba diving. The

THOSE MYSTERIOUS stone spheres

Although Costa Rica lacks the great cities, giant temples, and bas-relief carvings of the Maya, Aztec, and Olmec civilizations of northern Mesoamerica, its pre-Columbian residents did leave a unique legacy that continues to cause archaeologists and anthropologists to scratch their heads and wonder. Over a period of several centuries, hundreds of painstakingly carved and carefully positioned granite spheres were left by the peoples who lived throughout the Diquis Delta, which flanks the Térraba River in southern Costa Rica. The orbs, which range from grapefruit size to more than 2m (6½ ft.) in diameter, can weigh up to 15 tons, and many reach near-spherical perfection.

Archaeologists believe that the spheres were created during two defined cultural periods. The first, called the Aguas Buenas period, dates from around a.d. 100 to 500. Few spheres survive from this time. The second phase, during which spheres were created in apparently greater numbers, is called the Chiriquí period and lasted from approximately a.d. 800 to 1500. The "balls" believed to have been carved during this time frame are widely dispersed along the entire length of the lower section of the Téraba River. To date, only one known quarry for the spheres has been discovered, in the mountains above the Diquis Delta, which points to a difficult and lengthy transportation process.

Some archaeologists believe that the spheres were hand-carved in a very time-consuming process, using stone tools, perhaps aided by some sort of firing process. However, another theory holds that granite blocks were placed at the bases of powerful waterfalls, and the hydraulic beating of the water eventually turned and carved the rock into these near-perfect spheres. And more than a few proponents have credited extraterrestrial intervention for the creation of the stone balls.

Most of the stone balls have been found at the archaeological remains of defined settlements and are associated with either central plazas or known burial sites. Their size and placement have been interpreted to have both social and celestial importance, although their exact significance remains a mystery. Unfortunately, many of the stone balls have been plundered and are currently used as lawn ornaments in the fancier neighborhoods of San José. Some have even been shipped out of the country. The **Museo Nacional de Costa Rica** (p. 132) has a nice collection, including one massive sphere in its center courtyard. It's a never-fail photo op. You can also see the stone balls near the small **airports in Palmar Sur** and **Drake Bay,** and on **Isla del Caño** (which is 19km/12 miles off the Pacific Coast near Drake Bay).

The best place to see the spheres is the **Finca 6 Archeological Museum** ★★ (*©* **2100-6000;** daily 8am–4pm; $6), located between Palmar Sur and Sierpe. It is estimated that nearly 10 percent of all stone spheres produced in Costa Rica can be found on the 10 or so acres that comprise Finca 6. A small museum building provides background and displays of some smaller spheres and other artifacts. From here trails lead out to several excavations of archeological finds where a range of large stone spheres, stelae, and other relics are displayed in their natural and original positioning. Finca 6 is located 6km south of Palmar Sur. This unique archeological site is easily visited by anyone arriving or departing Drake Bay via Sierpe.

Snorkelers at Caño Island Biological Reserve.

island is about 19km (12 miles) offshore from Drake Bay and was once home to a pre-Columbian culture about which little is known. A trip to the island might include a visit to an ancient cemetery, and you'll also be able to see some of the stone spheres believed to have been carved by this area's ancient inhabitants (p. 470). Few animals or birds live on the island, but the coral reefs just offshore teem with life making this one of Costa Rica's prime **scuba diving sites ★★**. Visibility is often quite good, and the beach has easily accessible snorkeling. All of the lodges listed below offer trips to Isla del Caño. As of 2014, the Costa Rican National Park service has been severely restricting access to the island, and visiting groups are no longer allowed to picnic on the island. Typically, tours arrive in the morning, conduct their snorkel and scuba excursions, and then head back to the mainland for a picnic lunch and some beach time.

NIGHT TOUR   One of the most compelling tour options in Drake Bay is a 2-hour **night tour ★★★** (www.thenighttour.com; ✆ **8701-7356** or 8701-7462; $35 per person) offered by Tracie Stice, who is affectionately known as the "Bug Lady," and her partner Gianfranco Gómez. Equipped with flashlights, participants get a bug's-eye view of the forest at night. You might see reflections of some larger forest dwellers, but most of the tour is a fascinating exploration of the nocturnal insect and arachnid world, with the occasional discovery of some frogs, toads, or snakes. Consider yourself lucky if she finds the burrow of a trap-door spider or large tarantula. Any hotel in Drake Bay can book the tour for you. However, the travel distance makes it impossible for those staying at hotels outside of walking distance of the town.

WHALE-WATCHING   Drake Bay is one of the best places to go **whale-watching** in Costa Rica; humpback whales are commonly spotted in the area between late July and November and December through March. There are currently no dedicated whale-watching operators in the area, but all the hotels listed below can arrange whale-watching, as well as dolphin-spotting, trips. Two resident marine biologists, Shawn Larkin and Roy Sancho, are often hired by the better hotels, but depending on demand and availability, the hotels may send you out with one of their own guides and/or captains.

If you want more information on the local whale-watching scene, or to contact Shawn Larkin directly, head to the website **www.costa cetacea.com**. These folks also offer deep-water free diving and snorkel tours aimed at providing the chance to swim in close proximity to the large pelagic fish, mammals, and reptiles of the area.

Drake Bay Beach.

Where to Stay & Dine

Given the remote location and logistics of reaching Drake Bay, as well as the individual isolation of each hotel, nearly all the hotels listed below deal almost exclusively in package trips that include transportation, meals, tours, and taxes. I list the most common packages, although all the lodges will work with you to accommodate longer or shorter stays. Nightly room rates are listed only where they're available and practical, generally at the more moderately priced hotels.

In addition to the places listed below, **Guaria de Osa** ★ (www.guar iadeosa.com; ☎ **510/235-4313** in the U.S.) is a lovely lodge near the Río Claro that's a specialist in yoga, spiritual, and educational retreats.

EXPENSIVE

In addition to the places listed below, **Copa del Arbol** ★★ (www. copadearbol.com; ☎ **831/246-4265** in the U.S., or 8935-1212 in Costa

---

Where's the Beach?

While the beach at Drake Bay itself is acceptable and calm for swimming, it's far from spectacular. The most popular swimming beach is a pretty small patch of sand, known locally as Cocalito beach, about a 7-minute hike down from La Paloma Lodge. The nicest beaches around involve taking a day trip to either Isla del Caño or San Josesito. The latter is a stunning beach farther south on the peninsula with excellent snorkeling possibilities.

Rica) is another intimate jungle lodge located on the water's edge about midway between the village of Drake Bay and the San Pedrillo ranger station at the entrance to Corcovado National Park.

Aguila de Osa Inn ★   Set on a steep hillside that borders the Agujitas River right near the point where it empties out into Drake Bay, this is an expertly operated jungle lodge, with much of the credit going to owner Bradd Johnson, who is very much a hands-on proprietor. Personally, I prefer the set up at most of the other lodges listed in this section, as it can be a bit of a hike from the main lodge to the rooms, which are located at the highest point of the property. As well, this is one of the only high end lodges in this area without a swimming pool, a big drawback. But that said, rooms are airy and comfortable, the food is downright fabulous and the service attentive. The lodge has especially good scuba diving and sport fishing operations, with their own modern boats, top-notch equipment, and knowledgeable skippers and dive masters.

Drake Bay. www.aguiladeosa.com. © **866/924-8452** in the U.S. and Canada, 2296-2190 in San José, or 8840-2929 at the lodge. 13 units. $505–$665 for 3 days/2 nights; $715 and up for 4 days/3 nights. Rates are per person based on double occupancy and include round-trip transportation from Palmar Sur, and all meals. Closed Oct. **Amenities:** Restaurant; bar; free kayaks; free Wi-Fi.

Casa Corcovado Jungle Lodge ★   The closest of all the jungle lodges to Corcovado National Park, Casa Corcovado has a collection of well-appointed individual and duplex bungalows built on the site of a former cacao plantation. Most of the former farmland has been reclaimed and the whole operation is surrounded by dense primary forest. The property has two pretty swimming pools and a semi-private beach that is sometimes swimmable. Every afternoon, guests gather at "Margarita Sunset Point", a grassy bluff on a high point overlooking the Pacific Ocean, for cocktails, snacks and sunset saluting. Owner Stephen Lill, is a dedicated environmentalist and involved in numerous local conservation and sustainable development projects.

Osa Peninsula. www.casacorcovado.com. © **2256-3181.** 14 units. $825–$1,110 per person for 3 days/2 nights; $1,098–$1,395 for 4 days/3 nights. Rates are based on double occupancy and include round-trip transportation from San José, all meals, daily tours, park fees, and taxes. Closed Sept 1–Nov 14. **Amenities:** Restaurant; 2 bars; 2 outdoor pools.

La Paloma Lodge ★★★   This has long been one of my favorite nature lodges in Costa Rica, and for good reason. The views are to die for, the setting is sublime, and the wildlife viewing and adventure opportunities are as good as it gets. The best rooms here are the large Sunset ranchos. Each sits on a prominent high point overlooking the sea and backed by rainforest, with a massive master bedroom on the second floor featuring nothing but windows on three sides. But even the slightly more humble standard rooms are large and plush, with private balconies, and mesmerizing views. The food and service are top notch, as well. A small pool is set on the edge of a jungle-clad hillside; Cocolito Beach is a short hike down a winding trail through the rainforest. The lodge takes conservation seriously, and is actively involved in protecting the region.

Drake Bay. www.lapalomalodge.com. © **2293-7502.** 11 units. $990–$1,245 per person for 4 days/3 nights with 2 tours; $1,235–$1,575 per person for 5 days/4 nights with 2 tours. Rates are based on double occupancy and include all meals, park fees, and indicated tours. Rates slightly lower in off season. Closed Sept 15–Nov 1. **Amenities:** Restaurant; bar; small pool; free use of canoes and kayaks; free Wi-Fi.

MODERATE

In addition to the spot listed below, you might check out **Finca Maresia ★** (www.fincamaresia.com; © **2775-0279**), a pretty boutique property located between Drake Bay and the national park.

Drake Bay Wilderness Resort ★★   This is one of the best located of the lodges in Drake Bay, sitting on a large chunk of land with the Agujitas River on one side and the area's namesake Drake Bay on the other. Rooms feature hand-painted murals on concrete walls, and comfortable beds. A couple of budget rooms share bathrooms and shower facilities. The shoreline right at the lodge is a bit too rocky for swimming, but there's a good size pool naturally fed and filled with sea water. The owner Marlene's chocolate-chip cookies are regionally renowned.

Drake Bay. www.drakebay.com. © **2725-1715.** 20 units. $865 per person for 4 days/3 nights with 2 tours, including all meals and taxes. **Amenities:** Restaurant; bar; small saltwater pool; free use of canoes and kayaks; free Wi-Fi.

INEXPENSIVE

Hotel Jinetes de Osa ★   Just off the water at the far southern end of the footpath that runs along the Drake Bay shore, this has long been my top budget recommendation in the area. The superior rooms here are located higher up on the property and come with wonderful views of the bay, more space and air-conditioning. However, be prepared for the climb. Standard rooms are more hostel-like, and some can feel a little dark, and few have view to speak of. These folks specializes in dive trips and are recognized as a full-service PADI resort.

Drake Bay. www.jinetesdeosa.com. © **866/553-7073** in the U.S. and Canada, or 2231-5806 in Costa Rica. 9 units. $96–$160 double. Rates include breakfast. **Amenities:** Restaurant; bar; free Wi-Fi.

PUERTO JIMÉNEZ: GATEWAY TO CORCOVADO NATIONAL PARK

35km (22 miles) W of Golfito by water (90km/56 miles by road); 85km (53 miles) S of Palmar Norte

Don't let its small size and languid pace fool you. **Puerto Jiménez ★** is a bustling little burg, where rough jungle gold-panners mix with wealthy

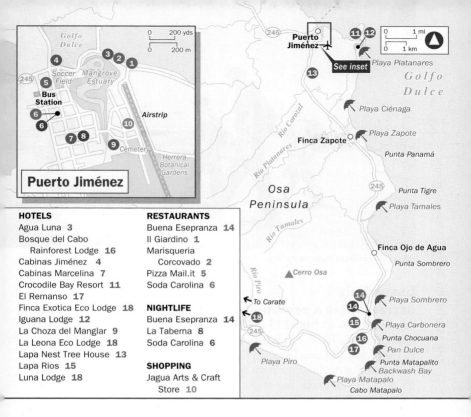

Puerto Jiménez

HOTELS
Agua Luna 3
Bosque del Cabo
 Rainforest Lodge 16
Cabinas Jiménez 4
Cabinas Marcelina 7
Crocodile Bay Resort 11
El Remanso 17
Finca Exotica Eco Lodge 18
Iguana Lodge 12
La Choza del Manglar 9
La Leona Eco Lodge 18
Lapa Nest Tree House 13
Lapa Rios 15
Luna Lodge 18

RESTAURANTS
Buena Esepranza 14
Il Giardino 1
Marisqueria
 Corcovado 2
Pizza Mail.it 5
Soda Carolina 6

NIGHTLIFE
Buena Esepranza 14
La Taberna 8
Soda Carolina 6

SHOPPING
Jagua Arts & Craft
 Store 10

ecotourists, budget backpackers, serious surfers, and a smattering of celebrities seeking anonymity and escape. Located on the southeastern tip of the Osa Peninsula, the town itself is just a couple of streets wide in any direction, with the ubiquitous soccer field, a handful of general stores, some inexpensive *sodas,* and several bars. Scarlet macaws fly overhead, and mealy parrots provide wake-up calls.

Corcovado National Park has its headquarters here, and this town makes an excellent base for exploring this vast wilderness area. Signs in English on walls around town advertise a variety of tours, including a host of activities outside of the park. If the in-town accommodations are too basic, you'll find several far more luxurious places farther south on the Osa Peninsula.

This is also a prime surf spot. **Cabo Matapalo** (the southern tip of the Osa Peninsula) is home to several dependable right point breaks. When it's working, the waves at Pan Dulce and Backwash actually connect, and can provide rides almost as long and tiring as those to be had in more famous Pavones (see "Playa Pavones: A Surfer's Mecca," p. 502).

Hiking in Corcovado National Park.

Essentials

GETTING THERE & DEPARTING   By Plane: Both **Nature Air** (www.
natureair.com; ✆ **800/235-9272** in the U.S. and Canada, or 2299-
6000 in Costa Rica) and **Sansa** (www.flysansa.com; ✆ **877/767-2672**
in the U.S. and Canada, or 2290-4100 in Costa Rica) have daily direct
flights to Puerto Jiménez from San José. The flight duration is around
55 minutes, although this flight often includes brief stops in Quepos,
Golfito, or Drake Bay. Fares range from $104 to $150, one-way.

Due to the remoteness of this area and the unpredictable flux of
traffic, both Sansa and Nature Air frequently improvise on scheduling.
Sometimes this means an unscheduled stop in Quepos, Drake Bay, or
Golfito, either on the way to or from San José, which can add time to
your flight. Less frequently, it might mean a change in departure time, so
it's always best to confirm.

Taxis are generally waiting to meet all incoming flights. A ride into
downtown Puerto Jiménez should cost around C1,500. If you're staying
at a hotel outside of downtown, it's best to have them arrange for a taxi to
meet you. Otherwise you can hire one at the airstrip. Depending upon
how far out on the peninsula you are staying, it could cost up to $80 for
a rugged four-wheel-drive vehicle that can carry up to four people.

By Car: Take the San José–Caldera Highway (CR27) to the first
exit past the Pozón toll booth, where you will pick up the Southern Highway, or Costanera Sur (CR34). Take this south through Jacó, Quepos,
and Dominical to Palmar Norte, where you'll meet up with the Interamerican Highway (CR2). Take this south to the turnoff for La Palma,
Rincón, and Puerto Jiménez.

By Bus: Transportes Blanco-Lobo express buses (℡ **2257-4121** in San José, or 2771-4744 in Puerto Jiménez) leave San José daily at 8am and noon from Calle 12, between avenidas 7 and 9. The trip takes 7 to 8 hours; the fare is C7,500. Buses depart Puerto Jiménez for San José daily at 5am and 9am.

By Boat: Several speedboats work as boat taxis between Puerto Jiménez and Golfito. The fare is C3,000, and the ride takes a little under 30 minutes. These boats leave four or five times throughout the day, or whenever they fill up, beginning at around 5am and finishing up at around 3pm. Ask around town, or at the docks for current schedules.

There is also a daily passenger launch. This slower boat takes 1½ hours and is C1,500. The ferry leaves the public dock in Golfito at 11:30am for Puerto Jiménez. The return trip to Golfito leaves Puerto Jiménez's municipal dock at 4pm. It's possible to charter a water taxi in Golfito for the trip across to Puerto Jiménez. You'll have to pay around $90 for an entire launch, some of which can carry up to 12 people.

VISITOR INFORMATION Puerto Jiménez is a dirt-lane town on the southern coast of the Osa Peninsula. The public dock is over a bridge past the north end of the soccer field; the bus stop is 2 blocks east of the center of town. You'll find a couple of Internet cafes in town; the best is **Cafe Net El Sol** (www.soldeosa.com; ℡ **8632-8150**), which is a great place to book tours and get information, and is also a Wi-Fi hot spot.

FAST FACTS Four-wheel-drive taxis are plentiful in Puerto Jiménez. You'll find them cruising or parked along the main street of town.

The Puerto Jiménez dock.

Cycling on the beach in Puerto Jiménez.

Alternatively, have your hotel call one. Or you can rent a car down here from **Solid Car Rental** (www.solidcarrental.com; © **800/390-7065** in USA and Canada, or 2442-6000 in Costa Rica).

Exploring Puerto Jiménez

While Puerto Jiménez has typically been a staging ground for adventures much farther out toward Carate and the park, quite a few activities and tours can be undertaken closer to town.

If you're looking to spend some time on the beach, head just east of town for a long, pretty stretch of sand called **Playa Plantanares.** The waves are generally fairly gentle, and quite a few hotels have begun to pop up here. If you head farther out on the peninsula, you'll come to the beaches of **Pan Dulce, Backwash,** and **Matapalo,** all major surf spots with consistently well-formed right point breaks. When the waves aren't too big, these are excellent places to learn how to surf.

Osa Aventura (www.osaaventura.com; © **2735-5758** or 8372-6135) is a local tour company that offers a host of guided tours and wildlife-watching expeditions around the Osa Peninsula and into Corcovado National Park. Rates run between $80 and $300 per person, depending upon group size and the tour.

AN APTLY NAMED ADVENTURE TOUR   For a real adventure, check in with **Psycho Tours ★★★** (www.psychotours.com; © **8353-8619**). These folks, who also call themselves Everyday Adventures, run a variety of adventure tours, but their signature combo trip features a free climb (with a safety rope attached) up the roots and trunks of a 60m-tall (200-ft.) strangler fig. You can climb as high as your ability allows, but most try to reach a natural platform at around 18m (60 ft.), where you take a leap of faith into space and are belayed down by your guide. This is preceded by an informative hike through primary rainforest, often wading through a small river, and followed by a couple of rappels down jungle waterfalls, the highest of which is around 30m (100 ft.). You can do either one of the above adventures separately, but I recommend the 5- to 6-hour combo tour, which costs $120.

CHOCOLATE TOUR Finca Kobo ★ (www.fincakobo.com; ✆ 8398-7604), near La Palma, 17km (11 miles) northwest of Puerto Jiménez, offers an informative tour through this organic cacao plantation. You'll learn about and see all the various stages involved in the process of growing cacao and transforming these precious beans into chocolate. At the end of the tour, you'll get to sample some of their handiwork, dipping some local fruit into fresh chocolate fondue. The tour costs $32; children 8 and under are half-price. Finca Kobo also has a few rooms and bungalows for rent.

KAYAKING Kayaking trips around the estuary, up into the mangroves and out into the gulf are very popular. **Aventuras Tropicales** (www. aventurastropicales.com; ✆ 2735-5195), which is set up in front of the soccer field, offers daily paddles through the mangroves, as well as sunset trips where you can sometimes see dolphins. More adventurous multiday kayak and camping trips are also available, in price and comfort ranges from budget to luxury (staying at various lodges around the Golfo Dulce and Matapalo).

SPORTFISHING If you're interested in doing some **bill-fishing** or **deep-sea fishing,** you'll probably want to stay at or fish with **Crocodile Bay Resort** (www.crocodilebay.com; ✆ 800/733-1115 in the U.S. and

A mangrove kayak tour near Puerto Jiménez.

Canada, or 2735-5631 in Costa Rica). This upscale fishing lodge is close to the Puerto Jiménez airstrip (airport code: PJM). Alternatively, you can ask at your hotel, or contact **Southern Costa Rica Sportfishing** (www. costaricasportsman.com; ✆ **2735-5298**). Rates run between $900 and $1,600 full day, or between $700 and $1,500 for a half-day, depending on the boat, tackle, number of anglers, and fishing grounds.

For a truly unique fishing adventure, try fishing for local game from the tenuous perch aboard a single, sit-atop kayak. **Costa Rica Kayak Fishing & Ecotours** (www.costaricakayakfishing.net; ✆ **6156-5949**) offers guided outings. Half-day tours, including fruit, water, snacks, gear, and tackle run between $100 and $150.

SURF & SUP LESSONS   **Pollo's Surf School** ★ (www.pollosurfschool. com; ✆ **8366-6559**) is located near some excellent learning waves on Pan Dulce beach. Pollo's is also the place to go to try your hand at some stand up paddling. A 2-hour lesson runs $55.

Exploring Corcovado National Park ★★★

Exploring Corcovado National Park is not something to be undertaken lightly, but neither is it the expedition that some people make it out to be. The weather is the biggest obstacle to overnight backpacking trips through the park. The heat and humidity are often quite extreme, and frequent rainstorms can make trails fairly muddy. Within a couple of hours of Puerto Jiménez (by 4WD vehicle) are several entrances to the park; however, the park has no roads, so once you reach any of the entrances, you'll have to start hiking. If you choose the alternative— hiking on the beach—you'll have to plan your hiking around the tides when often there is no beach at all and some rivers are impassable.

Corcovado National Park is amazingly rich in biodiversity. It is one of the only places in Costa Rica that is home to all four of the country's monkey species—howler, white-faced, squirrel, and spider. Its large size makes it an ideal habitat for wildcat species, including the endangered jaguar, as well as other large mammals, like the Baird's tapir. Apart from the jaguar, other cat species found here include the ocelot, margay, jaguarundi, and puma. More than 390 species of birds have been recorded inside the park. Scarlet macaws are commonly sighted here. Other common bird species include any number of antbirds, manakins,

A hummingbird, one of the many birds you might spot in Corcovado National Park.

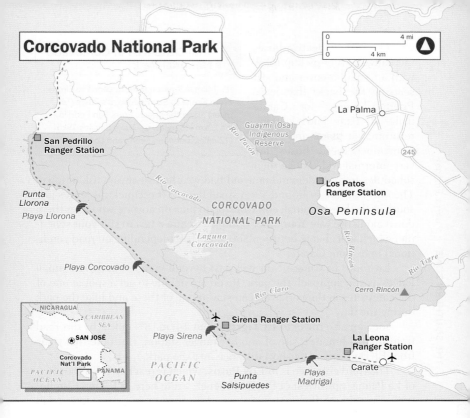

Corcovado National Park

San Pedrillo Ranger Station

Punta Llorona
Playa Llorona

La Palma

Guaymí (Osa) Indigenous Reserve

Río Pavón

Río Corcovado

Los Patos Ranger Station

CORCOVADO NATIONAL PARK

Osa Peninsula

Laguna Corcovado

Río Rincón

Playa Corcovado

Río Claro

Cerro Rincón

Río Tigre

NICARAGUA

CARIBBEAN SEA

SAN JOSÉ

Corcovado Nat'l Park

PANAMA

PACIFIC OCEAN

Sirena Ranger Station

Playa Sirena

PACIFIC OCEAN

Punta Salsipuedes

Playa Madrigal

La Leona Ranger Station

Carate

toucans, tanagers, hummingbirds, and puffbirds. Once thought extinct in Costa Rica, the harpy eagle has been spotted here as well. Most rivers in Corcovado are home to **crocodiles;** moreover, at high tide, they are frequented by **bull sharks.** For this reason, river crossings must be coordinated with low tides.

Because of its size and remoteness, Corcovado National Park is best explored over several days; however, it is possible to enter and hike a bit of it on day trips. The best way to do this is to book a tour with your lodge on the Osa Peninsula, from a tour company in Puerto Jiménez, or through a lodge in Drake Bay (see "Where to Stay & Dine," p. 472).

GETTING THERE & ENTRY POINTS The park has four primary entrances, which are really just ranger stations reached by rough dirt roads. When you've reached them, you'll have to strap on a backpack and hike. Perhaps the easiest one to reach from Puerto Jiménez is **La Leona ranger station,** accessible by car, bus, or taxi.

If you choose to drive, take the dirt road from Puerto Jiménez to Carate (Carate is at the end of the road). From Carate, it's a 3km (1.75-mile) hike to La Leona. To travel there by "public transportation," pick up one of the collective buses (actually, a 4WD pickup truck with a tarpaulin cover and slat seats in the back) that leave Puerto Jiménez for Carate daily at 6am and 1:30pm, returning at 8am and 4pm. Remember, these "buses" are very informal and change their

Trail Distances in Corcovado National Park

It's 14km (8.7 miles) from La Leona to Sirena. From Sirena to San Pedrillo, it's 23km (14 miles) along the beach. From San Pedrillo, it's 20km (13 miles) to Drake Bay. It's 19km (12 miles) between Sirena and Los Patos.

schedules to meet demand or avoid bad weather, so always ask in town. The one-way fare is around $9. A small fleet of these pickups leaves just south of the bus terminal, and will stop to pick up anyone who flags them down along the way. Your other option is to hire a taxi to suit your schedule, which will charge between $60 and $100 (depending on road conditions) to or from Carate.

En route to Carate, you will pass several campgrounds and small lodges as you approach the park. If you are unable to get a spot at one of the campsites in the park, you can stay at one of these and hike the park during the day.

You can also travel to **El Tigre,** about 14km (8¾ miles) by dirt road from Puerto Jiménez, site of another ranger station. But note that trails from El Tigre go only a short distance into the park.

The third entrance is in **Los Patos,** which is reached from the town of La Palma, northwest of Puerto Jiménez. From here, a 19km (12-mile) trail runs through the center of the park to **Sirena,** a ranger station and research facility (see "Beach Treks & Rainforest Hikes," p. 483). Sirena has a landing strip used by charter flights.

The northern entrance to the park is **San Pedrillo,** which you can reach by hiking from Sirena or by taking a boat from Drake Bay or Sierpe (p. 467). It's 14km (8¾ miles) from Drake Bay.

If you're not into hiking in the heat, you can charter a plane in Puerto Jiménez to take you to Carate or Sirena. A five-passenger plane costs between $200 to $450 one-way, depending on your destination. Contact **Alfa Romeo Air Charters** (www.alfaromeoair.com; ✆ **8632-8150**).

FEES & REGULATIONS Park admission is $15 per person per day. Only the Sirena station is equipped with dormitory-style lodgings and a simple soda; the others have basic campsites and toilet facilities. All must be reserved in advance by contacting the **ACOSA** (Area de Conservacion de Osa) in Puerto Jiménez (✆ **2735-5036;** pncorcovado@gmail.com). However, they are notoriously poor at answering emails and attending to reservations. Its offices are adjacent to the airstrip. Only a limited number of people are allowed to camp at each ranger station, so make your reservations well in advance. Your best bet is probably to contact **Osa Corcovado Tour & Travel** (www.corcovadoguide.com; ✆ **8632-8150**) or

A trail through Corcovado National Park.

Osa Aventura (www.osaaventura. com; ✆ **2735-5758** or 8372-6135), who will make the arrangements for you, for a small fee.

BEACH TREKS & RAINFOREST HIKES The park has quite a few good hiking trails. Two of the better-known ones are the beach routes, starting at either La Leona or San Pedrillo ranger stations. Between any two ranger stations, the hiking is arduous and takes all or most of a day, so it's best to rest for a day or so between hikes if possible. Remember, this is quite a wild area. Never hike alone, and take all the standard precautions for hiking in a rainforest. Be especially careful about crossing or swimming in any isolated rivers or river mouths. Most rivers in Corcovado are home to crocodiles; moreover, at high tide, some are frequented by bull sharks. For this reason, river crossings must be coordinated with low tides. During the wet months (July–Nov), parts of the park may be closed. One of the longest and most popular hikes, between San Pedrillo and La Sirena, can be undertaken only during dry season.

Sirena is a fascinating destination. As a research facility and ranger station, it's frequented primarily by scientists studying the rainforest. The network of trails here can easily keep you busy for several days. Just north of the station lies the mouth of the Río Sirena. Most days at high tide, bull sharks swarm and feed in this river mouth. Large crocodiles also inhabit these waters, so swimming is seriously discouraged. Still, it's quite a spectacle. The **Claro Trail** will bring you to the mouth of the Río Claro. A bit smaller, this river is also home to a healthy crocodile

---

Important Corcovado Tips

If you plan to hike the beach trails from La Leona or San Pedrillo, be sure to pick up a tide table at the park headquarters' office in Puerto Jiménez. The tide changes rapidly; when it's high, the trails and river crossings can be dangerous or impassable.

If you plan to spend a night or more in the park, you'll want to stock up on food, water, and other essentials in Puerto Jiménez. Carate has a minimarket with a limited selection. Although most of the stations have simple *sodas*, you need to reserve in advance if you plan to take your meals at any of these.

population, although allegedly fewer bull sharks. However, if you follow the Claro Trail upstream a bit, you can find several safe and appropriate swimming spots.

WHERE TO STAY & DINE IN THE PARK: CAMPSITES, CABINS & CANTINAS Reservations are essential at the various ranger stations if you plan to eat or sleep inside the park (p. 480). **Sirena** has a modern research facility with dormitory-style accommodations for 28 people, as well as a campground, *soda* and landing strip for charter flights. Camping is available at **La Leona, Los Patos,** and **San Pedrillo** ranger stations. Every ranger station has potable water, but it's advisable to pack in your own; whatever you do, don't drink stream water. Campsites in the park are $4/person per night. A dorm bed at the Sirena station will run $11— you must bring your own sheets, and a mosquito net is highly recommended—and meals here are $11 for breakfast, $15 for lunch, and $20 for dinner. Everything must be reserved in advance.

Where to Stay in Puerto Jiménez
EXPENSIVE
Crocodile Bay Resort ★ This high-end sportfishing resort features a fleet of top-notch boats, quality gear and excellent captains. Set on a large piece of land on the outskirts of town, the resort has its own 900-foot long pier jutting out into the Golfo Dulce. Rooms are fishy fun, too, with carved wooden marlin, tuna and wahoo hanging here and there (carved wooden animal bas reliefs adorn doors and cabinets). The resort's mid-size pool is fed by a tall stone waterfall, atop which sits an unheated Jacuzzi tub. Service is attentive, and in addition to fishing, a wide range of adventure tours are also offered. There's a well-equipped spa, as well.
Puerto Jiménez. www.crocodilebay.com. ✆ **800/733-1115** in the U.S. and Canada, or 2559-7990 in Costa Rica. 40 units. $299–$398 per person based on double occupancy. Rates include all meals and non-alcoholic beverages. A wide range of fishing and adventure tour packages are available. **Amenities:** Restaurant; bar; Jacuzzi; outdoor pool; large modern spa; watersports equipment rental; free Wi-Fi.

INEXPENSIVE
In addition to the places listed below, **Cabinas Marcelina** (✆ **2735-5007**) is a clean, dependable budget option right in the heart of town. **Agua Luna** (✆ **2735-5204**) is conveniently located, with rooms right at the foot of the town's public dock and close to a mangrove forest.

Cabinas Jiménez ★★ On the waterfront, this hotel offers 15 motel-style rooms with tile floors, fridges and even a deck with hammocks. They're enlivened, as are the common areas, by local arts and crafts, including hand-painted murals, carved animal sculptures, and complex iron works on the windows—an artistic variation on the typical grates meant to keep out burglars. The large, wood-and-bamboo rancho located just off the small kidney-shaped pool has a commanding view of the

Puerto Jiménez harbor. Down on the harbor shore, the hotel keeps kayaks, which are free for guest use, and they also maintain a fleet of bikes for guests, also complimentary. The owner has a few boats and offers excellent tours of the Golfo Dulce and into the nearby mangroves.

Downtown, 50m (165 ft.) north of the soccer field, Puerto Jiménez, Puntarenas. www.cabinasjimenez.com. ℂ **2735-5090.** 15 units. $65–$130 double. **Amenities:** Small outdoor pool; free Wi-Fi.

La Choza del Manglar ★   With expansive gardens and land, this hotel offers up rich wildlife viewing right on site. The large on-site restaurant and lounge are popular local gathering places, with ping pong, billiards and foosball tables. The rooms come in a wide range of shapes and sizes, and are clean if somewhat bare bones (colorful handpainted details adorn the walls and wooden furniture in some, giving them a bit more personality). The town and waterfront are each about 3 or 4 blocks away, in opposite directions.

125m (410 ft.) west of the airstrip, Puerto Jiménez. www.manglares.com. ℂ **2735-5002.** 11 units. $69–$99 double. **Amenities:** Restaurant; bar; free Wi-Fi.

Where to Stay in Playa Plantanares
EXPENSIVE

Iguana Lodge ★★   Located on the outskirts of Puerto Jiménez, this beachfront mini-resort fronts a calm section of beach where the Golfo Dulce and Pacific ocean meet. You'll find rooms in a wide range of prices here. I prefer the second-floor units of the two-story casitas, although the "club rooms" are an excellent value. All feature wood floors, bamboo and wicker furnishings, chairs and a hammock. With a massive second-story, open-air, wood-floor studio, yoga is a big attraction here, and there are often classes, or a visiting group conducting a retreat. The gardens are sumptuous, with plenty of open-air covered areas to chill, and gentle Playa Plantanares beach just steps away.

Playa Plantanares. www.iguanalodge.com. ℂ**800/259-9123** in the U.S. and Canada, or 8848-0752 in Costa Rica. 19 units. $180 double club room; $440 casita double; $650 3-bedroom beach house. Rates for club room include breakfast. Rates for the

---

Costa Rican Family Robinson

For a truly unique family vacation, consider renting the **Lapa's Nest Tree House** ★★ (www.treehouseincostarica.com; ℂ **508/714-0622** in the U.S., or 8372-3529 in Costa Rica), an impressive lodge built up and around a giant Guanacaste tree in the midst of thick forest. This gorgeous home, just 13km (8 miles) north of Puerto Jiménez, is chock-full of creative design touches. Spread over six levels, it features three bedrooms, two bathrooms, and a full kitchen. The price for all of this ranges from $1,350 to $1,900 per week, depending on the season. These folks also rent out a couple of other houses in the area.

casita include breakfast and dinner, while rates for the villa do not include any meals. All rates include taxes. **Amenities:** 2 restaurants; bar; Jacuzzi; outdoor lap pool; spa; watersports equipment rental.

Where to Stay & Dine Around the Osa Peninsula

As with most of the lodges in Drake Bay, the accommodations listed in this section include three meals a day in their rates and do a large share of their bookings in package trips. Per-night rates are listed, but the price categories have been adjusted to take into account the fact that all meals are included. Ask about package rates if you plan to take several tours and stay awhile: They could save you money.

In addition to the lodges listed below, other options range from small B&Bs to fully equipped home rentals. Surfers, in particular, might want to inquire into one of the several rental houses located close to the beach at Matapalo. Your best bet for alternative accommodations is to contact Isabelle at **Jiménez Hotels** (www.jimenezhotels.com; © **8632-8150**); she also handles a host of house rentals around the area.

Finally, Carate has several lodges. In addition to the lodges listed below, you can look into **Finca Exótica Eco-Lodge ★** (www.finca exotica.com; © **4070-0054**), a delightful oceanview lodge, and **La Leona Eco-Lodge ★** (www.laleonaecolodge.com; © **2735-5705**), a tent-camp option on the outskirts of the national park.

This is a very isolated area, with just one rough dirt road connecting all the lodges, nature reserves, and parks. Almost all visitors here take all their meals at their hotel or lodge. If you want to venture away for some good simple home cooking, head to Martina's **Buena Esperanza** (no phone), right there on the main road, near Matapalo.

The following lodges are some of the best ecolodges Costa Rica has to offer, and most are pretty pricey. However, keep in mind that despite paying top dollar, the rooms have no TVs, no telephones, no air-conditioning, and the town has no discos, very limited shopping, and no paved roads. Consequently, there are also no crowds and very few modern distractions. All of the lodges listed below are between 40 minutes to a little over an hour outside of Puerto Jimenez, along a rough dirt road, with several river crossings.

EXPENSIVE

Bosque del Cabo Rainforest Lodge ★★★   Considered by many to be the most spectacular of the Matalpo eco-lodges, Bosque del Cabo is perched some 500 feet over the water on more than 300 acres. It's at once rustic and elegant, with roomy bungalows and several houses. All are classily tarted up in hardwoods, cane and tile; some of the bungalows have thatched roofs. There are lots of nifty features—a nice pool and wildlife trails, of course, but also a thrillingly high bird-viewing platform set in a Manu tree, waterfall-rappelling courses, harnessed tree climbing, massage and reflexology treatments and more. Owners Phil and Kim Spier are often on hand, to make sure things run smoothly; it's thanks to their efforts that the resort has earned "4 Leaves" in the CST Sustainable Tourism program.

Osa Peninsula. www.bosquedelcabo.com. © **2735-5206** or 8389-2846. 17 units. $215–$325 per person. Rates include 3 meals daily and taxes. $30 per person, round-trip transportation from Puerto Jiménez Airport. **Amenities:** Restaurant; bar; midsize outdoor pool; surfboard rental.

El Remanso ★★

This magnificent collection of rooms, private cabins, and duplexes, is just up the road from Bosque del Cabo. The large main lodge and restaurant area is a tropical fantasy surrounded by towering rainforest trees and entirely open, with a soaring thatch roof. Rooms are spread around the sprawling gardens and grounds, and a few have ocean views. Families or groups will want to look at Casa Osa, which sleeps up to eight. For a real treat, be sure to ask to have breakfast atop the tree platform at least one time here. This place uses only renewable energy, and has earned "5 Leaves" in the CST Sustainable Tourism program.

Osa Peninsula. www.elremanso.com. © **2735-5569** or 8814-5775. 14 units. $170–$380 per person. Rates include 3 meals daily and all taxes. **Amenities:** Restaurant; bar; small outdoor pool.

Lapa Ríos ★★★

Led by owners John and Karen Lewis, this trailblazing lodge was one of the first to put ecotourism in the Osa Peninsula on the map. Each spacious room is totally private and oriented toward the

A bungalow at Lapa Rios.

view, with high-peaked thatch roof and open screen walls. A small tropical garden and large deck, complete with outdoor shower and hammock, more than double the living space. (There's also an indoor shower.) Rooms are housed in a series of duplex units stretching in a line down the spine of a mountain ridge. If you get one of the lower units, be prepared for a bit of a hike to and from the main lodge, restaurant, and pool area. As is common in the area, the main lodge and restaurant features a massive and high thatch roof overhead. Unique to Lapa Ríos is the spiral staircase leading up to a large

Bungalows at Luna Lodge.

lookout. Lapa Ríos sits on a 400-hectare (988-acre) private rainforest reserve, with a well-maintained trail system and abundance of flora and fauna.

Osa Peninsula. www.laparios.com. 🕐 **2735-5130.** 16 units. $430 double. Rates include 3 meals daily, 9 guided tours per stay, and round-trip transportation btw. the lodge and Puerto Jiménez. Discounts for children 11 and under. **Amenities:** Restaurant; bar; small outdoor pool; spa; all rooms smoke-free.

Luna Lodge ★ In an area renowned for its remote ecolodges, this is one of the most remote. It is literally beyond the "end of the road" located up a rugged dirt track high in dense rainforest above the tiny village of Carate, where roads end and Corcovado National Park begins. Would-be guests choose from three options: inexpensive, medium, and pricey. In the low-priced category are large, heavy platform tents that are surprisingly comfortable, with two twin or one queen bed, private bath and tiny little balcony. The newest units on property are the Spanish-colonial style rooms in the main lodge (the mid-priced pick). And for those seeking luxury—and with the deep pockets to pay for it—there are large octagonal cabins decorated with Balinese and Indonesian fabrics and artworks (each has a four-poster beds draped in cotton mosquito netting). Owner Lana Wedmore is almost always on hand to greet guests and provide insight into the area gained over decades living here. Luna Lodge is spread over a steep hillside, and some hiking is involved to and from some of the units. Yoga with a view is offered each morning on an outdoor platform.

Carate, Osa Peninsula. www.lunalodge.com. 🕐 **888/760-0760** in the U.S. and Canada, or 4070-0010 in Costa Rica. 16 units. $135 in tent; $175 in rooms; $195–$225 private bungalows. Rates are double occupancy, and include 3 meals daily and taxes. A range of package tours, including round-trip transportation btw. the lodge and Puerto Jiménez, spa treatments and yoga classes are also available. **Amenities:** Restaurant; bar; small spa; small outdoor pool; all rooms smoke-free; free Wi-Fi.

Where to Dine in Puerto Jiménez

In addition to the places listed below, you might head to the new waterfront **Marisquería Corcovado** (✆ **2735-5659**), a lively local joint serving up excellent seafood and local specialties. They'll even cook up your fresh catch for you if you have anything. You can also get excellent pizzas, pastas and fruit drinks at **Pizza Mail.it** (✆ **2735-5483**), fronting the soccer field, right next to the post office.

Il Giardino ★★ ITALIAN/INTERNATIONAL/SEAFOOD   This is the best fine dining experience available in Puerto Jimenez, although there's not much competition, and this place is far from fancy. (Think: lots of open-air seating, from tables under shade umbrellas to the open-air interior dining room.) The pastas and ravioli are all homemade and delicious, and the seafood is freshly caught and perfectly prepared. It's an odd combination, but these folks also frequently do sushi nights, and are even open for breakfast. Everything is made fresh to order, so the kitchen can be a bit slow at times.

On the beachfront, just down from the public pier, Puerto Jiménez. www.ilgiardinoitalianrestaurant.com. ✆ **2735-5129**. Main courses C5,000–C14,000. Daily 7am–10pm.

Soda Carolina ★ COSTA RICAN   This simple Costa Rican diner is the social and tourist hub of Puerto Jiménez. Bright rainforest scenes and animals are painted on the interior walls, while the open-air front walls open up to the city's main street. You can get filling *casados* (plates of the day), fresh grilled fish, and a number of other typical local dishes.

On the main street. ✆ **2735-5185**. Main courses C3,300–C9,800. Daily 6am–10pm.

Shopping

Jagua Arts & Craft Store ★★★ (✆ **2735-5267**) stocks excellent local and regional art and craft works, including some fine jewelry and blown glass. *Tip:* Many folks head to this store while waiting for their departing flight out of Puerto Jiménez as the store is near the airstrip. Be sure to give yourself enough time, as the store has a relatively extensive collection. They also have an inviting open-air lounge area with locally made ice cream for sale and free coffee, a great place to wait for a flight, or a transfer out to your remote lodge.

Entertainment & Nightlife

Any after-tours action in Puerto Jiménez, will be at **Soda Carolina** (see above), which is popular with locals, guides, and tourists. For a much more local scene, stop in for an Imperial beer at **La Taberna** (✆ **2735-9533**).

If you're staying in the Matapalo area farther out on the Osa and want to hang with locals, head to Martina Hoffmann's **Buena Esperanza** (no phone). This place can actually get pretty lively on a Friday or Saturday night. It's the only game in town, but they've got good game.

GOLFITO: GATEWAY TO THE GOLFO DULCE

87km (54 miles) S of Palmar Norte; 337km (209 miles) S of San José

Despite being the largest and most important city in Costa Rica's southern zone, Golfito, in and of itself, is neither a popular nor a particularly inviting tourist destination. In its prime, this was a major banana port, but following years of rising taxes, falling prices, and labor disputes, United Fruit pulled out in 1985. Things may change in the future, as rumors perennially abound about the potential construction of an international airport nearby, major marina right on the bay, or large-scale tuna farm just offshore. But for the moment, none of these megaprojects have gotten off the drawing board.

That said, Golfito is still a major sportfishing center and a popular gateway to a slew of nature lodges spread along the quiet waters, isolated bays, and lush rainforests of the Golfo Dulce, or "Sweet Gulf." In 1998, much of the rainforest bordering the Golfo Dulce was officially declared the **Piedras Blancas National Park ★★**, which includes 12,000 hectares (29,640 acres) of primary forests, as well as protected secondary forests and pasturelands.

Golfito is set on the north side of the Golfo Dulce, at the foot of lush green mountains. The setting alone gives it the potential to be one of the most attractive cities in the country. However, the areas around the municipal park and public dock are somewhat seedy and the

The Golfito shoreline.

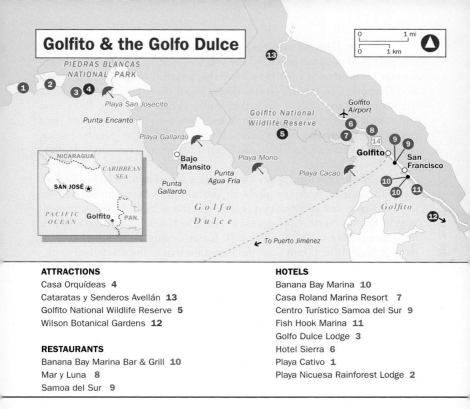

Golfito & the Golfo Dulce

PIEDRAS BLANCAS
NATIONAL PARK

Playa San Josecito

Punta Encanto

Golfito National
Wildlife Reserve

Golfito
Airport

Playa Gallardo

Bajo
Mansito

Playa Mono

Golfito

San
Francisco

Punta
Agua Fria

Playa Cacao

Punta
Gallardo

NICARAGUA

CARIBBEAN
SEA

SAN JOSÉ

PACIFIC
OCEAN

Golfito

PAN.

Golfo
Dulce

Golfito

To Puerto Jiménez

0   1 mi
0   1 km

ATTRACTIONS
Casa Orquídeas **4**
Cataratas y Senderos Avellán **13**
Golfito National Wildlife Reserve **5**
Wilson Botanical Gardens **12**

RESTAURANTS
Banana Bay Marina Bar & Grill **10**
Mar y Luna **8**
Samoa del Sur **9**

HOTELS
Banana Bay Marina **10**
Casa Roland Marina Resort **7**
Centro Turístico Samoa del Sur **9**
Fish Hook Marina **11**
Golfo Dulce Lodge **3**
Hotel Sierra **6**
Playa Cativo **1**
Playa Nicuesa Rainforest Lodge **2**

"downtown" section is quite run-down. Still, if you go a bit farther along the bay, you come to the old United Fruit Company housing. Here you'll find well-maintained wooden houses painted bright colors and surrounded by neatly manicured gardens. Toucans are commonly sighted. It's all very lush and green and clean—an altogether different picture from that painted by most port towns in this country. When a duty-free zone was opened here, these old homes experienced a minor renaissance and several were converted into small hotels. Ticos come here in droves on weekends and throughout December to take advantage of cheap prices on name-brand goods and clothing at the duty-free zone; sometimes all these shoppers make finding a room difficult.

Essentials

GETTING THERE & DEPARTING   By Plane: Both **Nature Air** (www. natureair.com; ℂ **800/235-9272** in the U.S. and Canada, or 2299-6000 in Costa Rica) and **Sansa** (www.flysansa.com; ℂ **877/767-2672** in the U.S. and Canada, or 2290-4100 in Costa Rica) have a couple of direct flights daily to the Golfito airstrip (airport code: GLF). The trip duration is around 1 hour; the fares run $135–$140 each way.

By Car: Take the San José–Caldera Highway (CR27) to the first exit past the Pozón toll booth, where you will pick up the Southern Highway, or Costanera Sur (CR34). Take this south through Jacó, Quepos, and Dominical to Palmar Norte, where you'll meet up with the Interamerican Highway (CR2). Take this south. When you get to Río Claro, you'll notice a couple of gas stations and quite a bit of activity. Turn right here and follow the signs to Golfito. If you end up at the Panama border, you've missed the turnoff by about 32km (20 miles). The complete drive takes about 6 hours.

By Bus: Tracopa buses (www.tracopacr.com; ✆ **2221-4214** or 2290-1308) leave San José daily for the southern zone throughout the day, between 5am and 6:30pm from Calle 9 and avenida 18. Almost all stop in Palmar Norte, but be sure to ask. The ride takes around 6 hours; fares range from C7,590 to C7,970. Buses depart Golfito for San José daily at 5am and 1:30pm from the bus station near the municipal dock.

By Boat: Several speedboats work as boat taxis between Golfito and Puerto Jiménez. The fare is C3,000, and the ride takes a little under 30 minutes. These boats leave five or six times throughout the day, or whenever they fill up, beginning at around 5am and finishing up at around 5pm. Ask at the *muellecito* (public dock) for current schedules.

There is also a daily passenger launch. This slower boat takes 1½ hours and is C1,500. The ferry leaves the public dock in Golfito at 11:30am for Puerto Jiménez. The return trip to Golfito leaves Puerto Jiménez's municipal dock at 4pm.

It's also possible to charter a water taxi in Golfito for the trip across to Puerto Jiménez. You'll have to pay around $90 for an entire launch, some of which can carry up to 12 people.

GETTING AROUND   Taxis are plentiful in Golfito, and are constantly cruising the main road all the way from the entrance of town to the duty-free port. A taxi ride anywhere in town should cost around C500. Local buses also ply this loop. The fare for the bus is C120.

If you drive down here and head out to one of the remote lodges on the gulf, you can leave your car at Samoa del Sur (see "Where to Stay," below) for around $12 per day.

If you need to rent a car in Golfito, check in with **Solid Car Rental Solid Car Rental** (www.solidcarrental.com; ✆ **800/390-7065** in USA and Canada; 2442-6000).

A sportfishing vessel in Golfito.

If you can't get to your next destination by boat, bus, commuter airline, or car, **Alfa Romeo Air Charters** (www.alfaromeoair. com; ℂ **8632-8150**) runs charters to most of the nearby destinations, including Carate, Drake Bay, Sirena, and Puerto Jiménez. A five-passenger plane costs around $200 to $450 one-way, depending on your destination.

Wilson Botanical Gardens.

Exploring Golfito & Surroundings

You won't find any really good swimming beaches right in Golfito. The closest spot is **Playa Cacao,** a short taxi boat ride away (around C3,000/person), although this is not one of my favorite beaches in Costa Rica. However, you might have to negotiate hard because these boatmen like to gouge tourists. If you really want some beach time, I recommend staying at one of the hotels in the Golfo Dulce (see "Where to Stay," p. 495) or heading over to **Playa Zancudo** (p. 497).

BOTANICAL GARDENS   About 30 minutes by boat out of Golfito, you'll find **Casa Orquídeas** ★★ (ℂ **8829-1247**; Sat–Thurs 8am–4pm), a private botanical garden lovingly built and maintained by Ron and Trudy MacAllister, who settled this remote piece of land in the 1970s. Most hotels in the area offer trips here, including transportation and a 2-hour tour of the gardens. During the tour, you'll sample fresh fruits picked right off the trees. If your hotel can't, you can book a trip out of Golfito with **Land Sea Tours** (ℂ **2775-1614**). If you decide to do it yourself, the entrance and guided tour is $10 per person, but it'll cost you between $80 and $100 to hire a boat for the round-trip ride. Regularly scheduled tours are on Thursdays and Sundays at 8:30am (three-person minimum).

If you have a serious interest in botanical gardens or bird-watching, consider an excursion to **Wilson Botanical Gardens** ★★★ at the **Las Cruces Biological Station** (www.threepaths.co.cr; ℂ **2524-0607** in San José or 2773-4004 at the gardens), just outside the town of San Vito, about 65km (40 miles) to the northeast. The gardens are owned and maintained by the Organization for Tropical Studies and include more than 7,000 species of tropical plants from around the world. Among the plants grown here are many endangered species, which make the gardens of interest to botanical researchers. Despite the scientific aspects of the gardens, with so many beautiful and unusual flowers amid the manicured grounds, even a neophyte can't help but be astounded. All this luscious flora has attracted at least 360 species of birds. A 4-hour guided walk costs $40; a shorter, 2-hour hike will run you $30. If you'd like to stay the night here, 12 well-appointed rooms are available. Rates include one guided walk, three meals, and taxes, and run $98 per person. Reservations are essential if you want to spend the night, and it's usually a good idea to make a reservation for a simple day visit and hike. The gardens are about 6km (3¾ miles) before San Vito. To get here from Golfito, drive out to the Interamerican Highway and continue south toward Panama. In Ciudad Neily, turn north. A taxi from Golfito should cost around $40 to $50 each way.

HIKING   With a trail head located just on the outskirts of town, the **Golfito National Wildlife Reserve ★** (daily 8am–4pm; $10 admission) is the closest place to Golfito for a hike in one of the area's typical local lowland rainforests. This reserve is home to much of the same wildlife and flora you'll find in other, more famous national parks in the region. A well-marked trail begins near the ranger station, just beyond the city's airstrip. You can hike it yourself or go as part of an organized tour with **Land Sea Tours** (✆ **2775-1614**). Sometimes admission doesn't get charged, and often the hours aren't enforced, either.

About a 20-minute drive over a rough dirt road from Golfito will bring you to the **Cataratas y Senderos Avellán** (www.avellancr.com; Avellán Waterfall & Trails; ✆ **8633-4768**; $5). Admission includes a 2-hour guided hike through the forests and a visit to a beautiful forest waterfall, with several refreshing pools perfect for swimming. A taxi should cost around $25 one-way. Horseback riding ($30) is available, and they even have a zip-line canopy tour ($40). Camping is allowed, and meals are served by the friendly owners of the land, the local Gamba family. However, for most folks, the best way to visit this site is to go as part of an organized trip with Land Sea Tours (see above).

SPORTFISHING   The waters off Golfito offer some of the best **sportfishing** in Costa Rica. Most game fish species can be caught here year-round, including blue and black marlin, sailfish, and roosterfish. November through May is the peak period for sailfish and blue marlin. If you'd like to try hooking a big one, contact **Banana Bay Marina** (www.bananabaymarinagolfito.com; ✆ **2775-0255**) or **Fish Hook Marina** (www.fish-hook-marina.com; ✆ **2775-1624** or 2775-2392 in Costa Rica). Both operations boast a full-service marina, waterside rooms for guests, and a fleet of sportfishing boats and captains. A full-day fishing trip costs between $950 and $1,800. You can also try the **Zancudo Lodge** (www.thezancudolodge.com; ✆ **800/854-8791** in the U.S. and Canada, or 2776-0008 in Costa Rica), based out of the Zancudo

Beach Resort (p. 501) in nearby Playa Zancudo. The lodge can arrange pickup in Golfito. I greatly prefer the Zancudo lodgings and scenery to what you'll find in Golfito.

Where to Stay

IN GOLFITO

Moderate

Casa Roland Marina Resort ★   This is easily the most modern and luxurious option available in Golfito, although that's not a high bar to clear. The hotel is located in the old United Fruit Company compound near the popular duty-free zone, and not on the water. Rooms are comfortable and attractive, featuring heavy wooden beds, wicker chairs and original paintings of rural Costa Rican scenes. Best rooms and suites are on the main floor, as those on the lower level have much less natural light. The main restaurant and bar area feature beautiful stained glass works. A lovely, large free-form pool is in a separate recreation area across the street from the main hotel.

Old American zone, near the duty-free zone, Golfito. www.casarolandgolfito.com. ✆ **888/398-6435** in the U.S. and Canada, or 2775-0180 in Costa Rica. 50 units. $125–$145 double; $185–$225 suites, $260 presidential suite. Rates include breakfast. **Amenities:** Restaurant; bar; outdoor pool; room service; spa; free Wi-Fi.

Hotel Sierra ★   Set right between the airstrip and duty-free zone, and within easy walking distance of each, this large resort-style hotel is one of the more popular options for Tico shoppers coming to Golfito to bargain hunt. Covered walkways connect a series of two-story pale yellow buildings with red zinc roofs. The rooms are spacious and feature clean tile floors, pure white walls, and large windows letting in lots of light. The large outdoor pool is ringed with chaise lounges and shade umbrellas, and features a busy swim-up bar. There's also a small children's pool. Don't be fooled by lingering web sites and reviews talking about a casino, that's been closed down for some time now.

Golfito. www.hotelsierra.com. ✆ **2775-0666.** 72 units. $80 double. Rates include breakfast. **Amenities:** Restaurant; bar; large outdoor pool; free Wi-Fi.

Inexpensive

Centro Turístico Samoa del Sur ★   This longstanding waterfront hotel is your best bet if you want to be right on the water in Golfito proper. The rooms are comfortable, if a bit worn, with red tile floors, hardwood furniture and a long shared veranda. The hotel features a popular bar and restaurant (French food), small marina, pool, and playground, which are open to the public for a fee. These folks run one of the more dependable parking lots for travelers with rental cars heading by boat to one of the more remote nature lodges of the Golfo Dulce.

100m (328 ft.) north of the public dock, Golfito. www.samoadelsur.com. ✆ **2775-0233.** 18 units. $85 double. **Amenities:** Restaurant; bar; midsize outdoor pool; room service; kayak rentals.

Where to Dine

Banana Bay Marina Bar & Grill ★★ INTERNATIONAL/SEA-FOOD Painted a bright yellow, and overlooking the marina and bay, this simple, open-air joint serves up fresh seafood, Continental standards, and typical bar food. The Bildge burger is popular as it's large and well-prepared, but those in the know opt for the fresh mahi-mahi burger, which comes either fried or grilled.

At the Banana Bay Marina, on the waterfront in downtown Golfito. ✆ **2775-0383.** Main courses $8–$25. Daily 6am–10pm.

Mar y Luna ★ COSTA RICAN/SEAFOOD This friendly bayfront restaurant serves up Tico fare, fresh seafood, and a mix of international dishes and bar food. The whole fried fish is the house specialty. The sunsets are lovely, and I like to enjoy them with some fresh ceviche and a cool drink on the main dining deck facing the water, under a plain zinc roof held up by roughhewn tree trunks. Inside, fishing buoys and mounted stuffed fish are hung on the walls and from the rafters. Some nights there's live music.

Km 3, on the waterfront, by INVU building. ✆ **2775-0192.** Main courses C3,500–C9,000. Daily 7am–10:30pm.

Entertainment & Nightlife

Golfito is a rough-and-tumble port town, and it pays to be careful here after dark. Most folks stick close to their hotel bar and restaurant. Of these, the bar/restaurants at **Samoa del Sur, Mar y Luna,** and the **Banana Bay Marina Bar & Grill** ★ are, by far, the liveliest. If you're feeling lucky, you can head to the **casino** at the **Hotel Sierra** (p. 495). Another popular, if somewhat oddly located, spot is the bar **La Pista** (✆ **2775-9015**), near the airstrip.

ALONG THE SHORES OF THE GOLFO DULCE

The lodges listed here are on the shores of the Golfo Dulce. This area has no roads, so you must get to the lodges by boat. I recommend that you have firm reservations when visiting this area, so your transportation can be prearranged. If worse comes to worst, you can hire a boat taxi at the *muellecito* (little dock), on the water just beyond the gas station, or La Bomba, in Golfito, for between $50 and $100, depending on your lodging destination. If driving a rental vehicle, you'll want to arrange for secure parking. See "Park It" below.

In addition to the lodges listed below, you might also check out **Playa Cativo** ★★ (www.playacativo.com; ✆ **2200-3131**), one of the first ecolodges I ever visited in Costa Rica, back when it was Rainbow Adventures. Closed for a few years, it has new owners, a major remodeling and is getting rave reviews as a prime ecolodge option in this area, with lovely rooms, great service and wonderful cuisine.

Golfo Dulce Lodge ★   This longstanding, Swiss-owned nature lodge is set just off the deeply curving beach that forms a quiet cove deep inside the Golfo Dulce. The lodge has a handful of airy, spacious cabins with hardwood floors, wood and rattan furnishings and private verandas with hammocks. Each one is named for a local animal that's hand-carved into the cabin's wooden entranceway. You're likely to see most of those critters live, especially if you're staying in the Toucan, Monkey or Macaw cabins. Three more economical, compact and basic rooms are in the main lodge building. The only neighbors the lodge has are Ron and Trudy from Casa Orquídeas (p. 493), an extensive botanical gardens located a few hundred yards away, along the beach. Golfo Dulce Lodge has been awarded "4 Leaves" by the CST Sustainable Tourism program.

Golfo Dulce. www.golfodulcelodge.com. © **8821-5398.** 8 units. $300–$360 per person double occupancy for a 3-night stay (the minimum). Rates include 3 meals daily and taxes. Add $30 per person for transportation to and from Golfito. Closed May 1–June 30 and Oct. No credit cards. **Amenities:** Restaurant; bar; outdoor pool.

Playa Nicuesa Rainforest Lodge ★★★   This exquisite lodge is one of the most remote ecolodges in the Southern zone, accessible only by boat, a 30-minute or so ride from Golfito deep inside the Golfo Dulce. The wildlife and nature viewing here is fabulous (it's a good place to find the endemic Golfo Ducle frog) as are the hikes through primary forest on the lodge's own 66-hectare (163-acre) private reserve adjoining the much larger Piedras Blancas National Park. Those who prefer water sports can kayaking and or take snorkel tours on the Golfo Dulce, where dolphins are common and whale sharks are occasionally spotted. As for the rooms, they're rich in local varnished hardwoods, and each has an element that makes the guest feel like they're one with nature. Tasty family-style meals are served in the large main lodge building, which soars and rambles over two floors featuring sitting areas, a library and reception that are all entirely open to the surrounding forest.

Golfo Dulce. www.nicuesalodge.com. © **866/504-8116** in the U.S., or 2258-8250 in Costa Rica. 9 units. $195–$255 per person per day, double occupancy. $125 children 6–12. Rates include all meals, taxes, and transfers to and from either Golfito or Puerto Jiménez. A 3-night minimum stay is required and a 4-night minimum stay is required during peak season. Closed Oct 1–Nov 15. **Amenities:** Restaurant; bar; unlimited free use of kayaks, snorkeling gear and fishing equipment.

PLAYA ZANCUDO ★

19km (12 miles) S of Golfito by boat; 35km (22 miles) S of Golfito by road

Playa Zancudo is one of Costa Rica's most undeveloped beach destinations. If you're looking for a remote and low-key beach getaway, it's hard to beat Zancudo. It's pretty far from just about everything, and with relatively few places to stay, it's virtually never crowded. However, the small number of hotel rooms to be had means that the better ones, such as those listed here, can fill up fast in the high season. The beach itself is long and flat, and because it's protected from the full force of Pacific waves, it's one of the calmest beaches on this coast and relatively good for swimming, especially toward the northern end. The beach has a splendid view across the Golfo Dulce, and the sunsets are hard to beat.

Essentials

A fishing vessel off Playa Zancudo.

GETTING THERE By Plane: The nearest airport is in Golfito. See "Golfito: Gateway to the Golfo Dulce," p. 490, for details. To get from the airport to Playa Zancudo, your best bets are by boat or taxi.

By Boat: Water taxis can be hired in Golfito to make the trip out to Playa Zancudo; however, trips depend on the tides and weather conditions. When the tide is high, the boats take a route through the mangroves. This is by far the calmest and most scenic way to get to Zancudo. When the tide is low, they must stay out in the gulf, which can get choppy at times. It costs around $15 to $20 per person for a water taxi, with a minimum charge of $40. If you can round up any sort of group, be sure to negotiate. The ride takes about 30 minutes.

Also, a passenger launch from the *muellecito* (little dock) in Golfito normally leaves daily at noon. Because the schedule sometimes changes, be sure to ask in town about current departure times. The trip lasts 40 minutes; the fare is C6,000. The *muellecito* is next to the town's principal gas station, La Bomba.

If you plan ahead, you can call **Zancudo Boat Tours** (www.los cocos.com; © **2776-0012**) and arrange for pickup in Golfito or Puerto Jiménez. The trip costs $20 per person each way from Golfito or Puerto Jiménez, with a $60 minimum. Zancudo Boat Tours also includes land transportation to your hotel in Playa Zancudo—a very nice perk because the town has so few taxis.

By Car: If you've got a four-wheel-drive vehicle, you can make it out to Zancudo even in the rainy season. To get here, follow the directions for driving to Golfito, but don't go all the way into town. The turnoff for playas Zancudo and Pavones is at El Rodeo, about 4km (2½ miles) outside of Golfito, on the road in from the Interamerican Highway. It's mostly rough, gravel and dirt roads. Follow the few signs and the flow of traffic (if there is any) or stick to the most worn route when in doubt.

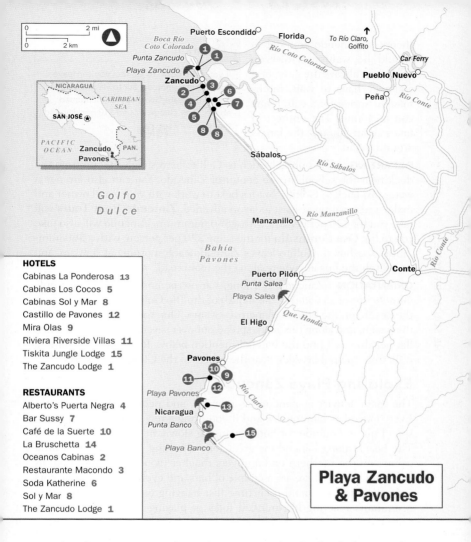

HOTELS

Cabinas La Ponderosa **13**
Cabinas Los Cocos **5**
Cabinas Sol y Mar **8**
Castillo de Pavones **12**
Mira Olas **9**
Riviera Riverside Villas **11**
Tiskita Jungle Lodge **15**
The Zancudo Lodge **1**

RESTAURANTS

Alberto's Puerta Negra **4**
Bar Sussy **7**
Café de la Suerte **10**
La Bruschetta **14**
Oceanos Cabinas **2**
Restaurante Macondo **3**
Soda Katherine **6**
Sol y Mar **8**
The Zancudo Lodge **1**

Playa Zancudo & Pavones

An alternative route from Paso Canoas (at the border) is via the towns of La Cuesta and Laurel. This route meets the route mentioned above at the small village of Conte.

A four-wheel-drive **taxi** costs around $75 from Golfito. It takes about 1 hour when the road is in good condition, and about 2 hours when it's not.

By Bus: It's possible to get to Zancudo by bus, but I highly recommend coming by boat from Golfito, or your own car. If you insist, there's one daily bus leaving Golfito for Zancudo at 3pm. Alternately, you can catch one of the Pavones buses and get off in the village of Conte. In theory, a Zancudo-bound bus should be waiting. However, this is not always the case, and you may have to wait, hitchhike, or spring for a cab, if any can be found. The entire trip takes about 3 hours; the fare is around $3.50.

> ### Park It
>
> If you drive down to Golfito, you can leave your car at Samoa del Sur (p. 495) and take one of the waterborne routes mentioned above. They charge around $10 per day, and the lot is very secure.

DEPARTING   The public launch to Golfito leaves daily at 7am from the dock near the school, in the center of Zancudo. You can also arrange a water taxi back to Golfito, but it's best to work with your hotel owner and make a reservation at least a day in advance. **Zancudo Boat Tours** will take you for $20 per person, with a $60 minimum. Zancudo will also take you to the **Osa Peninsula** for the same $20 per person, with a $60 minimum. The bus to Golfito leaves Zancudo each morning at 5:30am. You can catch the bus anywhere along the main road.

ORIENTATION   Zancudo is a long, narrow peninsula (sometimes only 90m/295 ft. or so wide) at the mouth of the Río Colorado. On one side is the beach; on the other a mangrove swamp. One road runs the length of the beach, and along this road, spread out over several kilometers of long, flat beach, you'll find the hotels I mention below. It's about a 20-minute walk from the public dock near the school to the Cabinas Sol y Mar.

Exploring Playa Zancudo

The main activity at Zancudo is relaxing, and people take it seriously. Every lodge has hammocks, and if you bring a few good books, you can spend quite a number of hours swinging slowly in the tropical breezes. The beach along Zancudo is great for swimming. It's generally a little calmer on the northern end and gets rougher (good for bodysurfing) as you head south. There are a couple of bars and even a disco, but visitors are most likely to spend their time just hanging out at their hotel or in restaurants meeting like-minded folks or playing board games. If you want to take a horseback ride on the beach, your hotel can arrange it.

Susan and Andrew England, who run Cabinas Los Cocos, also operate **Zancudo Boat Tours** (www.loscocos.com; ☏ **2776-0012**), which offers kayaking tours, trips to the Casa Orquídeas Botanical Garden, hikes on the Osa Peninsula, a trip up the Río Coto to watch birds and wildlife, and more. A boat trip through the Río Coto mangroves will turn up a remarkable number of sea and shore birds, as well as the chance to see a crocodile resting on a riverbank, or a white-faced monkey leaping overhead. Tour prices are $50 to $75 per person per tour, with discounts available for larger groups.

For fishing, ask at your hotel, or contact the **Zancudo Beach Resort** (see below). A full day of fishing with lunch and beer should cost between $950 and $1,600 per boat.

Because a mangrove swamp is directly behind the beach, mosquitoes and sand flies can be a problem when the winds die down, so be sure to bring insect repellent.

Where to Stay

Quite a few fully equipped beach houses are for rent here for long stays. Once again, Susan and Andrew at **Los Cocos** (www.loscocos.com; ☎ 2776-0012) are your best bet for lining up one of these houses.

EXPENSIVE

The Zancudo Lodge ★★★ The only upscale lodging in Playa Zancudo, this beachfront lodge is located towards the far northern tip of the peninsula, and caters predominantly to fishermen Each of the air-conditioned rooms has flat screen televisions, hardwood floors and handsome contemporary furnishings and decor. The resort also offers a salt-water fed swimming pool. The restaurant serves sophisticated cuisine, usually featuring at least some part of the daily catch, as well as the organic vegetables that are grown on-site. On the lagoon side of the peninsula the lodge maintains a marina, with a fleet of well-equipped open-cockpit fishing boats.

Playa Zancudo. www.thezancudolodge.com. ☎ **800/854-8791** in the U.S. or Canada, or 2776-0008 in Costa Rica. 15 units. $250 double; $325–$550 bungalow or suite. **Amenities:** Restaurant; bar; outdoor pool; free Wi-Fi.

MODERATE

Cabinas Los Cocos ★ Andrew and Susan Robertson homesteaded this lovely collection of four private cabins, set under tall trees and thick foliage, just steps from the beach. Two of the houses are reclaimed homes from the former United Fruit Company plantation in nearby Golfito. All feature thatch roofs and a private veranda, and offer a kitchen or kitchenette, encouraging longer stays. The Robertsons also run Zancudo Boat Tours, a topnotch operation providing waterborne transportation and tour activities around the region.

Playa Zancudo. www.loscocos.com. ☎ **2776-0012.** 4 units. $75 double. Weekly discounts available. No credit cards.

INEXPENSIVE

Cabinas Sol y Mar ★ Cozy and functional ocean-facing rooms with screened windows whose heavy wooden shutters swing open wide to let light and wind in—that's what you get at Cabinas Sol y Mar. And that, along with access to one of Zancudo's best restaurants (p. 502), is likely enough, especially with the fair pricing and the warm welcome you'll get from owners Rick and Lori. They're always on hand and have a knack for making guests feel like family. *Budgeteer tip:* They also allow on-site camping here, so don't be hesitant to ask.

Playa Zancudo. www.zancudo.com. ☎ **2776-0014.** 6 units. $46–$50 double. **Amenities:** Restaurant; bar; free Wi-Fi.

Where to Dine

In addition to the place listed below, you might try the tasty Italian meals at **Restaurante Macondo** (© **2776-0157**) or **Alberto's Puerta Negra** ★ (© **2776-0181**). If you want basic Tico fare and some local company, head to **Bar Sussy** (© **2776-0107**) or **Soda Katherine** (© **2776-0124**). For a good breakfast, lunch, or dinner, or perhaps just a midday ice-cream treat, check out the open-air restaurant at **Oceanos Cabinas** ★ (www.oceanocabinas.com; © **2776-0921**), which serves excellent freshly caught seafood and is locally famous for their *ceviche*.

Finally, for some refined dining or a special occasion, head to **The Zancudo Lodge** (p. 501).

Sol y Mar ★★ INTERNATIONAL/SEAFOOD   Most folks visiting Playa Zancudo end up here. Some never leave. This friendly, open-air restaurant and bar is undeniably the social (and culinary) center of this tiny beach town. The menu is long and varied, ranging from the fresh daily catch in a Thai coconut curry sauce to dry-rubbed beef served with basil butter. There's also plenty of bar food staples, as well as twice weekly barbeque nights. If there's live music in town, it's likely to be here, and the Sunday horseshoe tournament is a beloved tradition.

At Cabinas Sol y Mar. © **2776-0014.** Main courses C3,900–C8,600. Daily 8am–9pm.

PLAYA PAVONES: A SURFER'S MECCA ★

40km (25 miles) S of Golfito

Hailed as the world's longest rideable left point break, Pavones is a legendary destination for surfing. It takes around 1.8m (6 ft.) of swell to get this wave cranking, but when the surf's up, you're in for a long, long ride—so long, in fact, that it's much easier to walk back through town to where the wave is breaking than to paddle back. The swells are most consistent during the rainy season, but you're likely to find surfers here year-round. Locals tend to be pretty possessive of their turf, so don't be surprised if you receive a cool welcome.

Other than surfing, nothing much goes on here; however, the surrounding rainforests are quite nice, and the beaches feature some rocky coves and points that give Pavones a bit more visual appeal than Zancudo. If you're feeling energetic, you can go for a horseback ride or hike into the rainforests that back up this beach town, or stroll south on the beaches that stretch toward Punta Banco and beyond, all the way to the Panamanian border. This is a forgotten and isolated destination catering almost exclusively to backpackers. Be prepared—Pavones is a tiny village with few amenities, and most of the accommodations are quite basic.

The legendary left at Pavones.

Essentials

GETTING THERE & DEPARTING

By Plane: The nearest airport with regularly scheduled flights is in Golfito (p. 491). Tiskita Jungle Lodge (p. 504) has a private airstrip. Depending on space, you might be able to arrange transportation to Pavones on one of its charter flights even if you are not staying there.

By Car: If you've got a four-wheel-drive vehicle, you can make it out to Pavones even in the rainy season. To get here, follow the directions for driving to Golfito (p. 492), but don't go all the way into town. The turnoff for playas Zancudo and Pavones is at El Rodeo, about 4km (2½ miles) outside of Golfito, on the road in from the Interamerican Highway. It's mostly rough, gravel and dirt roads. Follow the few signs and the flow of traffic (if there is any) or stick to the most worn route when in doubt.

An alternative route from Paso Canoas (at the border) goes via the towns of La Cuesta and Laurel. This route meets the route mentioned above at the small village of Conte.

Be sure to pick up your tank in Golfito, Rio Claro or the small town of Laurel, as Pavones has no gas station.

By Bus: Two daily buses (no phone) go to Pavones from Golfito at 10am and 3pm. Trip duration is 2½ hours; the fare is C1695. Buses to Golfito depart Pavones daily at 5:30am and 12:30pm. This is a very remote destination, and the bus schedule is subject to change, so it always pays to check in advance.

Exploring Pavones

Surfing is the big draw in Pavones. For board rentals, head to **Sea Kings Surf Shop** (www.surfpavones.com; © **2776-2015**). If there are no waves, or you want some other form of exercise, check in with the folks at **Shooting Star Yoga** (www.yogapavones.com; © **2776-2107**).

If you're interested in a guided tour, call **Pavones Tours** (www.pavonestours.com; © **2776-2119**), which offers a wide range of adventure outings, including horseback rides on the beach and whale- and dolphin-watching cruises in small boats, as well as sportfishing, scuba diving, and kayak trips.

Alternately, you can do a day tour and guided hike at **Tiskita Lodge** (see below), for $25 per person, with advance reservation.

A WILD ride

Surfers first discovered the amazing wave off Pavones in the late 1970s. When conditions are right, this wave peels off in one continuous ribbon for over 2km (1.25 miles). Your skills better be up to snuff, and your legs better be in good shape, if you want to ride this wave.

Pavones got some good press in Allan Weisbecker's 2001 novel "In Search of Captain Zero: A Surfer's Road Trip Beyond The End of the Road." The word was out and surfers began flocking to Pavones from all over. On any given day—when the wave is working—you are likely to find surfers from the United

States, Brazil, Argentina, Israel, Australia, Peru, and any other number of countries.

However, the town and wave are not without controversy. Aside from the typical territorial spats that erupt over most popular waves, Pavones has been the site of a series of prominent squabbles and controversies that include land disputes, drug busts, fist fights, and even murders. For a unique and in-depth account of the town, its wave, and some of these controversies, check out Weisbecker's "Can't You Get Along with Anyone?: A Writer's Memoir and a Tale of a Lost Surfer's Paradise."

Where to Stay & Dine

In addition to the remote nature lodge listed below, **Riviera Riverside Villas** (www.pavonesriviera.com; ✆ **2776-2396**) offers modern, plush individual cabins, as well as several fully equipped house rentals, a block or so inland from the water, right alongside the Río Claro (Clear River). **Cabinas La Ponderosa ★** (www.laponderosapavones.com; ✆ **2776-2076**) is a small, beachfront collection of cabins and private, rustic villas, a bit outside of town, on the way to Punta Banco.

Right in Pavones, several very basic lodges cater to itinerant surfers by renting rooms for between $10 and $20 per night for a double room; most take walk-in reservations since they don't have phones. That said, for in-town budget lodgings, I recommend **Mira Olas** (www.miraolas.com; ✆ **2776-2006**), about 2 blocks uphill from the soccer field.

For dining, I recommend **Café de la Suerte ★** (www.cafedelasuerte.com; ✆ **2776-2388**), a lively little joint fronting the village soccer field that serves breakfasts and lunches and specializes in vegetarian items, freshly baked goods, and fresh-fruit smoothies. These folks serve dinner during the high season, and rent out cute, cozy A/C-equipped rooms. Heading out towards Punta Banco, **La Bruschetta ★** (✆ **2776-2174**) is another good option, with chef and owner Lela serving up excellent pizzas, pastas and other Italian-based fare.

EXPENSIVE

Tiskita Jungle Lodge ★★ This impressive ecolodge is the loving (and intense) handiwork of Peter and Lisbeth Aspinall. Carved into a rainforest-covered hillside with panoramic views to the Pacific Ocean, the lodge features nine bungalows offering up a total of 17 rooms. The bungalows are wood, wood, and more glowing wood, with dozens of windows letting the views in. Trails on the private reserve lead through thick rainforest to jungle waterfalls and idyllic swimming holes. The dark black volcanic sand beach is a relatively short hike downhill, but a good workout on the way back. Between the lodge and the shore lies a private airstrip with a grassy runway kept cut short by grazing cattle. A charter flight in is the quickest and most common means of reaching Tiskita. Peter is a pioneer in conservation and ecotourism in Costa Rica. He is also an avid farmer with an impressive and extensive collection of tropical fauna, including a wide range of exotic fruits, vegetables and nuts from around the globe. The lodge closes to all but groups in the off season.

6km (3¾ miles) southeast, down the road from Pavones. www.tiskita.com. © **2296-8125** reservation office in San José, or 2776-2194 at the lodge. 17 units. $570 per person for 3 nights. Additional nights $170 per person. Rates include all meals, 2 daily guided hikes, and taxes. Rates are based on double occupancy. 3-night minimum required. Discounts available for children 12 and under. **Amenities:** Restaurant; bar; small outdoor pool.

MODERATE

Castillo de Pavones ★   Set on a hillside just above the town and the famous break of Pavones, this is the best option for folks looking for easy access to the waves and a bit more in the way of creature comforts than you'll find at most of the other in-town options. There are only a few rooms here, but all are large, airy and feature plenty of windows. Some have private balconies with hand fashioned driftwood railings, and all feature a somewhat disorienting mix of odd, outdated furnishings and quirky stone and tile work. Still, the hotel's friendly staff, excellent restaurant and rooftop bar and lookout more than make up for any architectural or design flaws. The rooftop bar, by the way is the highlight of the building, completely open on three sides and featuring seating at a long plank hewn from a giant rainforest tree.

Suite at Castillo de Pavones.

4 blocks uphill from the center of town, Pavones. www.castillodepavones.com. © **2776-2191.** 5 units. $125-$200 double. Rates include full breakfast. **Amenities:** Restaurant; bar; free surfboard usage; free Wi-Fi.

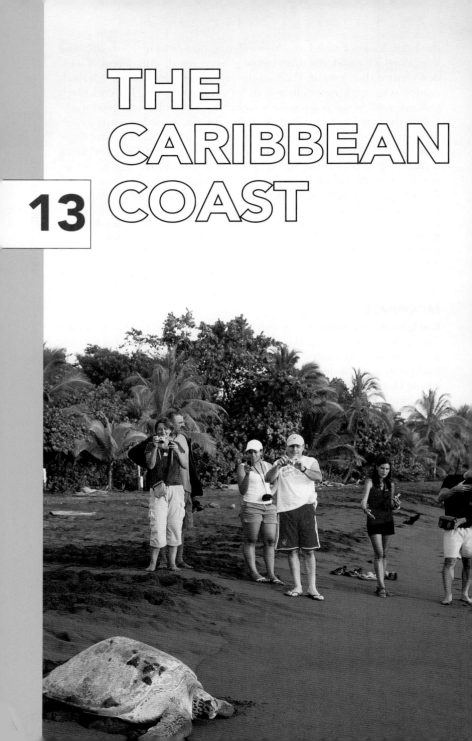

THE
CARIBBEAN
COAST

13

Costa Rica's Caribbean coast is a world apart from the rest of the country. The pace is slower, the food is spicier, the tropical heat is more palpable, and the rhythmic lilt of patois and reggae music fills the air. This remains one of Costa Rica's least discovered and explored regions. More than half of the coastline here is still inaccessible except by boat or small plane. This inaccessibility has helped preserve large tracts of virgin lowland rainforest, which are now set aside as **Tortuguero National Park ★★** and **Barra del Colorado National Wildlife Refuge ★**. These two parks, on the coast's northern reaches, are among Costa Rica's most popular destinations for adventurers and ecotravelers. Of particular interest are the sea turtles that nest here. Farther south, **Cahuita National Park ★★** is another popular national park, located just off its namesake beach village. It was set up to preserve 200 hectares (494 acres) of coral reef, but its palm tree-lined white-sand beaches and gentle trails are stunning.

So remote was the Caribbean coast from Costa Rica's population centers in the Central Valley that it developed a culture all its own. The original inhabitants of the area included people of the Bribri, Cabécar, and Kéköldi tribes, and these groups maintain their cultures on indigenous reserves in the Talamanca Mountains. In fact, until the 1870s, this area had few non-Indians. However, when Minor Keith (p. 25) built the railroad to San José and began planting bananas, he brought in black laborers from Jamaica and other Caribbean islands to lay the track and work the plantations. These workers and their descendants established fishing and farming communities up and down the coast. Today dreadlocked Rastafarians, reggae music, Creole cooking, and the English-based patois of this Afro-Caribbean culture give this region a quasi-Jamaican flavor, a striking contrast with the Spanish-derived Costa Rican culture.

The Caribbean coast has only one major city, **Limón,** a major commercial port and popular cruise ship port of call. However, the city itself is of little interest to most visitors, who quickly head south to the coast's spectacular beaches, or north to the jungle canals of Tortuguero.

FACING PAGE: **Tourists watching a turtle return to the sea after laying eggs.**

Over the years, the Caribbean coast has garnered a reputation as being a dangerous, drug-infested zone, rife with crime. And though there have been several high-profile crimes in the area and petty theft is a major problem overall this reputation is exaggerated. The same crime and drug problems found here exist in San José and most of the popular beach destinations on the Pacific coast. Use common sense and take normal precautions and you should have no problems on the Caribbean coast.

THE best CARIBBEAN COAST TRAVEL EXPERIENCES

- **Landing a Tarpon off Barra del Colorado:** Reaching lengths of between 1.8 and 2.8m (6–8 ft.), and often weighing in at well over 200 pounds, tarpon are a hard-fighting and high-jumping game fish. Barra del Colorado is a prime fishing ground for these fierce fish. See p. 509.

- **Cruising the Rainforest Canals of Tortuguero:** Lined by thick tropical rainforest and rich in wildlife, the canals surrounding Tortuguero are home to manatees, caimans, green macaws, and several monkey species. See p. 519.

- **Tasting Chocolate at the Source:** Taking you "from bean to bar," Caribeans Chocolate Tour starts with a walk through an organic cacao farm and ends with a tasting of freshly made, local organic chocolate. See p. 555.

- **Watching Surfers Challenge Salsa Brava:** Sometimes called "Little Pipeline," Puerto Viejo's Salsa Brava is a fast and steep wave that breaks over sharp, shallow coral. The wave is also pretty close to shore, which makes this a good place to watch some world-class surfing. See p. 546.

- **Snorkeling Off Manzanillo:** One of Costa Rica's most bountiful and beautiful coral reefs lies just off the coast of the small village of Manzanillo. In addition to coral, sponges, and reef fish, if you're lucky, you may also catch a glimpse of a dolphin or sea turtle. See p. 553.

BARRA DEL COLORADO ★

115km (71 miles) NE of San José

Most visitors to Barra del Colorado come for the fishing. Tarpon and snook fishing are world-class, or you can head farther offshore for deep-sea action. Barra del Colorado is part of the same ecosystem as Tortuguero National Park (p. 512); as in Tortuguero, an abundance of wildlife and rainforest fauna lives in the rivers and canals.

Named for its location at the mouth of the Río Colorado up near the Costa Rica–Nicaragua border, Barra del Colorado can be reached only by boat or small plane. No roads go in or out of Barra del Colorado. The town itself is a small, ramshackle collection of raised stilt houses, and it supports a diverse population of Afro-Caribbean and Miskito Indian residents, Nicaraguan emigrants, and transient commercial fishermen.

It's hot and humid here most of the year, and it rains a lot, so although some of the lodges have at times risked offering a "tarpon guarantee," they're generally hesitant to promise anything in terms of the weather.

Essentials

GETTING THERE & DEPARTING By Plane: Most folks come here on multiday fishing packages, and most of the area's lodges either include charter flights as part of their package trips or will book you a flight.

By Boat: It is also possible to travel to Barra del Colorado by boat from **Puerto Viejo de Sarapiquí** (see chapter 10). Expect to pay $400 to $600 each way for a boat that holds up to 10 people. Check at the

An angler pulling in a tarpon in Barra del Colorado.

public dock in Puerto Viejo de Sarapiquí or call **Oasis Nature Tours** (www.oasisnaturetours.com; ✆ **2766-6108**).

Río Colorado Lodge (www.riocoloradolodge.com; ✆ **800/243-9777** in the U.S. and Canada, or 2232-4063/2232-8610) runs its own launch between Barra del Colorado and San José. If you're staying at the Río Colorado Lodge, be sure to ask about this option (for at least one leg of your trip) when booking.

TOWN LAYOUT The Río Colorado neatly divides the town of Barra del Colorado. The airstrip is in the southern half of town, as are most of the lodgings. The lodges that are farther up the canals will meet you at the airstrip with a small boat.

Fishing, Fishing & More Fishing

Almost all the lodges here specialize in fishing packages. If you don't fish, you may wonder just what in the world you're doing here. Even though the area offers excellent opportunities for bird-watching and touring jungle waterways, most lodges merely pay lip service to ecotourists and would rather see you with a rod and reel.

Fishing takes place year-round. You can fish in the rivers and canals, in the very active river mouth, or offshore. Most anglers come in search of the tarpon, or silver king. **Tarpon** can be caught year-round, both in the river mouth and, to a lesser extent, in the canals; however, they are much harder to land in July and August—the two rainiest months—probably because the river runs so high and is so full of runoff and debris. **Snook,** an aggressive river fish, peak in April, May, October, and November; fat snook, or *calba,* run heavy from November through January. Depending on how far out to sea you venture, you might hook up with **barracuda, jack, mackerel** (Spanish and king), **wahoo, tuna, dorado, marlin,** or **sailfish.** In the rivers and canals, fishermen regularly bring in *mojarra, machaca,* and *guapote* (rainbow bass).

Following current trends in sportfishing, more and more anglers have been using fly rods, in addition to traditional rod-and-reel setups, to land just about all the fish mentioned above. To fish here, you'll need a fishing license, which covers both salt and fresh water. Fishing licenses can be bought for anywhere from 1 week to 1 year in duration and cost between $15 and $50 accordingly. The lodges in the area either include these in their packages or can readily provide the licenses for you.

Nonfishers should see whether their lodge has a good naturalist guide or canoes or kayaks for rent or use.

The Caribbean coast has only one major city, **Limón,** a major commercial port and popular cruise ship port of call. However, the city itself is of little interest to most visitors, who quickly head south to the coast's spectacular beaches, or north to the jungle canals of Tortuguero.

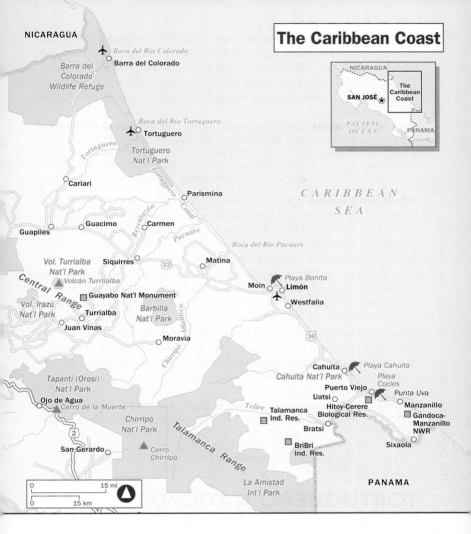

The Caribbean Coast

NICARAGUA

Boca del Río Colorado

Barra del Colorado

Barra del Colorado Wildlife Refuge

Boca del Río Tortuguero

Tortuguero

Tortuguero Nat'l Park

Cariari

Parismina

CARIBBEAN SEA

Guacimo

Carmen

Guapiles

Revantazón

Pacuare

Boca del Río Pacuare

Vol. Turrialba Nat'l Park

Siquirres

32

Matina

Volcán Turrialba

Playa Bonita

Moin

Limón

Guayabo Nat'l Monument

Westfalia

Vol. Irazú Nat'l Park

Turrialba

Barbilla Nat'l Park

Juan Vinas

Moravia

36

Tapanti (Orosi) Nat'l Park

Cahuita

Playa Cahuita

Cahuita Nat'l Park

Playa Cocles

Ojo de Agua

Cerro de la Muerte

Puerto Viejo

Uatsi

Punta Uva

Telire

Talamanca Ind. Res.

Hitoy-Cerere Biological Res.

Manzanillo

Chirripó Nat'l Park

Bratsi

Gandoca-Manzanillo NWR

San Gerardo

Cerro Chirripó

BriBri Ind. Res.

Sixaola

0   15 mi
0   15 km

La Amistad Int'l Park

PANAMA

Inset map: NICARAGUA · SAN JOSÉ · The Caribbean Coast · PACIFIC OCEAN · PANAMA

Where to Stay & Dine

Almost all of the hotels here specialize in package tours, including all your meals, fishing and tackle, taxes, and usually your transportation and liquor too, so rates are high. With no dependable budget hotels, Barra remains a remote and difficult destination for those looking to save.

Río Colorado Lodge ★ Founded in 1972 by the legendary fisherman and conservation activist Archie Fields, this fishing lodge can be a little rough around the edges, but nevertheless has been catering to discerning fishermen and women for over four decades. That's likely because both the food and the fishing guides are tip top and for anglers that's what matters. As for the property, its rambling complex of wooden structures with somewhat outdated but spotless rooms (time to get new curtains and sheets, folks!) connected by a network of raised walkways. The lodge has distinct bar, lounge and dining areas, where folks gather to tell their big fish tales. Current owner Dan Wise took over from Archie and is often on hand.

Barra del Colorado. www.riocoloradotarponfishing.com. **℗ 800/243-9777** in U.S. and Canada, or 2232-4063 or 2232-8610 in Costa Rica. 18 units. $2,813–$3,378/person double occupancy for 7 days/6 nights with 4 full days of fishing, 2 nights lodging in San José, all meals and drinks at the lodge, boat, guide, fuel and licenses. Non-fishing guests $175–$225/person per day. **Amenities:** Restaurant; bar; Jacuzzi; Wi-Fi.

Silver King Lodge ★★   For more comfort and pampering during the hours when you're not stalking some massive tarpon, this dedicated fishing lodge is the first choice. As at Rio Colorado Lodge (above), the large complex of rooms and common areas is built on pilings above the river and flood levels, and connected by a network of covered wooden walkways. But room quality, food and service are miles above anything else in the area. The whole place is awash in varnished hardwoods. In fact, the varnish is so well maintained you might reach for your sunglasses inside the rooms or bar and dining areas. The rooms themselves feel massive, and all come with two queen beds, and built-in racks for all your fishing gear. The lodge has a lovely outdoor pool and covered Jacuzzi, perfect for unwinding after a hard morning and hot afternoon fishing. Abundant and varied buffet meals are served. I'm not sure if I've ever had better coconut battered snook, anywhere.

Barra del Colorado. www.silverkinglodge.net. **℗ 877/335-0755** in the U.S. 10 units. $2,750–$3,960/person double occupancy for 3 full days of fishing, round-trip air transportation btw. San José and the lodge, all meals at the lodge, liquor, and taxes; $475–$545 per person per extra day, including all fishing, meals, liquor, and taxes. Closed June–Aug and Nov–Jan. **Amenities:** Restaurant; bar; Jacuzzi; small outdoor pool; small spa; free Wi-Fi.

TORTUGUERO NATIONAL PARK ★★

250km (155 miles) NE of San José; 79km (49 miles) N of Limón

Tortuguero is a tiny fishing village connected to the rest of mainland Costa Rica by a series of rivers and canals. This aquatic highway is lined with a mix of farmland and dense tropical rainforest that is home to howler and spider monkeys, three-toed sloths, toucans, and great green macaws. A trip through the canals surrounding Tortuguero is a lot like cruising the Amazon basin—on a much smaller scale.

"Tortuguero" comes from the Spanish name for the giant sea turtles (*tortugas*) that nest on the beaches of this region every year from early March to mid-October (prime season is July–Oct, and peak months are

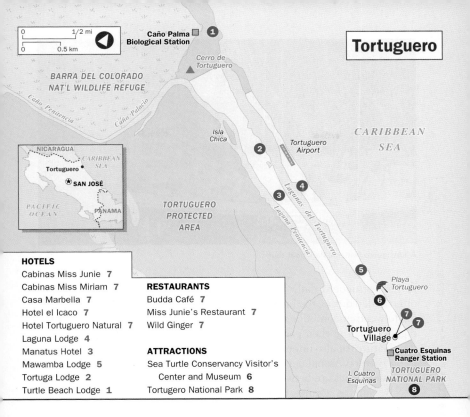

HOTELS

Cabinas Miss Junie **7**
Cabinas Miss Miriam **7**
Casa Marbella **7**
Hotel el Icaco **7**
Hotel Tortuguero Natural **7**
Laguna Lodge **4**
Manatus Hotel **3**
Mawamba Lodge **5**
Tortuga Lodge **2**
Turtle Beach Lodge **1**

RESTAURANTS

Budda Café **7**
Miss Junie's Restaurant **7**
Wild Ginger **7**

ATTRACTIONS

Sea Turtle Conservancy Visitor's
  Center and Museum **6**
Tortugero National Park **8**

Aug–Sept). The chance to see this nesting attracts many people to this remote region, but just as many come to explore the intricate network of jungle canals that serve as the region's main transportation arteries.

Independent travel is not the norm here, although it's possible. Most travelers rely on their lodge for boat transportation through the canals and into town. At most of the lodges around Tortuguero, almost everything (bus rides to and from, boat trips through the canals, and even family-style meals) is done in groups.

Very important: More than 508cm (200 in.) of rain fall here annually, so you can expect a downpour at any time of the year. Most of the lodges will provide you with rain gear (including ponchos and rubber boots), but it can't hurt to carry your own.

Essentials

GETTING THERE & DEPARTING **By Plane: Nature Air** (www.nature air.com; ✆ **800/235-9272** in the U.S. and Canada, or 2299-6000 in Costa Rica) has one daily flight at 6am for **Tortuguero** airstrip (no phone) from Juan Santamaría International Airport in San José. The flight takes approximately 30 minutes; the fare is $107 each way. The return flight

A Tortuguero National Park boat tour.

leaves Tortuguero daily at 7:05am for San José. Additional flights are often added during the high season, and departure times can vary according to weather conditions. In addition, many local lodges operate charter flights as part of their package trips.

Nature Air also offers a morning direct flight from Tortuguero airstrip to La Fortuna/Arenal departing at 7:05am. Frequency of this flight varies seasonally; fares are between $131 and $135 per person, one-way.

Be sure to arrange with your hotel to pick you up at the airstrip. Otherwise you'll have to plead with one of the other hotels' boat captains to give you a lift, which they'll usually do for free (or for a few dollars).

By Car: It's not possible to drive to Tortuguero. If you have a car, your best bet is either to leave it in San José and take an organized tour, or drive it to Limón or Moín, find a secure hotel or public parking lot, and then follow the directions for arriving by boat below. La Pavona has a secure parking lot useful for those meeting the boats plying the Cariari and La Pavona route outlined below.

By Boat: Flying to Tortuguero is convenient if you don't have much time, but a boat trip through the canals and rivers of this region is often the highlight of any visit. However, be forewarned: Although this trip can be stunning and exciting, it can also be long, tiring, and uncomfortable. You'll first have to ride by bus or minivan from San José to Moín, Caño Blanco, or one of the other embarkation points; then it's 2 to 3 hours on a boat, usually with hard wooden benches or plastic seats. All of the more expensive lodges listed offer their own bus and boat transportation packages, which include the boat ride through the canals. However, if you're coming here on the cheap and plan to stay at one of the less expensive lodges or at a budget *cabina* in Tortuguero, you will have to arrange your own transportation. In this case, you have a few options.

The most traditional option is to get yourself first to Limón and then to the public docks in **Moín,** just north of Limón, and try to find a boat on your own. You can reach Limón easily by public bus from San José (see "Getting There & Departing," p. 525). If you're coming by car, make sure you drive all the way to Limón or Moín, unless you have prior arrangements out of Cariari or Caño Blanco Marina.

If you arrive in Limón by bus, you might be able to catch one of the periodic local buses to Moín (C300) at the main bus terminal. Otherwise, you can take a taxi for around C7,000 to C8,500, for up to four people. At the docks, you should be able to negotiate a fare of between $60 and $90 per person round-trip with one of the boats docked here. These boats tend to depart between 8 and 10am every morning. You can stay as many days as you like in Tortuguero, but be sure to arrange with the captain to be there to pick you up when you're ready to leave. The trip from Moín to Tortuguero takes between 3 and 4 hours.

It is possible to get to Tortuguero by bus and boat from Cariari. For backpackers and budget travelers, this is the cheapest and most reliable means of reaching Tortuguero from San José.

To take this route, begin by catching the 9 or 10:30am direct bus to Cariari from the **Gran Terminal del Caribe,** on Calle Central, Avenida 13 (© **2222-0610**). The fare is C1,715. This bus will actually drop you off at the main bus terminal in Cariari, from which you'll have to walk 4 blocks east to a separate bus station, known locally as *"la estación vieja,"* or the old station. Here, you can buy your bus ticket for La Pavona, also known as Rancho El Suerte. The bus fare is around C1,300. Buses to La Pavona leave at 6am, 11am and 3pm.

A boat or two will be waiting to meet the bus at the dock at the edge of the river. These boats leave after a bus arrives, or when they fill up. The boat fare to Tortuguero is C1,600 each way. You can buy your ticket for the boat at the cashier of the very prominent (and only) restaurant at La Pavona. Return boats leave Tortuguero for La Pavona every morning at 6 and 11:30am, and 3pm, making return bus connections to Cariari.

Warning: Be careful if you decide to take this route. I've received reports of unscrupulous operators providing misinformation to tourists. Folks from a company called **Bananera** have offices at the Gran Terminal del Caribe and in Cariari, offering to sell you "packaged transportation" to Tortuguero. However, all they are doing is charging you extra to buy the individual tickets described above. Be especially careful if the folks selling you boat transportation aggressively steer you to a specific hotel option, claim that your first choice is full, or insist that you must buy a package with them that includes the transportation, lodging, and guide services. If you have doubts or want to check on the current state of this route, check out the site **www.tortuguerovillage.com**, which has detailed directions about how to get to Tortuguero by a variety of routes.

Finally, it's also possible, albeit expensive, to travel to Tortuguero by boat from **Puerto Viejo de Sarapiquí** (see chapter 10). Expect to pay $500 to $700 each way for a boat that holds up to 10 people. Check at the public dock in Puerto Viejo de Sarapiquí if you're interested. The ride usually takes about 3 to 4 hours, and the boats tend to leave in the morning.

VILLAGE LAYOUT Tortuguero is one of the most remote locations in Costa Rica. With no roads into this area and no cars in the village, all transportation is by boat or foot. Most of the lodges are spread out over several kilometers to the north of Tortuguero Village on either side of the main canal; the small airstrip is at the north end of the beachside spit of land. At the far northern end of the main canal, you'll see the **Cerro de Tortuguero (Turtle Hill),** which, at some 119m (390 ft.), towers over the area. The hike to the top of this hill is a popular half-day tour and offers some good views of the Tortuguero canal and village, as well as the Caribbean Sea.

Tortuguero Village is a small collection of houses connected by footpaths. The village is spread out on a thin spit of land, bordered on one side by the Caribbean Sea and on the other by the main canal. At most points, it's less than 300m (984 ft.) wide. In the center of the village, you'll find a small children's playground, the town's health clinic, and a soccer field.

A stilt house in Tortuguero.

LEFT: **A turtle hatchling heading to sea;** RIGHT: **Turtles in Tortuguero National Park.**

If you stay at a hotel on the ocean side of the canal, you'll be able to walk into and explore the village at your leisure; if you're across the canal, you'll be dependent on the lodge's boat transportation. However, some of the lodges across the canal have their own network of jungle trails that might appeal to naturalists.

FAST FACTS Tortuguero has no banks, ATMs, or currency-exchange houses, so be sure to bring sufficient cash in colones to cover any expenses and incidental charges. The local hotels and shops generally charge a commission to exchange dollars.

Exploring the National Park

According to existing records, sea turtles have frequented Tortuguero National Park since at least 1592, largely due to its extreme isolation. Over the years, turtles were captured and their eggs were harvested by local settlers; by the 1950s, this practice became so widespread that turtles faced extinction. Regulations controlling this mini-industry were passed in 1963, and in 1970 Tortuguero National Park was established.

Today, four different species of sea turtles nest here: the green turtle, the hawksbill, the loggerhead, and the giant leatherback. The park's beaches are excellent places to watch sea turtles nest, especially at night. As appealingly long and deserted as they are, however, the beaches are not appropriate for swimming. The surf is usually very rough, and the river mouths attract sharks that feed on the turtle hatchlings and many fish that live here.

Green turtles are the most common turtle found in Tortuguero, so you're more likely to see one of them than any other species if you visit during the prime nesting season from **July to mid-October** (Aug–Sept are peak months). **Loggerheads** are very rare, so don't be disappointed if you don't see one. The **giant leatherback** is perhaps the most spectacular sea turtle to watch laying eggs. The largest of all turtle species, the leatherback can grow to 2m (6½ ft.) long and weigh well over 1,000 pounds. They nest from late February to June, predominantly in the southern part of the park. See the "In Search of Turtles" box on p. 112.

You can explore the park's rainforest, either by foot or by boat, and look for some of the incredible varieties of wildlife that live here: jaguars, anteaters, howler monkeys, collared and white-lipped peccaries, some 350 species of birds, and countless butterflies, among others. Some of the more colorful and common bird species you might see in this area include the rufescent and tiger herons, keel-billed toucan, northern jacana, red lored parrot, and ringed kingfisher. Boat tours are far and away the most popular way to visit this park, although one frequently very muddy trail starts at the park entrance and runs for about 2km (1.25 miles) through the coastal rainforest and along the beach.

Although it's a perfect habitat, West Indian manatees (*Trichechus manatus*) are rare and threatened in the canals, rivers, and lagoons of Costa Rica's Caribbean coast. Hunting and propeller injuries are the prime culprits. Your chances of seeing one of these gentle aquatic mammals is extremely remote.

ENTRY POINT, FEES & REGULATIONS   The Tortuguero National Park entrance and ranger station are at the south end of Tortuguero Village. The ranger station is inside a landlocked old patrol boat, and a small, informative open-air kiosk explains a bit about the park and its environs. Admission to the park is $15. However, most people visit Tortuguero as part of a package tour. Be sure to confirm whether the park entrance is included in the price. Moreover, only certain canals and trails leaving from the park station are actually within the park. Many hotels and private guides take their tours to a series of canals that border the park and are very similar in terms of flora and fauna but don't require park

Turtle Tips

- Visitors to the beach at night must be accompanied by a licensed guide. Tours generally last between 2 and 4 hours.

- Sometimes you must walk quite a bit to encounter a nesting turtle. Wear sneakers or walking shoes rather than sandals. The beach is very dark at night, and it's easy to trip or step on driftwood or other detritus.

- Wear dark clothes. White T-shirts are not permitted.

- Flashlights, flash cameras, and lighted video cameras are prohibited on turtle tours.

- Smoking is prohibited on the beach at night.

entrance. When the turtles are nesting, arrange a night tour in advance with either your hotel or one of the private guides working in town. These guided tours generally run between $10 and $20. Flashlights and flash cameras are not permitted on the beach at night because the lights discourage the turtles from nesting.

ORGANIZED TOURS All of the lodges listed below, with the exception of the most inexpensive accommodations in Tortuguero Village, offer package tours that include various hikes and river tours; this is generally the best way to visit the area.

In addition, several San José-based tour companies offer budget 2-day/1-night excursions to Tortuguero, including transportation, all meals, and limited tours around the region. Prices for these trips range between $150 and $300 per person, and—depending on the price—guests are lodged either in one of the basic hotels in Tortuguero Village or one of the nicer lodges listed below. Reputable companies offering these excursions include **Exploradores Outdoors ★** (www.exploradores outdoors.com; © **646/205-0828** in the U.S. and Canada, or 2222-6262 in Costa Rica), **Jungle Tom Safaris** (www.jungletomsafaris.com; © **2221-7878**), and **Iguana Verde Tours** (www.iguanaverdetours. com; © **2231-6803**). Some operators offer 1-day trips in which tourists spend almost all their time coming and going but that do allow for a quick tour of the canals and lunch in Tortuguero. These trips are good for travelers who like to be able to say, "Been there, done that;" they generally run between $100 and $120 per person. However, if you really want to experience Tortuguero, I recommend staying for at least 2 nights.

Alternatively, you could go with **Fran and Modesto Watson ★** (www.tortuguerocanals.com; © **2226-0986**), who are pioneering guides in this region and operate their own boat. The couple offers a range of overnight and multiday packages to Tortuguero, with lodging options at most of the major lodges here.

BOAT CANAL TOURS Aside from watching turtles nest, the unique thing to do in Tortuguero is tour the canals by boat, keeping your eye out for tropical birds and native wildlife. Most lodges can arrange a canal tour for you, but you can also arrange a tour through one of the operators in Tortuguero Village. I recommend **Daryl Loth** (© **8833-0827;** http:// casamarbella.tripod.com), who runs the Casa Marbella (p. 523) in the center of the village. I also recommend **Ernesto Castillo** (© **8343-9565**). If neither of these guides is available, ask for a recommendation at the **Sea Turtle Conservancy Visitors' Center and Museum** (© **2767-1576**). Most guides charge between $20 to $25 per person for a tour of the canals. If you travel through the park, you'll also have to pay the park entrance fee of $15 per person.

Exploring Tortuguero Village

The most popular attraction in town is the small **Sea Turtle Conservancy Visitors' Center and Museum** ★ (www.conserveturtles.org; ✆ **2767-1576**). The museum has information and exhibits on a whole range of native flora and fauna, but its primary focus is on the life and natural history of the sea turtles. Most visits to the museum include a short, informative video on the turtles. All the proceeds from the small gift shop go toward conservation and turtle protection. The museum is open daily from 10am to noon and 2 to 5pm. Admission is $2, but more generous donations are encouraged.

In the village, you can also rent dugout canoes, known in Costa Rica as *cayucos* or *pangas*. Be careful before renting and taking off in one of these; they tend to be heavy, slow, and hard to maneuver, and you might be getting more than you bargained for.

You'll find a handful of souvenir shops spread around the center of the village. The **Paraíso Tropical Gift Shop** has the largest selection of gifts and souvenirs. But I prefer the **Jungle Shop,** which has a higher-end selection of wares and donates 10 percent of its profits to local schools.

Where to Stay

Although the room rates below may appear high, keep in mind that they usually include round-trip transportation from San José (which amounts to approx. $100 per person), plus all meals, taxes, and usually some tours. When broken down into nightly room rates, most of the lodges are really charging only between $60 and $150 for a double room. **Note:** When I list package rates below, I have always listed the least expensive travel

Tortuguero Village.

The pool at Tortuga Lodge.

option, which is a bus and boat combination both in and out. All of the lodges also offer packages with a plane flight, either one or both ways.

EXPENSIVE

Manatus Hotel ★★   Four words for you: air-conditioning and television. If those items are important to you, this is where you stay, because Manatus is the only hotel to offer those niceties. It continues with the creature comforts, in the form of pretty rooms (with hand-painted sinks and wall murals) with comfy four-poster beds bedecked in white muslin mosquito netting. The netting is actually mostly for show, funnily enough, as the net is entirely open at the top and the rooms are well-sealed off from the critters. The hotel also has a well-run little spa, as well as an exercise room and art gallery featuring local and regional artists and craftsman. Manatus is one of the smaller lodges in the area, allowing for a more intimate experience and more personalized service.

Tortuguero. www.manatushotel.com. © **2239-4854** reservations in San José, or 2709-8197 at the hotel. 12 units. $270 per person for 2 days/1 night; $383 per person for 3 days/2 nights. Rates are double occupancy, and include 3 meals daily, taxes, and daily tours. No children under 3 years of age allowed. **Amenities:** Restaurant; bar; outdoor pool; small spa and exercise room; free Wi-Fi.

Tortuga Lodge ★★★   This was one of the first upscale resorts to set up shop hereabouts, and like a Palm Beach socialite, it keeps up with the younger gals by having a touch of work done every so often. Like the other better lodges it's got amenities like ceiling fans (sorry, no A/C here) and landscaped gardens—and adds a snazzy stone-lined pool, a waterfront dining room (with some of the better local victuals), and 20 hectares

(50 acres) of grounds and jungle. Paths snake through for superb hiking. The bamboo-furnished rooms are class acts (the best are on the upper floor, all sleek varnished wood, with verandas and hammocks for lazing). The large, canal-front deck is built on several levels stepping up from the water and joining with the large, main dining room and bar, and serves as the social hub for the lodge. Service is impeccable. Costa Rica Expeditions, a leader in sustainable ecotourism in Costa Rica, owns and runs this property.

Tortuguero. www.tortugalodge.com. ℂ **2257-0766** for reservations in San José, or 2709-8136 at the lodge. 27 units. Starting at $166 double. More for packages including meals, tours and transportation. **Amenities:** Restaurant; bar; pool; free Wi-Fi.

Mawamba Lodge ★ Much like Laguna Lodge (see below) Mawamba is a collection of raised wooden buildings set amidst lush gardens on the ocean side of the main canal. This is the closest of the main nature lodges to the town, which is convenient for those looking to spend a bit more time picking up on the village's local flavor. The rooms are simple and tidy, with walls and floors of dark varnished hardwoods. All come with some sort of shared or private veranda, and most of these are equipped with hammocks or rocking chairs for some serious downtime. The four "superior" rooms are individual bungalows, featuring more space, king beds, large bathrooms with deep soaking tubs and river views. The lodge has a large pool, several bar and restaurant venues, including one of the main restaurants built on an old barge and moored just off the lodge's river bank. Butterfly, frog and iguana breeding projects insure great wildlife viewing opportunities.

Tortuguero. www.grupomawamba.com. ℂ **2293-8181.** 54 units. $230–$299 per person for 2 days/1 night; $321–$406 per person for 3 days/2 nights. Rates are double occupancy, and include round-trip transportation from San José, 3 meals daily, taxes, and some tours. Discounts for children 5–11. Children 4 and under free. **Amenities:** Restaurant; bar; free-form outdoor pool; free Wi-Fi.

Turtle Beach Lodge ★ Tucked away down a narrow canal on a thin strip of sand and jungle fronting the sea, this is the most isolated of the main Tortuguero nature lodges (it's about 5 miles from the village). It sits on 175 acres of private reserve with miles of private trails and deserted beachfront. During turtle nesting season, it offers superb night tours as guests have this section of beach all to themselves. The rooms are rustic affairs set on simple concrete foundations, with thin walls that are mostly fine mesh screening.

Caño Palma, Tortuguero. www.turtlebeachlodge.com. ℂ **2248-0707** in San José, or 2206-4020 at the lodge. 53 units. $284 per person for 2 days/1 night; $375 per person for 3 days/2 nights. Rates double occupancy, and include round-trip transportation from San José, 3 meals daily, taxes, and tours. **Amenities:** Restaurant; bar; free Wi-Fi; outdoor pool.

MODERATE

Laguna Lodge ★★ If you think of this as a "summer camp for adults"-type experience, you will be more than happy. Because rooms are about as basic as those you likely stayed in when you were 10, with screened rather than glass windows (which means that they can get noisy, as all the guestrooms are in a series of one-story buildings with shared verandas). It's also double the size of the other lodges in the area, so it can feel a bit too bustling. But does that really matter when you're surrounded by all of this glorious nature? Laguna Lodge sits on the ocean side of the main canal, about a 20- to 30-minute walk north of Tortuguero Village. It boasts splendiferous gardens (including a butterfly and a frog garden), and two pools; the beach is just a couple hundred yards away. Meals are served buffet-style in a large, covered, open-air dining room overlooking Tortuguero's main canal. The owner, Rodolfo "Popo" Dada is a well-known local poet and children's book author.

Tortuguero. www.lagunatortuguero.com. ⓒ **888/259-5615** in U.S. and Canada, or 2272-4943 in Costa Rica. 100 units. $235 per person for 2 days/1 night; $298 per person for 3 days/2 nights. Rates are double occupancy and include round-trip transportation from San José, tours, taxes, and 3 meals daily. Children 5–11 half-price. Children under 5 free. **Amenities:** Restaurant; 2 bars; 2 outdoor pools; free Wi-Fi.

INEXPENSIVE

Several basic cabinas in the village of Tortuguero offer budget lodgings for between $25 and $55 per person. **Cabinas Miss Junie** (ⓒ **2709-8102**) and **Cabinas Miss Miriam** (ⓒ **2709-8002**) are the traditional favorites, although in my opinion, you'll do better at Casa Marbella (below), with the second and third choices being **Hotel El Icaco** (www.hotelelicaco.com; ⓒ **2709-8044**), and **Hotel Tortuguero Natural** (www.hoteltortugueronatural.com; ⓒ **2767-0466**).

Casa Marbella ★ Co-owned by Daryl Loth, one of the most respected local guides around, this B&B occupies a converted clapboard home right on the canal in the heart of the village. All rooms come with one or two low-lying wooden beds, large windows, hardwood floors and little else. The best rooms have views of the water. There's a small covered canal-front patio where breakfast is served, and which also serves as a nice spot to relax or read or birdwatch. Beyond leading tours, Darryl can also help arrange a wide variety activities in the area.

Tortuguero, Limón. ⓒ **2709-8011** or 8833-0827. http://casamarbella.tripod.com. 11 units. $40–$45 double; $55–$65 superior. Rates include breakfast. No credit cards. **Amenities:** Small communal kitchen, free Wi-Fi.

Where to Dine

Most visitors take all their meals as part of a package at their hotel. The town has a couple of simple sodas and restaurants. The best of these is **Miss Junie's** (ⓒ **2709-8102**).

Budda Café ★ INTERNATIONAL   With an appropriately Zen atmosphere of canal-front outdoor seating—try and grab one of the tables on the over-the-water deck—this happy cafe has been in business for years, despite the fact that most visitors to the area take all three meals at their lodges. I'd say that speaks to the solid quality of the food here, which consists of fresh ceviche, pizzas, pastas, stuffed crepes, and a range of main dishes (plus excellent desserts).

On the main canal, next to the ICE building, Tortuguero Village. www.buddacafe. com. ✆ **2709-8084.** Main courses C4,500–C13,000. Daily Noon–9pm.

Wild Ginger ★★ INTERNATIONAL   Welcome to Tortuguero's one real fine dining option. Here that means "California meets Costa Rica" fare on a menu features everything from seasonal lobster and mango ceviche to a beef tenderloin in a coffee rub. As appropriate, the ginger-marinated chicken with a passion fruit sauce is a highlight. Wild Ginger also creates a number of options for vegetarians and vegans. The setting is cute: polished concrete floors, hand-painted murals, and lots of open air. Service is stellar (you'll feel like the owners are old friends by the time you pay the check).

On the ocean-side path, north end of Tortuguero Village. www.wildgingercr.com. ✆ **2709-8240.** Main courses C6.000–C13,000. Daily 12:30–3pm and 6–9pm.

LIMÓN: GATEWAY TO TORTUGUERO NATIONAL PARK & SOUTHERN COASTAL BEACHES

160km (99 miles) E of San José; 55km (34 miles) N of Puerto Viejo

It was just offshore from present-day Limón, in the lee of Isla Uvita, that Christopher Columbus is said to have anchored in 1502, on his fourth and final voyage to the New World. Believing that this was potentially a very rich land, he christened it Costa Rica ("Rich Coast"). While never supplying the Spanish crown with much in the way of gold or jewels, the spot where he anchored has proved over the centuries to be the best port on Costa Rica's Caribbean coast—so his judgment wasn't all bad. Today

A Fall Festival

Limón's biggest yearly event, and one of the liveliest festivals in Costa Rica, is **Carnaval,** around Columbus Day (Oct 12). For a week, languid Limón shifts into high gear for a nonstop bacchanal orchestrated to the beat of reggae, soca, and calypso music. During the revelries, residents don costumes and take to the streets in a dazzling parade of color. Festivities include marching bands, dancers, and parade floats. If you want to experience Carnaval, make your reservations early because hotels fill up fast. (This advice goes for the entire coast.)

Limón is a rough-around-the-edges port city that ships millions of pounds of bananas northward every year. It also receives a fair share of the country's ocean-borne imports and a modest number of cruise ship callings. On days when a cruise ship is in port, you'll find the city bustling far beyond the norm.

Limón is not generally considered a tourist destination, and few tourists take the time to tour the city, except those stopping here on cruise ships. Very few choose to stay here, and I don't recommend it except during Carnaval—even then you're better off in Cahuita or Puerto Viejo.

If you want to get in some beach time while you're in Limón, hop in a taxi or a local bus and head north a few kilometers to **Playa Bonita,** a small public beach. Although the water isn't very clean and is usually too rough for swimming, the setting is much more attractive than downtown. This beach is popular with surfers.

Essentials

GETTING THERE & DEPARTING By Plane: Nature Air (www. natureair.com; ℂ **800/235-9272** in the U.S. and Canada, or 2299-6000 in Costa Rica) and **Sansa** (www.flysansa.com; ℂ **877/767-2672** in the U.S. and Canada, or 2290-4100 in Costa Rica) both began daily flights into Limon's small seaside airstrip in 2015. Both have a very early morning flight, that leaves San Jose, and then heads to Tortuguero before returning to the capital. On Friday and Saturday, Nature Air also has an afternoon flight. Fares run between $80 and $120, one-way. The airport is located a few miles south of the city, on the coastal road to Cahuita and Puerto Viejo.

Local taxis are usually waiting for arriving flights. However, if you're looking to head down the coast to Cahuita or Puerto Viejo and beyond, I recommend arranging for transfer beforehand either with your hotel, or **Gecko Trail Adventures** (www.geckotrail.com; ℂ **2756-8412**), a Puerto Viejo–based tour agency and transfer company.

By Car: The Guápiles Highway (CR32) heads north out of San José on Calle 3 before turning east and passing close to Barva Volcano and through the rainforests of Braulio Carrillo National Park en route to Limón. The drive takes about 2½ hours and is spectacularly beautiful, especially when it's not raining or misty. Alternately, you can take the old highway, which is also scenic but much slower. It heads east out of San José on Avenida Central and passes through San Pedro and then Curridabat before reaching Cartago. From Cartago on, the narrow and winding road passes through Paraíso and Turrialba before descending out of the mountains to Siquirres, where the old highway meets the new. This route takes around 4 hours, more or less, to get to Limón.

By Bus: Transportes Caribeños buses (ℂ **2222-0610** in San José, or 2758-2575 in Limón) leave San José every hour daily between

5am and 7pm from the Caribbean bus terminal (Gran Terminal del Caribe) on Calle Central, Avenida 13. Friday and Sunday, the last bus leaves an hour later at 8pm. The trip duration is around 3 hours. The buses are either direct or

Along the Way

If you're driving to the Caribbean coast, you should consider combining the trip with a stop at the Rain Forest Aerial Tram (p. 104), or the Puerto Viejo de Sarapiquí area (p. 384).

local *(corriente),* and they don't alternate in any particularly predictable fashion. Local buses are generally older and less comfortable and stop en route to pick up passengers from the roadside. I highly recommend taking a direct bus, if possible. The fare is C3,260 one-way.

Buses leave Limón for San José every hour between 5am and 7pm, and similarly alternate between local and direct, with the last bus leaving 1 hour later on Sundays. The Limón bus terminal is on the main road into town, several blocks west of the downtown area and Parque Vargas.

Buses (© **2758-1572** for the terminal) to **Cahuita** and **Puerto Viejo** leave from here roughly every hour from 7:30am to 4:30pm daily.

Buses to **Punta Uva** and **Manzanillo,** both of which are south of Puerto Viejo, leave Limón daily at 5:30 6:30, 8:30, 10:30am, and 12:30, 3:30, 5:30, and 6:30pm from the same station.

CITY LAYOUT Nearly all addresses in Limón are measured from the central market, which is aptly located smack-dab in the center of town, or from Parque Vargas, which is at the east end of town fronting the sea. The cruise ship dock is just south of Parque Vargas. A pedestrian mall runs from Parque Vargas to the west for several blocks.

FAST FACTS A host of private and national banks are in the small downtown area. You can reach the **local police** at © 2758-1148 and the **Red Cross** at © 2758-0125. The **Tony Facio Hospital** (© 2758-0580) is just outside of downtown on the road to Playa Bonita.

Exploring Limón

Limón has little for tourists to do or see. The closest true attraction, **Veragua Rainforest Park** (p. 527), is about a 40-minute drive.

If you end up spending any time in Limón, be sure to take a seat in **Parque Vargas** along the seawall and watch the city's citizens go about their business. Occupying 1 city block on the waterfront, this is a quiet oasis in the heart of downtown. You may

Outdoor market in Limón.

Veragua Rainforest Park.

even spot some sloths living in the trees here. If you want to shop for souvenirs, head to the **cruise ship terminal** whenever a ship is in port, and you'll find more than your fair share of vendors. Finally, if you're interested in architecture, take a walk around town. When banana shipments built this port, local merchants erected elaborately decorated buildings, several of which have survived the city's many earthquakes, humid weather, and salty sea air. There's a certain charm in the town's fallen grace, drooping balconies, rotting woodwork, and chipped paint. One of the city's most famous buildings is known locally as the **Black Star Line** (© **2798-1948**), located on Avenida 5 and Calle 5. It was built in 1922, as the head-quarters for Marcus Garvey's United Negro Improvement Association. Restored several years ago, it serves today as the city's social and cultural meeting place, and houses a popular local restaurant (p. 528). Check here for traveling art exhibits, and the occasional live performances.

Just be careful: Limón is a rough and impoverished port town. Street crime and violence are problems. Tourists should stick to the very well-worn city center, and spots mentioned here. In addition, I don't rec-ommend walking anywhere at night. Even in the daytime, it's probably best to travel in small groups.

A ONE-STOP SHOP RAINFOREST TOURISM SPOT

Located outside of Limón in a patch of thick rainforest south of the banana town of Liverpool, **Veragua Rainforest Park** ★ (www.veraguarainforest.com; © **2296-5056**) is primarily a destination for cruise ship excursions. However, this extensive complex is a worthy stop for any-one visiting the area. Attractions include a serpentarium, butterfly garden and breeding exhibit, humming-bird garden, extensive insect exhibit, free-range rainforest frog room, zip-line canopy tour, and a short tram ride that takes you to their rainforest trail system. Along the trails, you'll find a beautiful little waterfall. A half-day tour runs $66–$125 per adult and $55–$110 per child, and a full-day tour runs

Marcus Garvey's Black Star Line building in Puerto Limón.

$99–$169 per adult and $99–$169 per child; these tour prices don't include transportation or lunch. The park is open daily from 8am to 3pm.

Where to Stay

Hotel Playa Westfalia ★   About 5 miles south of Limon proper, just beyond the city's tiny airport, Hotel Playa Westfalia's beachfront setting more than compensates for any lack of access to Limón's limited urban attractions. Rooms are forgettable but spacious, clean and kept cool with strong air conditioners. Each has either a balcony, patio or shared veranda. A mid-size pool is between the hotel and the beach, which is a large, long and almost always deserted stretch of dark sand running uninterrupted for miles in each direction.

Just south of Limón, just beyond the airstrip. www.hotelplayawestfalia.com. ✆ **4702-1861** or 4702-1852. 8 units. $90–$105 double; $105–$120 suite. Rates include full breakfast and taxes. **Amenities:** Restaurant; Jacuzzi; outdoor pool; free Wi-Fi.

Park Hotel ★   If you really must overnight in downtown Limón then this should be your first (and only) choice. The longstanding Park Hotel sits facing the water in the heart of downtown; a break wall and pedestrian promenade front the hotel. They've changed the exterior from a gaudy pink to a mellow yellow, and I hope it stays that way. Rooms are nothing to write home about, but spotless and blessed with air-conditioning and small outdated TVs. The popular restaurant here serves a mix of local Caribbean fare, traditional Tico standards and some Chinese dishes, perfectly reflecting the cultural mix of Limón.

Limón, Av. 3, btw. calles 1 and 3. www.parkhotellimon.com. ✆ **2758-4364.** 32 units. $72–$98 double. Rates include taxes and breakfast. **Amenities:** Restaurant; free Wi-Fi.

Where to Dine

Dining options are pretty limited in Limón. In addition to the place listed below, the restaurant at the **Park Hotel** (see above) is a good bet. Try to sample the local staple *paty*, a fried dough concoction that is stuffed with a slightly spicy ground meat filling. You'll find *paty* vendors all over downtown Limón.

If you're looking for a panoramic view head to **Bar & Restaurante El Faro** (✆ **2758-4020**) or the **Red Snapper** (www.redsnappercr.com; ✆ **2758-7613**), which are located near each other up on El Resbalón, the highest point in town, near all the city's cellphone towers. Both serve up traditional local fare and fresh seafood, and occasionally offer up live music on weekend nights.

Black Star Line ★ SEAFOOD/COSTA RICAN   History and good local cooking are the lures here. The former home to Marcus Garvey's famous steam ship company, The Black Star Line (p. 527), the restaurant is housed in well-preserved, bright green, two-story clapboard building with a white picket second-floor balcony railing. It has been declared a national historic monument. Inside you can get hearty plates of the local rice and beans, cooked in coconut milk, served along with freshly caught fish, or stewed chicken, and accompanied by fried plantains. This is also a good place to try the local specialty "pati," a spicy meat turnover. Be prepared for big crowds and slow service if a cruise ship is in town.

Corner of Avenida 5 and Calle 5, Limón. © **2798-1948.** Main courses C3,500–C9,000. Mon–Sat 7:30am–9pm; Sun 9:30am–5pm.

En Route South

Staying at the place listed below is a great way to combine some quiet beach time on the Caribbean coast with a more active ecolodge and bird-watching experience into one compact itinerary.

Selva Bananito Lodge ★★★ Selva Bananito provides many of the same types of experiences as those on offer at eco-lodges down on the Osa peninsula, at a lower cost and in close proximity to such highlights as Tortuguero and the many Caribbean beach towns. It's set high on the slopes of rainforest-covered mountains. A collection of spacious, stilt-raised cabins, each is blessed with large louvered windows and doors that swing wide open to let guests commune more closely with nature. Solar hot-water showers and large wraparound verandas or balconies are another lure as are the stunning views of the surrounding forests. On site are great opportunities for hiking and horseback riding, as well as tree-climbing, waterfall rappelling, and zip-line tours. Meals are served family-style in the large open-air main lodge building. The owners, the Stein family, are dedicated conservationists; the property was awarded "5 Leaves" in the CST Sustainable Tourism program.

Bananito. www.selvabananito.com. © **2253-8118.** 11 units. $128–$144 double. Rates include 3 meals daily, 1 tour daily, and all taxes. **Amenities:** Restaurant. You'll need a four-wheel-drive vehicle to reach the lodge itself, although most leave their rental cars in Bananito and let the lodge drive them the final bit. You can also arrange to be picked up in San José.

CAHUITA ★

200km (124 miles) E of San José; 42km (26 miles) S of Limón; 13km (8 miles) N of Puerto Viejo

Cahuita is a small beach village and the first "major" tourist destination heading south out of Limón. Nevertheless, the boom going on in Puerto Viejo and the beaches south of Puerto Viejo have in many ways passed Cahuita by. Depending on your point of view, that can be a reason to stay or to decide to head farther south. Any way you slice it, Cahuita is one of the more laid-back villages in Costa Rica. The few dirt and gravel streets here are host to a languid parade of pedestrian traffic, parted occasionally

A red-eyed tree frog in Cahuita.

by a bicycle, car, or bus. After a short time, you'll find yourself slipping into the heat-induced torpor that affects anyone who ends up here.

The village traces its roots to Afro-Caribbean fishermen and laborers who settled in this region in the mid-1800s, and today the population is still mainly English-speaking black Costa Ricans whose culture and language set them apart from the rest of the country.

People come to Cahuita for its miles of pristine beaches, which stretch both north and south from town. The southern beaches, the forest behind them, and the coral reef offshore (one of just a handful in Costa Rica) are all part of **Cahuita National Park ★★**. Silt and pesticides washing down from nearby banana plantations have taken a heavy toll on the coral reefs, so don't expect the snorkeling to be world-class. But on a calm day, it can be pretty good, and the beaches are idyllic every day. It can rain almost any time of year here, but the most dependably dry months are September and October.

Essentials

GETTING THERE & DEPARTING   **By Plane:** See p. 525 for Limon info. *Note:* While taxis do meet all incoming flights, I highly recommend you arrange a specific private transfer with your hotel if possible.

By Car: Follow the directions on p. 525 for getting to Limón. As you enter Limón, about 5 blocks before the busiest section of downtown, watch for a paved road to the right, just before the railroad tracks. Take this road (CR36) south to Cahuita, passing the airstrip and the beach on your left as you leave Limón. Alternatively, a turnoff with signs for Sixaola and La Bomba is several miles before Limón. This winding shortcut skirts the city and puts you on the coastal road (CR36) several miles south of Limón.

By Bus: Mepe express buses (www.mepecr.com; ✆ **2257-8129**) leave San José daily at 6 and 10am, noon, and 2 and 4pm from the Caribbean bus terminal (Gran Terminal del Caribe) on Calle Central, Avenida 13. The trip's duration is 4 hours; the fare is C4,670. During peak periods, extra buses are often added. However, it's wise to check because this bus line (Mepe) is one of the most fickle.

Alternatively, you can catch a bus to **Limón** (see above) and then transfer to a Cahuita- or Puerto Viejo–bound bus (✆ **2758-1572**) in Limón. These latter buses leave roughly every 2 hours between 7:30am and 4:30pm from the main Terminal Talamanca in Limón. Buses from

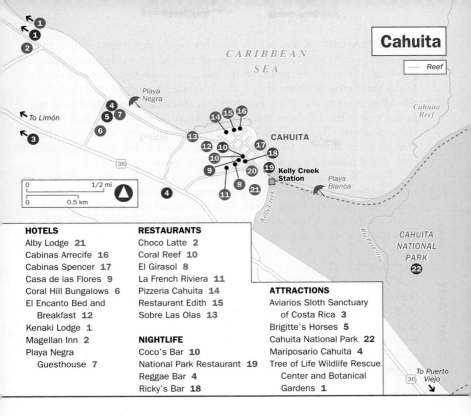

Cahuita

CARIBBEAN SEA

------ Reef

Playa Negra

To Limón

Cahuita Reef

CAHUITA

Playa Blanca

Kelly Creek Station

Kelly Creek

Río Perezoso

CAHUITA NATIONAL PARK
22

0   1/2 mi
0   0.5 km

To Puerto Viejo

HOTELS
Alby Lodge **21**
Cabinas Arrecife **16**
Cabinas Spencer **17**
Casa de las Flores **9**
Coral Hill Bungalows **6**
El Encanto Bed and
　Breakfast **12**
Kenaki Lodge **1**
Magellan Inn **2**
Playa Negra
　Guesthouse **7**

RESTAURANTS
Choco Latte **2**
Coral Reef **10**
El Girasol **8**
La French Riviera **11**
Pizzeria Cahuita **14**
Restaurant Edith **15**
Sobre Las Olas **13**

NIGHTLIFE
Coco's Bar **10**
National Park Restaurant **19**
Reggae Bar **4**
Ricky's Bar **18**

ATTRACTIONS
Aviarios Sloth Sanctuary
　of Costa Rica **3**
Brigitte's Horses **5**
Cahuita National Park **22**
Mariposario Cahuita **4**
Tree of Life Wildlife Rescue
　Center and Botanical
　Gardens **1**

Limón to Manzanillo also stop in Cahuita and leave from the same spot roughly every 2 hours between 6:30am and 6:30pm. The trip takes 1 hour; the fare is C2,420.

Interbus (www.interbusonline.com; ✆ **4100-0888**) has a daily bus that leaves San José for Cahuita at 7:50am. The fare is $50. Interbus buses leave Cahuita daily at both 6:30am and 2:30pm. Interbus will pick you up at most area hotels in both San José and Cahuita, and offers connections to various other destinations around Costa Rica.

Buses departing **Puerto Viejo** and Sixaola (on the Panama border) stop in Cahuita roughly every 2 hours between 7am and 7pm en route to San José. However, the schedule is far from precise, so it's always best to check with your hotel. Moreover, these buses are often full, particularly on weekends and throughout the high season. To avoid standing in the aisle all the way to San José, it is sometimes better to take a bus first to Limón and then catch one of the frequent Limón–San José buses. Buses to Limón pass through Cahuita regularly throughout the day. Another tactic I've used is to take a morning bus to Puerto Viejo, spend the day down there, and board a direct bus to San José at its point of origin, thereby snagging a seat.

VILLAGE LAYOUT   Cahuita only has about eight dirt streets. The highway runs parallel to the coast, with three main access roads running perpendicular. The northernmost of these access roads bypasses town and brings you to the northern end of Playa Negra. It's marked with signs for the Magellan Inn and other hotels up on this end. The second road in brings you to the southern end of Playa Negra, about 1km (a half-mile) closer to town. The third road is the principal entrance into town. The village's main street in town, which runs parallel to the highway, dead-ends at the national park entrance (a footbridge over a small stream).

Buses drop passengers off at a terminal at the back of a small strip mall on the main entrance road into town. Cabs will be waiting to take you to the lodges on Playa Negra. Alternately, you can head out walking north on the street that runs between Coco's Bar and the small park. This road curves to the left and continues 1.6km (1 mile) or so out to Playa Negra.

FAST FACTS   The police station (© **2755-0217**) is located where the road from Playa Negra turns into town. You'll find the post office (© **2755-0096**) as well as a well-equipped pharmacy, **Farmacia Cahuita** (© **2755-0505**), and a branch of the Banco de Costa Rica with an ATM in the small Arena Blancas strip mall in front of the bus station. Several Internet cafes are around the central downtown area of the village. If you can't find a cab in town, ask your hotel to call you one, or try **Alejandro** (© **8875-3209** or 8817-6571) or **Dino** (© **8340-2354**).

Exploring Cahuita National Park ★★

This little gem of a national park sits at the southern edge of Cahuita town. Although the pristine white-sand beach, with its picture-perfect line of coconut palms and lush coastal forest backing it, is the main draw here, the park was actually created to preserve the 240-hectare (787-acre) **coral reef** that lies just offshore. The reef contains 35 species of coral and provides a haven for hundreds of brightly colored tropical fish. You can walk on the beach itself or follow the trail that runs through the forest just behind the beach to check out the reef.

One of the best places to swim is just before or beyond the **Río Perezoso (Lazy River),** several hundred meters inside Cahuita

---

You Can Bring It with You

I recommend packing a picnic lunch, plenty of water, and some snorkel gear and hiking out along the inland rainforest trail, all the way out to Punta Cahuita. Once there, you can spread out a blanket or some towels, snorkel on the reef, and swim in the tide pools, before enjoying your lunch. You can walk along the beach for most of the return trip to town, and stop for a cooling dip or two if the mood strikes.

A trail through Cahuita National Park.

National Park. The trail behind the beach is great for bird-watching, and if you're lucky, you might see some monkeys or a sloth. The loud grunting sounds you'll hear off in the distance are the calls of howler monkeys, which can be heard from more than a kilometer away. Nearer at hand, you're likely to hear crabs scuttling amidst the dry leaves on the forest floor. A half-dozen or so species of land crabs live in this region—my favorites are the bright orange-and-purple ones.

The trail behind the beach stretches a little more than 9km (5.6 miles) to the southern end of the park at **Puerto Vargas** (© **2755-0302**), where you'll find a lovely white-sand beach. The best section of reef is off the point at Punta Cahuita, and you can snorkel here. If you don't dawdle, the 3.8km (2.35-mile) hike to Punta Cahuita should take a little over an hour each way—although I'd allow plenty of extra time to enjoy the flora and fauna, and take a dip or two in the sea. Bring plenty of mosquito repellent because this area can be buggy.

The beach in Cahuita National Park.

Although you can snorkel from the shore at Punta Cahuita, it's best to have a boat take you out to the nicest coral heads just off-shore. A 3-hour **snorkel trip** costs between $20 and $35 per person, with equipment. You can arrange one with any of the local tour companies listed below. **Note:** These trips are best taken when the seas are calm—for safety's sake, visibility, and comfort.

ENTRY POINTS, FEES & REGULATIONS   The **in-town park entrance** is just over a footbridge at the end of the village's main street. It has restroom facilities, changing rooms, and storage lockers. This is the best place to enter if you just want to spend the day on the beach and maybe take a little hike in the bordering forest.

The alternate park entrance is at the southern end of the park in **Puerto Vargas.** This is where you should come if you don't feel up to hiking a couple of hours to reach the good snorkeling spots. The road to Puerto Vargas is approximately 5km (3 miles) south of Cahuita on the left.

Officially, **admission** is $5 per person per day, but this is collected only at the Puerto Vargas entrance. You can enter the park from the town of Cahuita for free or with a voluntary contribution. The park is open from dawn to dusk for day visitors.

GETTING THERE   **By Car:** The turnoff for the Puerto Vargas entrance is clearly marked 5km (3 miles) south of Cahuita.

By Bus: Your best bet is to get off a Puerto Viejo– or Sixaola-bound bus at the turnoff for the Puerto Vargas entrance (well-marked, but tell the bus driver in advance). The guard station/entrance is only about 500m (1,640 ft.) down this road. However, the beach and trails are several kilometers farther.

Beaches & Activities Outside the Park

Outside the park, the best place for swimming is **Playa Negra** especially the stretch right in front of the Playa Negra Guesthouse (p. 537). The waves here are often good for bodysurfing, boogie-boarding, or surfing. If you want to rent a board or try a surf lesson, check in with Rennie at **Willie's Tours** (see below) or **Brigitte** (see below).

Cahuita has plenty of options for organized adventure trips or tours. I recommend **Cahuita Tours** (www.cahuitatours.com; ✆ **2755-0101**), **Willie's Tours** ★ (www.williestourscostarica.com; ✆ **2755-1024** or 8917-6982), and **Roberto Tours** (✆ **2755-0117**). All are located along Cahuita's main road, and offer a wide range of tours from snorkeling, to rainforest hikes, to visits to nearby indigenous reserves. Most also offer multiday trips to Tortuguero, as well as to Bocas del Toro, Panama.

A sloth at the Aviarios Sloth Sanctuary of Costa Rica.

HORSEBACK RIDING   Brigitte (www.brigittecahuita.com; © **2755-0053**) offers guided horseback tours for $35 to $85. She also rents mountain bikes and surfboards, and even has a few rooms available.

WILDLIFE VIEWING   Bird-watchers and sloth lovers should head north 11km (7 miles) to **Aviarios Sloth Sanctuary of Costa Rica ★★** (www.slothsanctuary.com; © **2750-0775**). Their signature tour features an informative visit to their sloth rehabilitation project and learning center, as well as a 1-hour canoe tour through the surrounding estuary and river system. More than 330 species of birds have been spotted here. You'll get an up-close look at a range of rescued wild sloths, both adults and babies, as well as several bred in captivity. After, you can hike their trail system and look for sloths in the wild. Tours begin at 8am, with the last tour of the day leaving at 2pm. Make reservations in advance. They are closed on Mondays. These folks also offer up a few cozy and quaint rooms right on site if you want to spend more time exploring the bird-watching and wildlife options, as well as the sloth rescue project.

Toward the northern end of the dirt road leading out beyond Playa Negra is the **Tree of Life Wildlife Rescue Center and Botanical Gardens ★** (www.treeoflifecostarica.com; © **2755-0014**). Stroll through extensive, well-maintained gardens, where a series of large cages house a range of rescued and recovering local fauna, including toucans, monkeys, coatimundi, deer, wild pigs, or peccaries. This place is typically open Tuesday through Sunday from 9am to 3pm; however, they often close for weeks or even months at a time. Admission is $15.

Where to Stay

In addition to the places listed below, **Coral Hill Bungalows** ★★ (www.coralhillbungalows.com; ✆ **2755-0479**) has three individual bungalows and a separate two-story house, in a garden setting, about a block or so inland from the beach at Playa Negra.

For a quiet and cozy retreat, also good for longer stays, check out **Kenaki Lodge** ★★ (www.kenakilodge.com; ✆ **2755-0485**), a small family-run operation several miles north of town, just across the road from the beach. These folks have a few rooms, as well as a few other kitchen equipped private one- and two-bedroom bungalows.

Another option is **Casa de las Flores** (www.lacasadelasfloreshotel. com; ✆ **2755-0326**), which has neat and cheery rooms set on the main road, right in the center of town, yet still close to the national park entrance. And **Cabinas Spencer** (✆ **2755-0027**) has a somewhat funky collection of rooms for true budgeteers. They're just a few feet from the water in the heart of town.

INEXPENSIVE

Alby Lodge ★★   German-owned Alby Lodge is a (forgive me) *wunderbar* surprise: beautifully manicured tropical gardens and four oh-so-Caribbean thatched-roof cabins on stilts with hammock-draped front porches. They're not luxurious, but they do have private baths, fans and a good bit of charm (wood beams, polished hardwood floors, nicely tiled baths). Guests have use of the communal kitchen; and Play Blanca beach, Cahuita's best, is just a few hundred feet away. One caution: Bring earplugs. Alby is home to a troop of early-rising howler monkeys. Cahuita. www.albylodge.com. ✆ **2755-0031.** 4 units. $60 double. $5 for extra person. No credit cards. **Amenities:** Free Wi-Fi.

Cabinas Arrecife ★   A seafront location and small pool give this very, very inexpensive backpacker haunt some appeal. Set facing the sea, this spartan place features a row of rooms in a low concrete building. The rooms themselves are kept acceptably tidy and come with one twin and one double bed, as well as a small television and table or floor fan. Next door is Restaurant Edith (see below). Cahuita (about 100m/328 ft. east of the Police station). www.cabinasarrecife.com. ✆ **2755-0081** or 8835-2940. 15 units. $30 double. **Amenities:** Outdoor pool; free Wi-Fi.

El Encanto Bed & Breakfast ★★   A short stroll from the beaches and main drag, the long popular El Encanto does seem to have a touch of enchantment to it. A tranquil, walled compound that's dominated by a whitewashed, colonial-style guesthouse it's an exotic mix of the tropical (lush bromeliads, heliconias, and orchids all over) and the indigenous Central American (seven guestrooms with arched doorways and windows, lively regional artworks on the walls, and varnished wood or red terra cotta floors). Modern conveniences aren't ignored: On-site is a small kidney shaped pool and gazebos that house a two-person Jacuzzi, and a pair of hanging chairs meant to lull you into a mid-afternoon siesta. Service is extremely friendly and accommodating.

Cahuita (just outside of town on the road to Playa Negra). © **2755-0113.** 7 units. $90 double; $110 studio, $200 studio suite. Rates include full breakfast. Rates slightly lower in off season; higher during peak weeks. **Amenities:** Restaurant, small outdoor pool; Jacuzzi, small spa and Wi-Fi.

Magellan Inn ★★ Terry Newton is the second-generation owner/manager of this quaint bed-and-breakfast and she's kept the balance of elements that makes this place so special. Service is friendly, but not intrusive; rooms are spacious and clean, but fairly priced (perhaps because they're not the most modern-looking of digs); and the grounds are Edenic, super green, with abundant flowers and a lovely pool built into the local coral. *Note:* Only about half of the rooms have A/C, and it's definitely worth this small upgrade. TVs, with satellite reception, are also an additional upgrade. The location is far enough from the Playa Negra beach that most guests have a rental car.

At the far end of Playa Negra (about 2km/1¼ miles north of Cahuita), Cahuita. www. magellaninn.com. © **2755-0035** or 8858-1140. 6 units. $65–$75 double; $130 deluxe. Rates include full breakfast. **Amenities:** Bar; lounge; small outdoor pool; free Wi-Fi.

Playa Negra Guesthouse ★★★ The best beachfront hotel in Cahuita by a long shot, Playa Negra Guesthouse is set just across a dirt-and-sand lane from a quiet and palm lined stretch of beach. The hotel has well-tended, exuberant gardens; and personality-filled rooms and plantation-style cottages (love the art on the walls and the unusual bed-spreads). A couple of these cottages, painted in Crayola colors and adorned with intricate, bright white gingerbread trim, come with full kitchens, making them ideal for families or those planning on an extended stay. Owners Pierre and Marise are always present to give advice and help in any way, and their friendly German Shepard is available for petting sessions. No meals are served here, but several restaurants are within easy walking distance, and the center of Cahuita is about 1.6km (1 mile) away by foot, bicycle, or taxi.

On Playa Negra (about 1.5km/1 mile north of town), Cahuita. www.playanegra.cr. © **2755-0127.** 6 units. $64–$79 double room; $99 cottage; $144 2-bedroom cottage. **Amenities:** Small outdoor pool; free Wi-Fi.

Where to Dine

Coconut meat and milk figure into a lot of the regional cuisine here. Most nights, local women cook up pots of various local specialties and sell them from the front porches of the two discos or from streetside stands around town; a full meal will cost you around $2 to $5.

In addition to the places listed below, for good, fresh Italian fare, try **El Girasol** (✆ **2755-1164**), a small, elegant family-run joint on the main road into town. Another popular Italian option is **Pizzeria Cahuita** (✆ **2755-0179**), located between the Police station and Restaurant Edith.

La French Riviera ★★ PIZZA/SANDWICHES/CREPES   Ooh la la, is this place ever a welcome change from the standard Tico eatery. Run by a friendly French couple, the specialties here are very well executed, especially the serious croque monsieur and both the sweet and savory crepes. Knowing their audience, the owners have branched out and bring Gallic flair to fab thin-crust pizzas and juicy burgers (served on a home-baked sesame seed bun with crisp, twice-cooked potatoes). The restaurant is open-air, with a thatched roof and loads of charm.

On the main road into town, across from the bus station. ✆ **2755-0050.** Main courses C3,000–C6,000; sandwiches C2,000–C3,000; pizzas C3,000–C3,800. No credit cards. Daily 10am–9pm.

Restaurant Edith ★ CREOLE/COSTA RICAN   Back when tourists were just starting to make their way to Cahuita, a well-known local lady named Miss Edith Brown started serving them down-home Caribbean cooking from her front porch. Now she and her daughters (and other family members) run Restaurant Edith, which may not be long on decor but delivers the goods, made to order. Dig in to flavorful local specialties like *rondon* (see "That Run-Down Feeling," p. 549) and jerk chicken. Keep in mind that service is Caribbean slow, and during high season you may have to share a table.

By the police station, Cahuita. ✆ **2755-0248.** Main courses C3,000–C18,000. No credit cards. Tue–Sun 7:30am–10pm.

Sobre Las Olas ★★★ SEAFOOD/ITALIAN   Both locals and visitors love this place (including a sloth that often travels through the trees right outside around dinner time, much to the delight of the diners). Not only does this small, oceanfront restaurant have one of the best settings in the region (if not the country), with the sea just steps away, and a stunning view down the coastline, but the food is excellent. The Italian owners prepare the freshest local seafood in a variety of ways, touching on their home-country heritage, and Caribbean cuisine, in equal measure. So you might choose between a ceviche or a carpaccio of fresh snapper to start, followed, perhaps, by Sicilian style pasta with locally caught shrimp, or a filet of mahi mahi in a coconut cream sauce. After eating, you can saunter onto the beach and commandeer one of the hammocks strung between the trees.

Just north of town on the road to Playa Negra. ✆ **2755-0109.** Main courses C5,000–C10,500. Wed–Mon noon–10pm.

Soda Chocolatte ★ COFFEEHOUSE/CREOLE   The town's best breakfast spot features darn good java drinks of all types, made-to-order eggs and house-baked croissants. You'll dine on these and more (it's also open for lunch) in an airy, slightly rickety old wooden raised-stilt building on main street near the center of the village.

On the main road in town, ½ block south of Coco's Bar. ℂ **2755-0010.** Main courses C3,000–C6,000. No credit cards. Daily 6:30am–2pm.

Shopping

For a wide selection of beachwear, local crafts, cheesy souvenirs, and batik clothing, try **Boutique Bambata,** on the main road near the entrance to the park. Folks also come here to have their hair wrapped in colorful threads and strung with beads. Heading north out of town, similar wares are offered at the **Cahuita Tours** gift shop. For something less organized, local and itinerant artisans in makeshift stands near the park entrance sell handmade jewelry and crafts.

If you're interested in the region, pick up a copy of Paula Palmer's "What Happen: A Folk-History of Costa Rica's Talamanca Coast." A history of Costa Rica's Caribbean coast, it's based on interviews with many of the area's oldest residents. It makes for a fun and interesting read, and you just might meet someone mentioned in the book.

Entertainment & Nightlife

Coco's Bar ★, a classic Caribbean watering hole at the main crossroads in town, has traditionally been the place to while away the nights (and days, for that matter). Cold beer and very loud reggae and soca music are the lures. Just across the street, the two-story **Ricky's Bar** tries to give Coco's a run for its money, and most folks simply ping-pong between the two. Toward the park entrance, the **National Park Restaurant** has a popular bar, with loud music and dancing on most nights during the high season and on weekends during the off season, while out toward Playa Negra, the **Reggae Bar ★** has a convivial vibe, with thumping tropical tunes blasting most nights. For gamesters, there's **Splash** (ℂ **8889-9668**), a restaurant and sports bar in the center of the village. These folks have billiard and foosball tables, as well as regular movie and Karaoke nights, live bands and DJs. They also have a small swimming

---

Cahuita's Calypso Legend

Walter "Gavitt" Ferguson, who turned 96 in 2015, is a living legend. For decades, Ferguson labored and sang in obscurity. Occasionally he would record a personalized cassette tape of original tunes for an interested tourist willing to part with $5. Finally, in 2002, Ferguson was recorded by the local label Papaya Music (www.papayamusic.com). Today, he has two CDs of original songs, "Babylon" and "Dr. Bombodee." Ask around town and you should be able to find a copy. If you're lucky, you might even bump into Gavitt himself.

Cahuita locals playing a friendly game of dominoes.

pool which is open to restaurant guests, and is especially refreshing on hot afternoons, although is often tempting to late night revelers as well.

PUERTO VIEJO ★★

200km (124 miles) E of San José; 55km (34 miles) S of Limón

Puerto Viejo is the Caribbean coast's top destination. Even though Puerto Viejo is farther down the road from Cahuita, it's much, much more popular, with a distinctly livelier vibe and many more hotels and restaurants to choose from. Much of this is due to the scores of surfers who come to ride the town's famous and fearsome Salsa Brava wave, and only slightly mellower Playa Cocles (p. 552) beach break. Nonsurfers can enjoy other primo swimming beaches, plenty of active adventure options, nearby rainforest trails, and a collection of restaurants.

This area gets plenty of rain, just like the rest of the coast (Feb–Mar and Sept–Oct are your best bets for sun, although it's not guaranteed).

Essentials

GETTING THERE & DEPARTING   By Plane: See the info for Limon on p. 525. **Note:** While taxis do meet all incoming flights, I highly recommend you arrange a specific private transfer with your hotel if possible

By Car: To reach Puerto Viejo, continue south from Cahuita on CR36 for another 16km (10 miles). Watch for a prominent and well-marked fork in the highway. The right-hand fork continues on to Bribri, Sixaola, and the Panamanian border. The left-hand fork (it actually

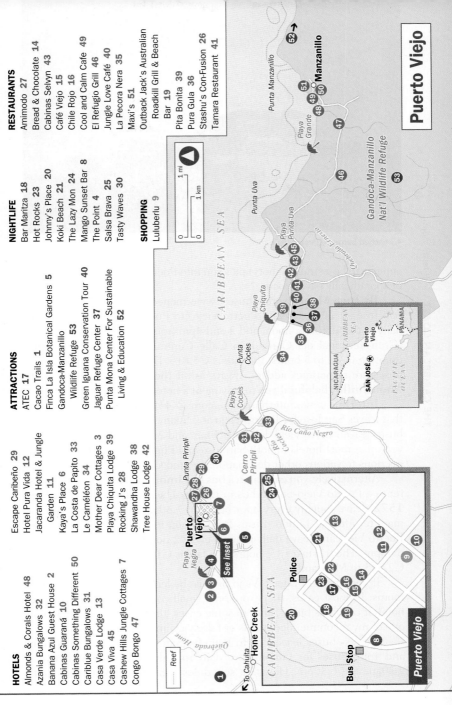

HOTELS

Almonds & Corals Hotel **48**
Azania Bungalows **32**
Banana Azul Guest House **2**
Cabinas Guaraná **10**
Cabinas Something Different **50**
Cariblue Bungalows **31**
Casa Verde Lodge **13**
Casa Viva **45**
Cashew Hills Jungle Cottages **7**
Congo Bongo **47**
Escape Caribeño **29**
Hotel Pura Vida **12**
Jacaranda Hotel & Jungle
    Garden **11**
Kaya's Place **6**
La Costa de Papito **33**
Le Caméléon **34**
Mother Dear Cottages **3**
Playa Chiquita Lodge **39**
Rocking J's **28**
Shawandha Lodge **38**
Tree House Lodge **42**

ATTRACTIONS

ATEC **17**
Cacao Trails **1**
Finca La Isla Botanical Gardens **5**
Gandoca-Manzanillo
    Wildlife Refuge **53**
Green Iguana Conservation Tour **40**
Jaguar Refuge Center **37**
Punta Mona Center For Sustainable
    Living & Education **52**

NIGHTLIFE

Bar Maritza **18**
Hot Rocks **23**
Johnny's Place **20**
Koki Beach **21**
The Lazy Mon **24**
Mango Sunset Bar **8**
The Point **4**
Salsa Brava **25**
Tasty Waves **30**

SHOPPING

Luluberlu **9**

RESTAURANTS

Amimodo **27**
Bread & Chocolate **14**
Cabinas Selvyn **43**
Café Viejo **15**
Chile Rojo **16**
Cool and Calm Cafe **49**
El Refugio Grill **46**
Jungle Love Café **40**
La Pecora Nera **35**
Maxi's **51**
Outback Jack's Australian
    Roadkill Grill & Beach
    Bar **19**
Pita Bonita **39**
Pura Gula **36**
Stashu's Con-Fusion **26**
Tamara Restaurant **41**

Puerto Viejo

A beached barge by Puerto Viejo.

appears to be a straight shot) takes you into Puerto Viejo on 5km (3 miles) of sporadically paved road.

By Bus: Mepe express buses (www.mepecr.com; ✆ **2257-8129** in San José, or 2758-1572 in Puerto Viejo) to Puerto Viejo leave San José daily at 6 and 10am, noon, and 2 and 4pm from the Caribbean terminal (Gran Terminal del Caribe) on Calle Central, Avenida 13. The trip's duration is 4½ to 5 hours; the fare is C5,815. During peak periods, extra buses are sometimes added. Always ask if the bus is continuing on to **Manzanillo** (helpful if you're staying in a hotel south of town).

Interbus (www.interbusonline.com; ✆ **4100-0888**) has a daily bus that leaves San José for Puerto Viejo at 7:50am. The fare is $50. Interbus buses leave Puerto Viejo daily at 6:50am and 2:30pm. Interbus will pick you up at most hotels in both San José and Puerto Viejo, and offers connections to various other destinations around Costa Rica.

Alternatively, you can catch a bus to **Limón** (p. 525) and then transfer to a Puerto Viejo-bound bus in Limón. These latter buses (✆ **2758-1572**) leave roughly every hour between 7:30am and 4:30pm from the main terminal in Limón. Buses from Limón to Manzanillo also stop in Puerto Viejo and leave daily roughly every 2 hours between 5:50am and 6:30pm. The trip takes 1½ hours; the fare is C1,860 to Puerto Viejo, and C2,535 to Manzanillo.

If you arrive in Puerto Viejo by bus, be leery of touts offering hotel rooms. In most cases, they work on a small commission from whatever hotel or *cabina* is hiring, and, in some cases, they'll steer you away from one of my recommended hotels or falsely claim that it is full.

Express buses leave Puerto Viejo for San José daily at 9 and 11am and 4pm. Buses for Limón leave daily roughly every 2 hours between 9:30am and 6:30pm. However, schedules are subject to change, so it's best to check with your hotel. Buses to **Punta Uva** and **Manzanillo** leave Puerto Viejo about a half-dozen times throughout the day.

GETTING AROUND Taxis are fairly easy to come by around Puerto Viejo. You'll either find them hanging around the *parquecito* (little park), or you can call **Taxi PV** (✆ **2750-0439**). You can rent scooters and bicycles from a handful of roadside operators around town.

If you need to rent a car, head to **Adobe Rent A Car** (www.adobe car.com; ✆ **2750-0290**).

TOWN LAYOUT The road in from the highway runs parallel to Playa Negra, or Black Sand Beach (not the beach in Cahuita), for a few hundred meters before entering the village of Puerto Viejo, which has all of about 10 dirt streets. The sea is on your left and forested hills on your right as you come into town. It's another 15km (9⅓ miles) south to Manzanillo. This road is paved all the way to Manzanillo, although many sections are nonetheless in fairly rough shape.

FAST FACTS You'll find a couple of banks and ATMs, as well as the **post office** (✆ **2750-0404**), near the entrance to town. A **police office** (✆ **2750-0230**) is on the beach, near Johnny's Place (p. 552).

Several self- and full-service Laundromats are around town. The one at **Café Rico** (✆ **2750-0510**) will give you a free cup of coffee, cappuccino, or espresso while you wait.

Exploring Puerto Viejo

CULTURAL & ADVENTURE TOURS The **Asociación Talamanqueña de Ecoturismo y Conservación** ★★ (**ATEC;** Talamancan Association of Ecotourism and Conservation; www.ateccr.org; ✆ **2750-0398**), across the street from the Soda Tamara, is a local organization dedicated to preserving the environment and cultural heritage of this area and promoting ecologically sound development. (If you plan to stay in Puerto Viejo for an extended period of time and would like to contribute to the community, ask about volunteering.) In addition to functioning as the local info center, Internet cafe, and traveler's hub, ATEC runs a little shop that sells T-shirts, maps, posters, and books.

ATEC also offers quite a few tours, including **half-day walks** that focus on nature and either the local Afro-Caribbean culture or the indigenous Bribri culture. These walks pass through farms and forests; along the way you'll learn about local history, customs, medicinal plants, and Indian mythology, and have an opportunity to see sloths, monkeys, iguanas, keel-billed toucans, and other wildlife. A range of different walks lead through the nearby **Bribri Indians' Kéköldi Reserve,** as well as more strenuous hikes through the primary rainforest. **Bird walks** and **night walks** will help you spot more of the area wildlife; there are even overnight treks. The local guides have a wealth of information and make a hike through the forest a truly educational experience. ATEC can arrange snorkeling trips to the nearby coral reefs, as well as snorkeling and fishing trips in dugout canoes, and everything from surf lessons to dance classes. ATEC can also help you arrange overnight and multiday **camping trips** into the Talamanca Mountains and through neighboring indigenous reserves, as well as trips to Tortuguero and even a 7- to 10-day transcontinental trek to the Pacific coast. Half-day tours (and night walks) are $25 to $60, and full-day tours run between $75 and $120. Some tours require minimum groups of 3 or 4 people and several days' advance notice. The ATEC office is open Monday through Saturday from 8am to 8pm and Sunday from 11am to 7pm.

A spa treatment at Pure Jungle Spa.

Local tour operators **Exploradores Outdoors ★★** (www.exploradoresoutdoors.com; ⓒ **2750-2020**), **Gecko Trail Adventures ★★** (www.geckotrail.com; ⓒ **2756-8412**), and **Terraventuras ★** (www.terraventuras.com; ⓒ **2750-0750**) all offer a host of half- and full-day adventure tours into the jungle or sea for between $40 and $280 per person. One especially popular tour is Terraventuras' zip-line canopy tour, which features 22 treetop platforms, a large harnessed swing, and a rappel.

HORSEBACK RIDING For horseback riding, check in with **Seahorse Stables** (www.horsebackridingincostarica.com; ⓒ **8859-6435**). A range of guided tours are offered, with rides along the beach, into the rainforest and multiday treks down to Punta Mona (p. 555).

SCUBA DIVING Scuba divers can check in with **Reef Runners Dive Shop** (www.reefrunnerdivers.com; ⓒ 2750-0480) or **Punta Uva Dive Center** (www.puntauvadivecenter.com; ⓒ 2759-9191). Both of these operations frequent a variety of dive sites between Punta Viejo and Punta Mona, and if you're lucky the seas will be calm and visibility good—although throughout most of the year, it can be a bit rough and murky here. Reef Runners has an office in downtown Puerto Viejo, while Punta Uva Dive Center has their operations center right off the beach in Punta Uva. Rates run between $80 and $110 for a two-tank boat dive.

LEFT: **Cacao fruit.** RIGHT: **Cacao beans drying in the sun.**

A LITTLE MIND & BODY REVITALIZATION Indulgence Spa ★★ (www.indulgencespa-salon.com; ℂ **2750-0536**), located at La Costa de Papito (p. 560), has a wide range of massage and treatment options at reasonable rates. They also have an in-house salon.

Pure Jungle Spa ★★ (www.purejunglespa.com; ℂ **2756-8413**) offers up a similar menu of treatment options in a lovely space close to downtown, just across from Rocking J's (p. 549). They make many of their own oils, masks, wraps, and exfoliants.

Better suited to a longer stay or organized retreat, **Samasati** (www. samasati.com; ℂ **800/563-9643** in the U.S., or 2737-3418 in Costa Rica) is a lovely jungle yoga retreat and spa, with spectacular hillside views of the Caribbean Sea and surrounding forests. Rates run between $190 and $260 per person per day, depending on occupancy and room type, and include two vegetarian meals per day. A wide range of tour, massage, and yoga packages are available. If you're staying elsewhere in Puerto Viejo or Cahuita, you can come up for yoga classes ($15), meditation ($5), or private massages ($130–$200) with advance notice. Samasati is located a few of kilometers before Puerto Viejo (near the turnoff for Bribri) and roughly 1.6km (1 mile) up into the jungle.

NOT YOUR EVERYDAY GARDENS One of the nicest ways to spend a day in Puerto Viejo is to visit the **Finca La Isla Botanical Gardens ★★** (www.samasati.com; ℂ **8886-8530**; Fri–Mon 10am–4pm), a few hundred meters inland from the Black Sand Beach on a side road just north of El Pizote lodge. Peter Kring and his late wife Lindy poured time and love into the creation of this meandering collection of native and imported tropical flora. The trails and experience are a bit rough around the edges, but you'll see medicinal, commercial, and just plain wild flowering plants, fruits, herbs, trees, and bushes. Visitors get to gorge on whatever is ripe at the moment. A rigorous rainforest loop trail leaves from the grounds. Entrance to the garden is $6 per person for a self-guided tour of the trails (you can buy their trail map for an extra $1), or $12 for a 2½-hour guided tour (minimum of three people).

Cacao Trails ★ (② 2756-8186) is a one-stop attraction featuring botanical gardens, an open-air museum demonstrating cacao cultivation and processing, and a series of trails, a large open-air restaurant, and a swimming pool. You can take canoe rides on the bordering Carbon River, and even watch leatherback sea turtles lay their eggs during the nesting season (p. 517). Admission is $25, including a guided tour. A full-day tour, including lunch and a canoe trip, as well as the guided tour, costs $50. During turtle nesting season, they offer night tours.

SUNNING & SURFING **Surfing** has historically been the main draw here, but increasing numbers of folks are coming for the miles of beautiful and uncrowded **beaches ★★**, acres of lush rainforests, and laid-back atmosphere. For swimming and sunbathing, locals like to hang out on the small patches of sand in front of the Lazy Mon @ Stanford's and Johnny's Place. Small, protected tide pools are in front of each of these bars for cooling off. The Lazy Mon has several hammocks; you're likely to stumble upon a pickup beach volleyball match or soccer game here.

If you want a more open patch of sand and sea, head north out to **Playa Negra,** along the road into town, or, better yet, to the beaches south of town around Punta Uva and all the way down to Manzanillo, where the coral reefs keep the surf much more manageable (p. 554).

Just offshore from the tiny village park is a shallow reef where powerful storm-generated waves sometimes reach 6m (20 ft.). **Salsa Brava ★★★**, as it's known, is the prime surf break on the Caribbean coast. Even when the waves are small, this spot is recommended only for very experienced surfers because of the danger of the reef. Other popular beach breaks are south of town on Playa Cocles.

Several operators and makeshift roadside stands offer bicycles, scooters, boogie boards, surfboards, and snorkel gear for rent. Compare prices and the quality of the equipment before settling on any one.

ANOTHER WAY TO GET WET & WILD **Exploradores Outdoors ★★** (www.exploradoresoutdoors.com; ② 646/205-0828 in the U.S., 2222-6262 in San José, or 2750-2020 in Puerto Viejo) runs daily white-water rafting trips on the Pacuare and Reventazón rivers. The full-day trip, including transportation, breakfast, and lunch, is $99. If you want to combine white-water rafting with your transportation to or from the Caribbean coast, they can pick you up at your hotel in San José or La Fortuna with all your luggage, take you for a day of white-water rafting, and drop you off at day's end at your hotel anywhere on the Caribbean

The beach in front of Lazy Mon @ Stanford's.

coast from Cahuita to Manzanillo. You can use this option in the other direction, as well. These folks also offer a combination kayaking and hiking tour to Punta Uva, as well as overnight tours to Tortuguero.

Where to Stay

For a longer stay, close to town, you might want to check out **Cashew Hill Jungle Cottages** (www.cashewhilllodge.co.cr; ✆ **2750-0001**). On a hill just on the outskirts of town, these are simple but immaculate individual one- and two-bedroom bungalows, with kitchenettes.

In addition to the places listed below, **Mother Dear Cottages ★★** (www.motherdearcr.com) offers two fully equipped, raised stilt cottages right on the beach in Playa Negra. And **Escape Caribeño** (www.escape-caribeno.com; ✆ **2750-0103**) is worth a look-see, located on the outskirts of town, just south of Salsa Brava.

MODERATE

Banana Azul Guest House ★★★   Colin from Canada and his partner Jorge (from Peru) run what they call a "straight friendly" hotel, and indeed half their clientele is straight. An adults-only lodging, it's located on the far northern end of Playa Negra, a vast stretch of undeveloped beach backed by thick forest (it stretches north from here all the way to Cahuita National Park). The decor? Well, call it "Queer Eye for the jungle lodge". There are such fabulous touches as a koi pond in the middle of the ceramic tiled common lounge and the "Red Frog" room has an open shower with a lovely frog mosaic. In fact, most of the suites include either a tub or Jacuzzi in a private bamboo enclosed patio. Their Azul Beach Club is a big hit, offering up a pool, chaise lounges, reclined seating, shade trees and umbrellas, and waiter service. The guys love to share their enthusiasm and knowledge of Puerto Viejo; on-site is a full-service tour desk and bicycles for rent.

Playa Negra Puerto Viejo, Limón. www.bananaazul.com. ☏ **2750-2035.** 16 units. $104–$165 double; $164–$207 suite or apt. Rates include full breakfast. No children 16 and under allowed. **Amenities:** Restaurant; bar; bike rental; Jacuzzi; outdoor pool; free Wi-Fi.

INEXPENSIVE

True budget hounds will find an abundance of basic hotels and *cabinas* in downtown Puerto Viejo in addition to those listed below. Of these, **Hotel Pura Vida** (www.hotel-puravida.com; ☏ **2750-0002**) and **Kaya's Place** (www.kayasplace.com; ☏ **2750-0690**) are recommendable.

Cabinas Guaraná ★   Clean, safe, and friendly—so what if the sheets are getting a bit worn here? Most visitors are so pleased with the prices, the friendly reception and the cheery decor (yellow walls with windows trimmed in bold purples and blues, louvered windows, low beds with slatted wooden headboards) that they forget to complain. The hotel is set a block inland from the town's main street, and features at least one tall old tree at the center of the complex giving it a quieter feel than you'd expect for such a centrally located lodging.

1½ blocks inland from Café Viejo, Puerto Viejo, Limón. www.hotelguarana.com. ☏ **2750-0244.** 12 units. $43 double. Rates include tax. Rates slightly lower in off season; higher during peak weeks. **Amenities:** Lounge; communal kitchen; free Wi-Fi.

Casa Verde Lodge ★★   Run by Swiss Rene Anton Kessler and his Tica wife Carolina Jimenez, Casa Verde has transformed from a simple hostel into a handsome mini-resort, with spa services and a lovely, land-scaped pool area. Budgeteers are still catered to in their Heliconia and Bromelia rooms, which come with shared bath facilities and are some-what spartan. Larger individual cabins and rooms with private baths are available to those who want more privacy. All have dark, well-worn wooden floors, and most have a private balcony or patio. The flowering gardens are lovely and the rooms, grounds and even the shared bath-rooms and showers, are immaculately maintained. In the town center.

Puerto Viejo, Limón. www.cabinascasaverde.com. ☏ **2750-0015.** 17 units, 9 with private bathroom. $60–$68 double with shared bathroom; $84 double with private bathroom. Rates include taxes. Discounts offered for cash payments. **Amenities:** Outdoor pool; massage hut; free Wi-Fi.

Jacaranda Hotel & Jungle Garden ★   Within walking distance of the center of town, this gated little resort has a welcome serenity. Rooms and individual cabins face inward, towards the well-tended garden area with its tall shade trees, which keeps them quiet. Alas, most of the digs are quite small and though they have cute painted murals and handsome rattan beds, some will find them a bit claustrophobic. All beds, by the way, come with mosquito netting, important as you'll need to keep your window open (there's no A/C). The friendly Trinidadian owner, Vera, is a wealth of local knowledge.

1½ blocks inland from Café Viejo, Puerto Viejo, Limón. www.cabinasjacaranda.net. © **2750-0069.** 12 units. $45 double. No credit cards. **Amenities:** Wi-Fi.

Rocking J's ★   If the countercultural party scene in Puerto Viejo has a headquarters, it's Rocking J's, kinda like an artsily done-up summer camp for recent college grads or a hippy commune-cum-beach resort for the backpacker set. Lodging options range from an open-air thatch-roofed communal hammock area to a second-floor covered camping plat-form where you can pop up your own tent or rent one of theirs. With each of these options you get a small locker area to keep your clothes and gear. There are also private rooms, and a treehouse suite, but the fun here is the communal living—bonfire parties on the beach out back; whipping up grub in the kitchen; downing pretty good (and cheap) bur-ritos in the restaurant; playing ping pong in the rec room. Fun!

Just south of downtown, Puerto Viejo, Limón. www.rockingjs.com. © **2750-0665** or 2750-0657. 35 units, 3 with private bathroom. $7–$12 per person in a tent or ham-mock; $11–$15 dorm room; $26–$35 double with shared bathroom; $70–$80 double with private bathroom. **Amenities:** Restaurant; bar; free Wi-Fi.

Where to Dine

To really sample the local cuisine, you need to look up a few local women. Ask around for **Miss Dolly, Miss Sam, Miss Isma,** and **Miss Irma,** who all dish out sit-down meals in their modest little *sodas.* In addition to locally seasoned fish and chicken served with rice and beans, these joints are usu-ally a great place to find *pan bon* (a local sweet, dark bread), ginger cakes, *paty* (meat-filled turnovers), and *rondon* (see "That Run-Down Feeling," below). Just ask around for these gals, and someone will direct you to them.

Puerto Viejo has a glut of excellent Italian restaurants; in addition to the places listed below, **Amimodo ★** (© **2750-0257**) serves an excel-lent lobster ravioli, as well as a *carpaccio* of home-smoked shark.

EXPENSIVE

Café Viejo Lounge Restaurant ★★ ITALIAN   Opened more than 16 years ago by three brothers from Rimini, Italy this local hot spot sits right on the main drag in the center of town. It's easy to spot, with white muslin drapes hanging from wooden posts and separating the open-air dining room from the busy streets beyond the veils. Wood-oven pizzas and a wide range of homemade pastas form the backbone of the extensive menu though you can also order up fresh whole fish, and an assortment of chicken and beef main dishes emphasizing the cuisine of Northern Italy,

> ### That Run-Down Feeling
>
> *Rondon* soup is a spicy coconut milk-based soup or stew made with anything the cook can "run down"—it usually includes a mix of local tubers (potato, sweet potato, or yucca), other vegetables (carrots or corn), and often some seafood. Be sure to try this authentic taste of the Caribbean.

but with other regional and local influences. The locally sourced fresh lobster ravioli are a house specialty. After the kitchen closes, this place transforms nightly into a hip, electronic European-style club. Final perk: an impressive wine list (and staff properly store their stock to protect it from the often oppressive Caribbean heat).

On the main road. ✆ **2750-0817.** Main courses C5,000–C25,000. Wed–Mon 6–11:30pm.

MODERATE

Stashu's Con-Fusion ★★★ INTERNATIONAL   Stashu is a local legend, and his cooking and restaurant have been a Puerto Viejo mainstay for years, albeit with a couple of different locations and names. The current incarnation serves up his classic mix of world fusion cuisines, with fresh fish, seafood, and vegetables featured in spicy curries or with Thai- or Mexican-tinged sauces. One of his more popular recurring blackboard specials is a macadamia-crusted fish filet with a white-wine-and-white-chocolate sauce. Thanks to the painted paper lanterns, creative artwork and sculptures, Stashu's is a good place for a romantic dinner despite being little more than a large, open-air space under an exposed zinc roof.

On the main road just south of downtown, about 1 block beyond Stanford's. ✆ **2750-0530.** Main courses C4,000–C18,000. Tues–Thurs 5–10pm.

INEXPENSIVE

Bread & Chocolate ★★ BREAKFAST/AMERICAN   Take your menu guidance from the name: The bread (biscuits, bagels, and such) is topnotch and baked on site; and the chocolate can't be beat, whether you have it as a drink, in a range of truffles or flavoring brownies. But this eatery also offers a range of tasty breakfast plates, as well as sandwiches, and salads. The open-air dining room is small, with just a handful of wooden tables and chairs, and it fills up fast. It's not uncommon to have to wait a little on weekends and during high season. If you don't want to wait, you can always get an order to go.

½ block south of Café Viejo. Downtown Puerto Viejo ✆ **2750-0723.** Main courses C3,200–C4,500. No credit cards. Tues–Sat 6:30am–6:30pm; Sun 6:30am–2:30pm.

Chile Rojo ★★ PAN-ASIAN/MEDITERRANEAN   From your perch on the second-floor balcony over the busiest section of the busiest street in Puerto Viejo you'll be able to watch the vacationing world parade by. As fun is chatting up Rojer, the gregarious owner, who always seems to be whipping up off-menu specials for diners. Not that the menu itself isn't solid, it is. I'm particularly partial to the Thai food on offer from Pad Thai to a raft of other curries, Chile Rojo also offers sushi, Indian Tikka-spiced fish, and a range of typical Middle Eastern classics like hummus, falafel and tabbouleh (vegetarians have many options here). Monday nights feature a sushi buffet, and weekends often include live music or a DJ.

2nd floor of shopping mall downtown. www.bestchilerojo.com. ✆ **2750-0025.** Main courses C3,000–C7,000. Wed–Mon 11:30am–10:30pm.

Outback Jack's Australian Roadkill Grill & Beach Bar ★ INTERNATIONAL   This restaurant gets around. Having set up shop first in Brasilito and later in Tárcoles, this boisterous, Australian-themed beach bar and grill has found a happy home in downtown Puerto Viejo. The ramshackle and colorful decor is gaudy and whimsical, and looks like it was created by team of painters and interior designers high on acid and working during a tornado. The menu features typical bar food appetizers, barbeque ribs, spicy chicken wings and "shrimp on the Barbie." You can also get whole fried red snapper, and a wide range of grilled meats, including a large, juicy T-bone steak. The mixed grill platter is ideal for sharing.

½ block south of the bus stop. www.outbackjacks.org. ✆ **8471-2622.** Main courses C3,500–C16,000. Tues–Fri and Sun 11am–1am; Sat 11am–11pm.

Tamara Restaurant ★ COSTA RICAN/CARIBBEAN   A handful of humble little restaurants around town serve local food made fresh by their namesake owner and chef. None is as popular as Tamara, which only recently went from calling itself a "soda" to a "restaurant." Occupying a prized spot near the water yet still on the town's main road, this open-air spot specializes in rice and beans (made with coconut milk) served with Caribbean-style chicken, fish or meat dishes. The low, wooden picket fence that separates this place from the street is painted in the bold red, green, yellow and black colors emblematic of the strong Jamaican influence and heritage of this coastline.

On the main road. ✆ **2750-0148.** Main courses C3,800–C26,000. Daily 11:30am–10pm.

Shopping

Puerto Viejo attracts a lot of local and international bohemians, who seem to survive solely on the sale of handmade jewelry, painted ceramic trinkets (mainly pipes and cigarette-lighter holders), and imported Indonesian textiles. You'll find them at makeshift stands set up by the town's *parquecito* (little park), which comprises a few wooden benches in front of the sea between Soda Tamara and Stanford's.

   In addition to the makeshift outdoor stands, a host of well-stocked gift and crafts shops are spread around town. **Luluberlu** ★ (✆ **2750-0394**), located inland across from Cabinas Guaraná, features locally produced craftwork, including shell mobiles and mirrors with mosaic-inlaid frames, as well as imports from Thailand and India.

   Tip: My favorite purchase here is locally produced chocolate, which is made by several local outfits, and can be found for sale at many gift shops and restaurants around town.

Nightlife & Entertainment

For a night of dancing, **Johnny's Place ★★** (✆ 2750-2000) near the Rural Guard station, is the place to be. The action spills out from the small dance floor and onto the beach most nights, where you'll find candle-lit tables set near the water's edge. Another popular waterfront spot, the **Lazy Mon @ Stanford's ★** (www.thelazymon.com; ✆ 2750-2116) has a bit more of a sports bar vibe to it, with a pool table, dartboard, and Xbox. The bar features regular live bands or DJs. Old timers like me, who still remember reggae nights at the long-lost Bambu Bar, are finding solace Wednesday, Friday and Sunday nights at the ocean front **Salsa Brava ★★** (✆ 2750-0241).

Right in the center of town, it's hard to miss **Hot Rocks** (✆ 8708-3183), with its massive stage, loud tunes, packed bar, and pool and foosball tables. Another option is the **Mango Sunset Bar ★★** (no phone), near the water, beside the bus station, and features either live music or a DJ most nights. For a more sophisticated ambience, try the oceanfront **Koki Beach ★** (www.kokibeach.com; ✆ 2250-0902).

For a laid-back beachfront sports bar, head to **The Point ★** (✆ 2756-8491), which is located right at the first point where the road in to Puerto Viejo hits Playa Negra. This convivial, open-air joint features six television screens, and offers up three different Costa Rican microbrews on tap. These folks often also feature live music.

Rocking J's (p. 549) sometimes features live music. Finally, for a more local scene, check out **Bar Maritza's** (✆ 2750-0443), in the center of town, right across from the basketball court, which is especially popular on Sunday nights.

Finally, heading south of town, at the start of Playa Cocles, **Tasty Waves Cantina** (✆ 2750-0507) has a very lively scene, with live bands, Karaoke, trivia nights and open jam sessions.

PLAYAS COCLES, CHIQUITA, MANZANILLO & SOUTH OF PUERTO VIEJO ★★★

200km (124 miles) E of San José; 55km (34 miles) S of Limón

South on the coastal road from Puerto Viejo, are several of Costa Rica's best beaches. Soft white sands are fronted by the Caribbean Sea and backed by thick rainforest. **Playa Cocles** is a popular surf spot, with a powerful and dependable beach break. South of here, the isolated **Playa Chiquita** is characterized by small pocket coves, and calm pools formed by dead coral reefs raised slightly above sea level by the 1991 earthquake. Beyond this lies **Punta Uva,** a long curving swath of beach punctuated by its namesake point (or *punta*), a rainforest-clad mound of land

The Punta Uva shoreline.

that looks vaguely like a bunch of grapes from the distance. If you come here, be sure to hike the short loop trail up and around the point. From Punta Uva the coastline stretches to **Manzanillo.** Along the way, the white sands are fronted by a living coral reef, which breaks up the waves and keeps the swimming here generally calm and protected. When it's calm (Aug–Oct), the waters down here are some of the clearest anywhere in the country, with good snorkeling among the nearby coral reefs. The tiny village of Manzanillo is literally the end of the road. The shoreline heading south from Manzanillo, located inside the **Gandoca–Manzanillo Wildlife Refuge,** is especially beautiful, with a series of pocket coves and small beaches, featuring small islands and rocky outcroppings offshore, and backed by thick rainforest. This park stretches all the way to the Panamanian border.

Essentials

GETTING THERE & DEPARTING   By Car: A single two-lane road runs south out of Puerto Viejo and ends in Manzanillo. A few dirt roads lead off this paved, but rutted road, both toward the beach and into the mountains.

By Bus: Follow the directions above for getting to Puerto Viejo. Local buses to Punta Uva and Manzanillo leave Puerto Viejo about a half-dozen times throughout the day.

GETTING AROUND   A taxi from Puerto Viejo should cost $8 to Punta Uva or $12 to Manzanillo. Alternatively, it's about 1½ hours each way by bike, with only two relatively small hills to contend with. Although the road is ostensibly paved all the way to Manzanillo, between the near-constant potholes and washed-out sections, it's almost like riding an off-road trail. Most of the hotels in this area either offer free bicycles, or will help arrange a rental.

It's also possible to walk along the beach all the way from Puerto Viejo to Manzanillo, with just a couple of short and well-worn detours inland around rocky points. However, I recommend you catch a ride down to Manzanillo and save your walking energies for the trails and beaches inside the refuge.

AREA LAYOUT   As you drive south, the first beach you will hit is **Playa Cocles ★**, which is 2km (1¼ miles) from Puerto Viejo. A little farther, you'll find **Playa Chiquita ★**, which is 5km (3 miles) from Puerto Viejo, followed by **Punta Uva ★★** at 8.4km (5¼ miles) away, and **Manzanillo ★★**, some 13km (8 miles) away.

FAST FACTS   There are no true towns, and no major services to be found along this stretch of coast. However, you can find a few scattered Internet cafes and small markets mixed in with the sporadic string of hotels, private homes, and restaurants that line the main road.

Exploring Playas Cocles, Chiquita, Manzanillo & South of Puerto Viejo

For all intents and purposes, this string of beaches is an extension of Puerto Viejo, and all of the tours, activities, and attractions mentioned above can be enjoyed by those staying here. For organized scuba diving, snorkeling, sportfishing excursions, or dolphin-sighting tours around Manzanillo and the beaches south of Puerto Viejo, check in with either **Abel Bustamante** (www.manzanillo-caribe.com; ✆ **2759-9043**) or **Omar Cook** (www.costa-rica-manzanillo.com; ✆ **2759-9143**).

MANZANILLO & THE GANDOCA–MANZANILLO WILDLIFE REFUGE ★★

13km (8 miles) south of Puerto Viejo

The **Gandoca–Manzanillo Wildlife Refuge ★★** encompasses the small village and extends all the way to the Panamanian border. Manatees, crocodiles, and more than 350 species of birds live within the boundaries of the reserve. The reserve also includes the coral reef offshore—when the seas are calm, this is the best **snorkeling** and **diving** spot on this entire coast. Four species of **sea turtles** nest on one 8.9km (5½-mile) stretch of beach within the reserve between March and July. Three species of dolphins (Atlantic spotted, bottlenose, and the rare tucuxi) also inhabit and frolic in the waters just off Manzanillo. This tucuxi species favors the brackish estuary waters, but has actually been observed in mixed species mating with local bottlenose dolphins. Many local tour guides and operators offer boat trips out to spot them.

If you want to explore the refuge, you can easily find the single, well-maintained trail by walking along the beach just south of town until you have to wade across a small river. On the other side, you'll pick up the trail head. Still, this is a wild and remote area, and I recommend doing the hike with one of the guides mentioned above.

SWEET STUFF ★★ **Caribeans Chocolate Tour** (www.caribean schocolate.com; ℂ **8836-8930** or 8341-2034; Mon 10am, Tues and Thurs 10am and 2pm, Fri and Sat 2pm; $30) explores a working organic cacao plantation and chocolate production facility. The tour illustrates the entire process of growing, harvesting, and processing cacao, and of course there's a tasting at the end. When you get around to the tasting, organic wine pairings are also available.

(ORGANIC) PEAS & LOVE ★ The **Punta Mona Center For Regenerative Design & Botanical Studies** (inside the Gandoca–Manzanillo refuge; www.puntamona.org) offers day visits to its fascinating organic permaculture gardens.

HORSEBACK RIDING ★★ **Caribe Horse Riding Club** (located between Punta Uva and Manzanillo; www.caribehorse.com; ℂ **8705-4250**; $50–$160/person) runs one of the better and more interesting horseback riding operations in the country. They offer a range of rides from short 90-minute beach jaunts to full day excursions into the mountains and nearby reserves. They even offer night rides. My favorite option is the Hippo Camp Tour, which feature a human and equine wade in the warm waters of the Caribbean Sea.

Wild and unspoiled coastline in Gandoca–Manzanillo Wildlife Refuge.

ESPECIALLY FOR KIDS

Several wildlife rescue centers and animal preservation centers operate in the area. The **Jaguar Refuge Center ★★** (www.jaguarrescue.com; ℂ **2750-0710;** guided tours Mon–Sat 9:30 and 10:30am; $18 adults, free for kids under 11) is the most extensive of the batch. This small center is located in Playa Chiquita and features a broad assortment of local critters, including monkeys, sloths, snakes, caimans, turtles, birds, and more. I have mixed feelings about the human-monkey interactions, but most guests are quite thrilled with the opportunity to enter an enclosure and have direct contact. Note that, despite the name, this place has never housed a jaguar.

Also down in Playa Chiquita, at the Tree House Lodge (see above), is the **Green Iguana Conservation Tour ★** (www.iguanaverde.com; ℂ **2750-0706;** Tues and Thurs at 8:30am; $15/person). This educational tour focuses on the life cycle, habits, and current situation of this endangered reptile. The tour features a walk around a massive natural enclosure, as well as a video presentation. Additional tours may be arranged by appointment.

You'll spot many iguanas on the Green Iguana Conservation Tour.

Where to Stay Between Puerto Viejo & Manzanillo

I recommend that you rent a car if you plan to stay at one of these hotels because public transportation is sporadic and taxis aren't always available. If you arrive by bus, however, a rented bicycle or scooter might be all you need to get around once you are settled.

On to Panama

Costa Rica's southern zone, particularly Puerto Viejo, is a popular jumping-off point for trips into Panama. The nearest and most popular destination is the island retreat of Bocas del Toro. Most tour agencies and hotel desks can arrange tours to Panama. The most reliable and easiest way to get to Bocas del Toro is to take the daily **Caribe Shuttle** (www.caribeshuttle.com; ℂ **2750-0626**), which will take you via land and boat for $32 each way; check the website or call for departure times.

Manzanillo's beach.

EXPENSIVE

Le Caméléon ★★   Contemporary comforts and style are the lure at Le Caméléon, by which I mean this is the place around where you'll find rooms with air-conditioning units, flat screen televisions and chic, contemporary design. The latter consists of minimalist, all-white rooms livened up by unusual lighting accents. On-site is a beach club with attentive waiter service, a small pool and Jacuzzi plus beachfront lounging options, set on the far southern end of Playa Cocles. The entire mini resort is connected by a network of wooden walkways and surrounded by thick forest. ***Room tip:*** I actually prefer the second floor "superior" rooms over the slightly larger first floor junior suites. The superior rooms have higher ceilings, larger balconies and a ceiling fan, in addition to the air-conditioning.

Playa Cocles, Puerto Viejo, Limón. www.lecameleonhotel.com. ✆ **2750-0501** reservations in San José or 2750-0501 at the hotel. 23 units. $240 double; $350–$400 suite. Rates include breakfast. **Amenities:** Restaurant; bar; beach club; Jacuzzi; small outdoor pool; free Wi-Fi.

MODERATE

In addition to the places listed below, **Casa Viva** (www.puntauva.net; ✆ **2750-0089**) offers beautiful, fully equipped one- and two-bedroom houses just steps from the sand on Punta Uva.

Almonds & Corals Hotel ★   Don't let the word "hotel" fool you. At Almonds & Corals you'll be staying inside a wildlife reserve in tent-cabin hybrids on stilts. Yup, this is "glamping", so your digs are tents with benefits like electric lamps, four poster beds and private baths (some private

Jacuzzis). Many, however, are overdue for a refurbishment (maintenance has been lax in the last 2 years, sadly). The biggest drawback here, aside from the upkeep, is the fact that the units are very close to each other, and with no solid walls, there's not a lot of privacy or sound insulation. The lodge is set in a patch of dense forest on the northern end of Playa Manzanillo. A maze of low wooden slat walkways connects the rooms to the main dining area and beach, although an onsite zip-line canopy tour is another popular way to reach the sand. Almonds & Corals has been awarded the maximum "5 Leaves" from the CST Sustainable Tourism program.

Manzanillo, Limón. www.almondsandcorals.com. © **888/373-9042** in the U.S. and Canada, or 2271-3000 reservations in San José, or 2759-9056 at the hotel. 24 units. $145 double. Rates include breakfast and taxes. Children 6–9 $40–$50; free for children 5 and under. **Amenities:** Restaurant; bar; bicycle rental; Jacuzzi; small spa; watersports equipment rental.

Cariblue Bungalows ★★   A posh mid-range option, Cariblue Bungalows has the feel of a tropical country club. The pool is the biggest in the region, with a thatched swim up bar; cobblestoned walkways cut through manicured grounds and gardens; and there are all sorts of amenities from the SoleLuna restaurant to a tropical bar, lounge area and game room. You'll find a range of room options, from budget rooms with no air-conditioning to deluxe rooms, individual bungalows, and large suites. I favor the Superior Bungalows, which are individual wooden cabins raised off the ground, and featuring a spacious private balcony. In 2014, Cariblue bought and took over the neighboring beachfront Totem Hotel, giving them a few ocean-view rooms, a separate beach bar and restaurant, and even better beach access. Cariblue is located directly in front of Playa Cocles, about 1.6km (1 mile) south of Puerto Viejo.

Playa Cocles, Puerto Viejo, Limón. www.cariblue.com. © **2750-0035** or 8814-1965. 29 units. $113–$147 double; $170–$249 suite. Rates include breakfast buffet. Rates slightly lower in off season. **Amenities:** Restaurants; bar/lounge; bike rental; Jacuzzi; 2 outdoor pools; free Wi-Fi.

Shawandha Lodge ★★   Set in a patch of thick forest on the inland side of the road near Playa Chiquita, this was one of the first boutique lodges in the area and it's still going strong. The individual wooden bungalows are simple, yet beautiful, and spread out amongst the trees and gardens, giving each a good sense of privacy and seclusion. They all feature high-pitched thatch roofs, a private veranda and mosaic tile creations in the bathrooms and showers. A short path leads to a usually deserted section of beach with tide pools and little coves stretching in either direction. If you don't want to walk all that way, there's a mid-size pool with a stone waterfall in garden setting just off the main lodge. The French owners have made the restaurant into one of the best in the area.

Puerto Viejo, Limón. www.shawandhalodge.com. © **2750-0018.** 13 units. $130 double. Rates include full breakfast. **Amenities:** Restaurant; outdoor pool; free Wi-Fi.

Tree House Lodge ★★★ Everything has a funky, fun Gilligan's Island feel to it here, and artistic touches and distinct architectural feats make each unit memorable. The namesake Tree House is built on high stilts and reached via a suspension bridge. It has a toilet plopped—so to speak—right in the middle of a hollowed out tree! The three-bedroom Beach Suite features a massive, domed bathroom lit by fanciful portholes and skylights of multicolored glass. Each of the four units has a full kitchen, but only two are air-conditioned. The whole compound is surrounded by tall rain forest trees, and anyone with a decent eye should be able to spot monkeys, and perhaps even a three-toed sloth. There's no pool, but right in front of the lodge lies a highly coveted section of white sand beach leading down to Punta Uva. The owners also run an iguana conservation project (p. 556) and have been awarded "4 Leaves" in the CST Sustainable Tourism program.

Punta Uva, Puerto Viejo, Limón. www.costaricatreehouse.com. © **2750-0706.** 4 units. $177–$345 double. Rates include taxes. No credit cards. **Amenities:** Free Wi-Fi.

INEXPENSIVE

In Manzanillo, the simple **Cabinas Something Different** (© **2759-9014**) are a good option, while **Congo Bongo** (www.congo-bongo.com; © **2759-9016**) offers fully equipped houses in a forest setting.

Azania Bungalows ★ This Argentine-owned lodge sits across from the beach, snuggled amid forest and densely planted gardens. It's comprised of 10 identical individual wooden cabins with high roofs, lots of space and a mix of one queen-size and two twin beds. One of these twin beds is actually located in a small loft area accessed by a steep and rustic

The Tree House Lodge.

wooden ladder—it's best for limber young'uns. Wooden lathe over the windows lets in mottled light, and is especially pleasing in the showers, where they let you feel connected to the surrounding forest, while still maintaining a sense of privacy. Each cabin comes with a private front porch hung with a cozy hammock. The restaurant serves up a mix of local fare, fresh seafood and Argentine specialties.

Playa Cocles, Puerto Viejo, Limón. www.azania-costarica.com. © **2750-0540.** 10 bungalows. $95 double. Rates include full breakfast. **Amenities:** Restaurant; bar; bike rental; outdoor pool; free Wi-Fi.

La Costa de Papito ★★ If there's such a thing as a "low-cost boutique jungle lodge" locally, it's this place. OK, it's right off the road, not deep in the jungle, but the feel is definitely there. On 2 hectares (5 acres) across from the beach stand a collection of stilt-raised bungalows, each individually decorated by owner and New York–transplant Eddie Ryan. Most of the furnishings here are handmade from local lumber, often using whole tree limbs or trunks. You practically need to be an Olympic weightlifter to lift or move the chairs in the restaurant. There's no pool here, but the beach is just across the street. The hotel's **Qué Rico Papito** restaurant is excellent, and sometimes features live music.

Playa Cocles, Puerto Viejo, Limón. www.lacostadepapito.com. © **2750-0704.** 13 units. $50–$103 double. Rates include breakfast. **Amenities:** Restaurant; bar; bike rental; watersports rental; small spa; free Wi-Fi.

Playa Chiquita Lodge ★ In the small, laid-back beach community of Playa Chiquita, you best bet, apart from renting a house, is the long-established lodge, about 300 feet from the water. It's a charming complex: Rooms are painted lively colors and housed in a series of wooden buildings that run in a line through thick gardens, connected by a raised wooden walkway. Tall rainforest trees tower above. Beds are a bit too hard, and the linens can be threadbare. But hot coffee and freshly harvested bananas are always on offer in the large thatch reception, breakfast and lounge area. A short trail through the rainforest lets you out onto **Playa Chiquita,** a pristine stretch of beach, broken up by several tide pools and coral outcroppings, and backed by thick forest.

Playa Chiquita, Puerto Viejo, Limón. www.playachiquitalodge.com. © **2750-0062.** 13 units. $95 double, $120 casitas double. Rates include breakfast and taxes. **Amenities:** Free Wi-Fi.

Where to Dine Between Puerto Viejo & Manzanillo

In addition to the restaurants listed below, **Pura Gula ★** (© **8634-6404**) is a chilled out open-air place in Playa Chiquita offering sushi, fresh fish, steaks and a range of salads and healthier fare. Their Pad Thai is actually quite good. Down the road, in Punta Uva, **Selvyn's** (© **2750-0664**) is an excellent option for local cuisine and fresh seafood, with

Playas Cocles, Chiquita, Manzanillo & South of Puerto Viejo

THE CARIBBEAN COAST

amiable hosts Selvyn and Blanca Brown. **Pita Bonita** (© 2756-8173) serves up wonderful Middle Eastern cuisine at an open-air spot between Playa Chiquita and Punta Uva.

Further south still, the **El Refugio Grill ★★** (© 2759-9007) is an Argentine-owned restaurant featuring perfectly grilled steaks, sausages, fresh tuna steaks, and other seafood in a romantic rainforest setting.

Finally, near the end of the line, where the road first hits the beach at Manzanillo, **Cool & Calm Café** (© 2750-3151) is winning faithful fans with its local cuisine and friendly atmosphere.

Jungle Love Café ★★ INTERNATIONAL   Excellent wood-oven pizzas, creative pasta dishes, healthy salads, and a mix of nightly specials keep the crowds coming (reservations definitely recommended). The owner's scrumptious signature dish is a family pasta recipe with carrots, leeks, and a spicy brandy-cream sauce, served here with fresh shrimp. I also like the Tokyo Tuna which adds a local twist to the traditional, Asian-style seared tuna, by adding fresh tamarind juice to the marinade. The main dining area is the compact front port of converted two-story wooden home, but there are also a few more tables in a detached gazebo in the nearby gardens.

Playa Chiquita. www.junglelovecafe.com. © **2750-0162.** Main courses C5,500–C8,000. Wed–Sun 5–9:30pm.

La Pecora Nera ★★★ ITALIAN   Whenever I'm asked to name my favorite restaurant in Costa Rica, I always answer, "La Pecora Nera." This place is that good. Chef/owner Ilario Gionnoni is a master and a marvel of perpetual motion. He is constantly innovating, raises his own chickens and pigs, and grows as much of his own fresh fruits, vegetables, and herbs as he can. The menu is long and varied, but I suggest not even reading it and simply asking Ilario what's best that day—he won't steer you wrong. Among the memorable dishes I've had here were shrimp cocktail with a beet-based spicy dipping sauce; and rooster ragù over homemade gnocchi. The large, multilevel, open-air dining room is dimly lit and romantic, with heavy wooden tables spread widely for privacy.

50m (164 ft.) inland from a well-marked turnoff on the main road south just beyond the soccer field in Cocles. © **2750-0490.** Reservations recommended. Main courses C6,000–C17,500. Tues–Sun 5:30–10pm.

Maxi's ★ COSTA RICAN/CARIBBEAN   This ramshackle two-story beachfront restaurant and bar is a local landmark, although food and service have suffered a bit since Ricky, the original owner, moved to San Jose in 2014. Good sized portions of rice and beans are served with freshly caught seafood and large, fried plantain chips, or *patacones*. Folks come mainly for the social scene and fabulous view of the beach and Caribbean sea just steps away.

On the beach, Manzanillo. © **2759-9073.** Main courses C3,500–C10,000; lobster C11,000–C25,000. Daily noon–10pm.

14

PLANNING YOUR TRIP TO COSTA RICA

C osta Rica is no longer the next new thing. Neither is it old hat. As Costa Rica has matured as a tourist destination, things have gotten easier and easier for international travelers. That said, most travelers— even experienced travelers and repeat visitors—will want to do some serious pre-trip planning. This chapter provides a variety of planning tools, including information on how to get there; tips on accommodations; and quick, on-the-ground resources.

GETTING THERE

By Plane

It takes between 3 and 7 hours to fly to Costa Rica from most U.S. cities, the origin of most direct and connecting flights. Most international flights still land in San José's **Juan Santamaría International Airport** (www.fly2sanjose.com; © **2437-2626** for 24-hr. airport information; airport code SJO). However, more and more direct international flights are touching down in Liberia's **Daniel Oduber International Airport** (www.liberiacostaricaairport.net; © **2668-1010;** airport code LIR).

Liberia is the gateway to the beaches of the Guanacaste region and the Nicoya Peninsula, and a direct flight here eliminates the need for a separate commuter flight in a small aircraft or roughly 5 hours in a car or bus. If you are planning to spend all, or most, of your vacation time in the Guanacaste region, you'll want to fly in and out of Liberia. However, San José is a much more convenient gateway if you are planning to head to Manuel Antonio, the Central Pacific coast, the Caribbean coast, or the Southern zone.

Numerous airlines fly into Costa Rica. Be warned that the smaller Latin American carriers tend to make several stops (sometimes unscheduled) en route to San José, thus increasing flying time.

By Bus

Bus service runs regularly from Panama City, Panama, and Managua, Nicaragua. If at all possible, it's worth the splurge for a deluxe or express bus. In terms of travel time and convenience, it's always better to get a direct bus rather than one that stops along the way—and you've got a better chance of getting a working restroom in a direct/express or deluxe bus. Some even have television sets showing movies.

Several bus lines with regular daily departures connect the major capital cities of Central America. Call **King Quality** (© **2258-8834**),

PREVIOUS PAGE: **A Costa Rican oxcart.**

Transnica (www.transnica.com; ℰ **2223-4242**), or **Tica Bus Company** (www.ticabus.com; ℰ **2296-9788**) for further information. All of these lines service Costa Rica directly from Managua, with connections to the other principal cities of Central America. Tica Bus also has service between Costa Rica and Panama. None of them will reserve a seat by telephone, and schedules change frequently according to season and demand, so buy your ticket in advance—several days in advance, if you plan to travel on weekends or holidays. From Managua, it's 11 hours and 450km (279 miles) to San José, and the one-way fare is around $30 to $50. From Panama City, it's a 20-hour, 900km (558-mile) trip. The one-way fare is around $42 to $58.

Whenever you're traveling by bus through Central America, try to keep a watchful eye on your belongings, especially at rest and border stops, whether they're in an overhead bin or stored below decks in a luggage compartment.

By Car

It's possible to travel to Costa Rica from North America by car, but it can be difficult. After leaving Mexico, the Interamerican Highway (Carretera Interamericana, also known as the Pan-American Hwy.) passes through Guatemala, El Salvador, Honduras, and Nicaragua before reaching Costa Rica. This highway then travels the length of Costa Rica before entering Panama. All of these countries can be problematic for travelers for a variety of reasons, including internal violence, crime, corrupt border crossings, and visa formalities. If you do decide to undertake this adventure, take the **Gulf Coast route** from the border crossing at Brownsville, Texas, because it involves traveling the fewest miles through Mexico. Those planning to travel this route should purchase a copy of "You Can Drive to Costa Rica in 8 Days!" by Dawn Rae Lessler, which is available from major online bookstores. You might also try to find a copy of "Driving the Pan-Am Highway to Mexico and Central America," by Audrey and Raymond Pritchard, which is harder to find. A wealth of information is also online at **www.sanbornsinsurance.com** and **www.drivemeloco.com**.

CAR DOCUMENTS You will need a current driver's license as well as your vehicle's registration and the original title (no photocopies) to enter the country.

CENTRAL AMERICAN AUTO INSURANCE Contact **Sanborn's Insurance Company** (www.sanbornsinsurance.com; ℰ **800/222-0158**), which has agents at various border towns in the United States. These folks have been servicing this niche for more than 50 years. They can supply you with trip insurance for Mexico and Central America (you won't be able to buy insurance after you've left the U.S.), driving tips, and an itinerary.

CAR SAFETY   Be sure your car is in excellent working order. It's advisable not to drive at night because of the danger of being robbed by bandits, especially in Mexico, Guatemala, El Salvador, and Honduras.

For information on car rentals and gasoline (petrol) in Costa Rica, see "Getting Around: By Car," later in this section.

By Boat

Some 350 cruise ships stop each year in Costa Rica, calling at Limón on the Caribbean coast, and at Puerto Caldera and Puntarenas on the Pacific coast. Many are part of routes that cruise through the Panama Canal.

GETTING AROUND
By Plane

Flying is one of the best ways to get around Costa Rica. Because the country is quite small, flights are short and not too expensive. Sansa and Nature Air are the country's domestic airlines. In the high season (late Nov to late Apr), be sure to book reservations well in advance. Both companies have online booking systems (see websites, below).

Sansa (www.flysansa.com; ✆ **877/767-2672** in the U.S. and Canada, or 2290-4100 in Costa Rica) operates from a private terminal at San José's Juan Santamaría International Airport (see above).

Nature Air (www.natureair.com; ✆ **800/235-9272** in the U.S. and Canada, or 2299-6000 in Costa Rica) operates from the main terminal at San José's Juan Santamaría International Airport (see above).

By Car

Renting a car in Costa Rica is no idle proposition. The roads are riddled with potholes, most rural intersections are unmarked, and, for some reason, sitting behind the wheel of a car seems to turn peaceful Ticos into homicidal maniacs. But unless you want to see the country from the window of a bus or pay exorbitant amounts for private transfers, renting a car might be your best option for independent exploring. (That said, if you don't want to put up with any stress on your vacation, it might be worthwhile springing for a driver.)

Be forewarned, however: Although rental cars no longer bear special license plates, they are still readily identifiable to thieves and are frequently targeted. (Nothing is ever safe in a car in Costa Rica, although parking in guarded parking lots helps.) Transit Police also seem to target tourists; never pay money directly to a police officer who stops you for any traffic violation.

Before driving off with a rental car, be sure that you inspect the exterior and point out to the rental company representative every tiny scratch, dent, tear, or any other damage. It's a common practice with many Costa

- **The *Tico Times*** (www.ticotimes.net): The English-language *Tico Times* makes it easy for *norteamericanos* (and other English speakers) to see what's happening in Costa Rica. It features the top story from its weekly print edition, as well as a daily update of news briefs, a business article, regional news, a fishing column, and travel reviews. There's also a link to current currency exchange rates.

- **Latin American Network Information Center** (http://lanic.utexas.edu/country/central): This site houses a vast collection of information about Costa Rica, and is hands-down the best one-stop shop for browsing, with helpful links to a diverse range of tourism and general information sites.

- **Costa Rica Maps** (www.mapcr.com): In addition to selling a wonderful waterproof map of the country, this site features several excellent downloadable nationwide, regional, and city maps, and a host of other useful information.

- **The U.S. Embassy in Costa Rica** (www.usembassy.gov): The official site of the U.S. Embassy in Costa Rica has a good base of information and regular updates of concern to U.S. citizens abroad, as well as about Costa Rica in general.

- **CostaRicaLiving E-Board** (www.costaricaliving.proboards.com): This is an information clearinghouse site put together by the folks at Costa Rica Living newsgroup. The site is chock-full of useful information, suggestions, reviews, and tips. If you want more information, feel free to join the newsgroup. The active newsgroup deals with a wide range of issues, and its membership includes many longtime residents and bona fide experts.

- **La Nación Digital** (www.nacion.com): If you can read Spanish, this is an excellent site to read regularly or simply browse. The entire content of the country's paper of record is placed online daily, and there's also an extensive searchable archive. It does maintain a small summary of major news items in English, although this section tends to run about a week behind current events.

Rican car rental companies to claim that you owe payment for minor dings and dents that the company finds when you return the car. Also, if you get into an accident, be sure that the rental company doesn't try to bill you for a higher amount than the deductible on your rental contract.

These caveats aren't meant to scare you off from driving in Costa Rica. Thousands of tourists rent cars here every year, and the large majority of them encounter no problems. Just keep your wits about you and guard against car theft and you'll do fine. Also, keep in mind that four-wheel-drives are particularly useful in the rainy season (May to mid-Nov) and for navigating the bumpy, poorly paved roads year-round.

Among the major international agencies operating in Costa Rica are Alamo, Avis, Budget, Hertz, National, Payless, and Thrifty. For a complete list of car rental agencies and their contact information, see the "Getting Around" sections of major tourist destinations in this book.

GASOLINE (PETROL)   Gasoline is sold as "regular" and "super." Both are unleaded; super is just higher octane. Diesel is available at almost every gas station as well. Most rental cars run on super, but always ask your rental agent what type of gas your car takes. When going off to remote places, try to leave with a full tank of gas because gas stations can be hard to find. If you need to gas up in a small town, you can sometimes get gasoline from enterprising families who sell it by the liter from their houses. Look for hand-lettered signs that say gasolina. At press time, a liter of super cost C536, or roughly $1.02 per liter, and $3.86 per gallon.

ROAD CONDITIONS   The awful road conditions throughout Costa Rica are legendary, and deservedly so. Despite constant promises to fix the problem and sporadic repair attempts, the hot sun, hard rain, and rampant corruption outpace any progress made toward improving the condition of roads. Even paved roads are often badly potholed, so stay alert. Road conditions get especially tricky during the rainy season, when heavy rains and runoff can destroy a stretch of pavement in the blink of an eye.

Note: Estimated driving times are listed throughout this book, but bear in mind that it might take longer than estimated to reach your destination during the rainy season or if roads have deteriorated.

Route numbers are somewhat sporadically and arbitrarily used. You'll also find frequent signs listing the number of kilometers to various towns or cities. Still, your best bets for on-road directions are billboards and advertisements for hotels. It's always a good idea to know the names of a few hotels at your destination, just in case your specific hotel hasn't put up any billboards or signs.

Most car rental agencies now offer the opportunity to rent out GPS units along with your car rental. Rates run between $8 and $15 per day. If you have your own GPS unit, several maps to Costa Rica are available. While you still can't simply enter a street address, most commercial GPS maps of Costa Rica feature hundreds of prominent points of interest (POI), and you should be able to plug in a POI close to your destination.

RENTER'S INSURANCE   Third Party Waiver, or Supplemental Liability Insurance (SLI) is mandatory in Costa Rica, regardless of your home policy or credit card coverage.

Even if you hold your own car-insurance policy at home or use a credit card that provides coverage, this coverage doesn't always extend abroad. Be sure to find out whether you'll be covered in Costa Rica, whether your policy extends to all persons who will be driving the rental car, how much liability is covered in case an outside party is injured in an accident, and whether the type of vehicle you are renting is included under your contract.

DRIVING RULES   A current foreign driver's license is valid for the first 3 months you are in Costa Rica. Seat belts are required for the driver and front-seat passengers. Motorcyclists must wear helmets. Highway police

PLANNING YOUR TRIP TO COSTA RICA

Getting Around

use radar, so keep to the speed limit (usually 60–90kmph/37–56 mph) if you don't want to be pulled over. Speeding tickets can be charged to your credit card for up to a year after you leave the country if they are not paid before departure.

To reduce congestion and fuel consumption, a rotating ban on rush-hour traffic takes place in the central core of San José Monday through Friday from 7 to 8:30am and from 4 to 5:30pm. The ban affects cars with licenses ending in the digits 1 or 2 on Monday; 3 or 4 on Tuesday; 5 or 6 on Wednesday; 7 or 8 on Thursday; and 9 or 0 on Friday. If you are caught driving a car with the banned license plate during these hours on a specified day, you will be ticketed.

BREAKDOWNS Be warned that emergency services, both vehicular and medical, are extremely limited outside San José, and their availability is directly related to the remoteness of your location at the time of break-down. You'll find service stations spread over the entire length of the Inter-american Highway, and most of these have tow trucks and mechanics. The major towns of Puntarenas, Liberia, Quepos, San Isidro, Palmar, and Golfito all have hospitals, and most other moderately sized cities and tour-ist destinations have some sort of clinic or health-services provider.

If you're involved in an accident, contact **National Insurance Institute** (INS) at © **800/800-8000.** You should probably also call the **Transit Police** (© **2222-9330**); if they have a unit close by, they'll send one. An official transit police report will greatly facilitate any insurance claim. If you can't get help from any of these, try to get written statements from any witnesses. Finally, you can also call © **911,** and they should be able to redirect your call to the appropriate agency.

If the police do show up, you've got a 50-50 chance of finding them helpful or downright antagonistic. Many officers are unsympathetic to the problems of what they perceive to be rich tourists running around in fancy cars with lots of expensive toys and trinkets. Success and happy endings run about equal with horror stories.

If you don't speak Spanish, expect added difficulty in any emergency or stressful situation. Don't expect that rural (or urban) police officers, hospital personnel, service station personnel, or mechanics will speak English.

If your car breaks down and you're unable to get well off the road, check your trunk for reflecting triangles. If you find some, place them as a warning for approaching traffic, arranged in a wedge that starts at the shoulder about 30m (98 ft.) back and nudges gradually toward your car. If your car has no triangles, try to create a similar warning marker using a pile of leaves or branches.

Finally, although not endemic, there have been reports of folks being robbed by seemingly friendly Ticos who stop to give assistance. To add insult to injury, there have even been reports of organized gangs who puncture tires of rental cars at rest stops or busy intersections, only to fol-low them, offer assistance, and make off with belongings and valuables. If you find yourself with a flat tire, try to ride it to the nearest gas station. If that's not possible, try to pull over into a well-lit public spot. Keep the doors of the car locked and an eye on your belongings while changing the tire, by yourself.

By Bus

This is by far the most economical way to get around Costa Rica. Buses are inexpensive and relatively well maintained, and they go nearly everywhere. **Local buses,** the cheapest and slowest, stop frequently and are generally a bit dilapidated. **Express buses** run between San José and most beach towns and major cities; these tend to be newer units and more comfortable, although very few are so new or modern as to have restroom facilities, and they sometimes operate only on weekends and holidays.

Two companies run regular, fixed-schedule departures in passenger vans and small buses to most of the major tourist destinations in the country. **Gray Line** (www.graylinecostarica.com; ✆ 800/719-3105 in the U.S. and Canada, or 2220-2126 in Costa Rica) has about 10 departures leaving San José each morning and heading or connecting to Jacó, Manuel Antonio, Liberia, Playa Hermosa, La Fortuna, Tamarindo, and playas Conchal and Flamingo. Return trips to San José are daily from these destinations and a variety of interconnecting routes. A similar service, **Interbus** (www.interbusonline.com; ✆ **4100-0888**) has a similar route map and connections. Fares run between $50 and $95, depending upon the destination. Gray Line offers an unlimited weekly pass for all of its shuttle routes for $198.

Beware: Both of these companies offer pickup and drop-off at a wide range of hotels. This means that if you are the first picked up or last dropped off, you might have to sit through a long period of subsequent stops before finally hitting the road or reaching your destination. Moreover, I've heard some shocking stories about both lines, concerning missed or severely delayed connections and rude drivers. For details on how to get to various destinations from San José, see the "Getting There" sections in the preceding chapters.

By Taxi

Taxis are readily available in San José and most popular tourist towns and destinations. In San José, your best bet is usually just to hail one down in the street. However, during rush hours and rain storms, and in more remote destinations, it is probably best to call a cab. Throughout the book, I list numbers for local taxi companies in the "Getting Around" sections. If no number is listed, ask at your hotel, or, if you're out and about, at the nearest restaurant or shop; someone will be more than happy to call you a cab.

All city taxis, and even some rural cabs, have meters (marías), although drivers sometimes refuse to use them, particularly with foreigners. If this is the case, be sure to negotiate the price up front. Always try to get drivers to use the meter first (say, "ponga la maría, por favor"). The official rate at press time is C590 per kilometer (½ mile). If you have a rough idea of how far it is to your destination, you can estimate how much it should cost from these figures, or you can ask at your hotel how much a specific ride should cost. After 10pm, taxis are legally allowed to add a 20 percent surcharge. Some of the meters are programmed to include the extra charge automatically, but be careful: Some drivers will use the evening setting during the daytime or (at night) to charge an extra 20 percent on top of the higher meter setting.

By Thumb

Although buses serve most towns in Costa Rica, service can be infrequent in the remote regions, so local people often hitchhike to get to their destinations sooner. If you're driving a car, people will frequently ask you for a ride. In remote rural areas, a hitchhiker carrying a machete is not necessarily a great danger; use your judgment. Hitchhiking is not recommended on major roadways or in urban areas. In rural areas, it's usually pretty safe. (However, women should be extremely cautious about hitchhiking anywhere in Costa Rica.) If you choose to hitchhike, keep in mind that if a bus doesn't go to your destination, there probably aren't too many cars going there, either. Good luck.

TIPS ON WHERE TO STAY

When the Costa Rican tourist boom began in the late 1980s, hotels popped up like mushrooms after a heavy rain. By the 1990s, the country's first true megaresorts opened, and then more followed, and now still more are under construction or in the planning phase. Except during the few busiest weeks of the year, there's a relative glut of rooms in Costa Rica. That said, most hotels are small to midsize, and the best ones fill up fast throughout much of the year. You'll generally have to reserve well in advance if you want to land a room at any of the more popular or highly rated hotels. Still, in broader terms, the glut of rooms is good news for travelers and bargain hunters. Less popular hotels that want to survive are being forced to reduce their rates and provide better service.

Your best bet in Costa Rica is to negotiate directly with the hotels themselves, especially the smaller ones. Almost every hotel in Costa Rica has e-mail, if not its own website, and you'll find the contact information in this book. However, be aware that response times might be slower than you'd like, and many of the smaller hotels might have some trouble communicating back and forth in English.

Throughout this book, I separate hotel listings into several broad categories: Expensive, $200 and up; Moderate, $100 to $200; and Inexpensive, under $100 for a double. Rates given in this book do not include the 13 percent room taxes, unless otherwise specified. These taxes will add considerably to the cost of your room.

Throughout Costa Rica, rates generally fluctuate somewhat according to season and demand, with a majority of hotels offering lower rates in the off season and charging higher rates during peak periods.

Hotel Options

Costa Rica has hotels to suit every budget and travel style. In addition to the Four Seasons, Andaz Papagayo and JW Marriott, the host of amazing boutique hotels around the country will satisfy the high-end and luxury traveler.

Still, the country's strong suit is its moderately priced hotels. In the $100-to-$200

> ### Skip the Motel
>
> You'll want to avoid motels in Costa Rica. To a fault, these are cut-rate affairs geared toward lovers consummating their affairs—usually illicit. Most rent out rooms by the hour, and most have private garages with roll-down doors outside each room, so that snoopy spouses or ex-lovers can't check the cars or license plates.

price range, you'll find comfortable and sometimes outstanding accommodations almost anywhere in the country. However, room size and quality vary quite a bit within this price range, so don't expect the kind of uniformity that you may find at home.

If you're even more budget- or bohemian-minded, you can find quite a few good deals for less than $100 for a double. But beware: Budget-oriented lodgings often feature shared bathrooms and either cold-water showers or showers heated by electrical heat-coil units mounted at the shower head, affectionately known as "suicide showers." If your hotel has one, do not adjust it while the water is running. Unless specifically noted, all rooms listed in this guide have private bathrooms.

Note: Air-conditioning is not necessarily a given in many midrange hotels and even in some upscale joints. In general, this is not a problem. Cooler nights and well-placed ceiling fans are often more than enough to keep things pleasant, unless I mention otherwise in the hotel reviews.

Bed-and-breakfasts are also abundant. Although the majority are in the San José area, you'll also find B&Bs (often gringo-owned and -operated) throughout the country.

Costa Rica has many small nature-oriented ecolodges. These lodges offer opportunities to see wildlife (including sloths, monkeys, and hundreds of species of birds) and learn about tropical forests. They range from spartan facilities catering primarily to scientific researchers to luxury accommodations among the finest in the country. Keep in mind that although the nightly room rates at these lodges are often quite moderate, prices start to climb when you throw in transportation (often on chartered planes), guided excursions, and meals. Also, just because you can book a reservation at most of these lodges doesn't mean that they're not remote. Be sure to find out how to get to and from the ecolodge and which tours and services are included in your stay. Then think long and hard about whether you really want to put up with hot, humid weather (cool and wet in the cloud forests), biting insects, rugged transportation, and strenuous hikes to see wildlife.

A couple of uniquely Costa Rican accommodations types that you might encounter are the apartotel and the cabina. An apartotel is just what it sounds like: an apartment hotel where you'll get a full kitchen and one or two bedrooms, along with daily maid service. Cabinas are Costa Rica's version of cheap vacation lodging. They're very inexpensive and very basic—often just cinder-block buildings divided into small rooms. Occasionally, you'll find a cabina in which the units are actually cabins, but these are a rarity. Cabinas often have clothes-washing sinks (pilas), and some come with kitchenettes; they cater primarily to Tico families on vacation.

STAYING HEALTHY

Staying healthy on a trip to Costa Rica is predominantly a matter of being a little cautious about what you eat and drink, and using common sense. Know your physical limits, and don't overexert yourself in the ocean, on hikes, or during athletic activities. Respect the tropical sun and protect yourself from it. As you climb above 3,000m (10,000 ft.), you may feel the effects of altitude sickness. Be sure to drink plenty of water and not overexert yourself. Limit your exposure to the sun, especially during the first few days of your trip and, thereafter, from 11am to 2pm. Use sunscreen with a high protection factor, and apply it liberally. Remember that children need more protection than adults. I recommend buying and drinking bottled water or soft drinks, but the water in San José and in most of the country's heavily visited spots is safe to drink.

General Availability of Healthcare

In general, Costa Rica has a high level of medical care and services for a developing nation. The better private hospitals and doctors in San José are very good. In fact, given the relatively budget nature of care and treatment, a sizable number of Americans come to Costa Rica each year for elective surgery and other care.

Pharmacies are widely available, and generally well stocked. In most cases, you will not need a doctor's script to fill or refill a prescription.

If You Get Sick

Your hotel front desk should be your best source of information and assistance if you get sick while in Costa Rica. In addition, your local consulate in Costa Rica can provide a list of area doctors who speak English. I list the best hospitals in San José in "Fast Facts: San José," in chapter 6; these have the most modern facilities in the country. Most state-run hospitals and walk-in clinics around the country have emergency rooms that can treat most conditions, although I highly recommend the private

red TIDES

Also known as harmful algal blooms (HAB), red tides are a natural phenomenon occurring in oceans worldwide. Red tides can arise from natural, as well as man-made causes. Some are seasonal; while others may be provoked by pollution or chemical waste. Some are toxic, while others are benign. Harmful algal blooms are often accompanied by dead fish and sea life. Rising sea temperatures have been cited as a cause of an increase in HAB occurrences, although they have been recorded in frigid arctic waters. Some can turn ocean waters a deep red, while color changes from deep green to murky brown have also been documented. Some, in fact, do not affect the water color at all. Tidal changes have no causal link to red tides, so the name is more than a bit of a misnomer.

All red tides are characterized by rapid and massive reproduction of algae or phytoplankton. Anecdotally, Costa Rica may be experiencing an increase in long lasting red tides. Pacific coast beaches have been hardest hit, especially those along the Nicoya Peninsula. Still, red tides have been recorded all along both of the country's coastlines. In Costa Rica, red tides tend to be more common near the start of the rainy season. Most only last a day or so, although some have lasted as long as a couple of weeks. It's extremely hard to tell for certain if a red tide is a dangerous algal bloom or not. If you notice a deep red or unnatural brown tint to the water, it is best to refrain from swimming. Due to dark sands and benign river runoff, many of Costa Rica's beaches often appear to have brownish water that is perfectly safe for swimming. Ask around locally to find out the current water conditions.

hospitals in San José if your condition is not life threatening and can wait for treatment until you reach one of them.

Regional Health Concerns

TROPICAL ILLNESSES   Your chance of contracting any serious tropical disease in Costa Rica is slim, especially if you stick to the beaches or traditional spots for visitors. However, malaria, dengue fever, and leptospirosis all exist in Costa Rica, so it's a good idea to know what they are.

Malaria is found in the lowlands on both coasts and in the northern zone. Although it's rarely found in urban areas, it's still a problem in remote wooded regions and along the Caribbean coast. Malaria prophylaxes are available, but several have side effects, and others are of questionable effectiveness. Consult your doctor regarding what is currently considered the best preventive treatment for malaria. Be sure to ask whether a recommended drug will cause you to be hypersensitive to the sun; it would be a shame to come down here for the beaches and then have to hide under an umbrella the whole time. Because malaria-carrying mosquitoes usually come out at night, you should do as much as possible to avoid being bitten after dark. If you are in a malaria-prone area, wear long pants and long sleeves, use insect repellent, and either sleep under a mosquito net or burn mosquito coils (similar to incense, but with a pesticide).

Of greater concern is dengue fever, which has had periodic outbreaks in Latin America since the mid-1990s. Dengue fever is similar to malaria and is spread by an aggressive daytime mosquito. This mosquito seems to be most common in lowland urban areas, and Puntarenas, Liberia, and Limón have been the worst-hit cities in Costa Rica. Dengue is also known as "bone-break fever" because it is usually accompanied by severe body aches. The first infection with dengue fever will make you very sick but should cause no serious damage. However, a second infection with a different strain of the dengue virus can lead to internal hemorrhaging and could be life threatening.

One final tropical fever that I think you should know about (because I got it myself) is leptospirosis. There are more than 200 strains of leptospires, which are animal-borne bacteria transmitted to humans via contact with drinking, swimming, or bathing water. This bacterial infection is easily treated with antibiotics; however, it can quickly cause very high fever and chills, and should be treated promptly.

If you develop a high fever accompanied by severe body aches, nausea, diarrhea, or vomiting during or shortly after a visit to Costa Rica, consult a physician as soon as possible.

Costa Rica has historically had very few outbreaks of cholera. This is largely due to an extensive public-awareness campaign that has promoted good hygiene and increased sanitation. Your chances of contracting cholera while you're here are very slight.

DIETARY RED FLAGS   Even though the water in San José and most popular destinations in Costa Rica is generally safe, and even if you're careful to buy bottled water, order *frescos en leche* (fruit shakes made with milk rather than water), and drink your soft drink without ice cubes, you still might encounter some intestinal difficulties. Most of this is just due to tender stomachs coming into contact with slightly more aggressive Latin American intestinal flora. In extreme cases of diarrhea or intestinal discomfort, it's worth taking a stool sample to a lab for analysis. The results will usually pinpoint the amoebic or parasitic culprit, which can then be readily treated with available over-the-counter medicines.

Except in the most established and hygienic of restaurants, it's also advisable to avoid ceviche, a raw seafood salad, especially if it has any shellfish in it. It could be home to any number of bacterial critters.

BUGS, BITES & OTHER WILDLIFE CONCERNS   Although Costa Rica has Africanized bees (the notorious "killer bees" of fact and fable) and several species of venomous snakes, your chances of being bitten are minimal, especially if you refrain from sticking your hands into hives or under rocks in the forest. If you know that you're allergic to bee stings, consult your doctor before traveling.

At the beaches, you'll probably be bitten by pirujas (sand fleas). These nearly invisible insects leave an irritating welt. Try not to scratch because this can lead to open sores and infections. Pirujas are most active at sunrise and sunset, so you might want to cover up or avoid the beaches at these times.

Snake sightings, much less snakebites, are very rare. Moreover, the majority of snakes in Costa Rica are nonpoisonous. If you do encounter a snake, stay calm, don't make any sudden movements, and do not try to touch the snake. Avoid sticking your hands under rocks, branches, and fallen trees.

Scorpions, black widow spiders, tarantulas, bullet ants, and biting insects of many types can all be found in Costa Rica. In general, they are not nearly the danger or nuisance most visitors fear. Watch where you stick your hands; in addition, you might want to shake out your clothes and shoes before putting them on to avoid any unpleasant and painful surprises.

TROPICAL SUN Limit your exposure to the sun, especially during the first few days of your trip and, thereafter, from 11am to 2pm. Use a sunscreen with a high protection factor, and apply it liberally. Remember that children need more protection than adults.

RIPTIDES Many of Costa Rica's beaches have riptides: strong currents that can drag swimmers out to sea. A riptide occurs when water that has been dumped on the shore by strong waves forms a channel back out to open water. These channels have strong currents. If you get caught in a riptide, you can't escape the current by swimming toward shore; it's like trying to swim upstream in a river. To break free of the current, swim parallel to shore and use the energy of the waves to help you get back to the beach.

[Fast FACTS] COSTA RICA

Area Codes Costa Rica doesn't have area codes. All phone numbers are eight-digit numbers.

Business Hours Banks are usually open Monday through Friday from 9am to 4pm, although many have begun to offer extended hours. Post offices are generally open Monday through Friday from 8am to 5:30pm, and Saturday from 7:30am to noon. (In small towns, post offices often close on Sat.) Stores are generally open Monday through Saturday from 9am to 6pm (many close for 1 hr. at lunch), but stores in modern malls generally stay open until 8 or 9pm and don't close for lunch. Most bars are open until 1 or 2am, although some go later.

Customs Visitors to Costa Rica are permitted to bring in all manner of items for personal use, including cameras, video cameras and accessories, tape recorders, personal computers, and music players. Customs officials in Costa Rica seldom check tourists' luggage.

Doctors Your hotel front desk will be your best source of information on what to do if you get sick and where to go for treatment. Most have the number of a trusted doctor on hand. In addition, your local consulate in Costa Rica can provide a list of area doctors who speak English. Also see "Staying Healthy," earlier in this chapter.

Drinking Laws Alcoholic beverages are sold every day of the week throughout the year, with the exception of the 2 days before Easter and the 2 days before and after a presidential election. The legal drinking age is 18, although it's only sporadically enforced.

Liquor—everything from beer to hard spirits—is sold in specific liquor stores, as well as at most supermarkets and even convenience stores.

Electricity   The standard in Costa Rica is the same as in the United States and Canada: 110 volts AC (60 cycles). However, three-pronged outlets can be scarce, so it's helpful to bring along an adapter.

Embassies & Consulates   The following are located in San José: **United States Embassy,** Calle 98 and Avenida Central, Pavas (✆ **2519-2000;** http://costarica.usembassy. gov); **Canadian Embassy,** Oficentro Ejecutivo La Sabana, Edificio 5 (www.costarica.gc.ca; ✆ **2242-4400**); and **British Embassy,** Edificio Colón, 11th Floor, Paseo Colón between calles 38 and 40 (www.gov.uk/government/world/costa-rica; ✆ **2258-2025**). San José does not have an Australian, Irish, or New Zealand embassy.

Emergencies   In case of any emergency, dial ✆ **911** (which should have an English-speaking operator); for an ambulance, call ✆ **1028;** and to report a fire, call ✆ **1118.** If 911 doesn't work, you can contact the police at ✆ **2222-1365** or 2221-5337, and hopefully they can find someone who speaks English.

Family Travel   Hotels in Costa Rica often give discounts for children, and allow children to stay for free in a parent's room. Still, discounts for children and the cutoff ages vary according to the hotel; in general, don't assume that your kids can stay in your room for free.

Some hotels, villas, and cabinas come equipped with kitchenettes or full kitchen facilities. These can be a real money-saver for those traveling with children, and I list many of these accommodations in the destination chapters in this book.

Hotels offering regular, dependable babysitting service are few and far between. If you will need babysitting, make sure that your hotel offers it, and be sure to ask whether the babysitters are bilingual. In many cases, they are not. This is usually not a problem with infants and toddlers, but it can cause problems with older children.

Insurance   For information on traveler's insurance, trip-cancellation insurance, and medical insurance while traveling, please visit www.frommers.com/planning.

Internet & Wi-Fi   Cybercafes can be found all over Costa Rica, especially in the more popular tourist destinations. Moreover, an ever-increasing number of hotels, restaurants, cafes, and retailers around Costa Rica are offering high-speed Wi-Fi access, either free or for a small fee. Throughout the book, I list which hotels provide Wi-Fi free, or for a fee.

Language   Spanish is the official language of Costa Rica. However, in most tourist areas, you'll be surprised by how well Costa Ricans speak English. See chapter 15 for some key Spanish terms and phrases.

Legal Aid   If you need legal help, your best bet is to first contact your local embassy or consulate. See "Embassies & Consulates," above, for contact details.

LGBT Travelers   Costa Rica is a Catholic, conservative, macho country where public displays of same-sex affection are rare and considered somewhat shocking. Public figures, politicians, and religious leaders periodically denounce homosexuality. However, gay and lesbian tourism to Costa Rica is quite robust, and gay and lesbian travelers are generally treated with respect and should not experience any harassment.

If you speak Spanish, you'll want to connect with the **Comunidad Arco Iris** (**CARI;** www.caricr.com), which serves as a meeting place and information clearinghouse for the entire LGBT community.

Mail   At press time, it cost C365 to mail a letter to the United States, and C435 to Europe. You can get stamps at post offices and at some gift shops in large hotels. Given the Costa Rican postal service's track record, I recommend paying an extra C550 to have anything of any value certified. Better yet, use an international courier service or wait until you get home to post it. DHL, on Paseo Colón between calles 30 and 32 (www.dhl.com; ✆ **2209-6000**); EMS Courier, with desks at most post offices nationwide (www.correos.go.cr; ✆ **2223-9766**); FedEx, which is based in Heredia but will arrange pickup anywhere in the metropolitan area (www.fedex.com; ✆ **2239-0576**); and United Parcel Service, in Pavas (www.ups.com; ✆ **2290-2828**), all operate in Costa Rica.

Medical Requirements No shots or inoculations are required to enter Costa Rica. The exception to this is for those who have recently been traveling in a country or region known to have yellow fever. In this case, proof of a yellow fever vaccination is required. Also see "Staying Healthy," earlier in this chapter.

Mobile Phones Costa Rica uses GSM (Global System for Mobile Communications) networks. If your cellphone is on a GSM system, and you have a world-capable multiband phone, you should be able to make and receive calls in Costa Rica. Just call your wireless operator and ask for "international roaming" to be activated on your account. Per-minute charges can be high, though—up to $5 in Costa Rica, depending upon your plan.

Costa Rica has three main cellphone companies and a couple of smaller outfits. The main providers are the government-run ICE/Kolbi and the international giants Claro and Movistar. All offer a range of prepaid and traditional phone plans. Pricing and coverage are competitive, and I don't recommend one over the other.

You can purchase a prepaid SIM card for an unlocked GSM phone at the airport and at shops all around the country. A prepaid SIM card costs around $2 to $4. Cards usually come loaded with some minutes, and you can buy additional minutes separately either online or at cellphone stores and ICE offices around the country.

If you don't have your own unlocked GSM phone, you might consider buying one here. Shops around the country offer basic, functional phones with a local line, for prices beginning at around $35.

In addition, most of the major car rental agencies offer cellphone rentals. Rates run around $5 to $7 per day or $25 to $50 per week for the rental, with charges of 50¢ to $1.50 per minute for local calls and $1 to $3 per minute for international calls.

Money & Costs The unit of currency in Costa Rica is the colón. In this book, prices are listed in the currency you are most likely to see quoted. Hence, nearly all hotel prices and most tour and transportation prices are listed in dollars, since the hotels, airlines, tour agencies, and transport companies quote their prices in dollars. Many restaurants do, as well. Still, a good many restaurants, as well as taxis and other local goods and services, are advertised and quoted in colones. In those cases, prices listed are in colones (C).

The colón is divided into 100 céntimos. You'll find gold-hued 5-, 10-, 25-, 50-, 100-, and 500-colón coins.

Paper notes come in denominations of 1,000, 2,000, 5,000, 10,000 and 20,000 colones. You might hear people refer to a "rojo" or "tucán," which are slang terms for the 1,000- and 5,000-colón bills, respectively. One-hundred-colón denominations are called "tejas," so "cinco tejas" is 500 colones. I've yet to encounter a slang equivalent for the 2,000, 10,000, and 20,000 bills.

Forged bills are not entirely uncommon. When receiving change in colones, it's a good idea to check the larger-denomination bills, which should have protective bands or hidden images that appear when held up to the light.

THE VALUE OF THE COLÓN VS. OTHER POPULAR CURRENCIES

Colones	Aus$	Can$	Euro (€)	NZ$	UK £	US$
530	A$1.28	C1.25	€.90	NZ$1.32	65p	$1.00

You can change money at all banks in Costa Rica. Since banks handle money exchanges, Costa Rica has very few exchange houses. One major exception to this is the Global Exchange (www.globalexchange.co.cr; *C* **2431-0686**) offices at the international airports. However, be forewarned they exchange at more than 10 percent below the official exchange rate. Airport taxis accept U.S. dollars, so there isn't necessarily any great need to exchange money the moment you arrive.

Hotels will often exchange money and cash traveler's checks, as well; there usually isn't much of a line, but they might shave a few colones off the exchange rate.

If you plan on carrying around dollars to pay for goods and services, be aware that most Costa Rican businesses, be they restaurants, convenience stores, or gas stations, will give a very unfavorable exchange rate.

Your best bet for getting colones is usually by direct withdrawal from your home account via a bank card or debit card, although check in advance if you will be assessed any fees or charges by your home bank. In general, ATMs in Costa Rica still don't add on service fees. Paying with a credit card will also get you the going bank exchange rate. But again, try to get a credit card with no foreign transaction fees.

Be very careful about exchanging money on the streets; it's extremely risky. In addition to forged bills and short counts, street money-changers frequently work in teams that can leave you holding neither colones nor dollars. Also be very careful when leaving a bank. Criminals are often looking for foreigners who have just withdrawn or exchanged cash.

The currency conversions provided in the "Value of the Colón vs. Other Popular Currencies" box were correct at press time. However, rates fluctuate, so before departing, consult a currency exchange website such as www.oanda.com/currency/converter to check up-to-the-minute rates.

MasterCard and Visa are the most widely accepted credit cards in Costa Rica, followed by American Express. Most hotels and restaurants accept all of these, especially in tourist destination areas. Discover and Diners Club are far less commonly accepted.

Beware of hidden credit card fees while traveling. Check with your credit or debit card issuer to see what fees, if any, will be charged for overseas transactions. Recent reform legislation in the U.S., for example, has curbed some exploitative lending practices. But many banks have responded by increasing fees in other areas, including fees for customers who use credit and debit cards while out of the country—even if those charges were

WHAT THINGS COST IN COSTA RICA	US$	COSTA RICAN COLONES
Taxi from the airport to downtown San José	25.00–40.00	C13,250–C21,200
Double room, moderate	120.00	C63,600
Double room, inexpensive	70.00	C37,100
Three-course dinner for one without wine, moderate	20.00–30.00	C10,600–C15,900
Bottle of beer	1.50–3.00	C795–C1,590
Cup of coffee	1.00–1.50	C530–C795
1 gallon/1 liter of premium gas	3.86 per gallon; 1.02 per liter	C2,029 per gallon; C536 per liter
Admission to most museums	2.00–5.00	C1,060–C2,650
Admission to most national parks	15.00	C7,950

made in U.S. dollars. Fees can amount to 3 percent or more of the purchase price. Check with your bank before departing to avoid any surprise charges on your statement.

Costa Rica has a modern and widespread network of ATMs. You should find ATMs in all but the most remote tourist destinations and isolated nature lodges. In response to several "express kidnappings" in San José, in which folks were taken at gunpoint to an ATM to clean out their bank accounts, both Banco Nacional and Banco de Costa Rica stopped ATM service between the hours of 10pm and 5am. Other networks still dispense money 24 hours a day.

It's probably a good idea to change your PIN to a four-digit PIN. While many ATMs in Costa Rica will accept five- and six-digit PINs, some will only accept four-digit PINs.

Newspapers & Magazines   Costa Rica has a half-dozen or so Spanish-language dailies, and you can get *Time* magazine and several U.S. newspapers at some hotel gift shops and a few of the bookstores in San José. If you read Spanish, *La Nación* is the paper you'll want. Its "Viva" and "Tiempo Libre" sections list what's going on in the world of music, theater, dance, and more.

Packing   Everyone should be sure to pack the essentials: sunscreen, insect repellent, camera, bathing suit, a wide-brimmed hat, all prescription medications, and so forth. You'll want good hiking shoes and/or beach footwear, depending upon your itinerary. I also like to have a waterproof headlamp or flashlight and refillable water bottle. Lightweight, long-sleeved shirts and long pants are good protection from both the sun and insects. Surfers use "rash guards," quick-drying Lycra or polyester shirts, which provide great protection from the sun while swimming.

If you're just heading to Guanacaste between December and March, you won't need anything for the rain. Otherwise, I recommend an umbrella, some rain gear, or both. Most high-end hotels provide umbrellas. If you plan to do any wildlife-viewing, bringing your own binoculars is a good idea, as is a field guide (p. 31).

Passports   Citizens of the United States, Canada, Great Britain, and most European nations may visit Costa Rica for a maximum of 90 days. No visa is necessary, but you must have a valid passport, which you should carry with you at all times while you're in Costa Rica. Citizens of Australia, Ireland, and New Zealand can enter the country without a visa and stay for 30 days, although once in the country, visitors can apply for an extension.

It is advised to always have at least one or two consecutive blank pages in your passport to allow space for visas and stamps that need to appear together. It is also important to note when your passport expires. Many countries require your passport to have at least 6 months left before its expiration in order to allow you into the destination.

See "Embassies & Consulates," above, for whom to contact if you lose your passport while traveling. For other information, contact the following agencies:

Australia   Australian Passport Information Service (www.passports.gov.au; ✆ **131-232**).

Canada   Passport Office, Dept. of Foreign Affairs and International Trade, Ottawa, ON K1A 0G3 (www.ppt.gc.ca; ✆ **800/567-6868**).

Ireland   Passport Office, Setanta Centre, Molesworth Street, Dublin 2 (www.foreignaffairs. gov.ie; ✆ **01/671-1633**).

New Zealand   Passports Office, Dept. of Internal Affairs, 109 Featherston St., Wellington, 6140 (www.passports.govt.nz; ✆ **0800/225-050** or 04/463-9360).

United Kingdom   Visit your nearest passport office, major post office, or travel agency or contact the Identity and Passport Service (IPS), 89 Elston Sq., London, SW1V 1PN (www. ips.gov.uk; ✆ **0300/222-0000**).

United States   To find your regional passport office, check the U.S. State Department website (www.travel.state.gov/passport) or call the National Passport Information Center (✆ **877/487-2778**) for automated information.

Petrol   Please see "Getting Around: By Car," earlier in this chapter.

Police   In most cases, dial ⓒ **911** for the police, and you should be able to get someone who speaks English on the line. Other numbers for the **Judicial Police** are ⓒ **2222-1365** and 2221-5337. The numbers for the **Traffic Police (Policía de Tránsito)** are ⓒ **800/8726-7486** toll-free nationwide, or 2222-9245.

Safety   Although most of Costa Rica is safe, petty crime and robberies committed against tourists are endemic. San José, in particular, is known for its pickpockets, so never carry a wallet in your back pocket. A woman should keep a tight grip on her purse (keep it tucked under your arm). Thieves also target gold chains, cameras and video cameras, prominent jewelry, and nice sunglasses. Be sure not to leave valuables unsecured in your hotel room, or unattended—even for a moment—on the beach. Given the high rate of stolen passports in Costa Rica, mostly as collateral damage in a typical pickpocketing or room robbery, it is recommended that, whenever possible, you leave your passport in a hotel safe, and travel with a photocopy of the pertinent pages. Don't park a car on the street in Costa Rica, especially in San José; plenty of public parking lots are around the city.

Rental cars generally stick out and are easily spotted by thieves. Don't leave anything of value in a car parked on the street, not even for a moment. Be wary of solicitous strangers who stop to help you change a tire or take you to a service station. Although most are truly good Samaritans, there have been reports of thieves preying on roadside breakdowns. See "Getting Around: By Car," above, for more info.

Inter-city buses are also frequent targets of stealthy thieves. Try not to check your bags into the hold of a bus if they will fit in the rack above your seat. If it can't be avoided, keep your eye on what leaves the hold. If you put your bags in an overhead rack, be sure you can see the bags at all times. Try not to fall asleep.

Single women should use common sense and take precaution, especially after dark. I don't recommend that single women walk alone anywhere at night, especially on seemingly deserted beaches or dark, uncrowded streets.

Senior Travelers   Be sure to mention that you're a senior when you make your travel reservations. Although it's not common policy in Costa Rica to offer senior discounts, don't be shy about asking for one anyway. You never know. Always carry some kind of identification, such as a driver's license, that shows your date of birth, especially if you've kept your youthful glow.

Many reliable agencies and organizations target the 50-plus market. **Road Scholar,** formerly known as Elderhostel (www.roadscholar.org; ⓒ **800/454-5768** in the U.S. and Canada), arranges Costa Rica study programs for those ages 55 and older, as well as intergenerational trips good for families. **ElderTreks** (www.eldertreks.com; ⓒ **800/741-7956** in the U.S. and Canada; 0808-234-1714 in the U.K.) offers small-group tours to Costa Rica, restricted to travelers 50 and older.

Smoking   Many Costa Ricans smoke, but in March 2012, Costa Rica's legislature passed a strict anti-smoking law. Under this law, smoking is prohibited in all public spaces, including restaurants, bars, offices, and such outdoor areas as public parks and bus stops. The law also raises taxes on cigarettes and places restrictions and controls on advertising.

Most higher-end hotels are either entirely nonsmoking, or have at least some nonsmoking rooms. However, many midrange hotels and most budget options are pretty laissez-faire when it comes to smoking. Whenever possible, the presence of nonsmoking rooms is noted in hotel listing description information.

Student Travelers   Although you won't find any discounts at the national parks, most museums and other attractions around Costa Rica do offer discounts for students. It always pays to ask.

Taxes   The national 13-percent value added tax (often written as IVA in Costa Rica) is added to all goods and services. This includes hotel and restaurant bills. Restaurants also add on a 10-percent service charge, for a total of 23 percent more on your bill.

The airport departure tax is $29, and must be purchased prior to check-in. By the time this book goes to print this tax should automatically be included in the airline ticket price at time of purchase. If not, you will be able to pay it at check-in.

Telephones   Costa Rica has an excellent and widespread phone system. A phone call within the country costs around C10 per minute. Pay phones are relatively scarce. If you do find one, it might take a calling card or 5-, 10-, or 20-colón coins. Calling cards are much more practical. You can purchase calling cards in a host of gift shops and pharmacies. However, there are several competing calling-card companies, and certain cards work only with certain phones. CHIP calling cards work with a computer chip and just slide into specific phones, although these phones aren't widely available. Better bets are the 197 and 199 calling cards, which are sold in varying denominations. These have a scratch-off PIN and can be used from any phone in the country. Generally, the 197 cards are sold in smaller denominations and are used for local calling, while the 199 cards are deemed international and are easier to find in larger denominations. Either card can be used to make any call, however, provided that the card can cover the costs. Another perk of the 199 cards is the fact that you can get the instructions in English. For local calls, it is often easiest to call from your hotel, although you may be charged around C150 to C300 per call.

You might also see about getting yourself a local mobile phone; for information on this, see "Mobile Phones" (p. 577).

To call Costa Rica from abroad:
1.   Dial the international access code: 011 from the U.S. and Canada; 00 from the U.K., Ireland, or New Zealand; or 0011 from Australia.
2.   Dial the country code 506.
3.   Dial the eight-digit number.

To make international calls: First dial 00 and then the country code (U.S. or Canada 1, U.K. 44, Ireland 353, Australia 61, New Zealand 64). Next dial the area code and number. For example, if you want to call the British Embassy in Washington, D.C., you would dial 00-1-202-588-7800.

For directory assistance: Dial 1113 if you're looking for a number inside Costa Rica, and dial 1024 for numbers to all other countries.

For operator assistance: If you need operator assistance in making a call, dial 1116 if you're trying to make an international call, and 0 if you want to call a number in Costa Rica.

Toll-free numbers: Numbers beginning with 0800 or 800 within Costa Rica are toll-free, but calling a 1-800 number in the States from Costa Rica is not toll-free. In fact, it costs the same as an overseas call.

Time   Costa Rica is on Central Standard Time (same as Chicago and St. Louis), 6 hours behind Greenwich Mean Time. Costa Rica does not use daylight saving time, so the time difference is an additional hour from early March through early November.

Tipping   Tipping is not necessary in restaurants, where a 10-percent service charge is always added to your bill (along with a 13-percent tax). If service was particularly good, you can leave a little at your own discretion, but it's not mandatory. Porters and bellhops get around C500 to C1,000 per bag. You don't need to tip a taxi driver unless the service has been superior; a tip is not usually expected.

Toilets   These are known as "sanitarios," "servicios sanitarios," or "baños." They are marked damas (women) and hombres or caballeros (men). Public restrooms are hard to come by. You will almost never find a public restroom in a city park or downtown area. Public restrooms are usually at most national park entrances, and much less frequently inside the national park. In towns and cities, it gets much trickier. One must count on the generosity of some hotel or restaurant. The same goes for most beaches. However, most restaurants, and, to a lesser degree, hotels, will let you use their facilities, especially if you buy a soft drink or something else. Bus and gas stations often have restrooms, but many of these are pretty grim. In some restrooms around the country, especially more remote and natural areas, it's common practice not to flush any foreign matter, aside from your business, down the toilet. This includes toilet paper, sanitary napkins, cigarette butts, and so forth. You will usually find a little sign advising you of this practice in the restroom.

Travelers with Disabilities   Although Costa Rica does have a law mandating Equality of Opportunities for People with Disabilities, and some facilities have been adapted, in general, there are relatively few buildings, bathrooms, public buses or taxis specifically designed for travelers with disabilities in the country. In San José, sidewalks are particularly crowded and uneven, and they are nonexistent in most of the rest of the country. Few hotels offer wheelchair-accessible accommodations. In short, it can be difficult for a person with disabilities to get around San José and Costa Rica.

Many travel agencies offer customized tours and itineraries for travelers with disabilities. Among them are **Eco Adventure International** (www.eaiadventure.com; ✆ **888/710-9453** in the U.S. and Canada); **Flying Wheels Travel** (www.flyingwheelstravel.com; ✆ **612/381-1622**); and **Accessible Journeys** (www.disabilitytravel.com; ✆ **800/846-4537** or 610/521-0339).

Access-Able Travel Source (www.access-able.com; ✆ **303/232-2979**) has a comprehensive database of travel agents around the world with experience in accessible travel; destination-specific access information; and links to such resources as service animals, equipment rentals, and access guides.

Another great organization that offers a vast range of resources and assistance to travelers with disabilities is **SATH** (Society for Accessible Travel & Hospitality; www.sath.org; ✆ **212/447-7284**).

Visitor Information   In the United States or Canada, you can get basic information on Costa Rica by contacting the **Costa Rican Tourist Board** (ICT, or Instituto Costarricense de Turismo; www.visitcostarica.com; ✆ **866/267-8274** in the U.S. and Canada, or 2299-5827 in Costa Rica). Travelers from the United Kingdom, Australia, and New Zealand will have to rely primarily on this website, or call direct to Costa Rica, because the ICT does not have toll-free access in these countries.

You can pick up a map at the ICT's information desk at the airport when you arrive, or at their downtown San José offices (although the destination maps that come with this book are sufficient for most purposes). Perhaps the best map to have is the waterproof country map of Costa Rica put out by **Toucan Maps** (www.mapcr.com), which can be ordered directly from their website or any major online bookseller, like Amazon.com.

Water   Although the water in San José is generally safe to drink, water quality varies outside the city. Because many travelers have tender digestive tracts, I recommend playing it safe and sticking to bottled drinks as much as possible. Also avoid ice.

Women Travelers   For lack of better phrasing, Costa Rica is a typically "macho" Latin American nation. Single women can expect catcalls, hisses, whistles, and car horns, especially in San José. In most cases, while annoying, this is harmless and intended by Tico men as a compliment. Nonetheless, women should be careful walking alone at night throughout the country. Also, see "Safety," earlier in this section.

SPANISH TERMS & PHRASES

Costa Rican Spanish is neither the easiest nor the most difficult dialect to understand. Ticos speak at a relatively relaxed speed and enunciate clearly, without dropping too many final consonants. The *y* and *ll* sounds are subtly, almost inaudibly, pronounced. Perhaps the most defining idiosyncrasy of Costa Rican Spanish is the way Ticos overemphasize, and almost chew, their *r*'s.

BASIC WORDS & PHRASES

English	Spanish	Pronunciation
Hello	Buenos días	**bweh-nohss dee-ahss**
How are you?	¿Cómo está usted?	**koh-moh ehss-tah oo-stehd**
Very well	Muy bien	**mwee byehn**
Thank you	Gracias	**grah-syahss**

English	Spanish	Pronunciation
Goodbye	Adiós	**ad-*dyohss***
Please	Por favor	**pohr fah-*vohr***
Yes	Sí	**see**
No	No	**noh**
Excuse me (to get by someone)	Perdóneme	**pehr-*doh*-neh-meh**
Excuse me (to begin a question)	Discúlpeme	**dees-*kool*-peh-meh**
Give me	Deme	***deh*-meh**
Where is . . . ?	¿Dónde está . . . ?	***dohn*-deh ehss-*tah***
the station	la estación	**la ehss-*tah*-syohn**
the bus stop	la parada	**la pah-*rah*-dah**
a hotel	un hotel	**oon oh-*tehl***
a restaurant	un restaurante	**oon res-tow-*rahn*-teh**
the toilet	el servicio	**el ser-*vee*-syoh**
To the right	A la derecha	**ah lah deh-*reh*-chah**
To the left	A la izquierda	**ah lah ees-*kyehr*-dah**
Straight ahead	Adelante	**ah-deh-*lahn*-teh**
I would like . . .	Quiero . . .	***kyeh*-roh**
to eat	comer	**ko-*mehr***
a room	una habitación	**oo-nah ah-bee-tah-*syohn***
How much is it?	¿Cuánto?	***kwahn*-toh**
When?	¿Cuándo?	***kwan*-doh**
What?	¿Qué?	**keh**
Yesterday	Ayer	**ah-*yehr***
Today	Hoy	**oy**
Tomorrow	Mañana	**mah-*nyah*-nah**
Breakfast	Desayuno	**deh-sah-*yoo*-noh**
Lunch	Almuerzo	**ahl-*mwehr*-soh**
Dinner	Cena	***seh*-nah**
Do you speak English?	¿Habla usted inglés?	***ah*-blah oo-*stehd* een-*glehss***
I don't understand Spanish very well.	No entiendo muy bien el español.	**noh ehn-tyehn-do mwee byehn el ehss-pah-nyohl**

NUMBERS

English	Spanish	Pronunciation
zero	cero	**ser-oh**
one	uno	**oo-noh**
two	dos	**dohss**
three	tres	**trehss**
four	cuatro	**kwah-troh**
five	cinco	**seen-koh**
six	seis	**sayss**
seven	siete	**syeh-teh**
eight	ocho	**oh-choh**
nine	nueve	**nweh-beh**
ten	diez	**dyehss**
eleven	once	**ohn-seh**
twelve	doce	**doh-seh**
thirteen	trece	**treh-seh**
fourteen	catorce	**kah-tohr-seh**
fifteen	quince	**keen-seh**
sixteen	dieciséis	**dyeh-see-sayss**
seventeen	diecisiete	**dyeh-see-syeh-teh**
eighteen	dieciocho	**dyeh-see-oh-choh**
nineteen	diecinueve	**dyeh-see-nweh-beh**
twenty	veinte	**bayn-teh**
thirty	treinta	**trayn-tah**
forty	cuarenta	**kwah-rehn-tah**
fifty	cincuenta	**seen-kwehn-tah**
sixty	sesenta	**seh-sehn-tah**
seventy	setenta	**seh-tehn-tah**
eighty	ochenta	**oh-chehn-tah**
ninety	noventa	**noh-behn-tah**
one hundred	cien	**syehn**
one thousand	mil	**meel**

DAYS OF THE WEEK

English	Spanish	Pronunciation
Monday	lunes	**loo-nehss**
Tuesday	martes	**mahr-tehss**

English	Spanish	Pronunciation
Wednesday	miércoles	***myehr*-koh-lehs**
Thursday	jueves	***wheh*-behss**
Friday	viernes	***byehr*-nehss**
Saturday	sábado	***sah*-bah-doh**
Sunday	domingo	**doh-*meen*-goh**

SOME TYPICAL TICO WORDS & PHRASES

Birra   Slang for beer.

Boca   Literally means "mouth," but also a term to describe a small appetizer served alongside a drink at many bars.

Bomba   Translates literally as "pump," but is used in Costa Rica for "gas station."

Brete   Work, or job.

Buena nota   To be good, or have a good vibe.

Casado   Literally means "married," but is the local term for a popular restaurant offering that features a main dish and various side dishes.

Chapa   Derogatory way to call someone stupid or clumsy.

Chepe   Slang term for the capital city, San José.

Choza   Slang for house or home. Also called *chante*.

Chunche   Knickknack; thing, as in "whatchamacallit."

Con mucho gusto   With pleasure.

De hoy en ocho   In 1 week's time.

Diay   An untranslatable but common linguistic punctuation, often used to begin a sentence.

Estar de chicha   To be angry.

Fria   Literally "cold," but used to mean a cold beer—*una fria, por favor.*

Fut   Short for *fútbol,* or soccer.

Goma   Hangover.

Harina   Literally "flour," but used to mean money.

La sele   Short for *la selección,* the Costa Rican national soccer team.

Limpio   Literally means "clean," but is the local term for being broke, or having no money.

Macha or **machita**   A blond woman.

Mae   Translates like "man"; used by many Costa Ricans, particularly teenagers, as frequent verbal punctuation.

Maje   A lot like *mae,* above, but with a slightly derogatory connotation.

Mala nota   Bad vibe, or bad situation.

Mala pata   Bad luck.

Mejenga   An informal, or pickup, soccer game.

Pachanga or **pelón**   Both terms are used to signify a big party or gathering.

Ponga la maría, por favor   This is how you ask taxi drivers to turn on the meter.

Pulpería   The Costa Rican version of the "corner store" or small market.

Pura paja   Pure nonsense or BS.

Pura vida   Literally, "pure life"; translates as "everything's great."

Qué torta   What a mess; what a screw-up.

Si Dios quiere   God willing; you'll hear Ticos say this all the time.

Soda   A casual diner-style restaurant serving cheap Tico meals.

Tico   Costa Rican.

Tiquicia   Costa Rica.

Tuanis   Similar in usage and meaning to *pura vida,* above.

Una teja   100 colones.

Un rojo   1,000 colones.

Un tucán   5,000 colones.

Upe!   Common shout to find out if anyone is home; used frequently since doorbells are so scarce.

Zarpe   Last drink of the night, or "one more for the road."

MENU TERMS
FISH

Almejas   Clams

Atún   Tuna

Bacalao   Cod

Calamares   Squid

Camarones   Shrimp

Cangrejo   Crab

Ceviche   Marinated seafood salad

Dorado   Dolphin or mahimahi

Langosta   Lobster

Lenguado   Sole

Mejillones   Mussels

Ostras   Oysters

Pargo   Snapper

Pulpo   Octopus

Trucha   Trout

MEATS

Albóndigas   Meatballs

Bistec   Beefsteak

Cerdo   Pork

Chicharrones   Fried pork rinds

Chorizo   Sausage

Chuleta   Literally chop, usually pork chop

Cordero   Lamb

Costillas   Ribs

Delmonico   Rib-eye

Jamón   Ham

Lengua   Tongue

Lomo   Sirloin

Lomito   Tenderloin

Pato   Duck

Pavo   Turkey

Pollo   Chicken

Salchichas   Hot dogs, but sometimes refers to any sausage

VEGETABLES

Aceitunas Olives
Alcachofa Artichoke
Berenjena Eggplant
Cebolla Onion
Elote Corn on the cob
Ensalada Salad
Espinacas Spinach
Frijoles Beans

Lechuga Lettuce
Maíz Corn
Palmito Heart of palm
Papa Potato
Pepino Cucumber
Tomate Tomato
Yuca Yucca, cassava, or manioc
Zanahoria Carrot

FRUITS

Aguacate Avocado
Banano Banana
Carambola Star fruit
Cereza Cherry
Ciruela Plum
Durazno Peach
Frambuesa Raspberry
Fresa Strawberry
Granadilla Sweet passion fruit
Limón Lemon or lime
Mango Mango

Manzana Apple
Maracuya Tart passion fruit
Melón Melon
Mora Blackberry
Naranja Orange
Papaya Papaya
Piña Pineapple
Plátano Plantain
Sandía Watermelon
Toronja Grapefruit

BASICS

Aceite Oil
Ajo Garlic
Arreglado Small meat sandwich
Azúcar Sugar
Casado Plate of the day
Gallo Corn tortilla topped with meat or chicken
Gallo pinto Rice and beans
Hielo Ice
Mantequilla Butter
Miel Honey
Mostaza Mustard

Natilla Sour cream
Olla de carne Meat and vegetable soup
Pan Bread
Patacones Fried plantain chips
Picadillo Chopped vegetable side dish
Pimienta Pepper
Queso Cheese
Sal Salt
Tamal Filled cornmeal pastry
Tortilla Flat corn pancake

DRINKS

Agua purificada Purified water
Agua con gas Sparkling water
Agua sin gas Plain water
Bebida Drink

Café Coffee
Café con leche Coffee with milk
Cerveza Beer
Chocolate caliente Hot chocolate

Jugo   Juice

Leche   Milk

Natural   Fruit juice

Natural con leche   Milkshake

Refresco   Soft drink

Ron   Rum

Té   Tea

Trago   Alcoholic drink

OTHER RESTAURANT TERMS

Al grill   Grilled

Al horno   Oven-baked

Al vapor   Steamed

Asado   Roasted

Caliente   Hot

Cambio or vuelto   Change

Cocido   Cooked

Comida   Food

Congelado   Frozen

Crudo   Raw

El baño   Toilet

Frío   Cold

Frito   Fried

Grande   Big or large

La cuenta   The check

Medio   Medium

Medio rojo   Medium rare

Muy cocido   Well-done

Pequeño   Small

Poco cocido or rojo   Rare

Tres cuartos   Medium-well-done

OTHER USEFUL TERMS

HOTEL TERMS

Aire acondicionado   Air-conditioning

Almohada   Pillow

Baño   Bathroom

Baño privado   Private bathroom

Caja de seguridad   Safe

Calefacción   Heating

Cama   Bed

Cobija   Blanket

Colchón   Mattress

Cuarto or Habitación   Room

Escritorio   Desk

Habitación simple/sencilla   Single room

Habitación doble   Double room

Habitación triple   Triple room

Llave   Key

Mosquitero   Mosquito net

Sábanas   Sheets

Seguro de puerta   Door lock

Silla   Chair

Telecable   Cable TV

Ventilador   Fan

TRAVEL TERMS

Aduana   Customs

Aeropuerto   Airport

Avenida   Avenue

Avión   Airplane

Aviso   Warning

Bus   Bus

Cajero   ATM, also called *cajero automatico*

Calle   Street

Cheques viajeros   Traveler's checks

Correo   Mail, or post office

Cuadra   City block

Dinero or plata   Money

Embajada   Embassy

Embarque   Boarding

Entrada   Entrance

Equipaje Luggage
Este East
Frontera Border
Lancha or bote Boat
Norte North
Occidente West
Oeste West

EMERGENCY TERMS

¡Auxilio! Help!
Ambulancia Ambulance
Bomberos Fire brigade
Clínica Clinic or hospital
Doctor or **médico** Doctor
Emergencia Emergency
Enfermo/enferma Sick
Enfermera Nurse

Oriente East
Pasaporte Passport
Puerta de salida or **puerta de embarque** Boarding gate
Salida Exit
Sur South
Tarjeta de embarque Boarding pass
Vuelo Flight

Farmacia Pharmacy
Fuego or **incendio** Fire
Hospital Hospital
Ladrón Thief
Peligroso Dangerous
Policía Police
¡Váyase! Go away!

15

Other Useful Terms

SPANISH TERMS & PHRASES

Index

PHOTO CREDITS

p. i: Vilainecrevette; p. iii: Adrian Hepworth; p. 1: oleksajewicz; p. 2: lvalin ; p. 3, top: Courtesy Tabacon Grand Thermal Resort; p. 3, bottom left: worldswildlifewonders; p. 3, bottom right: Nacho Such; p. 4: Pattie Steib; p. 5: IrinaK; p. 6: Hugh Lansdown; p. 7: Coral Blanche Hummer; p. 8: Dan McWeeney; p. 11, bottom: Steffen Foerster; p. 11, middle: kuma chan; p. 12: Max Herman / Shutterstock.com; p. 13, top: Martin Garrido; p. 13, middle: Adrian Hepworth; p. 14, top: N K; p. 14, middle: boivin nicolas; p. 15: Chad Rosenthal; p. 16, left: Thornton Cohen; p. 16, right: Thornton Cohen; p. 18: Mark Caunt; p. 19: lvalin; p. 21: Don Fink; p. 23, top: Adrian Hepworth; p. 23, middle: Olaf Speier ; p. 27: Adrian Hepworth; p. 28: Rodtico21; p. 29: Jolanda ; p. 32: Gail Frederick; p. 35: Ken Cedeno; p. 36, top: Roberto Rodríguez; p. 36, middle: Maxim B.; p. 37, left: The LEAF Project; p. 37, right: Everjean; p. 38: Toh Gouttenoire; p. 40: The LEAF Project; p. 45: David Berkowitz; p. 48: Thornton Cohen; p. 49: Chris Wronski; p. 51, top: Vytautas Š'rys; p. 51, middle: Jarno Gonzalez Zarraonandia; p. 53, top: Bill Green; p. 53, middle: Jennifer Morrow; p. 54: Nao Iizuka; p. 56: Colin D. Young; p. 58, left: colacat ; p. 58, right: Wouter Tolenaars; p. 60: mervas ; p. 61: Kristin & Jordan Hayman; p. 62: Thornton Cohen; p. 66, top: Ken Cedeno; p. 66, bottom: Don Henise; p. 68: DeLoyd Huenink; p. 70: Vilainecrevette; p. 71, left: Phoo Chan; p. 71, right: Timur Kulgarin; p. 72: Sergey Uryadnikov; p. 73: Adrian Hepworth; p. 75: Thornton Cohen; p. 76: Thornton Cohen; p. 81: lvalin; p. 82, top: Sarah Murray; p. 82, second from top: Miguel Vieira; p. 82, middle: Jerry Kirkhart; p. 82, second from bottom: Thornton Cohen; p. 82, bottom: Sergei Scurfield; p. 83, top: Kim; p. 83, bottom: Adrian Hepworth; p. 84, top left: Adrian Hepworth; p. 84, top right: Adrian Hepworth; p. 84, bottom: Adrian Hepworth; p. 85, top: Frank Wasserfuehrer ; p. 85, second from top: Adrian Hepworth; p. 85, middle: Adrian Hepworth; p. 85, second from bottom: Adrian Hepworth; p. 85, bottom: Adrian Hepworth; p. 86: Chris Ison ; p. 87, top: Adrian Hepworth; p. 87, middle: Adrian Hepworth; p. 87, bottom: Thornton Cohen; p. 88, top: Thornton Cohen; p. 88, second from top: Thornton Cohen; p. 88, middle: Adrian Hepworth; p. 88, bottom left: Adrian Hepworth; p. 88, bottom right: Jason Patrick Ross ; p. 89, top: Adrian Kaye ; p. 89, middle: Leonardo Gonzalez ; p. 89, bottom: IrinaK ; p. 90, top left: Adrian Hepworth; p. 90, top right: Ethan Daniels ; p. 90, middle: Matt9122 ; p. 91, top: FineShine ; p. 91, middle: Adrian Hepworth; p. 91, bottom: Ken Cedeno; p. 92, top left: RHIMAGE ; p. 92, top right: wendybwalke/ Frommers.com Community; p. 92, bottom left: YuryZap ; p. 92, bottom right: Adrian Hepworth; p. 93, top left: Adrian Hepworth; p. 93, top right: Lee Prince ; p. 93, bottom: Adrian Hepworth; p. 94, top left: Adrian Hepworth; p. 94, top right: Mark Carthy ; p. 94, bottom left: meaofoto ; p. 94, bottom right: Stephen Therres ; p. 95: dog4aday; p. 116: Mihai-Bogdan Lazar / Shutterstock.com; p. 118: Meredith P.; p. 122: Ken Cedeno; p. 123: Adrian Hepworth; p. 125: Daniel Korzeniewski / Shutterstock.com; p. 128: Richie Diesterheft; p. 129, top: De Jongh Photography / Shutterstock.com; p. 129, bottom: Ken Cedeno; p. 132, top: Ken Cedeno; p. 132, bottom: Ken Cedeno; p. 133: Rodrigo Fernández; p. 134: Adrian Hepworth; p. 136, left: Bogdan Migulski; p. 136, right: Adrian Hepworth; p. 137, top: Adrian Hepworth; p. 137, bottom: Bernal Saborio; p. 138: ElTico68; p. 140: Derek Blackadder; p. 142: Courtesy Hotel Grano de Oro; p. 145: Ken Cedeno; p. 152: Ken Cedeno; p. 153: Ken Cedeno; p. 155: Ken Cedeno; p. 156: Adrian Hepworth; p. 157: Kenneth Hong; p. 158: Ken Cedeno; p. 159: Ken Cedeno; p. 162: Thornton Cohen; p. 164: Courtesy of Calypso Cruises; p. 166, top: Tami Freed ; p. 166, bottom: William Berry ; p. 168: The LEAF Project; p. 172: Adrian Hepworth; p. 176: Ken Cedeno; p. 178, top: Ken Cedeno; p. 178, middle: Ken Cedeno; p. 181, top: Adrian Hepworth; p. 181, bottom: Andy Rusch; p. 182: Adrian Hepworth; p. 183: Courtesy of Marriott; p. 185: Jason Walsh; p. 186: Courtesy of Villa San Ignacio; p. 188: Adrian Hepworth; p. 189: Adrian Hepworth; p. 190: Courtesy Finca Rosa Blanca Coffee Plantation; p. 193, top: Adrian Hepworth; p. 193, bottom: Adrian Hepworth; p. 195: Olaf Speier ; p. 198: Ken Cedeno; p. 199: Jolanda; p. 200: Sergey Uryadnikov; p. 201: Adrian Hepworth; p. 202, top: The LEAF Project; p. 202, middle: Adrian Hepworth; p. 203: Adrian Hepworth; p. 204: Adrian Hepworth; p. 205: Raul Rosa; p. 208: EQRoy / Shutterstock.com; p. 210: EQRoy / Shutterstock.com; p. 212: Thornton Cohen; p. 214: Thornton Cohen; p. 215: Thornton Cohen; p. 216: PatrickRohe; p. 217: Thornton Cohen; p. 220: Thornton Cohen; p. 221: Adrian Hepworth; p. 223: Thornton Cohen; p. 226: justinknabb; p. 228: Thornton Cohen; p. 230, left: Marissa Strniste; p. 230, right: Jaan; p. 231: Courtesy of Dreams Las Mareas; p. 233: Didier Baertschiger; p. 237: Courtesy of Four Seasons; p. 242: PatrickRohe; p. 244: Gary J. Wood; p. 250: Thornton Cohen; p. 251: Colin D. Young; p. 252: Adrian Hepworth; p. 253: Paul Kehrer; p. 256: Thornton Cohen; p. 257: Adrian Hepworth; p. 258: Thornton Cohen; p. 261: Amoslisa/ Frommers.com Community; p. 264: riekephotos / Shutterstock.com; p. 266: